Collective Wisdom
Principles and Mechanisms

James Madison wrote, "Had every Athenian citizen been a Socrates, every Athenian assembly would still have been a mob." The contributors to this volume discuss and for the most part challenge this claim by considering conditions under which many minds can be wiser than one. With backgrounds in economics, cognitive science, political science, law, and history, the authors consider information markets, the Internet, jury debates, democratic deliberation, and the use of diversity as mechanisms for improving collective decisions. At the same time, they consider voter irrationality and paradoxes of aggregation as possibly undermining the wisdom of crowds. Implicitly or explicitly, the volume also offers guidance and warnings to institutional designers.

Hélène Landemore is a graduate of the École Normale Supérieure in Paris, Sciences Po Paris, and Harvard University (PhD 2008). After holding postdoctoral positions at the Collège de France in Paris, Brown University, and MIT, she is now an assistant professor of political science at Yale University. She is the author of *Hume: probabilité et choix raisonnable* and *Democratic Reason: Politics, Collective Intelligence, and the Rule of the Many*. Her work has appeared in the *Journal of Moral Philosophy*, *Raison Publique*, *Synthese*, *Journal of Public Deliberation*, *Critical Review*, and *Political Psychology*.

Jon Elster is Robert K. Merton Professor of Political Science at Columbia University. He was previously a professor at the University of Chicago. From 2005 to 2011, he held the Chaire de Rationalité et Sciences Sociales at the Collège de France in Paris. He is a member of the American Academy of Arts and Sciences, Academia Europaea, and the Norwegian Academy of Science and is a Corresponding Fellow of the British Academy. He holds honorary doctorates from the universities of Valencia, Stockholm, Trondheim, Bogotá, Torcuata di Tella, and Louvain-la-Neuve. Elster is the author of twenty-three monographs, which have been translated into eighteen languages. The most recent of these include *L'Irrationalité*; *Alexis de Tocqueville: The First Social Scientist*; *Le Désintéressement*; *Explaining Social Behavior*; *Agir contre soi*; *Closing the Books*; and *Alchemies of the Mind*.

Collective Wisdom

Principles and Mechanisms

Edited by

HÉLÈNE LANDEMORE
Yale University

JON ELSTER
Columbia University and (Emeritus) Collège de France

CAMBRIDGE
UNIVERSITY PRESS

CAMBRIDGE
UNIVERSITY PRESS

32 Avenue of the Americas, New York NY 10013-2473, USA

Cambridge University Press is part of the University of Cambridge.

It furthers the University's mission by disseminating knowledge in the pursuit of education, learning and research at the highest international levels of excellence.

www.cambridge.org
Information on this title: www.cambridge.org/9781107630277

First published 2012
First paperback edition 2014

A catalogue record for this publication is available from the British Library

Library of Congress Cataloguing in Publication data

Collective wisdom : principles and mechanisms / [edited by] Hélène Landemore, Jon Elster.
    p.   cm.
Includes bibliographical references and index.
ISBN 978-1-107-01033-8 (hardback)
1. Group decision making.   2. Social choice.   I. Landemore, Hélène, 1976–
II. Elster, Jon, 1940–
HM746.C654   2012
302.3–dc23   2011036711

ISBN 978-1-107-01033-8 Hardback
ISBN 978-1-107-63027-7 Paperback

Contents

Contributors

Daniel Andler is Professor of Philosophy of Science and Epistemology at Université Paris–Sorbonne and a senior member of Institut Universitaire de France. He taught in mathematics departments before moving to positions in philosophy. His main interests lie in cognitive science, extending from foundational issues to the impact on social science and on societal issues, education in particular. He is the author and/or editor of several books (including *Philosophie des sciences*, Gallimard, 2002; *Introduction aux sciences cognitives*, Gallimard, 2004) and numerous papers. His new book, *Critical Naturalism*, will be published in 2012.

Bryan Caplan is Professor of Economics at George Mason University and blogger for EconLog. He is the author of *The Myth of the Rational Voter: Why Democracies Choose Bad Policies* (Princeton University Press, 2007), named the "best political book of the year" by the *New York Times*, and *Selfish Reasons to Have More Kids: Why Being a Great Parent Is Less Work and More Fun Than You Think* (Basic Books, 2011). He has published in the *New York Times*, *Washington Post*, *Wall Street Journal*, *American Economic Review*, *Economic Journal*, *Journal of Law and Economics*, and *Intelligence*.

Jon Elster is Robert K. Merton Professor of Social Sciences at Columbia University. He was previously a professor at the University of Chicago and the Collège de France in Paris. Elster is the author of twenty-three monographs translated into eighteen languages. The most recent of these include *L'Irrationalité* (Seuil, 2010); *Alexis de Tocqueville: The First Social Scientist* (Cambridge University Press, 2009); *Le Désintéressement* (Seuil, 2009); *Explaining Social Behavior* (Cambridge University Press, 2007); *Agir contre soi* (Odile Jacob, 2006); *Closing the Books* (Cambridge University Press, 2004); and *Alchemies of the Mind* (Cambridge University Press, 1999).

David Estlund is Lombardo Family Professor of Humanities in the Departments of Philosophy and Political Science at Brown University, where he has been teaching since 1991. He edited the collection *Democracy* (Blackwell, 2001) and is the author of *Democratic Authority: A Philosophical Framework* (Princeton University Press, 2008). He is the editor of the *Oxford Handbook in Political Philosophy* (Oxford University Press, 2012) and is writing a book about whether normative political theories must be realistic.

John Ferejohn is the Samuel Tilden Professor of Law at New York University. He was formerly a Professor of Social Sciences at the California Institute of Technology (1972–83) and a Professor of Political Science at Stanford University and a Senior Fellow of the Hoover Institution (1983–2009). He is the author of *Pork Barrel Politics* (Stanford University Press, 1974), as well as many scholarly articles in political science, economics, and philosophy, and the coeditor of *Information and Democratic Processes* (University of Illinois Press, 1990), *Constitutional Culture and Democratic Rule* (Cambridge University Press, 2001), and *The New Federalism: Can the States be Trusted?* (Hoover Institution Press, 1997). He recently coauthored *A Republic of Statutes* (Yale University Press, 2010).

Lu Hong is Professor of Economics in the Loyola University Graduate School of Business. She writes on implementation theory and mechanism design. Her work has appeared in leading economic theory journals as well as in the proceedings of the National Academy of Sciences.

Hélène Landemore is Assistant Professor of Political Science at Yale University. She is the author of *Hume: probabilité et choix raisonnable* (Presses Universitaires de France, 2004) and *Democratic Reason: Politics, Collective Intelligence, and the Rule of the Many* (Princeton University Press, 2012). Her work has appeared in the *Journal of Moral Philosophy*, *Raison Publique*, *Synthese*, *Journal of Public Deliberation*, *Critical Review*, and *Political Psychology*.

Christian List is Professor of Political Science and Philosophy at the London School of Economics. He works on the theory of democracy, individual and collective agency, and the relationship between reductive and nonreductive explanations in the social sciences. He was awarded a Philip Leverhulme Prize, the Fifth Social Choice and Welfare Prize (jointly with Franz Dietrich), a Laurence S. Rockefeller Visiting Fellowship at Princeton University, and a Visiting Fellowship of the Swedish Collegium for Advanced Study. Jointly with Philip Pettit, he recently published *Group Agency: The Possibility, Design, and Status of Corporate Agents* (Oxford University Press, 2011).

Gerry Mackie is Associate Professor of Political Science and founding Co-director of the Center on Global Justice at the University of California, San Diego. He is a political theorist interested in contemporary political theory, the history of political thought, and problems of collective action. His main area of interest is democracy, particularly democratic voting. He is the author of *Democracy Defended* (Cambridge University Press, 2003). Since 1998 he has worked with the nongovernmental organization Tostan in Senegal, which has organized unprecedented mass abandonment of female genital cutting (FGC) in 6,200 communities in seven countries. Since 2004 he has worked closely with UNICEF on the issue, helping devise an internationally distributed best-practices publication and a global abandonment strategy. The "common approach" to the practice endorsed in 2009 by eleven United Nations agencies was influenced by his scholarship. The work on FGC leads him to further study of the sociology of norms, moral psychology, and international human rights.

Hugo Mercier is a Postdoctoral Fellow in the Philosophy, Politics, and Economics Program at the University of Pennsylvania. His work has focused on reasoning and argumentation. He has written a series of articles that cover this issue from different perspectives – moral, developmental, cross-cultural, and political.

Josiah Ober, Constantine Mitsotakis Professor of Political Science and Classics at Stanford University, works on political institutions, culture, and theory, especially the thought and practice of the ancient Greek world. His 2008 book, *Democracy and Knowledge: Innovation and Learning in Classical Athens* (Princeton University Press), analyzes ancient Athenian democracy as a system for aggregating, aligning, and codifying useful knowledge. The book seeks to explain the close correlation between the development of democratic institutions and state performance in the age of Thucydides, Plato, and Aristotle. His current projects concern the relationship between cooperation and knowledge in Greek political thought, the relationship between civic and human dignity, and the role of expertise in democratic decision making.

Gloria Origgi is a tenured researcher at the Institut Nicod, Centre National de la Recherche Scientifique, Paris. Her main areas of interest are social epistemology, philosophy of social and cognitive sciences, and Web studies. Among her most recent publications are *Qu'est-ce que la confiance?* (VRIN, 2008) and (with Frédéric Darbellay) *Repenser l'interdisciplinarité* (Slatkin, 2010). She has conceived and is the chief editor of the platform for virtual conferences www.interdisciplines.org.

Scott E. Page is the Leonid Hurwicz Collegiate Professor of Complex Systems, Political Science, and Economics at the University of Michigan–Ann Arbor. He works on questions related to the role of diversity in institutional design and performance. He is the author of *The Difference: How the Power of Diversity Creates Better Groups, Firms, Schools, and Societies* (Princeton University Press, 2007). His most recent book, *Diversity and Complexity* (Princeton University Press, 2010), explores the role of diversity in complex systems.

Emile Servan-Schreiber founded and ran the NewsFutures prediction market from 2000 to 2010. He is now a managing director of Lumenogic, a consulting firm specializing in corporate applications of collective intelligence and prediction markets. Trained in the cognitive sciences at Carnegie Mellon University (PhD, 1991), he is the coauthor of two award-winning multimedia CD-Roms featuring the collective intelligence of dozens of world-class scientists: *The Challenge of the Universe* (Hypermind/Oxford University Press, 1996) and *Secrets of the Mind* (Hypermind/Montparnasse, 1998).

Dan Sperber is Professor of Philosophy and Cognitive Science at the Central European University (Budapest) and Directeur de Recherche Emeritus at the Institut Jean Nicod (CNRS, ENS, and EHESS, Paris). He is the author of *Rethinking Symbolism* (Cambridge University Press, 1975), *On Anthropological Knowledge* (Cambridge University Press,1985), and *Explaining Culture* (Blackwell, 1996); the coauthor with Deirdre Wilson of *Relevance: Communication and Cognition* (Blackwell, 1986; 2d ed., 1995) and *Meaning and Relevance* (Cambridge University Press, 2012); the editor of *Metarepresentations: A Multidisciplinary Perspective* (Oxford University Press, 2000); the coeditor with David Premack and Ann James Premack of *Causal Cognition: A Multidisciplinary Debate* (Oxford University Press, 1995) and, with Ira Noveck, of *Experimental Pragmatics* (Palgrave Macmillan, 2004).

Philippe Urfalino is a Senior Researcher at the French Centre National pour la Recherche Scientifique and Professor at the École des Hautes Etudes en Sciences Sociales in Paris. He is also Director of the Raymond Aron Center for Political and Sociological Studies (UMR CNRS/EHESS). Urfalino has written several books on French cultural policies and on pharmaceutical agencies. His most recent books are *L'invention de la politique culturelle* (Pluriel-Fayard, 2004) and *Le grand méchant loup pharmaceutique* (Textuel, 2005). He is currently writing a book on collective decision conceived as a normative phenomenon.

Adrian Vermeule is John H. Watson Professor of Law at Harvard Law School. His research has examined problems in constitutional law and theory, administrative law, and collective decision making. His most recent book is *The System of the Constitution* (Oxford University Press, 2011).

Collective Wisdom

Old and New

Hélène Landemore

The idea of collective wisdom presented in this volume is both old and new. It is old because Aristotle is generally credited with having first taken seriously the idea that "many heads are better than one." He himself was in fact rehearsing an argument that the Sophists were using in defense of democracy. In a much-quoted passage in the *Politics*, Aristotle thus remarks that

the many, who are not as individuals excellent men, nevertheless can, when they have come together, *be better than the few best people, not individually but collectively*, just as feasts to which many contribute are better than feasts provided at one person's expense. (*Politics* III, 11, 1281a41–1281b2 (1998): 83, my emphasis)

Jeremy Waldron (1995) has felicitously labeled this argument "the doctrine from the wisdom of the multitude." Most commentators agree that the mechanism accounting for the superiority of a group over any of its members is, in Aristotle's view, the pooling of information and arguments that occur in deliberation.

The idea of collective wisdom is new, on the other hand, to the extent that it has resurfaced in the past eight to ten years in a substantially different guise in the literature on the "wisdom of crowds" sparked in part by, or concomitant with, the success of James Surowiecki's *New York Times* best seller by the same title.[1] Some other landmarks are Howard Rheingold's (2003) *Smart Mobs: The Next Social Revolution*, Don Tapscott and Anthony D. Williams's (2006) *Wikinomics: How Mass Collaboration Changes Everything*, Cass Sunstein's

[1] See Surowiecki (2004).

This volume is based on the contributions to an international conference that took place at the Collège de France in Paris, May 24–25, 2008. Jon Elster and I would like to thank Karen Kroxson, Stéphanie Novak, Pierre Rosanvallon, and Yves Sintomer for their crucial role as discussants on this occasion. Videos of the presentations are available at http://www.cerimes.education. fr/sagesse-collective-principes-mecanismes-catalogue-college-france-philosophie-fiches-a223154s 100001017t24_.html. Special thanks to Austin Baik for his work on the index and invaluable help throughout the editing process.

(2006) *Infotopia: How Many Minds Produce Knowledge,* and a more specific management literature, such as Jeff Howe's (2008) *Crowd-Sourcing: How the Power of the Crowd Is Driving the Future of Business,* as well as collectively authored books such as Charles Leadbeater's (2008) *We-think: The Power of Mass Creativity* and Barry Libert and John Spector's (2008) *We Are Smarter Than Me: How to Unleash the Power of Crowds in Your Business.*[2]

The novelty here, compared with what Aristotle was describing, is at least threefold. The first novelty lies in the sheer scope of collective wisdom, involving millions of individuals rather than the few thousand at best that Aristotle had in mind (assuming, plausibly, that he was thinking of Athenian assemblies).

The second novelty is that many of these phenomena – for example, the predictive accuracy of information markets – do not depend on or involve any kind of deliberation or direct and conscious communication among the participants. In Surowiecki's book, the opening and paradigmatic example of the wisdom of the crowds is Francis Galton's statistical experiment at a country fair, in which many individuals wrote down their best guess about the weight of an ox once slaughtered and dressed, and the median guess of the eight hundred participants turned out to fall within one pound of the right answer. Another example is that of the *Scorpion,* a lost submarine found only after all the individual guesses of a diverse group of mathematicians, submarine specialists, and salvage men had been averaged out, without any prior deliberation among them. When deliberation is at play – for example, in the case of Wikipedia – it takes forms that depart from the classical exchange of arguments that Aristotle had in mind, being more fragmented but also more cooperative and creative in many ways.

As a result, it is dubious that the mechanisms at play in the wisdom of crowds have much to do with the type of deliberation as exchange of arguments in a public forum that Aristotle was most likely thinking of. Indeed, the literature on the wisdom of crowds generally focuses on information markets, polling, voting, or the logic of search engines like Google that do not involve any form of communication among the participants and that do not even require that they either know one another or are in each other's physical presence. What seems more likely to account for the emergence of collective wisdom in such cases is not so much classical deliberation as other forms of judgment and preference aggregation procedure.

---

[2] Collective books on collective intelligence are particularly interesting from a formal and procedural point of view (although they have not always been particularly successful from the substantive point of view). *We Are Smarter Than Me,* for example, involved the collaboration of thousands of business professionals and scholars, who all get equal credit inside the book's cover, as does an uncredited "crowd" of more than a million students. All participants contributed Wikipedia-style, co-writing and sharing insights on a wiki page. In France, Marc Foglia's (2008) collaborative volume on Wikipedia consists of multiple entries by the main author, which are supplemented by longer articles by other contributors. Our own edited volume is a much more traditional and conservative attempt at tapping the collective wisdom of many authors by simply juxtaposing their contributions to a common topic.

Notice that further differentiation among nondeliberative judgment aggregation procedures is needed. In voting, for example, participants not only do not communicate with others as they vote, but also are not supposed to be influenced by the concomitantly emerging collective wisdom of the rest of the voters, which is why, say, Canadian law forbids election returns from the East Coast to be publicized before the polls close on the West Coast. This is to be contrasted with the logic of Google or Amazon, where collective wisdom emerges as a result of stigmergy – a phenomenon of self-organization first observed in societies of insects that refers to a situation in which entities leave meaningful trails in the environment that have an impact on subsequent entities passing that way. Google illustrates this phenomenon in that it involves iterative feedback through which the existing popularity of a site increases its chances of being seen and linked to, further magnifying its apparent popularity on Google. In the case of Amazon, the program has a function "People who bought this book also bought these other books," a statement that reinforces itself over time as customers take the hint and buy the other books that are popular among persons of their type. The collective wisdom emerging from the Google and Amazon programs lies in the fact that they translate individual clicks and purchases into an informational trace for subsequent visitors, in a way that is comparable to the way ants use the chemical clues left on the soil by previous ant traffic to make decisions about where to go next.[3]

Of course, one might want to make the case that all these apparently nondeliberative procedures are in fact parts or the expression of a more general process of decentralized and distributed deliberation, one in which ideas circulate among masses of people in ways similar to what deliberation does among individuals, although the process does not take place among all the participants at once but mere clusters of them and does not involve all there is to deliberate but only subtopics or elements. Supplemented by large-scale ways to aggregate the views of the many, this initially decentralized process of deliberation may amount to the kind of collective wisdom that Aristotle had in mind – only disindividualized (distributed over both smaller and larger entities than individuals) and writ larger.

A third novelty of the contemporary idea of collective wisdom lies in the importance of the notions of network and connectedness, which captures the fact that information is transmitted and distributed across diversely connected individuals rather than centralized in one specific public sphere. This volume touches only tangentially on that aspect of collective wisdom, but I should mention the existence of an exploding body of scientific work on the properties of networks. The boom in this realm in the past ten years has included work done by physicists, computer scientists, and sociologists (for a survey see the introductory chapters of Newman, Baribasi, and Watts 2006).[4] Furthermore, little if anything is mentioned in the volume about the related but distinct question of

---

[3] I thank Tom Atlee for suggesting these distinctions and comparisons.
[4] I thank Robert Laubacher for bringing this literature to my attention.

social networks (such as MySpace, Facebook, Google+, and Twitter) and their implications in terms of collective wisdom. The point of such networks may not explicitly be to produce any kind of collective answer to a given individual or collective problem, but it does not seem far-fetched to suppose that they can contribute to the formation of such answers in indirect ways. I would hypothesize that these networking interactions and the information they convey can contribute to reducing pluralistic ignorance[5] and dispelling some common yet erroneous beliefs among communities that extend beyond the traditional circle of friends living in the same neighborhood or the same city.[6] It might be, of course, that under some circumstances, these social interfaces actually amplify polarization and biases, but it is by no means necessary. On the contrary, the multiplication of "weak ties" (Granovetter 1973) to very different people that these networks favor makes it unlikely. For example, Facebook's loose definition of who counts as a "friend" actually ensures that you include in your network not just close people who think exactly like you, but a lot of vague acquaintances whose views may be extremely diverse. It is through these weak ties that individuals can gain access to information from distant parts of the social system rather than be confined to the news and views of their close friends. One could thus argue that social networks prepare the ground for higher-quality collective decisions. Unfortunately, the owl of academia takes its flight too late in these times of lightning-speed technological change, and we perhaps spared ourselves the discomfort of utter outdatedness by not taking on that extra dimension of the topic, although the question of social networks and "networked publics" (Varnelis 2008) is definitely in need of more research.[7]

All in all, I would argue that the new "collective wisdom" is not just the old one writ large. The Internet-based technological revolution that has taken place over the past twenty years is changing the reality of human affairs and interactions. The explosion of the literature on collective intelligence has already affected the way business and politics are conducted, spreading the view that, in an increasingly complex and connected world, knowledge and smart solutions are more likely to emerge from the bottom up, among groups of regular

---

[5] "Pluralistic ignorance" refers to a situation in which a majority of group members privately reject a norm but assume incorrectly that most others accept it, which provides support for a norm that may in fact be disliked by a majority of people. For example, most people, prior to their experience on Facebook, probably thought that everyone else morally objected to the exhibition of one's private life, through pictures, among other things, as a form of despicable narcissism.

[6] Such as, trivially, the belief that you cannot be both a serious employee and a goofy person or, more significantly, the belief that other citizens subscribe to repressive government policies when in fact they share a common rejection and fear of the existing authorities. For an example of the usefulness of Facebook in reducing pluralistic ignorance in potentially revolutionary ways, see its usage in the Arab world: http://www.nytimes.com/2009/01/25/magazine/25bloggers-t.html?_r=5&pagewanted=1&emc=eta1.

[7] For a recent, exciting take on social networks, see papers by danah boyd, e.g., her doctoral thesis, "Taken Out of Context" (2008), http://www.danah.org/papers/TakenOutOfContext.pdf.

people, than to be produced at the top by a few experts.[8] It is now time for the theory to catch up with the practice.

The goal of this edited volume is to go beyond the accumulation of anecdotes and vague intuitions about collective wisdom and to offer the first attempt at a systematic and scholarly inquiry into the nature of the phenomenon. The focus is more specifically on the "principles" and "mechanisms" of collective wisdom. Very roughly speaking, one can say that the principles are at least two: individual intelligence (or, depending on the contributors, ability, sophistication, or epistemic competence) and cognitive diversity. The mechanisms involved are many (also depending on what the contributors mean by "mechanisms"), but they roughly fall into either of two categories: deliberative practices, on the one hand, and aggregation procedures that do not require actual communication or an exchange of views among the participants, such as information markets and voting, on the other. The volume also includes contributions concerned with applications and institutional design.

Let me say a word here about the importance of "cognitive diversity" as a principle of collective wisdom. To some, the idea that a multiplicity of points of view, in which cognitive diversity seems immediately to translate, matters to the quality of the outcome will seem fairly intuitive, and in fact it has been established at least since John Stuart Mill's celebration of freedom of thought in *On Liberty*. We are better off in our collective pursuit of truth, Mill argued, if all of us are free to speak our minds, so that (1) we do not risk silencing true opinions by mistaking them for false ones; (2) the bits of truth often contained in wrong opinions can rise to the surface and supplement our received but partial truths; (3) complete and established truths themselves do not turn into dead dogma for lack of having to be proved over and over again against falsehoods; and (4) for lack of being constantly vivified in the mind and soul of individuals by the need to refute critics (*On Liberty*, ch. 2, p. 53). While arguably qualifying as an epistemic liberal, that is, a liberal who thinks that a regime of individual freedoms is conducive to truth, Mill does not elucidate sufficiently the logic that produces truth out of the coexistence and clash of conflicting points of view. The same could be said of James Surowiecki's (2004) book, which certainly lists diversity as a key factor but lumps together all sorts of diversity and merely registers some factual evidence in favor of these forms of diversity. Similarly, Cass Sunstein (2002, 2006) suggests that social diversity is conducive to a more diverse pool of arguments, which is useful to avoid polarization effects, but ends up registering a mere correlation, not a causal effect. I would argue that Lu Hong and Scott Page's work, on the other hand, goes some notable way toward elucidating the puzzle of why a diversity of viewpoints matters for the quality of collective outcomes. By looking closely at the microfoundations of collective intelligence, their work emphasizes that only a certain type of diversity is good: what they call "cognitive diversity," or the existence in a group

---

[8] See, e.g., the work conducted by Tom Atlee and his peers at the Co-Intelligence Institute. http://www.co-intelligence.org/index.html.

of different interpretive and predictive models used by individuals to navigate the world. This fundamental diversity in the way people treat information and produce arguments will often translate into a variety of viewpoints but is not reducible to them, no more than a variety of processes can be reduced to the variety of outcomes they may result in. Hong and Page also crucially distinguish among different contexts for collective intelligence. They show that, in predictive settings, cognitive diversity matters as much as individual ability. For problem solving, however, cognitive diversity matters *more* than individual ability.[9] In other words, in some contexts, ensuring enough cognitive diversity may offset the lack of brilliant minds in a group. These rather counterintuitive conclusions are not just new and mind-boggling. They open new avenues for research and, if true, entail far-reaching social, economic, legal, and political implications.

In the remainder of this introduction, I will explain the choice of "collective wisdom" as the title of the volume and then give a brief overview of each contribution and point out ways in which the essays respond to each other or leave room for further research.

COLLECTIVE WISDOM

As the editors of this collection of essays, Jon Elster and I have used the term "collective wisdom" rather than "collective intelligence" or "wisdom of the crowds" or "wisdom of the multitude." Although some of the authors in this volume use these expressions interchangeably, we do think that there is a distinction between the terms "wisdom" and "intelligence," as there is a distinction between a group and a crowd or between a collective and a mere multitude.

We first privileged "wisdom" over "intelligence" because it seemed to us that the notion of wisdom – however vague and antiquated in some ways – was a more encompassing notion than the apparently more technical concept of intelligence, offering as a result more common ground for people coming from different disciplines. To an extent, we also wanted to avoid suggesting that the volume is about information technologies or computer sciences, which are the disciplines often associated with the concept of intelligence (as in "artificial intelligence"). While the questions raised in those fields should certainly be on the horizon of any study of collective wisdom, we for the most part steered clear of that more technical path.[10]

---

[9] In other words, when the issue is to solve a collective problem of some complexity, it matters more for the emergence of a good collective answer that we add diversely thinking individuals to the group than yet another member of "the best and the brightest."

[10] See instead the work of researchers at the MIT Center for Collective Intelligence, who specifically focus on the interface between human intelligence and the computer: http://cci.mit.edu/.

This is not to say, far from it, that we reject the concept of intelligence, at least understood broadly as the ability to comprehend one's surroundings and to figure out what to do, as opposed to mere book learning or test-taking smarts (i.e., intelligence as mere IQ). Some of the essays in this volume thus resort to a concept of "collective intelligence" as such a complex notion of intelligence premised of groups as opposed to individuals.

Another advantage of the notion of "wisdom" over that of "intelligence" is that whereas intelligence may seem to refer to the here and now, wisdom evokes a larger temporal horizon. The idea of wisdom suggests the intelligence of a collective extending not just through space (including many people) but through time as well (including many generations), thus making room for both experience and memory – as they are transmitted, for example, in proverbs and sayings or preserved by institutions such as constitutions or museums – and perhaps making room also for the ability to project the impact of one's actions into the future. Few of the essays develop the temporal or diachronic dimension of collective wisdom, but it is clearly an element of the problem. Another question oriented toward the future would be: How do we maximize our chances that apparently intelligent decisions taken today will turn out to be wise for the seventh generation after us?

The concept of wisdom was also chosen over that of rationality. Never a serious contender in our view, the concept of rationality has a major pull in disciplines like economics, political sciences, and the law. Yet it seems to us that rationality is not the most adequate concept to describe phenomena such as the predictive accuracy of information markets, the descriptive correctness of Wikipedia entries, or the rightness of decisions and choices made by deliberating groups or majorities. The notion of wisdom implies a commitment to the view that there is something substantially right or correct, perhaps even "true," about the decisions reached. In effect, it implies some judgment about the morality of the content of those decisions. Rationality, by contrast, is more often used in contexts where coherence and formal correctness, rather than substantive (moral) truth or rightness, are all that matters. The concept of rationality also gives too central a role to the faculty of reason, whereas wisdom makes room for habit, tradition, perhaps even certain forms of emotions or, as Hume would put it, "calm passions."

As to the adjective "collective" in "collective wisdom," the term needs a justification of its own, especially in relation to the rival notions of "wisdom of the crowds" or "distributed intelligence." First, it should be noted that a collective can refer to the sum of its parts or something else altogether. Our title leaves both interpretations open. Many of the contributors, however, defend collective wisdom as more than a direct function of individual wisdom and in effect something of an emergent or supervenient phenomenon, of a different nature or quality than what may or may not be observed at the level of individuals. As Lu Hong and Scott Page argue, for example, an essential ingredient of collective wisdom is the cognitive diversity of the group, a property that, by definition and unlike individual ability, cannot be found in individuals.[11]

Second, "collective" wisdom can also be understood as a distributed phenomenon. In computer sciences and cognitive sciences, distributed intelligence or distributed cognition refers to a decentralized way of processing information and solving problems. More specifically, in cognitive sciences, distributed intelligence refers to cognitive processes that are stretched across individuals and their different components (mind, body, and activity) as well as culturally organized settings, including groups and institutions (Lave 1981: 1).[12] Distributed cognition thus refers to an emergent phenomenon that cannot be traced simply to individual minds, but rather to the interaction between those minds and between them and their constructed environment (which plays the role of extending their cognitive capacities).

Conceptualizing collective wisdom as a potentially distributed phenomenon is important in two respects. First, it suggests that collective wisdom is an emergent phenomenon rather than the amplification of individual wisdom.

As mentioned earlier, collective wisdom can be understood as an amplification of individuals' cognitive abilities, performing for individuals' wisdom what a megaphone, say, does for an individual's voice, namely intensifying it. This intensity is, perhaps, what a certain type of deliberation is meant to achieve, publicizing as an end result of debates among individuals the knowledge of a few members of the group and enlightening the rest about the nature of a problem and its potential solutions. In this case, collective wisdom is just the wisdom of an individual appropriated by the group. Or collective wisdom can be understood as something different from individual wisdom publicized and writ large and, indeed, as an emergent and systemic property that can be distributed across the members of a group and their institutional environment, their culture, their historical heritage, as well as their communication technologies, their media, and their information systems.

Viewing collective wisdom as a distributed phenomenon also precludes the view of collective wisdom as necessarily involving a central authority. Whereas a particular mechanism – whether an information market yielding a prediction, an algorithm, or a decision procedure – is required to express a particular

---

[11] Notice that while emphasizing that the diversity of a group cannot be found in individuals, I am not ruling out the possibility that individuals themselves can be wise to the extent that they have themselves a form of internal cognitive diversity, being, for example, able to view things from multiple perspectives and even to hold as equally valid seemingly contradictory propositions. One might further hypothesize that individuals are "wise" to the extent that they have internalized the collective wisdom of the group they belong to, as opposed to being merely "intelligent" in a narrowly individualistic sense (I owe this idea to Hugo Mercier).

[12] A famous study by the cognitive anthropologist Edwin Hutchins (1995) shows, for example, how the computation involved in steering a large ship does not take place in the head of any particular individual, not even the captain, but in the coordination of the minds of different individuals equipped with navigational artifacts, such as landmarks, maps, phone circuits, and organizational roles. The relevant cognitive unit in this case is no particular individual, but the system "crew + relevant cognitive artifacts" as a whole.

result or view produced by collective intelligence, collective wisdom itself need not be located in any particular unified center, whether a central committee or the head of a particular individual. The expression "collective wisdom" should thus be understood as a broad umbrella for both decentralized "wisdom of the crowds" phenomena, such as information markets and Google, and more classically centralized deliberative exchanges, such as those of a panel of experts. Intermediary scenarios – where collective wisdom is partly centralized, partly decentralized – are also conceivable. Wikipedia probably falls into the latter category, involving decentralized clusters of deliberating groups.

Wisdom and Truth

This volume for the most part leaves outside of its scope an important philosophical problem, which is that of the standard for wisdom and more specifically the standard for wise choices, decisions, or answers. Not every group decision or collective phenomenon is wise, and in that sense, there must be a procedure-independent standard by which to assess where and when the crowd or the group goes right or wrong. As said earlier, the idea of wisdom, collective or not, does seem to commit us to a thick standard by which to assess the quality of a decision or a judgment – something more than mere coherence or formal rationality. In most of the essays, the standard is simply posited and assumed without being further discussed. It is implicitly defined by the context: the reality of verifiable events for information markets; factual, historical, and scientific truth for Wikipedia entries; actual quality of the references and products for Google or eBay; actual quality of the decisions for deliberating groups. As we move from factual to moral and political questions, however, the standard becomes fuzzier and it becomes harder to assess whether it has been met. In the case of information markets, Oscars or election predictions are verified or fail to be verified empirically at a given point in time. In the case of Wikipedia, the degree of accuracy can be measured by comparing Wikipedia entries with those found in expert-written encyclopedias. For some entries, however, an expert-produced proxy for the "right" answer might not be readily available (expert-written encyclopedias rarely include entries on Paris Hilton or the latest hot political issue). Finally, there are questions where what we are trying to ascertain is not just the facts of the matter, or some causal relationship on which there might exist or come to exist a consensus among experts, but the moral validity of certain judgments. In such cases, the procedure-independent standard can only be postulated, not a priori identified.[13] It can be tempting in such cases to deny that it makes sense to speak of a procedure-independent standard of correctness. In politics, in particular, this might seem to mean that there is no truth beyond what the local consensus of a given people is at any

---

[13] One could perhaps assume that the immorality of torture or racism serves as a local "fixed point" (to borrow Rawls's terminology) of our moral reasoning. Yet most moral and political questions are located in a gray zone where such fixed points are not available.

given time or, to put it in the words of contemporary Sophist Stephen Colbert, there is nothing but "truthiness."[14]

Some of the essays in this volume that specifically address the question of collective wisdom in relation to democracy endorse an epistemic approach to democracy – that is, a view of democracy premised on the assumption that there exists a procedure-independent standard by which to assess the quality of collective decisions. None of these contributions, however, devote much space to defending this assumption or interpreting all the potential meanings of a procedure-independent standard of correctness in moral and political matters. The standard for moral and political wisdom is generally posited to be a necessary premise, but it is in general little more than a placeholder and does not commit the contributors to a specific moral or metaphysical view. In particular, most of the authors remain agnostic as to whether the standard should be considered a universally valid truth, and what the relevant conception of truth would be in that case, or a context-dependent social construction.[15]

Principles and Mechanisms

This volume sets out to uncover the principles and mechanisms of collective wisdom. By "principles," we mean the theoretical logic and rules undergirding

[14] Abramowicz makes the interesting suggestion in his book *Predictocracy: Market Mechanisms for Public and Private Decision-Making* (2007) that we should use as a proxy for the standard of the "right" moral decision the actual decision to be made in the distant future by the head of some respected political institution or administration, which we think is moving in the direction of what we have to assume is moral progress of some kind. In the same diachronic vein, one could imagine that the standard could be the consensus of a more advanced society similar to ours. These ideas, of course, presuppose that there is such a thing as moral progress and an ability to agree on which institutions or societies embody it, at least for a given question.

[15] For a more direct treatment of these questions in democratic theory, see, e.g., the work of David Estlund (1997, 2008), Alvin Goldman (1999, ch. 7 on democracy), Joseph Raz (1990), and Robert Talisse (2009). I would also mention my own work on the topic (Landemore in press, specifically the chapter entitled "Political Cognitivism: A Defense"). For an empirical approach to the standard of expert political judgments on foreign policy that can prove suggestive in assessing the judgments of groups of nonexperts, also see Philip Tetlock (2005). Finally, a large philosophical literature in the field of social epistemology addresses, among other things, the question of the meaning of truth in both the sciences and morality. For deeper philosophical investigations into the meaning of knowledge, information, and truth, and debates between "classical" social epistemologists (who focus on the epistemic goal of having true or at least justified beliefs) and "anticlassical" or postmodernist social epistemologists (who have no use for the concepts of truth and justification), see the landmarks in that field (e.g., Steve Fuller 1987, 1988, 1999; Alvin Goldman 1986, 1987, 1999; Philip Kitcher 1990, 1993, 2001), as well as publications in relevant journals (*Synthese, Episteme: A Journal of Social Epistemology*, and *Social Epistemology: A Journal of Knowledge, Culture, and Policy*). While many essays in this volume, and perhaps the volume as a whole, qualify as contributions to social epistemology, neither the contributions nor the volume as a whole were intended specifically as such. For a survey and discussion of the questions addressed by social epistemologists, see Goldman's (2006) article, "Social Epistemology," in the *Stanford Encyclopedia of Philosophy*, http://plato .stanford.edu/entries/epistemology-social/.

the phenomenon. Those are best expressed in theorems and models and anything that can count as the microfoundations of collective wisdom. Three main theoretical accounts are considered: (1) the Condorcet Jury Theorem, which is generally used in defense of the epistemic properties of majority rule; (2) the "miracle of aggregation," or the idea that symmetric mistakes around the right answer cancel each other out in the aggregate; and (3) Lu Hong and Scott Page's modeling of collective wisdom as a function of both individual ability and cognitive diversity.

The Condorcet Jury Theorem (CJT) is perhaps the most well known of the three. It establishes that among large electorates voting on some yes or no question, majoritarian outcomes are virtually certain to track the "truth," so long as three conditions hold: (1) voters are better than random at choosing true propositions; (2) they vote independently of each other; and (3) they vote sincerely or truthfully.[16] The CJT, first formulated by the Marquis de Condorcet in 1785 and rediscovered by Duncan Black in the 1950s, has spawned many formal analyses in recent decades. These analyses, however, usually fall short of drawing substantive normative implications, in part because the CJT is generally considered of little relevance to the real world. Its assumptions are analyzed as pure mathematical technicalities with no matching real-life application (e.g., Ladha 1992). Meanwhile, philosophers remain unsure of the usefulness of the Condorcet theorem for democratic theory. Even David Estlund, an unambiguous advocate of an (at least partially) epistemic theory of democracy, who repeatedly mentions the CJT in support of the superiority of majoritarian decisions over alternative decision rules, ends up distancing himself from the theorem as "less than trustworthy" (Estlund 1997: 189) and more recently as entirely "irrelevant" (Estlund 2008: ch. 12).

The "miracle of aggregation" (Converse 1990) is another statistical explanation, distinct from the CJT, although also dependent on the law of large numbers. The most established version of the "miracle of aggregation" explains collective intelligence as the statistical phenomenon by which a few informed people in a group are all it takes to guide the group to the right answer, if uninformed people's answers are randomly distributed around the right answer and thus cancel each other out. This "elitist" version goes back perhaps to Berelson et al. (1954). Here collective intelligence actually depends on extracting the information held by an informed elite (say "the attentive public," which represents at best 10 percent of the population) from the mass of "noise" represented by other people's random opinions.

A more democratic version of the miracle of aggregation, however, presents things slightly differently. On Page and Shapiro's account (1992), for example,

---

[16] To briefly illustrate the power of large numbers harnessed by majority rule according to the CJT, consider 10 voters, each of whom has a .51 probability of being correct on any yes or no question. A majority of 6 will have a 52% chance of being right. Expand now the group to 1,000 people, and a majority of 600 is almost 100% sure to be right. This is merely an implication of what is also known as the "Central Limit Theorem."

there are meaningful opinions within each individual surrounded by noise, and aggregation across individuals is what produces an aggregation of those real opinions. While the idea of "distributed intelligence" hardly applies to the elitist model of the miracle of aggregation (since technically the "intelligence" is concentrated in a few individuals only), it applies well to this latter, democratic version. In any case, the miracle of aggregation is sometimes presented as a better explanation of collective intelligence than the traditional explanation in terms of deliberation and the pursuit of rational consensus (e.g., Sunstein 2007: "Deliberating Groups versus Prediction Markets [or Hayek's Challenge to Habermas]").

Some critics, however, have raised serious doubts as to the plausibility of the miracle of aggregation, doubts that seem to apply to both the democratic and the elitist version. The main problem with the miracle of aggregation scenario is that in order for the "miracle" to occur, one has to assume that there is a symmetrical distribution of errors around the right answer. Bryan Caplan (2007) suggests that this assumption is wildly implausible and that people are more likely to be systematically biased in the same direction (suffering among other things from "antimarket" and "protectionist" biases). At the collective level, these individual biases can aggregate into massive political mistakes.

Scott Page has offered a third account in a book that sees "cognitive diversity" as key to group intelligence (Page 2007). By cognitive "diversity," Page means the fact that people come equipped with different ways of seeing the world and interpreting problems and questions in it. Cognitive diversity cashes out in different cognitive tools, called "perspectives" and "heuristics." In his book, Page presents an elegant "Diversity Trumps Ability Theorem," according to which cognitive diversity *always* trumps ability when the problem is hard, the people are smart and diverse, and the group is bigger than a handful and chosen from a large population (Page 2007: 162; see also Hong and Page 2001, 2004). I mention this result because in Lu Hong and Scott Page's essay in this volume, they focus only on the problem of prediction and information aggregation, where cognitive diversity matters just as much as (and not more than) individual ability. In any case, what is symptomatic of their approach is the fact that so far as information aggregation and prediction are concerned, neither the Condorcet Jury Theorem nor the miracle of aggregation features prominently in their theoretical explanation of collective intelligence.[17]

"Mechanisms" is a loose term by which we mean to refer to the concrete institutions that channel collective wisdom, such as expert committees, deliberative assemblies, deliberative communities like Wikipedia, majority rule, information markets, or the ranking algorithms of search engines such as Google.

---

[17] Page is particularly skeptical of the "averaging-of-noise model," which, according to him "fails as a model of prediction" because it leaves unexplained why one should make the heroic assumption that people's guesses are drawn from a distribution that has the correct mean and independent errors (Page 2007: 194).

Since Aristotle, deliberation has perhaps been the most frequently considered mechanism. Deliberative synergies are supposed to appear when many people pool their information and arguments, thus guiding each other to the most accurate picture of the situation, and/or the best argument or "rational consensus," and/or the "global optimum" of a given situation (e.g., Nino 1996; Habermas 2006; Page 2007; Estlund 2008). In contexts where no deliberation is feasible or relevant, however, other practices or mechanisms have to do the work. All the essays in this volume explore the potential of different mechanisms.

A REVIEW OF THE ESSAYS

There is no unique or clear principle behind the order of the contributions, which follows for the most part the order in which the papers were given at the conference on which this book is based. The volume begins with concrete contemporary examples of collective wisdom – information markets, Google, eBay, Wikipedia – in the essays by Emile Servan-Schreiber and Gloria Origgi. Most of these examples are aggregative in nature, with the exception of Wikipedia, which presents some central deliberative features. Lu Hong and Scott Page's essay turns to the study of the microfoundations of the aggregative side of collective wisdom. Daniel Andler's and John Ferejohn's essays then take a philosophical step back to shed some light on the meaning of, respectively, the terms "wisdom" and "collective" in the idea of "collective wisdom." They are followed by what may count as three case studies of a number of institutions channeling collective wisdom: the institutions of Athenian democracy in Josiah Ober's essay, constitutional assemblies in Jon Elster's, and expert committees in Philippe Urfalino's. In these case studies, deliberation is the central mechanism of collective wisdom. Christian List's essay changes the focus from the question of the accuracy of collective wisdom to that of its coherence. The group of essays by David Estlund, Hélène Landemore, Gerry Mackie, Bryan Caplan, and Adrian Vermeule center more specifically on the application of the idea of collective wisdom to democracy and the institutional reforms that the possibility of collective wisdom may or may not suggest. Finally, Dan Sperber and Hugo Mercier's essay offers an evolutionary twist to the idea of collective wisdom, suggesting that human reasoning is, first and foremost, an individual competence best deployed in social contexts.

AN INTRODUCTION TO THE ESSAYS

In Chapter 1, Emile Servan-Schreiber focuses on information markets, a particular judgment and information aggregation procedure capable of predicting future events – such as weather, a movie's opening income, or election results – by pooling the guesses of many individuals. Emphasizing the economic, mathematical, and neurological foundations of this form of collective wisdom, he argues that although the design of the trading mechanism matters, the ultimate driver of predictive accuracy is the betting proposition itself. A wager at the same time attracts contrarians who introduce a diversity of opinions into the mix, leading to a collective prediction and promoting dispassionate thinking (because of the financial incentive), which increases the quality of each aggregated opinion.

In Chapter 2, Gloria Origgi examines "reputation" as a key ingredient of collective processes of knowledge. She studies the mechanisms of "rating" and "ranking" information on the Web, taking as examples the functioning of Google, eBay, Amazon, and Wikipedia. She predicts that the information age will ultimately give way to a more sophisticated "reputation age," in which reputation serves as a rational criterion of information extraction. According to Origgi, those collective wisdom systems that have access to individuals' judgments and ranking of information are most effective at producing relevant knowledge in an increasingly complex, uncertain, and networked environment.

In Chapter 3, Lu Hong and Scott Page build on their previous work on the microfoundations of collective wisdom to account mathematically for the conditions that sustain or undermine collective wisdom. Their essay further unpacks their claim on the particular question of judgment aggregation – rather than problem solving, which they developed in their earlier work. They argue that from a synchronic perspective (without prior or further deliberation), the group will always be more "wise," that is, accurate, than its *average* member (a result that obtained in their previous work) and, in some circumstances, *more* accurate than *any* of its members (a new result). As in their previous work, they use what they call a "cognitive model" of collective wisdom, which complicates and extends traditional statistical approaches in social science. This difference allows their model to bring out the importance of cognitive diversity for the emergence of collective wisdom.

In Chapter 4, Daniel Andler addresses the meaning of "wisdom" in "collective wisdom" from a philosophical angle. Is collective wisdom, or the wisdom of crowds, really the same as the wisdom of an individual, just writ larger? Andler's answer is largely negative: collective wisdom has not much to do with wisdom, beyond differing from individual intelligence. According to him, the only thing that "collective wisdom" can meaningfully refer to is a set of culturally transmitted beliefs and practices – the wisdom of past generations as it has been accumulated over time and inherited by each of us. He objects to calling "wisdom" the kind of judgment accuracy reached by the crowds operating, for example, in information markets.

John Ferejohn's philosophical inquiry in Chapter 5 bears on the "collective" aspect of "collective wisdom." He addresses the question of whether it is meaningful to think of "collective intentions," such as the intention of a nation, the Supreme Court, or – his focus – the legislature. Ferejohn argues in favor of the meaningfulness of such collective concepts, although he falls short of committing himself to a holistic ontology. He presents his theory of legislative intention as a more classical theory of democratic deliberation.

Josiah Ober, in Chapter 6, identifies diversity and sophistication as crucial to the production of collective wisdom, but he demonstrates this on the basis of a detailed historical analysis of some of the most important Athenian institutions. Ober strikingly describes ancient Athens as a "participatory epistemic democracy" and argues that it outperformed its thousand or so rival city-states, including Sparta, thanks to its superior ability to tap into collective wisdom, whether in terms of problem solving, knowledge and information aggregation, predictive abilities, or mere social cooperation. Ober shows that the Athenian constitution incorporated (consciously or not) design features promoting the aggregation of knowledge. He also shows how, specifically, two democratic institutions – the Council of 500 and the practice of "ostracism" – worked as mechanisms of collective wisdom. The Council of 500 functioned as a deliberative mechanism for solving collective problems. Ostracism functioned as a "preclusive prediction market," whereby a plurality of guesses could preclude a possible future that was regarded by most Athenians, at a given moment, as particularly dangerous. Ober emphasizes that the size of Athens and the importance of social diversity were key ingredients of collective wisdom in the context of such democratic institutions.

In Chapter 7, Jon Elster focuses on the process and conditions leading to the production of a good constitution and is thus interested in the question of institutional design. Although Elster professes to remain agnostic as to the nature of the optimal constitution, he identifies a number of features of the constitution-making process likely to induce biases. Among the features that it is important to control for are the number of delegates, the mode of (s)election of the delegates, the diversity of preferences and information, and the presence of passions and interests. His main recommendations are to control for those factors and to complement the constitution-making process with two deliberative moments prior to and subsequent to the constitutional moment: a wide public deliberation before the assembly meets and a referendum on the ensuing proposal.

In Chapter 8, Philippe Urfalino analyzes the tension between numbers and reason within two expert committees, which he calls "areopagi": the French drug approval committee and the U.S. Food and Drug Administration. In order to ensure that cooperation among several experts culminates in a collective decision or opinion of high quality, Urfalino argues that two problems must be solved: one must first pick a judgment aggregation procedure and then maximize the epistemic performance of that procedure. In addition to the comparative dimension between an American and a French areopagus, Urfalino develops a comparison across time, between those two areopagi, on the one hand, and the Catholic Church, on the other. One of the interesting conclusions of that two-dimensional comparison is that the common point between the French approach of "exhausting objections" and the U.S. practice of "public balloting" is that both combine the medieval use of sanior pars (reason) and maior pars (number).

In Chapter 9, Christian List addresses the question of collective wisdom from the angle of "coherence" rather than "correspondence" (or rationality rather than knowledge or accuracy or truth). List argues that a necessary condition for wisdom is not just to produce judgments that are "accurate" or "true" in the sense of meeting some procedure-independent standard (the concern of most of the other essays), but to produce judgments that are coherent among each other. By "coherence," List means a minimal logical consistency. According to List, even a good factual accuracy of some of the judgments of a panel of experts, for example, would not be enough to compensate for certain violations of coherence. In other words, List argues that coherence as a form of rationality must be part of collective wisdom. Armed with that claim, he goes on to demonstrate that the apparently dispiriting results of the literature on judgment aggregation (which he distinguishes from and opposes to the literature on the Condorcet Jury Theorem) need not threaten the possibility that collective judgments can be wise in the sense of coherent.

David Estlund's essay (Chapter 10) is a philosophical reflection on the moral significance of numbers in normative democratic theory. Equating democracy with inalienable popular sovereignty, he argues that this definition does not say anything in terms of the number of decision makers. In other words, democracy need not translate into rule of all, the many, or even the majority. Estlund considers a series of expanding and shrinking factors in light of their epistemic properties and their democratic credentials. The aim is to exhibit some of the complexity about numbers that remains even when the principle of democracy is taken for granted.

Starting from a different definition of democracy as a collective decision rule involving the many, Hélène Landemore argues in Chapter 11 that, under the right conditions, democracy is epistemically superior to any variant of the rule of the few because of the maximal cognitive diversity that democratic inclusiveness entails. In order to support this strong epistemic claim, Landemore considers several accounts of the complementary epistemic properties of two democratic mechanisms (inclusive deliberation and majority rule), including the Condorcet Jury Theorem, the miracle of aggregation, and – the account Landemore ultimately privileges – Lu Hong and Scott Page's cognitive model of problem solving and prediction. In the process, she takes aim at Caplan's attack on democratic decision making as flawed by the problem of systematic biases and "rational irrationality," arguing that Caplan's approach is intrinsically elitist and begs the question of who has authority to rule in politics in the first place.

Gerry Mackie, in Chapter 12, focuses specifically on the theory of the rationally ignorant voter, criticizing economic theory more generally for drawing a false opposition between the market and politics. Whereas economists believe that the wisdom of crowds nicely applies to the logic of the market, they generally oppose the application of the same idea to politics, assuming on the part of the average voter either "rational ignorance" or, more recently with Bryan Caplan, "rational irrationality." After tracing the history of that antidemocratic argument in a tradition running from Plato to Gustave Le Bon and Schumpeter, Mackie proposes a "contributory model" of voting, which he opposes to the dominant "pivotal" approach, in which it is irrational for an individual to vote unless he or she is pivotal to the outcome of the election. Unlike the pivotalist model, Mackie argues, the contributory model is compatible with the empirical fact that many people vote and the actual reasons given by these same individuals for voting. Using this contributory model, Mackie challenges the economic hypothesis of rational ignorance and rational irrationality.

Bryan Caplan's essay (Chapter 13) is a three-part reply to his critics: Estlund, Landemore, and Mackie. Against Estlund, Caplan argues that he cannot accept a noninstrumental justification of political authority. Against Landemore, Caplan expresses skepticism toward the claim that democracy is epistemically superior to the rule of the few, asking for more empirical and theoretical evidence and rejecting the idea of a procedure-independent standard of good or right political judgments that would be distinct from expert judgment. In his reply to Mackie, Caplan admits that more empirical research must be conducted on the comparison between voters' and consumers' rationality and knowledge, but he remains unconvinced by the actual evidence adduced by Mackie, further objecting to Mackie's defense of the rationality of certain religious dogmas.

Adrian Vermeule's essay (Chapter 14) proposes legal institutional reforms meant to generate and exploit collective wisdom where it exists. Assuming that the social goal is to maximize the epistemic quality of the laws, Vermeule argues for a shift of constitutional lawmaking authority from courts to Congress and the executive, for the appointment of nonlawyers to the Supreme Court, and for an expansion of Congress's membership. He also outlines the trade-offs between epistemic and nonepistemic values, such as the costs of decision making, the aggregation of preferences, and the perceived legitimacy of the legal system.[18]

In Chapter 15, Dan Sperber and Hugo Mercier argue that contrary to what is generally taken for granted, the function of reasoning is not to enhance individual cognition – individuals are often better off following their intuition than reasoning; rather, reasoning is primarily social. In other words, its function is to produce arguments in order to convince others and to evaluate arguments others use in order to convince us. They show how this view of reasoning as a

---

[18] Adrian Vermeule came to the conference skeptical of what he called at the time, after Sunstein, "many-minds arguments" and delivered a paper in which he expressed his doubt about their usefulness for legal theory ("Many-Minds Arguments in Legal Theory," http://papers .ssrn.com/sol3/papers.cfm?abstract_id=1087017, now Vermeule 2009a). It is worth noting that in his entirely rewritten contribution to the volume, as well as in his later book (2009b), Vermeule has changed his mind and advocates democratizing representative institutions, including the Supreme Court, for some of the epistemic reasons that were discussed at the 2008 Paris conference (in particular the role of cognitive diversity). Vermeule acknowledges the role of the conference in "clarifying some key points" in a note at the end of his book (Vermeule 2009b: 195).

form of social competence correctly predicts both good and bad performance in the individual and in the collective case, and helps explain a variety of psychological and sociological phenomena.

Bibliography

Aristotle. 1998. *Politics*. Trans. C. D. C. Reeve. Indianapolis: Hackett.

Abramowicz, Michael. 2007. *Predictocracy, Market Mechanisms for Public and Private Decision-Making*. New Haven, CT: Yale University Press.

Atlee, Tom. 2002/2003. *The Tao of Democracy: Using Co-intelligence to Create a World That Works for All*. North Charleston, SC: Imprint Books.

Berelson, Bernard R., Paul F. Lazarsfeld, and William N. McPhee. 1954. *Voting: A Study of Opinion Formation in a Presidential Campaign*. Chicago: University of Chicago Press.

boyd, danah. 2008. "Taken Out of Context: American Teen Sociality in Networked Publics." PhD dissertation, University of California–Berkeley, School of Information.

Caplan, Bryan. 2007. *The Myth of the Rational Voter: Why Democracies Choose Bad Policies*. Princeton, NJ: Princeton University Press.

Converse, Philip. 1990. "Popular Representation and the Distribution of Information." In J. A. Ferejohn and J. H. Kuklinski (eds.), *Information and Democratic Processes*, 369–88. Urbana: University of Illinois Press.

Estlund, David. 2008. *Democratic Authority: A Philosophical Framework*. Princeton, NJ: Princeton University Press.

1997. "Beyond Fairness and Deliberation: The Epistemic Dimension of Democratic Authority." In James Bohman and William Rehg, eds., *Deliberative Democracy*, 173–204. Cambridge, MA: MIT Press.

Foglia, Marc (ed.). 2008. *Wikipédia, média de la connaissance démocratique. Quand le citoyen lambda devient encyclopédiste*. Paris: FYP Éditions.

Fuller, Steve. 1999. *The Governance of Science: Ideology and the Future of the Open Society*. London: Open University Press.

1993. *Philosophy, Rhetoric, and the End of Knowledge*. Madison: University of Wisconsin Press.

1988. *Social Epistemology*. Bloomington: Indiana University Press.

1987. "On Regulating What Is Known: A Way to Social Epistemology." *Synthese* 73 (1): 145–83.

Goldman, Alvin. 1999. *Knowledge in a Social World*. Oxford: Oxford University Press.

1987. "Foundations of Social Epistemics." *Synthese* 73: 109–44.

1986. *Epistemology and Cognition*. Cambridge, MA: Harvard University Press.

Gottfredson, L. S. (ed.). 1997. "Intelligence and Social Policy." *Intelligence* 24 (1) (Special issue).

Granovetter, M. S. 1973. "The Strength of Weak Ties." *American Journal of Sociology* 78 (6): 1360–80.

Habermas, Jürgen. 2006. "Political Communication in Media Society: Does Democracy Still Enjoy an Epistemic Dimension? The Impact of Normative Theory on Empirical Research." *Communication Theory* 16 (4): 411–26.

Hong, Lu, and Scott Page. 2009. "Interpreted and Generated Signals." *Journal of Economic Theory* 144 (5): 2174–96.

2004. "Groups of Diverse Problem Solvers Can Outperform Groups of High-Ability Problem Solvers." *Proceedings of the National Academy of Sciences* 101 (46): 16385–89.

2001. "Problem Solving by Heterogeneous Agents." *Journal of Economic Theory* 97 (1): 123–63.

Howe, Jeff. 2008. *Crowd-Sourcing: Why the Power of the Crowd Is Driving the Future of Business*. New York: Random House.

Hutchins, Edwin. 1995. *Cognition in the Wild*. Cambridge, MA: MIT Press.

Kitcher, Philip. 2001. *Science, Truth, and Democracy*. Oxford: Oxford University Press.

1993. *The Advancement of Science*. Oxford: Oxford University Press.

1990. "The Division of Cognitive Labor." *Journal of Philosophy* 87: 5–22.

Ladha, Krishna. 1992. "The Condorcet Jury Theorem, Free Speech, and Correlated Votes." *American Journal of Political Science* 36 (3): 617–64.

Landemore, Hélène. In press. *Democratic Reason: Politics, Collective Intelligence, and the Rule of the Many*. Princeton, NJ: Princeton University Press.

Lave, Jean. 1988. *Cognition in Practice: Mind, Mathematics, and Culture in Everyday Life*. New York: Cambridge University Press.

Leadbeater, Charles. 2008. *We-think: The Power of Mass Creativity*. London: Profile Books.

Libert, Barry, John Spector, and thousands of contributors. 2008. *We are Smarter Than Me: How to Unleash the Power of Crowds in Your Business*. Philadelphia: Wharton School Publishing.

Nambisan, Satish, and Mohanbir Sawhney. 2008. *The Global Brain: Your Roadmap for Innovating Faster and Smarter in a Networked World*. Philadelphia: Wharton School Publishing.

Newman, Mark, Albert-Laszio Baribasi, and Duncan J. Watts (eds.). 2006. *Structure and Dynamics of Networks*. Princeton, NJ: Princeton University Press.

Nino, Carlos S. 1996. *The Constitution of Deliberative Democracy*. New Haven, CT: Yale University Press.

Page, Benjamin, and Robert Y. Shapiro. 1992. *The Rational Public: Fifty Years of Trends in Americans' Policy Preferences*. Chicago: University of Chicago Press.

Page, Scott. 2007. *The Difference: How the Power of Diversity Creates Better Groups, Firms, Schools and Societies*. Princeton, NJ: Princeton University Press.

Raz, Joseph. 1990. "Facing Diversity: The Case of Epistemic Abstinence." *Philosophy and Public Affairs* 19 (1): 3–46.

Rheingold, Howard. 2003. *Smart Mob: The Next Social Revolution*. Cambridge, MA: Perseus.

Sunstein, Cass. 2007. "Deliberating Groups versus Prediction Markets (or Hayek's Challenge to Habermas)." *Episteme: Journal of Social Epistemology* 3: 192–213.

2006. *Infotopia: How Many Minds Produce Knowledge*. Oxford: Oxford University Press.

2002. "The Law of Group Polarization." *Journal of Political Philosophy* 10 (2): 175–95.

Surowiecki, James. 2004. *The Wisdom of Crowds: Why the Many Are Smarter Than the Few and How Collective Wisdom Shapes Business, Economies, Societies and Nations*. New York: Random House.

Talisse, Robert. 2009. *Democracy and Moral Conflict*. Cambridge: Cambridge University Press.

Tapscott, Don, and Anthony D. Williams. 2006. *Wikinomics: How Mass Collaboration Changes Everything*. New York: Penguin Group.

Tetlock, Philip. 2005. *Expert Political Judgment: How Good Is It? How Can We Know?* Princeton, NJ: Princeton University Press.

Varnelis, Kazys (ed.). 2008. *Networked Publics*. Cambridge: MIT Press.

Vermeule, Adrian. 2009a. "Many-Minds Arguments in Legal Theory." *Journal of Legal Analysis* 1: 1–45.

2009b. *Law and the Limits of Reason*. Oxford: Oxford University Press.

Waldron, Jeremy. 1995. "The Wisdom of the Multitude: Some Reflections on Book 3, Chapter 11 of Aristotle's *Politics*." *Political Theory* 23 (4): 563–84.

1

Prediction Markets

Trading Uncertainty for Collective Wisdom

Emile Servan-Schreiber

INTRODUCTION

Collective intelligence in insect societies had long been a source of wonder for the educated mind, but in the first decade of this new century, something remarkable happened: the wide cultural realization that collective intelligence can be efficiently and successfully leveraged in human societies as well.

The notion that, as the Japanese proverb says, "none of us is smarter than all of us" is disturbing to many, perhaps because it knocks the human brain off its pedestal as the most intelligent thing in the universe and thus devalues the *individual* intellect. Indeed, the "discovery" of human collective intelligence may yet launch a revolution of thought as profound as those initiated by Copernicus and Darwin, although, appropriately, no single individual's name may be attached to it.

It is the World Wide Web that has enabled human collective intelligence to burst into the public consciousness. Google, Wikipedia, and online prediction markets are the three poster children of what James Surowiecki (2004) termed "the wisdom of crowds."

For years now, billions of humans have experienced the power of Google's PageRank search algorithm, which relies primarily on the rich network of links from one Web site to another that result from countless individual Webmasters' assessments of which pieces of information are related and worth linking to. Wikipedia, the collaborative encyclopedia, has confounded skeptics with its breadth and depth, so much so that its entries are often found at the top of Google searches.

But whereas Google and Wikipedia are content to aggregate *existing* knowledge, prediction markets take up the challenge of generating reliable knowledge about what is fundamentally unknowable: the future. At this ancestral human pursuit they have proved consistently more adept than the existing alternatives, such as individual experts and opinion polls. This *relative* success has captured the public's imagination and given them a slight aura of "magic"

(Pethokoukis, 2004; Stuart, 2005). It is the purpose of this essay to investigate the sound economic, mathematical, and neurological foundations of this particular form of collective wisdom. It describes various prediction market designs, documents their record of successes, and identifies the ultimate drivers of their performance.

PREDICTION MARKET DESIGN

A prediction market is, at its core, a betting venue. It differs from a classic bookmaker's operation in that it removes the middleman and allows people to bet against each other through a trading system borrowed from the financial stock markets.

A Classic Design: Binary Contracts

One of the most popular market designs proposes "binary contracts" that pay $1 if an event happens or $0 if it does not. People can offer to buy or sell a contract in various quantities at their preferred prices, in a process known as a "continuous double auction." For instance, one trader may offer to buy 15 contracts at $0.60 a piece, while another offers to sell 30 contracts at $0.65. When a buyer and a seller agree on the quantity and the price, the transaction happens. The buyer can then later turn around and resell her contracts at a higher price if she finds a willing buyer, or she can hold onto them until the outcome is decided and the market operator buys back all outstanding contracts at the expiry price of $1 (event happened) or $0 (event did not happen).

While the market is open for trading, speculative profits can be made by anticipating shifts in the collective opinion, buying low and then selling high, or selling high (on credit, also called "shorting") and buying low later.

Rational Trading Behavior

How would a rational trader behave in such a market? At any point in time, he could calculate the expected value of the contract as follows:

$$\textit{Expected value of contract} = \textit{Probability that the event happens} \\ \times \textit{expiry price if it does}$$

So, for instance, if he gave the event a 65 percent chance of happening,

$$\textit{Expected value of contract} = .65 \times \$1 = 65 \textit{ cents}$$

Accordingly, he would be willing to buy contracts that are offered at lower prices and to sell contracts that receive higher bids.

How many contracts he would be willing to buy or sell at the market price would then depend on at least on five things: (1) how much his estimate of the contract's expected value differs from the market price, (2) how certain he is of her estimate, (3) how many contracts are actually available to buy or sell at the market price, (4) how much cash (to buy) or how many contracts (to sell) he has at his disposal, and (5) the opportunity cost of trading this particular outcome's contracts rather than contracts for other outcomes that might be listed concurrently. Different combinations of these factors may yield exactly the same trading behavior, making it difficult for an observer to tell them apart. In practice it is very challenging to infer with any precision what a trader's belief actually is simply by observing her trading behavior.

For instance, if a trader buys contracts at $0.65, all we may infer is that she expects those contracts to be worth more, but we can't tell how much more. All other things being equal, she may be *very confident* that they will be worth *a little bit more*, or she may be *somewhat confident* that they will be worth *a lot more*. In reality, the situation is even more complex because the trade may just be speculative – that is, driven by expectations of how the market will move in the near term rather than by anticipation of the ultimate expiry price.

To Profit: Be Right, Before Others

So long as a trader disagrees with the market price, he has incentives to trade. But he also has incentives to trade as soon as he disagrees with the market price, because the more he waits, the more others are likely to find out what he knows and to take advantage of the market themselves before he does, thereby erasing the profit opportunity. In a prediction market, as in any financial market, it is not enough to *be right* to make a profit; you must also be right *before others*. In this way, the prediction market provides incentives for both timely and truthful revelation of trader opinions.

Market Price as Consensus

As noted before, so long as a trader disagrees with the market price, he has incentives to trade. But it is important to note that each of those trades will tend to move the market price closer to his estimate. In this way, just by trying to profit from a "wrong" market price, the trader shares his opinion with the other traders. In effect, it is impossible to seek to profit from the market without broadcasting information to other traders. That is what enables markets to aggregate the knowledge that is privately held by each trader.

With many traders coming to the market with different probability assessments and different degrees of confidence in their estimates, the trading price eventually settles down to where people "agree to disagree": the equilibrium price at which no one is willing or able to buy or sell. That consensus price holds until some new traders join the market or some new information makes existing traders change their probability assessments, which leads to a new equilibrium. The more disturbing the new information is, the more dramatic the change in price.

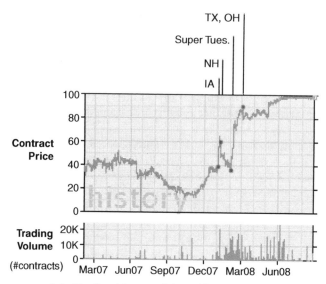

FIGURE 1.1. Trading history of the "Obama to win the Democratic nomination" contract on NewsFutures, from early February 2007 to the Democratic Convention at the end of August 2008. The contract would be worth 100 points if Obama became the nominee or 0 otherwise. Key milestones in the campaign were the Iowa primary (IA), which Obama unexpectedly won, then New Hampshire (NH), which he unexpectedly lost just a week later, then Super Tuesday, when Clinton failed to crush him, then Ohio and Texas, which Clinton both won, but too late. Points indicate trading prices just *before* each milestone.

An Example

Figure 1.1 displays the actual trading history of the "Obama to win the Democratic nomination" contract on NewsFutures, a popular "play-money" prediction market where people trade for prizes and bragging rights. The price of this contract experienced some dramatic changes as the primary race developed and as Obama's various successes and setbacks impacted traders' perception of his prospects.

Binary Contract Price = Event Probability

What is the proper way to extract a prediction from the price of a binary contract? Well, if at any point in time the trading price captures the collective estimation of the contract's expected value, we can directly derive from it the crowd's estimation of the event's probability. For instance, when the contract is trading at 65 cents (or points), it must mean that the market currently "believes" that the event has a 65 percent chance of happening. Empirical evidence that such predictions correlate well with observed event frequencies in the real world will be presented later in the chapter.

When looking at a price chart such as Figure 1.1 that exhibits dramatic price changes, one might wonder if the market is really predicting anything. Since Obama did finally win the nomination, shouldn't his contracts have traded very high, at least higher than 50 percent, or perhaps just higher than all its rivals, *throughout* the campaign? Wasn't the market wrong when it priced Obama in the teens in the fall of 2007? Well, no. At any point in time, the market cannot be faulted for not taking into account *future* developments. In other words, only in a fully deterministic universe could you fault the market for not divining right away the ultimate outcome. Rather, at each point in time there were possible futures in which Obama would win and others in which he would lose, and all of these futures were just as valid, if not as probable. So it may well be that the market was right that, in November 2007, Obama had less than one in five chances of winning and then was right again a few weeks later when, after his victory in Iowa, it gave him two in three chances.

Other Designs: Index Contracts and Winner-Take-All Markets

Other prediction market designs are meant to extract other types of predictions. The two other common designs are the "index" contract and the "winner-take-all" market.

The expiry price of an index contract, instead of being a binary 0 or 1 variable, is a continuous variable that depends on the value of an outcome. For instance, the Iowa Electronic Markets[1] (IEM), a political prediction market run by the University of Iowa's Tippie College of Business, features "vote-share" contracts: each candidate's contract pays 1 cent per percentage of the vote that she obtains. So if 56 percent vote for this candidate, the contract expires at 56 cents (Foresythe et al. 1992). In this design, the trading price captures the mean consensus estimate for a specific variable. Besides vote share, it has been used in various contexts to forecast a company's quarterly sales, the number of bug reports for a software product, or the completion date of a large industrial project. Any continuous quantity can be forecasted in this manner.

In some situations, however, it may be insufficient to forecast just the mean estimate for a variable. One may instead want to extract the full probability distribution for the outcome. The winner-take-all design makes that possible through a combination of several binary contracts. For instance, to predict the sales of a widget, the full range of possible sales outcomes is divided into adjacent intervals, and the market proposes a binary contract for each interval that pays $1 if the interval includes actual sales or $0 otherwise. Since each contract is traded according to the probability that it captures actual sales, the set of prices reveals a probability distribution over the continuum of possible sales outcomes (Chen and Plott 2002).

Whichever design is chosen, the prediction market performs three tasks: it provides incentives for research and knowledge discovery (the more informed

---

[1] http://www.biz.uiowa.edu/iem/.

you are, the more you can profit), it provides incentives for timely and truthful revelation (the sooner you act on your information, the more profit you can make), and it provides an algorithm for aggregating opinions (into the trading price). Its accuracy depends on how well it performs these tasks.

EVIDENCE OF MARKET PREDICTION ACCURACY

In its prospective special issue "The World in 2008," the magazine *The Economist* anointed prediction markets as today's "most heeded futurists," to the chagrin of the certified pundit whose glory days now seem past (Cottrell 2007). Theory alone or mere laboratory experiments could not buy this level of public respect. It has been earned with a record of success in the field.

Prediction markets have been available online to the general public since the mid-1990s, in both real-money (gambling) and play-money (game) formats, and a few have developed large communities of regular traders. Researchers have closely studied the predictions implied by prices in these markets, using the various designs previously described, and have found them to be remarkably accurate, whether they operate with real money or play money.

Price–Probability Calibration

The prices of binary contracts, which imply event probabilities, are closely correlated with observed event frequencies. This is verified by pooling a number of events that have contracts trading around a particular price, say 30 cents, and observing that about 30 percent of these events actually do happen. Figure 1.2 illustrates this with data from Servan-Schreiber et al. (2004), who looked at market predictions for the winner of 208 National Football League games. Two markets were actually investigated, one using real money (TradeSports)[2] and the other using play money (NewsFutures), but in both cases the correlation was very high: .96 for TradeSports and .94 for NewsFutures.

The calibration of contract price to observed frequency is a robust finding that has been reproduced in a variety of domains and prediction market venues. For instance, Pennock et al. (2001a, b) documented it in Hollywood Stock Exchange[3] (HSX) predictions about Oscar, Emmy, and Grammy awards, as well as in Foresight Exchange[4] (FX) predictions about future developments in science and technology. An internal market operated by Google to pool the guesswork of its employees about various business issues also exhibits this calibration (Cowgill et al. 2008).

Note, however, that prediction markets are not immune to the classic "favorite–longshot bias," whereby high-probability events are somewhat underpriced, while low-probability events are somewhat overpriced. This bias is apparent in the TradeSports and NewsFutures data in Figure 1.2, as well

---

[2] http://www.tradesports.com.
[3] http://www.hsx.com.
[4] http://www.ideosphere.com.

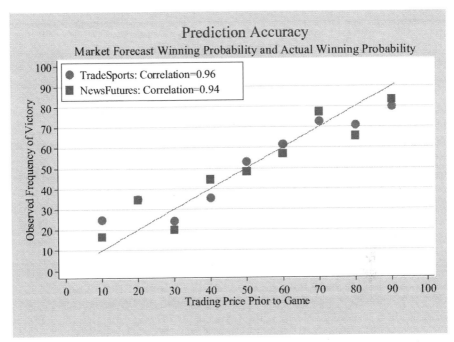

FIGURE 1.2. Calibration of market prices to observed event frequencies. Pre-game home-team prices for 208 games (416 teams) are rounded to the nearest ten percentage points, and the observed frequency of victory is plotted against these prices.

as in the HSX, FX, and Google data already mentioned. Erikson and Wlezien (2008) have also detected it in IEM election prices. Snowberg and Wolfers (2008) argue that this miscalibration is due to traders' actual misperceptions of the probabilities of events of very high and very low frequency rather than to some form of "risk love" that might be encouraged by the wagering format. In any case, it is clear that the probabilities implied by very high or very low prices are to be taken with a grain of salt.

Index contracts, which directly forecast specific quantities, have also performed well in the real world. For instance, HSX "movie stocks" are indexed on the box office receipts of a movie over the first four weeks of its release. Looking at data from 280 movies, Elberse and Anand (2007) found a .94 correlation between forecasted and actual receipts. Evidently, despite the fact that, as everyone knows in Hollywood, *nobody* can consistently identify blockbusters or flops in advance, HSX is able to do just that by aggregating the insights of many nobodies.

Political Markets versus Polls

In the political domain, the IEM's "vote-share" contracts have become well known for outperforming polls, both on election eve and in the long run (Berg, Nelson, and Rietz 2008). Market forecasts are also typically more stable over time than poll numbers. Although the advantage is small – a fraction of a percentage point, on average – these results are impressive because, contrary to polls, markets make no effort to recruit traders who are "representative" of the U.S. voting population as a whole: IEM traders are typically young, male, Caucasian, well educated, and so on.

Arguably, the farther back in time from election day one looks at the data, the more awkward the comparison of market predictions with raw poll numbers becomes, because the polls are meant only to provide a snapshot of today's voting preferences rather than a prediction of the ultimate outcome. However, in practice, this comparison is fair game because the latest poll numbers are so often reported by the media, and understood by the public, as being themselves predictive of the outcome.

A less naive interpretation of polling data, Erikson and Wlezien (2008) argue, entirely dissipates the market's advantage, and even reverses it. Drawing poll *projections* from simple linear regressions on polling data gathered during all U.S. presidential elections since 1952, they show them to be superior forecasts of vote share than the IEM prices. Again, the advantage is small: a trader armed with their model would be able to profit from trading on the IEM by a modest 1.4 percent return on investment. A similar comparison of IEM implied probabilities for winning an election versus educated projections drawn from historical polling data confirms the wisdom of trusting the poll-based projections rather than the markets.

What this critique demonstrates is that there is a wealth of information in the historical record of polling data that are not priced into the IEM and that the popular perception that IEM prices are more predictive than polls misses part of the story: the IEM may beat the *raw* poll numbers, but it doesn't beat educated *projections* from the polling data. In fact, the advantage that the IEM has claimed over polls in the United States has not been consistently reproduced elsewhere in the world (Bruggelambert 1999; Servan-Schreiber 2007), presumably because U.S. polling organizations report *raw* poll numbers whereas polling organizations in other countries publish educated *projections* instead.

However, if Erikson and Wlezien's critique helps dissipate some of the magic aura that has surrounded the political stock markets, it hardly reduces their practical merit. On a daily basis during a presidential campaign, the IEM and other markets of its kind still provide a better calibrated summary of the candidates' prospects than what is reported by polling organizations and the media.

Markets versus Individual Experts

Outperforming individuals is what collective intelligence is all about. Servan-Schreiber et al. (2004) repeatedly matched the probabilistic predictions of NewsFutures and TradeSports against those of 1,947 individual prognosticators of 208 NFL game winners. As the season developed, week by week, the predictions were scored by a proper scoring rule, which allowed the participants and the markets to be ranked according to their cumulative performance. In the first week, the markets were already performing better than 85 percent of the participants. By week 12, they were both in the top 1 percent, and they ended the twenty-one-week season ranked sixth and eighth, outdone by only 0.26 percent of the participants.

Enterprise Markets versus Official Company Forecasts

As the Google study mentioned earlier suggests, leading companies have started adopting prediction markets to pool the guesswork of their employees, and such markets have been consistently found to improve on the company's internal forecasts.[5] Popular market applications include forecasting sales of existing products, identifying promising new products, ranking projects, monitoring project deadlines, and measuring various business risks.

In a series of experiments that would later inspire many other companies to kick the tires of this technology, researchers at Hewlett-Packard enrolled a few dozen of the company's employees as prediction traders and found that their forecasts of product sales outperformed the official ones 75 percent of the time (Chen and Plott 2002).

Over many years of practice as a provider of collective intelligence solutions for businesses, Lumenogic has found that HP's pioneering result is quite robust across companies and products. Within Eli Lilly, for instance, a dozen sales people were recruited in November 2004 to trade contracts indexed to sales of three of the company's drugs two weeks ahead, six weeks ahead, and ten weeks ahead (so nine contracts in all). As Figure 1.3 illustrates, the market beat the official forecast two times out of three in each time period, and this advantage was larger for forecasting targets that were farther into the future. The HP and Eli Lilly experiments also show that, remarkably, prediction markets can work well even when the number of traders is quite small (compared with the public markets that were discussed earlier).

WHAT DRIVES MARKET PREDICTION ACCURACY?

Most of the research to date has focused on documenting accuracy in various contexts rather than trying to understand what produces it. In fact, trying to understand performance by looking at the trading data is very difficult because, despite being specifically designed to draw informed traders and to have them trade truthfully, real-world prediction markets like IEM, NewsFutures, Trade-Sports, FX, and HSX are populated by human beings who behave not at all like

---

[5] Besides Google, some well-known companies that have implemented internal markets to date include Hewlett-Packard, Eli Lilly, Pfizer, Siemens, Cisco, Best Buy, Motorola, Google, General Electric, Microsoft, and Electronic Arts.

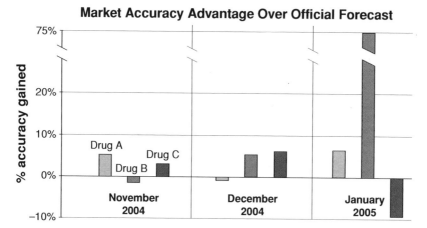

FIGURE 1.3. Sales forecasting at Eli Lilly for three drugs. All forecasts were made in early November 2004, for that same month, and for the two following months (December and January). The market beats the official forecast two-thirds of the time, and its advantage, combined over the three drugs, grows for targets farther into the future.

the rational trader that was discussed earlier. That makes market performance all the more remarkable, but also more mysterious.

Irrational Trading

One of the best-documented biases in people's decision making under risk (aka prospect theory; see Kahneman and Tversky, 1979) is called "loss aversion": people would rather avoid a risk than seek a reward of equivalent size. Typically, the subjective impact of losing money is perceived as *twice* that of winning an equivalent amount. In a prediction market context it means that traders will, for instance, avoid trades that present a 50/50 chance of winning $1 if their exposure is more than 50 cents. Or they will require a profit opportunity of at least $2 if they take a 50/50 chance of losing $1.

Another source of behavioral asymmetry is known as the "endowment effect" (Kahneman, Knetch, and Thaler 1991): people often demand much more to give up an object they have received for free than they would have been willing to pay to acquire it in the first place. Consistent with this, Oliven and Rietz (2004) have observed that traders in the IEM make fewer pricing mistakes on the selling side than they do on the buying side.

In a prediction market, even these well-known biases are hard to isolate because they interact with risk/reward computations that are dynamic in time. In contrast to a standard betting venue where someone risks something and then waits for the outcome to decide if he loses the entire investment or wins the entire reward, a prediction market allows the trader much more risk control: if the price starts going down, she can resell at a loss without losing all his investment. Similarly, he can take a partial profit on his investment by reselling at any time when the price is rising. For instance, a trader who buys a binary contract at 60 cents might consider that, for a chance to win 40 cents, she is really risking only 10 cents, rather than 60 cents, because, if worse came to worst, she could always liquidate her position at 50 cents instead of taking a complete loss. An observer, however, would not be able to deduce what risk/reward computation the trader conducted before buying the contract.

Another source of asymmetry in the market is that some traders usually command more, sometimes vastly more, monetary resources than others, and that gives them more power to move the price in their preferred direction. When the resources that a trader commands are unrelated to how informed or knowledgeable he is, knowledge aggregation should suffer. Servan-Schreiber et al. (2004) cite this as a possible reason that some play-money prediction markets, which correlate trader wealth with past performance, can achieve prediction accuracy comparable to that of real-money markets, where this correlation is unlikely to hold. Consistent with that, Oliven and Rietz (2004) report that higher-income participants in the IEM tend to be more careless with their trades, presumably because for them the limited stakes[6] are lower. In general, when monetary resources differ, it is not reasonable to assume that a $10 bet represents the same perceived risk for everyone.

Market Makers

Despite the daunting complexity of real-world prediction market ecosystems, a few researchers have delved deep inside trading data to try to understand what drives performance. An early proposal from Foresythe et al. (1992) is the "marginal trader hypothesis": in a sea of biased, emotional, error-prone traders, there exists a core group of traders whose behavior is more rational, and they are the ones who truly set the market prices. For instance, Oliven and Rietz (2004) observe that in the IEM there are essentially two types of traders: those who tend to propose prices to others (market makers or marginal traders) and those who tend to accept those offers (price takers). The roles are self-selected and may shift back and forth in the course of the market, but most people tend to stick to their preferred role. Looking closely at thousands of orders from hundreds of traders, the researchers found that market makers tend to behave much more rationally than price takers, making five times fewer trading errors (i.e., suboptimal trades). They conclude that because market makers have, by definition, a much more durable impact on market prices than price takers, their superior rationality helps the market as a whole overcome the wilder behavior of the other traders.

However, as Berg et al. (2008) note, a rational trader who doesn't possess good information cannot take advantage of others' biases, so the marginal trader hypothesis isn't sufficient to explain market performance. To complete

---

[6] Even though the IEM is a real-money market, its stakes are limited: each trader can invest only up to $500.

the explanation, they propose that markets are more accurate than publicly available predictions *when* those predictions possess a known bias. People who are aware of this bias are naturally attracted to a market where they can take advantage of their superior knowledge for profit. They self-select into the rational, marginal trader role and help the market settle on the appropriate price.

It's Not about the Market Mechanism Itself

On higher grounds, there is reason to doubt that any explanation that, like the marginal trader hypothesis, is rooted in particular trading mechanics can really get at the heart of a phenomenon that is reproducible across a diverse set of trading schemes. Indeed, while markets like IEM, TradeSports, NewsFutures, and FX let traders negotiate prices directly with each other through a continuous double auction, HSX and a host of more recent venues rely on various automated market makers to set the price in response to traders' buy and sell orders.[7] Although the accuracy of these various trading schemes has yet to be formally compared, the wisdom of the trading crowds seems to emerge in every case.

Several nonmarket *betting* schemes have also been shown to perform just as well as prediction markets when matched head to head. For instance, Chen et al. (2005) compared the prediction accuracy of NewsFutures and Trade-Sports with the simple averages of predictions elicited from 1,966 individuals regarding the outcomes of 210 U.S. football games. Those predictions were scored by the quadratic scoring rule, one of the so-called proper scoring rules designed to elicit honest forecasts. Although the collective intelligence emerged forcefully in each case – outperforming all but a few individuals – there was no advantage for the markets over a simple arithmetic average of the individual predictions. Limited laboratory experiments have shown that when the number of people in a crowd is particularly small, say around a dozen, some simple betting schemes may even beat the market (Chen, Fine, and Huberman 2003).

So if prediction accuracy isn't manufactured by the market mechanism itself, where does it come from?

Attracting Diversity

Scott Page's "Diversity Theorem" provides an elegant mathematical foundation for the wisdom of a crowd (Page 2007):

Collective error = Average individual error − diversity of Predictions

Or more precisely:

$$(P - O)^2 = \text{average}(p_i - O)^2 - \text{average}(p_i - P)^2$$

---

[7] See, for instance, the Logarithmic Market Scoring Rule (Hanson 2003) and the Dynamic Pari Mutuel algorithm (Mangold et al. 2005).

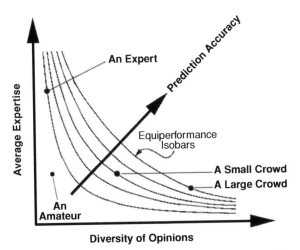

FIGURE 1.4. Page's Diversity Theorem applied to forecasting. The curves represent equiperformance isobars, so that every point on a particular isobar is a combination of average expertise and total diversity that yields the same prediction accuracy. In a crowd of one, diversity is null and an expert will outpredict an amateur. However, a small group of amateurs endowed with diverse opinions may outpredict an expert. Even as the average amount of expertise decreases when a crowd grows, it may more than make up for it with increased diversity.

Where p_i are the individual predictions, P is the average of those predictions, that is, the consensus, and O is the observed outcome.

In layperson terms, when we average individual predictions, each of which contains bits of truth mixed with various misconceptions, the bits of truth add up to a larger truth, whereas the misconceptions and biases cancel each other. (That is because bits of truth tend to be positively correlated, whereas biases tend to be independent.) So the more diverse opinions are represented, the more complementary bits of truth can be combined, while the extra biases still get canceled.

One implication is that you may obtain the same prediction accuracy from a crowd of amateurs that you can from a much smaller group of experts, so long as the individuals in the crowd hold sufficiently diverse opinions. In other words, the diversity in a crowd can make up for lapses in individual expertise. This trade-off is illustrated in Figure 1.4.

The power of diversity is beautifully illustrated by a study of 2,231 football amateurs making predictions about 267 NFL games (Pennock 2007; Reeves and Pennock 2007). Again, the predictions were scored by the quadratic scoring rule. They found that the number of individuals able to outpredict a group decreased as a power function of the size of the group. For instance, while 64 percent of the participants scored above the average individual score, 16 percent scored better than the average group of five, and only 5 percent scored better than the average group of ten.

So one fundamental factor in the performance of any forecasting system is its ability to attract a crowd of people with diverse information and opinions. However, in the real world, it is often difficult or expensive to recruit diverse expertise. Budgets may severely constrain a manager's ability to solicit and aggregate the opinions of more than a handful of experts. Polling organizations need to keep up with fast-changing communication trends, such as cell phones, email, and instant messaging, to maintain their ability to recruit "representative" panels of consumers or voters.

In contrast, prediction markets excel at attracting diverse expertise because they incentivize disagreement and confrontation rather than conformity. If anyone has any reason to disagree with the market price, she has incentives to self-select into the pool of traders to contribute her contrary opinion. And, as noted earlier, the more she disagrees with the market, the more incentives she has to join it because of the larger profit opportunity.

Promoting Objectivity

Perhaps the "explanation" that is given most often for the power of prediction markets is that, contrary to punditry and polls, they require participants to "put their money where their mouth is" (e.g., Hanson 1999). As valid an insight as that may be, it needs some fleshing out before it can claim explanatory power.

First of all, it is necessary to qualify the use of the loaded word "money." As the comparative studies of play-money and real-money markets have shown, the presence of real currency in the market is not necessary to obtain the best performance: play-money markets may perform as well as real-money ones (Servan-Schreiber et al. 2004; Gruca, Berg, and Cipriano 2008) so long as they provide *real incentives*, of which there are various sorts besides currency – for instance, prizes, knowledge, professional advancement, or social recognition.

From a different perspective, brain-imaging studies show that the mere prospect of risk and reward mobilizes cognition-specific brain modules. In particular, behavioral "loss aversion" seems to be driven by the activation or inhibition of specific neurons deep in the brain (striatum) as well as in the prefrontal cortex (Tom et al. 2007). Neuroscientists have also found evidence that, when under stress to perform a demanding task for monetary rewards, the brain inhibits signals from its emotional modules in order to maximize cognitive performance: the more important the rewards are, the more inhibition is observed (Pochon et al. 2002). In summary, when the brain contemplates a gamble, it literally *thinks differently* than when there is no perceived risk or reward: it becomes more risk averse and tunes out the emotional signals that might interfere with cognitive performance. "A true Englishman doesn't joke when he's talking about such serious a thing as a wager," remarks the hero of Jules Verne's *Around the World in Eighty Days*. Nor, apparently, do the rest of us.

Much of the advantage of prediction markets – indeed, of any betting institution – over pundits and polls may then simply come from framing the predictions as wagers rather than unaccountable opinions.

CONCLUSION

Prediction markets have captured the public's imagination with their ability to pool the guesswork of many to outperform venerable institutions such as individual experts and polls. Typical explanations for why they work so well entail the efficiency of markets or the insight that participants must "put their money where their mouth is." Ultimately, though, it seems that the forecasting accuracy of prediction markets has little to do with any specific trading mechanism or even with trading in any way. Nor is hard currency necessarily involved.

The key driver of accuracy seems to be the betting proposition itself: on the one hand, a wager attracts contrarians, which enhances the *diversity* of opinions that are aggregated; on the other hand, the mere prospect of reward or loss promotes more objective, less passionate thinking, thereby enhancing the *quality* of the opinions that are aggregated.

We can speculate about the reasons this conclusion is rarely voiced by advocates of this technology. In the United States, where most of the research on prediction markets has been done and where most of the applications have been fielded, "bets and wagers" have much social stigma attached to them – they destroy families – and antigambling laws are strictly enforced. Markets, on the other hand, are respected institutions at the core of the national economy.[8] This encourages proponents to argue, or lets them believe, that more than betting is involved in a prediction "market," as when a score of high-profile economists, including several winners of the Nobel Prize, recently called for their legalization (Arrow et al. 2008). In Europe, where betting is more institutionalized, a more visible part of the social fabric, people simply use the phrase "betting exchange" to refer to the same thing.

Vocabulary aside, many practitioners have already recognized that the financial trading metaphor, which is so much a part of the concept of a prediction market, is not always the best approach to harnessing the collective wisdom. On the one hand, it is customary nowadays to encounter forecasting systems that loosely call themselves "prediction markets" or "forecasting markets" for marketing purposes but that really are just sophisticated betting venues involving no trading. The chip maker Intel and the steelmaker Arcelor Mittal, for instance, have relied on such systems to forecast product sales with apparent success (Llera 2006; Hopman 2007). On the other hand, even some of the most dedicated operators of prediction markets are themselves fielding applications that go to great lengths to hide the trading mechanics in order to reduce the user experience to a simple bet. For instance, the creators of the IEM have chosen this strategy when fielding their Influenza Prediction Market, populated by doctors who are mostly unfamiliar with financial trading (Polgreen, Nelson, and Neumann 2007).

---

[8] Although the level of public respect for markets may have taken a hit as a result of Wall Street's subprime-fueled implosion.

A prediction market, then, is one of many betting-based methods for aggregating forecasts. In some contexts, for some purposes, it is an elegant solution, while in other situations it may be cumbersome. In any case, the ability of betting crowds to predict the future is a robust phenomenon that doesn't seem to be bottled up in any one particular contraption.

References

Arrow, Forsythe, Gorham, Hahn, Hanson, Ledyard, Levmore, Litan, Milgrom, Nelson, Neumann, Ottaviani, Schelling, Shiller, Smith, Snowberg, Sunstein, Tetlock, Tetlock, Varian, Wolfers, and Zitzewitz (2008). The promise of prediction markets. *Science*, 320: 877–78.

Berg, J. E., Nelson, F., and Rietz, T. A. (2008). Prediction market accuracy in the long run. *International Journal of Forecasting*, 24(2): 285–300.

Bruggelambert, G. (1999). Information efficiency in political stock markets: An electronic market experiment. Working paper, University of Essen.

Chen, Y., Chu, C. H., Mullen, T., and Pennock, D. M. (2005). Information markets vs. opinion pools: An empirical comparison. *Proceedings of the 6th ACM Conference on Electronic Commerce (EC'05)*, 58–67.

Chen, K. Y., Fine, L. R., and Huberman, B. A. (2003). Predicting the future. *Information Systems Frontiers*, 5(1): 47–61.

Chen, K. Y., and Plott, C. R. (2002). Information aggregation mechanisms: Concept, design and implementation for a sales forecasting problem. Social Science Working Paper No. 1131, California Institute of Technology, Pasadena.

Cottrell, R. (2007). The future of futurology. *The Economist – The World in 2008*, December 2007: 104–105.

Cowgill, B., Wolfers, J., and Zitzewitz, E. (2008). Using prediction markets to track information flows: Evidence from Google. http://www.bocowgill.com/Google PredictionMarketPaper.pdf.

Elberse, A., and Anand, B. (2007). The effectiveness of pre-release advertising for motion pictures: An empirical investigation using a simulated market. *Information Economics and Policy*, 19(3–4): 319–43.

Erikson, R. S., and Wlezien, C. (2008). Are political markets really superior to polls as election predictors? *Public Opinion Quarterly*, 72(2): 190–215.

Foresythe, R., Nelson, F. D., Neumann, G. R., and Wright, J. (1992). Anatomy of an experimental political stock market. *American Economic Review*, 82(5): 1142–61.

Gruca, T. S., Berg, J. E., and Cipriano, M. (2008). Incentive and accuracy issues in movie prediction markets. *Journal of Prediction Markets*, 2(1): 29–73.

Hanson, R. (1999). Decision Markets. *IEEE Intelligent Systems* (May–June 1999): 16–19.

   (2003). Combinatorial Information Market design. *Information Systems Frontiers*, 5(1): 107–19.

Hopman, J. W. (2007). Using forecasting markets to manage demand risk. *Intel Technology Journal*, 11(2): 127–35.

Kahneman, D., Knetsch, J. L., and Thaler, R. H. (1991). Anomalies: The endowment effect, loss aversion and status quo bias. *Journal of Economic Perspectives*, 5(1): 193–206.

Kahneman, D., and Tversky, A. (1979). Prospect theory: An analysis of decision under risk. *Econometrica*, 47(2): 263–91.

Llera, J. (2006). Sparc: Arcelor's prediction market. Presentation at the First European Prediction Market Summit, Vienna, November.

Mangold, B., Dooley, M., Flake, G. W., Hoffman, H., Kasturi, T., and Pennock, D. M. (2005). The tech buzz game. *IEEE Computer*, 38(7): 94–97.

Oliven, K., and Rietz, T. (2004). Suckers are born but markets are made: Individual rationality, arbitrage and market efficiency on an electronic futures market. *Management Science*, 50(3): 336–51.

Page, S. (2007). *The Difference: How the Power of Diversity Creates Better Groups, Firms, Schools, and Societies*. Princeton, NJ: Princeton University Press.

Pennock, D. M. (2007). The wisdom of the ProbabilitySports crowd. *Oddhead Blog*, http://blog.oddhead.com/2007/01/04/the-wisdom-of-the-probabilitysports-crowd/.

Pennock, D. M., Lawrence, S., Giles, C. L., and Nielsen, F. A. (2001a). The real power of artificial markets. *Science*, 291(5506): 987–88.

Pennock, D. M., Lawrence, S., Nielsen, F. A., and Giles, C. L. (2001b). Extracting collective probabilistic forecasts from web games. *Proceedings of the 7th ACM SIGKDD International Conference on Knowledge Discovery and Data Mining (KDD-2001)*, 174–83.

Pethokoukis, J. M. (2004). All seeing, all knowing. *US News & World Report*, August 22, 2004.

Pochon, J. B., Levy, R., Fosati, P., Lehericy, S., Poline, J. B., Pillon, B., Le Bihan, D., and Dubois, B. (2002). The neural system that bridges reward and cognition in humans: An fMRI study. *Proceedings of the National Academy of Sciences*, 99(8): 5669–74.

Polgreen, P. M., Nelson, F. D., and Neumann, G. R. (2007). Use of prediction markets to forecast infectious disease activity. *Clinical Infectious Diseases*, 44(2): 272–79.

Reeves, D., and Pennock D. M. (2007). How and when to listen to the crowd. *Overcoming Bias Blog*, http://www.overcomingbias.com/2007/02/how_and_when_to.html.

Servan-Schreiber, E. J. (2007). Results of the Dutch political stock market. *NewsFutures blog*, http://newsfutures.wordpress.com/2007/02/22/results-of-the-dutch-political-stock-market/.

Servan-Schreiber, E. J., Wolfers, J., Pennock, D. M., and Galebach, B. (2004). Prediction markets: Does money matter? *Electronic Markets*, 14(3): 243–51.

Snowberg, E., and Wolfers, J. (2008). The favorite–longshot bias: Examining explanations of a market anomaly – Preferences or perceptions? In D. B. Hausch and W. T. Ziemba (eds.), *Handbook of Sports and Lottery Markets*, 103–36. Amsterdam: Elsevier.

Stuart, A. N. (2005). Market magic. *CFO*, November 1, 2005.

Surowiecki, J. (2004). *The Wisdom of Crowds*. New York: Doubleday.

Tom, S. M., Fox, C. R., Trepel, C., and Poldrak, R. A. (2007). The neural basis of loss aversion in decision-making under risk. *Science*, 315(5811): 515–18.

2

Designing Wisdom through the Web

Reputation and the Passion for Ranking

Gloria Origgi

> Civilization rests on the fact that we all benefit from knowledge we do not possess.
> Friedrich Hayek

The so-called Web 2.0 invites the possibility of aggregating socially distributed information to obtain intelligent outcomes, ones more sophisticated and precise than could be produced by a single expert mind. For much of the history of thought, such a genuinely collective intelligence was either a curiosity or a fantasy.[1] If collective intelligence is not yet realized in all of our knowledge systems, it certainly affects much of our daily lives. Google searches, Wikipedia entries, eBay transactions, CiteULike libraries: none is a genuine collective intelligence, but each might form the building blocks of one. Collective intelligence is a tantalizing prospect, one that epistemologists should take seriously.

One way to take collective intelligence seriously is to focus on issues of institutional design. Each of the systems just mentioned filters data (often through elaborate forms of aggregation) to generate informational products. Yet for each system, control over aggregation can be poor and prospects for beneficial interventions limited by features of design. Appreciating the importance of institutional design is critical, not only for assessing the products of these epistemic systems, but also for appreciating the possibility of their misuse. The ways that we aggregate lay judgments affect the kind of society we live in. Regardless of how many people are involved in an epistemic system, institutional design constrains and helps determine the *epistemic quality* of its products. The central *design question* I will consider is this: assuming we can evaluate

---

[1] As Adrian Vermeule notes in Chapter 14, this volume, the idea of collective intelligence has an impressive pedigree. In the *Politics*, Aristotle conjectured that "the many are better judges than a single man of music and poetry; for some understand one part, and some another, and among them they understand the whole" (*Politics*, bk. 3, ch. XI). Aristotle's insight applied to political and evaluative judgments rather than the broader epistemic topic of the collective construction of knowledge.

the truth-tracking capacity of systems that generate results from the aggregation of individual opinions, how (if at all) can we design such systems so that
their products are more reliable?

The importance of design is, of course, well known to policymakers and
constitutional theorists. In Chapter 14, Adrian Vermeule offers a "catalogue"
of design mechanisms for harnessing the collective wisdom of corporate political bodies like courts and assemblies.[2] Yet institutional design is also important
for knowledge systems (like the Web) based on the collection of diffuse information or involving hidden rules. Both political and knowledge systems are
threatened by strategic manipulations of their inputs. Further, the epistemic
quality of a (political or epistemic) system's products can be compromised
by inherent flaws in the system's aggregation mechanism. These flaws might
not be appreciable from the limited, ex ante perspective of those who design
the relevant algorithm. Institutional design, then, is at least as pressing and
omnipresent a topic for epistemic systems like the Web as it is for political
ones.

The centrality of institutional design might surprise some. In the halcyon
days of the 1990s, the Web was the paradigmatic "disruptive technology,"[3]
one that would overturn all of our practices for accessing knowledge and
empower users to collaboratively produce, access, and distribute content in
previously unimagined ways.[4] Over the past decade, this enthusiasm has been
replaced by a more nuanced attitude. Replacing our practices for accessing
knowledge is not simple. Moreover, not all crowds are wise. Some are subject
to group polarization, information cascades, and conformity.[5] How can we tell
which crowds are wise and which are not?

This theoretical question has everyday importance. To take one common
example, how do we know that our Google search will display the "best"
information related to a query? Usually, this is a matter of personal experience.
After many trials with Google searches, we either arrive at or reject the conclusion that the results of search inquiries should be believed. This information
is collectively produced, but we do not have independent ways to verify it.[6]
This scenario suggests one difference between evaluating epistemic and political systems. In the domains of law and politics, officials can point to shared
expectations (e.g., the "original intention of the framers," the "common interest") to evaluate a system's products and (by implication) the quality of its
design. Moreover, in most such cases, we can readily identify which officials
are in charge of the design and reform of the system. For knowledge production
systems, by contrast, external standards are not as ready to hand. Moreover,

---

[2] See Vermeule, Chapter 14, this volume.
[3] See Bower and Christensen (1995); see also Christensen (1997).
[4] Many enthusiasts speak of a "digital empowerment" across a variety of contexts, such as political participation, access to information by previously underserved populations, and business
creation; see Mäkinen (2006). For a forerunner of these enthusiastic views, see Kurzweil (1990).
[5] On group polarization and information cascades, see Sunstein (2006).
[6] See Origgi (2010b).

although the Web reflects a design, many features lack a discernible designer. Because it is designed, the Web is influenced by motivations, values, and intentions that are embedded in its architecture; because this design is diffuse, there is nobody to query when these features manifest.

The Web presents an acute example of problems that all collective wisdom systems face. In what follows, I describe some these problems and the design features that underlie them. I also argue for the centrality of ranking to the epistemic value of a collective wisdom system generally, and the Web in particular. The success of the Web as an epistemic practice is due not to its nearly infinite storage capacity so much as its potential to improve the reliability of diffuse information through filtering mechanisms like ranking and rating. The true possibility of the Web is less as a harbinger of some novel "information age" than as an extension of our long-standing practice of extracting information from reputation (i.e., how others value and rate an item).[7] To be sure, the Web dramatically expands the first-order information on which reputation is built. But in an information-dense environment like ours, first-order information is useful only in conjunction with reputation. Reputational devices like rankings and ratings, then, are central to the epistemic value of any collective wisdom system.

INTELLIGENCE, WISDOM, TRADITION, AND REPUTATION

To defend this thesis, it will help to clarify what I mean by "wisdom" and how collective systems can be wise. As Hélène Landemore points out in her introduction to this volume, many authors use the terms "wisdom" and "intelligence" interchangeably. Yet "collective wisdom" is subtly different from the idea of intelligence.[8] To this end, Daniel Andler offers definitions that illuminate the relevant differences between these concepts. *Intelligence*, as Andler says, is "to a large extent a matter of getting the job done, that is, of solving problems in finite time."[9] On the other hand, *wisdom*, at least in the sense relevant to epistemology, aims at drawing a balanced conclusion, all things considered. That is, wisdom ideally produces a judgment that properly accounts for both an agent's experiences and her limited perspective for judgment (a feature that Andler calls *inclusiveness*).[10] If we limit ourselves to what Andler calls *epistemic wisdom*, I think that the definition he proposes is very close to the traditional identification of wisdom with experience and reliance on the authority of the past. The idea of wisdom appeals to a standard of epistemic quality that is already there, that has been already established (as in the case of the "right" Google answer), whereas intelligence can generate a new standard of quality. Wisdom appeals to an already known quality, one that is often selected by

---

[7] See Origgi (2010b).
[8] See the introduction to this volume by Landemore.
[9] Andler, Chapter 4, this volume.
[10] Ibid.

previous experience. I will adopt this traditional view, according to which wisdom is a complex of values, judgments, and preferences that are developed in the past and refined over time. The authority of wisdom is thus intimately connected with the authority of tradition.[11]

Consider Edmund Burke's remarks about tradition and wisdom. For Burke, the process of refining our traditions was the essence of civilization. These traditions comprise a thick lore of judgments, values, and opinions, one that penetrates the minds of individuals through education and socialization. Such traditions were a necessary background to wisdom, since they not only organize our conception of the world but also suggest which institutions are required to live in it. Burke's renowned antipathy to revolutions reflected his suspicion that they risked wiping out these traditions and compromising civilization. Without access to these sources, we are (collectively and individually) condemned to reinvent the wheel at each generation. As he says:

> We are afraid to put men to live and trade each on his own private stock of reason, because we suspect that this stock in each man is small, and that the individuals would do better to avail themselves of the general bank and capital of nations, and of ages.[12]

We might reject Burke's reactionary political conclusions while admitting that he had an insight about epistemology. Not all traditions are worth preserving. The institutional biases and the social pressures that ensure the survival of a political tradition might be so partisan that it is wiser to rethink our traditions wholesale. However, from an epistemic point of view, Burke captures the high costs of this rethinking, especially if it proceeds divorced from the experiences that are embedded in a culture's knowledge traditions. Of course, there are "good" and "bad" knowledge traditions, and what makes a knowledge tradition worth preserving is different than what makes a political tradition authoritative.

Yet Burke's central insight remains. We need filters to access our knowledge traditions. These filters are the standards for our epistemic judgments. We can never have a "pure" access to information. Unvarnished interaction with the external world, the subject contacting reality without the filter of others, is a central image in epistemology. It is also an unrealistic limit case. Without the filters of our corpuses of knowledge, we would face the impossible task of Bouvard and Pécuchet, the two heroes of Flaubert who decide to retire and to go through every known discipline. We, like them, would never be able to learn anything. This insight evokes W. V. O. Quine's well-known metaphor from his discussion of Carnap:

> The lore of our fathers is a fabric of sentences. In our hands it develops and changes, through more or less arbitrary and deliberate revisions and additions of our own. . . . It is a pale gray lore, black with fact and white with convention. But I have found no

---

[11] Vermeule, Chapter 14, this volume.
[12] Burke (1790).

substantial reasons for concluding that there are any quite black threads in it, or any white ones.[13]

To say that our lore is part of the "fabric of sentences" is to say that it transmits not merely fact-data, but also a sophisticated ensemble of judgments and conventions that shape the way facts will be extracted and classified. The preferences, conventions, and values of our traditions thus play a critical role in the fashioning of collective wisdom. These shape the reputational landscape that we use to organize our own heuristics in order to extract information and provide a (sometimes reliable, sometimes biased) shortcut to what is worth keeping, remembering, and preserving as knowledge.

Past evaluations are a way of tracking records of an item, that is, of attaching a reputation to it. The evaluative dimension of our social life, the generation of opinions on each other's actions, is reputation. "Reputation" derives from the Latin verb *putare*, to know. The prefix "re-" indicates that reputation develops over iterations. Reputation also has a fundamentally social dimension. As Marcel Proust says, reputation, even when it is true, is always made by other people's ideas.[14] Attributing reputations is part of mapping a domain. This task is particularly important when we confront new domains.[15] To summarize a vast game-theoretical[16] and epistemological[17] literature on reputation, reputations are central to coordinated and cooperative social phenomena. We can use the term "reputation" broadly to denote widely accepted positive or negative opinion. This broad sense is often used in the study of animal behavior.[18] A more precise (and, for our purposes, appropriate) definition sees reputation as a complex phenomenon involving the emergence of a normative judgment from ranking or rating systems and the distribution of this judgment as common knowledge.[19]

Reputation both helps fashion collective processes of knowledge and is a central criterion for extracting information from these systems. It is a fundamental shortcut for cumulating knowledge in processes of collective wisdom. It is also an ineluctable filter. In an environment where sources are in constant competition for attention and direct verification is unavailable, rankings and ratings allow us to have and use information. While this effect is striking in contemporary societies characterized by information overload, I think it is a permanent feature of the task of extracting knowledge from a corpus. Some corpuses are organized, maintained, and transmitted over populations via culture. But culture is not the only constraint on the construction of reputation.

[13] See Quine (1961).

[14] See M. Proust: "Ces réputations là, même varies, sont faites avec les idées des autres." *Du coté de chez Swann*, ed. Pléiade, Gallimard, Paris, p. 313.

[15] See Origgi (2010c).

[16] See, e.g., Tirole (1996); Origgi (2007b).

[17] See, e.g., Henrich et al. (2006); Mathew and Boyd (2009).

[18] Subiaul et al. (2008).

[19] On reputation as a social belief, see Sperber et al. (2010).

Cognitive constraints also force us to utilize reputational cues. These include *conformism*, or the tendency to adopt mainstream judgments, and *emulation*, which enables fast and efficient social learning of cognitively opaque cultural knowledge.[20] Thus, both cognitive and social factors explain the importance of traditions and reputations. What I want to stress here is that there is no ideal knowledge that we can evaluate or adjudicate hermetically from the evaluations and adjudications of others. Our minds can never investigate or manipulate the world in solitude. The greater our uncertainty about the content of information, the stronger our reliance on the opinions of others to evaluate this content. Just as our lore is woven into the fabric of our sentences, our concern for reputation is woven into the fabric of our collective wisdom systems. This claim is in part conceptual, in part empirical. Even if not all such systems reflect this passion for ranking, we can expect those that do will generate more epistemically reliable products than those that do not. This insight drives many of our Web-based collective wisdom systems (like eBay and CiteULike). When reputational mechanisms like rankings and ratings are introduced, the products of these systems are more reliably true (in that the ratio of true outcomes to false outcomes is higher). Moreover, individual participants can more productively access these products in deciding for themselves what to believe. Meeting these goals is in large part a matter of institutional design.

Rankings may seem to have the opposite effect, since these devices introduce bias in the way information is categorized and classified.[21] Yet mechanisms that bias judgment can still produce epistemic gains. Some biased judgments add epistemic value by allowing participation in a stabilizing tradition of knowledge. Other biased judgments sustain prejudicial information and should be wiped out. However, if (as my argument suggests) no information is completely independent of bias, the aim of a second-order epistemology like the one I advocate here should be to keep the biases worth keeping and eliminate those worth eliminating. Yet this delineation might be especially difficult in environments like the Web, where rankings arise from diffuse activities. As a result, many users might be in the vulnerable position of relying on the reputational outputs of a dynamic, machine-based process that is incomprehensible to them and over which they have no control. Consider, for example, a 2002 study revealing that fully 60 percent of users were unaware that companies pay for inclusion or "preferred placement" in search engine inquiries.[22]

---

[20] On the cognitive heuristics of social learning, see Boyd and Richerson (2005); Csibra and Gergely (2009).

[21] I mean the term "bias" in its statistical sense, which denotes an inclination to hold a partial perspective at the expense of equally valid alternatives. The term is used also in psychology and sociology to denote the tendency toward prejudicial perspectives (e.g., "cognitive bias," "cultural bias").

[22] Princeton Survey Research Associates, "A Matter of Trust: What Users Want from Websites," Princeton, NJ, January 2002, at http://www.consumerWebwatch.com/news/report1.pdf. The case is reported in Rogers (2004).

The centrality of reputational mechanisms like ranking and rating to our collective wisdom systems raises a series of epistemological questions:

1. Why do (and should) people trust these rankings?
2. Why might the collective filtering of preferences produce wiser results?
3. Which heuristics and biases of collective wisdom systems on the Web should people be aware of?

Each of these questions has both descriptive and normative aspects. I will here focus more on the descriptive aspects, although my analysis will also have implications for the normative aspects.

There are many ways to account for the judgments of others. Some methods are more reliable than others. Some are maintained for cultural reasons that are unrelated to their epistemic value – for example, rating systems in idiosyncratic cultural domains like wine.[23] Some methods might be maintained entirely for their cognitive function or their epistemic optimality. It is probable that no ranking system is purely cultural. Even the practice of wine ranking must be recalibrated to fit people's actual preferences and values in order to maintain its usefulness. Likewise, no useful system could be purely "rational," in the sense of avoiding all cultural biases and contemporaneous values. Even PageRank has to distinguish the hubs of the Web or special sites whose influence is given disproportionate influence.[24] Further, there are no completely naive users of Web ranking systems. We all have personal filters for encountering the judgments of others, although these filters might be based on our background cultural values.

Thus, appreciating the Web's epistemic possibilities requires appreciating the possible biases that are woven into the fabric of our collective wisdom systems. Maintaining an awareness of these biases is part of competent institutional design, just as awareness of the limits and biases of our perceptual mechanisms is part of our individual epistemic competence.[25]

COLLECTIVE INTELLIGENCE OUT OF INDIVIDUAL CHOICES

People – and other intelligent agents[26] – often think better in groups. Sometimes, groups enable thinking that is simply not possible in isolation. The Web is surely an example of this, which perhaps explains the celebratory expectations about the emergence of a new form of thought described earlier. The possibility of genuinely collective intelligence inspired a variety of metaphors: the Internet as an extended mind, as distributed digital consciousness, even as

[23] See Origgi (2007a).
[24] I discuss the implications of this requirement in the subsection on PlayRank.
[25] I have called this awareness "epistemic vigilance." See Origgi (2010a); see also Sperber et al. (2010).
[26] Conradt and List (2009) provide a useful survey of collective intelligence outside the human species.

a higher-order intelligent being.[27] Yet the epistemic power and promise of the Web does not rest on anything so exotic. Rather, it draws from the mechanisms (including the aggregation of choices and preferences) that characterize other forms of collective cognition. However, unlike these more hidebound forms, the Web makes possible new (and spectacular) forms of aggregation. Before exploring some of these new forms, let us start with some basic facts about the design of the Web.

The Internet and the Web

The Web provides new ways to articulate individual choices and filter preferences. Here it is useful to distinguish between the Internet as a networking phenomenon and the Web as a specific technology based on this network. The Internet is a network whose beginnings go back to the 1960s, when U.S. scientists at AT&T, the RAND Corporation, MIT, and the Defense Communication Agency started to think of an alternative model of transmitting information through a network. In the early 1970s, the first decentralized network, Arpanet, achieved the transfer of messages by spreading and reassembling them through networks.

Part of the Internet's power lay in its decentralized architecture. The Internet used preexisting wires (like telephone networks) to connect computers, and nonpropriety protocols[28] (such as transmission control protocol [TCP] with Internet protocol [IP]) enabled communication among each new user with all other users. Each new application drew on these basic protocols. Internet protocols are thus *commons*,[29] that is, goods that cannot be traded. Freedom in the use of protocols not only facilitated the growth of the network, but also expanded the variety of applications that could utilize it. Appreciating this basic, scalar architecture is crucial for appraising the wisdom of the Web. Without the political choice to keep these protocols free, neither the decentralized growth of the Web nor the collaborative knowledge practices that characterize it would have been possible. The World Wide Web, a more recent invention than the Internet, utilized the same ethos of open protocols (like http://). This format allows and encourages interconnection through the technique of "hyperlinks." What drives the growth of the Web differs from what drives the growth of the Internet; the former's proliferation might be explained by the lack of technical competence required to make an effective hyperlink. However, the Web could not exist without the Internet, and its flourishing demonstrates how

---

[27] Examples of these metaphors can be found in Clark (2003) and Lévy (2000).

[28] Internet protocols are standards of transmission that allow two end points in a network to communicate with each other. Keeping them nonproprietary was an important political choice by the U.S. government (especially supported by Albert Gore, Jr., who worked as a senator on the High Performance Computing and Communication Act of 1991 [HPCA], leading to the development of the National Information Infrastructure Act, which guarantees the nonproprietary status of the Internet protocols).

[29] On this point, see Lessig (2001).

an Internet application can thrive because of the openness of the underlying protocols. Yet although the structure of the Web is fundamentally open, the collaborative sharing that occurs over the Web is not necessarily equitable. Indeed, informational free-riding is rampant on the Web, as many more people take advantage of shared information than actually share.[30]

The Web, Collective Memory, and Meta-Memory

What is special about the aggregation of individual preferences through the Web? The Web presents unparalleled opportunities for the storage, dissemination, and retrieval of information. Like other major cultural revolutions, the Web also affects the distribution of memory. The Web has often been compared to the invention of writing or printing. Both comparisons have merit. Writing, introduced at the end of the fourth millennium B.C. in Mesopotamia, is an external memory device that enabled a massive reorganization of intellectual life and a new structuring of thoughts, neither of which is as fully possible in oral cultures.[31] With the introduction of writing, one part of our cognition "leaves" the brain to be distributed among external supports. Visual representation allows the reorganization of knowledge in a more useful, "logical" fashion, for example, by lists, tables, calendars, or genealogical trees. It also allows such information to be transmitted across generations. These transmission possibilities give rise to "managerial" castes that oversee cultural memory, including scribes, astrologists, and librarians. Transmission also gives rise to *meta-memory*, or the set of processes for accessing and recovering transmitted cultural memory. Printing, which was introduced in our culture at the end of the fifteenth century, redistributes cultural memory by changing the configuration of the informational "pyramid," that is, the hierarchical structure of the diffusion of information in a society.

In what sense is the Web revolution comparable to the invention of writing and printing? Like these two earlier revolutions, the Web increases the efficiency of recording, recovering, reproducing, and distributing cultural memory. Like writing, the Web is an external memory device, although the Web is a more "active" mechanism than writing. Like printing, the Web is a device for redistributing the cultural memory within a population; however, the Web crucially modifies the costs and time of distribution. Unlike these other two forms, the Web presents a radical change in the conditions for accessing and recovering cultural memory because it introduces new devices for managing meta-memory.

Culture, to a large extent, is the conception, organization, and institutionalization of an efficient meta-memory – that is, a system of rules, representations,

---

[30] For an interesting example of free-riding on information sharing in the case of sharing music files on the Web, see Adar and Huberman (2000).

[31] On the reorganization of knowledge made possible by the introduction of writing, see Goody (1986).

and rankings that enable us to usefully orient ourselves in the collective memory. A good part of our education consists in internalizing the systems of meta-memory of our culture. For example, it might be important to know the basics of rhetoric in order to rapidly "classify" a line of verse as belonging to a certain style, and hence to a certain period, so as to efficiently locate it within the corpus of literature. Meta-memory thus serves both a cognitive function of retrieving information from a corpus and a social epistemic function of organizing information in ways that embody the "lore" of the corpus. The retrieval of information is an epistemic activity that proceeds via the previous classifications of cultural authorities. With the advent of technologies that automate the functions of accessing and recovering memory, meta-memory converges with external memory. What was a central task of cultural organization becomes another "outsourced" cognition. If I have in mind a line of poetic verse, say, "Let us go then, you and I," but can recall neither the author nor the period and am unable to classify the style, these days I can simply write the line of verse in the text window of a search engine and look at the results. The results are a list of Web sites ranked by an algorithm that considers both relevance and accessibility. This list serves a meta-mnemonic function. The highly improbable combination of words in a line of verse makes possible a sufficiently relevant selection of information that yields the poem from which the line is taken as the first result in the search inquiry.

This meta-memory is part of the fabric of the Web. The Web uniquely allows a user to leave a mark that is immediately reusable by others. (This system resembles the trails that snails leave on the ground, which reveal to other snails the path to be followed, a phenomenon called "stigmergy" in ethology.)[32] These patterns of use have informational content that can influence the preferences and actions of users. This corpus of knowledge is built and maintained by the individual behavior of users, and it is automatically filtered by aggregative systems.

To illustrate this dynamic, I will analyze two types of meta-memory devices. Both devices select and sort information in a way that informs and influences the behavior of others, albeit in slightly different ways. This difference is worth considering more carefully.

COLLABORATIVE FILTERING: WISDOM OUT OF ALGORITHMS

Knowledge Management Systems

Collaborative filtering is a way of drawing inferences about the preferences of one user on the basis of patterns of behavior of others. It is used mainly for commercial purposes in Web applications, although it has been extended to other domains. A well-known example of a collaborative filtering system is Amazon.com. Amazon.com is both a commercial Web application and a

---

[32] See the introduction to this volume by Landemore (this volume).

knowledge management system that tracks users' interactions. This tracking component displays correlations between patterns of purchases in a way that projects a user's preferences. The best-known feature of this system makes predictions with the format "Customers who buy X also buy Y." The matching between X and Y is, in a sense, bottom-up, although the design of the inferential thresholds is fixed by the information architecture of the system. For example, say that you bought James Surowiecki's book *The Wisdom of Crowds*. The Amazon page for Surowiecki's book will recommend other books, like Ian Ayers's *Super Crunchers*, via an algorithm that divines correlations from the aggregated preferences of other users who bought *The Wisdom of Crowds*. It is a unique feature of these interactive systems that new categories are created by the automatic transformation of human actions into visible rankings. The collective intelligence of the system is due to a division of cognitive labor between the algorithms that compose and visualize information, and the users who interact with the system. These inferences are not themselves the products of previous cultural knowledge, but rather emerge from the patterns of individual interactions with the system. Of course, biases are possible within the system. The weights associated with each item are fixed so that some items have a greater chance of being recommended than others. However, because the system is alimented by the repeated actions of the users, an overly biased recommendation (i.e., one that will not reliably motivate user activity) will not be replicated enough times to stabilize as an equilibrium.

PageRank

Search engines are another collective wisdom system that performs meta-memory functions. Search engines have transformed (and, in some cases, revolutionized) our epistemic practices. Indeed, these tools are useful because of the social structure of the Web,[33] a network from which much can be divined about the preferences and habits of users. Second-generation search engines, most prominently Google's, exploit this structure to gain information about the distribution of knowledge. The PageRank algorithm interprets a link from page A to page B as equivalent to page A voting for page B. But while the Web may be a democracy, not every vote counts the same. Votes from certain sites – called "hubs" – have more weight than others, which is reflected in a reputational hierarchy. A link from my home page to the page of Harvard University counts much less than a link to my page from Harvard's. To borrow an expression from social network theorists, the Web is an "aristocratic" network, one in which the "rich get richer."[34] The more links a page receives, the higher the probability that it will receive more links. This disparity of weights creates a "reputational landscape" that informs the result of future queries. The PageRank algorithm is nourished by the local knowledge and preferences of individual users, and in turn it generates plausibly relevant results for the user.

[33] Kleinberg (2001).
[34] See Newman, Barabasi, and Watts (2006).

This system is not a knowledge management system, though, since PageRank knows nothing about the particular pattern of activities of each individual. A *click* from a page to another is opaque information for PageRank, whereas a *link* between two pages contains a lot of information about users' knowledge that PageRank is able to extract. Still, PageRank resembles knowledge management systems in that its design facilitates an aggregated collective intelligence from uncoordinated inputs. Whatever collaboration occurs is the result of automated systems rather than human agents.[35] Knowledge management systems draw inferences from unwitting information, search engines from the links between pages. In both cases, the collective intelligence emerges from individually motivated actions.

The bias of search engines has been a major subject of discussion recently. As a result of political interventions, second-generation search engines like Google's now mark paid inclusions and preferred placements. From an epistemic standpoint, perhaps a more interesting topic is the tendency of aristocratic networks to reinforce the prominence of the most powerful, or the so-called *Matthew effect*.[36] Yet the effect of these biases can be muted, and if users are informed about such biasing tendencies they should be less vulnerable to them. For example, recent work[37] shows that search engines favor their own services (videos, images, etc.) in displaying results. We would expect (and hope) that users gain awareness of this bias for interconnected services.

REPUTATION SYSTEMS: WISDOM OUT OF STATUS ANXIETY

The collaborative filtering of information may sometimes require more active communal participation than the preceding examples suggest. In *Information Politics on the Web*, the sociologist Richard Rogers classifies Web dynamics as *voluntaristic* or *nonvoluntaristic* on the basis of the comparative role of humans and machines in generating information feedback. The systems described earlier are highly nonvoluntaristic. *Reputation systems*, by contrast, are more voluntaristic, involving a special kind of collaborative filtering algorithm that determines ratings for a collection of agents based on the agents' opinions of each other. Reputation systems thus collect, distribute, and aggregate information about participants' past behavior.

One of the best-known and most straightforward large-scale reputation systems is the one for auction sales at www.eBay.com. eBay allows commercial interactions among more than 200 million registered users. A buyer bids on

---

[35] Knowledge management systems like Amazon.com have some collaborative filtering features that require cooperation, like reviews and direct rankings of books. Yet these cooperative activities are not essential to the functioning of the collaborative filtering process.

[36] The Matthew effect, coined by the great sociologist of science Robert Merton, posits that credit is disproportionately given to those who have it already. The expression refers to a well-known passage in the Gospels: "For unto every one that hath shall be given, and he shall have abundance: but from him that hath not shall be taken away even that which he hath" (Matt. 25:29).

[37] Edelman and Lockwood (2011).

items and, if successful, enters a commercial transaction with the seller. Both buyers and sellers may leave feedback about the quality of the transaction. This information is automatically aggregated into a feedback profile, which includes positive feedback and negative feedback (coupled with some narrative comments). The reputation revealed by one's profile informs one's future interactions with buyers and sellers. Reputation thus has an immediate commercial value: in a market with fragmented offers and restricted information about sellers, reputation is tightly intertwined with trustworthiness. Note that eBay generates an economic or game-theoretic, rather than epistemic, form of reputation, one that tracks the histories of and is specifically attached to particular agents.[38] Indeed, because of the value of reputation in this environment, some buyers and sellers engage in sham transactions in order to enhance their reputations. Although the collective result of this dynamic is to facilitate cooperation, the feedback system itself is collaborative behavior that does not require any participant to value cooperation as such. Users who do not comply with the norms of the feedback system can be sanctioned in a variety of ways; sometimes they are evaluated negatively, not because of the quality of the transaction, but because of their refusal to participate in the evaluation dynamic. In some cases, those who violate the norms of evaluative participation are excluded from the community entirely. Active participation from the users thus arises, in part, because of each user's fear of being ostracized by the community (and, as a result, losing valuable business opportunities). Here, too, the possibility for bias is significant: one's reputation is vitally important, but caring too much about it (in the form of engaging in reputation-enhancing tactics) can actually undermine one's reliability. Similar reputational features are used by noncommercial systems. For example, consider Flickr (www.flickr.com), a Yahoo service that consists of a collaborative platform for sharing photos. Users choose to share photos and, for any given photo, can track which other users have viewed and approved it.

These Web-based reputation systems differ from other systems measuring reputation, such as citation analysis of the Science Citation Index. This system uses scientometric techniques to measure the impact of a publication based on how it is cited by other publications. Here measuring reputation does not require any special participation by agents, nor does it take into account preferences or behaviors other than citation.[39] However, these systems might soon evolve new ways to measure reputation and influence based on the evaluative judgments of those who consume these informational products. Many efforts to include this social dimension in evaluation promise to dramatically improve our systems of measuring academic reputation and impact.[40]

---

[38] For game-theoretic approaches to reputation, see Mailath and Samuelson (2006). For a collection of essays on the economics of reputation, see Klein (1997).

[39] On the Science Citation Index, see Origgi (2007b).

[40] See, e.g., the new European Commission project, Liquidpublication, http://wiki.liquidpub.org/, whose aim is to promote an alternative Web-based system of scientific production that takes

OPEN COLLABORATIVE SYSTEMS: WISDOM OUT OF COOPERATION

In the future, collaborative filtering on the Web may become even more voluntaristic, although whether such systems produce intelligent outcomes will still depend crucially on their architecture. Two prominent examples of collaborative systems owe their success to active human cooperation: first, "open-source" communities of software development, like the one supporting the operating system Linux; second, "open-content" projects like Wikipedia. In both cases, the filtering process is completely human-made: code or content is made available to a community and filtered according to local standards. These communities are, for the most part, composed of amateurs rather than professionals. Collective wisdom thus emerges when individual efforts are filtered through the cooperative norms of the enterprise.

I will not extensively discuss biases on Wikipedia; these are both well known and complex enough to warrant a separate essay. It is notable that Larry Sanger, one of Wikipedia's founders, currently promotes an alternative project, www.citizendum.org, which includes a mechanism for evaluating individual contributors. Wikipedia, of course, lacks such a mechanism. As a result, self-promotion, ideology, and targeted attacks on reputation threaten to bias entries. Yet for the most part, these threats have not materialized, and the fear that Wikipedia is a fount of tendentious information has been largely disconfirmed. Thanks to its scale and the differentiated perspectives of contributors, Wikipedia entries have been found to be roughly as reliable as their counterparts in the *Encyclopaedia Britannica*[41] (although the validity of this study has been questioned).[42] In this case, democracy and size are not the only drivers of reliability. Wikipedia enjoys a core group of members who are committed to its values and aims and disproportionately participate in efforts to police the quality of entries. As Florence Devouard, the former president of the French Wikimedia Foundation, pointed out,[43] Wikipedia works because it is organized around a multiplicity of communities (usually sorted by language, nation, or focus of interest), each of which is strongly animated by a group of so-called glue people or bridge people, who develop the best practices within communities and facilitate their spread to other communities. Wikipedia also works because it transmits cultural information. This transmission function allows a division of labor, as a diffuse group of contributors can add discrete bits of information to a single entry. Rules and norms of cooperation thus enable the growth and maintenance of this collective wisdom system. Yet they do not

---

into account credits established by the scientific community as well as credits accumulated through the opinions expressed by the readers of the articles.

[41] See "Internet Encyclopedias Go Head to Head," *Nature*, 438 (December 15, 2005).

[42] See the reply to L. Giles's *Nature* inquiry written by the Encyclopaedia Britannica at http://corporate.britannica.com/britannica_nature_response.pdf, and Nicolas Carr's critical analysis of the results at http://www.roughtype.com/archives/2006/03/britannicas_ind.php.

[43] See Florence Devouard's speech at the *World Knowledge Dialogue* (Crans, Switzerland, September 2008), http://www.wkdnews.org/webcast?clip=9.

invariably reinforce democracy. The institutional architecture of Wikipedia is extremely complex and hierarchical, especially given the increasing professionalization of the Wikimedia Foundation, which oversees the project. This foundation, like all foundations, is subject to pressure from donors and stakeholders. The danger is, as one former employee of Wikimedia France, who prefers to remain anonymous, told me, that this capacity for more centralized control will create a cadre that can usurp the distributed network of contributors. Such a consolidation of power might threaten the epistemic productivity of the system.

SHARING FOLKSONOMIES: WISDOM OUT OF TAGGING INFORMATION

Many of the most interesting and promising collective wisdom systems are *social computing systems,* in which social software facilitates individual organization into groups for the pursuit of collective goals. Many such systems are based on social "tagging," or the organization of information according to spontaneous, user-generated categorizations. Tagging involves the addition of keywords or markers to digital resources. These markers are then accessible to the user and (often) to others, and can be used to search for content. A variety of content can be tagged, including blogs (Technorati), books (Amazon), photos (Flickr), podcasts (Odeo), videos (YouTube), Web pages (Delicious), to tags themselves. Tags are both metadata and content. Tagging also allows social groups to coalesce around shared interests and points of view, so it is inherently social. Social tagging is one of the most powerful tools of Web 2.0, one that both harnesses the "wisdom of crowds" and facilitates connections among users.[44] An example of a social tagging system is CiteULike, a free online service for sharing academic papers within scientific communities. CiteULike allows users to find out who is reading similar papers and organize libraries around tags. Preferences are voluntarily shared by users, who are asked to rate items, express a comparative preference between two items, or create lists of highly rated items. The result is a collaborative filtering technique, albeit with an active component: preferences are expressed rather than inferred from behavior. Yet such active filtering mechanisms may affect the epistemic reliability of the information products. It is well known in psychology[45] that we often lack introspective access to our own preferences, routinely expressing preferences that are inconsistent with our behavior. If asked, I might express a preference for classical music. However, if I keep a weekly record of how often I listen to classical music compared with other genres of music in a week, I would probably realize that my preferences are quite different.

[44] See G. Veltri, "Social Computing and Social Science," TGE Adonis CNRS report, December 2008.

[45] The phenomenon is known in social psychology as *introspection illusion* and *bias blind spot.* See Nisbett and Wilson (1977), Pronin and Kugler (2007).

Folk taxonomies produced by social tagging are "traditions" in the Burkean sense described earlier: they provide filtered, evaluative information that can be used to improve our classifications of the world. Yet these "high-tech traditions" are instantaneously produced rather than institutionally reinforced: they can be created and re-created anew. If they last, it is most likely because they serve a cognitive function, not merely an ideological one. The more information that falls under these systems, the better their products. If we carefully attend to their design, open collaborative systems promise a virtuous circle, a "cornucopia of the commons" in which use brings overflowing abundance.[46]

CONCLUSIONS

Web tools can promote collective wisdom by aggregating individual choices and preferences. However, to borrow a slogan common among promoters of the social Web, "architecture is politics." The design features that I have highlighted here generate dramatically different collective wisdom systems. In some systems, there is no community at all (or, in the case of Google, none that is normatively interesting). In other systems (e.g., eBay), the community is more normatively demanding, as widespread participation is necessary for the system's survival. These differences must be accounted for in order for Web 2.0 to provide generalizable results for the design of collective wisdom procedures.

Let me end with an epistemological claim about the kind of knowledge that is produced by these tools. As I have argued throughout this essay, collective wisdom systems work insofar as they provide access to rankings, ratings, and other ways of classifying and evaluating information. Even Wikipedia, which does not avail itself of any explicit rating device, works on the principle that, if an entry has survived the editing rigors of other wikipedians, it is likely to be reliable. This is an implicit rating device, and one that many think should be more explicit.[47] In my opinion, the survival of egalitarian projects like Wikipedia depends on their capacity to incorporate rankings in order to orient the choices of users. Without the general reputation of Wikipedia, the epistemic success of that project would be much more doubtful.

The Web is not only a powerful reservoir of labeled and unlabeled information, but also a powerful reputational tool that draws on the rankings, ratings, tags, weights, and biases that are integral to our knowledge practices. In our information-dense world, knowledge is a cacophony that, without evaluation, we would encounter as mutes. Knowledge systems grow and survive by generating evaluative tools. Cultural traditions arise from, transmit, and are sustained by their labeling systems. Reputational tools like rankings and ratings play the same role for collective wisdom systems like the Web. In the Web era, our

---

[46] On the idea of "cornucopia of the commons," which echoes G. Hardin's well-known article, "The Tragedy of the Commons," *Science*, 162, no. 3859 (1968), 1243–46, see Dan Bricklin's blog: http://www.bricklin.com/cornucopia.htm.

[47] See Sanger (2007) and my reply to him, Origgi "Why Reputation Matters," www.edge.org.

inevitable evaluations proceed through tools that can challenge our received views and reflect a more democratic way of selecting knowledge. To appreciate how institutional design might harness these reputational devices, we must first appreciate that they are part of the fabric of our digital sentences.

References

E. Adar and F. Huberman (2000), "Free Riding on Gnutella," *First Monday*, http://firstmonday.org/htbin/cgiwrap/bin/ojs/index.php/fm/article/view/792/701.

J. L. Bower and C. M. Christensen (1995), "Disruptive Technologies: Catching the Wave," *Harvard Business Review*, 73(1): 43–53.

R. Boyd and P. Richerson (2005), *Not by Genes Alone: How Culture Transformed Human Evolution*, University of Chicago Press.

E. Burke (1790), *Reflections on the Revolution in France*, vol. 8 in *Writings and Speeches of Edmund Burke*, gen. ed. P. Langford, Clarendon Press, Oxford, 1981–97.

C. M. Christensen (1997), *The Innovator's Dilemma*, Harvard Business Press, Cambridge, MA.

A. Clark (2003), *Natural Born Cyborgs*, Oxford University Press.

L. Conradt and C. List (2009), "Group Decisions in Humans and Animals: A Survey," *Philosophical Transactions of the Royal Society B*, 364: 719–42.

G. Csibra and G. Gergely (2009), "Natural Pedagogy," *Trends in Cognitive Science*, 13(4): 148–53.

B. Edelman and B. Lockwood (2011), "Measuring Bias in 'Organic' Web Search," http://www.benedelman.org/searchbias/.

J. Goody (1986), *The Logic of Writing and the Organization of Society*, Cambridge University Press.

J. Henrich and R. Boyd (1998), "The Evolution of Conformist Transmission and the Emergence of Between-Group Differences," *Evolution and Human Behavior*, 19: 215–41.

J. Henrich et al. (2006), "Costly Punishment Across Human Societies," *Science*, 312(5781): 1767–70.

D. Klein (ed.) (1997), *Reputation*, University of Michigan Press, Ann Arbor.

J. Kleinberg (2001), "The Structure of the Web," *Science*, 294: 1849–50.

R. Kurzweil (1990), *The Age of Intelligent Machines*, MIT Press, Cambridge, MA.

L. Lessig (2001), *The Future of Ideas*, Vintage, New York.

P. Lévy (2000), *Worldphilosophie*, Éditions Odile Jacob, Paris.

G. J. Mailath and L. Samuelson (2006), *Repeated Games and Reputation*, Oxford University Press.

M. Mäkinen (2009), *Digital Empowerment in Community Development*, PhD thesis, Tampere University Press.

S. Mathew and R. Boyd (2009), "When Does Optional Participation Allow the Evolution of Cooperation?" *Proceedings of the Royal Society (B)*, 276: 1167–74.

M. Newman, A. L. Barabasi, and D. J. Watts (2006), *The Structure and Dynamics of Networks*, Princeton University Press.

R. Nisbett and E. Wilson (1977), "Telling More Than We Can Know: Verbal Reports on Mental Processes," *Psychological Review*, 84(3): 231–59.

G. Origgi (2007a), "Wine Epistemology: The Role of Reputation and Rating Systems in the World of Wine," in B. Smith (ed.), *Questions of Taste: The Philosophy of Wine*, 236–53, Oxford University Press.

(2007b), "Un certain regard. Pour une épistémologie de la réputation," Paper presented at the workshop *La réputation*, Fondazione Olivetti, Rome, April.

(2008), *Qu'est-ce que la confiance*, VRIN, Paris.

(2010a), "Epistemic Vigilance and Epistemic Responsibility in the Liquid World of Scientific Publications," *Social Epistemology*, 24 (3): 147–57.

(2010b), "The Age of Reputation," in J. Brockman (ed.), *This Will Change Everything: Ideas That Will Shape the Future*, 173–74, Harper, New York.

(2010c), "Rational Trust and Reputation: For a Second-Order Epistemology," Paper presented at the Workshop on Epistemic Trust, University of Copenhagen.

(2011), "Collective Quality: How to Design Collective Standards of Knowledge?" in J. Billotte, M. Cockell, F. Darbellay, and F. Waldvogel (eds.), *Common Knowledge: The Challenge of Transdisciplinarity*, 197–204, Presses Polytechniques et Universitaires Romandes, Lausanne.

(in press), "Reputation" in B. Kaldys (ed.) *SAGE Encyclopedia of Philosophy of Social Science*, SAGE Publications, New York.

E. Pronin and M. Kugler (2006), "Valuing Thoughts, Ignoring Behavior: The Introspection Illusion as a Source of the Bias Blind Spot," *Journal of Experimental Social Psychology*, 43: 565–78.

W. V. O. Quine (1961), "Carnap and Logical Truth," reprinted in *The Ways of Paradox and Other Essays*, Harvard University Press, Cambridge, MA.

R. Rogers (2004), *Information Politics of the Web*, MIT Press, Cambridge, MA.

L. Sanger (2007), "Who Says We Know: On the New Politics of Knowledge," at www.edge.org and my reply at www.edge.org.org: http://www.edge.org/3rd_culture/sanger07/sanger07_index.html.

F. Subiaul, J. Vonk, S. Okamoto-Barth, and J. Barth (2008), "Do Chimpanzees Learn Reputation by Observation? Evidence from Direct and Indirect Experience with Generous and Selfish Strangers," *Animal Cognition*, 11: 611–23.

D. Sperber et al. (2010), "Epistemic Vigilance," *Mind and Language*, 25 (4): 359–93.

C. R. Sunstein (2006), *Infotopia*, Oxford University Press.

J. Tirole (1996), "A Theory of Collective Reputations," *Review of Economic Studies*, 63 (1): 1–22.

3

Some Microfoundations of Collective Wisdom

Lu Hong and Scott E. Page

In describing the benefits of democracy, Aristotle observed that when individuals see distinct parts of the whole, the collective appraisal can surpass that of individuals. Centuries later, von Hayek, in describing the role of information in decentralized markets, made a related argument suggesting that the market can accurately determine prices even if the average person in the market cannot (von Hayek 1945). To be sure, institutional structures such as democracies and markets rest substantially on the emergence of collective wisdom. Without a general tendency for groups of people to make reasonable appraisals and decisions, democracy would be doomed. The success of democracies, and for that matter markets, provides broad-stroke support that collective wisdom often does exist. Abundant anecdotal and small- to large-scale empirical examples also suggest at least the potential for a "wisdom of crowds" (Surowiecki 2004).

Collective wisdom, as we shall define it here, exists when the crowd outperforms the people in it at a predictive task. This is a restrictive notion. Wisdom often has a broader conception than mere accuracy. A society deliberating on laws or common purpose must exercise wisdom in judgment. The task is much richer and nuanced than estimating the value of a stock or the weight of a steer. And yet if we see wisdom in these contexts, and anticipating multiple implications and interactions, then we might also think of wisdom as the ability to recognize the multiplicity of effects and to accurately predict the magnitude of each. If so, we might see our conception of collective wisdom as less circumscribed.

The logical statistical foundations for collective wisdom are well known. First, a straightforward mathematical calculation demonstrates that the average prediction of a crowd *always* outperforms the prediction of the crowd's average member (Page 2007). Second, this same calculation implies that, with some regularity, crowds can outperform *any* member or all but a few of their members. We describe how that can be the case in detail.

Mathematics and lofty prose not withstanding, the claim that the whole of a society or group somehow exceeds the sum of its parts occurs to many to be overidealized. Any mathematician or philosopher who took a moment to venture out of his or her office would find no end of committee decisions, jury verdicts, democratic choices, and market valuations that have proved far wide of the mark. Collective wisdom, therefore, should be seen as a potential outcome, as something that can occur when the right conditions hold, but it is in no way guaranteed.

The gap between theory and reality can be explained by the starkness of existing theory. The core assumptions that drive the mathematical necessity of collective wisdom may be too convenient. In particular, the idea that people receive independent signals that correlate with the truth has come to be accepted without thought. And as we shall argue, it is this assumption that creates the near inevitability of collective wisdom.

In this essay, we describe a richer theoretical structure that can explain the existence of collective wisdom as well as the lack thereof. In this model, individuals possess predictive models. Hong and Page (2007) refer to these as *interpreted signals* to capture the fact that these predictions can be thought of as statistical signals but that their values depend on how people interpret the world. The prediction of a crowd of people can be thought of as some type of average of the models contained within those people's heads. Thus, collective wisdom depends on characteristics of the models people carry around in their heads. We show that for collective wisdom to emerge, those models must be sophisticated or they must be diverse. Ideally, crowds will possess both.

These two features refer to different units of analysis. Diversity refers to the collection seen as a whole. The people within it, or their models, must differ. Sophistication/expertise refers to the capabilities of individuals within the collection. The individuals must be smart. There need not be a trade-off between these two aspects of a crowd. Crowd members can become both more sophisticated and more diverse. They can also become less sophisticated and less diverse. In the former case, the crowd becomes more accurate, and in the latter case, it becomes less so. A trade-off does exist in the necessity of these characteristics for an accurate crowd. Homogeneous crowds can be accurate only if they contain extremely sophisticated individuals, and groups of naive individuals can be collectively accurate only if they possess great diversity.[1]

The intuition that collective wisdom requires sophisticated individuals when those individuals are homogeneous should be straightforward. We cannot expect an intelligent whole to emerge from incompetent parts. The intuition that diversity matters, and matters as much as it does, proves more subtle, so much so that several accounts misinterpret the mechanism through which diversity operates and others resort to hand waving. The logic of why diversity matters requires two steps. First, diverse models tend to produce negatively

---

[1] Our approach borrows ideas from ensemble learning theory. In ensemble learning, collections of models are trained to make a prediction or a classification. The predictions of the individual models are then aggregated to produce a collective prediction.

correlated predictions.[2] Second, negatively correlated predictions produce better aggregate outcomes. If two predictions are negatively correlated, when one tends to be high the other tends to be low, making the average more accurate.

The model we describe differs from the standard approach in political science and economics, or what we call the *statistical model* of aggregation. As mentioned earlier, in the statistical model, individuals receive signals that correlate with the value or outcome of interest. Each individual's signal may not be that accurate, but in aggregate, owing to a law of large numbers logic, those errors tend to cancel. In the canonical statistical model, errors are assumed to be independent. More elaborate versions of the model include both negative and positive correlation, a modification we take up at some length, as negative correlation proves to be crucial for collective wisdom.

In what follows, we first describe the statistical model of collective wisdom. This approach dominates the social science literature on voting and markets, as well as the early computational literature on ensemble learning. That said, the computational scientists do a much more complete job of characterizing the contributions of diversity. Social science models tend to sweep diversity under the rug – calling it noise. In fact, we might even go so far as to say that social scientists consider diversity to be an inconvenience more than a benefit.

We then formally define *interpreted signals* (Hong and Page 2007). These form the basis for what we will call the *cognitive model* of collective wisdom. This approach dominates the current computational science models. This cognitive model does not in any way contradict the statistical model. In fact, we rely on the statistical model as a lens through which to interpret the cognitive model. In characterizing both types of models, we consider a general environment that includes both binary-choice environments, that is, simple yes or no choices, and cardinal estimation, such as when a collection of people must predict the value of a stock or the rate of inflation. When necessary for clarity, we refer to the former as *classification problems* and to the latter as *estimation problems*. The analysis differs only slightly across the two domains, and the core intuitions prove to be the same. We conclude our analysis with a lengthy discussion of what the theoretical results imply for the existence or lack thereof of collective wisdom in markets and democracies; we also discuss what we call the *paradox of weighting*. That discussion is by no means exhaustive but is meant to highlight the value of constructing deeper microfoundations.

Before beginning, we must address two issues. First, a growing literature in political science and in economics considers the implications of and incentives for strategic voting. For the most part, we steer clear of strategic considerations. When they do come into play, we point out what their effect might be. We want to make clear from the outset that regardless of what motivates the way votes

---

[2] In the case of a yes or no choice, Hong and Page (2007) show that when people use maximally diverse models (we formalize this in the paper), their predictions are necessarily negatively correlated.

are cast, the possibility of collective wisdom ultimately hinges on a combination of collective diversity and individual sophistication/expertise.

Second, we would be remiss if we did not note the irony of our model's main result: that collective wisdom requires diverse or sophisticated models. Yet in this essay, we have constructed just two models – a statistical model and a model based on individuals who themselves have models. If our theory is correct, these two cannot be enough. Far better that we have what Page (2007) calls "a crowd of models." Complementing these models with historical, empirical, sociological, psychological, experimental, and computational models should provide a deeper, more accurate picture of what conditions must hold for collective wisdom to emerge. Clearly, cultural, social, and psychological distortions can also bias aggregation. We leave to other essays in this volume the task of fleshing out those other perspectives on collective intelligence. We note in passing that historical accounts, such as that of Ober (Chapter 6, this volume), also identify diversity and sophistication as crucial to the production of collective wisdom.

THE STATISTICAL MODEL OF COLLECTIVE WISDOM

The statistical model of collective wisdom considers the predictions or votes of individuals to be *random variables* drawn from a distribution. That distribution can be thought of as generating random variables conditional on some true outcome. In the most basic models, the accuracy of the signals is captured by an *error term*. In more elaborate models, signals can also include a *bias*. In the canonical model, the signals are assumed to be independent. This independence assumption can be thought of as capturing diversity, but how that diversity translates into the signals is left implicit. More nuanced theoretical results will allow for degrees of correlation, as we shall show.

In all of the models that follow, we assume a collection of individuals of fixed size:

*The **set of individuals**:* $N = \{1, \ldots, n\}$.

The voters attempt to predict the *outcome*. As previously mentioned, that outcome can be either a simple yes/no or a numerical value:

*The **outcome** $\theta \in \Theta$. In classification problems $\Theta = \{0, 1\}$, and in estimation problems $\Theta = [0, \infty]$.*

As mentioned, individuals receive signals. A signal can be thought of as the prediction or opinion of the individual. To distinguish these signals from those produced by cognitive models, we refer to this first type as *generated signals* and to the latter as *interpreted signals*. This nomenclature serves as a reminder that in the statistical model the signals are generated by some process that produces signals according to some distribution, whereas in the cognitive model the signal an individual obtains depends on how he or she interprets the world:

*Individual i's **generated signal*** $s_i \in \Theta$ *is drawn from the distribution* $f_i(\cdot \mid \theta)$.

The notation allows for each individual's signals to be drawn from a different distribution function. The collection of all signals can be characterized by a *collective distribution function*:

> *The **collective distribution function*** $g(s_1, s_2, \ldots, s_n \mid \theta$ *describes the joint distribution of all of the signals conditional on* θ,
>
> $g_i(s_1, s_2, \ldots, s_n \mid \theta) = f_i(s_i \mid \theta)$.

The *squared error* of an individual's signal equals the square of the difference between the signal and the true outcome:

> *The **sq-error** of the ith individual's signal* $SqE(s_i) = (s_i - \theta)^2$.

> *The **average sq-error*** $SqE(\vec{s}) = \frac{1}{n} \sum_{i=1}^{n} (s_i - \theta)^2$.

In what follows, we assume that the *collective prediction* equals the average of the individuals' signals. In the last section of the essay, we take up differential weighting of signals:

> *The **collective prediction*** $c = \frac{1}{n} \sum_{i=1}^{n} s_i$.

We denote the squared error of the collective prediction by $SqE(c)$. The squared error gives a measure of the accuracy of the collective. We can measure the *predictive diversity* of the collective by taking the variance of the predictions:

> *The **predictive diversity** of a vector of signals* $\vec{s} = (s_1, s_2, \ldots, s_n)$ *equals their variance.*

$$PDiv(\vec{s}) = \frac{1}{n} \sum_{i=1}^{n} (s_i - c)^2.$$

Statistical Model Results

With this notation in hand, we can now state what Page (2007) calls the *Diversity Prediction Theorem* and the *Crowds Beat Averages Law*. These widely known results provide the basic logic for the wisdom of crowds. The first theorem states that the squared error of the collective prediction equals the average squared error minus the predictive diversity. Here we see the first evidence that collective accuracy depends both on expertise (low average error) and on diversity.

Theorem 1 (Diversity Prediction Theorem). *The squared error of the collective prediction equals the average squared error minus the predictive diversity:*

$$SqE(c) = SqE(\vec{s}) - PDiv(\vec{s}).$$

Proof. Expanding each term in the expression, it suffices to show that

$$(c - \theta)^2 = c^2 - 2c\theta + \theta^2$$

$$= \left[\sum_{i=1}^{n} \frac{s_i^2}{n}\right] - 2c\theta + \theta^2 - \left[\sum_{i=1}^{n} \frac{s_i^2}{n}\right] + 2c^2 - c^2$$

$$= \frac{1}{n}\left[\sum_{i=1}^{n}(s_i^2 - 2s_i\theta + \theta^2)\right] - \frac{1}{n}\left[\sum_{i=1}^{n}(s_i^2 - 2s_i c + c^2)\right]$$

$$= \frac{1}{n}\left[\sum_{i=1}^{n}(s_i - \theta)^2\right] - \frac{1}{n}\left[\sum_{i=1}^{n}(s_i - c)^2\right].$$

Note that in the proof the third equality follows from the second by the definition of c. A corollary of this theorem states that the collective squared error must always be less than or equal to the average of the individuals' squared errors.

Corollary 1 (Crowd Beats Averages Law). *The squared error of the collective's prediction is less than or equal to the averaged squared error of the individuals that make up the crowd.*

The fact that predictive diversity cannot be negative implies that the corollary follows immediately from the theorem. Nevertheless, the corollary merits stating. It provides a clean description of collective wisdom. In aggregating signals, the whole cannot be less accurate than the average of its parts.

The previous two results beg the question: How do we ensure diverse predictions? We now describe more general results from the statistical model of collective wisdom to address this. That characterization will get us partway there, but to fully understand the basis of diverse predictions, we need a cognitive model, a point we take up in the next section. Now, however, we focus on the statistical foundations of diverse predictions.

We first note that the previous two results describe a particular instance. Here, we derive results in expectation over all possible realizations of the generated signals given the outcome. Before, we considered a single instance, so we could think of each signal as having an error. Now, we average over a distribution, and errors can take two forms. A person's signal could be systematically off the mark, or it could just be off in a particular realization. To differentiate between the systematic error in an individual's generated signal and the idiosyncratic noise, statisticians refer to these as the *bias* and the *variance* of the signal:

> Let $\mu_i(\theta)$ denote the **mean** of individual i's signal conditional on θ.
> Individual i's **bias**, $b_i = (\mu_i - \theta)$.
>
> The **variance** of individual i's signal $v_i = E[(s_i - \mu_i)^2]$.

We can also define the *average bias* and the *average variance* across the individuals:

> The **average bias**, $\bar{b} = \frac{1}{n}\sum_{i=1}^{n}(\mu_i - \theta)$.
>
> The **average variance** $\bar{V} = \frac{1}{n}\sum_{i=1}^{n} E[s_i - \mu_i]^2$.

To state the next result, we need to introduce the idea of covariance. The covariance of two random variables characterizes whether they tend to move in the same direction or in opposite directions. If covariance is positive, when one signal is above its mean the other is likely to be above its mean as well. Negative covariance implies the opposite. Thus, negatively correlated signals tend to cancel out one another's idiosyncratic errors.

> The **average covariance** $\bar{C} = \frac{1}{n(n-1)}\sum_{i=1}^{n}\sum_{j\neq i} E[s_i - \mu_i][s_j - \mu_j]$.

Note the implicit mode of thinking that underpins this analysis. Each person has an associated distribution function that generates signals. Any one prediction can be thought of as a random draw from that distribution.

To evaluate a prediction's accuracy prior to a random draw, we use the measure of expected squared error, $E[SqE(s_i)]$. Mathematically, it is straightforward that the expected squared error can be decomposed into the systematic error and the idiosyncratic noise:

$$E(s_i - \theta)^2 = (\mu_i - \theta)^2 + E(s_i - \mu_i)^2.$$

The expected squared error for the collective has the same decomposition:

$$E[SqE(c)] = \left(\frac{1}{n}\sum_{i=1}^{n}\mu_i - \theta\right)^2 + E\left[\frac{1}{n}\sum_{i=1}^{n}(s_i - \mu_i)\right]^2.$$

Note that $c = \frac{1}{n}\sum_{i=1}^{n} s_i$, and the mean of the collective prediction is equal to the average of the individual means, $\frac{1}{n}\sum_{i=1}^{n}\mu_i$.

This decomposition reveals the key to collective wisdom in the statistical model. First, the collective's systematic error (the first term on the right side) is smaller if individuals bias in different ways – some bias upward and others bias downward. This is because the bias for the collective is the average of the individuals' biases. In the collective, biases get averaged out. Second, for any realization of the signals, the collective's deviation from its mean is the average of the individual deviations from their respective means. So if individuals deviate in different ways – if some deviate by being too high and others deviate by being too low – then the deviation of the collective is reduced, leading to a smaller idiosyncratic error. In other words, in the collective, idiosyncratic errors get averaged out. Finally, if enough such realization happens, taking expectation over the distributions, idosyncratic error for the collective is small. We characterize these situations with variance and covariance in the following result, commonly known as the *bias–variance–covariance decomposition*.

Theorem 2 (Bias–Variance–Covariance (BVC) Decomposition). *Given n generated signals with average bias $\bar{b}$, average variance $\bar{V}$, and average covariance $\bar{C}$, the following identity holds:*

$$E[SqE(c)] = \bar{b}^2 + \frac{1}{n}\bar{V} + \frac{n-1}{n}\bar{C}$$

Proof. From the discussion of the previous decomposition, we need only show that $E[\frac{1}{n}\sum_{i=1}^{n} i = 1^n (s_i - \mu_i)]^2 = \frac{1}{n}\bar{V} + \frac{n-1}{n}\bar{C}$.

$$E\left[\frac{1}{n}\sum_{i=1}^{n}(s_i - \mu_i)\right]^2 = \frac{1}{n^2}E\left[\sum_{i=1}^{n}(s_i - \mu_i)^2 + \sum_{i=1}^{n}\sum_{j=1, j\neq i}^{n}(s_i - \mu_i)(s_j - \mu_j)\right]$$

$$= \frac{1}{n}\left[\frac{1}{n}\sum_{i=1}^{n}E(s_i - \theta)^2 + (n-1)\right.$$

$$\left. \cdot \frac{1}{n(n-1)}\sum_{i=1}^{n}\sum_{j=1, j\neq i}^{n}E(s_i - \mu_i)(s_j - \mu_j)\right]$$

$$= \frac{1}{n}\left[\bar{V} + (n-1)\bar{C}\right]$$

$$= \frac{1}{n}\bar{V} + \frac{n-1}{n}\bar{C}.$$

At first glance, according to the BVC decomposition, increasing the variance of signals increases expected error. This seems to contradict the Diversity Prediction Theorem, which implies that variation in predictions reduces error. There is in fact no contradiction. First, the impact of the variance of signals on the collective error can not be analyzed alone. A change in the variance of signals often changes covariance, and therefore the impact of the variance of signals should be analyzed along with the impact of the covariance.

Consider a collective consisting of two people. The signals of these two people have the same variance, denoted by v. So $\overline{V} = v$. However, their signals are perfectly negatively correlated, which means that anytime one person's prediction deviates by being too high, the other deviates by being too low. Since the correlation is perfect, the magnitude of their covariance equals the variance. So $\overline{C} = -v$.

According to the BVC decomposition, the idiosyncratic error for the collective is equal to zero. This makes sense because, with each realization of the signals, the average deviation is also zero – one person's deviation cancels out the other's. Now let the variance increase, but keep everything else the same. Then the idiosyncratic error for the collective remains zero. That is, even though each individual signal is less accurate due to the increased variance, the collective does equally well.

Second, in the Diversity Prediction Theorem, variance is defined differently – it measures the difference between the individual signal realization and the resulting collective prediction. For the expected predictive diversity to be high, it has to be that for most of any given realizations, high deviations to the right by some are balanced out by high deviations to the left by others simply because the collective prediction is the average of individual signals. When bias is taken out of the picture, this implies negative correlations in signals, which lowers the expected squared error of the collective according to the BVC decomposition.

Taking the biases as given, if we consider generated signals that are negatively correlated to be diverse, then the theorems provide two alternative ways of seeing the benefits of accuracy and diversity for collective prediction.

We conclude our analysis of the statistical model with a corollary that states that as the collective grows large, if generated signals have no bias and bounded variance and covariance, then the expected squared error goes to zero.

Corollary 2 (Large Population Accuracy). *Assume that for each individual average bias $\overline{b} = 0$, average variance $\overline{V}$ is bounded from above and that average covaraince $\overline{C}$ is weakly less than zero. As the number of individuals goes to infinity, the expected collective squared error goes to zero.*

Proof. From the BVC decomposition, we have that

$$E[SqE(c)] = \overline{b}^2 + \frac{1}{n}\overline{V} + \frac{n-1}{n}\overline{C}.$$

By assumption, $\overline{b} = 0$ and there exists a T such that $\overline{V} < T$. Furthermore, $\overline{C} \leq 0$. Therefore, $E[SqE(c)] < T/n$, which goes to zero as n approaches infinity.

Note that *independent unbiased generated signals* are a special case of this corollary. If each individual's generated signals equal the truth plus an idiosyncratic error term, then as the collective grows large, it necessarily becomes wise.

THE COGNITIVE MODEL OF COLLECTIVE WISDOM

We now describe a cognitive model of collective wisdom. This cognitive model allows us to generate deeper insights than does the statistical model. In this section we show that for collective wisdom to emerge, the individuals must have relatively sophisticated models of the world; otherwise, we cannot expect them collectively to come to the correct answer. Furthermore, the models that people have in their heads must differ. If they don't, if everyone in the collective thinks the same way, the collective cannot be any better than the people in it. Thus, collective wisdom must depend on moderately sophisticated and diverse models. Finally, sophistication and diversity must be measured relative to the context. What is it that these individuals are trying to predict?

When we think of collective wisdom from a cognitive viewpoint, we begin to see shortcomings in the statistical model. The statistical model uses accuracy as a proxy for sophistication or expertise as well as for problem difficulty and uses covariance as a proxy for diversity. The cognitive model that we describe considers expertise, diversity, and sophistication explicitly. To do so, the model relies on signals of a different type, called *interpreted signals*. These signals come from predictive models.

Interpreted Signals

Interpreted signals can be thought of as model-based predictions that individuals make about the outcome.[3] Those models, in turn, can be thought of as approximations of an underlying *outcome function*. Therefore, before we can define an interpreted signal, we must first define the outcome function that the models approximate. To do this, we first denote the set of all possible states of the world:

The *set of states of the world X.*

The *outcome function F* maps each possible state into an outcome:

The **outcome function** $F : X \rightarrow \Theta$.

Each individual has an *interpretation* (Page 2007), which is a partition of the set of states. An interpretation partitions the states of the world into

---

[3] For related models, see Barwise and Seligman (1997), Al-Najjar, Casadesus-Masanell, and Ozdenoren (2003), Aragones et al. (2005), and Fryer and Jackson (2008).

distinct categories. These categories form the basis for the individual's predictive model. For example, one individual might partition politicians into two categories: liberals and conservatives. Another voter might partition politicians into categories based on identity characteristics such as age, race, and gender.[4]

> Individual i's **interpretation** $\Phi_i = \{\phi_{i1}, \phi_{i2}, \ldots, \phi_{im}\}$ *equals a set of* **categories** *that partition* X.

We let $\Phi_i(x)$ denote the category in the interpretation to which the state of the world x belongs. Individuals with finer interpretations can be thought of as more sophisticated. Formally, we say that one individual is more sophisticated than another if every category in its interpretation is contained in a category of the other's:[5]

> Individual i's interpretation is **more sophisticated** than individual j's interpretation if, for any x, $\Phi_i(x) \subseteq \Phi_j(x)$, with strict inclusion for at least one x. A collection of individuals **becomes more sophisticated** if every individual's interpretation becomes more sophisticated.

Individuals have what we call *predictive models* that map their categories into outcomes. Predictive models are coarser than the outcome function. Whereas the objective function maps states of the world into outcomes, predictive models map sets of states of the world, namely categories, into outcomes. Thus, if an individual places two states of the world in the same category, the individual's predictive model must assign the same outcome to those two states:

> Individual i's **predictive model** $M_i : X \to \Theta$ s.t. if $\Phi_i(x) = \Phi_i(y)$ then $M_i(x) = M_i(y)$.

An individual's prediction equals the output of his or her predictive model. The predictive model of an individual can be thought of as a signal. However, unlike a *generated signal*, this signal is not a random variable drawn from a distribution. It is produced by the individual's interpretation and predictive

---

[4] An interpretation is similar to an information partition (Aumann 1976). What Aumann calls an information set, we call a category. The difference between our approach and Aumann's is that he assumes that once a state of the world is identified, individuals know the value of the outcome function.

[5] Admittedly, this strong restriction may often fail to hold across individuals, but it is the natural definition if we think of an individual as becoming more sophisticated.

model. To distinguish this type of signal, we refer to it as an *interpreted signal*. The *collective prediction* of a population of individuals we take to be the average of the predictions of the individuals:

$$\text{The \textbf{collective prediction} } \bar{M}(x) = \sum_{i=1}^{n} M_i(x).$$

The ability of a collection of individuals to make an accurate prediction depends on their predictive models. Intuitively, if those models are individually sophisticated (i.e., they partition the set of states of the world into many categories), and collectively diverse (i.e., they create different partitions), then we should expect the collective prediction to be accurate. The next example shows how this can occur.

> **Example.** Let the set X consist of three binary variables. Each state can therefore be written as a sequence of 0s and 1s of length 3. Formally, $X = (x_1, x_2, x_3)$, $x_i \in \{0, 1\}$. Assume that each state is equally likely and that the outcome function is just the sum of the variables, that is, $F(x) = x_1 + x_2 + x_3$. Assume that individual i partitions X into two sets according to the value of x_i, which the individual can identify; $M_i(x) = 1$ if $x_i = 0$ and $M_i(x) = 2$ if $x_i = 1$. The following table gives the interpreted signals (the predictions) for each realization of x, as well as the collective prediction and the value of the outcome function.

State	$M_1(x)$	$M_2(x)$	$M_3(x)$	$\bar{M}(x)$	$F(x)$	$SqE(\bar{M})$
000	1	1	1	1	0	1
001	1	1	2	$4/3$	1	$1/9$
010	1	2	1	$4/3$	1	$1/9$
100	2	1	1	$4/3$	1	$1/9$
011	1	2	2	$5/3$	2	$1/9$
101	2	1	2	$5/3$	2	$1/9$
110	2	2	1	$5/3$	2	$1/9$
111	2	2	2	2	3	1

We can view these interpreted signals using the statistical framework. Though each prediction results from the application of a cognitive model, we can think of them as random variables. Since the statistic model presented before is with regard to any given outcome, we compute the interpreted signal's bias and squared error conditional on a given value of $F(x)$. In what follows, we do our computation and comparison conditional on $F(x) = 1$. The case for $F(x) = 2$ is similar, and the cases for $F(x) = 0$ $F(x) = 3$ are trivial since there is no randomness in the signals. By symmetry, it suffices to consider a single interpreted signal to compute bias and squared error, as in the following table.

State	$F(x)$	$M_1(x)$	Error(M_1)	$SqE(M_1)$	$\overline{M}(x)$	Error($\overline{M}$)	$SqE(\overline{M})$
001	1	1	0	0	$\frac{4}{3}$	$\frac{1}{3}$	$\frac{1}{9}$
010	1	1	0	0	$\frac{4}{3}$	$\frac{1}{3}$	$\frac{1}{9}$
100	1	2	1	1	$\frac{4}{3}$	$\frac{1}{3}$	$\frac{1}{9}$
Expectation	1	$\frac{4}{3}$	$\frac{1}{3}$	$\frac{1}{3}$	$\frac{4}{3}$	$\frac{1}{3}$	$\frac{1}{9}$

As can be seen from the table, the bias of the interpreted signal equals $\frac{1}{3}$. A straightforward calculation shows that the variance of the interpreted signal equals $\frac{2}{9}$. Notice that each individual has an expected squared error equal to $\frac{1}{3}$, but the collection has an expected squared error equal to just $\frac{1}{9}$. So in this case, the collective is more accurate, in expectation, than any of the individuals. This is a result of negative correlation in each pair of interpreted signals. Covariance of interpreted signals 1 and 2 (or 2 and 3 or 1 and 3) = $\frac{1}{3}[(1 - \frac{4}{3})(1 - \frac{4}{3}) + (1 - \frac{4}{3})(2 - \frac{4}{3}) + (2 - \frac{4}{3})(1 - \frac{4}{3})] = -\frac{1}{9}$. In the collective, idiosyncratic errors of individuals cancel each other out. The remaining error comes from the squared average bias.

In the example, each individual considered a distinct attribute. Hong and Page (2007) refer to these as independent interpreted signals:

> *The interpreted signals of individual* 1 *and* 2 *are based on **independent interpretations** if and only if for all i and j in* $\{1, 2, \ldots, m\}$
>
> $\text{Prob}(\phi_{1j} \cap \phi_{2i}) = \text{Prob}(\phi_{1j}) \times \text{Prob}(\phi_{2i})$.

If two individuals use independent interpretations, they look at different dimensions given the same representation. Hong and Page (2007) show that for classification problems, that is, problems with binary outcomes, independent interpreted signals must be negatively correlated. The theorem requires mild constraints on the individuals' predictive models – namely that they predict both outcomes with equal probability and that they are correct more than half the time.[6]

> **Theorem 3.** *If* $F : X \rightarrow \{0, 1\}$, *if each outcome is predicted equally often and if each individual's prediction is correct with probability* $p > \frac{1}{2}$ *then independent interpreted signals are negatively correlated.*

Proof. See Hong and Page (2007).

This theorem provides a linkage between the models that individuals use and statistical properties of their predictions. For classification problems, model diversity implies negatively correlated predictions conditional on outcomes,

---

[6] Extending the theorem to arbitrary outcome spaces would require stronger conditions on the predictive models and on the outcome function.

which we know from the statistical models implies more accurate collective predictions.

The statistical approach focuses on the size of the expected error as a function of bias, error, and correlation of generated signals. The cognitive model approach does not assume any randomness in the prediction, although uncertainty about the state of the world does exist. Therefore, a natural question to ask within the cognitive model approach is whether a collection of individuals can, through voting, produce the correct outcome. In other words, we can ask: What has to be true of the individuals and of the outcome function in order for collective wisdom to emerge?

The answer to that question is surprisingly straightforward. Individuals think at the level of category. They do not distinguish among states of the world that belong to the same category. Therefore, we can think of each individual's interpretation and predictive model as producing a function that assigns the same value to any two states of the world in the same category. If a collection of people vote or express an opinion about the likely value of an outcome, what they are doing is aggregating these functions.

If the outcome function can be defined over the categories of individuals, it would seem possible that the individuals can combine their models and approximate the outcome function. However, suppose that the outcome function assigns an extremely high value to states of the world in the set S but that no individual can identify S; that is, for each individual i, S is strictly contained within a category in Φ_i. Then we should not expect the individuals to be able to approximate the outcome function. Thus, a necessary condition for collective wisdom to arise is that, collectively, the interpretations of the individuals be fine enough to approximate the outcome function. In addition, the outcome function must be an additive combination of the predictive models of the individuals (for a full characterization see Hong and Page 2008). This additivity assumption should be seen as especially strong. It limits what outcomes a crowd can always predict correctly.

SOPHISTICATION AND DIVERSITY IN COGNITIVE MODELS

In the statistical model, bias and error are meant to be proxies for sophistication and correlation is thought to capture diversity (Ladha 1992). In the cognitive model framework, sophistication refers to the number and sizes of the categories. Interpretations that create more categories produce more accurate predictions. And as just described, the ability of a collection of people to make accurate appraisals in all states of the world depends on their ability to identify all sets that are relevant to the outcome function. Therefore, as the individuals become more sophisticated, the collective becomes more intelligent.

As for diversity, we have seen in the case of classification problems that independent interpretations produce negatively correlated interpreted signals. That mathematical finding extends to a more general insight: more *diverse interpretations tend to produce more negatively correlated predictions.* Consider first the extreme case. If two individuals use identical interpretations and make the best possible prediction for each category, their predictive models will be identical. They will have no diversity. Their two heads will be no better than one. If, on the other hand, two people categorize states of the world differently, they will likely make different predictions at a given state. Thus, diversity in predictions comes from diversity in predictive models.

Even with a large number of individuals, we might expect some limits on the amount of diversity present. In the statistical model, as the number of individuals tends to infinity, in the absence of bias the collective becomes perfectly accurate. That will not happen in the cognitive model unless we assume that each new individual brings a distinct predictive model.

DISCUSSION

In this essay, we have provided possible microfoundations for collective wisdom. We have contrasted this approach with the standard statistical model of collective wisdom that dominates the literature. While both approaches demonstrate the importance of sophistication and diversity, they do so in different ways. The statistical model makes assumptions that might be expected to correlate with sophistication and diversity, while the cognitive model approach includes sophistication and diversity directly.

The cognitive microfoundations that we have presented also help to explain the potential for the madness of crowds. A collection of people becomes more likely to make a bad choice if the individuals rely on similar models. This idea aligns with the argument made by Caplan (2007) that people make systematic mistakes. Note, though, that in other venues where collections of individuals do not make mistakes, they are not necessarily more accurate individually; they may just be more diverse collectively.

The causes of diversity and sophistication are manifold and diverse. Diversity can be produced by differences in identity (see Nisbett 2003). It can also result from different sources of experience and information (Stinchcombe 1990). Sophistication derives from experience, attention, motivation, and information. It is important, however, to recall that ramping up individual-level sophistication can have costs: decreases in diversity can more than offset increases in individual accuracy.

Finally, we have yet to discuss the potential for persuasion within a group. In the statistical model, persuasion places more weight on some individuals than on others. Ideally, the weight assigned to each generated signal would be proportional to its accuracy. In any particular group setting, we have no guarantee that such weighting will emerge. And, in fact, improper weightings may lead to even worse choices. In our cognitive model, persuasion can have a similar effect. However, instead of changing weights, people may abandon models because they find another person's model more convincing. Often such behavior makes the collective worse off. It is better for the collective to contain a different and less accurate model than to add one more copy of any existing model, even if that existing model is more accurate.

References

Al-Najjar, N., R. Casadesus-Masanell, and E. Ozdenoren (2003), "Probabilistic Representation of Complexity," *Journal of Economic Theory* 111 (1), 49–87.

Aragones, E., I. Gilboa, A. Postlewaite, and D. Schmeidler (2005), "Fact-Free Learning," *American Economic Review* 95 (5), 1355–68.

Aumann, Robert (1976), "Agreeing to Disagree," *Annals of Statistics* 4, 1236–39.

Barwise, J., and J. Seligman (1997), *Information Flow: The Logic of Distributed Systems*, Cambridge Tracts in Theoretical Computer Science, Cambridge University Press, New York.

Caplan, Bryan (2007), *The Myth of the Rational Voter: Why Democracies Choose Bad Policies*, Princeton University Press, Princeton, NJ.

Hong, L., and S. Page (2007), "Interpreted and Generated Signals," Working paper.

Hong, L., and S. Page (2008), "On the Possibility of Collective Wisdom," Working paper.

Jackson, M. A., and R. G. Fryer, Jr. (2008), "A Categorical Model of Cognition and Biased Decision-Making," *B. E. Journal of Theoretical Economics (Contributions)* 8 (1), 1–42.

Ladha, K. (1992), "The Condorcet Jury Theorem, Free Speech, and Correlated Votes," *American Journal of Political Science* 36 (3), 617–34.

Nisbett, R. (2003), *The Geography of Thought: How Asians and Westerners Think Differently . . . and Why*, Free Press, New York.

Page, S. (2007), *The Difference: How the Power of Diversity Creates Better Firms, Schools, Groups, and Societies*, Princeton University Press, Princeton, NJ.

Stinchcombe, A. (1990), *Information and Organizations*, California Series on Social Choice and Political Economy I, University of California Press, Berkeley.

Surowiecki, James (2004), *The Wisdom of Crowds*, Doubleday, New York.

von Hayek, F. (1945), "The Use of Knowledge in Society," *American Economic Review* 4, 519–30.

4

What Has Collective Wisdom to Do with Wisdom?

Daniel Andler

Conventional wisdom holds two seemingly opposed beliefs. One is that groups are often much better than individuals at dealing with certain situations or solving certain problems. The other is that groups are usually, and some say always, at best as intelligent as their average member and at worst even less intelligent than the least of their members.

Consistency would seem to be easily reestablished by distinguishing between advanced, sophisticated social organizations that afford the supporting communities a high level of collective performance, and primitive, moblike structures that pull the group toward the lower end of the achievement scale. But this reconciliation meets with some objections. The most familiar ones concern the mixed record of elaborate social systems, which are said to occasionally or even, according to some accounts, systematically produce wrong decisions, poor assessments, disastrous plans, counterproductive measures, and so on. A more recent set of objections rests on cases where "crowds," that is, groups *not* organized in a sophisticated way, produce good results, in fact, results that better those of most, or even all, members of the group. Many such cases are collected in James Surowiecki's book *The Wisdom of Crowds*, which argues more generally in favor of an "order out of chaos" view of collective thinking: whether sophisticated or simple, social organizations for the production of knowledge or problem solving can benefit from the absence of certain individualistic constraints that are traditionally thought to foster excellence in cognitive tasks.

This flavor of paradox is enhanced by Surowiecki's choice of phrase: at the surface level, "wisdom of crowds" conflicts with the well-entrenched cliché of the folly[1] of crowds; but at a deeper level, Surowiecki seems to appeal to one frequent connotation of "wisdom," which is precisely its paradoxical character. Whether Surowiecki actually intended to exploit this connotation is not entirely clear, as he uses "wisdom," "intelligence," or even sometimes "knowledge" and

---

[1] Or "madness"; see the title of Mackay (1852), quoted in Surowiecki (2005: 285).

similarly, "wise," "intelligent," and even "smart" interchangeably.[2] However, and despite the fact that a lot of attention is given throughout to "group" (or "collective") "intelligence," the book, as I read it, also strongly suggests that the wisdom of crowds should be seen as more than mere collective intelligence and be thought of instead as partaking of wisdom. Indeed, wisdom of crowds does seem to share with the ordinary concept of wisdom some important features, which in particular do not typically belong to intelligence. Thus, as a concept and as a project, wisdom of crowds invites us to take a closer look at wisdom, in particular in its relation to intelligence or rationality, quite in the way artificial intelligence invited us decades ago,[3] and in a new guise today invites us again,[4] to take a closer look at (human, ordinary) intelligence, in particular in its relation to cognition or logic, for example.

This essay is organized as follows. It starts with a brief clarification of the target phenomenon: wisdom of crowds, in Surowiecki's book, covers a wide variety of phenomena that cannot be encompassed within a single approach, and I will spell out where my focus lies, namely in the "mindless" processes of aggregation of individual cognitive competences that tend to result in cognitive progress. I will then propose a contrastive characterization of rationality, intelligence, and wisdom, as they apply to individuals. Next I will examine the possibility of extending these terms to collective entities or processes (leaving rationality to the side, for reasons that will become clear) and ask to what extent wisdom of crowds can be regarded as a form or realization of collective intelligence and/or collective wisdom. The answer will turn out to depend on which variety of collective processes one is considering: wisdom of crowds in the sense that is central to Surowiecki's argument will qualify as collective intelligence, not as collective wisdom. I will argue, on the other hand, that there exists a more familiar kind of collective process that does meet the requirements on a reasonable extension of the concept of wisdom to the collective level, but is at best distantly related to what Surowiecki reports on and commends.

WISDOM OF CROWDS AND COLLECTIVE COGNITIVE PROCESSES

Processes that pool, in one way or another, the cognitive resources of a plurality of human beings, are anything but rare and unusual. Humans have forever been discussing and settling matters collectively. From day-to-day decisions about what, where, and when to hunt, pluck, or fish, cook, sow, or graze, to the most elaborate systems of knowledge production (such as contemporary science) and deliberation (such as contemporary advanced democracies), people attempt to pool their intellectual resources in order to come up with answers they hope, quite reasonably, to be on the average better than any of those they would have reached individually had they proceeded on their own. Such cognitive

---

[2] See also his reference (Surowiecki 2005: 286) to H. Rheingold's 2002 book, *Smart Mobs*.
[3] See, e.g., Haugeland (1981) and Dennett (1978).
[4] Goertzel and Pennachin (2007).

processes, in which potentially all the cognitive and communicative resources of the individual participants are on call, I propose to call *thickly collective*.

In contrast, processes in which individual agents, far from deliberating or exchanging information and arguments, simply provide their own conclusions, which are then fed to some aggregating algorithm or mechanism, I will label *thinly collective*. Most forms of collective cognition studied by legal theorists, political scientists, and historians are of the thick sort. These fall under the wisdom-of-crowds concept in its widest extension, but the emphasis, in Surowiecki's book as well as related work in the recent scholarly literature, is on thin collective processes (examples follow presently).

The main contrasts between the two sorts are the following. (1) Individuals participating in thick processes typically interact; in thin processes they do not. (2) During the course of interaction that is characteristic of thick processes, individuals can, and often do, change their minds or go from indecision or confusion to a firm opinion and a relatively clear view. In thin processes, there is no place for such intra-individual dynamics. (3) The aggregating procedure of a thin process is insensitive to everything but certain data delivered in a predetermined format, and that format is fixed throughout the procedure. In particular, the procedure is insulated from the participating individuals' views on the process; for example, it cannot be improved or modified in any way as the process unfolds. In contrast, thick processes allow, except perhaps in highly formalized settings, for changes in the procedure. In particular, as the process unfolds, participants usually have an opportunity to form and revise their understanding of the procedure and may argue in favor of changing it.

In fact, the two types of processes are polar opposites, between which intermediate cases arise. Classical thick procedures can be simplified so as to limit interactions to a more or less restricted set,[5] and symmetrically thin procedures can be enriched so as to allow "thicker" information to be transmitted and aggregated. Locating a particular collective process on this scale can be difficult, a challenge for the historian, the political scientist, or the cognitive scientist. Sometimes there is no obvious way to individuate a process. For example, an election can be seen as a thin process if it is limited to the voting procedure, while it appears to be thick, or somewhat thicker, if the campaign is included.

One condition, however, is essential to thinly collective processes: the aggregating function must be filled by a computational, automatic mechanism. The central agency must be essentially "dumb," or rather "semantically blind,"[6] in

---

[5] An example might be the Delphi method; see, e.g., Linstone and Turoff (1975).

[6] The disputed conceivability of genuine artificial intelligence makes this point hard to put concisely: "dumb" computers may turn out to be "intelligent." Yet they remain, on the classical analysis, "syntactic" machines, with no direct, "first-person" access to the semantic content of the symbolic structures they process – hence the appeal to "semantic blindness." In practice, however, there is in most cases no difficulty involved in locating a given collective cognitive process on the "blindness" or automaticity axis and in locating it accordingly on the thin–thick axis.

order for the "wisdom of crowds" effect to be fully expressed. In the simplest case, the individual inputs are numerical quantities (the estimated weight of a prize ox, a preference order, a one- or two-dimensional interval expressing the agent's estimate of the location of some unknown, etc.), and the aggregation is performed by averaging or some comparably simple operation. More complex cases are prediction markets, with the bookmaker implementing a possibly non-strictly algorithmic procedure,[7] yet still restricted to the odds on offer, and accepting no further information or rational consideration bearing directly on the situation under scrutiny.

Surowiecki distinguishes, within the genus of "collective wisdom," three species of collective processes according to whether they aim at acquiring knowledge, at coordinating a group, or at getting its members to cooperate. Although quite different in many ways, as problem-solving mechanisms they share a common core (coordination and cooperation involving an extra layer of collective processes). Like Surowiecki, I will restrict myself to the first kind of process, which should help keep the discussion focused. I will call these processes cognitive collective processes (CCPs).

RATIONALITY, INTELLIGENCE, AND WISDOM

Wisdom and intelligence are inextricably intertwined in common parlance. This is especially true for the adjectival forms "wise" and "intelligent": in many cases, exchanging one for the other in a proposition seems to preserve its core meaning, although not necessarily all the connotations. On the other hand, saying of someone that she is a wise person is not the same as saying she is intelligent or remarkably intelligent. The substantives lend themselves even less to interchange: wisdom is typically associated, in folk psychology, to age and experience; intelligence is found also in the very young. Such intuitions based on ordinary usage are not to be taken on board uncritically. I will try to show, however, that (1) there is a distinction and (2) it does not rest solely on a difference in domains of deployment.

"Wisdom" and "intelligence" are not only notoriously slippery concepts; they are also extraordinarily loaded terms. Analytic philosophers, by and large, have all but ruled them out of bounds;[8] they have thought of them as too loose for theoretical purposes, leaving them for popular writers, psychologists, and computer scientists to discuss. Intelligence has been represented, on the contemporary philosophical scene, by rationality, cognition, or knowledge. Wisdom has split into two very unequal parts: practical wisdom is extensively scrutinized by moral philosophers under labels such as "flourishing," "the good life," and "prudence"; theoretical wisdom appears in epistemology under the

---

[7] I don't know enough about prediction markets to feel any confidence on this point.

[8] Characteristically, Lalande's *Vocabulaire* (1902–23, 5th ed., 1947) has entries for both terms, while the comparably sized *Cambridge Dictionary of Philosophy* (Audi 1995) has neither.

guise of "judgment" or "reasonableness."[9] Wisdom as a term of art is definitely philosophically outdated. As for intelligence, its theoretical status has been put into question, due to its less than stellar (some would say disastrous) scientific track record, and also for ethical and political reasons. Yet we cannot avert our gaze from these contested topics if we want to get clearer on the purported "wisdom" of the phenomena described by Surowiecki.

In contrast, "rationality" is all the more philosophically respectable, as it is a term of art that only philosophers and social scientists use, although the adjectival forms ("rational," "irrational") have been incorporated into common parlance. As just mentioned, it is closely connected to intelligence. Perhaps rationality is just the philosopher's code word for intelligence. Let us take a closer look, first at one, then at the other.

Rationality

As an area of research, rationality is fairly well defined. As a concept, however, it is not; there is no consensus on what it covers.[10] There is nothing alarming about this; the important thing is that there exists a rich set of overlapping theories of rationality, whose precise articulation constitutes a stimulating goal for the entire field.[11] For present purposes, however, a working definition can be offered, at the cost of some methodological decisions that will remain unmotivated here for reasons of space. The first is to restrict the concept to mental entities (states, processes, dispositions, etc., as opposed, in particular, to laws, rules, customs, institutions), with occasional extensions to individuals harboring such entities. The second decision is to regroup all current conceptions of rationality under three headings.

N-rationality (N for "narrow") consists in a demand for consistency and coherence among the beliefs of an agent, or between his beliefs and his goals, at any moment in time or over an extended period. Consistency in turn is cashed in as absence of contradiction, and coherence, a more problematic notion, aims at characterizing the unity of the set under consideration, the extent to which its various elements are connected, and the principled or systematic nature of the connections.

R-rationality (R for "resistance") consists in the capacity to resist distorting factors in the formation of one's beliefs, intentions, and the like. Rationality on this general view is an active avoidance of subjectivity, dogma, prejudice, bias such as discounting of less salient or less favorable evidence, disregard of base rate, reliance on surface features of wordings, wishful thinking, bad faith, and so on.

---

[9] This traditional division between two kinds of wisdom will be questioned in the sections that follow.

[10] See, e.g., Mele and Rawling (2004). For another piece of lexicographic evidence, as of this writing there is no "rationality" entry in the *Stanford Encyclopedia of Philosophy*.

[11] As argued and illustrated by Spohn (2002).

Finally, B-rationality (B for "broad") is a commitment to the deliveries of reason. Reason in turn stands for a variety of demands: objectivity, reproducibility across contexts and persons, conformity to recognized norms, rules and methods of reasoning, respect for evidence, openness to and curiosity about new facts, preference for comprehensiveness, consistency, coherence, careful weighing of relevant factors, and, significantly, acceptance of the dispassionate critical game of public giving and taking of reasons.

The third decision is to give prominence to B-rationality, on the grounds that the connection of rationality with reason seems to be part of any nonarbitrary definition: B-rationality seems to be the most basic as well as the most inclusive concept, and this leads me to propose the following working definition:

> A set of mental entities (states, processes, dispositions, . . .) is rational to the extent that it accords with the demands of reason: objectivity, communicability, public reason-giving and -taking, including honest acceptance of critical argument, regard for evidence, and openness to novel facts, comprehensiveness, consistency, and coherence.

Intelligence

As remarked earlier, "intelligence," unlike "rationality," is a household word with a thousand and one uses, and intelligence judgments often seem to say at least as much about the judge's tastes and abilities as about the person being judged. Cognitive science has all but discarded the notion as nonscientific, in large part because it seems to rest on a view of the mind as a homogeneous system, whose performance can be assessed along a single dimension.[12] On the other hand, intelligence is universally seen as an almost priceless commodity and has been the focus of enormous quantification efforts on the part of psychology, working in tandem with educational and military authorities, as well as human resources departments of businesses and administrations. This work has also had momentous consequences in penal practices.[13] Finally, as is well known, Turing and the artificial intelligence movement have defined intelligence for their own purposes, drawing on an essentially unanalyzed reference to human intelligence: intelligence is whatever is exercised by a human agent in order to accomplish a task generally considered to require . . . intelligence; and a machine that can carry out such a task is thereby considered to exhibit some degree of intelligence.[14]

This gives us a lead. First, intelligence is to a large extent a matter of getting the job done, that is, of solving problems in finite time. Second, this performance cannot be the outcome of a series of strokes of luck; it results from enduring properties of the intelligent entity, which result in the capacity to understand the

---

[12] See, e.g., Piatelli-Palmarini (1980) and Barkow, Cosmides, and Tooby (1992). For a dissenting view regarding the cognitive-scientific standing of intelligence, see Sternberg and Pretz (2005).

[13] As illustrated, e.g., in Flynn (2007).

[14] Turing (1950), Newell and Simon (1976).

world or the way "things are." The two dimensions are not wholly independent. The understanding is an important factor of the problem-solving capacity, and at the same time it is heavily dependent on it: one comes to understand the world in part by solving problems of categorization, causal attribution, and so on. Yet they are distinct: understanding is also brought about by cultural transmission (in particular formal and informal learning, imitation), by experience, and for some aspects of the human world by empathy; conversely, the solution to certain problems seems to require very little, if any, world understanding – that would seem to be the case of abstract logic, mathematics, and other formal setups such as chess, go, and other games and puzzles.

Intelligence comes in degrees. Although sometimes the term of reference is left unstated, it is an essentially comparative notion. On this count, the two dimensions of intelligence are also correlated, but only partly so. It is hard to imagine a very deep understanding of the world accompanied by a very low problem-solving capacity, and the reverse seems true: except for ill-understood and rare cases of prodigy-level performance in some restricted kinds of problem solving, accompanied by a very feeble understanding of the world (idiots savants, certain forms of autism), a high problem-solving capacity is a good predictor of a fair level of world understanding. However, one may score high on understanding and modestly on problem solving, and conversely. All of this remains true if one chooses to break down intelligence into domain-specific abilities.[15]

How do psychologists view intelligence? Problem solving is directly or indirectly involved in their characterization of intelligence, but it is not usually complemented by "world understanding." Instead, they list elementary capacities, such as those that form the WISC IQ test: information, arithmetic, vocabulary, comprehension (a very elementary form of world understanding), picture completion, object assembly, coding, picture arrangement, similarities.[16] Alternatively, R. J. Sternberg proposes to complement "analytic intelligence" (abstract problem solving) with "creative intelligence" and "practical intelligence" (deployed when applying concepts to real-world situations).[17]

In contrast, J. R. Flynn suggests that before we can start to make sense of the famous Flynn effect (the robust and steady increase of IQ in all populations, during the twentieth century, at a rate on the order of 0.3 IQ point per year), "we must dissect intelligence into solving mathematical problems, interpreting the great works of literature, finding on-the-spot solutions, assimilating the scientific worldview, critical acumen, and wisdom."[18] This is remarkable in two ways: first, it features world understanding prominently; second, the view

---

[15] There is no need here to open a debate about forms of intelligence and the independent reality of general intelligence (the psychologists' "g factor").

[16] See Flynn (2007: 5).

[17] Sternberg (1988), as summarized in Flynn (2007: 79).

[18] Flynn (2007: 10). Flynn defends a three-pronged approach to intelligence, based on "Brain, Individual Differences, and Social Trends" (Flynn 2007: 56–57).

of intelligence it proposes is externalist in part, in the sense that what counts as "understanding" and what counts as "the world" are not determined on purely individualistic grounds, but have a crucial social-cultural component. The internal component Flynn attempts to explicate, later in the book, by proposing a pre-theoretical concept of intelligence in the form of "*an answer to a question: what traits affect our ability to solve problems with cognitive content?*" He lists mental acuity ("the ability to provide on-the-spot solutions" to novel problems), habits of mind, attitudes (which "lay the foundations for acquiring habits of mind"), knowledge and information, speed of information processing, and memory retrieval.[19]

Psychologists thus waiver between, or combine, internalist or partly externalist functional definitions of intelligence and "chemical" definitions, which list elementary "ingredient" properties and/or sources of intelligence.

Faced with this rather complicated background, on the one hand, and the question of whether CCPs qualify as intelligent and/or wise, on the other, we find ourselves in a situation similar to that of Turing. We can follow his example, by offering a functional definition of intelligence, but cannot avail ourselves of a pre-theoretical unanalyzed notion of (human, individual) intelligence. The stipulative definition I propose is this:

> Intelligence is the capacity to understand the world and to use this understanding in order to find in due time acceptable solutions to an unlimited variety of pressing problems, including problems arising from the need to better understand (describe, explain, predict) the world.

The definition is to be understood comparatively, thus allowing for degrees of intelligence in different individuals and relative to different realms, and partly dependent on the cultural context. In particular, it is intended to make room for a modulation of performance according to the region to which someone's mind is attuned and according to the degree of versatility achieved – the breadth of problems that can be successfully attacked and the fluid passage from one kind to another.

The Link between Rationality and Intelligence

As could be expected, under the stipulative definitions I have proposed, rationality and intelligence come out to be closely connected. Intelligence enlists rationality. Reason is the best proven resource for accomplishing the typical tasks facing intelligence: it is a rare problem that does not benefit from the recommendations of reason for its resolution. These recommendations can be positive – for example, coherence and comprehensiveness are often good heuristics. The instrumental role of rationality also comes into play: wanting to solve a problem and believing that this requires solving some subproblem lead one to a course of action that is conducive to the solution of that subproblem.

---

[19] Flynn (2007: 53–54), emphasis added.

But reason's recommendations can also be, and arguably are, more often used negatively: rationality *rules out* erroneous solutions, for example, those that violate the consistency requirement or that succumb to one or another kind of bias. Here the R-side of rationality is on full display: intelligence enrolls R-rationality to prune its search tree. Altogether, intelligence is a rational employer of reason, and in particular tends to deploy typically rational methods.

Connected as they are, rationality and intelligence are nevertheless distinct. This is common sense: someone may be highly rational and of average intelligence. Rationality, however developed, is compatible with poor memory or a low level of activity, contrary to intelligence. Most important, intelligence seems to rely on a kind of grasp that allows it to see the problem situation as a foreground/background structure and to zero in on a promising direction. Intelligence piggybacks on serendipity: it is able to discern, in a chance encounter, the long-sought solution to a seemingly unrelated problem.[20] Intelligence would thus appear to be rationality *supplemented* by certain further abilities or virtues. But this is an oversimplification, for at least two reasons. First, as common sense never tires of noticing and cognitive psychologists have documented, intelligence can coexist with at least a certain amount of irrationality, that is, clear breaches of rationality. Second, more controversially, intelligence seems compatible with a degree of a-rationality; that is, there may be cases where intelligence floats free of rationality altogether, as when the solution to a given problem immediately "springs" to the mind, without any systematic search, reasoning, or deliberation. There is no doubt that this happens frequently. It has been abundantly documented in grandmaster-level chess, and it is a feature often seen as characteristic of expertise. What makes these cases moot is the role played by unconscious processes: there is no guarantee that the agent is not, after all, performing very fast rationality-sanctioned operations, in part due to a huge repertory of memorized situations and a well-trained "similarity module." But then, there is *always* a level at which conscious processes bottom out, including rational deliberation.

However it may be, we can summarize the differences between rationality and intelligence as follows. First, intelligence, unlike rationality, contains a success clause; in this respect, intelligence stands to rationality somewhat in the way performance stands to competence in the realm of language. Second, it cannot be ruled out that intelligence occasionally deploys nonrational procedures to reach its goals.

Should we then reject our initial view of intelligence and rationality as being strongly connected? Hardly. Despite being possibly (if some of my arguments are roughly correct) an *oversimplification*, the model of intelligence that first emerged, in which intelligence by and large includes rationality and supplements it with performance factors (such as swift application of a judicious

---

[20] The history of science provides many well-known examples of so-called chance discoveries, such as the rediscovery of penicillin by Alexander Fleming in 1928.

and efficient problem-solving or proof-seeking procedure, prompt memory retrieval, etc.) remains *basically* correct. As for the last suggested discrepancy, which has to do with the possibility of nonrational shortcuts, it can be argued that although intelligence may not always *proceed* in explicit agreement with rationality, its *end products* can always be accounted for in rational terms. To put the point more vividly, although intelligence may not always proceed stepwise, with reasons provided for every step, it typically yields trajectories that can be reconstructed as a series of reasoned steps.

Wisdom

There is a traditional conception of wisdom that makes it obviously distinct from intelligence but that is of no relevance for our present purpose. The wisdom of crowds (thin CCPs) has clearly not much to do with the higher ends of human existence, with flourishing, or with the proper way to "meet with Triumph and Disaster." In contrast, wisdom is often understood precisely as the art of living a life worth living. Intelligence might then be considered, to put it briefly, the art of knowing (explaining, predicting, discovering, planning, etc.), and so the two would appear to be distinct by virtue of applying to different domains, and "wisdom of crowds" would appear to be a simple misnomer.

On this traditional view, wisdom and intelligence also differ in nature: while wisdom is seen as a virtue of character (exemplified by the Stoic philosopher, or the philosopher *tout court* in the popular imagination, or the Zen master, or again Kipling's "man"), intelligence is a virtue of reason. Wisdom is about controlling one's desires, emotions, ultimate goals, and mustering courage and moral strength; intelligence about controlling one's belief fixation procedures and determining one's action plans in a rationally optimal way.

This view, which is at least roughly Platonic, aligns therefore two contrasts: (1) knowledge/life and (2) reason (or intellect)/character. Aristotle however saw, against Plato, that leading the good life is not merely a matter of character and that it *also* requires a special sort of *intellectual* virtue: character is not enough to ensure the competence required for practical purposes, even supplemented by theoretical knowledge. What is needed is *phronêsis*, which sits next to *sophia* (theoretical wisdom) among the intellectual virtues (i.e., those attached to that part of the soul to which reasoning properly belongs).[21] On this view, wisdom and intelligence both belong to reason, and thus do not differ in nature, but only in their domains of competence.[22]

---

21 *Nichomachean Ethics* VI, 2. I am indebted to J. Labarrière's article on wisdom and temperance in Canto-Sperber (1996: 1326).

22 Thus, Robert Nozick writes, "Wisdom is what you need to *understand* in order to live well and cope with the central problems and avoid the dangers in the predicaments human beings find themselves in" (Nozick 1989: 267, quoted in Ryan 2008; my emphasis), and proceeds to give a long list of pieces of knowledge, of kinds of know-how, and of instances of understanding that are all required for wisdom. Sharon Ryan calls this conception "Wisdom as Knowing How to Live Well."

I would like to propose a symmetrical move, and thus complete the four-place logical space created by crossing, instead of aligning, the two aforementioned contrasts. Just as the pursuit of a life worth living calls on two distinct resources, one purely intellectual (practical wisdom in the Aristotelian sense) and the other pragmatic (character: courage, temperance, justice, etc.), I tentatively propose to regard the pursuit of knowledge as resting on two pillars, intelligence (closely related, as we saw, to reason via rationality) and *epistemic wisdom*, as I will call it. In the following table, the key feature is the presence of two elements on the "knowledge" line; the choice of terms in the other boxes, which might cause concern, is best left unexamined here:

Domain Faculty → ↓	Rational/Intellectual Skills (*Theoria*)	Pragmatic Skills (*Praxis*)
Life	*Phronêsis*, or practical wisdom	Character
Knowledge	*Sophia*, or intelligence	Epistemic wisdom

The task before us now is to make a case for epistemic wisdom as an ability or skill not already included in intelligence. The discussion can hardly be conclusive, given the highly elastic semantics of the words under consideration, and its purpose is to motivate a stipulative definition needed to ground an answer to my title question. The motivation, in rough outline, is straightforward enough: intuitively, putting aside many complexities, one step beyond rationality is intelligence, and one step beyond intelligence is wisdom – after all, wisdom has been associated, since the beginning of philosophy, with the notion of ultimate or supreme quality, and this association remains clearly central to the everyday use of the word. I will attempt to separate wisdom from intelligence by following three clues.

(1) A good starting point may be to think of those cases where intelligence runs out. In the moral domain, the analogue might be the cases where one's powers run out, where there is nothing one can do to prevent or repair misfortune. Traditionally, this is where wisdom takes over: the sage draws the fundamental distinction between what depends on us and what doesn't, and turns this intellectual insight into fortitude; it allows her to live through the storm while remaining true to herself. In the theoretical domain, epistemic wisdom consists in the inquirer's recognition and acceptance of his epistemic finitude and his ability to live with it without renouncing his epistemic ideal. This is the "humility" criterion, first put forward by the wisest of Athenians, Socrates.

It is quite important not to confuse the humility criterion with the notion of bounded rationality.[23] As Jon Elster remarks, the inflexible demand for optimal rationality is not true rationality but "addiction to reason."[24] The key insight

---

[23] See Simon (1957), Gigerenzer and Selten (2002).
[24] Elster (1989: 117–22, 1999: 290–91).

incorporated into the notion of bounded rationality is that the truly rational being or system takes into account the finiteness of its resources (including the time available before a decision must be made) and consequently settles for suboptimal answers. More generally, intelligence is supposed to regulate our epistemic agenda: it is clearly within its purview to evaluate the difficulty of certain tasks and to recommend not to take them on.[25] But bounded rationality, or self-aware intelligence, is still rationality or intelligence. "Wisdom," Elster rightly insists, "is not the ability to terminate deliberation at the right moment, but the ability to know that there may be no (knowable) right moment combined with the serenity to be unaffected by this indeterminacy."[26]

How do we go from humility to mastery? What makes wisdom different from mere acceptance of defeat? The answer is that wisdom is "a man for all seasons"; it is in charge come what may, triumph as well as disaster and everything in between; or, in the epistemic realm, it countenances equally a complete solution to a given problem, a total blank, and all partial solutions. Wisdom's function is to take in the creature's predicament in its entirety and, having let the normal processes of rationality, emotion, and intelligence run their course, to draw a conclusion *all things considered*, one that it proposes or bets will turn out to be the best possible *in the fullness of time*. In other words, while intelligence seeks answers that are optimal given a *local* problem situation and a *limited* horizon of evaluation, epistemic wisdom is answerable to the *global* problem situation and aims for vindication *in the long run*.

This feature of epistemic wisdom (henceforth simply "wisdom") I will call *inclusiveness*. I take it to be one of two key attributes of wisdom. Inclusiveness accounts for several other traits commonly attributed to wisdom. The most common is the possession of considerable experience (of experiential knowledge): one common use of "wise" makes it all but synonymous with "(very) experienced" and closely linked to "knowledgeable." Indeed, inclusive judgment, in the sense just outlined, cannot be caught by surprise: it had better have learned from extended exposure to previous cases what might turn out in the situation at hand.

(2) Wisdom has an air of mystery; its phenomenology is somewhat paradoxical and markedly different from that of intelligence.[27] It is part of the

---

[25] Note in passing that the exclusive focus on limitations characteristic of the bounded rationality movement misses about half of the phenomenon: the ability to realize that some difficult task, contrary to first impression, is within the range of possible accomplishments is also a mark of intelligence, in fact, a mark of high intelligence.

[26] Personal communication.

[27] Under a construal of intelligence that, like the one I propose, strongly links it to rationality. Flynn, in the passage quoted earlier, makes wisdom a component of intelligence; to me, this confuses the issue. Elsewhere in the book, he seems to deploy a different concept of wisdom, one more consonant with the one I am expounding. For example, he writes: "[Wisdom] exists only when human beings integrate the intellectual and moral virtues into a functional whole" (Flynn 2007: 159).

commonsense use of wisdom that it defies a fully rationalistic account, that it sometimes at least seems to work like magic, unaccountably yielding superior results with none of the exertions of intelligence working full blast. It seems to operate without intermediate steps, appearing as a kind of intellectual vision: it is holistic and intuitive.[28] Wisdom seems to have a synoptic view of the reasons and solutions procured by intelligence, yet to follow its own agenda, putting an end to fact-finding, reason-giving, argument-weighing. Like the folk-theoretical concept of vision, wisdom has an air of passivity: while intelligence is active, busy, wisdom requires a form of letting go; it seems to consist in a return to immobility.

Note that the *phenomenology* of wisdom need not be taken as an indication of its underlying nature. It provides no reason to deny the possibility that wisdom supervenes, in some sense, on natural properties and processes. To seem to work like magic is not the same as to be magical; to seem immobile is not the same as to be immobile; and so on. Indeed, we know from cognitive science and other fields such as immunology that complex dynamic systems can exhibit counterintuitive behaviors that share some of the traits (e.g., holism, absence of intermediate steps, return to equilibrium, "unearned" success) of the phenomenology of wisdom.

(3) Wisdom and intelligence are often hard to tell apart on the basis of their particular pronouncements (as was remarked earlier). The reason is that the globality of inclusiveness can be approximated by a sufficiently broad form of locality. Intelligence can, and its higher form does in fact extend its horizon to a very large perimeter and delivers solutions that are indistinguishable on the spot from those sanctioned by wisdom. It may be only in the very long run, over a very large series of episodes, and from a very wide perspective that wisdom may pull apart, so to speak, from intelligence. Nor is eventual success, in any form, guaranteed. In fact, the wise person can die unrecognized and utterly defeated, because fate denied her the temporal horizon in which her wisdom would have become manifest.

Indeed, wisdom is not omnipotence, nor is inclusiveness omniscience.[29] Wisdom implies risk taking, that is, responsibility. The second cardinal trait of wisdom as I see it is its irreducibly moral character. Even when restricted to cognitive or theoretical matters rather than applied to the broader pursuit of a life worth living, wisdom is an attribute of a self. Nothing short of a self can take responsibility for putting an end to deliberation, on the basis of a willful and conscious (be it partly intuitive) taking-in of the entire situation. To use another vocabulary, nothing short of a self can pass judgment. Nothing short

---

[28] "Wisdom must be intuitive reason combined with scientific knowledge – scientific knowledge of the highest objects which has received as it were its proper completion" (*Nichomachean Ethics* VI, 1141b). This brief sentence manages to combine three of the features listed in the text: knowledge (experience), completion (close to what I call inclusiveness), and intuitive character.

[29] God's "infinite wisdom" is not a good model or paradigm of human wisdom.

of a self can face the possible consequences of its decisions and accept them when the time comes.

Epistemic wisdom, in the logical space I have proposed, stands at the intersection of knowledge and praxis. As partaking of knowledge, its distinguishing mark is inclusiveness. As partaking of praxis, its distinguishing mark is responsibility. Selfhood, the necessary rooting of wisdom in a human individual, is presupposed by both: inclusiveness is relative to the unifying assessment of an individual, and responsibility is relative to the pragmatic, normative involvement of an individual.

To sum up, I propose the following definition:

> (Epistemic) wisdom is the capacity to guide the epistemic trajectory of an individual by taking, in the space of reasons and in the temporal horizon, the broadest possible perspective and to take responsibility for the individual's final, "all things considered" decisions regarding his beliefs and other epistemic attitudes and dispositions, by drawing on extensive experience, as well as on the constraints of rationality and the fruits of intelligence, which decisions tend to lead to the best possible outcomes, as evaluated in the fullness of time.

As in the cases of rationality and of intelligence, this definition is meant to allow for comparative assessments based on the eventual judgment borne by the community on the outcome: wisdom is not taken here to be an all-or-nothing affair.

INTELLIGENCE AND WISDOM IN COLLECTIVE COGNITIVE PROCESSES

Is it helpful to regard a glass eye as an eye? A computer virus as a virus? Synthetic urea as urea? There is, of course, no determinate answer to such questions. They begin to make sense once one fixes a further aim; for example, a glass eye is an eye of sorts for the purposes of restorative medicine; it is an eye-for-the-sake-of endowing a human face with a normal appearance, in a way comparable to the way a regular eye contributes to the appearance of a typical face. Synthetic urea is urea of sorts inasmuch as it can play in organic chemistry and in biochemistry the very role played by naturally produced urea. A computer virus is a virus of sorts inasmuch as it spreads among computers and tends to harm them in ways comparable to the ways biological viruses spread among organisms and harm them.

The concepts of rationality, intelligence, and wisdom are rather more slippery than those of eye, virus, or urea, making the matter of their extensions more involved. Still, we now have working definitions that circumscribe their use in relation to individuals or individual minds. On the other hand, we are presented with two broad families of collective cognitive processes: thick and thin. The label given to these processes by Surowiecki invites us to ask in what sense it might be helpful to regard them as rational, intelligent, or wise. I shall leave aside the issue of collective rationality, which has received extensive treatment in philosophy and the social sciences, and is not directly at stake in the wisdom-of-crowds literature. Rationality came in as a close relative of intelligence, and it was useful to clarify the connection between them before examining the properties of CCPs, but there is no novel problem raised by the distinction at the collective level.

Collective Intelligence

So let us begin with the sense in which CCPs can be said to be intelligent. Turing's argument in favor of the notion of machine intelligence was in large part pragmatic:[30] stripping the received notion of intelligence of some of its familiar traits results in a function that is central to human intelligence but can conceivably be attributed, under suitable conditions, to certain machines.[31] Can a similar move vindicate the notion of collective intelligence that is put forward by a small but growing intellectual *cum* social-political movement, drawing on a variety of sources: ethology and "swarm intelligence," distributed artificial intelligence and computer science, social science, media studies?

The ground has been cleared: according to the working definition proposed earlier, an entity has intelligence to the extent that it has an understanding of the world that allows it to find in due time solutions to a large variety of pressing problems, in particular to expand the understanding itself. The part of the definition that lends itself easily to an extension is the solution-finding capacity; indeed, this is the path chosen by AI: if a machine can solve a problem (a problem being the search for a nonobvious solution, one that "normally" requires human intelligence), it is ipso facto intelligent.

A crucial question awaited early AI. What should count as a solution? Does merely getting the *end result* qualify? Or is something more required: should the *process* leading the machine to the solution be similar to the path taken by human intelligence? The first criterion was named "weak equivalence," the second "strong equivalence," and a subsidiary question was, If weak is not good enough, how strong should strong be? The grain at which similarity should be demanded could not be too fine, as clearly the microstructure of a computer is vastly different from that of a brain. On the other hand, the weak-equivalence criterion makes a soap bubble intelligent, insofar as it "solves" a highly nontrivial problem of energy minimization, and a sufficiently rich, well-indexed conversation book "solves" the question-and-answer problem in a straightforward way. The weak versus strong conundrum blended into the better-known problem of *genuine* understanding, made famous by Searle's Chinese Room argument:[32] neither the soap bubble nor the conversation book

---

[30] Turing (1950).

[31] In a similar spirit, Harsanyi (1977) shows to what end it might be useful to extend the notion of rational behavior to a robot.

[32] Searle (1980).

has any real understanding of the problem situation, which they can deploy in order to come up with a solution.

It is fair to say that AI is still struggling with these problems, and this should warn us against too facile an answer to our question. Our definition does indeed present us with a difficulty, which concerns the understanding clause. While it is easy to say that a CCP may, under certain conditions, provide a solution to a given problem, the sense in which it uses its "understanding" of the (relevant aspects of the) world in order to come up with the solution is anything but obvious. What does it mean for a group of people to collectively understand anything?

For thick collective processes, there is an answer such that these processes come out as endowed with collective intelligence. Their products and inner workings are such that they can in principle be reproduced or simulated by an individual. So even though they may not be equivalent to individual processes to an unlimited fineness of grain, they can be reconstructed so as to exhibit considerably more similarity to individual processes than mere equivalence of final results. This makes it plausible to attribute collective understanding to the group, inasmuch as a sufficiently tightly connected series of intermediate steps are individually understood and acted upon by various individuals in the group.

Actually it is far from obvious that this condition is met, particularly in the case of science. As recent work in social epistemology has shown, trust, authority, and the division of labor play a large role. Both inference and reference are distributed so that no single scientist could in practice know with some precision what all the terms she uses refer to, according to the best available theories, or how to conduct the necessary inferences leading to propositions she accepts.[33] But I will leave these rather subtle issues to the side,[34] for they pale in comparison with the problem posed by thin collective processes.

What gets in the way in that case is the fact that agents have no access either to each other's reasons or to the aggregation function that produces the final, "intelligent" outcome of their joint labors. Even when the aggregation is performed by a human being relying on his ordinary rational resources, the thinness of the procedure by definition implies that he is barred from judging his constituents' estimates on their merits: he must accept them at face value and treat them as partial evidence in favor of a particular value or hypothesis regarding the outcome of an unknown or uncertain process. It is precisely this voluntary blindness that makes the results so surprising in some cases. Not only are the participants not in a position to ascertain the evidence available to the others in the group or the validity of the aggregating function, they may not even know that they are participating in an episode of collective intelligence, let alone that they are successful. As Surowiecki says, sometimes "the people

---

[33] Hardwig (1985), Schmitt (1994), Goldman (2002).
[34] Pursuing this track might lead one to place contemporary science closer to the thin than to the thick end of the spectrum.

in the group aren't...aware that [they are making decisions or solving a problem]."[35]

Thin collective processes may nonetheless, I submit, be regarded as exhibiting collective intelligence in a suitably extended sense, on two distinct interpretations, which I will call *internalist* and *externalist*, respectively.

On the internalist interpretation, the one that immediately comes to mind, a thin CCP is, so to speak, Minsky's "society of mind" writ large.[36] Just as Minsky, and cognitive science more generally,[37] attempt to show how intelligence emerges from an assemblage of nonintelligent components, each one in charge of a narrowly defined task, thin CCPs produce intelligent behavior, or intelligent effects, by interconnecting in specific ways agents that are deliberately used as mere "sensors" of a certain narrow segment of the world. One might be tempted to say that, in contradistinction to thick CCPs, there is no intelligence *in* a thin CCP, but intelligence *of* the process. This would not be quite right, however, for the components of a thin CCP are not assumed to be entirely devoid of intelligence: the "sensing" they accomplish can be complex[38] and involve inner workings that are those of a fully intelligent creature. So there is, after all, some intelligence *in* the system, *plus* a specific intelligence *of* the system. Thus, a thin CCP is more akin to the hybrid models favored in AI today, which are networks of complex, rather than simple, components.

The upshot is that a thin CCP may be regarded as intelligent if one is prepared to sever the link between the two components of intelligence: the world understanding is achieved, in a distributed fashion, by the individual members of the group (each one possessing a partial yet genuine understanding), while the search for a solution is achieved by the architecture of the system in a purely formal (i.e., semantically blind) fashion. Examples that come to mind are search engines such as Google[39] and other Internet-based tools, or perhaps the entire Web itself.

On the externalist interpretation,[40] a thin CCP is viewed as a sophisticated tool in the hands of a discerning agent or agency. Somewhat like the advanced software used in design, investment, forecasting, and the like, such a setup is recruited by an intelligent individual in order to achieve a cognitive end that is presumably superior to what she would have obtained without it. The intelligence here consists in setting up and making good use of a complex tool. A fine example is provided, according to Surowiecki's account, by John Craven's search for the lost submarine *Scorpion*.[41] In such examples, the intelligent system comprises the tool and its user.

---

[35] Surowiecki (2005: xviii).

[36] Minsky (1985).

[37] Dennett (1978), Hofstadter (1985).

[38] In fact, according to Hong and Page (Chapter 3, this volume), they must be, at least to the extent that the variety of the individual contributors doesn't make up for their low competence.

[39] See Origgi, Chapter 2, this volume.

[40] Clark and Chalmers (1998).

[41] Surowiecki (2005: xx–xxi), Sontag and Drew (1998: 146–50).

The two interpretations are not mutually exclusive. In fact, the externalist one depends on the internalist one, as it would not be an intelligent strategy to set up and use a complex, expensive tool if it didn't deliver, in the case at hand, an "intelligent" assistance. The reverse is not true: a thin CCP may conceivably operate without some exterior operator harnessing it for his own purpose. In fact, this is the situation of the invisible hand of free market economy and, more generally, of self-organized social systems. It might be doubted that such a system is self-aware in the way in which individual intelligence appears to be. But what we mean by self-awareness and what might correspond to it from a scientific standpoint are far from clear; besides, there is no reason to demand that collective intelligence resemble ordinary intelligence in every way.

To sum up, we may offer the following stipulative definition of collective intelligence:

> A system exhibits collective intelligence insofar as there exists within the system fragments of world understanding that are exploited by the system in such a way as to produce in due time solutions to a large variety of pressing problems, including problems arising from the need to further world understanding.

The definition does not demand that the solutions be the outcome of an intention of the system to find them. Under this definition, then, both thick and thin CCPs, albeit for different reasons, may be said to be collectively intelligent.

The conceptual question has been answered. The empirical question has not: it makes sense to inquire whether some CCPs do in fact possess collective intelligence. We can regard, as I have proposed, the idea of thin collective intelligence as conceptually coherent without thereby assuming that it is empirically sound. Compare: Turing convinced many that we would eventually accept the idea that machines *might* be able to think or that they *might* be considered intelligent. But this did not settle the question of the *actual* intelligence of the real machines that we can in fact build. Many agree that, as far as our present machines are concerned, it is still at best very primitive, and the new wave of "artificial general intelligence"[42] is an attempt to remedy this. For thin CCPs as for traditional AI systems, we must ask how "intelligent" they can be, under sufficiently general conditions.[43] Further, we may want to ask how close they are to becoming *truly* intelligent, in the sense of meeting the versatility criterion: applicability to a wide variety of problem situations and fluid transfer from one to the other. This last question is precisely the one that the artificial general intelligence movement thinks has not been answered in the case of machines.

---

[42] Goertzel and Pennachin (2007).

[43] Hong and Page (Chapter 3, this volume) provide general, formal conditions under which a CCP can be expected to behave "intelligently."

Collective Wisdom

We can approach the problematic notion of collective epistemic wisdom from two sides. On the one hand, we have a pre-theoretical notion provided by a familiar collective process that might be thought to partake of wisdom. On the other hand, we have a specification of the concept by way of its relation to neighboring concepts. Specifically, we have a "fourth proportional" description: collective epistemic wisdom (if it exists) is the notion that stands to collective intelligence in the way individual (epistemic) wisdom stands to individual intelligence, and that stands to individual (epistemic) wisdom in the way collective intelligence stands to individual intelligence;[44] it is an x such that

(E1) x / collective intelligence = individual wisdom / individual intelligence

(E2) x / individual wisdom = collective intelligence / individual intelligence

Note that the inexact nature of the relations prevent (E1) and (E2) from being equivalent, as they would be in the case of numbers; they are distinct equations.

We would like to know whether thin CCPs deserve the name given them by Surowiecki: "wisdom of crowds." Does it make sense to credit them with (collective) wisdom? We can seek an answer either by comparing them with the familiar pre-theoretical instance or by checking whether they satisfy equations (E1) and/or (E2). We can also combine the two strategies and ask, first, how the traditional entity fares with respect to the equations and, second, how thin CCPs compare on that count.

So, first, what is the traditional entity that I have in mind? It is made up of a wide array of real-life social processes whose main purpose or effect is to produce within the community an increase in world understanding and epistemic capacities. It includes fairly organized bodies of explicit, fully articulated beliefs, which are widely shared and are to a large extent common knowledge, serving as a reservoir of epistemic and other behavior-guiding resources for both individual and collective tasks, ensuring in particular an essential function in coordination and cooperation: scientific practices, but many other things besides, such as formal and informal education and training, expert panels, media and publishing, formalized discussions and informal conversations, literary traditions, and so on. But it also includes unarticulated assumptions, social norms, inculcated (rather than explicitly taught) skills, practices, and perspectives, which serve the function of an invisible guardian angel for the community. Most of these processes will be typically thick, in our technical sense, although some "thinness" may appear in the guise of nonconscious constraints or habits that contribute to the outcome unbeknownst to the participants and are thus insensitive to their consciously held beliefs and preferences.

---

[44] I am indebted to Jon Elster for suggesting this formulation.

This heterogeneous lot largely overlaps with culture but includes only its beneficial parts.[45] Besides, for the sake of parity, we should restrict ourselves, at the cost of some arbitrariness, to those cultural processes whose main function is epistemic. Now we can ask, first, why this set of cultural processes might be thought, pre-theoretically, to partake of wisdom and, second, whether it satisfies our equations.

The first question is easily answered. Just as the wise person has drawn the lessons of prolonged experience, accumulated a wealth of dos and don'ts, and weeded out false beliefs, destructive desires, and utopian plans, the culture of a community comprises a shared set of maxims and skills that shield it from disastrous enterprises and keep its members from coming to grief. On the positive side, just as her wisdom allows a person to zero in on the right answer, the plan to follow, and forgo the slow and laborious process of examining and eventually rejecting a whole series of inferior hypotheses or plans, culture (in favorable cases) proceeds directly to the heart of the problem at hand, guiding the community toward the best response.

Now does this form of cultural wisdom satisfy equations (E1) and (E2)? As for (E2), the answer is fairly straightforward. The passage from individual to collective intelligence involves (1) lifting the obligation of co-location of the epistemic resources and thus (2) allowing "blind" processes to play a part in the processes leading to a solution of the problems at hand (the blindness may extend to the solution itself, which may not necessarily appear as such in any conscious mind). The kind of process we are examining now seems to stand to individual wisdom in a similar relation: those epistemic resources that result in the culture's wisdom are not located in any single member of the community, and the end result relies to a large extent on processes such as division of labor and responsibilities, confrontations of opinions, which can be partially blind (as when the confrontation terminates without explicit agreement), or again tacit exclusion of certain potential solutions.

Whether equation (E1) is also satisfied is a more involved matter. Going from individual intelligence to individual wisdom implies a coordinated series of changes, three of which appear to be crucial: the spatial and temporal horizons expand from local to global; inference and computation give way to holistic decision; impersonal, objective problem solving takes second place to personal responsibility. If we start from collective intelligence, we have no concept of a person ready at hand. The challenge then is to retrieve a functional equivalent of a person, a self of sorts, in collective processes. The concept of a collective self is contentious, but for present purposes we can perhaps

---

[45] In contradistinction to so-called popular wisdom (in French, *sagesse des nations*) in at least two respects. First it is not limited to maxims and sayings or to shared beliefs, public norms, etc. Second, it is restricted to those practices considered by the community to foster its essential interests, all things considered and in the fullness of time. By contrast, popular wisdom is often used with derisive intent, as referring to empty or erroneous generalizations or (in a wider sense) as sanctioned practices that in fact have a deleterious effect.

bypass the controversy. The set of processes under consideration belong to the core of the community's culture: it contributes to the self-perpetuation of the community across inessential changes as well as hard times. It is a commonplace that a society's culture either defines, constitutes, or enables that society's identity. If we accept that view, the set of cultural epistemic goods of the community is constitutive of the group's identity. We retrieve the needed functional equivalent of the self, and the "all things considered" goodness of wisdom falls out as well: what is good for the group as such is precisely the perpetuation of its culture, hence its identity, across change, and it is wisdom again that steers the group in the "right" direction. Cultures that fall apart as a result of endogenous or exogenous factors simultaneously lose their wisdom and their identity.

The upshot is that one may indeed regard traditional, "thick" CCPs embedded in culture as satisfying both equations and thus fully deserving of the label.

Finally, how do thin CCPs, the focus of the wisdom-of-crowds movement, fare? Again, (E2) can be regarded as satisfied, for much the same reasons, and again the serious problem concerns (E1), due to the requirement of some analogue of personhood. And here comes the rub: this requirement would seem to directly contradict the essential "blindness" of thin collective processes. Even if we were prepared to grant some form of collective personhood to the participants in a given thin CCP, on the mere basis of their participation in the process, the resulting ersatz self would lack essential attributes of selfhood such as self-reflection and responsibility. A stronger form of selfhood would perhaps result from a "common spirit," such as binds together a tightly knit community, something like a rowing team, a drama company, or an orchestra performing, or an army brigade in action, constantly coordinated and recalibrating their mutual expectations, blending into a "we" capable of we-thoughts, we-intentions, we-actions. But such a collective would be maximally distant from the sort of group that can support thin CCPs, because it would lack precisely the diversity and independence required of a well-functioning wisdom-of-crowds setup. It would fall prey to a form of "groupthink."

We have thus finally reached an answer to our initial question: the wisdom of crowds has not much to do with wisdom, beyond differing from individual intelligence. There does exist something that may deserve the name of collective wisdom, but it is nothing other than a set of culturally transmitted beliefs and practices that are at considerable distance from the wisdom of crowds in the focal sense (thin CCPs) that makes it interesting to Surowiecki.

Of course, this is not to rule out the possibility that recommending a thin CCP to settle or regulate a particular issue, or to systematically favor such setups in a wide variety of situations, may be regarded as wise, either on the part of a single social or political engineer or on the part of a group. But the wisdom would not belong to the thin processes proposed.

References

Audi, R., ed., *The Cambridge Dictionary of Philosophy*, Cambridge: Cambridge University Press, 1995.

Barkow, J., Cosmides, L., and Tooby, J., eds., *The Adapted Mind: Evolutionary Psychology and the Generation of Culture*, New York: Oxford University Press, 1992.

Canto-Sperber, M., ed., *Dictionnaire d'éthique et de philosophie morale*, Paris: Presses Universitaires de France, 1996.

Clark, A., and Chalmers, D. J., The extended mind, *Analysis* 58 (1998), 7–19.

Dennett, D. C., *Mindstorms*, Cambridge, MA: MIT Press, 1978.

Elster, J., *Alchemies of the Mind*, Cambridge: Cambridge University Press, 1999.
   Solomonic Judgments, Cambridge: Cambridge University Press, 1989.

Flynn, J. R., *What Is Intelligence?* Cambridge: Cambridge University Press, 2007.

Gigerenzer, G., and Selten, R., eds., *Bounded Rationality: The Adaptive Toolbox*, Cambridge, MA: MIT Press, 2002.

Goertzel, B., and Pennachin, C., eds., *General Artificial Intelligence*, Berlin: Springer, 2007.

Goldman, A., *Pathways to Knowledge, Private and Public*, Oxford: Oxford University Press, 2002.

Hardwig, J., Epistemic dependence, *Journal of Philosophy* 82, no. 7 (1985), 335–49.

Harsanyi, J. C., Advances in understanding rational behavior, in R. E. Butts and J. Hintikka, eds., *Foundational Problems in the Special Sciences*, Dordrecht: Reidel, 1977, 315–43.

Haugeland, J., ed., *Mind Design*, Cambridge, MA: MIT Press, 1981.

Hofstadter, D., *Metamagical Themas*, New York: Basic Books, 1985.

Lalande, A., *Vocabulaire technique et critique de la philosophie*, 5th ed., Paris: Presses Universitaires de France, 1947.

Linstone, F., and Turoff, H., eds., *The Delphi Method: Techniques and Applications*, Reading, MA: Addison-Wesley, 1975; 2002 reprint can be downloaded at http://is.njit.edu/pubs/delphibook/.

Mackay, C., *Extraordinary Popular Delusions and the Madness of Crowds*, 1852; repr. New York: Harmony, 1980.

Mele, A., and Rawling, P., eds., *The Oxford Handbook of Rationality*, Oxford: Oxford University Press, 2004.

Minsky, M., *The Society of Minds*, New York: Simon & Schuster, 1985.

Newell, A., and Simon, H. L., Computer science as empirical inquiry: Symbols and search, *Communications of the Association for Computing Machinery* 19 (1976), 113–16; repr. in Haugeland (1981).

Nozick, Robert, *The Examined Life*, New York: Touchstone, 1989.

Piatelli-Palmarini, M., ed., *Language and Learning: The Debate between Jean Piaget and Noam Chomsky*, London: Routledge & Kegan Paul, 1980.

Rheingold, H., *Smart Mobs*, Boston: Perseus, 2002.

Ryan, Sharon, Wisdom, in E. N. Zalta, ed., *The Stanford Encyclopedia of Philosophy*, Fall 2008 edition.

Schmitt, F., ed., *Socializing Epistemology: The Social Dimensions of Knowledge*, Lanham, MD: Rowman & Littlefield, 1994.

Searle, J. R., Minds, brains, and programs, *Behavioral and Brain Sciences*, no. 3 (1980), 417–57.

Simon H. A., *Models of Man*, New York: Wiley, 1957.

Sontag, S., and Drew, C., *Blind Man's Bluff*, New York: Public Affairs, 1998.

Spohn, W., The many facets of rationality, *Croatian Journal of Philosophy* 2 (2002), 247–62.

Sternberg, R. J., *The Triarchic Mind: A New Theory of Human Intelligence*, New York: Penguin, 1988.

Sternberg, R. J., and Pretz, J. E., eds., *Cognition and Intelligence*, Cambridge: Cambridge University Press, 2005.

Surowiecki, J., *The Wisdom of Crowds*, New York: Doubleday, 2004; Anchor Books, 2005.

Turing, A. M., Computing machinery and intelligence, *Mind*, 59 (1950), 236, 433–60.

5

Legislation, Planning, and Deliberation

John Ferejohn

INTRODUCTION

Any government must protect its subjects and allow them a chance to live tolerable lives. These tasks require the occasional threat of force to coordinate the actions of its citizens and officials around policies to secure these effects. A liberal democratic government asks more of itself, insisting that the people play some role in directing (possibly coercive) state policies and providing legal and political space for people to take private actions to determine the course of their own lives. In a modern (representative) democracy, the legislature normally directs and regulates coercive state power by making laws and directing their enforcement, and anyone subject to legal force is entitled to a justification, in a suitable forum, as to why her interests are to be subordinated to those of others or the public interest. This justificatory burden requires that a statute be seen as intentionally aimed at furthering some genuine public interest.[1]

When someone complains in a court about the application of a law, he poses three questions. First, (in a constitutional regime) was the legislature authorized to enact the statute? Second, is the state's interest – the aim or intention of the statute – sufficient to justify its coercive application? And third, are the particular coercive measures authorized by the statute proportionate to that interest?[2] Thus, as part of discharging its burden of justification, a democratic government must convince a court that the statute is aimed at achieving a legitimate public interest. That is, it seeks to provide the court with a kind of intentional explanation of the law, attributing an intention to the legislature itself.

---

[1] What counts as a valid or legitimate purpose is a complex topic that I do not address here beyond saying that validity would include both procedural elements – that the statute was enacted according to established and fair procedures – and substantive ones (including constitutional and possibly other criteria).

[2] This is a complex question that is resolved in various ways in different legal systems.

Why? Why not just point to the configuration of individual intentions held by the members of the legislature that enacted the law or those who voted for it? Such an account might explain the existence of structure of the law, but it would fall short of justifying it. Members could have voted for all kinds of nonpublic reasons – to advance their electoral or partisan interests or because of logrolls or other kinds of bargains. Are all statutes passed for such reasons inapplicable or without force if members were moved by interests of these kinds? This seems too strong a requirement for democratic law to meet. I think there is a better foundation for the burden of justification. We want government to act wisely: to determine public interests democratically and to pursue them in ways that can be justified to citizens and others affected by this pursuit. This requires, at minimum, that the government, and specifically the legislature, be understood as an intentional agent, able to act for reasons in the way that ordinary persons do.

For government to act wisely in this way requires that the "legislature" be seen as an entity that continues over time. When justifying the application of force at a moment in time, we need to claim that legislative intentions normally persist and are not merely manifestations of a particular congress in the past. This is so for three reasons. First, when the state has exerted force on someone evoking a legal complaint, the legislature that enacted the law has normally disappeared. If its intention was to have vanished along with the legislature, then there would be no state purpose behind the application of force and no justification for it. That is a recipe for tyranny or anarchy. Second, the characteristic duties of the state generally persist over time: the public will always need police and fire protection, a system of national defense, some provisions for social security and health care (at least for the old and dependent), and a stable framework within which markets can operate. And the statutes aimed to deal with these issues are likely to be enduring. Third, a legislative statute is merely a string of words by which the actions of many different people and officials are to be coordinated. Just as the members of the state apparatus (the police and other civil servants) must know what each is to do and not do, so too must ordinary people be able to coordinate their actions either to conform with or possibly to change the law. In this sense, statutes need to encourage the development of complex systems of interrelated and widely distributed beliefs that allow the coordinated solution of persisting social problems and, for these reasons, be relatively stable over time. Any statutory scheme is therefore likely to be imperfect: to fall short of fulfilling its "intended" purposes and to require, for that reason, amending and tinkering to allow it to accomplish its aims. If that is the way that laws normally operate, it seems unlikely that the justification for a statute could plausibly be tied to the transitory intentions of some particular legislature operating at a particular moment in time. Rather, the more likely conclusion is that a statute is aimed to further a stable intention, attributable to the legislature itself, aimed at resolving or managing a persistent social problem. At least this seems the case for big and important statutes.

This is not to deny that events at the moment of enactment are significant in some way. The text enacted by the original legislature and the debates that produced it have evidentiary authority as to how members of the enacting legislature understood the problem and how they thought the statute would address it. That legislature presumably focused on the problem in its specific political context and incurred political costs involved in trying to resolve it as best they could. But these "original" intentions depend on the beliefs and expectations that members held at the time. For this reason, notions of original intent – because they privilege the intentions of the enacting legislature – will not generally produce the right kind of guidance about the intentions that should direct the application of the statute today, when the beliefs will have evolved. Later lawmakers (and citizens too) will have had the chance to learn much more about the circumstances of application of the original statute. Since they have the benefit of experience in applying the law, their expectations and beliefs are likely to be more accurate than those of the original legislature.[3] And they will have had many opportunities to update or change or even abolish the statute in light of these new developments. So as long as a subsequent parliament does not cancel the statutory scheme altogether, it seems to me plausible to think of it as retaining the intention of the original legislature, possibly revised in light of new information, that produced the original legislation.

This stance may seem to commit us to a philosophically controversial view of legislative intent. One can distinguish between a *realist* notion of legislative intent, which sees intentions as playing a causal role of some kind in the enacting of a statute, and an *instrumentalist* notion, which sees legislative intent merely as a "posited" entity, one that merely provides an ex post rationale for the statute rather than a causal account of it. There are two kinds of realist theories of legislative intent: *aggregative* theories, which see legislative intention as some kind of aggregation of the actions and intentions of the individual members – perhaps those of the majority that prevailed in a particular vote or that of the "median voter," if one exists – and *holistic* theories, which see the legislative intentions as irreducible to individual actions or intentions.

Aggregative theories often produce legislative intentions that are incomplete or incoherent. Such a theory might be able to explain a statute, in the sense of showing why it was enacted (a majority voted for it) or took the shape it did (that was what the majority could agree on), but it generally cannot explain it as the action of an intentional agent. By contrast a holistic theory sees the legislature itself as capable of having an intention of the kind that individuals do. But it may seem implausible that a legislature can actually form real intentions capable of playing a causal role.[4]

---

[3] The text of the statute, which was produced by that legislature, is another matter. Any theory of legislation – normative or positive – must take account of text both as something that is fought over in the legislature and as having constraining effects on what the law can be subsequently.

[4] Christian List and Philip Pettit, *Group Agency* (Oxford: Oxford University Press, 2004).

Ontological doubts of this kind have led some to argue that the only plausible candidates for a holistic idea of legislative intention are instrumental or interpretive,[5] which "construct" legislative intent as the best explanation of the legislative materials (text, history, applications, etc.). This kind of instrumentalism lacks explanatory force unless it is claimed that that intention actually existed and was the reason the legislature enacted the statute (which amounts to a retreat to realism). I shall argue that there is a plausible realist construction that can play the appropriate role in shaping statutes as well as providing interpretations of them. The idea is to see statutes as *plans* of a certain kind.

There are reasons that notions of *continuing* legislative intentions of the kind discussed here may be resisted. These reasons are normative rather than ontological. Legislatures, for example, are not supposed to be able to bind their successors.[6] The idea that new legislation could be constrained by previous legislation seems undemocratic in interfering with the capacity of the present generation to govern itself. While I think there is something to this belief, it is often too crudely stated to be correct.[7] In any case, my construction sees the current legislature as sharing the relevant intention, so there is no sense that the current legislature is constrained by an earlier one. Indeed, legislative intentions do not generally bind by constraining a future congress from taking some action. Rather, these intentions are a source of reasons for action, in just the way that a person's intentions provide reasons for her to act in certain ways.[8] The power of intentions to shape actions is normative in that sense.

The language of collective intent is already familiar to anyone who has read an opinion of the Supreme Court: when writing an opinion, a justice typically refers to what "we" or "this Court" decided when referring to decisions a century old (and with which the current opinion writer may disagree). The idea is that those previous decisions establish a continuing policy of the Court itself that is normally understood to be binding on the current Court in any sufficiently similar case.[9] For the Court, this is not a mere manner of speaking, but a recognition by members of the current Court that they have duties to

---

[5] One could also imagine an instrumentalist aggregative view. Such a view may have scientific value, I suppose, in permitting the attribution of intentions to members or coalitions.

[6] Formal precedents that govern how a legislature conducts its business are often important, of course. The procedural rules of both the United States House and Senate are often found in precedents.

[7] In the areas of taxes and appropriations, Congress frequently sees itself as bound by its previous commitments. This is also the case with government contracts. Legislative "entitlements" represent, perhaps, a weaker sense of bindingness, since Congress does sometimes adjust entitlements. For a detailed treatment of this issue see Eric Posner and Adrian Vermeule, "Legislative Entrenchment: A Reappraisal," *Yale Law Journal*, 111 (May 2002), 1665–1705.

[8] If you intend to drive to the store from your house, that intention gives you reasons to get in the car, back out of your driveway, and turn left or right at various intersections. You could refuse to do these things, but then the chances are you would not fulfill your intention.

[9] While the notion of the Supreme Court, as a multimember body, acting as an intentional agent may be familiar, it is no less mysterious, in the terms of this essay, than the idea of a legislature having an intent.

present the Court as a continuing body, as a unified agent acting over time, capable of offering to present and future litigants a coherent account of their legal rights and duties. The notion that "horizontal" precedent has binding force on the current Court is obviously a normative claim. It is an expression of an ethical notion of how a judge on a court operating over time ought to behave.[10] I argue that similar commitments and concomitant supporting norms can be traced in the legislature as well.[11] In response to the ontological objections, I shall argue that the notion of a statute as a kind of partial plan plays the key explanatory role.

I shall try to accomplish three things in this essay. First I want to sketch an account of statutes as plans and ask about the implications of that idea for the notion of legislative intentions. Second, I will argue that the planning perspective on statutes is not really committed to any particular theory of group intentions but can leave room for the major philosophical competitors. Third, I will develop a theory of legislative deliberation that builds on the assumption that members of the legislature have some motivation to make their statutes at least somewhat coherent. But coherence is one value and is sometimes in conflict with others. And (as we will see) making an incoherent statute more coherent entails giving up some other value. But insofar as members want their statutes to have effects and to survive legal challenges, they have reasons to make them somewhat coherent. Moreover, coherence may help in building majorities and in constructing stable legal regimes – ones that will last over time.

An Example

The issues discussed here can be illustrated by the recent debate over how to reform the Social Security program. The Social Security Act of 1935 arose out of a deliberate campaign by President Roosevelt to persuade Congress and the people to embrace a new program for economic security – one that would create a new kind of economic right or entitlement to income during retirement. He explained that a new economic right was necessary because structural changes in the economy had undermined the capacity of families to support their older members. He established a commission made up mostly of economists and insurance experts to come up with a legislative blueprint for the new program. His allies engaged in extensive congressional debates aimed at crafting and

---

[10] My view is that such norms are widely shared among judges and normally have explanatory value. Certainly others have taken a reductionist view that such expressions merely stand in for something else – ideology, material interest, whatever. I don't deny that such factors can be causally important but claim only that previous decisions or doctrine are a source of reasons for the current Court and that as such can play a role determining what it actually does.

[11] Kornhauser and Sager urge caution in comparing courts and legislatures in respects under discussion in this essay. Lewis Kornhauser and Laurence Sager, "The One and the Many: Integrity and Group Choice in Paradoxical Cases," *Philosophy and Public Affairs*, 32 (2004), 249–76.

justifying the new legislation, which was then enacted. Subsequently, Congress revisited the program several times (most notably in 1939, 1950, 1972, and 1983) to amend and usually to expand it, as well as to make its promises more credible and secure. Each revisiting was predicated on the notion that the United States had undertaken a long-term commitment, in the Social Security Act, to provide certain kinds of "guarantees" to its citizens that would enable them to plan their lives, and that it (the Congress) recognized an obligation to ensure that the program was structured in a way to redeem the promises it made in the act.

Changing external facts arising from demography and fiscal constraints, as well as from the automatic cost-of-living adjustments in the benefits formula, have made Social Security reform more pressing. Republicans, especially in the House of Representatives, have long been encouraging leaders to push for reforming the original program by introducing private accounts that would be "owned" and perhaps controlled by individuals. On its face, a system based on private accounts seems to depart from the social insurance principle of the traditional system. Should we therefore understand the position of the Republicans in this debate to be simply a call to put an end to the Social Security program altogether and put some new program in its place? Or should we see the Republican advocacy of private accounts as somehow fitting in with long-standing congressional intentions and merely representing a more efficient set of means to achieve it? On the latter account, the Republican proposal of private accounts would be offered as a better interpretation of an abstract congressional intention to provide retirement income as applied to modern conditions.

This posture – framing the argument as one about ongoing congressional or even popular intentions – offers powerful rhetorical leverage. It casts arguments about the policy as appropriately guided by a long-standing intention to provide for Social Security. Insofar as this framing succeeds, advocates of private accounts must therefore seek to persuade others that to adopt private accounts does not amount to abandoning prior intention but is, rather, a way to achieve it most effectively. Conversely, defenders of the current system can oppose this interpretation of collective intentions on the ground either that it is insincere or that it fails to ensure adequate guarantees of security and is therefore inconsistent with long-standing congressional intent. That is to say, they reject the notion that private accounts would be a better way to fill in the partial plan embodied in existing Social Security laws. Thus, for supporters as well as opponents of the proposed reform, the argument centers on congressional intentions and the best way they can be implemented by amending (or abolishing) Social Security laws.

PLANS AND LEGISLATION

Like individuals, legislatures need to decide what to do. But as collectivities they are large and complex organizations that are distinctive in having little control over their membership, and they need to coordinate the actions of their diverse members through time in order to gather information, make decisions, and take action. Moreover, legislative actions are not usually self-executing but rather establish programs and policies that extend through time and that have the aim of coordinating the actions of millions of other people, among them judges and executive officials, as well as the actions of future congresses. Statutes, on this view, are plans for the future, and legislating amounts to deliberating about plans.

This conception of deliberation arises from seeing the legislature as a "planning agent." According to Michael Bratman, deciding what to do – practical reasoning – generally involves forming an intention to take some course of action.[12] He argues that as part of forming an intention, we commit to a course of action or *partial plan*. Thus, rather than taking the Aristotelian view of practical reasons (in which beliefs and desires determine actions syllogistically), he suggests that there is something that comes in between beliefs and desires, on the one side, and action, on the other, and that this something can be described either as an intention or as a partial plan.[13] In effect he posits a duality relation between intentions and plans, which will be useful to us later on.

We might intend, in one of Bratman's examples, to present a paper at a professional meeting in Boston in October. In adopting this intention, we have already (at the same time) adopted a partial plan to arrive, somehow, at the meeting in Boston on the appointed date. This plan may be very incomplete: for example, it may not yet involve a commitment to go by plane or train, to buy a ticket, to arrange for a trip to the airport or train station, and so on. Still, the intention itself already involves a part of a plan: to arrive in Boston on the appointed day, with a paper to present. As we go forward in time, assuming that we retain the intention, we are moved, somehow, to fill in the partial plan by planning on doing the required things to make the intended state of affairs come about.

In this respect, Bratman sees planning as central to deliberating over what to do, and we do it because it helps us to coordinate our activities over time. Partial plans represent commitments to courses of action, and they provide reasons that enter into our choice of actions over time. Plans are relatively stable in the sense that we do not constantly reconsider them as our beliefs and temporal location changes; if we did, plans would not help us coordinate our actions and intentions over time. And because they are relatively stable, plans help us to structure our further deliberations by permitting us also to

---

12 Michael Bratman, *Intentions, Plans and Practical Reasoning* (Cambridge, MA: Harvard University Press, 1987).

13 Bratman partly grounds the idea of planning on limited cognitive capacities. The adoption of a partial plan early in the deliberative process reduces the complexity of the decision problem, And because this simplification is valuable, an agent will have reason to hold onto a plan even if there is some evidence that the plan is suboptimal. Bratman recognizes other reasons for sticking with a plan rather than jettisoning it at the first sign that it is not the best possible course of action.

consider a manageable set of options (train, plane, boat) to decide among.[14] They also make our future actions more predictable both to ourselves and to others. Knowing that I intend to be in Boston at the professional meeting helps me make other decisions about how to spend my time (writing the paper, etc.) and permits others who may want to see me to form their own intentions. Plans help, in these ways, to coordinate or organize our deliberations over time. It is important to note that plans exert normative or critical pressure on our actions and on our other intentions and actions: if I plan to go to Boston, there is reason for me to decide about mode of transport, to see about getting a ticket, and so on. I can, of course, abandon my plan, so this normative pressure is defeasible, but so long as my plan remains in place, it (along with other considerations) generates reasons for action. I want to call this idea "weak normativity" to distinguish it from such things as obligations to others.[15]

In any case, whether or not they can form intentions, groups can make plans in very much the same way that individuals do. Indeed, insofar as interpersonal coordination problems are more difficult than the intrapersonal ones faced by individuals, groups have stronger reasons to plan. An important aspect of a group plan is that there is a need for the plan to "fit" with the personal intentions or plans of its members. Because of this requirement of "fit," the plans of a group and its members have to adjust to each other. If you and I plan to paint a house, at some point one of us had better get some paint and brushes and, in this way, adjust our personal plan to permit this.

Bratman thinks that once we have formed a partial plan to paint the house, that plan then structures a further negotiation over a choice of color. He doesn't say very much about how this process might proceed. I might simply buy some blue paint and get started, and you, while preferring a yellow house to a blue one, still decide to go along with my choice rather than paint over my blue with yellow. Or the process could involve more explicit bargaining and agreement. The point is that our group plan imposes various kinds of coherence constraints. Joint plans are constrained in the same way that personal plans are (to be coherent, etc.) and, in addition, must fit or mesh with personal plans of group members (and with other joint plans involving group members). How this coherence or harmonization is brought about cannot be specified in advance but must be negotiated.

This idea that partial plans provide a basis for further negotiating, bargaining, and deliberation seems especially important for large and heterogeneous

---

[14] On the cognitive limitations view, failure to adopt plans would be a failure of at least second-best rationality. It is not an option to act as though we could plan synoptically, taking every conceivable option into account, so a refusal to plan would tend to lead us to worse outcomes than those we could achieve if we took account of our limitations.

[15] The authority of our plans over our further deliberations takes the form of exclusionary reasons in Raz's sense. That is, if I am considering taking an action and I have adopted a plan that excludes taking that action, I have a reason to take the plan's constraint as a reason for not performing the action in question. I do not look behind the plan for the reasons that led to adopting the plan in the first place; rather, the plan itself provides reasons for action or restraint.

groups. There are bound to be many disagreements in such groups, and these make it difficult to achieve full coherence. In heterogeneous groups, therefore, full coherence might often remain a goal or aspiration rather than an achievement. For example, an ethnically diverse group might be willing to tolerate some degree of inconsistency in its plans in order to recognize values important to various subgroups. Or to take a more pedestrian example, we might have a policy of subsidizing tobacco farmers while at the same time discouraging or even forbidding smoking. Such a policy recognizes both the value of a traditional agrarian lifestyle for the farmers whose land might be suitable only for tobacco cultivation and a public concern about the malign effects and addictive qualities of tobacco consumption. Obviously such policy combinations are vulnerable to criticism from a coherence viewpoint.[16]

What, then, is the force of coherence on a group plan? Bratman's house painters suggest two different kinds of force or pressure. First, if neither of us undertakes to get the paint and brushes – if neither of us plans to do our part – there may be a sense in which we have not really committed ourselves to a group plan to paint the house. Let's call that a constitutive constraint. A second source of constraint is perhaps more interesting in that it arises from the desires or values of the group members. We could, sensibly, paint the house both blue and yellow, but if each of us prefers either a blue or yellow house to a multiply colored one, there is a reason for us to bargain or negotiate over the color so that we can decide on a single color plan. We can call this a regulatory or normative constraint.

I don't think that it is necessary to assume that the direction of these normative forces is fixed. A normative constraint arising between a group plan and a personal plan of a group member requires only that one or the other intention give way – at least a little. Which intention is to be altered or abandoned is another question. If a joint intention requires, for example, that one of the group members act immorally, the pressure would probably be to reinterpret or abandon the joint intention.

Legislatures are very different than the small groups that Bratman has discussed: internal (partisan or other) divisions are both legitimate and sharp, and are often institutionalized in various ways. Indeed, legislatures are designed in ways that encourage social divisions to manifest themselves inside the legislature. For that reason, electoral results can give the legislature special democratic

---

[16] These examples are supposed to illustrate aspects of value pluralism circumstances of tragic choice that may prevent either groups or individuals from acting with full coherence. A related issue arises when a policy might be explained or justified in terms of two conflicting principles. Here the policy itself, as a partial plan, might be seen as coherent when viewed in either of two ways: as pursuing goal A or goal B. But if A and B are incompatible in the sense that each would fill in the partial plan in different ways, then to fill in the plan requires a choice between A and B. The adherents of each interpretation will argue that their principle gives the better explanation or justification of the policy and, therefore, gives the better recommendations as to how the plan should be completed. So long as the underlying issue remains unresolved, the authority that the plan exerts on future actions will remain controversial.

reasons to abandon plans (and intentions). On the other hand, the coordination value of plans seems more important for large heterogeneous groups like a legislature than for smaller ones. Thus, there is good reason to think that legislative deliberation can be understood as planning activity, that statutes are (incomplete or partial) plans, and that subsequent legislators have reason to regard themselves as participants in ongoing planning activity. To allege that legislatures are planning agents is to claim that they can act in some respects in the same way a person would, so we need to have an account of how this is possible.

I emphasized earlier that Bratman posits a duality relationship between plans and intentions. To form an intention is to adopt a partial plan consistent with achieving that intention, although, since it is only a partial plan, it would also be consistent with achieving many other intentions as well. And presumably, as this partial plan is filled in, each new partial plan is consistent with the intention but consistent with fewer and fewer other possible intentions. In the limit, a completed plan might be consistent with only a single intention. Ideally, therefore, *complete* plans and intentions map onto each other in a one-to-one fashion. In this respect, filling out plans involves forward and backward aspects: forward, filling in the current partial plan; and backward, narrowing the range of intentions that the current partial plan could be understood to advance.

While we might normally think that an individual actually has a particular intention, so that the negotiations involved in completing a partial plan mostly involves deciding how to go forward, legislative deliberation often seems to require backward deliberation. That is, part of what a legislature must do when filling in a plan (amending a statute) is to eliminate those possible intentions (perhaps held by some members) that are inconsistent with the amended plan. Moreover, the backward view suggests that when thinking about heterogeneous groups, we might revise the connection between intentions and plans. The legislature might, for example, be able to agree on a partial plan even though it might not be able to agree on an intention; different members could agree to the plan, each seeing it as consistent with his own intention.[17] This suggests that when thinking about legislation, the planning perspective may come apart from the intentional perspective. Indeed, it might suggest that we can leave aside, to some extent, the question of what the best theory of group intention might be. This is a good thing, because there is a good deal of philosophical controversy over that question.

GROUP INTENTIONS: TWO THEORIES

Michael Bratman's approach is to develop a conception of group intentions that can serve to guide planning. His theory develops group intentions from

---

[17] This view is similar to the one advanced by Cass Sunstein in *Legal Reasoning and Political Conflict* (Oxford: Oxford University Press, 1996).

the "ground up," in the sense that group intentions are constituted by appropriate configurations of personal intentions of the members. This is an ontological move, in that Bratman presents an account of what group intentions are as a way to account for how planning works. On his account, group intentions are not to be regarded as actual "mental" states of the group but as configurations of mental states held by group members. Thus, while group intentions (like individual intentions) are propositional attitudes, they do not themselves represent the mental states of an agent; rather, they correspond to complex combinations of the mental states of the group's members.[18] This construction has the virtue of being "ontologically conservative," in that in order to account for group intentions, there is no need to posit any new autonomous entities such as group minds. But as economical as is Bratman's strategy in the examples he explores (usually involving groups of two to five people), it is not clear that this construction is plausible for large and complex groups such as legislatures.

A joint or shared or group intention (I shall use these expressions interchangeably) is different from a personal intention in the following way. We can understand personal intentions as intentions to "do" something. This formulation takes account of the fact that one can only intend to do something that one is able to accomplish – at least in more or less normal circumstances (assuming one is not struck by lightening, etc.). But Bratman wishes to avoid introducing a wholly new entity – for example, a group that can form intentions in just the same way that individuals can – and so he connects group intentions to more basic individual intentions.[19] There are some complications for group intentions: individual members cannot normally form ordinary intentions – intentions "to" X – on behalf of the group because individual members are not normally in control of a group's actions in this way. But a member can intend "that" the group take some action, where having a "that" intention requires the individual to do her part in bringing about X. And in Bratman's account, if members have the right combination of "that" intentions, the group will have a shared or group intention.[20]

Intending "that" will involve the same kind of constraints that intending "to" does. These constraints, arguably, follow from features of planning agency. Thus, Bratman's principle of agglomerativity implies that a group

---

18 "Shared intentions are intentions of the group. . . . [W]hat they consist in is a public, interlocking web of intentions of the individuals" (Michael Bratman, *Faces of Intention*, [Cambridge: Cambridge University Press, 1999], 43). Thus, as with the social choice theory account, Bratman's theory reduces group intentions to individual intentions; however, the kind of reduction is not aggregative in the sense of social choice theory – at least not obviously so – but constitutive.

19 Whether individual attitudes are rightly thought to be simpler or more primitive is a controversial matter.

20 "Shared intention, as I understand it, is not an attitude in any mind. It is not an attitude in the mind of some fused agent, for there is no such mind; and it is not an attitude in the mind of either or both participants. Rather, it is a state of affairs that consists primarily in attitudes . . . of the participants and interrelations between those attitudes" (Bratman, *Faces of Intention*, 122–23).

member cannot (knowingly) intend that the group achieve two contradictory results, and so the group itself cannot have a shared intention to achieve
inconsistent objectives. Moreover, group members cannot intend the group
to do something that the group cannot normally bring about, and so shared
intentions seem subject to further practical constraints in the same way that
individual intentions are.

In addition there are vertical relations among shared and personal intention
and actions. If I intend "that" we (our group) do x, I would normally have
appropriate personal intentions to do my part in bringing x about.[21] Or at
least, I must be disposed to form such personal intentions along with others
in order that the group's intention (my intention that) be realized. The part
I am to play in the plan has to "mesh" with the plan. And you would have
to have similar individual intentions to do your part.[22] Meshing also requires
that both of us will feel normative pressure to bring our other plans into line
with our shared intention. Finally, in some way, we must each know that these
considerations are satisfied.

Bratman's formal account of shared intention goes like this. (1) I intend that
we X and you intend that we X. (2) I intend that we X by means of (1) (including
meshing subplans of (1)). And you intend that we X by means of (1) (including
meshing subplans of (1)). (3) All of this is common knowledge between us.
An important aspect of this definition is that it defines shared intention in
terms of a complex interlocking set of individual attitudes (intentions and
beliefs). Moreover, shared or group intentions require unanimous personal
intentions "that." This condition implies that properties of shared intentions
"to" – including coherence properties – will be inherited from the properties
of the individual attitudes.

Thus, Bratman's definition of a shared intention seems delicate precisely
because it requires that an elaborate set of interlocking attitudes of beliefs and
intentions be held by the group's members. In larger and more complex groups,
it is difficult to believe that such conditions could be achieved very often or
at all. Some writers have attempted to relax these conditions somewhat while
keeping the idea of shared or group intention. This may be a fruitful path, but
I cannot pursue it here. Instead I want to explore a different theory of group
intentions.

Margaret Gilbert argues that the creation of a shared intention entails, first
of all, the creation of a "plural subject" – essentially by a kind of agreement
among the members – which is an entity that can have intentions in just the
same way that individuals can. The intentional attitudes of this subject are

---

[21] Where not everyone has to do something to implement the intention, the requirement might be
minimal.

[22] What "my part" and "your part" amount to is a complex issue. Our parts may be fully specified
in the partial plan in some cases. In others there may be some background idea of fairness that
would play a role in determining what our individual obligations are. I owe this observation to
Seana Shiffrin. Liam Murphy's work is relevant here.

somewhat independent of those of its constituent members. Second, the relationship between group members and the plural subject is normative – something like obligations to keep "agreements" with others. Her account envisions in this sense a new psychological entity that enters into causal and normative interactions in the world.

For a group to "agree," in Gilbert's sense, to form a plural subject, there must (already) be a convention to mark what counts as "agreeing." Her story about how two people come to be walking together describes a kind of elaborate signaling ritual in which separate walkers converge (perhaps wordlessly) on a joint commitment to walk "together" and not merely in parallel. In the case of a two-person interaction, such conventions operate implicitly and probably have the feature that forming a plural subject requires unanimous assent. We are not walking together unless both of us have somehow committed ourselves to walking together. Gilbert's shared intentions, once formed, are autonomous from the mental attitudes of group members. Two people walking together constitute themselves as a "plural subject," capable of having intentions and other mental states, and capable of responding to new circumstances as any rational agent would be.

In larger and more complex organizations, things are more ambiguous. We cannot generally expect to have implicit background conventions that would permit all of us to recognize when we have acted as a plural subject. Moreover, the formation of an intention by a plural subject cannot plausibly require unanimous agreement or anything as strong as Bratman's meshing condition. We should expect that, in the case of larger groups, more formalized norms will be relied on to describe the circumstances in which a plural subject has been acted. A large corporation, for example, can be committed to a course of action by acts of its CEO or of its board of directors. Legislatures can take action through their formal rules for proposing and accepting proposals, which usually require the assent of only a part of the body. Still, Gilbert would think the actions and policies of a corporation or a legislature are the acts of plural subjects.

Bratman and Gilbert agree that joint intentions put normative pressures on the actions and intentions of the group members. Bratman thinks this pressure is weak in the sense that it is grounded in the same kind of stabilizing or coordinating pressures generated by individual intentions. If you and I have a shared intention (and have adopted a partial plan) to X, then that gives us reason to coordinate our actions and intentions on pain of being indecisive or inconstant, or perhaps of acting suboptimally in disregarding our cognitive limitations. Gilbert argues that additional and stronger kinds of interpersonal obligations come into play at the group level, so that failing to keep up our part of a joint intention essentially involves failure to fulfill the obligations that arise from the shared intention itself.[23]

---

[23] One of Gilbert's criteria for identifying a joint intention is the existence of obligations (or at least a sense of obligation) to pursue and help the others in the group pursue the joint intention. These

The plural-subject view offers the prospect of a realist conception of legislative intent. Plural subjects, on Gilbert's account, have genuine intentions and these intentions are autonomous from the intentions of group members. Gilbert's conditions may trigger philosophical worries. Shared intentions are supposed to be mental states and such states are supposed to require minds, and perhaps minds require brains. Bratman's solution is attractive precisely in that shared intentions are seen as (complex configurations of) individual mental states, and those (individual) states are linked to brains in the ordinary way. Gilbert's view breaks the link between group and individual mental states, and so it raises questions about the status of group mental attitudes and indeed about group minds. She could argue that positing group minds is objectionable only if group minds are considered to be very much like individual human minds. But group minds may simply lack much of the power of human minds and simply be places where quite sparse and primitive mental attitudes are housed.[24]

In any case, the intentions of a plural subject are supposed to respond rationally to other group attitudes, desires, and beliefs, in more or less the ways that individual intentions normally do: we expect a plural subject's intentions to be rationally related to its beliefs and desires. But whatever it is that regulates the relations among group mental attitudes may be very different from the processes that work for individuals. That regulation may work through normatively guided social processes rather than neurophysiological ones. If that is right, Gilbert's group intentions lack some key features of individual mental attitudes. They are not realized in any kind of neural machinery, and they may lack what might be called "subjectivity" in the sense that the group as such may not have any privileged access to them in the way that ordinary individuals might be thought to have special access to their own attitudes. More important, the way group and individual intentions interact may be completely different from the way individual intentional attitudes do: normatively rather than chemically.

Because Gilbert's group intentions are not reducible, as Bratman's are, to complex sets of individual mental attitudes and are built instead on the public actions (virtual "agreements") of the members, her theory seems to offer a plausible basis for a realist theory of legislative intent. Her "agreements" could be realized both through institutionalized rituals such as votes in a legislature and in the less formal ways she discusses. Moreover, her idea that group intentions are the intentions of an autonomous subject forces us to ask how it is that group mental attitudes are made coherent. Specifically it requires us to focus

---

obligations have something of the same force as the obligation to keep promises. Even so, if such obligations conflict with individual intentions or other commitments, such obligations might be overridden, even at the price of being rebuked by other group members.

[24] For an exploration of these issues see Philip Pettit, "Groups with Minds of Their Own," in Frederick Schmitt, ed., *Socializing Metaphysics*, 167–93 (Landham, MD: Rowan & Littlefield, 2003).

directly on the normative (rather than constitutive) relationships among group members and the intentions of their plural subject. That is, it permits us to ask directly about the normative obligations group members may have to help the group pursue its purposes. These features make the notion of a plural subject a possible grounding for a realist notion of legislative intent.

While both of these approaches have attractions as theories of legislative intention, each has weaknesses too. It appears to be very hard for a legislature (or any large heterogeneous group) to meet Bratman's existence conditions and therefore to actually have a shared intention. Thus, it is unlikely that a statute could be construed as the intentional act of the legislature as a body and, therefore, it would be difficult to give the kind of justification for its application that we sketched in the introduction. On his account, state actions would be hard to justify.[25] Gilbert's theory seems politically unattractive in the opposite way. It permits the ready creation of autonomous moral agents (plural subjects), based on implicit or tacit "agreements," which can give rise to new moral obligations and rights that are unconnected to preferences or values of group members. Her theory risks overjustifying state coercion and, in this way, threatens both liberal rights and democratic rule. So maybe it is best to sidestep the philosophical issues associated with group intention and try to exploit Bratman's duality argument, to start from plans and planning and try to derive a theory of legislative intention from there.

A THEORY OF LEGISLATIVE INTENTION

The idea is this: we can describe a legislative plan as "extensionally" equivalent to the set of intentions compatible with it. While I cannot fully explore the consequences of this view here, the idea is simple: rather than trying to determine the intention of the legislature, we could look at the set of intentions it might plausibly have had given the statute it enacted. Note that these intentions may include those that were actually held by members of the enacting legislature. But this set will usually include many other intentions – ones that were held by no one at the time but that, had any been held, might have led to the adoption of the statute that was enacted.

---

[25] Annie Stilz has attempted another path: to see a democratic state itself as an instance of what Bratman called "Shared Cooperative Activity." Bratman's meshing conditions are then applied to the operation of the state as such, and state actions are given more or less wholesale prima facie justification (more or less of the kind that consent theories seek to provide). This largely avoids my objection, since it seems plausible that citizens could see their relation to their government in a way that might satisfy the meshing conditions (at least if the people are fairly homogeneous). And it provides a convincing way to answer a fundamental question: showing why people have a prima facie obligation to obey the law of their well-functioning democracy. But Stilz's theory is coarse rather than fine-grained. It cannot say why a particular statute or an application of a statute is justified against someone making a rights-based objection. So it doesn't seem useful as a normative theory of law. Annie Stilz, *Liberal Loyalty* (Princeton, NJ: Princeton University Press, 2009).

The set of compatible intentions might also be interpreted as the set of plausible *interpretations* of the statute. Such interpretations may be advanced by a judge seeking to interpret the statute. But an interpretation might also be advanced by someone, in the legislature or outside, who recommends a possible way in which the statutory plan might be perfected or amended.

Moreover, this view generates a plausible causal story about statutes. Remember, the account of causation we want must see legislative actions as causally connected to reasons, and regard agent intentions as a source of reasons for action, namely reasons for amending the statute in one way rather than another. The duality story retains this causal story: if a member's intention is compatible with the current plan, that intention will normally provide reasons for completing the plan as his intention directs rather than in some other way. And if his arguments prevail and the statute is amended in this way, his intentions may be (partly) causally responsible for changes in the statute. In this respect, intentions play a causal role in explaining how the statute is amended, as a realist theory requires. The intentions that play this role, however, are individual rather than group intentions. However, it is important to see that the set of intentions that can play a causal role is restricted by the compatibility requirement, which is fixed by the current statute: as the legislative plan is filled in, the set of intentions that can play a causal role narrows, possibly converging to something that might be called the legislative intention. Thus, there is a vague sense in which legislative "intention" – which is a limit concept – is causally relevant to explaining how the statute changes over time. But this is so only because the individual intentions that do the causal work are approximated by the constructed legislative intention.

Bratman duality also generates an attractive account of statutory interpretation. When reading an incomplete statute, an interpreter should determine its extension – the set of intentions compatible with it – which would then limit the range of plausible interpretations. What I called the original intent of the statute might be in the extension – presumably that intention was held by supporters of the actual statutory language and explains why the statute took its current form. But there would be many other intentions in the extension as well, any of which could serve as a valid way to resolve ambiguities or conflicts in the statute. Given that any argument in the extension "fits" the statute, determining which interpretation is best requires further argument, perhaps historical arguments as originalists urge or perhaps moral arguments of the kind Dworkin recommends.

LEGISLATIVE DELIBERATION

In this section I want to sketch an account of legislative deliberation as a kind of planning in the context of the Social Security reform debate introduced earlier. The members disagree as to whether the existing Social Security system is viable and some are open to taking radical steps. But others disagree. For illustrative purposes I restrict attention to a three-person legislature with only

TABLE 5.1

SS "Bankrupt"	Private Accounts Work	Adopt Reform
A	Yes	No	No
B	No	Yes	No
C	Yes	Yes	Yes

two issues, but the considerations are general and can be extended to more complex situations.[26] Consider the following hypothetical pattern of judgments about Social Security reform.[27] Member A thinks the Social Security system is bankrupt but doubts whether private accounts will work.[28] She may think that they will be too expensive or will result in unacceptable risks to some. Member B doubts that Social Security is in fact bankrupt, but considers private accounts a feasible way of providing adequate guarantees of financial security. And C thinks both that the current system is bankrupt and that the proposed new system is workable in the sense given in the preceding sentence.[29] I assume that a member would favor adopting private accounts only if she accepted both premises, as C does, so that the decision structure is "conjunctive."[30]

How might deliberation proceed in the circumstance described in Table 5.1? One possibility is that the members simply vote on whether to adopt the reform. Presumably, member C would vote for the reform, while neither A nor B would; both are skeptical about one of the reform's supporting premises. We call this way of deciding "results-oriented" voting. Note that if the information in Table 5.1 were to be revealed during the debate or if the legislature were actually to take public votes on the premises, the majority outcome (rejection of the reform) would be unsupported by majority views

[26] For a more developed argument, see John Ferejohn, "Conversibility and Deliberation," in Geoffrey Brennan, Robert Goodin, and Michael Smith, eds., *Common Minds: Themes from the Philosophy of Philip Pettit* (Cambridge: Cambridge University Press, 2007).

[27] This arrangement of the debate into an issue structure is admittedly not "given" by the record but represents a simplified version of the deliberation.

[28] The private accounts proposal must be packaged with associated benefit reductions and tax increases. Such accounts may be said to work if they are fiscally feasible and if they provide "adequate" guarantees of financial security. In other words, "work" in this context is interpretive in that it includes some notion of what such adequate guarantees would require.

[29] Preference distributions of this kind have been called a "doctrinal paradox" by Lewis Kornhauser and Larry Sager; see their "The One and the Many: Adjudication in Collegial Courts," *California Law Review*, (1993) 91: 1–51. Philip Pettit terms them instances of a "discursive dilemma."

[30] This assumption is certainly open to challenge: a member could vote for the reform if she thinks it workable even while thinking that the current system is not bankrupt. I ignore that possibility here. I suppose one could claim that this exclusion could be justified on the basis of a kind of political rationality: that proposing to replace the current system, which appears to be working well enough and on which people have relied, is so politically costly that no representative would try it.

on each of the premises – there are majorities in favor of the proposition that Social Security is bankrupt and that private accounts are workable. Indeed, we can imagine another way of proceeding: the legislature could take votes on the premises and then decide on the result in the way consistent with the vote on the premises. Philip Pettit calls this procedure "premise-oriented" and notes that it has the virtue of picking an outcome that is supported by majority-endorsed premises.[31]

An important feature of the pattern of judgments in Table 5.1 is that each member is "pivotal" to the pattern of outcomes: any member could change her votes in a way that would alter the outcome and, in effect, bring about a coherent result.[32] If member A were convinced that Social Security is not bankrupt, her vote on that premise would then switch to negative, as would the collective judgment on the premise, which would then produce a negative result. Similarly, if either of the other members took a different view of one premise, the dilemma would disappear. In this sense each member can be thought of as bearing some kind of responsibility for the overall outcome, in the sense that if she could be persuaded to change her views on one issue, a coherent result would be produced.

I distinguish two models of deliberation: *pure* and *impure*. In pure deliberation, the group deliberates about all of its judgments in a symmetric way, giving no priority to judgments about one issue over another or to the question on the result. The aim is to produce an outcome that is acceptable to a majority and is coherent, and to accomplish this each member is deliberatively disposed to reconsider his own judgments as to the premises and the result, and so each is engaged in a process of reflective equilibration. There may be substantive reasons for the fact that it is more difficult to adjust some judgments than others – certain beliefs, for example, may be tethered closely to empirical evidence. But each of the judgments in Table 5.1 embodies normative as well as empirical judgments: the judgment that the current system is bankrupt is offered not as mere description but as a reason to do something to correct or reform it. Similarly, the judgment that private accounts are workable implies a judgment that they would constitute an adequate substitute for the current system of providing Social Security.

---

[31] A doctrinal paradox of the kind in Table 5.1 can arise only for nonunanimous decision procedures (such as majority rule). And if the dilemma is conjunctive (as in Table 5.1), the paradoxical outcome must be one in which the results-oriented vote is negative, while the premise-based outcome would be positive. In effect, results-oriented voting advantages the "status quo," and this status quo "bias" grows as the number of premises increases.

[32] A member might also, strategically, propose a switch from premise-based to result-based procedures, or vice versa, to get her preferred outcome chosen. There is some work on this by J. F. Bonnefon, "How Do Individuals Solve the Doctrinal Paradox in Collective Decisions?" *Psychological Science*, 18 (2007), 753–55. *Psychological Science* 2007. List and Pettit in their discussions often expand Table 5.1 to include this option. I have simplified the example for the present discussion.

Impure deliberation proceeds sequentially, making a decision on one issue and then taking up further issues in sequence, without reconsidering the initial decision. In Table 5.1, the legislature might first decide whether the Social Security system is bankrupt and then deliberate about private accounts without revisiting the previous decision. Proceeding in the impure way amounts to an "institutional" resolution of the paradox: the structure of the procedure guarantees that a coherent pattern will be produced. It seems clear enough why such a deliberative procedure would be called impure: the result depends on an arbitrary fixing of the order of decisions.

Impure procedures may be adopted for reasons of practicality. Some decision institutions (e.g., courts) have their decisions set exogenously with limited opportunities to reopen old debates; some may adopt precedent-based decision making in such circumstances. Other groups might choose to parcel out decision tasks to subgroups, which are expected to honor the prior determinations of other subgroups. Such examples are familiar in legislative, judicial, and executive branch decision-making groups.

Impure Deliberation

Decision making is impure if the order in which issues are considered is fixed in advance. We assume the members are sequentially rational, which means that at each point at which a member has to make a decision, that decision must be best for her from that point on. Each is free to alter her judgments in light of the outcome of earlier votes. For a start, let's assume that each legislator is more committed to her views as to what the final outcome should be – whether the reform should be adopted – than she is to her premise judgments[33] and that the decision on the workability of private accounts is to be taken after the issue of bankruptcy is voted on. And so before voting on workability, each member will know if the legislature has decided affirmatively on the bankruptcy issue. Under the premise-based procedure, the overall outcome will depend on whether the legislature decides that private accounts are workable. On this issue, members B and C are pivotal, in that if either one votes no, the final outcome will be negative. We assumed that B is convinced that the reform is unwise; so she has a strong (coherence-driven) reason to reconsider her judgment on workability, which would lead to the reform's defeat.

Thus, if the legislature adopts the sequential premise-based procedure and its members are result-oriented and sequentially rational in the way assumed here, the outcome would be to reject the reform and preserve the current system. And there would be a coherent and public explanation for that result. Note that had the votes occurred in the other order, the result would have been the same in this respect, although the voting pattern – and therefore the public justification for it – would have been different.

---

[33] I used the term "committed" to indicate how sure they are of their judgment.

There is no need to consider the question of coherence independently of the decision itself – the sequential premise-based procedure itself guarantees that the pattern of votes will cohere. But the outcome is the opposite of what Pettit hypothesizes under premise-based voting. This is not surprising in that we assumed that each member is result-oriented (i.e., more confident in her judgment about the outcome than she is in her premise judgments). Had each been more confident in her views about the premises than she was about the final outcome, perhaps none would have been willing to revise her initial premise judgments, so that premise votes would have been positive and the reform would have been adopted.[34]

It may seem that sequential rationality is too strong an assumption because it makes the voting order inordinately important. In any case, the deliberative practices described here may be troubling if they are thought to imply that voters are actually concealing their own best judgments (on the premises) in order to try to get their preferred outcome. But if individuals are convinced as to what the right outcome would be, why should they not be willing to reconsider their premise judgments and votes in order to try to get the best outcome? Moreover, insofar as the premise judgments are (partly) evaluative, why isn't this a case of deciding how to balance conflicting values? Why should they privilege their initial premise judgments over their views as to the best outcome rather than be willing to revise them in the course of deliberation? Still, one might think that the arbitrariness of sequential deliberation forces artificial choices on some people and leaves many alternatives unexamined.

Pure Deliberation

In pure deliberation, all the issues – premise judgments as well as the final result – are decided simultaneously. The legislature might, in effect, take repeated straw votes on each of the issues so that individual legislators could reconsider their judgments over time, in light of the pattern of collective judgments. The pure procedure is less institutionally constrained than impure

---

[34] This argument extends to more general cases. Assume that there are k premises and n voters, that the underlying or prior judgments form a discursive dilemma of the kind in Table 5.1, and that the premises are voted on and the final result is determined by the pattern of collective premise judgments. Thus, at a final node following a sequence of $k - 1$ positive premise votes, each person who prefers a negative result would have a reason to vote no on the kth vote, and since this group is a majority, the final result would be negative and there would be a coherent justification for it.

  If the result itself were to be voted as one of the first k votes, it would fail, as there is no premise-based reason not to vote initial outcome preferences in the first k votes. And on every one of the $k - 1$ premise votes, the judges are free to vote their initial judgments. Only the last premise judgment is to be implicitly fixed in a way that supports previous votes. What if we assume that the members are premise- rather than result-oriented, in the sense of being more confident in their premise judgments than in their views about the outcome? A parallel argument suggests that members should not alter their initial premise judgments, and the result will be that the reform is adopted.

procedures because it treats the issues symmetrically. The principle of pivotality, introduced earlier, permits each legislator to see the consequences of changing his vote in view of how others are voting and thereby helps to focus deliberation. While the impure procedure and sequential rationality will automatically produce a coherent justification for each decision, with pure deliberation members have to take coherence into account explicitly – by seeing it as a reason for action during the deliberations. I assume that each member places great value on producing a coherent pattern of results as well as on getting a good result, so that each sees failure of coherence (a pattern of premise judgments that does not support the final result) as a reason to continue deliberating.[35]

Is there anything objectionable about the idea of members seeing all of their judgments, on premises as well as on results, as being in play during the deliberative process? These judgments are normative judgments as to what the group ought to do – they are not private in the way that preferences are often thought to be. And insofar as their normative judgments conflict, there is reason for each member to be open to reconsidering them in light of arguments raised by others. Moreover, as in the example, judgments may have empirical contents too: legislators may learn new information during deliberation that may cause them to reassess their own empirical views.

We can start by partitioning the set X of outcomes into the following subsets: Let YC be the set of voting patterns that would produce a yes on the result and a coherent set of premise judgments, NC a negative result with coherent preference judgments, YI a yes vote with an incoherent set of premise judgments, and NI a no vote with incoherent judgments. So NI is the set of initial discursive dilemma preferences. We have already remarked that in the case described in Table 5.1, YI is empty, so we need consider only three subsets. We may suppose that the members have initial rankings of the elements in X and that these rankings may be revised or adjusted in deliberation.

We shall say that an outcome $x \, \varepsilon \, X$ is deliberatively unstable if someone may alter her expressed judgments in such a way as to achieve either a preferred outcome or a coherent voting pattern supporting the same outcome. The first thing to notice is that the pattern of initial judgments in Table 5.1 is deliberatively unstable. Member A could alter her judgment on bankruptcy from Y to N and thereby produce a coherent pattern of judgments in support of the negative result. Or she could change her views about private accounts from N to Y (and therefore her judgment on the final result from N to Y) to produce a coherent judgment pattern in support of a positive result.[36]

---

[35] This does not imply any commitment to the notion of a common or general will shared or held by the members. Rather I simply assume not only that each member cares about the result that is achieved, but also that there is a coherent justification for it (revealed in the outcomes of the premise votes). These values are in some conflict, according to the initial pattern of premise judgments, so that each member may need to adjust her premise judgment in order to bring about a majority-acceptable outcome together with a coherent justification for it.

[36] Indeed, this seems to be a general result for a three-person group with any number of premises: every judgment pattern in NI is unstable. The argument would go like this: for any $x \, \varepsilon \, NI$,

It is easy to see that there will always be many deliberatively stable profiles, and so in a sense the legislators must solve a "coordination" problem in order to settle on one rather than another. Each of the stable profiles reflects a different way in which the members may adjust their views on the premises and outcomes. And as the investigation here remains at a formal or nonsubstantive level, there seems no natural way to narrow this set of possible deliberative results. In specific cases there may well be substantive reasons for the legislature to choose one deliberatively stable profile over another. And we have said nothing about the dynamics of the deliberative process that might lead to one particular outcome over others.

The point of thinking through these models of deliberation is to illustrate how members of a legislative body might try to take considerations of coherence into account. I claimed that they would be and ought to be disposed to reconsider their initial judgments in light of the consequences of exercising these judgments. If they do that, depending on other assumptions, legislators will sometimes have reason to modify their "expressed" judgments in the course of deliberation. I don't have the space to investigate the general effects of such deliberations, but it seems likely that its effects would be to diminish the heterogeneity of expressed judgments relative to initial judgments. In the language of social choice theory, deliberation produces a restriction on the domain of preference configurations.

More to the point, deliberation, if it proceeds in the way outlined here, will tend to produce a coherent plan and therefore a legislative intention (via Bratman duality). Because pure deliberation is nonsequential and supports many different outcomes, it is impossible to say in advance which partial plan will emerge from a pure deliberative process. There are generally many deliberatively stable voting profiles, and which one emerges depends on how competing values are weighed.

DISCUSSION

The planning perspective offers a democratic account of legislation in two senses. First, as in traditional theories of representation, legislators receive their rule-making authority in democratic elections and are obliged to represent the people's interests. Second, making rules that bind others gives rise to a

---

there is at least one individual who is voting Y on a premise and N on the outcome and whose vote is pivotal on the premise. If she changes from Y to N on the premise, the resulting pattern is in NC, which is the better result for her. But the case of three voters is special in that for any profile in NI, there is always at least one player who is pivotal. If each of the rows in Table 5.1 were to represent three people, none would be pivotal and the nine-person judgment pattern would be stable. For this reason it makes sense to require each judge to express her judgment on a question, presuming that she is pivotal to deciding it. The presumption of pivotality is, in this setting, a device for focusing responsibility and organizing deliberation. It is an explicitly normative posture since, in the nine-person case, since it requires that members take their votes to be pivotal even if (as in the nine-person example) they are not.

normative obligation to show that those rules further valid social purposes and infringe on people's rights only in ways that are necessary to accomplish those purposes. And this explanatory duty is owed to everyone equally.

These two sets of normative obligations, or at least some interpretations of them, may come into conflict: a narrow understanding of the duty to represent might direct legislators to pursue only those views expressed by their constituents and to be unwilling to compromise in this pursuit. But such an uncompromising posture will require that legislation be produced by aggregation, and this will often lead to incoherent legislation for which there is no coherent public account. This is a reason to reject such a narrow understanding of representation and to say, instead, that the legislator's duty is to balance the interests of his constituents with the public interests of the polity generally.

In this respect, the planning view of legislation sees statutes as rationally directed to furthering common purposes or legislative intentions. These purposes remain, in most cases, matters of continuing conflict and dispute. The planning view regards a statute as a partial and incomplete expression of those intentions – partly because their content is not completely agreed upon – and sees a statute as needing further development and specification as new circumstances arise. It presumes that individual legislators regard statutes as imposing normative pressures on their personal actions and intentions – reasons to take or restrain from action or to adjust their own plans – as well as on the actions and intentions of many outside the legislature. There is pressure in the other direction as well – pressure to refine or redirect the legislative intention. Central to these normative pressures is the notion that those involved in the statute ought to seek to present it as rationally directed to further a shared intention or policy of the statute and as coherent or exhibiting integrity. These normative pressures will normally be manifested in other legislative deliberations – certainly in deciding how much funding ought to be provided and in considering which amendments should be proposed in light of experience – but in administrative and judicial proceedings as well. I think that they will also be articulated in elections when candidates compete for positions in the legislature on the basis of pledges to pursue certain policies or to alter or reject them.

Finally, it is important to remark that as important as coherence is, it is one value to be weighed and considered against others. Sometimes, full coherence or integrity is not worth achieving, because it would entail sacrificing other values of greater importance. This is true for individuals too; the writings on tragic choice or incommensurability are relevant in this connection. No one thinks that such examples undermine the possibility of human integrity or agency; indeed, some might argue that such cases provide particularly good examples of what integrated moral agency actually requires. So I am not sure that failures of complete coherence undercut group agency claims – at least if the failures are of the right kind.

6

Epistemic Democracy in Classical Athens

Sophistication, Diversity, and Innovation

Josiah Ober

I. INTRODUCTION: A SUCCESSFUL EPISTEMIC DEMOCRACY

A democracy may be said to be "epistemic" to the degree to which it employs collective wisdom to make good policy.[1] Lu Hong and Scott Page (Chapter 3, this volume) offer a formal model of collective wisdom, in the sense of accurately predicting or characterizing an outcome, which is produced by two factors: the individual sophistication of participants and the diversity of their perspectives. The city-state of Athens, from the late sixth through the late fourth century B.C. is a case study of a participatory epistemic democracy: an intensively studied historical example of a community whose remarkable success can, at least in part, be explained by Hong and Page's two factors of sophistication and diversity.

Democratic Athens depended directly and self-consciously on actively deploying the epistemic resources of its citizenry to hold its place in a highly competitive multistate environment. While the Athenian case cannot, in and of itself, prove the general validity of Hong and Page's model, it may offer some insight into how, in the real world, increased sophistication and sustained diversity of participants produce positive results over time. To be successful, real-world epistemic democracies (like other governments) must indeed accurately predict and characterize outcomes. But they must also (inter alia) create institutions for setting agendas and implementing policy. The Athenian case suggests that, along with outcome prediction and characterization, an

---

[1] On epistemic features of democracy, see E. Anderson (2006), Ober (2008: ch. 1), and Estlund (2008: 232), who states that "it is very natural and plausible to think that if democracy has any epistemic value it is partly to do with the sharing of diverse perspectives." Page (2007) emphasizes both the epistemic potential and the problems associated with socially diverse groups of decision makers. Of course, even successful democracies experience epistemic failures; an epistemic democracy ought to be able to learn from its failures and to design institutions that make similar failures less likely in the future. Sections II–V of this chapter are adapted from Ober (2008), especially chapter 4.

enhanced capacity for institutional innovation in the face of environmental change is a central feature of epistemic democracies. The capacity for institutional innovation is promoted by growing sophistication and sustained diversity of participants, while sophistication and diversity are, in turn, promoted by well-designed institutions.

In Athens, collective wisdom produced useful knowledge – a matrix of experience, expertise, and information that in turn reliably (if not invariably) yielded good (if imperfect) solutions to complex problems. Knowledge that is useful to collectivities like Athens is possessed by individuals, but it is also located in social networks and reproduced by institutionalized processes.[2] Athens outperformed its city-state rivals at least in part because of its citizens' superior capacity to produce new solutions to the ever-changing menu of challenges confronted by the Greek city-states. Athens beat its rivals by more effectively aggregating, aligning, and codifying the vast store of social and technical knowledge distributed across its large, diverse, and increasingly sophisticated population.[3]

A variety of statistical measures of comparative city-state performance across the classical era (ca. 500–325 B.C.) indicate that Athens was preeminent among the thousand or more Greek city-states. Moreover, Athenian state capacity (measured as a composite of military activity, public building, and domestic programs) was strongly and positively correlated with the development of Athenian democracy (measured as a composite of the percentage of adult males holding full participation rights, the power of the *demos* to effect policy, and the authority of law). Athenian state capacity was considerably lower both before and after the democratic era.[4]

With the exception of two brief oligarchic interludes, arising at least in part from the democracy's epistemic failures (411/10 and 404 B.C.), classical Athens

---

2 The terms "data," "information," and "knowledge" are variously defined by organizational theorists. Davenport and Prusak (1998: 1–6) suggest that data are facts about events, information is data that have been given relevance and purpose, and knowledge is a matrix of experience, values, insight, and contextual information that allows for the incorporation of new experiences and information. See also Dixon (2000: 13) and Brown and Duguid (2000: 119–202). On expertise as an unusually high level of mastery of a particular domain of endeavor, see Ericsson (1999).

3 For a detailed description of Athenian democracy, its history and institutions, see Hansen (1999). Athens is a good case study because its documented history includes pre- and post-democratic eras, as well as a long (185-year) period of democratic self-government. Athenian history can readily be subdivided into multiple phases, allowing us to assess democracy's origins, recovery, persistence, and demise. The evidence base is rich: a substantial number of government documents (in the form of inscriptions) enable us to trace institutional changes. A large corpus of public speeches allows analysis of democratic ideology. Athenian democratic government was subjected to probing critical-theoretical scrutiny by prominent contemporary intellectuals (e.g., Thucydides, Plato, and Aristotle).

4 On comparative Athenian performance, see Ober (2008: ch. 2); the statistical measures of Athenian success confirm the *communis opinio* of specialists in ancient Greek history. Athens stood out in a high-performing environment: Compared with other premodern societies, the Greek city-states were densely populated, highly urbanized, and characterized by high rates of economic growth (Ober 2010).

was governed directly "by the people" – participation was widespread across a relatively large citizen body (about thirty thousand adult native males). Levels of active participation became more egalitarian over time: higher percentages of poorer and nonurban citizens took part in state governance in the fourth century B.C. than in the fifth. Participation promoted social learning (mastery of institutions and political culture) across a citizenship that was socially diverse in terms of wealth, geography, and occupation (if not in religion, language, ethnicity, or gender). Yet Athens avoided the ossification and institutional stagnation that can accompany deep social learning. The democracy learned from its epistemic failures; new institutions were designed and implemented in the aftermath of the late-fifth-century crises. Athens's rate of institutional innovation remained high throughout the democratic era, as attested by ancient opinion and the historical record.[5]

The conjunction of a highly participatory democracy with outstanding competitive success is surprising, in light of claims by social and organizational theorists (e.g., R. Michels 1962 [1911]; O. Williamson 1975, 1985) that no truly participatory democratic organization can survive in a competitive environment. Athenian success cannot be explained by denying the reality of democracy through positing the existence of a cryptic ruling elite. Individual orators and generals certainly played important leadership roles – Pericles provides a paradigm case, although he was hardly unique. Leaders were drawn from elites of education and wealth, but elite individuals gained and kept precarious leadership positions on the basis of their proven ability to secure public goods; there was no entrenched "elite ruling class." Athens's distributed authority structure and lack of formal patronage structures denied organized groups of elites the usual mechanisms of political domination. It was the reality of the demos's control of public affairs that drew the critical attention of Greek political theorists. Democratic ideology, promoted by public discourse, and the emergence of a vibrant culture of political dissent (subjects of my earlier work on Athens) were essential to the system's functioning, but these factors, in and of themselves, are inadequate to explain why or how Athens did so well in such an intensely competitive environment.[6]

Aristotle points to an epistemic explanation for "unexpected" democratic success in an important passage in the *Politics*, in which he discusses conditions under which the "wisdom of the many" may outdo individual expertise. His point is that a "multitude [*plêthos*] is like a single person, yet many-footed and many-handed and possessing many sense-capacities [*aisthêseis*]." With its diverse perspectives, such a multitude may, under the right conditions,

[5] On greater egalitarian participation in the fourth than the fifth century, see Taylor (2007, 2008); on the danger of ossification, Levitt and March (1988); on Athenian diversity, Ober (2005: ch. 4).

[6] On the Athenian political elite, see Hansen (1983, 1984); on the lack of a ruling elite, Ober (1989). On the lack of formal patronage, see Millett (1989); on democratic ideology, Ober (1989); on dissent, (Ober 1998).

judge better than any individual: "for some judge a particular aspect [*of the matter*], while all of them judge the whole."[7] But if we are to understand the basis of Athens's success, we need to go beyond Aristotle's compressed account of collective wisdom, to focus on how institutional design promoted the aggregation of the useful knowledge possessed by many diverse individuals, the alignment of people's efforts based on their common knowledge, and the codification of rules that expanded access to institutions and increased the reliability and procedural fairness of legal judgments.[8]

This chapter focuses on the aggregation of knowledge, which is distinct from the aggregation of preferences, interests, opinions, or data. Knowledge aggregation, in the sense in which I am using it here, means bringing together, in a single "solution space," a diverse array of useful information and expertise. Suppose, for example, that a state confronts an enemy attack by sea. Organizing an appropriate defense requires mobilizing expertise and accurate information in the domains of (inter alia) military strategy, shipbuilding, public finance, and manpower availability. The totality of the relevant knowledge necessary to address a complex problem (e.g., naval defense policy) is unlikely to be possessed by any one individual. Of course, only certain kinds of social and technical knowledge will be useful for solving a given problem. Much of the knowledge possessed by residents of the state is strictly irrelevant to naval defense; Plato's Socrates (*Protagoras* 319b–c) claims that when the subject before the citizen Assembly was shipbuilding, the "wise Athenians" refused to listen to anyone lacking expertise in naval architecture.

No two problems faced by a state will be exactly alike (next year, the big problem may be a flood), and so there is a constant demand for innovative solutions: last year's armada is not the answer if this year we need to rebuild levies. Yet each problem is likely to present certain features that are relevantly similar to the features of other problems (some of the manpower and finance issues will cross over from naval defense to flood relief), and so there is a constant demand for social learning and the cross-appropriation of expertise among domains (Spinosa, Flores, and Dreyfus 1997).

If the premises laid out in the previous paragraphs are correct, then the following will hold. (1) A better solution will emerge if (a) the specialized knowledge possessed by multiple sophisticated individuals is brought into the solution space, (b) irrelevant information and expertise are excluded from that space, and (c) each relevant knowledge input is given its appropriate weight in the final policy. (2) No fixed and limited set of experts will possess the range of knowledge necessary for addressing the multiplicity of problems that will

---

[7] 3.11 = 1281a40–b10, trans. C. Lord, adapted. Waldron (1995) underlines the importance of this passage and emphasizes its deliberative character. See Ober (1998: 319–24, 2008: 110–14) for discussion and bibliography. Estlund (2008: ch. 12) contrasts Condorcet's theorem (and variations thereof) to Aristotle's diverse-perspectives approach.

[8] Ober (2008) devotes individual chapters to the epistemic processes of knowledge aggregation (4), alignment (5), and codification (6), arguing that it is the integration of these three processes, over time, that produced the superior Athenian performance.

confront a state (or other organizations) over time. (3) Adapting the aggregated knowledge relevant in one solution space to different but relevantly similar problems in another space will speed the process of innovating new solutions. Yet in order for these results to be achieved, certain conditions must pertain (Section II).

This chapter argues that the constitutional reform that inaugurated democracy in Athens (in or shortly after 508/ 507 B.C.) incorporated (consciously or not) design features that promoted individual sophistication and the aggregation of diverse perspectives (Section III). It focuses on an institution that was a key part of the new regime: the Council of 500 (Sections IV and V). The deliberative Council of 500 played a prominent role in agenda setting, day-to-day administration, policy implementation, and certain legal matters. The Council employed techniques of lottery, rotation, and representative sampling to bring together groups of geographically and socially diverse decision makers – persons with very different life experiences and knowledge sets. The experience of service on the Council tended to increase the political sophistication of individual citizens: they became more expert in the conduct of public affairs. The institutional rules by which the Council was selected and governed gave each individual councilor good reasons (in the form of strong social incentives) to share his knowledge with his fellows, and to attend in turn to what they knew, when deliberating in advance of making highly consequential public decisions.

II. CONDITIONS FOR KNOWLEDGE AGGREGATION

Knowledge aggregation is grounded in joint action (Bratman 1999) and complicated by political scale and social diversity. The information relevant to a given outcome, along with the social and technical knowledge necessary for processing it, is lodged in the minds of a great many individuals from many walks of life (Hayek 1945). Collecting knowledge in a large (beyond face-to-face) participatory democracy demands communication among people who are, at least in the first instance, strangers to one another. Communication among strangers requires overcoming a basic collective action problem (Olson 1965): Why should a rational individual freely communicate potentially valuable information to someone who might prove to be a free-rider? If the problem of knowledge aggregation is to be solved, individuals possessing potentially useful information must have some reason for sharing it. Moreover, they must have access to appropriate communications technology – a low-cost means of bringing forward what they know and making it available to the community. The community, for its part, must employ a sorting method, a means of discriminating between bits of information that are more and less useful in any given decision-making context.

Because knowledge has exchange value it can profitably be hoarded under conditions of scarcity. Unique information and technical expertise may, for example, take the form of proprietary trade secrets that are valuable only so long as those in the know are few (e.g., the secret formula for Coca Cola).

Ancient examples of proprietary knowledge might include sources of raw materials, trading partners, weather patterns, craft techniques, even military formations and tactics (in the fourth century B.C., there was a ready "international market" for Greek mercenary soldiers and generals). In other cases (for example open source computer software – or, in antiquity, improved rowing techniques for propelling many-oared warships), information gains in value when it is widely known and used. In either case, if a productive epistemic equilibrium is to be achieved, incentives for communicating useful information must somehow correspond to the value of what is shared.[9]

Incentives need not be material. An implied contract between the knowing agent and those who desire access to her knowledge may be built into the common culture. Information sharing may be promoted by established relationships of reciprocity in an "economy of esteem" (Brennan and Pettit 2004). In a competitive culture, like that of ancient Greece, in which the publicly expressed esteem of others was an important part of individual utility, some incentives for knowledge communication could be cast in the form of public honors for winning victories in state-sponsored "knowledge-aggregation contests" – that is, competitions that could be won only by those willing to share what they knew and capable of persuading others to do likewise. The general point is that public incentives for knowledge sharing must be valuable because knowledge is recognized as having value to individuals and groups, as well as to the community as a whole. The first principle of institutional design for an organization attempting to solve epistemic collective action problems should be providing incentives to knowledgeable individuals such that they will choose to share what they know.[10]

Next, the communication technology – the means available to agents for communicating useful knowledge – should be as nearly costless (i.e., easy to use and ready to hand) as possible because the greater the costs associated with the act of communicating, the higher the incentives must be for doing so. Reducing the cost of public communications means lowering the cost to individuals of communicating what they know by compensating them for the burdens they incur in moving information to the point in an organization at which it will do some good.

Finally, there must be an epistemic sorting device, a means for distinguishing not only truth from falsity, but what sorts of expertise and what information

---

[9] On trade secrets, see Davenport and Prusak (1998: 16–17); on incentives as essential for effective knowledge sharing, Sunstein (2006: 69–70, 201, 203–5); on open-source software and related forms of nonmarket productivity, Benkler (2006).

[10] On the vocabulary of "honor-loving" and Athenian public practices associated with it, see Whitehead (1983, 1993); on nonmaterial incentives for knowledge sharing, Davenport and Prusak (1998: 22–51) (internal "knowledge markets") and Osterloh and Frey (2000). Walker 2004 discusses modern "word of mouth" marketing techniques, suggesting that for at least some people the experience of sharing some kinds of information (in this case about new products) with others is valued in itself and that material incentives are relatively less important. Also see Dixon (2000: 6–7).

may (in any given context) actually prove useful. If those involved in decision making are incapable of weeding out false or irrelevant information and disregarding inappropriate expert knowledge, they will be unable to produce good policy. The sorting mechanisms must be context-sensitive: some technical knowledge that is of great value to a national assembly deliberating on matters of foreign policy will be useless to a village assembly discussing lease arrangements for communally owned land. In the participatory Athenian context, social knowledge served as a sorting device. Experienced citizens learned habits of discrimination, of recognizing who to attend to and whose opinion to trust in what context. Sections IV and V seek to specify how.

The conjoined imperatives of incentives, low communication costs, and sorting mean that designing an aggregation process is inherently difficult. The difficulty increases with the complexity of what must be decided, the volume and diversity of the information necessary for decision making, and the multiplication of kinds of expert knowledge that must be brought to bear. Knowledge collection becomes more complicated as organizations grow larger and more diverse. Yet the costs to an organization of *failing* to collect and attend to the right kind of information before making major policy choices can be extraordinarily high, as the Athenians were reminded, for example, in the course of the catastrophic Sicilian expedition (415–413 B.C.) – a series of events that, if we are to trust the account of Thucydides (book 6; with Ober 1998, 104–20), resulted in large part from an epistemic failure and certainly contributed substantially to the crisis of the late fifth century.

One solution to the problem of collecting knowledge is routinization: capturing the organization's past experience by archiving data, establishing standard protocols, and socializing members into "the ways we do things around here." Routinization can build expertise and thereby make work processes more efficient, and thus more productive. Yet oversocialization in established routines becomes counterproductive when circumstances change. Making effective use of archived data is difficult, and an overemphasis on routines can lead to process ossification and a decline of productive capacity. In order for an organization to remain competitive in the long run and under new conditions, it must be able to innovate: it must break with established routines and draw on information sources outside the standard banks of data. Innovation depends on tapping latent knowledge held by people who have not been fully socialized into routine patterns of behavior. This in turn means that organizations in competitive and fast-changing environments will pay a heavy price if they fail to maintain a diversity of experience, expertise, and social knowledge among their members.[11]

Athenian democratic institutions and practices, when viewed in their social context, can be understood as a kind of machine (see Elster, Chapter 7, this

---

[11] On the difficulty of making effective use of archived data, see Brown and Duguid (1991, 2000); on routinization versus innovation in organization theory, Levitt and March (1988).

volume) whose design facilitated the aggregation of useful knowledge and produced benefits of routinization while maintaining a capacity for innovation. The machine of Athenian government was fueled by incentives, oiled by low communication costs and efficient means of information transfer, and regulated by formal and informal sanctions. The machine served to build, over time, special kinds of social knowledge among a large segment of the Athenian population: an increased capacity to discriminate among sources of expertise and information, and to cross-appropriate relevant knowledge from one domain of application (e.g., a deliberative council) to another (e.g., a court of law). Those heightened capacities can be understood to be a sort of political sophistication or expertise, an expertise in the operations of self-government.

This essay argues that the Athenian machine performed better over time for the reasons specified in Hong and Page's formal model: more citizens became more sophisticated while preserving diversity of perspectives; growth in sophistication did not entail homogenization of perspectives. As a result, learning and innovation were simultaneously supported, and Athens thrived, over time, in its competitive environment. In order to understand how the machine came into existence, we need to attend to the origins of Athenian democracy in the late sixth century B.C.: the constitutional reforms associated with Cleisthenes that were enacted, by the Athenian demos, in the aftermath of the Athenian Revolution.

III. CLEISTHENES' REFORMS: DEMES AND TRIBES AS SOCIAL NETWORKS

Consider a typical village (*deme*) of Athens near the end the sixth century B.C., just before the Athenian Revolution of 508 B.C. and the institution of the democratic political order.[12] Prasiai was a settlement on the east-central coast of Attica. Farming, supplemented by some fishing and local trade, formed the economic base. The total free population of Prasieis was probably in the range of 700 persons. Of these, perhaps 180 to 200 were adult native males – citizens of Athens who had enjoyed limited privileges in regard to participation and certain legal immunities since the reforms of Solon in 594 B.C.[13]

After the democratic revolution of 508, the adult male Athenian residents of Prasiai, as in the other villages and urban neighborhoods of Athens, were full citizens with extensive rights of participation in the central institutions of *polis* government. They had the opportunity to meet periodically in a local village assembly in order to vote on admitting new citizens and to decide on various matters of local concern. By the late sixth century, many of the families

---

[12] On the revolution and the constitutional reforms, see note 17, this chapter. Osborne (1990) answers the question What is a deme and why does it matter? This is discussed further later in the chapter.

[13] On Prasiai see Vanderpool, McCredie, and Steinberg (1962), Whitehead (1986: index s.v.), and Camp (2001: 281).

of the village had lived there for generations. A century and a half later, by the middle of the fourth century, a number of Prasieis had moved away, to the city or elsewhere in Athenian territory. Yet by Athenian constitutional law, they maintained membership in their ancestral deme and many of them still attended deme meetings.[14]

As a result of their long history of steady interaction – social, economic, and religious, if not yet extensively political – the men of late-sixth-century Prasiai knew a lot about each other. By comparative reference to other small and relatively egalitarian premodern rural communities, we can assume that many of the ties between adult male citizens of Prasiai were "strong," in the sense that the term is used by modern theorists of social networks. That is to say, the local social network by which the Prasieis were connected to one another was based on regular face-to-face interaction and featured a good deal of overlap and redundancy. In a strong-tie network, an individual's friends are also one another's friends.

As a result of this strong-tie-linked network of social relationships, the level of mutual social knowledge in Prasiai was high. People for the most part knew, for example, who was technically skilled in various domains, who could be counted on and in what circumstances, whose advice was valuable on what topics. Social norms of reciprocity and propriety were clear and dictated who shared what sort of information with which others and under what circumstances. Since network ties were strong both in the ordinary sense of the word (i.e., dependable) and in the network-theory sense that a person's friends were friends with one another, social norms were correspondingly strong. Commitments made in this context were credible because people knew a lot about each other's business and, when necessary, free-riders were sanctioned. The environment was "safe" in that cooperation was socially mandatory and defection was difficult. The key thing, from the point of view of organizational performance, is that small-scale networks based primarily on strong ties are very good at distributing information internally, but they are poor conduits for importing or disseminating useful knowledge *outside the local network itself*. As a result of their inherently small scale and lack of diversity, closed strong-tie networks tend to be relatively unproductive. The problem is a lack of weak "bridging ties." A weak tie is defined as a friendship (which may be close: weak ties need not be superficial relationships) between two individuals whose friends are not one another's friends.

In a classic article, the sociologist Mark Granovetter (1973) demonstrated that small-scale networks based on strong ties between individuals promote intensive interaction but do not allow for extensive bridging from one network to another. In the limit case, in which each of my friends is also each other's friend, there may be no space for bridging at all – every new tie I form must necessarily be a tie shared by all of my existing friends. There is, consequently,

---

[14] On deme life and the diachronic history of residence patterns in rural Attica, see Osborne 1985, 1987), Whitehead (1986), and Jones 1999.

no feasible way for me to bridge to another strong-tie network of persons. Strong-tie networks tend to operate as small and closed cliques. Lacking bridges to other networks, these cliques are resistant to the free flow of information outside the local network. Cliques render large-scale cooperation more difficult and impede coordination across an extended social network. As a result, it is harder to aggregate knowledge or to align action at larger scales. The gains potentially reaped from extensive cooperation remain limited – and the problem of scale looms as unsolvable.[15]

If we imagine late-sixth-century Prasiai as characterized primarily by strong ties (either as a single strong-tie network or as a collection of such networks), the residents of Prasiai would have had relatively few bridging ties outside their local community; relatively few men from Prasai (and fewer women) would have had reason to make connections with men from other towns or neighborhoods in Attica. Of course, the hypothetical limit case in which *everyone's* friends were one another's friends is unlikely ever to have existed in practice. But to the extent that strong-tie networks were a general social norm in the many villages scattered across Athenian territory, overall Athenian capacity for effective joint action was likewise limited. Relatively low Athenian state capacity in the areas of military, building, and domestic policy in the pre-democratic period is consistent with the hypothesis that sixth-century Prasiai (and other Athenian villages and neighborhoods) were characterized, in the first instance, by strong-tie networks.[16]

It seems very likely that, with a degree of local variation, this hypothetical "Prasiai situation" was replicated many times over in the pre-democratic era and throughout much of the territory of Athens. It certainly cannot be true that all sixth-century Athenians were living out their lives entirely within local strong-tie networks; we know, for example, that some Athenians were involved in regional and overseas trade, so we can assume the existence of some weak ties. But it seems safe to say that something like the Prasiai model sketched here was the seventh- and sixth-century Athenian norm – just as it was the norm throughout most of Greece. That social norm was the central problem faced by Cleisthenes in the months after the Athenian Revolution of 508 B.C.

At the moment of the revolution, the people of Athens demonstrated a capacity for at least short-term collective action in the face of extreme national danger: confronted by the double specter of foreign domination and a return

---

[15] Granovetter (1973). See, further, Granovetter (1983, 1985), Krackhardt (1992), Gargiulo and Benassi (2000), and Diani and McAdam (2003). Padgett and Ansell (1993) and Gould (1995) are notable examples of how social network theory can be used to explain an actual historical situation. Morten T. Hansen (2002) explores knowledge networks in multiunit firms, an organizational situation with striking analogies to Athens and its constituent demes. Chang and Harrington (2005) emphasize the need for persistent diversity within networks and quality of ties for effective network performance based on both innovation and learning.

[16] Purcell (1990) rightly warns against overstating the insularity of archaic Greek villages. The point is that, in comparison with later Athenian history, Prasiai of the late sixth century is likely to be relatively lacking in bridging ties.

to the pre-tyrannical oligarchic rule of a handful of "big men," many of the ordinary people of Athens gathered in the city and forced the surrender of a Spartan-led army after a three-day siege of the Acropolis. They recalled Cleisthenes, who had been exiled by the would-be oligarchic rulers of the city after having "taken the people as his comrades" and proposing popular institutional changes. Back in Athens and with expectations running high, Cleisthenes took on the task of rapidly creating a new government. Whatever else it accomplished, Cleisthenes' new order had to be able to put a large and highly motivated military force into the field – and to do so very quickly. This was no mean feat, given that in all probability Athens had never had an organized "national army." Earlier Athenian military actions had depended on ad hoc cooperation among the relevant local big men, but after the revolution, their authority was thrown into doubt.[17]

Cleisthenes' comrade-constituents, the demos that had recalled him from exile, expected a system of government suited to their newly expressed identity as participating members of a political community. Oligarchy and tyranny, the familiar modes of archaic Greek political organization, had been discredited by the events leading up to the uprising. Although other Greek *poleis* experienced political upheavals in the sixth century and there was much experimentation with institutional forms (Robinson 1997), there was no "off the shelf" organizational model for Cleisthenes to follow. The "Prasiai situation," the cliquish strong-tie local networks that characterized ordinary Athenian social life, rendered it difficult to achieve the large-scale joint action necessary to defeat the expected Spartan attack – and then to sustain a flourishing community so that Athens's great potential (relative to its rivals) in terms of human and natural resources would be realized in fact.

If "Prasiai" was the problem, the revolutionary uprising itself pointed to the solution. Cleisthenes had been recalled to Athens after the demos had demonstrated its potential for large-scale joint action in the three-day siege of the Acropolis. Athenians clearly now thought of themselves as sharing an Athenian identity, which could potentially come to mean belonging to an extended network that included the entire polis. The design opportunity for Cleisthenes was building on a capacity revealed in a moment of crisis and based on a shared Athenian identity. The challenge was creating institutional conditions for a productive equilibrium that would enable the Athenians to reap the individual and collective benefits of social cooperation. Although Cleisthenes lacked the theoretical apparatus of modern social science, the solution he devised makes sense when it is described in terms of social network theory. Cleisthenes created institutions that employed the principles of incentives for knowledge sharing, lowering communication costs, and context-sensitive information sorting. A key to the new system (although probably an unintended consequence of

---

[17] On the Athenian Revolution, see Ober (1996: ch. 5), Forsdyke (2005), Pritchard (2005), and Raaflaub, Ober, and Wallace (2007). On the lack of an Athenian regular army before 508, Frost (1984) and Siewert (1982).

institutional design) was the emergence of many bridging weak ties between members of local strong-tie networks.

Granovetter (1973) showed that, in contrast to strong ties, weak ties (i.e., the case in which my friends are unlikely to be friends with one another) *do* promote bridging across extended networks. Weak ties break down the claustrophobic environment of cliques by efficiently transferring information across an extended network. Weak ties are therefore an essential complement to strong-tie networks for social mobilization and for overall organizational cohesion. Granovetter's key conclusion (1973: 1376) was that "the more local bridges... in a community and the greater their degree, the more cohesive the community and the more capable of acting in concert." In the terminology used by ancient commentators on his reforms, Cleisthenes "sought to intermix" (Aristotle, *Ath. Pol.* 21.2–3) the residents of Athenian territory.[18]

Cleisthenes accomplished this intermixing by inaugurating ten new and blatantly artificial "tribes." These new tribes would play important roles in the new political system. They would also become key markers of Athenian identity. Each of the ten new tribes was named after an Athenian mythical hero; according to Athenian memory, the ten heroes were chosen by Apollo's priestess at Delphi from a much more extensive list. Notably, the new tribes would not be territorially contiguous; each tribe drew about a third of its membership from communities located in coastal, inland, and urbanized regions of Athenian territory.[19]

As a result of Cleisthenes' tribal reform, Prasiai now became one of the eleven demes – that is, towns, villages, or urban neighborhoods – constituting the newly created tribe of Pandionis. Prasiai was designated a *coastal deme* – as were three other nearby villages, each located near the eastern coast of Attica. These four coastal demes of the tribe Pandionis made up the coastal "third" (*trittys*) of the tribe. They were administratively joined to four inland demes to the west (the inland trittys) and to three city demes: neighborhoods in or near the main city of Athens (the city trittys). The citizens of the eleven demes, grouped in these "thirds," were now officially the tribe Pandionis. The same organizational principles were used in constituting the other nine tribes. The new system is represented schematically in Figure 6.1.

Cleisthenes' organizational design was at once radical and practical. It was predicated on conjoining long-standing, familiar "natural" units – the existing villages and neighborhoods of Athens – with new, unfamiliar, and highly artificial units – the ten new tribes. The tribes and their constituent "thirds" were the institutional bridges by which a stable local identity ("resident of Prasiai") was linked to a desired national identity ("participatory citizen of Athens").

---

[18] The value of social networks in building "communities of practice," and thus to organizational performance, is well attested in business literature; see Wenger (1998), Davenport and Prusak (1998: 37–39, 65–67), Brown and Duguid (2000: 142–43, 157–59), and Benkler (2006).

[19] G. Anderson (2003) offers a detailed review of Cleisthenes' program, with bibliography.

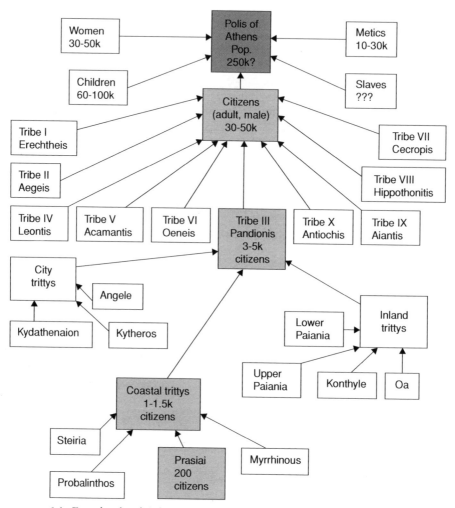

FIGURE 6.1. Four levels of Athenian civic subdivisions: status groups, tribes, trittyes, demes.

Tribes would now be the basis for mustering a newly created national army. The core of the army comprised heavily armed infantrymen (hoplites). Roughly speaking, these were the wealthiest one-third of the Athenian population. In the aftermath of Cleisthenes' reforms, some sixty or seventy men of Prasiai might be expected periodically to march into battle as hoplites along with hoplite-villagers from nearby towns in the coastal district. This would not be anything new; we can assume that the big men of the central Athenian coast had been mustering their heavily armed supporters against pirates and other local threats for generations. But now the men of Prasiai would also muster alongside members of tribe Pandionis, who hailed from far away inland and city demes (Siewart 1982; Christ 2001).

Likewise, much of Athenian ritual life was now restructured on a tribal basis – the Prasieis would sacrifice and eat ritual meals, march in parades, and dance in ritual contests with their fellow tribesmen, the Pandioneis. As a result, people with very different life histories and different sets of social and technical knowledge frequently found themselves in close social proximity to people they never would have otherwise known. The system very literally intermixed Athenians from different geographic/economic zones in a variety of psychologically powerful activities. Over time, the experience of marching, fighting, sacrificing, eating, and dancing together in this newly intermixed grouping would, according to Cleisthenes' plan, lead to a strengthened collective identity at the level of the polis. As we shall see, the system also promoted extensive bridge building across the existing strong-tie networks, and these bridges were essential to the process of knowledge aggregation.[20]

IV. THE COUNCIL OF 500: STRUCTURAL HOLES AND BRIDGING TIES

Among key political institutions introduced or restructured in conjunction with the new deme/tribe system was a new Council of 500, a linchpin institution that was given control of the vital agenda-setting function, deciding what matters should be discussed in the full Assembly of Athenian citizens. The Assembly, which all Athenian citizens in good standing were entitled to attend whenever they pleased, was a potentially chaotic legislative body. In the democratic era, thousands of citizens attended its frequent meetings (forty per year in the fourth century). The Assembly was the embodied citizenry – the demos – and as such decided all important matters of state policy, including finance and matters of diplomacy, war, and peace. The Council met regularly in Athens, eventually in a purpose-built architectural complex. In addition to its vital function of setting the Assembly's agenda, the Council had responsibility for the day-to-day administration of state affairs, including meeting foreign delegations and reviewing the performance of outgoing Athenian magistrates. The Council also played an important executive role in ensuring that policy dictated by the Assembly was properly carried out.[21]

According to Cleisthenes' plan, the new Council of 500 was to be made up of ten delegations of fifty men each – one delegation from each of the ten newly

---

[20] On the intertwining of ritual, financial, and civic life in the Athenian tribe, see Osborne (1994); on sacrificing and eating, Schmitt-Pantel (1992); on marching, Maurizio (1998); on dancing, Wilson (2000: esp. 56–57, 75–76), *contra* Pritchard (2004). Tribal networks were also helpful, especially for nonelite Athenians, in legal disputes (Rubinstein 2000).

[21] Rhodes (1985) gives an indispensable description of the Council of 500, its origins, and its role in Athenian government; see esp. chapter 3 for an analysis of the Council's main areas of responsibility: finance, army and navy, public works, and religion.

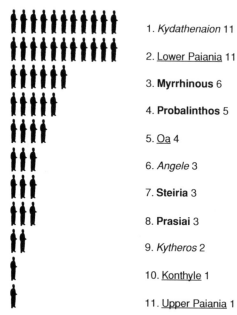

1. *Kydathenaion* 11

2. Lower Paiania 11

3. **Myrrhinous** 6

4. **Probalinthos** 5

5. Oa 4

6. *Angele* 3

7. **Steiria** 3

8. **Prasiai** 3

9. *Kytheros* 2

10. Konthyle 1

11. Upper Paiania 1

FIGURE 6.2. Tribe Pandionis's delegation of councilors for one year (quotas by deme). City demes, italic type; inland, underlined; coastal, bold.

created tribes.[22] The members of each tribal delegation were in turn selected at deme level. Each year every deme sent forward a certain number of councilors, based on the deme's citizen population.[23] Prasiai annually sent three councilors as part of Pandionis's fifty-man delegation. Meanwhile, the large inland deme of Lower Paiania and the city deme of Kydathenaion each sent eleven men, while tiny Upper Paiania and Konthyle each sent only one. Tribe Pandionis's annual delegation to the Council of 500 is represented schematically in Figure 6.2.

What choices, made by an individual member of the Council, might either promote or hinder the Council's overall capacity for joint action? Lacking any detailed first-person narrative from antiquity, a thought experiment must suffice. So imagine a councilor (*bouleutês*) from Prasiai, let us call him Posei-dippos (at least one man of that name did later live in Prasiai), embarking on a

[22] Rhodes (1985: 17–18), favors a later date (ca. 462 B.C.) for the introduction of the tribal delegations serving in rotation as "presidents" of the Council, but he notes that the scholarly *communis opinio* is that the tribal teams were a Cleisthenic innovation.

[23] Quotas are based on fourth-century evidence. Here I assume that the system was put into place in the immediate postrevolutionary period (see next note) and (with Traill 1975: 101–103) remained essentially unchanged through 322 B.C. The main lines of the argument I develop here would not be much affected by the kinds of changes that have been proposed to date, e.g., by Hansen et al. (1990).

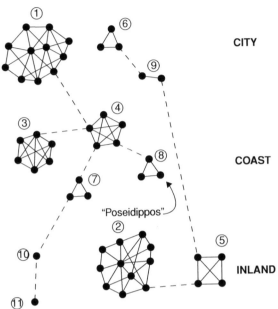

FIGURE 6.3. Pandionis's tribal team as a social network: starting position. Solid lines within deme networks (numbered 1–11) are hypothetical strong ties. Dashed lines between deme networks are hypothetical weak ties. Prasiai is deme 8.

year's service on the Council in the first year after the Council was founded.[24] Poseidippos was probably selected by lot for service; this was, in any event, the later selection procedure. He took up temporary quarters in the city, rightly expecting to spend a great deal of time serving on the Council; in later years, at least, the Council met some three hundred days each year (Rhodes 1985: 30). Let us stipulate, on the basis of our description of late-sixth-century Prasiai, that among the forty-nine other members of the tribal team, Poseidippos had strong ties with his two fellow Prasieis but no bridging ties to any of his other fellow councilors. The point is that when the year's new group of councilors first took up their office, many of the deme delegations that made up each tribal delegation of fifty were already likely to be strong-tie-networked, but there were relatively few bridging "weak ties" between the strongly tied local deme networks. This is a microcosm, at the level of fifty men, of the large-scale problem Cleisthenes faced as he embarked on his reform plan. The hypothetical "starting point" situation of the fifty members of the Pandionis team as they entered into their year of service on the Council in 507 B.C. is represented in Figure 6.3.

---

[24] I am assuming here that the Council, along with the deme/tribe system, came into existence in the immediate aftermath of the Athenian Revolution of 508; an alternative view holds that the system was not fully functional until 501/500 (Rhodes 1985: 1, 191–93; Badian 2000).

As he takes up his office, Poseidippos is (ex hypothesi) connected by strong-tie bonds with his two fellow Prasieis. He has no preexisting connections to his other fellow councilors from tribe Pandionis. Yet he knows that he must work closely with forty-seven men with whom he has no current ties, weak or strong, and then with the other 450 councilors from the nine other tribes. According to Cleisthenes' plan, the fifty-man tribal teams were responsible for much of the work of the Council – each tribe would take a leading role in directing the Council's business for a tenth of the year in rotation with the other nine teams. During the period when a tribe-team was exercising its presidency, a third of its delegate-members were on twenty-four-hour duty. In later generations, in the fifth and fourth centuries, they would eat together (using vessels carefully labeled "public property") and sleep in a public building located in the Agora, Athens's public square.[25]

If Poseidippos had known the terminology of contemporary network theory, he would have described the Pandionis team as a network riddled with "structural holes." That is to say, there were many substantial gaps, bridged by few or no weak ties, between the eleven deme networks, each of which featured a dense matrix of strong ties. The holes are evident in Figure 6.3; there are no existing weak-tie bridges, for example, between demes 1 and demes 6 and 9 or between deme 8 and demes 7, 2, and 5. In one sense, these holes are an institutional design problem, in that, as we have seen, they represent the absence of the sort of dense networking via weak ties that Granovetter identified as a prerequisite for effective joint action. And so the holes represent a problem that Cleisthenes needed to solve by his new organizational design. Yet these same structural holes also represent opportunities – both for the individual willing to take the effort to bridge them and for the organization as a whole. The presence of so many structural holes offered a key incentive to an ambitious and entrepreneurial councilor.

As Ron Burt demonstrated in a series of influential studies (esp. Burt 1992, 1997), in a networked structure, the holes between densely linked sub-networks are points of entrepreneurial opportunity because the individuals who bridge those holes gain social capital. They do so simply by taking up a strategic position in respect to the flow of useful information and social knowledge: they become the conduit through which information passes, and they reap rewards accordingly. Burt showed that, in modern business firms, the social capital accumulated by diligent bridgers of structural holes translates into material gain (e.g., higher salaries) – and thus individuals have strong incentives to identify structural holes and to establish bridging ties across them. The social capital that accumulates from bridging holes potentially benefits all members of the network, although the original bridge builders do especially well. Among Burt's important general points is that networked organizations with many structural holes also present many opportunities for entrepreneurial gain by

---

[25] On the Tholos as the headquarters of the presiding tribal delegation, see Rhodes (1985: 16). Cf. Camp (2001: 69–70).

individuals willing and able to occupy bridge positions. There is, therefore, a correlation between being "full of holes" and the development and maintenance of an entrepreneurial, innovation-prone, organizational culture.[26]

Because a given Athenian councilor's term was limited to a year, the value of networking on the Council was likewise limited when it is compared with institutions (e.g., the U.S. Senate) in which continuous membership may span decades. The wealthiest and most socially prominent councilors might regard network building under these conditions as unlikely to reward the effort. Let us stipulate, therefore, that Poseidippos is among the poorest and least well connected councilors on his tribal team. Like other Athenian fathers, Poseidippos seeks good marriages for his sons and daughters, but he cannot offer large dowries to suitors.[27] The hope of advancing his family's position gives Poseidippos a strong incentive to try to build social capital, which might stand in lieu of larger cash settlements. Let us stipulate further that Poseidippos is the sort of individual who intuitively recognizes the social capital gains (and the associated utility gains over time) available to a bridge builder. As such he will use opportunities offered by the frequent meetings of Pandionis's tribal team of fifty to build bridges to men from other demes, starting perhaps on the basis of shared occupational interests, distant kinship relations, or common cult membership. The personal interactions within the tribal delegation are intense, as its members struggle to accomplish their duties – and thereby, since the assumed context is 507 B.C., to save their polis and themselves from destruction at the hands of the angry Spartans. That intensity facilitates rapid tie formation, and thus makes it easier for Poseidippos to form friendship ties with strangers. The result is illustrated in Figure 6.4.

As the year goes on, Poseidippos becomes an increasingly well respected and highly valued member of his tribal team because of his bridging position. He has a handle on more and more useful information – that is, he learns what people in other demes know. He learns something, for example, about pottery manufacture from his city-deme contacts and something about upland olive farming from his inland contacts. He also accumulates more and more social knowledge. He knows who among the members of his Pandionis team are trustworthy and on what topics, who are friends and enemies with whom, and so on. He is therefore in a position to aggregate important items of information and social knowledge: to bring disparate pieces of knowledge together for problem solving. The social capital he stands to gain is a strong incentive to reveal his own latent knowledge – that is, the expertise and experience he has gained in the course of his life – and to share his newly aggregated knowledge with others. The intimate conditions of service on the Council reduce the costs of communication. Meanwhile, Poseidippos's growing social knowledge promotes greater discrimination in respect to information sorting. As a source and a conduit of useful aggregated knowledge, Poseidippos assumes the role

---

[26] On structural holes, see Burt (1992: 1997, 2004) and Gargiulo and Benassi (2000).

[27] Dowries were very substantial expenses (Cox 1998).

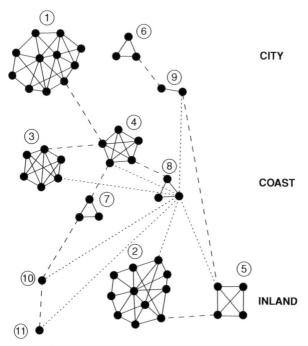

FIGURE 6.4. Pandionis's tribal team network, stage 2. Dotted lines represent hypothetical new weak ties established by "Poseidippos."

of informed leader in deliberations. He thereby accrues advantages for himself and he enables his tribal team to get its job done.

Of course, Poseidippos is not the only one to see the advantages of building bridging links across local networks. Many others on his team imitate his example. As a consequence, the Pandionis delegation is soon densely networked by weak links, as illustrated in Figure 6.5. The tribe-team never becomes a strong-tie network – it is not the case that everyone is everyone else's friend. But the multiple weak-tie bridges ensure that information can flow readily from one strong-tie network to another.

Tribe Pandionis is not special, of course – according to Cleisthenes' design, each of the ten tribes features similar demographic diversity. Thus, structural hole opportunities exist in each tribal team and on the Council as a whole. As a result, the bridge building we have hypothesized for Pandionis went on within each of the ten tribal teams. Moreover, unlike strong-tie networks, weak-tie networks are scalable. The same bridge-building process went on at an extensive network level *between* tribal teams of the Council. If the social capital for being a tribal team-level bridger of local networks and aggregator of knowledge was considerable, it was that much greater at the level of an intertribal bridge builder. And so we can postulate that over the course of the year, the membership of the Council as a whole became linked by weak ties and came to function as a single, extended network. The upshot is that the five hundred

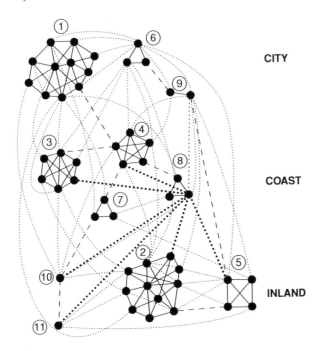

FIGURE 6.5. Pandionis's tribal team network, stage 3. Dotted lines represent hypothetical new weak ties established by various team members.

members of the Council became more capable of working cooperatively, both at the level of the tribal delegations of fifty and as a committee of the whole.

The networking process I have hypothesized, based on the social composition and governmental responsibilities of the Council of 500, directly addresses the public action problems affecting knowledge aggregation. As weak-tie bridges, formed by entrepreneurial individuals, link existing strong-tie local networks across regions, across kinship groups, across occupational groups, and across social classes, useful knowledge flows across the extended network with increasing ease. As the network becomes more dense and social capital grows, social knowledge is exchanged ever more freely. As they witness and experience the social capital gains that come with communication, experts in various technical domains are more willing to share proprietary information about sources of materials, trading partners, weather patterns, and so on. Others realize that their tacit knowledge of people and processes, formerly simply taken for granted as a sort of obvious "common sense" among the members of a strong-tie network, is valuable when brought to the surface and made explicit within a diverse group of people possessing very different sorts of tacit knowledge.

As the year goes on, both the latent specialized technical knowledge and the generalized tacit knowledge necessary to making good decisions, which had formerly been isolated inside individual minds and in closed networks, becomes increasingly accessible to the deliberations of the group as a whole. As councilors become clearer about who is good at what and whom to go to for what sort of information, they can be more discriminating about their recommendations, and as a result the whole Council becomes increasingly capable of doing its difficult job well.

Moreover, as the Council overcomes its collective action problems and learns to work cooperatively toward its common goal, it can potentially gain access to external knowledge resources distributed through the entire population of Athens – and beyond. Because each councilor has a network of contacts *outside* the Council, each councilor is a bridge between the Council and a local subset of the larger population. As a result, the Council, as a body, can gain access, at fairly low cost, to a good deal of the total knowledge available to the extended Athenian community. As a result, at least potentially, "Athens knows what the Athenians know."

Finally, because councilors ordinarily serve for only a year and are judged, and potentially rewarded, on the basis of how well they serve the public purposes of the polis, the Council as an institution never develops a self-serving identity or corporate culture.[28] The rules of order remain sufficiently simple and transparent to be learned by each year's incoming class. Because each year's turnover is complete, all councilors enter into their year on something approaching equal footing; there is no in-group of "old Council hands" controlling the agenda. As councilors build their extended networks and work together over the course of the year on problems of polis governance, they come to better grasp the larger governmental system of which they are (for a year) one part. Government ceases to be regarded as a black box, and councilors can quite quickly become fairly expert at the work of politics.

Their growing system-level expertise conjoins with the councilors' growing social knowledge–based information-sorting capacity, and so they are better able to judge the value of available knowledge to the larger purposes of the polis – and thus better able to make good decisions in the exercise of their office. As a result, better agendas are set, the government is better run from day to day, and so Athens does better overall. We can thereby begin to understand how participatory democratic institutions could help promote growth in productive capacity and overall organizational success.

V. ORGANIZATIONAL AND INDIVIDUAL LEARNING

So far we have focused on the first year after Cleisthenes' establishment of the Council of 500 – and so we have been assuming that Poseidippos and his 499 fellow *bouleutai* entered their first tribal team meetings and first full Council sessions innocent of what to expect and with few preexisting weak-tie bridges. Let us next imagine Poseidippos's son, call him Poseidippos II for simplicity's

---

[28] This key insight was developed by Gomme (1951).

sake, as he enters into a year's service on the Council some time in the mid-470s. Like his father, Poseidippos II lives in Prasiai. He had been formally voted on by his father's demesmen when he reached age eighteen; because he had been accepted by them as a legitimate son of an Athenian man, the vote was positive and thus Poseidippos II became at once a demesman of Prasiai and a citizen of Athens. Like his father, as a councilor, Poseidippos II is confronted with a new challenge – the city had been sacked by the Persians in 480–479. Rebuilding would be expensive. It would be more difficult because Sparta had opposed Athens's plan to refortify and would be of no help in building and maintaining the long-term anti-Persian alliance that most Athenians saw as essential to long-term security and prosperity.

Unlike his father, Poseidippos II had a sense of what to expect on the Council – he knew in advance many of the rules (written and unwritten) governing work on the Council. He had his father's recalled experience to draw on, but also the experience of a full generation of Prasieis who had served, three each year, and brought back to the village much of what they had learned. Over time, every Athenian citizen who cared to avail himself of it had easy and redundant access to men who had served on the Council and had faced a variety of crises and impasses. Both their successes and their failures became part of the general lore passed on across local social networks. Former councilors' accounts of their experience served as an incentive to future councilors. Because he had observed men upon their return from government service over the years, Poseidippos II knew that increased status and recognition could come with a year on the Council. He recognized that the work would be hard and at times frustrating and that he would be taken away from the pleasures and opportunities offered by his ordinary life. Yet these negative considerations were outweighed by Poseidippos II's anticipation of gaining honors and social capital by playing a bridge-building role and by the substantial and long-term benefits associated with that gain.[29]

Within Poseidippos II's own lifetime, the growing aggregate experience of Council service would have changed the structure of local and cross-polis social networks. Poseidippos II had grown up in a Prasiai in which social conditions were deviating from the tightly bounded world into which his father had been born. If we stipulate that Poseidippos I's gain in social capital had enabled him to marry one of his daughters to a somewhat wealthier tribesman from an urban deme to whom he had "bridged" in the course of his Council service, Poseidippos II would have kinship ties to a different social stratum and in a different region of the polis as a result of his father's Council year.[30] The point

---

[29] There is no obvious way to test whether the independent variable of Council service led to a rise in the dependent variable of individual or family utility. The question deserves further study; see also Taylor (2008).

[30] On inter-deme marriages, see Osborne (1985: 27–38, documenting 32 intra-deme and 131 extra-deme marriages), with Cox (1998: 38–67). More research is needed on the question of how public service might have affected marriage patterns.

here is that the weak-tie friendships that were forged in a year's service (as well as in other tribal activities: war, religious ritual, etc.) had ramifications in the lives of many individual Athenians and thereby across the polis as a whole. As a result, each year's group of councilors began their work in a social environment featuring more preexisting weak ties between deme delegations. Local strong-tie networks were supplemented at a polis level by an increasingly rich and complex network of strong and weak links.

As an extensive social network of weak *and* strong ties, the polis as an organization had an enhanced opportunity to build a store of collective social capital and thus gained the ability to work more cooperatively and more effectively in addressing public action problems. At the same time, the Athenian population was large and (at least in the early to middle fifth century) growing quite rapidly. As a result, even as the density of bridges across the extended network grew, there were always structural holes opening up and thus always new opportunities for entrepreneurial bridge builders – the relatively great size of Athens and its constant exposure to demographic change (a function of, inter alia, war casualties, disease, immigration, and emigration) meant that there was no meaningful risk of network ossification – the ties within the extended polis network never became so dense and overlapping as to threaten the entrepreneurial culture Poseidippos I first experienced in the late sixth century.

We can now jump ahead to 325 B.C., near the end of the democratic era of Athenian history. Assuming the family line of Poseidippos I continued, his great-great-great-great-grandson, Poseidippos VI, might have served on that Council. Perhaps, like many Athenians over the generations, he has moved away from his home deme and now lives in the city. But he still attends deme meetings (some of which are held in the city), and he literally wears his deme identity around his neck – as a bronze citizen's identification tag used (inter alia) in lotteries for service on boards of magistrates (Kroll 1972).

Poseidippos VI still feels the pull of the network incentives that had motivated his ancestors. But over the generations, the material incentives for Council service had been formalized. He was paid a daily wage for his service and the Pandionis tribal team competed for a prize offered by the demos, honoring the year's best team.[31] When serving as the Council's presidents, Pandionis's tribal delegation (and the other nine in rotation) still met in the Tholos, which was being planned during Poseidippos II's term of service. But when he attended meetings of the full Council, Poseidippos VI usually sat in the New Bouleuterion. As before, most Council meetings were open to the Athenian public. The Old Bouleuterion, in which Poseidippos II had deliberated over the rebuilding of the city, was now dedicated to the Mother of the Gods and used to house the state archives. Here, councilors and other Athenians could consult the record of Athenian laws and decrees. A small staff of public slaves and citizen-clerks

---

[31] The pay was 5 obols/day for ordinary service, 6 obols (1 drachma)/day for service while the members of the tribal team were serving as presidents (Rhodes 1985: 16–17). On the annual prize for best tribal delegation, offered by the Council in the early fourth century and by the demos by the mid–fourth century, see Rhodes (1985: 8, 22–23).

was available to help with archives and technical matters, yet this staff never amounted to anything like a professionalized bureaucracy; the main work of the Council was still done by the councilors themselves.[32]

By 325 B.C., the accumulated and transmitted knowledge of 180 years of institutional experience and policy experiments, and the results of 180 years of networking among Athenians, were potentially available, orally or in written form. The councilors of the later fourth century, the age of Aristotle, had a substantial store of knowledge to draw on. In sum, because of a structured capacity for passing on what was learned, the Athenian Council had developed the character of a learning organization. As valuable experience accumulated over time, a formal archival system was developed and many of the work routines for accomplishing the Council's work were codified.[33] Yet the regular turnover of Council membership and the diversity of experiences new councilors brought to the table ensured that the socialization of the members of the Council never approached the level at which innovative solutions were likely to be suppressed in favor of ossified routinization. The Council was manned by amateurs, in that their experience as councilors was limited to two terms. In practice and perhaps, therefore, in principle, terms were always nonconsecutive. Yet the apparent seamlessness with which knowledge, both innovative and routinized, could be aggregated and made available to decision makers on the Council enabled them to manifest some of the characteristics associated with experts who have thousands of hours of personal experience to call on. The decision-making process of the Council itself had, over time, evolved into a sort of "expert system," capable of addressing a wide variety of problems.[34]

VI. CONCLUSIONS

The Council is only one example of how knowledge aggregation was facilitated by the "machine" of democratic governance in Athens; other Athenian institutions can also be better understood by reference to the role of incentives and sanctions, communication costs, and sorting within a knowledge-based

---

[32] On the Old and New Bouleuteria, see Rhodes (1985: 31–33) and Camp (2001: 44, 127); on meetings open to the public, Rhodes (1985: 40–43). Before the 360s a principal "secretary to the council" and, after the 360s, other three citizen-secretaries were annually assigned to the Council, but their tenure (like that of all Athenian citizen-clerks) was annual. On secretaries, see [Aristotle], *Ath. Pol.* 54.3–5 with Rhodes (1985: 16, 134–42), Morten T. Hansen (1999: 123–24, 244–45), and Henry (2002). Public slaves (*huperetai*) looked after records in the Metroon and the records of the *poletai*, and perhaps a half-dozen other public slaves were available to assist the Council. Rhodes (1985: 142–43) emphasizes the modest size of the Council's staff; there is no warrant for imagining a substantial professionalized bureaucracy, comparable to that typical of parliamentary democracies, working in the background.

[33] The formulaic language of enactment and disclosure typical of Athenian decrees (Hedrick 1999) is one piece of evidence for routinization.

[34] The term "expert system" ordinarily refers to electronic computing techniques that seek to simulate (and thereby regularize and make easily accessible to end users) the decision-making processes of experts (Jackson 1999).

system.[35] The Athenian system of government both encouraged (through incentives) and required (in order to broaden the range of information and expertise) participation in decision making and problem solving from a diverse population. Equality of opportunity for public participation was a cherished Athenian value (Raaflaub 1996). The institutional design model established by Cleisthenes and elaborated through subsequent institutional innovations was based on offering substantial incentives (honorary, social, and material) for public service. These incentives made public service possible and more desirable across class lines. Formerly inexperienced men had the chance to become experienced in political affairs, indeed, to become quite expert at the work of democratic politics. By gaining experience and therefore confidence in their own capacities, Athenian citizens *lost* a substantial *disincentive* to engage in political activity. Substantial power inequalities remained between elite and nonelite social strata. But opportunities for political activity were to some degree equalized across class lines by the use of the lot (Taylor 2007) and pay for service.

The model I have presented here predicts that, over the course of time, the population of "politically active citizens" should be increasingly representative of, and indeed functionally coextensive with, the citizen population as a whole. An initial overrepresentation of wealthy citizens and of those with easy geographical access to the city center should lessen as poorer and more geographically distant citizens come to appreciate the potential value of their own participation, both to themselves and to their community. This prediction is borne out by Claire Taylor's demographic analysis of some twenty-two hundred politically active Athenians in the fifth and fourth centuries. In the fifth century, 19 percent of identifiable politically active citizens were wealthy (i.e., from the liturgy-paying class: ca. 4 percent of the total population) and 58 percent came from near-city demes (aggregate bouleutic quota 123 out of 500 members: ca. 25 percent of the total membership). In the fourth century, by contrast, only 11 percent of citizens known to be politically active were wealthy and 31 percent were from near-city demes. Taylor's numbers do not prove that citizens' growing experience with government processes (or any other candidate variable) *caused* the trend toward equalization in levels of participation. Her results are, however, consistent with the model offered here. The opposite result (growing inequality of participation) would, by contrast, falsify it.[36]

---

[35] Lyttkens (1992, 1994, 2006) (taxation), Quillin (2002) (amnesty) Schwartzberg (2004, 2007) (law and diplomacy), Fleck and Hanssen (2006) (agricultural economy), Kaiser (2007) (trierarchies), and Teegarden (2007) (antityranny legislation) are notable examples of explanatory approaches to various aspects of Athenian institutions, which emphasize rational action and incentives, although they do not focus in the first instance on dispersed knowledge.

[36] Taylor (2008) argues persuasively that exogenous factors (e.g., demographic changes due to disease, war, rural migration to the city) are inadequate to explain the growth in participation. Taylor's figures fit well with the conclusions of Morris (1998: 235–36), who notes that in comparative terms, and especially in comparison with the pre-democratic period, the pattern of landholding among citizens in fourth-century Athens was "*extremely* egalitarian" (Morris's emphasis; Gini coefficient of 0.382–0.386); on Greek rule egalitarianism, see further Ober (2010: 270–75).

The social context of knowledge-aggregation processes explains how Athenian institutional design promoted learning – both organizational learning, so that the system as a whole became more expert, and individual learning by citizens engaged in a lifelong civic education. The principles of representative sampling through a lottery and rotation inhibited the emergence of a limited elite of entrenched policy experts. The circulation through various kinds of public service (military, judicial, magisterial) by a great many citizens, who remained diverse in terms of age, geographic home, economic class, and occupation, facilitated innovative problem solving. Innovations emerged continuously as teams of citizen-magistrates brought into being new constellations of social and technical knowledge by aggregating an ever-changing repertoire of diverse information and expertise. Innovation was stimulated though cross-appropriation of knowledge between domains of expertise and from one solution space to another.

Like all decision-making processes, the Athenian system was fallible and sometimes produced bad policy. Yet overall and over time, democratic Athens fared well enough to outdo all of its city-state rivals. The postulated value of aggregated knowledge, drawn from a large and diverse population, to problem solving in the fluid and competitive environment of the Greek city-states solves the riddle of unexpected Athenian success. It offers at least a partial explanation of why Athenian democracy, with its costly participatory decision-making institutions, is so strongly correlated with improved state capacity and superior competitive performance.

Bibliography

Anderson, Elizabeth. 2006. "The Epistemology of Democracy." *Episteme: Journal of Social Epistemology* 3: 8–22.

Anderson, Greg. 2003. *The Athenian experiment: Building an imagined political community in ancient Attica, 508–490 B.C.* Ann Arbor: University of Michigan Press.

Badian, E. 2000. "Back to Kleisthenic Chronology." In *Polis and politics [Festschrift Hansen]*, edited by P. Flensted-Jensen, T. H. Neilsen, and L. Rubinstein, pp. 447–64. Copenhagen: Museum Tusculanum Press, University of Copenhagen.

Benkler, Yochai. 2006. *The wealth of networks: How social production transforms markets and freedom.* New Haven, CT: Yale University Press.

Bratman, Michael, and University of Toronto, Faculty of Law. 1999. *Reflection, planning, and temporally extended agency and valuing and the will.* [Toronto:] University of Toronto, Faculty of Law.

Brennan, Geoffrey, and Philip Pettit. 2004. *The economy of esteem: An essay on civil and political society.* Oxford: Oxford University Press.

Brown, John Seely, and Paul Duguid. 1991. "Organizational Learning and Communities-of-Practice: Toward a Unified View of Working, Learning, and Innovation." *Organization Science* 2: 40–57.

2000. *The social life of information.* Boston: Harvard Business School Press.

Burt, Ronald S. 1992. *Structural holes: The social structure of competition.* Cambridge, MA: Harvard University Press.

1997. "The Contingent Value of Social Capital." *Administrative Science Quarterly* 42: 339–65.

2004. "Structural Holes and Good Ideas." *American Journal of Sociology* 110: 349–99.

Camp, John M., II. 2001. *The archaeology of Athens*. New Haven, CT: Yale University Press.

Chang, Myong-Hun, and Joseph E. Harrington. 2005. "Discovery and Diffusion of Knowledge in an Endogenous Social Network." *American Journal of Sociology* 110: 937–76.

Christ, Matthew R. 2001. "Conscription of Hoplites in Classical Athens." *Classical Quarterly* 51 (2): 398–422.

Cox, Cheryl Anne. 1998. *Household interests: Property, marriage strategies, and family dynamics in ancient Athens*. Princeton, NJ: Princeton University Press.

Davenport, Thomas H., and Laurence Prusak. 1998. *Working knowledge: How organizations manage what they know*. Boston: Harvard Business School Press.

Diani, Mario, and Doug McAdam (eds.). 2003. *Social movements and networks: Relational approaches to collective action*. Oxford: Oxford University Press.

Dixon, Nancy M. 2000. *Common knowledge: How companies thrive by sharing what they know*. Boston: Harvard Business School Press.

Ericsson, Anders. 1999. "Expertise." In *The MIT encyclopedia of the cognitive sciences*, pp. 298–300. Cambridge, MA: MIT Press.

Estund, David M. 2008. *Democratic authority: A philosophical framework*. Princeton, NJ: Princeton University Press.

Fleck, Robert K., and F. Andrew Hanssen. 2006. "The Origins of Democracy: A Model with Application to Ancient Greece." *Journal of Law and Economics* 49: 115–46.

Forsdyke, Sara. 2005. *Exile, ostracism, and democracy: The politics of expulsion in ancient Greece*. Princeton, NJ: Princeton University Press.

Frost, Frank J. 1984. "The Athenian Military before Cleisthenes." *Historia* 33: 283–94.

Gargiulo, Martin, and Mario Benassi. 2000. "Trapped in Your Own Net? Network Cohesion, Structural Holes, and the Adaptation of Social Capital." *Organization Science* 11: 183–96.

Gomme, A. W. 1951. "The Working of the Athenian Democracy." *History* 36: 12–28.

Gould, Roger V. 1995. *Insurgent identities: Class, community, and protest in Paris from 1848 to the Commune*. Chicago: University of Chicago Press.

Granovetter, Mark S. 1973. "The Strength of Weak Ties." *American Journal of Sociology* 78: 1360–80.

1983. "The Strength of Weak Ties: A Network Theory Revisited." *Sociological Theory*, 1: 201–33.

1985. "Economic Action and Social Structure: The Problem of Embeddedness." *American Journal of Sociology* 91: 481–510.

Hansen, Mogens Herman. 1983. "*Rhetores* and *Strategoi* in Fourth-Century Athens." *Greek, Roman, and Byzantine Studies* 24: 151–80.

1984. "The Number of *Rhetores* in the Athenian *Ecclesia*, 355–322 B.C." *Greek, Roman, and Byzantine Studies* 24: 227–38.

1999. *The Athenian democracy in the age of Demosthenes: Structure, principles and ideology*. Norman: University of Oklahoma Press.

Hansen, Mogens Herman, H. L. Bjertrup, T. H. Nielsen, L. Rubinstein, and T. Vestergaard. 1990. "The Demography of the Attic Demes: The Evidence of the Sepulchral Inscriptions." *Analecta Romana* 19: 24–44.

Hansen, Morten T. 2002. "Knowledge Networks: Explaining Effective Knowledge Sharing in Multiunit Companies." *Organization Science* 13: 232–49.

Hayek, F. A. 1945. "The Use of Knowledge in Society." *American Economic Review* 35 (4): 519–30.

Hedrick, Charles W. 1999. "Democracy and the Athenian Epigraphic Habit." *Hesperia* 68: 387–439.

Henry, Alan S. 2002. "The Athenian State Secretariat and Provisions for Publishing and Erecting Decrees." *Hesperia* 71: 91–118.

Jackson, Peter. 1999. *Introduction to expert systems*. Reading, MA: Addison-Wesley.

Jones, Nicholas F. 1999. *The associations of Classical Athens: The response to democracy*. New York: Oxford University Press.

Kaiser, Brooks A. 2007. "The Athenian Trierarchy: Mechanism Design for the Private Provision of Public Goods." *Journal of Economic History* 67: 445–80.

Krackhardt, David. 1992. "The Strength of Strong Ties: The Importance of Philos in Organizations." In *Networks and organizations: Structure, form, and action*, edited by Nitin Nohria and Robert G. Eccles, pp. 216–39. Boston: Harvard Business School Press.

Kroll, John H. 1972. *Athenian bronze allotment plates*. Cambridge, MA: Harvard University Press.

Levitt, Barbara, and James March. 1988. "Organizational Learning." *Annual Review of Sociology* 14: 319–40.

List, Christian, and Philip Pettit. 2004. "An Epistemic Free-Riding Problem?" In *Karl Popper: Critical appraisals*, edited by Philip Catton and Graham Macdonald, pp. 128–58. London: Routledge.

Lyttkens, Carl Hampus. 1992. "Effects of the Taxation of Wealth in Athens in the Fourth Century B.C." *Scandinavian Economic History Review* 40: 3–20.

——— 1994. "A Predatory Democracy? An Essay on Taxation in Classical Athens." *Explorations in Economic History* 31: 62–90.

——— 2006. "Reflections on the Origins of the Polis: An Economic Perspective on Institutional Change in Ancient Greece." *Constitutional Political Economy* 17: 31–48.

Maurizio, Lisa. 1998. "The Panathenaic Procession: Athens' Participatory Democracy on Display?" In *Democracy, empire, and the arts in fifth-century Athens*, edited by Deborah Dickmann Boedeker and Kurt A. Raaflaub, pp. 297–317. Cambridge, MA: Harvard University Press.

Michels, Robert. 1962. *Political parties: A sociological study of the oligarchical tendencies of modern democracy*. New York: Collier Books.

Millett, Paul C. 1989. "Patronage and Its Avoidance in Classical Athens." In *Patronage in ancient society*, edited by A. Wallace-Hadrill, pp. 15–48. London: Routledge.

Morris, Ian. 1998. "Archaeology as a Kind of Anthropology (A Response to David Small)." In *Democracy 2500? Questions and challenges*, edited by Ian Morris and Kurt A. Raaflaub, pp. 229–39. Dubuque, IA: Kendall/Hunt.

Ober, Josiah. 1989. *Mass and elite in democratic Athens: Rhetoric, ideology, and the power of the people*. Princeton, NJ: Princeton University Press.

——— 1996. *The Athenian revolution: Essays on ancient Greek democracy and political theory*. Princeton, NJ: Princeton University Press.

——— 1998. *Political dissent in democratic Athens: Intellectual critics of popular rule*. Princeton, NJ: Princeton University Press.

——— 2005. *Athenian legacies: Essays in the politics of going on together*. Princeton, NJ: Princeton University Press.

2007. "Natural Capacities and Democracy as a Good-in-Itself." *Philosophical Studies* 132: 59–73.

2008. *Democracy and knowledge: Learning and innovation in Classical Athens.* Princeton, NJ: Princeton University Press.

2010. "Wealthy Hellas." *Transactions of the American Philological Association* 210: 241–86.

Olson, Mancur. 1965. *The logic of collective action: Public goods and the theory of groups.* Cambridge, MA: Harvard University Press.

Osborne, Robin. 1985. *Demos, the discovery of classical Attika.* Cambridge: Cambridge University Press.

1990. "The Demos and Its Divisions in Classical Athens." In *The Greek city: From Homer to Alexander*, edited by Oswyn Murray and S. R. F. Price, pp. 265–93. Oxford: Clarendon Press.

1994. "Ritual, Finance, Politics: An Account of Athenian Democracy." In *Ritual, finance, politics: Athenian democratic accounts presented to David Lewis*, edited by Robin Osborne and Simon Hornblower, pp. 1–24. Oxford: Clarendon Press.

Osterloh, Margit, and Bruno S. Frey. 2000. "Motivation, Knowledge Transfer, and Organizational Form." *Organization Science* 11: 538–50.

Padgett, John F., and Christopher K. Ansell. 1993. "Robust Action and the Rise of the Medici, 1400–1434." *American Journal of Sociology* 98: 1259–1319.

Page, Scott E. 2007. *The difference: How the power of diversity creates better groups, firms, schools, and societies.* Princeton, NJ: Princeton University Press.

Pritchard, David. 2004. "Kleisthenes, Participation, and the Dithyrambic Contests of Late Archaic and Classical Athens." *Phoenix* 58: 208–28.

2005. "Kleisthenes and Athenian Democracy: Vision from Above or Below?" *Polis* 22, no. 1: 136–57.

Purcell, Nicholas. 1990. "Mobility and the Polis." In *The Greek city: From Homer to Alexander*, edited by Oswyn Murray and S. R. F. Price, pp. 29–58. Oxford: Clarendon Press.

Quillin, James. 2002. "Achieving Amnesty: The Role of Events, Institutions, and Ideas." *Transactions of the American Philological Association* 132: 71–107.

Raaflaub, Kurt. 1996. "Equalities and Inequalities in Athenian Democracy." In *Dēmokratia: A conversation on democracies, ancient and modern*, edited by Josiah Ober and Charles W. Hedrick, pp. 139–74. Princeton, N.J.: Princeton University Press.

Raaflaub, Kurt, Josiah Ober, and Robert W. Wallace. 2007. *The origins of democracy in ancient Greece.* Berkeley: University of California Press.

Rhodes, P. J. 1985. *The Athenian Boule.* Oxford: Clarendon Press.

Robinson, Eric W. 1997. *The first democracies: Early popular government outside Athens.* Stuttgart: F. Steiner.

Rubinstein, Lene. 2000. *Litigation and cooperation: Supporting speakers in the courts of classical Athens.* Wiesbaden: Franz Steiner.

Schmitt-Pantel, Pauline. 1992. *La cité au banquet: Histoire des repas publics dans les cités grecques.* Rome: École française de Rome.

Schwartzberg, Melissa. 2004. "Athenian Democracy and Legal Change." *American Political Science Review* 98: 311–25.

2007. *Democracy and legal change.* Cambridge: Cambridge University Press.

Siewert, Peter. 1982. *Die Trittyen Attikas und die Heeresform des Kleisthenes.* Munich: C. H. Beck.

Spinosa, Charles, Fernando Flores, and Hubert L. Dreyfus. 1997. *Disclosing new worlds: Entrepreneurship, democratic action, and the cultivation of solidarity.* Cambridge, MA: MIT Press.

Sunstein, Cass R. 2006. *Infotopia: How many minds produce knowledge.* New York: Oxford University Press.

Taylor, Claire. 2007. "An Oligarchy of the City? The Sociological Impact of Election and Lot in Athenian Democracy." *Hesperia* 76: 323–46.

———. 2008. "A New Political World." In *Debating the Athenian cultural revolution: Art, literature, philosophy, and politics, 430–380 BC,* edited by Robin Osborne, pp. 72–90. Cambridge: Cambridge University Press.

Teegarden, David. 2007. "Defending Democracy: A Study of Ancient Greek Anti-Tyranny Legislation." PhD dissertation, Department of Classics, Princeton University.

Traill, John S. 1975. *The political organization of Attica: A study of the demes, trittyes, and phylai, and their representation in the Athenian Council.* Princeton, NJ: American School of Classical Studies at Athens.

Vanderpool, Eugene, James McCredie, and A. Steinberg. 1962. "Koroni: A Ptolemaic Camp on the East Coast of Atica." *Hesperia* 31: 26–61.

Waldron, Jeremy. 1995. "The Wisdom of the Multitude: Some Reflections on Book III, Chapter 11 of the *Politics." Political Theory* 23: 563–84.

Walker, Rob. 2004. "The Hidden (in Plain Sight) Persuaders." *New York Times Magazine* 5 (December): 69–76ff.

Wenger, Etienne. 1998. *Communities of practice: Learning, meaning, and identity.* Cambridge: Cambridge University Press.

Whitehead, David. 1983. "Competitive Outlay and Community Profit: *Philotimia* in Democratic Athens." *Classica et Mediaevalia* 34: 55–74.

———. 1986. *The demes of Attica, 508/7–ca. 250 B.C.: A political and social study.* Princeton, NJ: Princeton University Press.

———. 1993. "Cardinal Virtues: The Language of Public Approbation in Democratic Athens." *Classica et Mediaevalia* 44: 37–75.

Wilson, Peter. 2000. *The Athenian institution of the Khoregia: The chorus, the city, and the stage.* Cambridge: Cambridge University Press.

Williamson, Oliver E. 1975. *Markets and hierarchies, analysis and antitrust implications: A study in the economics of internal organization.* New York: Free Press.

———. 1985. *The economic institutions of capitalism: Firms, markets, relational contracting.* New York: Free Press.

7

The Optimal Design of a Constituent Assembly

Jon Elster

I. INTRODUCTION

If there is one task for which "wisdom" would seem highly desirable, it is that of writing a constitution that is intended to last for the indefinite future. In fact, wisdom is not only desirable in light of the importance of the issues, but also necessary in light of their complexity. Writing to his son soon after the opening of the Federal Convention in Philadelphia, George Mason confessed that "to view through the calm, sedate medium of reason the influence which the establishment now proposed may have upon the happiness or misery of millions yet unborn, is an object of such magnitude, as absorbs, and in a manner suspends, the operations of the human understanding" (in Farrand 1966: vol. 3, 33).

A good constitution is a complex piece of machinery, a set of interlocking parts that are finely adjusted to each other. A priori, one might think that the task of writing it is best entrusted to a single individual who can weigh all the relevant considerations without having to accept the compromises that are inevitable in any collective decision-making process. In stylized form, whereas both [A, B] and [A', B'] might be viable combinations, the committee compromise $[(A + A')/2, (B + B')/2]$ might not be. The first reasonably well documented constitution, that of Solon, was in fact the accomplishment of a single individual. Although details are shrouded in obscurity, it seems to have been remarkably successful. Other examples of constitutions essentially handed down by a single person include the French Charter of 1815, the "octroyed" Prussian constitution of 1848, and the constitution of the Fifth French Republic. These can hardly, however, be said to have been uncontroversially successful.

In this essay I do not address the issue of whether a constitution is best written by a single person or by an assembly of citizens but rather focus on the optimal mode of decision making by assembly. Let me nevertheless mention

I am grateful to Hélène Landemore for many helpful discussions and comments.

one obvious objection to the idea of singly authored constitutions, namely that in the absence of a reliable procedure for finding a person with the requisite wisdom, the proposal is too fragile to be taken seriously. In fact, this observation also applies to the analysis I propose here. I analyze the *conditions* that make for optimal constitution making, without looking into the *processes* by which these conditions might be realized. Actual constitution making is often a messy business, triggered by crises of one kind or another and rarely governed by the "calm, sedate medium of reason." The cliché that constitutions are chains imposed by Peter when sober on Peter when drunk is, in fact, seriously misleading. Overstating the case somewhat, one might say that the conditions for optimal constitution making are the very same as those in which the need for adopting a constitution will not be felt.

In the spirit of Bentham (1999: 15), I take a purely procedural approach to the issue of the optimal design of the constituent assembly, in the sense that I remain agnostic as to the nature of the optimal constitution. There is no specific outcome that the process is supposed to be tracking. In Rawls's terminology, I am proposing neither perfect nor imperfect procedural justice (Rawls 1999: 74–75). At the same time, it would not be accurate to say that I am proposing a scheme for pure procedural justice (Rawls 1999) in which the outcome is ipso facto optimal if the correct procedure has been followed. I believe not only that in a given context some constitutional schemes may be better than others, but also that the best procedures may lead to a suboptimal outcome. The relevant question, however, is whether it is possible to eliminate or minimize the features that, from the ex ante point of view, are likely to lead to bias of one kind of another. If one were to succeed in that task and the constitution that resulted still had flaws, these might simply be attributable to the undue influence of strong but misguided delegates, against whom no procedural safeguards can be erected.

I proceed as follows. In Section II, I set out the basic framework of interest, reason, and passion that will guide much of the discussion. In the following sections, I address issues of institutional design: the tasks of the constituent assembly (Section III), the size and duration of the assembly (Section IV), the location of the assembly (Section V), the election of delegates to the assembly (Section VI), the question of secrecy versus publicity of the proceedings of the assembly (Section VII), the internal organization of the assembly (Section VIII), and the embeddedness of the assembly in broader upstream and downstream processes (Section IX). Section X summarizes the main ideas of the essay. To a surprising or maybe unsurprising extent, a good constitution-making process turns out to consist of mutually interlocking parts much in the way a good constitution does.

I rely throughout on historical examples, notably on the two eighteenth-century cases I know best, to flesh out the implications of the various proposals. In some cases, I also rely on historical illustrations to show that constitution makers had some awareness of the normative desirability of the criteria I propose. Although some of the historical episodes have little direct relevance to contemporary constitution making, my hope is that they will contribute to the general framework I present.

I conclude this introduction by mentioning the two main theoretical analyses of the topic, both from the late eighteenth century. First, there are the well-known works by Condorcet (1785/1986, 1788). Second, there are the less well known but remarkable writings in French by Bentham (1788/2001, 1789/2001) that purport to advise the French on the organization of the upcoming Etats-Généraux. Although I return briefly to these writings later, my comments will not in any way do them full justice.

II. INTEREST, REASON, AND PASSION

As I have spelled out this framework at some length elsewhere (Elster 1999: ch. 5; Elster 2007a: chs. 4 and 5), I offer only a bare-bones account, supplemented by a few remarks motivated by the question at hand.

In their analysis of human motivations, the seventeenth-century French moralists made a fruitful distinction among interest, reason, and passion. Interest is the pursuit of personal advantage, be it money, fame, power, or salvation. Even action to help our children counts as the pursuit of interest, since our fate is so closely bound up with theirs. A parent sending his children to an expensive private school where they can get the best education is not sacrificing his interest but pursuing it. The passions may be taken to include emotions as well as other visceral urges, such as hunger, thirst, and sexual or addictive cravings. The ancients also included states of madness within the same general category because, like emotions, they are involuntary, unbidden, and subversive of rational deliberation. For many purposes, we may also include states of intoxication among the passions. From the point of view of the law, anger, drunkenness, and madness have often been treated as being on a par.

Reason is a more complicated idea. The moralists mostly understood it as the desire to promote the public good rather than private ends. Occasionally, they also used it to refer to long-term (prudential) motivations as distinct from short-term (myopic) concerns. Both ideas can be summarized under the heading of *impartiality*. In designing public policy, one should treat individuals impartially rather than favor some groups or individuals over others. Individuals, too, may act on this motivation. Parents may sacrifice their interest by sending their children to a public school, because they believe in equality of opportunity. At the same time, policymakers as well as private individuals ought to treat outcomes occurring at successive times in an impartial manner by giving each of them the same weight in current decision making rather than privileging outcomes in the near future. When, as Mason wrote to his son, one is trying to organize the lives of "millions yet unborn," the importance of this consideration is obvious.

In negative terms, the constituent assembly ought to be organized to minimize the influence of individual or group interest, including that of the current generation. At the same time, the process ought to be designed to insulate the framers from the influence of passions, be it their own or those of others in a position to influence or pressure them. In positive terms, the assembly ought to be designed to maximize the influence of what Madison in *Federalist* 42 called "the mild voice of reason."

To these summary remarks I now want to add two considerations. First, some of my earlier writings may have left the misleading impression that reason is only a matter of impartial *motivation*. On reflection, it is clear that the intuitive idea of reason also has a cognitive or *epistemic* element, in that it requires decisions to be based on rational beliefs (Elster 2006). My preferred conception of wisdom (individual or collective), therefore, is that of *impartial motivations conjoined with rational beliefs*. Generally speaking, rational belief formation requires both optimal processing of available information and optimal gathering of information. In the context of decision making by an assembly, these two requirements translate, roughly speaking, into optimal deliberation (Sections VII and VIII) and optimal representation (Section VI). The purpose of these processes is partly to improve the understanding of factual problems (where the shoe pinches) and partly to improve the quality of solutions (how to make good shoes).

Second, the claim that passion ought, as far as possible, to be eliminated is somewhat problematic. Hegel wrote that "[n]othing great in the world has been accomplished without passion." That impartiality does not exclude passion was demonstrated by the French framers in 1789, who, in the words of the biographer of one of them, were "drunk with disinterestedness" (Lebègue 1910: 261). One of the most impressive of them, the Comte de Clermont-Tonnerre, said that "[a]narchy is a frightening yet necessary passage, and the only moment one can establish a new order of things. It is not in calm times that one can take uniform measures" (AP 9: 461). To overcome petty interests, reason may have to form an alliance with passion. The decrees of the night of August 4, 1789, are often cited as an example, although the facts are a bit more complicated (Elster 2007b).

More recently, Jeb Rudenfeld has made a systematic argument to this effect. To assess it, we may note once more that constitutions are usually written in times of transition, turbulence, and even violence. The Peter who writes the constitution is more likely to be drunk than sober. This fact does not, of course, prove that he is engaged in an act of "hot" (emotional) precommitment against his future "cold" (dispassionate but not necessarily disinterested) state. Rudenfeld takes that additional step when distinguishing between precommitment and commitment. "Ulyssean precommitment appeals to rationality against the seduction of transient passion, . . . commitment appeals to passion against the seduction of rationality" (Rudenfeld 2001: 129). Constitution makers enlist the help of passion to entrench the common good against private interest (not, as he misleadingly says, against rationality).

This may all be true. Yet even if we were to accept that constitution making is unlikely to occur without passion and unlikely to succeed without it, it would be absurd to claim that passion ought to be built into the constitution-making process. The passions that have constructive potential derive from the general political context, not from within the assembly itself, although the latter often acts as an amplifier. Moreover, these passions can also have destructive and distorting effects. For one thing, they may make participants afraid of speaking their mind. For another, even though enthusiasm may provide admirable ends, it also tends to undermine the clearheaded thinking needed to realize them. Even in the best of cases, the impact of passion on collective wisdom is ambiguous: while enhancing impartiality, it impedes rational belief formation.

In the following, then, I focus on three issues: how to minimize the role of interest, how to minimize the role of passion, and how to maximize the epistemic quality of the decisions. It is a question not only of substituting arguing for bargaining (Elster 2000), but also of reducing the scope of fear, anger, malice, vanity, and other emotions that may interfere with the quality of the arguments.

III. THE TASK OF THE CONSTITUENT ASSEMBLY

It might seem obvious that the task of constituent assemblies is to adopt (or propose) a constitution. While certainly *a* task, it has rarely, however, been their only task. One may in fact distinguish four varieties of constituent assemblies:

- constitutional conventions (conventions, for short)
- mandated constituent legislatures
- self-created constituent legislatures
- self-created legislating assemblies

In the following I argue that conventions are superior to the other three (mixed) regimes. I first characterize the various regimes, then discuss and reject arguments purporting to show the superiority of mixed regimes to conventions, and conclude by offering some arguments against the mixed regimes.

A constitutional convention is elected for the sole purpose of adopting the constitution and does in fact carry out only that task. The best-known instances are the Federal Convention (with current affairs being handled by the Continental Congress) and the Parliamentary Council that elaborated the 1949 Bonn constitution (with current affairs being handled by the occupational powers). The American states have also used this format on many occasions (Hoar 1917). Later, I discuss some recent Latin American instances.

A mandated constituent legislature is explicitly elected with the double task of adopting a constitution and performing the task of an ordinary legislature. Thus, in the election of the first French parliament after 1945, the voters were asked, "Do you want the assembly elected today to be a constituent assembly?" Fully 96 percent of the voters answered yes. In 1776 John Scott argued that the existing Provincial Congress in the state of New York "had the power to [frame] a government, or at least, that it is doubtful whether they have not that power." Gouverneur Morris argued strongly, however, for the calling of a constitutional convention, and a compromise was reached in the form of the election of a mandated constituent legislature, which took care of Morris's concern for the legitimacy of the new constitution (Kline 1978: 54–56). In Delaware, by contrast, the need for a constitutional convention was seen as more important than the need for a mandate (Kruman 1997: 28–29).

A self-created constituent legislature is elected as an ordinary parliament and then turns itself into a constituent assembly. This was a very common pattern among the American states during the revolutionary years. Among the constituent assemblies convened in this period, eight fell in this category (Hoar 1917). The Second Continental Congress, too, was a self-appointed constituent body when it enacted the Articles of Confederation. The Hungarian parliament of 1989–90 was also self-appointed. It had been created under Communist rule, but took it upon itself to destroy that regime by piecewise constitutional amendments that amounted to a wholly new constitution.

A self-created legislative assembly is elected as a constitutional convention and then assumes legislative powers, following either of two principles: "He who can do more can do less" (Le Pillouer 2003: 98, 130, 133) and "He who can create a power can also exercise it" (143). Examples include the Frankfurt parliament of 1848, which dissolved the Assembly of the German Confederation and arrogated its powers to itself, and the Indian constituent assembly of 1946. In the nineteenth century, a number of American states called conventions that authorized themselves to legislate (Hoar 1917: 140–48).

As a practical matter, a country usually needs a body or an organ to handle current affairs. That body may be (1) the constituent assembly, (2) another elected legislative body, or (3) an unelected body such as an occupational power or a provisional government. Disregarding the relatively few cases in the third category (Italy, 1946; Germany, 1949), the first solution is by far the most common one. To my knowledge, concurrent constituent and legislative bodies have been found only in America (1787), Colombia (1991), and Venezuela (1999). In the last two cases, a president essentially declared war on his legislature by calling elections to a constituent assembly in ways not provided for by the existing constitution. The "cohabitation" of the two assemblies proved to be highly unstable. In Colombia, the constitutional convention ordered the dissolution of the legislature and elected an interim legislature from within its own body. In Venezuela, the constitutional convention took it upon itself to "assume the functions of the legislators . . . when these do not . . . carry out their tasks or delay their execution" (*Le Monde*, September 1, 1999). These events correspond to the analysis of Robespierre in a speech of 1793, in which he said: "A double representation contains the germ of civil war. . . . One assembly would appeal to the existing constitution and the other to the keener interest that a people takes in new representatives; the struggle would be engaged and the rivalry would excite hatred" (cited after Le Pillouer 2003: 127).

The two Latin American cases and Robespierre's dubious authority do not prove that dual assemblies are disastrous. After all, the Federal Convention and the Continental Congress did coexist without friction. One might argue, perhaps, that constituent legislatures are desirable because of the scarcity of competent legislators. If a country opts for the concurrent operation of a legislature and a constitutional convention, the quality of debates and decisions in one or both will suffer. Against this argument one may cite the claim by Bryce (1905: 62) that "[e]xperience has shown ... in the United States, the country in which this method [conventions] has been largely used for redrafting, or preparing amendments to, the Constitutions of the several States, that a set of men can be found for the work of a Convention better than those who form the ordinary legislature of the State."

In Canada, the Beaudoin-Edwards Special Joint Committee argued that constituent legislatures are superior because the framers can be held accountable at the next election. It is certainly desirable that self-created constituent legislatures be held accountable in some way, either by election or by downstream ratification of the constitution. If these were to arrogate the constituent power to themselves without being accountable to anyone, it would amount to a legislative coup d'état. It is less clear why conventions (or constituent legislatures with an upstream mandate) would also need a downstream approval. If this should be thought desirable, ratification can obviate the need to hold the ax of reelection over the head of the framers. I return to these questions in Section X.

One might argue, furthermore, that conventions are inferior to constituent legislatures because, in their inability to legislate, they might write matters into the constitution that ought, by the nature of the subject matter, to be left to statute. This has, in particular, been common in many American state conventions. Although "this subterfuge of including legislation in the constitution has not always gone unchallenged by the courts," still "many of our State constitutions today [1917] consist for the most part of legislative details which ought to have been left to the ordinary legislature" (Hoar 1917: 143–44). Yet this temptation is matched by the temptation of a majority in constituent legislatures to constitutionalize clauses that by their nature belong to statute, to make it more unlikely that future majorities will overturn them. Along similar lines, as soon as the Assemblée Constituante had imposed the principle that statutes but not constitutional provisions were subject to the royal veto, the deputies had a clear incentive to present each of their decisions as a constitutional one (de Staël 2000: 243).

As an argument against mixed regimes one may cite the fact that it is easier to keep proceedings secret in a single-task constituent assembly than in a dual-task one. As this argument depends on the premise that secrecy is a good thing, I postpone discussion until Section VII. Another argument against mixed regimes is that decisions made by the assembly wearing its legislative hat may unduly affect the decisions it makes wearing its constitutional hat (a form of path dependence). An example from the Assemblée Constituante will illustrate the problem.

In the fall of 1789, Mirabeau twice addressed the issue of the relation between the king's minister and the assembly. In September, his proposal that ministers chosen from the assembly could retain their seat (or stand for reelection) might have been adopted had it been put to a vote, which for technical reasons it was not (AP 9: 212). When the issue came up again in November, he argued for the more limited proposal that the ministers be allowed to have a "consultative voice" in the assembly until "the constitution shall have fixed the rules which shall be followed with regard to them" (AP 9: 711). Had the vote not been postponed until the next day, the proposal might have been adopted. As the delay gave Mirabeau's enemies time to gather their forces, it was defeated. Among the arguments offered against it, the most relevant for my purposes was made by Pierre-François Blin, a deputy of the third estate: "The issue may seem detached from the constitution and to be merely provisional; but the authority of the past on the future binds the facts at all times" (AP 9: 716). Although the appeal to the danger of precedent setting was probably a pretext for excluding Mirabeau from the ministry, the argument itself is plausible and, in fact, applies directly to Blin's own successful motion that "[n]o member of the National Assembly shall from now on be able to enter the ministry during the term of the present session." It is likely that the article in the constitution of 1791 banning members of any assembly from the ministry during their tenure, and in the two years following it, can be traced back to his motion. Although it was adopted mainly for the purely tactical purpose of stopping the ascent of Mirabeau, the assembly could then hardly disavow the lofty principle on which it pretended to rest.

A constituent legislature may also be subject to a self-enhancing bias, in the sense of creating an excessively strong legislative branch with correspondingly weak executive and judicial branches. The bias might stem from one of two sources. First, if the framers expect or hope to be elected to the first post-constitutional assembly, they have a direct interest in being able to promote their interest – or just to exercise power – at that later stage. In 1780 the voters in Massachusetts turned down a constitution proposed by a constituent legislature partly because of a perception that the legislators had "Prepossessions in their own Favor" (Kruman 1997: 32). The constitution proposed by a subsequent convention was, however, ratified. When Robespierre proposed the famous (and disastrous) self-denying ordinance that the French framers adopted on May 16, 1791, he justified it by the need to ensure disinterestedness. Second, as members of the legislature, they might naturally come to think that the institution to which they belong is a particularly important one, partly because they have more intimate knowledge about it than about the other branches and partly because there is a natural human tendency to enhance one's own importance in the scheme of things.

Finally, as further discussed in Section VI, if one and the same assembly is entrusted with both writing the constitution and forming a government, it is liable to perform one of the tasks suboptimally, depending on the mode of election of delegates. In the terminology explained later, either governability or representativeness will suffer.

IV. THE OPTIMAL SIZE AND DURATION OF A CONSTITUENT ASSEMBLY

The number of delegates to constituent assemblies varies considerably, with the Federal Convention (55 delegates) and the Assemblée Constituante (1,200 delegates) being at the two extremes. The Parliamentary Council in Bonn, with 65 delegates, is close to the lower extreme, whereas the French and German assemblies of 1848, with respectively 800 and 649 members, are the ones I have found that come closest to the upper extreme.

The optimal number is clearly related to the size and homogeneity of the country. The larger and the more diverse the population, the more delegates are needed to ensure a broadly representative assembly. For the time being, I bracket that issue, which I shall discuss in Section VI.

Let me first cite the locus classicus on the subject, *Federalist 55* by Madison:

Sixty or seventy men may be more properly trusted with a given degree of power than six or seven. But it does not follow that six or seven hundred would be proportionably a better depositary. And if we carry on the supposition to six or seven thousand, the whole reasoning ought to be reversed. The truth is that in all cases a certain number at least seems to be necessary to secure the benefits of free consultation and discussion, and to guard against too easy a combination for improper purposes; as, on the other hand, the number ought at most to be kept within a certain limit, in order to avoid the confusion and intemperance of a multitude. In all very numerous assemblies, of whatever character composed, passion never fails to wrest the sceptre from reason. Had every Athenian citizen been a Socrates, every Athenian assembly would still have been a mob.

A lower limit is imposed by the need to prevent "elected oligarchies," who would be able to use the "given degree of power" to promote their private interests. More generally, a lower limit is needed to prevent bargains and logrolling, assuming (perhaps controversially) that these are in general undesirable activities (see Stratmann 1997; Mueller 2003: 104–12). Before the rise of the modern political party, it was indeed very hard to strike bargains among a large number of unregimented *individuals*. The experience from the French Assemblée Constituante, with its shifting alliances formed around this or that leader, offers an example. The best-known attempted logrolling, proposed by the "triumvirate" (Barnave, Duport, and A. Lameth) to Mounier in August 1789, came to nothing. By contrast, at the much smaller Federal Convention hard bargains between the large states and the small states, and between slave-holding southern states and the seafaring northern states, were struck and (for the most part) kept.

Assuming, again controversially (Dowding and van Hees 2007), that strategic or sophisticated voting is undesirable, small assemblies would also be undesirable. The reason is that as the number of voters "grows large the likelihood of a voter's knowing the preferences of the others grows small, and thus so do the chances of successfully manipulating the outcome" (Mueller 2003: 155–56). Once again, this argument holds only for the period preceding the rise of political parties.

Madison's argument that an upper limit is needed "to avoid the confusion and intemperance of a multitude" may also seem to be confirmed by the Assemblée Constituante, which did indeed at times exhibit an utterly chaotic style. It is not clear, however, whether this fact was due to the large number of delegates or to the public character of the debates (see Section VII). I cannot see in principle why a numerous assembly debating behind closed doors could not enforce some discipline on itself, except for the fact that with many delegates there is a near certainty that some of them would leak the contents of the debates to the public and create public commotion that would render calm debate impossible. As I note in Section V, a judicious choice of location for the assembly might reduce this problem.

Condorcet's Jury Theorem might seem to offer an argument for large assemblies, assuming that the conditions for the theorem (independence, individual competence, sincere voting) are empirically validated. In his writings, however, Condorcet shows himself to be quite aware of the dangers of large assemblies. In the essay where he first states the Jury Theorem, he notes (Condorcet 1785: 166ff.) that in large assemblies most people will be only marginally competent, that is, will be able to reach the correct decision in a dichotomous choice with probability only slightly larger than one-half. As a result, he claims, the likelihood that the majority will reach the right decision may be "below the limit that has been assigned for it." The remedy, in his opinion, consists in two-stage elections, since even the marginally competent "will be sufficiently enlightened, not to state with any probability which individual among many has the greatest merit, but to choose as the most enlightened one of those who are [in my terminology, J.E.] more than marginally competent." Elsewhere, he makes a more sociological argument for an interior optimum:

> If a body is not numerous enough, it is necessarily weak, because, in the occasions where courage is needed, everyone will fear to be personally compromised. But the problem of too numerous a body is that it has a strength independent from that which it owes to its quality of a representative assembly, that is a strength based on the particular credit of its members and resulting from their union only. The numerous body can abuse this strength; it can derive from it a form of independence. There thus exists a middle-ground that it is important, and sometimes hard, to grasp. (Condorcet 1788: 366)

I do not know whether Bentham, at the time he wrote his two essays for the Estates-General, was aware of Condorcet's 1785 essay. (The reference in Bentham 1808/1843: 19 shows that he knew about it in 1808.) Internal evidence suggests, however, that he was. In his first essay, he admits that "[i]t is certain that with a larger number [of delegates] there is also a larger probability of a good rather than a bad decision" (Bentham 1788/2001: 35). Yet, he goes on to say, experience from the British Parliament suggests that "the greater the number of voters the less the weight and the value of each vote, the less its price in the eyes of the voter, and the less of an incentive he has in assuring that it conforms to the true end and even in casting it at all." In the second essay, he first states the argument for a large assembly: "With the number of members increases the chances of wisdom (*sagesse*). So many members, so many sources of enlightenment"; he then objects that "the reduction that this same cause brings in the strength of the motivation to exercise one's enlightenment offsets this advantage" (Bentham 1789: 122).

Condorcet, as noted, assumed that assembly members would be unequally competent and, like Aristotle, saw the different levels of competence as exogenously given. Bentham's twist is that he saw competence as endogenous, that is, as a function of assembly size. In large assemblies, the incentive for any given individual to inform herself is small, and the temptation to free-ride on the information gathering of others correspondingly large. This remarkable observation was rediscovered by Karotkin and Paroush (2003), who do not, however, cite Bentham's work. It provides, in my opinion, perhaps the best argument for a low upper limit on the size of the constituent assembly. As a guess, I'd say that an assembly with less than fifty members is dangerously vulnerable to strategic behavior, and one with more than a hundred dangerously vulnerable to free-riding in information gathering. The second claim must, however, be counterbalanced by the need for diversity, to be discussed shortly.

The duration of constituent assemblies is also subject to considerable variation. The Norwegian assembly of 1814 sat for five weeks, and the Assemblée Constituante for more than two years. Between these extremes we find the Federal Convention (three months), the 1948–49 German Parliamentary Council (six months), the 1848 Paris assembly (six months), the 1848–49 Frankfurt assembly (one year), and the 1988 Brazilian constitutional assembly (two years).

There are two relevant normative issues: Should the assembly be subject to a time limit? If so, what is the optimal duration? To my (limited) knowledge, there are few cases of firm and credible time limits, perhaps because constituent assemblies often ignore the constraints that upstream actors try to impose on them (Elster 1993). External events may create a pressure to finish quickly, but – like the passions they trigger (as mentioned earlier) – these can hardly be included in an institutional design. One example of a firm time limit is nevertheless offered by the 1994 interim South African constitution, which laid down that the final constitution had to be adopted within two years.

If the constituent assembly is not subject to a firm time constraint, some actors may be able to benefit from dragging their feet. Thus, in the work on the 1949 Bonn constitution, "[t]he major parties had different attitudes with regard to the time schedule of the work of the Council.... The sooner the elections took place the better for the SPD, whereas the CDU hoped to gain time until the new economic policy and the seasonal upward turn in employment might produce a shift to the right" (Merkl 1963: 96). In a situation of this kind, the more patient actor should be able to obtain a substantive concession from the impatient part in exchange for an early adoption of the document. From a normative point of view, this effect is clearly undesirable. Note, however, that bargaining of this kind may occur even with a time limit, unless the assembly is under the constraint that the constitution be adopted by time t, *and no earlier*. Yet the relevance of this observation is somewhat reduced by the general tendency in negotiations for the final agreement to be reached only under the pressure of an impending deadline. Assuming, then, that time limits will in fact be binding constraints, they ought to be part of the optimal design.

There is not much one can say on the question of the optimal duration of the assembly. If secrecy is a desideratum (as discussed later), a short-lived assembly may be necessary. A smaller assembly will usually be able to write the constitution more quickly than a large one. The Federal Convention illustrates both ideas. If the country is large and/or federally organized, more time may be needed. The issue is also related to the optimal length of the constitutional document (Section VIII). If the plan is to write a short and general constitution, it can be done more quickly; conversely, a short time limit may be a way of inducing conciseness (although we know the apology of the letter writer: "I am sorry I did not have the time to be brief").

V. THE OPTIMAL LOCATION OF THE CONSTITUENT ASSEMBLY

If the proceedings of the constituent assembly are secret, it does not matter where it meets. If, however, the debates are open to and reported in the press, or even open to visitors, the location can matter a great deal. Once individuals with strong interests in one or another outcome of the process know which solutions seem to be emerging, they may try to influence the votes by bribes or threats. The constituent assemblies in Versailles/Paris (1789), Paris (1848), and Frankfurt (1848) show that this is not simply an abstract possibility, but a real and sometimes decisive factor in shaping the outcome. Under such circumstances, "the coercion-less force of the better argument" (Habermas) may not stand much of a chance. To reduce the danger of the problem occurring, one may choose to locate the assembly in a small town remote from any major urban agglomerations. Thus, in 1919 the Germans deliberately chose to hold the constituent assembly in Weimar, well away from the street rioting in Berlin. During the 2007–2008 constituent process in Ecuador, framers were sequestered in a small village. They could leave it, but visitors needed a special permit, which was hard to get, to pass the police roadblocks (Adam Przeworski, personal communication).

In the discussions leading up to the Estates-General, the danger was only dimly understood. In 1788 there were several options on the table: Paris, Versailles at 13 km from Paris, or a more distant town such as Soissons at 100 km or Compiègne at 80 km (Kessel 1969: 74–76; Egret 1975: 249–50). Among these options, the queen and the *garde des sceaux* (minister of justice), Barentin, preferred the more distant locations because they feared the influence of the Parisian agitators on the deliberations of the assembly. The king's principal minister, Necker, preferred Paris because he thought the proximity to the capital market in Paris would have a moderating influence on the assembly. Officials of the court advised against leaving Versailles, because of the extra costs involved in moving the 15,000 to 16,000 members of the royal retinue (Brette 1902: 299). The king decided in favor of Versailles because he did not want his hunting habits disrupted. After July 14, however, it became impossible to ignore the dangerous presence of Paris. In September, an ill-assorted deputation of moderates and royalists, with the approval of Necker and the foreign minister, Montmorin, proposed the transfer of the assembly to Compiègne or Soissons. The moderates wanted to remove the assembly from the threat of popular interference, and the royalists to remove the protection against military threats that Paris had just shown it could offer (Mathiez 1898: 272). When the ministers put the proposal to the king, he refused. He was drowsy after hunting and slept through most of the council.

As implied by the last comment on the motives of the royalists, popular crowds are not the only threat to an assembly: troops can be equally dangerous. The events leading up to July 14 underline the importance of this fact. As Sieyes reminded the Assembly on July 8, the provincial estates in Brittany did not deliberate if there were troops within 40 km. The assembly had not forgotten the lessons from July 13–14 (and from the events on October 5–6) when it laid down, in the constitution of September 3, 1791, that "[t]he executive power [i.e., the king] cannot cause any body of troops to pass or sojourn within thirty thousand toises [60 km] of the legislative body, except upon its requisition or its authorization." As we see, the "separation of powers" can have a literal physical meaning as well as its usual institutional meaning.

VI. THE OPTIMAL MODE OF ELECTION TO THE CONSTITUENT ASSEMBLY

The optimal mode of election to any assembly depends on the task the assembly has to perform. In electing a legislature that is to vote a government into power, a system that tends to give a clear-cut majority to one party is preferable to one that will produce many small parties. This criterion of "governability" favors majority voting or proportional voting with a high threshold. In electing a constituent assembly, a system that tends to reflect, in miniature, the diversity of the nation is preferable to one that risks excluding significant minorities. This criterion of "representativeness" favors proportional voting with a low threshold or no threshold. As already briefly noted, a mixed assembly that is to perform both tasks may therefore fail in one of them. Whereas governability does not require an extensive suffrage, representativeness obviously does.

The argument for representativeness rests on epistemic rather than on normative grounds. It is not a question of the individual's right to influence the choice of delegates, but of the community's need for the individual's knowledge. In the words of Barnave (AP 29: 366), voting is a *function*, not a right.

The delegates do not represent interest, but the knowledge of interest (where the shoe pinches). Between them, they might even have knowledge of how to satisfy those interests (how to make better shoes). At the Federal Convention, where the delegates had experiences with twelve very different state political systems, they could *pool solution proposals* with, in some cases, remarkable results. By contrast, because of the poor representation of the backcountry at the Convention (according to McGuire 2003: 69, the average distance from the place of residence to navigable water was 16 miles with a maximum of 200), the framers may not have felt all the places where the shoe pinched (see also McDonald 1992: 37).

In the contemporary French assembly, the utter lack of practical political experience of most delegates made them inept as cobblers. They could, nevertheless, tell where the shoe pinched. In 1789 Louis XVI (or his minister) devised electoral rules that made the parish priests rather than the bishops the main representatives of the clergy to the Estates-General. He did so, he asserted in the electoral rules announced on January 24, 1789, because "the good and useful pastors, who assist the people in their needs on a close and daily basis . . . know their sufferings and apprehensions most intimately" (AP 1: 544). The lower clergy "thus were to represent the peasantry as well as the clerical assemblies that had elected them" (Necheles 1974: 427). We may note in passing that the king's enlightened choice also became his undoing when, in May–June 1789, the priests allied themselves with the third estate to undermine the estate system itself and ultimately the royal power.

Along (somewhat) similar lines, the "economic interpretation" of the American constitution proposed by Charles Beard does not amount, as is often said, to a claim that the delegates to the Federal Convention were influenced, in casting their votes, by their personal economic interests. Rather the question was: "Did they represent distinct groups whose economic interests they understood and felt in concrete, definite form through their own personal experience with identical property rights, or were they working merely under the guidance of abstract principles of political science?" (Beard 1986: 73). In opting for the former answer, he looked to the qualitative experience of the framers rather than to their quantitative interest. "That is, he makes no distinction between, say, a planter who had land of $20,000 and incidentally a few dollars in securities, and a financier who had invested most of his resources in securities. Each is classified as a security older, and no weight is attached to the relative importance of the securities of each. This practice is consistent with Beard's explicit concentration on the significance of holdings of various forms of property as giving the delegates experience with the tribulations of each, rather than as inspiring them to act in certain ways out of self-interest" (McDonald 1992: 12–13).

This argument, to be sure, is not quite the same as the one I made with regard to Louis XVI. It is one thing to justify an electoral system ex ante by its knowledge-representing (rather than interest-aggregating) effects; it is another to explain the adopted document by the knowledge (rather than the interests) of the delegates. I am only making the point that in the normative perspective of optimal design, the composition of the delegations at the Federal Convention may have served a desirable epistemic function. In the Assemblée Constituante, with two-thirds of the third estate being magistrates and lawyers "working merely under the guidance of abstract principles of political science," lack of practical economic experience was a severe handicap.

Let me cite two other episodes in which the conveners of a constituent assembly opted, to their detriment, for representativeness rather than governability. For the election of delegates to the 1919 Weimar assembly, the provisional Socialist government under the leadership of Friedrich Ebert adopted proportional voting together with female suffrage, consistent with long-standing positions of the Social Democratic Party. These two features "prevented the Majority [section of the] Socialists from gaining an absolute majority in the national assembly" (Huber 1978: 1067). It is not clear whether the Socialist leaders would have been able to impose majority voting or whether they predicted the likely outcome of the law. Be this as it may, the outcome was disastrous. "While it is clearly unjust to lay the parliamentary defeat of the Republic at the feet of the Social Democrats alone, the *failure of the Reichstag's largest party to secure its own electoral self-interest* between 1918 and 1928 was indisputably a major contribution to the comprehensiveness of that defeat" (Hodge 1987: 186–87; my emphasis).

In 1990 Vaclav Havel imposed a similarly *counter-interested* proportional system to allow a place for his former Communist enemies in the constituent assembly (Elster 1995a). One of Havel's close associates told me in 1994 that "this decision will be seen either as the glory or the weakness of the November [1989] revolution: we were winners that accepted a degree of self-limitation." Like Louis XVI and the German Socialists before him, Havel paid a high price for his impartiality. The Communists, notably the deputies from Slovakia, ended up as constitution wreckers rather than as constitution makers.

Similar arguments apply to the extent of the suffrage. There is a tendency for a wider suffrage in electing deputies to conventions than in choosing representatives to legislatures (for the American state constitutions, see Hoar 1917: 203–207). In the elections to the 1780 constituent legislature in Massachusetts (as discussed earlier), the general court (lower house) "enfranchised all free adult male town inhabitants for the duration of the constitution-making process" (Kruman 1997: 30–31). The enfranchisement held from the election of delegates to a constituent legislature up to (not, as we shall see shortly, beyond) the ratification of the document. The act for the holding of the Indiana convention in 1918 temporarily extended the vote to women for the ratification (Hoar 1917: 205).

Where delegates to a constituent assembly have been elected by universal or wide suffrage, the assembly may nevertheless write a more restricted suffrage into the constitution. The Massachusetts charter that governed elections prior to the adoption of the 1780 constitution limited suffrage to those who had "an estate of freehold in land . . . to the value of 40 shillings per Annu . . . or other estate to the value of forty pounds sterling." In the election to the convention that succeeded the unsuccessful constituent legislature, all freemen could vote and, later, participate in the ratification. The constitution adopted by the convention, however, increased the property qualifications by 50 percent compared with the charter (Hoar 1917: 206).

There is indeed nothing intrinsically contradictory in a convention elected by universal suffrage adopting a limited suffrage for future legislatures. For an analogy, consider the outcome when revisions in the Danish constitution were submitted to referendum in 1953. Each voter cast two votes, one for or against the proposed constitution and one for a change in the voting age. The alternatives for the second vote were to lower the age from 25 to 23 or to 21 years. In the first vote, only citizens older than 25 could cast a vote. In the second, everybody older than 21 could vote. The result of the referendum was that the extended extraordinary electorate refused a corresponding extension of the ordinary electorate. A majority of the voters older than 21 decided to lower the voting age from 25 to 23 rather than to 21. "We the people" may collectively decide that only some of "us" shall be entrusted with day-to-day political decisions. Conversely, the 1830 Virginia constitution was "ratified in an election open to all who were prospectively enfranchised by it" (Pole 1966: 332).

VII. SECRECY VERSUS PUBLICITY

To discuss whether secrecy of the proceedings is desirable, one has to assume that it is feasible. As mentioned earlier, it may not be possible to keep proceedings secret if the assembly is large. Also, the longer the duration of the assembly, the harder it will be to keep secrecy. There may, of course, be trade-offs among these factors. One may, for instance, think that secrecy is so important that one has to sacrifice representativeness if the latter would lead to an unmanageably large assembly. I do not claim, however, to be able to address this issue. I shall try only to address arguments for and against the use of closed proceedings, assuming that other factors are constant.

Judge Brandeis said that "[s]unlight is the best disinfectant, and electric light the most efficient policeman." Bentham (1999: 29) wrote, "The greater the number of temptations to which the exercise of political power is exposed, the more necessary is it to give to those who possess it, the most powerful reasons to resist it. But there is no reason more constant and more universal than the superintendence of the public." In 1781 Necker noted in a memorandum on the provincial assemblies to the king that "the publicity of the debates will force honesty" (Castaldo 1989: 304). These are strong arguments that remain valid in many contexts. With regard to ordinary legislatures, at least, they appear self-evident today. They reflect what J. R. Pole (1966: 140) calls a shift from "the politics of trust" to "the politics of vigilance." Bentham (1999: 37), too, is explicit on this point: "Is it objected against the régime of publicity that it is a system of *distrust*? This is true, and every good political institution is founded upon that base." Political constitutions, in particular, may be viewed as systems of organized distrust (Elster 2007a: 434–39).

It does not follow, however, that the process of *establishing* the constitution ought to be "founded upon that base." Let me begin by making a minor point. Among the many arguments for publicity made by Bentham, one concerns the issue of accountability: "In an assembly elected by the people, and renewed from time to time, publicity is absolutely necessary to enable the electors to act from knowledge. For what purpose renew the assembly, if the people are always obliged to choose from among men of whom they know nothing?" (Bentham 1999: 33). This argument does not apply to constituent assemblies, which meet only once. As noted earlier, the ax of reelection that might be applied to a constituent legislature is not needed if the people can ratify the constitution.

To go into more central matters, we first need to spell out the possible forms that publicity may take. The following categories refer mainly to what happens during the tenure of the assembly, although we shall see later that information divulged at later times may also constitute an issue:

- Access of visitors to the galleries of the assembly
- Publication of speeches by the delegates
- Publication of the names of delegates who voted for and against a given proposal
- Publication of the number of delegates who voted for and against a given proposal

Again, the Federal Convention and the Assemblée Constituante stand at opposite extremes. In the former there were no visitors; the speeches were first published (in Madison's abridged versions) more than fifty years after the event; and we do not know how individual delegates voted. (We do not know, however, how the state delegations voted on each of the 569 roll call votes.) In the latter, there were large crowds in the galleries, which could accommodate more than a thousand visitors (Versailles) or more than five hundred (Paris). The speeches were widely reported and often published. Although the names of delegates who voted for and against a given proposal were not published in the technical sense of appearing in print, the fact that any member could ask for roll call vote on any issue (instead of the usual method of voting by standing and sitting) implied that nobody could count on his vote going unnoticed. Although roll call votes obviously established the size of the majority and the minority, these numbers did not appear in print, due to the Rousseauist ideology according to which the function of the vote was to discover the general will (Castaldo 1989: 273).

As the assemblies in Paris (1789–91 and 1848) and Frankfurt (1848) demonstrate with particular force, the first and the third form of publicity may interfere seriously with the quality of the debates and of the decisions. Vanity can prevent people from changing their mind as a result of argument, and fear can prevent them from speaking (and voting) their mind in the first place.

On the first point, we may cite what Madison is reported to have said many years after the Federal Convention: "[H]ad the members committed themselves publicly at first, they would have afterwards supposed consistency required them to maintain their ground, whereas by secret discussion no man felt himself obliged to retain his opinions any longer than he was satisfied of their propriety and truth, and was open to the force of argument. Mr. Madison thinks no constitution would ever have been adopted by the convention had the debates been public" (Farrand 1966: vol. 3, 479). Conversely, the vanity of the French framers and notably their desire for popularity made for cant and grandstanding on many issues. On the second point, the presence of an audience that can note the names of delegates who vote against popular proposals may, in a heated situation, have a chilling effect. The defeat of bicameralism and of the executive veto in Paris (September 1789) was due partly to the fact that many delegates feared for their lives if they voted in favor of these proposals (Egret 1950).

The principal argument in favor of publicity is that it prevents delegates from striking self-interested bargains and constrains them to argue for their proposals in terms of the public good. In an early development of this idea (Elster 1986: 113), I claimed that by virtue of being forced to argue in terms of the common good "one will end up having the preferences that initially one was faking." Today, I would claim only that hypocrisy has a certain *civilizing force* in that it takes the most self-serving proposals off the agenda. Be this as it may (I'm still not sure), it seems clear that publicity (or transparence) prevents the kind of bargaining in "smoke-filled backrooms" that have repeatedly been the bane of Canadian constitution making (Russell 1993: 134–45, 191, 219–27).

I have argued elsewhere (Elster 1995b) that whereas secrecy tends to induce bargaining and publicity to induce arguing, secrecy also improves the quality of whatever arguing takes place behind closed doors. The net impact of the choice of one or the other mode of decision making on the quality of the decisions seems, therefore, to be indeterminate. In general, this seems right. In the particular case of constitution making, however, the dangers of secrecy may be reduced to the extent that the framers limit themselves to general institutional issues *on which self-interest has no purchase*. According to Calvin Jillson (1988: 16), the American framers were generally guided by their interest except when it came to such matters as unicameralism versus bicameralism and life tenure versus fixed-term tenure for judges or for the executive. "This was not because the constitution-makers disregarded their personal interests in favor of broader social interests when considering questions at the 'higher' level of constitutional choice, but because they were unlikely to see what difference choices concerning such broad structural questions would make to them as individuals, or to their states and region."

At the Federal Convention, there were plenty of issues at the "lower" constitutional level at which interest does have a purchase. The constitutional clauses favoring creditors over debtors, small states over large states, and the prohibition of export duties certainly reflect interest. In any constitution-making setting, there will obviously be issues of this kind. If we compare constituent assemblies with ordinary legislatures, however, we will see that the latter has a much stronger focus on interest-relevant issues and therefore a much greater need for the disinfectant of publicity.

Moreover, the agenda of the framers is not *given*, but to some extent up to them. They can choose to write a short and concise constitution that focuses on broad principles of institutional design and avoids the kind of absurdly detailed clauses that we find, for example, in the Brazilian constitution. In other words, a joint regime of secrecy and brevity might limit the impact of interest and enhance the role of reason.

VIII. THE INTERNAL ORGANIZATION OF THE ASSEMBLY

The issue of secrecy versus publicity can be restated as the issue of the optimal combination of secrecy and publicity. In this section, I discuss combinations within the assembly as well. In the next section, I consider the combination of secrecy and publicity at the national level. In the present section, I also consider some other aspects of the internal organization of the assembly. Should it be unicameral or bicameral? How are debates to be organized? Should decisions be taken by simple or by qualified majority voting? Ought votes to be secret or public?

Beginning with the Assemblée Constituante, many assemblies have been based on a division of labor between closed committees and plenary debates that are open to the public. In modern assemblies, this is invariably the case. Even if the members of the committee should be tempted to strike a deal based on their private interests, they are constrained by the fact that the terms of the bargain will have to be defended in public-interest terms before the plenary assembly. In technical matters, the assembly may show some deference to the committee, provided that this constraint is satisfied. In broader matters of policy – should elections be held every three, every four, or every five years? – there is no reason to expect such deference. A populist politician who is the focus of media attention might successfully propose frequent elections and severe term limits on plausible-sounding public-interest grounds (there are many such). Hence, my tentative preference would be for a system combining closed committees and *closed* plenary sessions.

Unicameralism versus bicameralism is often an issue on the agenda of a constituent assembly. In addition, one may ask whether the assembly itself should have one or two houses. In the Assemblée Constituante, Clermont-Tonnerre argued that bicameralism had its place in the constitution but not in the constituent assembly: "To create everything, a single Chamber with its irresistible force and energy is needed. *The three-headed hydra* [king, first chamber, and second chamber] would never have allowed the making of a constitution; but all that must change in the future: more is needed to conserve than to establish; and haste must be avoided in a legislative body" (AP 8: 574).

We note that of the many possible arguments for bicameralism, he singles out the cooling-down and slowing-down effect of the system.

One might ask, however, whether haste cannot also be a problem for constituent assemblies. The history of the Assemblée Constituante shows in fact that even at the constitution-making stage there may be some justification for a divided assembly. According to the *règlement* of the assembly, "Any proposal in legislative or constitutional matters must be brought to discussion on three different days." In the rush of decisions on the night of August 4, however, the assembly ignored this self-imposed constraint. In a letter to his constituency, the Comte d'Antraigues complained that in order to "engage the . . . assembly to consent to all the decrees of August 4 one had to . . . destroy the wisest rules of the assembly itself, which put a brake on hasty deliberations" (Kessel: 1969: 127). The Comte de Roys wrote to his constituency in similar terms (Kessel 1969: 200). Having tried to stem the tide on August 4, the Marquis de Foucauld also referred to the violation of the rules in a speech on August 6 (Kessel 1969: 200). In response, those who wanted immediate action said that "an élan of patriotism does not need three days" and "since one cannot vary in such sentiments, the three days would be a pointless waste of time" (*Courrier de Provence* 24).

The episode illustrates a general phenomenon: one who can bind can also unbind. Hence, "the legislative . . . , in order to its being restrained, should absolutely be divided. For, whatever laws it can make to restrain itself, they never can be, relatively to it, any thing more than simple resolutions: as those bars which it might erect to stop its own motions must then be within it, and rest upon it, they can be no bars" (De Lolme 1807: 219). Étienne Dumont makes the same point in a passage he inserted into Bentham's *Political Tactics*: "[A] single assembly may have the best rules, and disregard them when it pleases. Experience proves that it is easy to set them aside; and urgency of circumstances always furnish a ready pretext, and a popular pretext, for doing what the dominant party desires. If there are two assemblies, the forms will be observed; because if one violate them, it affords a legitimate reason to the other for rejection of everything presented to it after such suspicious innovation" (Bentham 1999: 26).

Although De Lolme and Dumont had in mind the ordinary legislative process, the episode of the night of August 4, 1789, shows that their argument applies equally to a constituent assembly. The question is whether it applies to the ideal assembly I am trying to construct in this essay. It is not obvious to me that it does. The "urgency of circumstances" that might provide a "popular pretext" for the assembly to ignore its self-imposed constraints did indeed obtain on the night of August 4, but only by virtue of the extremely intense interaction among the assembly, the audience, and Paris. An assembly working behind closed doors, insulated from strong and urgency-generating emotions, would have less need for protection against impulsiveness.

The question of how to organize the debates in the assembly presupposes that the delegates do not come with bound mandates. Although some delegates at the Federal Convention, in the Assemblée Constituante, and in the Frankfurt assembly claimed to be bound by the instructions from their constituencies, the actual proceedings respected Burke's principle that a national assembly "is not a *congress* of ambassadors from different and hostile interests [but] a deliberative assembly of *one* nation, with *one* interest, that of the whole."

Once this principle has been established, the optimal rules of debate for a constituent assembly would seem to be more or less the same as for any other assembly. To ensure the quality of the debates, one might (following de Staël 2000: 179) ban the use of speaking from manuscripts. As in the partly similar case of voting, the president of the assembly should recognize speakers on the principle that speaking is a function, not an individual right (Jouvenel 1961). The tenor of the actual debates will no doubt be different from those in ordinary legislatures, since (assuming secrecy) the delegates will speak only to one another and not to their audience or their constituency.

By contrast, it is arguable that *voting* in a constituent assembly ought to proceed differently from voting in an ordinary legislature. Consider first the question of ordinary majority voting versus supermajority voting. It might seem tempting to argue that by virtue of the importance of the issues, decisions in a constituent assembly ought to be taken by a qualified majority. If amendments to the constitution require supermajorities, as they very often do, should not the same requirement a fortiori be imposed on the adoption of the constitution itself? On reflection, however, only simple majority will do. Qualified majorities are possible only when there is a status quo that will remain in place if a given proposal does not achieve the requisite majority, but this condition cannot obtain in a constituent assembly that starts from tabula rasa. The relevant comparison is to voting the annual budget, not to amending the constitution. It may seem paradoxical – and is in some ways undesirable – that an assembly should be able to impose by simple majority a law that later generations can undo only with a qualified majority. A small majority may be able to "lock in" its preferences and exercise a de facto dictatorship over the future. Yet the overall effect of the alternative – making the constitution amendable by simple majority – is likely to be worse.

Consider next the issue of public versus secret voting in the assembly. In an ordinary legislature, votes are casts in public so that the electorate can hold their representatives accountable. As a by-product, logrolling is made possible. If one decides that vote trading is undesirable on normative grounds (as described earlier), one can block that option simply by enforcing the secret ballot. Under conditions of secret voting, nobody can make a credible promise to vote this way or that. This question is independent of the issue of the secrecy or publicity of debates. In theory, one might envisage any of the four possible combinations of public or secret debates and votes. If the debates are public, perhaps because the need for diversity requires a large assembly that will not be able to maintain secrecy, one might in fact impose secret voting both to eliminate interest-based logrolling and to make the delegates unafraid of voting the wrong way on popular proposals. Note how, in the preceding sentence, size, diversity, publicity, secrecy, interest, and passion interact in a way that illustrates the interlocking nature of the elements of the optimal assembly.

IX. IS THE OPTIMAL PROCESS HOURGLASS-SHAPED?

At the beginning of the preceding section I mentioned how secrecy and publicity may be combined with the constituent assembly. Here I discuss how they may be combined at the broader national level. The idea is that the closed assembly may be supplemented by upstream and downstream public consultations, generating an overall "hourglass-shaped" procedure (Russell 1993: 191).

In the process of electing delegates to the assembly, one may also create a national debate over the main constitutional issues. In 1789 the French people expressed their grievances and proposed remedies for them in the *cahiers de doléances*, which take up four thousand double-column small-print pages of the *Archives Parlementaires*. Before the adoption of the South African constitution in 1996, the constituent assembly invited suggestions from the citizens and received 1.2 million responses. In neither case, however, is there any evidence that the opinions expressed in this way made much of a difference to the constitution that was finally adopted. The most influential upstream process is probably the debates that take place among the candidates to the assembly rather than direct citizen involvement.

The downstream process of ratification by the citizens, following a national debate, is more important. Generally speaking, one would think that most constitutions submitted to referendum would be approved, simply because members of the assembly will be sufficiently rational and well informed to anticipate the views of the electorate. The debates at the Federal Convention are very revealing in this respect, with their constant references to what might or might not be approved by the ratifying conventions. Perhaps because they anticipated that these conventions would be elected with a broad suffrage (as discussed earlier), the framers proposed a constitution that was more democratic than the one they would have chosen in the absence of ratification (Amar 2005: 279–80). Moreover, the anticipation of ratification probably caused the framers to *internalize each other's concerns*. A delegate from state A might vote for a proposal to which he was opposed because the ratifying convention in state B might otherwise reject the document, with the possible consequence that the required number of nine ratifying states would not be reached. In the process of arguing and bargaining at the Convention, the *warning of nonratification* was probably as effective as the *threat of leaving the convention*.

The ratification of the U.S. constitution was a very close affair. It could easily have derailed. In quite a few cases, proposed subnational, national, or international constitutions have in fact been turned down by the ratifiers. The Australian constitution of 1898 had to be revised after it failed a referendum in New South Wales. In France in 1946, voters turned down the first proposal for a new constitution, probably because it was perceived to give too much power to a parliament that might be dominated by the Communists. In 1992 a proposed constitution for Canada was turned down by voters in Quebec because they thought it gave too little to Quebec, and by voters in other provinces because they thought it gave too many concessions to Quebec. In 1994 Albanian voters turned down a proposed constitution. In 2005 a new constitution was voted down in Kenya. And the proposed EU constitution was, of course, turned down by voters in France and Holland (for multiple reasons). At the subnational level, Lenowitz (2007) shows that among the twelve constitutions submitted by conventions (not mixed assemblies) to referendum in the American states in the 1960s and 1970s, seven were rejected, in two cases by a high margin (4:1 in Rhode Island and 3:1 in New York State). These are striking and puzzling findings, which are hard to reconcile with "the law of anticipated reactions."

In some of these cases (Canada, New York State), the failures seem to have reflected an aversion of the electorate to the bargaining style of constitution making. If politicians go about constitution making in the mode of politics as usual, the voters will punish them. Moreover, when politicians are in that mode, they may be unable to perceive the difference. In this perspective, the downstream ratification process serves as a corrective device when politicians are unable to adopt a normatively proper constitutional framework.

X. SUMMARY

In this essay I have tried to argue that the task of constitution making implies a number of normative demands that can, to some extent at least, be resolved by institutional design.

Minimizing the Role of Interest. To exclude logrolling, bargaining, and strategic voting, assuming these to be undesirable, the assembly should not be too small. To exclude logrolling, one might also impose secret voting. Bound mandates should be excluded. The assembly should focus on issues of broad constitutional design, with regard to which individual or group interests are neutral. To prevent the more patient parties from gaining an unfair bargaining advantage, the assembly should work under a time limit. To exclude a self-enhancing "legislature-centric" bias, the assembly should not at the same time serve as an ordinary legislature.

Minimizing the Role of Passion. To exclude audience pressure that might bring delegates under the sway of emotion (vanity or fear), the assembly should debate in secret or, alternatively, vote in secret. An isolated location of the assembly may serve the same end. To prevent the assembly from giving in to impulses, a bicameral organization might or might not be needed.

Maximizing Epistemic Quality. (1) Optimal information gathering: Elections to the assembly should be organized to ensure diversity and representativeness. The idea – close to the eighteenth-century notion of "virtual representation" – is to have many epistemic perspectives and a variety of experiences represented, not to have each of them represented in proportion to its numerical importance in the electorate. (2) Optimal information processing: To prevent free-riding on the information of others, the assembly should not be too large. The rules of debating should favor exchanges rather than prepared speeches. Speaking should be viewed as a function serving the needs of the assembly, not as an individual right.

References

Amar, A. (2005), *America's Constitution*, New York: Random House.

AP (*Archives Parlementaires*), Ser. I: 1787–99, Paris, 1875–88.

Beard, C. (1986), *An Economic Interpretation of the Constitution of the United States*, New York: Free Press.

Bentham, J. (1788/2001), "Lettre d'un Anglois à M. le C. de M. sur l'objet soumis aux notables de 1788," in Bentham, *Rights, Representation and Reform*, Oxford University Press.

(1789/2001), "Considérations d'un Anglois sur la composition des Etats-Généraux y compris réponses aux questions proposées aux notables," in Bentham, *Rights, Representation and Reform*, Oxford University Press.

(1808/1843), "Scotch reform," in J. Bowring (ed.), *The Works of Jeremy Bentham*, vol. 5, Edinburgh: William Tait.

(1999), *Political Tactics*, Oxford University Press.

Brette, A. (1902), *Histoire des édifices où ont siégé les assemblées parlementaires de la Révolution Française*, Paris: Imprimerie Nationale.

Bryce, J. (1905), *Constitutions*, Oxford University Press.

Castaldo, A. (1989), *Les méthodes de travail de la constituante*, Paris: Presses Universitaires de France.

Condorcet, Marquis de (1785/1986), "Essai sur la constitution et les fonctions des assemblées provinciales," in Condorcet, *Sur les elections*, Paris: Fayard.

(1788), "Essai sur l'application de l'analyse à la probabilité des decision rendues à la pluralité des voix," in Condorcet, *Sur les elections*, Paris: Fayard.

De Lolme, J. L. (1807), *The Constitution of England*, London.

Dowding, K., and van Hees, M. (2007), "In praise of manipulation," *British Journal of Political Science* 38: 1–15.

Egret, J. (1950), *La révolution des notables*, Paris: Armand Colin.

(1975), *Necker, Ministre de Louis XVI*, Paris: Champion.

Elster, J. (1986), "The market and the forum," in J. Elster and A. Hylland (eds.), *Foundations of Social Choice Theory*, 103–32, Cambridge University Press.

(1993), "Constitutional bootstrapping in Paris and Philadelphia," *Cardozo Law Review* 14: 549–76.

(1995a), "Transition, constitution-making and separation in Czechoslovakia," *Archives Européennes de Sociologie* 36: 105–34.

(1995b), "Strategic uses of argument," in K. Arrow et al. (eds.), *Barriers to the Negotiated Resolution of Conflict*, 236–57, New York: Norton.

(1999), *Alchemies of the Mind*, Cambridge University Press.

(2000), "Arguing and bargaining in two constituent assemblies," *University of Pennsylvania Journal of Constitutional Law* 2: 345ff.

(2006), *Raison et raisons*, Paris: Fayard.

(2007a), *Explaining Social Behavior*, Cambridge University Press.

(2007b), "The night of August 4 1789: A study of social interaction in collective decision-making," *Revue Européenne des Sciences Sociales* 45: 71–94.

Farrand, M., ed. (1966), *Records of the Federal Convention*, New Haven, CT: Yale University Press.

Hoar, R. S. (1917), *Constitutional Conventions*, Boston: Little, Brown.

Hodge, C. (1987), "Three ways to lose a republic: The electoral politics of the Weimar SPD," *European History* 17: 165–93.

Huber, E. R. (1978), *Deutsche Verfassungsgeschichte seit 1789*, vol. 5, Stuttgart: Kohlhammer.

Jillson, C. (1988), *Constitution Making: Conflict and Consensus in the Federal Convention of 1787*, New York: Agathon Press.

Jouvenel, B. de (1961), "The chairman's dilemma," *American Political Science Review* 44: 368–72.

Karotkin, D., and Paroush, J. (2003), "Optimum committee size: Quality-versus-quantity dilemma," *Social Choice and Welfare* 20: 429–41.

Kessel, P. (1969), *La nuit du 4 août 1789*, Paris: Arthaud.

Kline, M.-J. (1978), *Gouverneur Morris and the New Nation, 1775–1788*, New York: Arno Press.

Kruman, M. (1997), *Between Authority and Liberty: State Constitution Making in Revolutionary America*, Chapel Hill, NC: University of North Carolina Press.

Lebègue, E. (1910), *Thouret*, Paris: Felix Alcan.

Lenowitz, J. (2007), "Rejected by the people: Failed U. S. state constitutional conventions in the 1960s and 70s," Unpublished manuscript, Department of Political Science, Columbia University.

Mathiez, A. (1898), "Étude critique sur les journées des 5 & 6 octobre 1789," *Revue Historique* 67, 241–84.

McDonald, F. (1992), *We the People: The Economic Origins of the Constitution*. New Brunswick, NJ: Transaction.

McGuire, R. (2003), *To Form a More Perfect Union*, Oxford University Press.

Merkl, P. (1963), *The Origins of the West German Republic*, Oxford University Press.

Mueller, D. (2003), *Public Choice III*, Cambridge University Press.

Necheles, R. F. (1974), "The Curés in the Estates General of 1789," *Journal of Modern History* 46: 425–44.

Pillouer, A., le (2003), *Les pouvoirs non-constituants des assemblées constituants*, Paris: Dalloz.

Pole, J. R. (1966), *The Gift of Government*, Athens: University of Georgia Press.

Rawls, J. (1999), *A Theory of Justice*, rev. ed., Harvard, MA: Cambridge University Press.

Rudenfeld. J. (2001), *Freedom and Time*, New Haven, CT: Yale University Press.

Russell, P. (1993), *Constitutional Odyssey: Can Canadians Become a Sovereign People?* rev. ed., University of Toronto Press.

Staël, Mme de (2000), *Considérations sur la Révolution Française*, Paris: Tallandier.

Stratmann. T. (1997), "Logrolling," in D. Mueller (ed.), *Perspectives on Public Choice*, 322–41, Cambridge University Press.

8

Reasons and Preferences in Medicine Evaluation Committees

Philippe Urfalino

How can collective wisdom best be fostered in collectives of the wise? This question is directly relevant for a number of commissions or committees with important decisions to make for a social group, decisions requiring that the members who participate in making them have specific competence or expertise. It is in this sense that such committees are composed of sages, "the wise." The competence of group members is the first guarantee of a high-quality group decision. But since the decisions or formal opinions of these groups are arrived at collectively, one question at least has to be asked: How can it be ensured that cooperation among several sages will culminate in a high-quality collective decision or opinion? To satisfy this requirement, two problems must be resolved: choosing a method for merging individual opinions into a single collective opinion and making sure that this method will enable the group to make good decisions.

When the entity called upon to give an opinion or make a decision is a group, there can be no certainty that all group members will reach the same opinion. The group must therefore have a decision-making rule. Given that lot drawing and delegating judgment to a single member are not relevant means of proceeding in this type of committee, there is a good chance it will use a voting procedure. Any such technique implies the expression of members' opinions and some means of counting them.

But while voting allows for reaching a decision collectively by aggregating individual opinions, it does not guarantee the quality of the decision made. Voting, then, raises concerns that are probably as old as the practice. How can it be guaranteed that the decision that results from voting is a good one? What relation obtains between numbers and reason? These questions are particularly relevant for the committees of sages that concern us here: their collective decisions or recommendations have to be justified by argumentation. I will call

Warm thanks to Jon Elster, Bernard Manin, Stéphanie Novak, and Gudrun Urfalino for their comments on an earlier version of this text; also to Amy Jacobs for the English translation.

such expert committees "the areopagus."[1] Because the areopagus has to reach a collective decision, it has to attend to the number of members whose opinions converge toward a single option. But because it also has to produce arguments to justify the decision it makes, it cannot settle for numbers only. The areopagus is therefore subject to a difficulty that can be expressed by paraphrasing a comment from Pliny the Younger often cited in critical discussions of voting (*Letters*, II, 12): How can votes be simultaneously counted and weighed?

The Catholic Church was confronted with this problem throughout the Middle Ages when it came to appointing monastery heads, bishops, as well as the pope. The Church developed a whole series of solutions, all of which involved a compromise between wisdom and numbers, between what were called the *sanior pars* and the *maior pars*: the sounder part and the greater part.

Here I present two very different examples of contemporary means of reaching a compromise between *sanior pars* and *maior pars*. The examples are taken from the area of medicine evaluation. I studied committees called upon to present opinions either on the value of proposed medicinal remedies – the committees determine if and under what conditions a molecule can acquire the official status of medicine and be put on the market – or, for molecules already on the market, on whether they should be withdrawn or whether changes should be made regarding the conditions for prescribing them. I discuss two such bodies: France's drug approval committee and the advisory committees appointed by the United States Food and Drug Administration (FDA).

The presentation is mainly descriptive; the point is to see how the problem of the quality of the collective decisions made by expert bodies whose opinions have major implications for public health is conceived and handled in these two contrasting cases. In the first section, I describe the characteristics of what I have called the areopagus. In the second, I present a few of the methods invented by the Catholic Church during the Middle Ages and the lessons they convey. In the third, I examine the French drug approval committee, whose particular decision-making rule may be defined as reaching decisions by exhausting objections. In the fourth, I discuss the use of public balloting by the advisory committees of the drug section of the FDA. Finally, in the fifth section, I demonstrate how the decision-making rules used respectively in the two contemporary expert committees reflect the main characteristics of the medieval combination of *sanior pars* and *maior pars*.

I. WHAT IS AN AREOPAGUS?

By the term "areopagus," I mean a specific class of collective decision-making situations that I will try to isolate bit by bit and through iteration in a combined,

[1] The term "areopagus" comes from the "council of the Areopagus," a major institution of Athenian democracy. Here, however, I am using it in the somewhat vaguer sense it acquired later of a "council of sages or eminent personalities." This allows me to avoid using a more specific or technical term and therefore to refer to constitutional courts as well as technical and scientific committees.

detailed examination and comparison of empirical cases. I refer in particular to constitutional courts and drug approval committees – my most direct knowledge is of the second – but I hope the characteristics I have identified will prove applicable to other committees as well. Those characteristics are as follows:

1. An areopagus is a group that deliberates in order to make decisions (or to present opinions to help other authorities make decisions) that will concern a larger group, in some cases the entire population of a given country.

2. Members of an areopagus are appointed rather than elected. They are chosen for their competence in the field of the decision aimed for and recognized for their knowledge related to this field.

3. Members are supposed to be independent. The general understanding is that the appointment process, the conditions under which the areopagus acts, and even in some cases members' earlier professional trajectory will ensure that they have a sufficient degree of independence when it comes to using their expertise within that body. Furthermore, they are not supposed to have any personal or professional vested interests in the matters they handle.

4. Areopagus decisions are partially predefined by the nature of the institution in which they are inscribed. In this the areopagus is different from political assemblies, whose decisions may affect all components and dimensions of a political entity's social life; areopagus decisions concern only certain components or dimensions of social life. The terms of those decisions may be strictly formatted. A constitutional court determines whether or not this or that part of a law complies with the constitution. An expert committee in a health agency does or does not grant its approval with extremely detailed specifications, including the health problem(s) targeted by the drug, dosage, length of treatment, type of prescribing physician, and so on. While areopagus decisions can have a wide impact, the formulation of the decisions follows a strict format.

5. The collective work of the areopagus bears on both the decision itself and the arguments advanced to support and justify that decision. The areopagus members are called upon to formulate the reasons that a decision appeared to be right or necessary. As a consequence, the decision has to have the status of the conclusion of a line of reasoning. The relative impact of reasons and the decision varies by case:
   - At a maximum, the line(s) of reasoning justifying the decision is/are of greater consequence than the decision itself. This is the case for courts, as the reasons cited may be used in later decision making;
   - At a minimum, the justification requirement is as important as the requirement of reaching a decision. In this case, even if the justification does not affect other decisions, it may have an impact on the body that made that decision, in the sense that it may leave it open to criticism.

6. Individual areopagus members have to practice the discipline of arguing their position in accordance with certain validity requirements, in
   particular when the last phase of the decision-making process is a
   deliberation.

Areopagus members are constrained by discipline bearing on their reasons
and arguments. Four types of demands appear to be operative in argumentative
discipline:

1. *Justification: reasons override motives.* X cannot simply say he wants
   or prefers option A to option B; he has to mention reasons Y and Z
   (Pasquino 2007).
2. *The justification has to be substantial; one reason does not suffice – an
   entire line of reasoning is required.* It was in these terms that Aristotle
   distinguished between dialectic and rhetoric. In dialectic an argument
   must hold over a long chain of reasons, whereas in rhetoric it is enough
   for the orator to say he supports X for reason Y (Bodéüs 1992). The
   requirements for substantiating justifications vary greatly from one institution to another. We can say that those requirements are especially strict
   in the areopagus.
3. *The argumentation has to be appropriate; this is specialized argumentation adapted to the matters handled by the given areopagus.* This
   requirement has a positive component: the argumentation has to follow the canons of reasoning recognized as relevant to the given issues
   and for the areopagus itself. Legal reasoning and a certain legal corpus
   are relevant for constitutional courts; areopagus work in health agencies
   requires the types of reasoning and knowledge used in evaluating the
   quality of medicines, as well as the particular rules in effect for comparatively weighting decision-making criteria. The requirement also has a
   negative component: certain types of arguments are not only irrelevant
   but prohibited because they are understood to have a damaging effect
   on collective deliberation. "Gag rules" may exist (Holmes 1988), such
   as the one in effect in the French drug approval committee's prohibition
   on mentioning medicine costs: in this committee's evaluations, health
   questions alone may be taken into account.
4. *Contextual validity: arguments have to be adapted to the case at hand.*
   It is not enough to meet requirement 3; the matter under study calls for
   certain types of arguments *only*, among all those that may legitimately
   be used in the given areopagus. In a constitutional court, the recognized
   relevance of using a given text or precedent varies greatly from case to
   case. In the evaluation of medicines, an argument bearing on the value
   of the indicator used to measure how effective a medication is ("end
   points" in clinical trials) may be particularly relevant when it comes
   to advocating or advising against marketing that medication; in other
   cases, an argument on expected consumer behavior will be more to the
   point.

II. *SANIOR PARS* AND *MAIOR PARS*

The following analysis of some of the concepts and methods once used by the Catholic Church to resolve its collective decision-making problems should shed light on how the two modern-day medicine evaluation committees operate.

A. Counting and Weighing Votes in the Middle Ages

Throughout the Middle Ages, the matters of designating heads of monasteries, bishops, and the pope represented critical moments for the Church and its various institutions.[2] When outgoing officials were not authorized to designate their successors, as was often the case in the early Church period and in later periods, this task fell to electoral bodies whose contours were only gradually stabilized: monks of a given monastery elected their head; chapter members elected bishops; the pope was elected first by bishops, then cardinals. Disagreements as to the outcomes of these collective decision-making processes led to disputes, cases of nondecision, unfilled positions, and positions for which more than one candidate had been elected (as regularly happened in the case of popes). These situations divided the Church and exposed it to the danger of losing decision-making autonomy to other powers. In response to this danger, all sorts of dispute-resolution arrangements, rules, and interpretations were developed.

Disputes occurred and were resolved in a context strongly marked by two features:

- There was a concern to reach consensus, or at least consent; consensus was supposed to be the norm. It was only an ideal, however: although voters were thought to receive divine inspiration for making the right decision, there was not always unanimity as to what that right decision was. But an absence of unanimity was a problem only if certain voters refused to accept the victory of the candidate they had not supported. Decisions were ultimately reached – and the decision-making process concluded – more by means of consent than by the application of a clearly defined rule.[3]
- Disagreements, appeals to other bodies, and arbitration were organized in accordance with the Church's hierarchical division into statuses and institutions. In the case of disagreement, one of the parties would turn to a higher-level authority to arbitrate. Sometimes the arbitration was also contested, and the case was submitted to a third, still higher institution.

The crucial notions mobilized to resolve these conflicts were *sanior pars* and *maior pars*, the sounder part and the greater part, two ways of dividing up

---

[2] For an overview of the question, see Gaudemet (1990); for a vision of these Church practices from the standpoint of social choice theory, see McLean, Lorrey, and Colomer (2008).

[3] The consensus ideal was not exclusive to the Church; it was a political ideal in ancient Rome and throughout the Medieval West (Hurlet 2002), and it persisted to the beginning of modern political thought (Przeworski 2006).

the electoral body and enabling one party – either with the greater number or the wiser – to override the other, with the understanding that the wiser might be fewer in number. We find an expression of this in Saint Benedict's rule for how monks should designate the head of their monastery. Benedict envisioned three possible solutions: unanimous choice of the right candidate; unanimous or majority choice of a wrong candidate; a wise minority that would favor the right candidate. Curiously, he did not imagine a *majority* of voters making the *right* decision. In Benedict's judgment, if not everyone could agree on the right candidate, it was necessary to appoint "the one chosen by a part of the community, even if [those belonging to] that part are fewer in number [than the majority], as long as its judgment is wiser [than that of the majority]" (Saint Benedict, quoted by Moulin 1958a: 376–77).

The idea of simultaneously and complementarily taking both "parts" into account dates back much farther than Church history. But when using the number and weight of opinions to justify a given position during electoral conflicts, Church members fit them together with great analytic and combinatory sophistication. First, "saniority" was assessed in terms of two parameters: the quality or "merit" of voters, conceived in terms of authority, dignity, and holiness; and the quality of their votes or their "zeal," that is, the good or bad intentions governing their choices. Second, the combination of voter numbers, merit, and zeal – and in some cases an evaluation of the quality of the winning candidate (likewise in terms of merit and zeal) – made it possible to draw up a long list of types of cases[4] and determine the legitimate winner for each one or else to conclude that the case had to be submitted to a higher authority.

Despite a family resemblance, the notions of *sanior pars* and *maior pars* cannot be likened to our modern decision-making rules, understood in the limited sense of aggregation rules that allow for reaching a collective decision on the basis of individual preference distribution. (Some similarities and differences between the two are discussed later.) The two notions are not really decision-making rules strictly speaking but rather a set of principles that intervene in a system for arbitrating disputes case by case. Moreover, none of these case lists enabled those in charge to determine with absolute certainty what to do in the case of a dispute. Canon 24 of the Fourth Council of the Lateran, assembled in 1215 to determine doctrine on the point, leaves open the choice of the primary decision-making criterion: "After collation, the one elected will be the one who has obtained the consent of all, or of the majority of the chapter, or of its most qualified components" (quoted in Gaudemet 1990: 323).

Finally, we have to take into account the material means for expressing choices. Secret ballot techniques (using beans or writing the preferred candidate's name on a sheet of paper) were not used until the fifteenth century (Gaudemet 1990: 333). Before that, the dominant practice by far was public

---

[4] For several examples see Jörg Peltzer (2008), who shows the concern of Norman ecclesiastics to assemble compilations of canon law from all of Europe that could serve as conflict-resolution instruments.

voting, and this meant voters could be influenced or pressured into choosing whatever or whomever was considered the wiser option by a segment of them (Gaudemet 1990: 324; Moulin 1958b: 501; Llull 2001: 8). It is important to specify that with regard to saniority criteria and the practice of evaluating public votes, wisdom tended to be closely linked to hierarchical superiority, even if it could not be reduced to this factor.

B. The Specific Weight of Reasons, a Doubling of the Collective Decision-Making Process, and the Hierarchic Principle

With these concepts, practices, and their contexts in mind, we should be able to identify general characteristics that will be helpful in studying the contemporary areopagus. While it may seem a risky undertaking to try to link decision-making modes in effect in hierarchical societies with our societies, committed as we are to the notion that all votes are equal, opinions may legitimately be considered unequal in value in situations where the general understanding is that decisions must be founded on expertise. Justifying decisions by citing reasons implies a possible hierarchy of lines of argument; one such line can be judged better than another. Also, the skill of mobilizing appropriate reasons or arguments is likely to make acceptable the idea and practice of attributing different values to the individual participants in a collective decision-making process.

To grasp the specificity of the Church's experiences of collective decision making, it is useful to break down and identify the activities they involved, the stages in the process, and the hierarchical levels:

- The first hierarchical level and the first stage involved each voter's *vote*, that is, the succession of individually expressed opinions and preferences with regard to the candidates. The voting was oral and public. In most cases, each voter was also called upon to justify his choice.
- The second stage, also at the level of the voters, was *public observation of the results*, that is, a public statement of the number of votes each candidate had gained and how each participant voted.[5]
- This opened the way for the third stage, which once again involved the voter level: *evaluating the results*. It was at this stage that the combined use of *sanior pars* and *maior pars* came into play, bringing with it a second type of activity: weighing votes and evaluating candidates. We can summarize the results of this operation by considering two contrasting outcomes.
  1. Most of the persons perceived as "the most qualified components" have voted with the majority, and the minority agrees, for a couple of reasons (low intensity of preference, no resources for contesting the decision), to join the majority. The decision is thus confirmed, and the whole process has taken place at the first hierarchical level – the electoral body.

---

[5] The first two stages were clearly distinguished from each other in a procedure known as the *scrutinum* (see Gaudemet, 1990: 322–27). In simple public voting, however, the two stages may become indistinguishable.

2. The votes of members of the "most qualified component" are divided between the majority and minority camps, and the minority does not agree, for a couple of reasons (high intensity of preference, some resources for contesting the decision – namely the number of "qualified" persons in their group and the importance of those persons' authority or reputation), to join the majority. A dispute begins involving conflicting assessments of the quality of the voters ("merit") and their intentions ("zeal") and conflicting judgments about the candidates' "suitability."

Either the dispute gets resolved at this point, or there is a second vote, which will open up a new cycle of the process and may bring it to completion. But if the dispute is not resolved, the group submits the matter to a higher level:

• *Arbitration* is now requested from the hierarchical level immediately above the electoral body, and this leads to the fourth stage. The authority to which one or all of the parties has turned must declare one of the candidates the winner while referring in its turn to voter number and quality, voter attitude during the voting, and suitability of the competing candidates. This arbitration could also be contested, leading to an appeal to a yet higher authority, and so on all the way to the pope.

From this overview of how elections proceeded in the medieval Catholic Church, we can identify three general features:

1. As in all collective decision making, preferences are expressed and an outcome reached. But the reasons, justifications, and evaluations that individual participants put forward have specific weight alongside their votes. We can say that the expression of preferences and the numerical aggregation of preferences are constantly being "doubled" by practices of justifying votes, evaluating voter "saniority" and voter intentions, and assessing candidate "suitability."
2. Next, we see a division into two parts of the collective decision being made: to the first stage of preference expression is added an evaluation of the opinions expressed and of how they have been aggregated. Vote "weighing" remains strictly qualitative. If it were numerical, votes could be counted and weighed at the same time.[6] This first instance of division is repeated if the next-higher level is called in to arbitrate.
3. Finally, hierarchy is omnipresent: there is a hierarchy of decision-making levels, a status hierarchy, and the possible superiority of one line of argument over another.

It will be useful to keep these three characteristics in mind when we examine the two contemporary medicine evaluation committees.

---

[6] This is the case, for example, in decision making by condominium owners, where the numerical value of each vote is determined by the size of building surface the voter owns, or in decision making by a company's board of directors, where the value of each member's vote is proportional to how much of the company she owns.

C. *Sanior Pars* Sensitivity to the Clash of Interests

The *sanior pars–maior pars* combination ultimately yielded to strict numerical majority rule (either absolute or qualified). This proves that it could not stand as a *rule* for reaching collective decisions and concluding the decision-making process. The only way of ending disputes and reaching decisions was to have the dispute arbitrated by one or more higher authorities. This point brings to light – by contrast, as it were – the importance in the contemporary areopagus of members having no personal or professional interest in the matters at hand.

The *sanior pars* was overrun by the majority rule in the Church for different reasons in the case of papal elections than in other types of Church appointments. The specificity of papal elections is obviously that there is no authority above that voter level that could arbitrate between opposed camps (Colomer and McLean 1998). At the other levels, the majority rule for elections was systematically adopted only later, because it was less imperative. In fact, its use spread as it began to seem desirable to reduce the number of disputes submitted to arbitration. This is particularly clear in the mendicant orders, namely among the Dominicans, who, in the thirteenth century, were not as willing as others to allow the *sanior pars* to challenge majority numbers. Gradually secret balloting and the absolute majority rule were adopted by all orders and hierarchical levels (Gaudemet 1990; Moulin 1958b). As soon as it became clear that the higher authorities were no longer willing to arbitrate disputes, and/or as soon as a more egalitarian, decentralizing spirit began to spread among the institutions (mendicant orders were more democratic than the others), the concern to get the decision made at the voter level became uppermost. Along with this, it became more attractive to have a decision-making rule whose result could no longer be contested (except on the grounds of some voting irregularity) – that is, majority rule (Elster 2007: 326).

But the *sanior pars* idea did not "lose the contest" for decision-making rule for exclusively cognitive reasons (i.e., the wisdom of a choice is open to several competing evaluations). It lost out, above all, because there were interests at stake. Important power and career issues were involved in choosing one candidate rather than another to head a monastery or bishopric, and those decisions could have an impact on the wealth of the individuals and groups involved. Disputes around different interpretations of the "wisdom" of voters and winning candidates, and thus different evaluations of election "worthiness," were fueled at least in part by clashing interests.

These last observations lead us to the contemporary areopagus and one of its characteristics: the absence of any connection between the affairs handled and the handlers' personal or professional interests. Qualitative evaluation in these expert committees is thus not subject to the kind of turbulence that the Church encountered in its earlier history, when the clash of interests came into play. Opinions may diverge, of course, even when members do not have any vested interests and even when they practice the discipline of arguing and defending their choices. And those divergences may be sharpened by passions or the pursuit of a cause. Still, the fact that there are no personal or professional interests at stake can reasonably be assumed to allow for greater stability, on average, in the delicate exercise of conjointly counting and weighing votes.

III. MAKING DECISIONS BY EXHAUSTING OBJECTIONS: THE CASE OF THE FRENCH DRUG APPROVAL COMMITTEE

In the 1960s, Western states began creating rights and organizations that would enable them to control the quality of medications. They entrusted to government administrations and to agencies the tasks of approving or declining to approve proposed remedies for marketing, monitoring their effects as knowledge of them evolved, and restricting their use or taking them off the market altogether if deemed necessary. Agencies have to make reasoned use of available scientific data in reaching decisions and transmitting what they consider useful information to prescribers and patients. These decisions and actions must all be founded on reasons; that is, they must be supported by arguments and made in the service of public health, a certain idea of the collective good.

In this section, I describe the collective decision-making mode used by the committee in charge of drug approval in France; Section IV presents that of the American equivalent of this committee in the U.S. Food and Drug Administration.

A. Conditions for Creating the French Drug Approval Committee

The drug approval committee was created in 1978, together with a new department in the national-level administration of the French Health Ministry. The minister of health had realized that France was behind other countries – such as the United States, Great Britain, and Sweden – in the evaluation of medicines.[7]

The creation of the committee was motivated by the following observation: the administration did not have competent personnel of the sort required for the modern evaluation of medicines; it therefore had to turn to a new generation, the first generation of doctors and hospital officials with any knowledge of clinical pharmacology or the competence required for this new type of evaluation. But the health administration did not have the funds needed to hire a sufficient number of full-time experts. The solution was to create a committee made up of private physicians and research hospital doctors who in many cases headed hospital sections, were representatives of the new generation, and would work only part time and temporarily for the health administration in exchange for modest compensation. At any given time between 1978 and 2000, the

---

[7] All information on the history and functioning of the French drug approval committee is from a study based on documents, archives, and interviews. In 2000, as part of this study, Emmanuelle Bonetti conducted approximately twenty interviews of standing drug approval committee members and former members who had belonged to the committee at various periods since its creation.

committee was made up of approximately thirty members, including a chair-person, all appointed by the health administration for a three-year renewable term. Over time, there were major changes in the number of applications for drug approval and in the time required to make decisions. The average length of time for handling a drug approval application in 1990 was 600 days; by 2000 it had fallen to nearly 200 days. The number of applications went from 722 in 1991 to 1,185 in 1997. However, the committee has held its plenary sessions every two weeks since 1978.[8]

While the minister used to have the last say on drug approval (in 1993 this became the prerogative of the director of the Agence Française du Médicament (French drug agency), which in 1998 was named the Agence Française de Sécurité Sanitaire des Produits de Santé (French agency for the safety of medical products, or AFSSAPS), the drug approval committee is responsible for the final evaluation. No health administration body reassesses that committee's findings.

It should be specified that the content of committee decisions consists in more than an answer to the yes/no question "Should this medicine be approved for marketing?" Indeed, when a medication is approved, the committee has to specify what kinds of health problems it is indicated for, what types of patients, the dosages, and what information about proper use and possible side effects should be indicated on the notice that accompanies all medicines sold in France. It also has to define what kinds of doctors can legally prescribe the medicine: general practitioners, specialists, or hospitals only. If the marketing application is rejected, the committee has to explain why and in some cases specify what further studies should be done by the drug company that owns the patent before submitting its product for approval a second time. In sum, the result of the committee's deliberations is a series of decisions on all these points.

B. Rejection of Voting

The newly created committee was made up of young specialists appointed for their competence, although they had no particular authority in the medical milieu. Conversely, a doctor enjoying great medical authority, but without any particular expertise on medicines per se, was appointed to head the committee. The committee's first chair, Professor Legrain, imposed a decision-making rule that remains in effect thirty years later.

Professor Legrain set up a style of collective work that involved discussion, attentive listening, and reaching decisions by consensus rather than voting. This quest for a consensus that would reflect the opinion of the given scientific community had two defensive aspects: first, it was a response to the fear that the new arrangement might be contested by pharmaceutical firms and the medical milieu; second, collective discussion seemed the best means of collectively

---

[8] The number of committee member task forces preparing these plenary sessions has considerably increased, as has their workload; this has helped the committee reduce the time required to make decisions.

mobilizing recent knowledge and practices. The use of decision making by consensus, the extensive use of experts from outside the health administration, and the fact that the committee was granted relatively full decision-making power constitute original features of the French drug approval. And the fact that that decision-making mode, characterized by the quest for consensus, has been made permanent suggests the need for a careful definition.

What emerges from the statements collected by interviews is that a decision has been made when a consensus is reached, that is, when everyone shares the same view of the decisions to be made. With rare exceptions, reaching decisions by voting is rejected.[9] These medicine experts therefore seem to reach decisions according to Jürgen Habermas's communicative action model, which starts with interaction among specific, co-present interlocutors and introduces Pierce's idea that consensus is the horizon of the ongoing, indefinitely extensive progress of scientific knowledge. According to this model, the only thing that should count is the strength of an argument, and participants should be granted all the time needed to exchange arguments, the purpose being to resolve or absorb differences. Participants' remarks are congruent with this interaction model:[10]

In most cases there is no voting. That may seem surprising; it's fundamentally very good. This is supposed to be scientific decision-making, so it's got to be consensus. If it isn't, that means mysterious things remain.... If we can't manage it, we postpone it rather than voting. For X [a medicine], it took us a year to reach consensus. (E1)

Usually we manage to agree – if we don't, we haven't worked together enough.... We proceed by going around the table.... On many subjects, there's a tendency, broad directional lines, though maybe not on everything. But consensus has to be consensus. If there are some who don't agree, they have to say so. There's nothing worse than secret ballot voting. (E2)

Clearly, the fact that decision making by consensus was adopted and maintained is linked to the understanding that voting is not an appropriate means of reaching decisions of a strongly epistemic nature and that discussion of medicine applications can culminate in the convergence of opinion.[11]

---

[9] All interviewees mentioned – and approved – the fact that the committee rejects voting. Voting is reserved for the extremely rare case of major disagreement lasting over several months. Our observations confirm interviewees' statements: in the five sessions we attended in 2000 (we chose the sessions), there was not a single instance of voting. Since March 2006, reports of drug approval sessions can be consulted on the Web site of the AFSSAPS. In the spring of 2008, thirty-seven reports were accessible: voting was used only once, and the result was "unanimity minus 2 abstentions." However, the voting process *has* been used to give solemnity to committee decisions upon presentation to outside observers (we can cite the case of a pharmaceutical company that had threatened to sue). It is not used to resolve any deep internal disagreement.

[10] Interviewees are cited anonymously; each has been arbitrarily assigned a number: E1, E2, etc.

[11] As explained later, FDA advisory committees use voting to answer exactly the same questions. This means that the scientific dimension of medicine evaluation is compatible with more than one collective decision-making rule. When the French committee was created, the idea that voting was ill adapted to the work to be done was accepted without any real debate. But

Still, the notion of a gradually emerging consensus that works as a stop rule, allowing decisions to be reached and the process concluded, raises at least one question: If there is indeed consensus, how do participants realize it has been reached? For drug approval committee members, as for political philosophers and political scientists who apply communicative action to decision-making situations, consensus seems a way of indicating that the collective decision-making process has been brought to conclusion – exactly what happens when a matter is put to a vote, but instead of voting, participants have put forward arguments until they all agree. This description leaves out one important step, however: *recognizing* that the collective decision has been reached and that the process has therefore been concluded. Collective decision making necessarily includes a phenomenological dimension, in the first sense of the word "phenomenon": that which *appears*. In order for the collective decision-making process to be concluded, not only does an intention to act have to be determined or fixed, but the fact that it has been fixed has to be perceived and attestable by each and all. In voting, reaching a decision occurs simultaneously with the perception that the decision has been reached. But saying a decision has been reached by consensus generally does no more than indicate the means of arriving at that decision; that is, its content has been accepted by all. This is at best an incomplete description of what happens in consensus decision making, for the question remains as to how, without a vote, participants manage to realize that their opinions have finally converged.

The interviews alone do not allow for identifying the decision-making mode used, for while participants' statements justify the use of consensus and mention opposition to voting, they do not describe the exact means of decision making involved in this process understood as distinct from voting. In fact, without some form of voting, even something highly informal – head nods, for example – experts cannot know whether or not they have reached consensus, simply because they are not transparent to each other. They therefore cannot know if the discussion is over or must be pursued. Direct observation of how the French drug approval committee proceeds, rather than interviewee answers, enables us to resolve this enigma and grasp the exact nature of this decision-making mode.

Once any nonmember reporters have left the room, committee deliberation begins with the purpose of reaching a decision. After an exchange of views on the application at hand as a whole and its most debatable points, discussion takes off from a proposal by the committee chair running the meeting. Some features of that proposal elicit reactions, expressions of disagreement or doubt, specifications, suggested additions. The arguments presented in support of the reactions are then discussed by the chair himself or other members. The chair then makes another proposal which is meant to be a synthesis of the preceding

---

the example of the FDA and more recently the European Medicine Agency, whose marketing approval committee practices absolute majority voting, have not shaken the French committee's attachment to its consensus-reaching mode of decision making.

discussion. That second proposal may again elicit partial objections or suggestions of ways to improve it. Discussion progresses thus, punctuated and pushed forward by the chair's successive proposals. The deliberation acquires the status of a decision reached when it appears that none of the participants has any more objections. It should be noted that when the chair calls for reactions to what will soon become his last proposal, some participants overtly approve, but most abstain from overtly expressing their opinion in any way.

C. Reaching Decisions by Exhausting All Objections

Despite the fact that the decision-making mode used by French drug approval experts is not very well known – and often inaccurately designated "consensus or unanimity" decision making – it is in fact quite widespread and used currently in a variety of contexts. It can be defined as follows: a decision is understood to have been reached when there are no longer any objections expressed to a proposal for action, a proposal itself understood to reflect the preceding discussion.

Apparent Consensus. I have suggested calling this practice and decision-making rule "apparent consensus decision making."[12] It follows a specific sequence and presents three major characteristics:

1. In a typical procedure, (a) a member presents to the assembly the nature of the problem requiring a decision, together with an initial formulation of already stated options; (b) members discuss this presentation of the issue; (c) the same member or another synthesizes the discussion and indicates which option seems to him or her to have emerged out of it; (d) at this point there are two possibilities: (i) no one speaks out against the consensus proposal just presented, in which case even if most participants remain silent and only a few explicitly manifest their approval, that proposal becomes the decision, or (ii) at least one participant explicitly or implicitly contests the synthesis proposal, in which case discussion starts up again until the same member or another one offers a new synthesis, which once again gives rise to situation (i) or (ii); (e) if all successive consensus proposals are contested, the decision-making process for that particular matter may be postponed until a later meeting.
2. There is no systematic expression or counting of opinions. This aspect of decision making by apparent consensus makes it radically different from voting. In apparent consensus decision making, the fact that the decision has been reached – that is, that an intention to act has been determined – is attested by collective noting of an *absence*: the absence of any overt opposition. The consensus is thus apparent in two ways.

[12] For a detailed analysis of what characterizes this decision-making mode and the problems of description that often get in the way of apprehending and defining it clearly, see Urfalino (2007).

First, it clearly *appears* that no one objects to the proposal – in order for that proposal to acquire the status of a reached decision, the absence of opposition must be observable; it must become *apparent*. Second, the consensus that can be assumed to have been reached on the basis of this absence is in fact *only* apparent – that is, it may be misleading – since those who remain silent do not necessarily approve the proposal.

3. Apparent consensus is distinct from unanimity. Not explicitly rejecting a proposal is not the same thing as visibly unanimously approving it. In apparent consensus decision making, each participant has veto power since she can contest the synthesis proposal and thereby prevent it from becoming the decision. Reaching the decision does not require unanimity; what is required is that, for whatever motive, those who disapprove the proposal no longer contest it.

These are the identifying features of decision making by apparent consensus. In fact, the French drug approval committee uses a variant of that mode, for there are at least two ways of using it, deemed relevant or not depending on context.

Rejection or Objection. The variations have to do with *how* the proposal is contested. A proposal may be *rejected*, in which case the validity of the rejection will be unconditional, or it may be *objected to*, with the understanding that the validity of the objection is in turn open to discussion.

In African "palaver," for example, participants have a veto power de jure. This means that any instance of disagreement, however discreet or indirect and regardless of whether any argument is presented to support it, has the effective value of a veto. But for various reasons, participants may choose not to use their veto power. The status and resources that an assembly member has at his disposal strongly determine his ability to reject a proposal. He might expose himself to retaliation from members in favor of a proposal likely to be adopted, members with resources that may not be related to the affair being debated but that would (or would not) allow them to buy the silence of potential opponents. In this case, decision making by apparent consensus opens up a wide range of explicit or implicit negotiations for producing or preventing rejection of a given proposal (El-Hakim 1978; Coleman 1990: 857–58).

In the case that interests us here, speaking out against the proposal constitutes an objection but does not necessarily amount to a veto. In order for the objection to be a veto, it has to be accepted; that is, the other members have to deem it valid. Here, as specified earlier, the context is one in which deliberating members are not supposed to have any interests at stake and in the vast majority of cases do not; they have nothing to negotiate and nothing to fear or hope from speaking out – except in connection with the value that will be attributed to what they say. Use of the option to contest a proposal is not conditioned here by any resource external to the decision-making process; rather, the value of the objection, its veto power, is conditioned by whether or not the arguments used against the proposal are recognized as valid.

There seem, then, to be two dominant variants of apparent consensus decision making, depending on how a stated proposal is contested:

- by outright rejection, rejection permitted by the rules in effect in the context in question; this is the equivalent of de jure veto power, and the possibility of using it is conditioned by statuses and outside resources not necessarily related to the decision being made; or
- by objection, a move permitted both a priori and by context rules; however, the degree to which a given objection is effective is conditioned by its argumentative content and by the other members' explicit or tacit recognition of its validity.

D. The Dynamic of Objecting and the Specific Weight of Reasons

What becomes of an objection? It may be deemed invalid by at least part of the assembly and become itself the focus of a debate to determine whether it should be accepted or rejected. Or it may be accepted immediately – or at least tacitly recognized as valid in that its substance is integrated into the discussion that follows. In any case, in order for an objection to be distinguished clearly from rejection, members must practice what I have called the argumentative discipline characteristic of the areopagus. In sum, recognition of an objection as valid, and any contesting of that objection, are framed and made possible not only by members' competence but by argumentative discipline, discipline that each member imposes on herself but also – and above all – on the others.[13]

It follows from this that the silence of a member who says nothing when the session chair proposes a decision – a silence that may help turn that proposal into a decision – reflects one of the following three situations:

1. The silent member is convinced that the proposal is good and should become the decision.
2. The silent member does not really know whether the proposal is good or bad, and for some reason – inattention, fatigue, not having worked much on this particular application, feeling less competent than others with regard to the medicine in question – he implicitly delegates his judgment, counting on the others to see whether the proposal is inadequate and to contest it if it is.[14]
3. The silent member is not convinced by the proposal and may even feel the committee is not moving toward the right decision, but he does not have a good argument – that is, an argument that complies with areopagus argumentative discipline and is likely to be judged acceptable (or that was actually accepted earlier).

---

[13] Argumentative discipline presupposes that there are no strongly divergent approaches to evaluating medicines, a point addressed in Section V.

[14] The issue of judgment delegation is considered in greater detail in Section V.

To better grasp the specificity of this decision-making rule, it is useful to see what happens when we apply voting categories to it. Projecting voting vocabulary on a decision-making rule that differs from voting in that there is no counting of opinions brings out a clarifying contrast. We can say that at every step in the process of decision making by the exhaustion of objections, the majority comprises three groups: those voting in favor of the proposal (the persuaded), abstainers (their silence amounts to delegation of judgment), and opponents who cannot vote against because they do not have any valid arguments. This unusual distribution of yes votes, abstentions, and no votes with or without arguments – I am deliberately using voting vocabulary here – is due to the specific constraints on preference expression and the value of preference expression operative in the decision-making mode, as at least partially illustrated by the following table:

Number	A Virtually Silent Majority	An "Objecting" Minority
Value of the expressed opinion	In favor of the proposal as it stands	Against the proposal as it stands
Expression	Explicit approval or no expression	Explicit disapproval
Mental state and reasons	Persuaded Undetermined = delegation of judgment Not convinced but having no objection that one feels can be validated or having made an objection deemed invalid by the others	Not persuaded and having an objection that one feels can be validated or that has already been validated by the others

If we continue to project voting categories on decision making by the exhaustion of objections, we have to add that the "election" is always won either by a minority (temporarily) or unanimously (apparent unanimity, defined by the absence of opposition) since, as explained, the objection of any one participant, if deemed valid according to the committee's validity requirements, is enough to counterbalance those who approve the proposal or do not manifest their opinion of it; and when there are no more objections, the proposal becomes the decision thanks to what may be called negative unanimity, that is, an absence of observable objections. In any case, "saniority" – wisdom – prevails over number: the explicitly recognized validity of an objection is all that is needed for successive proposals to be rejected, and the proposal that is ultimately arrived at is considered wise because it was the one that exhausted all objections, *not* because it would have won everyone's vote.

Clearly the objection procedure and the transformation of the quest for convergence through counted instances of approval (voting) into a quest for the absence of observable disapproval – a double negative that does not produce mere affirmation – constitute a system in which *sanior pars* and *maior pars* – reasons and number – are constantly working together.[15]

IV. PUBLIC VOTING BY ADVISERS: THE CASE OF FDA-APPOINTED ADVISORY COMMITTEES

The procedure for determining a collective finding at the FDA is much simpler and more transparent than that of the French drug approval committee.[16]

A. Conditions for the Emergence and Use of Advisory Committees

The FDA began using advisory committees after World War II, and then only on a small scale. It was not until the 1970s that they came to be used systematically, a development explained by at least three factors: the increasing complexity of the technologies involved in products overseen by the FDA, new laws, and the growth of consumer activism, including the oversight and critique of agency decisions. Advisory committees serve to enrich agency decision making and to ensure that views external to the agency's will be represented. In controversial situations, these committees may also function to protect the agency, as it can then turn to them as an outside source of counsel (Sherman 2004).

In sum, the role of the advisory committees is to provide the FDA with independent advice from outside experts on issues deemed difficult or sensitive because the available scientific data render decision making difficult and/or because the issue at hand is controversial. The agency mobilizes advisory committees only for this kind of issue; many of its decisions on drugs are made without such committees. And when it does to turn to them, it is not bound by their recommendations.

The FDA is composed of six centers; here we are interested in the Center for Drug Evaluation and Research (CDER), which elicits the opinions of sixteen to eighteen advisory committees (the number varies slightly as new committees are created and existing ones redefined). Nearly all committees specialize in a major type of disease linked to a group of organs or a physiological function. There is an Arthritis Drugs Advisory Committee, a Cardiovascular and Renal Drugs Advisory Committee, and so on. At times, there have also been one or two horizontal committees – for example, the Drug Safety and Risk Management Advisory Committee, created in 2002.

---

[15] It is interesting that, consistent with the typology of Saint Benedict noted in Section II, A and usually considered rather odd, there is no "wise" majority: the *sanior pars* takes the form of either a minority, often amounting to a sole objector, or unanimity.

[16] My study of FDA-appointed advisory committees is based, among other things, on the many documents available on the agency's Web site. For vote analysis, I used Zuckerman's study (2006), which examines meetings of six advisory committees, randomly selected from among the sixteen that evaluated drugs from 1998 to 2005. Also cited is an analysis I did with Pascaline Costa of the entire set of votes for all joint committee meetings of the Drug Safety and Risk Management Advisory Committee plus another specialized committee, from the time the Safety Committee was created in 2002 through 2007.

Each advisory committee is made up of members appointed for four years with the status of "special government employees" (SGEs). Most committees have eleven members, all appointed for their special expertise; three of the members have a representative function. Committees usually include a chair, several academics or practitioners, as well as a consumer and an industry representative and, in some cases, a patient representative. Industry representatives are not SGEs and do not have the right to vote. Additional experts with specialized knowledge may be added for individual meetings as needed. Depending on the committee, the number of guest specialists called in to lend their expertise on a given pathology or drug, and absences, the number of voting members varies from six to eighteen.

For each advisory committee meeting, usually lasting a day, the FDA and the firm that owns the drug in question first present the relevant data and their analyses. The guest specialists are then given an opportunity to present their interpretation of the question. Meetings are open to the public, and prescreened audience members are permitted to take the floor. This is followed by public collective deliberation, in which advisory committee members only participate, on each of two to six questions previously formulated by the FDA. A vote is held on some of these questions. The entire process is characterized by a marked concern for transparency, as attested by the presence of an audience of ordinary citizens and, above all, by the fact that all meeting materials can be consulted on the FDA Web site. One month after the carefully recorded meeting, a full transcript (on average, five hundred pages long) is published online.

In fact, FDA advisory committees may be said to contrast with the French drug approval committee both in terms of the situations leading to the creation of committees and the rules used. Not all high-level expertise is concentrated in these committees, nor do they do all the evaluating. In fact, they are not really decision makers; instead, each committee constitutes a kind of "multiple adviser."

B. The Public Balloting of a "Multiple Adviser"

After a discussion in which reasons for a positive or negative response are put forward, advisory committee members vote on each of the FDA questions. When the discussion is over, the chair asks each member to vote yes, vote no, or abstain.

In 2007 the voting procedure was reformed. Before that date, the chair went around the table asking each member successively and by name to give an oral response, together with a commentary if the member wished to do so. The 2007 reform was designed to eliminate the effects of sequential voting, the fear being that later votes would be influenced by earlier ones (Food and Drug Administration 2007).[17] The current procedure is for the chair to ask for all

---

[17] The FDA document entitled *Draft Guidance* cites Callander (2007) on sequential voting.

in favor to raise their hands. He proceeds in the same way for no votes and abstentions. Then he asks each in turn to repeat her vote orally (so that the yes, no, and abstain votes can be recorded); at that time, members may make a comment when they vote.

The FDA stresses that while it takes advisory committee opinions very seriously, it is the FDA that makes the decision. It also insists that it pays close attention to deliberations as well to the voting results. The FDA requires voting to bear on specific questions, such as, "Given current knowledge, does this medicine have a demonstrated benefit?"; "Do the available data support the conclusion that this medicine increases cardiac ischemic risk?"; "Do the data presented support an acceptable risk–benefit profile for the 4 mg dose of this medicine?" Clearly, the yes/no answers to these questions furnish quite direct indications as to what the desirable decision is. For example, if the advisory committee deems the risk–benefit profile acceptable, the medication can be approved or reconfirmed for marketing.

While emphasizing the fact that votes on these questions cannot be interpreted without being linked to the discussion that preceded them and the associated commentaries, the FDA is insistent on voting tallies. This means it will not settle for discussion alone. The advisory committees, then, could conceivably serve only to enrich deliberations among FDA officials. This is not the case, however. What the FDA wants is for a collective advisory committee to be analogous to a single adviser. And for the committee to be so, its questions have to be voted on.

Once again, however, collective advising is not collective decision making. In voting, the advisory committee mimics collective decision making but does not actually perform it. This fact is patent in the rare cases of a tie vote.[18] What happens when there is a tie? Nothing. The chair may feel awkward and ask the FDA representative at the meeting if this is a problem. The FDA representative will answer that a vote resulting in the same number of yes and no opinions requires no particular procedure or corrective measure. Still, there is a sense of confusion about the result and the situation may elicit some joking remarks:

Dr. Fong (committee chair): We have a split vote, six for yes and six for no. Is there anything else that the FDA or the sponsor would like...

Dr. Chambers (FDA representative): Nothing from the FDA's perspective, except to thank you very much for your time and efforts."[19]

---

[18] In the fifty instances of voting observed by Zuckerman in her study of the meetings of six FDA advisory committees, there was only one tie vote (Zuckerman 2006), and we encountered only one tie vote in our study of nine joint committees made up of a particular area committee plus the Drug Safety and Risk Management Advisory Committee. In the latter case the count proved inaccurate because one member's ambiguously expressed position was interpreted as a no vote by the chair when it was in fact a yes vote, as clarified later by the member in question.

[19] From the transcript of the Dermatologic and Ophthalmic Drug Advisory Committee, March 17, 2007, pp. 192–93.

Dr. Swenson (committee chair):... What this means is that we have a tie vote. Dr. Albrecht, how do we proceed here with the second portion to this question?

Dr. Albrecht (FDA representative): I think next time we will invite an odd number of consultants [*laughter*].[20]

Since they do not make the definitive choice, advisory committees do not have a decision-making rule that would allow them to break the tie, that is, majority rule. One original feature of these committees, then, linked to their advisory status, is that they practice voting without a decision-making rule conceived as a stop rule. Instead, the vote may indicate a dominant orientation in advisers' thinking on the question.

This explains the apparently nonproblematic status of tie votes. If there were many such votes, the FDA would have to turn to the arguments put forward by yes and no voters. But in that case the advisory committee orientation function would be lost, and all the involved parties seem to value that function – the FDA and those on the outside concerned about its decisions, namely those eager to criticize them. This concern for being able to isolate collective advice through voting is manifested among other things in the indirect presence of majority rule, which, while not explicitly part of the procedure, is nonetheless present in the minds of all involved (Vermeule 2007).

V. CONVERGENCE AND DIVERGENCE OF EXPERTS' OPINIONS

In this last section I first show how the functioning of the French and American medicine evaluation committees illustrates the main characteristics of *sanior pars* and *maior pars* use identified in Section II. I then examine why, in direct contrast to what we saw in the decision making of the medieval Catholic Church, these evaluation arrangements succeed in bringing the decision-making process to fruitful conclusion without a need for arbitration at a higher level.

A. *Sanior Pars* and *Maior Pars* in the Two Evaluation Committees

In both medicine evaluation committees, we find the three previously identified features for determining a balance between wisdom and the majority, namely the weight of reasons, a double decision-making process, and a hierarchic principle.

In the French drug approval committee, first, reaching a decision by exhausting objections ensures that reasons are more important than preferences. This is due to the norm that by definition applies to every areopagus – that is, the requirement of justifying preferences, which is the first rule of argumentative discipline – but also to the fact that there are only two ways of expressing preferences: either not contesting the proposal or opposing it with reasoned

---

[20] From the transcript of the Pulmonary-Allergy Drugs Advisory Committee, June 6, 2005, p. 314.

arguments. The only thing that can be explicitly put forward against the reasons for supporting a proposal are other reasons – those for rejecting it. This means that votes are indeed "weighed" before being "counted." And once again, counting is only implicit.

Second, the collective decision making is clearly a dual process. But this occurs within the assembly itself and during the same sequence. Each newly formulated proposal may elicit silence, approbation, or objection. A classic collective decision-making process would at this point apply an aggregation rule that would transform the individual preference distribution into a collective preference. But in the French drug approval committee, that distribution is only the starting point, which could be followed by a minority critique of the majority's judgment.

Third, the hierarchic principle involved in *sanior pars* is operative in the committee's decision-making rule in that members are legitimately recognized as having unequal influence. Indeed, the fact that certain participants are recognized as having greater authority than others corresponds to the fact that greater weight is attributed to reasons than preferences. Consensus seeking thus permits the play of legitimate inequality of influence, that is, inequality related to differences in competence:

Voting's not good because it gives everyone the same weight. If we're handling an application for a heart medicine, my cardiologist colleague should have more weight than me. (E3)

We always reach a consensus, that's much better. There's never been a vote. It's preferable for people to explain what they mean. Let those who know explain. We've got official members representing the Medical Academy, the Pharmacology Academy, INSERM [Institut National de la Santé et de la Recherche Médicale]. They're representative, but they haven't got any particular qualifications. The experts, on the other hand, are qualified. The problem with voting is that it gives everybody equal weight. (E4)

It is important to specify that inequalities in competence or authority among members are not fixed. Several medicines are examined in the same session, and the assessments often involve different medical specialties, so the distribution of inequality in competence varies with the drug in question.

Conversely, the collective decision-making unit of analysis extends beyond the FDA-appointed advisory committees, since the final decisions are made by the FDA's Center for Drug Evaluation and Research (CDER) after receiving the relevant committee's recommendations. We therefore have to take into account both the CDER and the advisory committees.

First, the division into two parts of the decision-making process here is more explicit than in the French case. It has even been institutionalized: the advisory committee produces a recommendation with respect to the medicine to be decided on and the CDER makes the decision.

Second, the hierarchic principle is reflected in relations between the two bodies: the CDER is by right and in fact hierarchically superior to the advisory committee. It decides whether or not to call in an advisory committee for a given medicine, and whenever an advisory committee gives its recommendation, it reiterates that while it pays close attention to the committee's advice, it is not bound by it.

In this connection the question arises as to how often CDER decisions are consistent with advisory committee recommendations. The FDA followed the advisory committee in forty-five of the fifty cases studied by Zuckerman (2006). In all five cases of divergence, the committee had recommended that the FDA turn down the marketing application. In our study of the drug safety committee, the FDA followed committee recommendations of seven of the nine meetings in which committees voted. One of the two cases of divergence cannot be counted as a disagreement because new information came out after the advisory committee meeting, which led to a different evaluation of the medicine. In the second case, the FDA pulled an anti-inflammation drug off the market despite the committee's recommendation that it remain there. On the basis of these figures, we can say that the CDER is likely to follow committee recommendations; it does so roughly nine times out of ten, but not systematically.

Third, in both advisory committee functioning and CDER behavior, we see the specific weight of evaluations and reasons. To begin with, advisory committee members do more than vote. Because voting is public and oral,[21] each member is asked to specify the main reason she ultimately favors a negative or positive answer to the question. Second, the CDER always specifies that it is attentive to both votes and arguments. Finally, when the FDA justifies its own decisions, the fact that a majority or all of the members of an advisory committee voted consistently with the FDA decision is cited as only one of the factors that the FDA took into account. If the FDA decision goes against the advisory committee opinion and if the advisory committee's vote was split, the FDA will always point out that split, as if to stress the difficulty of evaluating the medicine in question. FDA experts also emphasize the factors that they feel justify the decision *they* have ultimately reached.

Given that our modern evaluation committees display the three characteristics of decision-making arrangements found in the medieval Church, we have to ask why in their case the compromise between numbers and reasons does not constitute an obstacle to reaching decisions and concluding the process. In direct contrast to Church members, who were called on to elect the heads of their institutions, medicine evaluation committee members do not have personal or professional interests at stake – which in their case would be a direct interest in what becomes of the medications they evaluate. Still, the absence of such interests is not enough to explain the fact that the modern areopagus is able to reach decisions. We must therefore examine how it solves the problem of a possible divergence of expert opinions.

---

[21] Advisory committee meetings are open to the public and are recorded and transcribed in full; meeting transcripts are then put on the FDA's Web site.

B. Two Ways of Resolving the Problem of Diverging Opinions

In both the U.S. and French cases, decisions about medications are reached without major difficulties. This is quite remarkable in the French case given that the approval committee has never really decided by voting; in reality, only the "exhausting objections" procedure is used (see Section III, B and note 10). It is also remarkable that the many decisions made – as many as ten per daylong meeting – are usually reached without any postponements and without extending the deliberation time. In the 1980s, one or two delicate decisions were reached only after a year of deliberation.[22] However, since 1993, when the French drug approval agency was founded, and even more rigorously since the 1995 creation of the European agency, which relies in part on the various national agencies' work (Hauray and Urfalino 2009), marketing approval applications have been handled within a tight schedule that does not allow for postponement.[23]

The answer seems more obvious in the U.S. case, because the FDA is the only decision maker and the advisory committees practice voting. Still, given that the FDA calls in an advisory committee only in cases where evaluation is a delicate matter, it is useful to consult such a committee only if the concluding vote brings out a clear collective inclination in one direction or the other.

A convergence of expert opinions is, of course, desirable in both the French case, where it alone allows for reaching a decision, and the U.S. case, where it facilitates decision making and helps render the decision itself acceptable. In the former case, convergence is required; in the latter, there cannot be too many cases of sharp divergence.

Advisory Committee Voting Patterns: Strong Expert Convergence. The fact is that FDA committee votes are often unanimous, or else they result in a strong qualified majority. This is the conclusion I draw from two soundings of the mass of FDA advisory committee meetings and votes, all allowing for one of three responses: yes, no, abstain.

The first sounding is again Zuckerman's (2006). She examined meetings of six advisory committees, randomly selected from among the sixteen that evaluated drugs from 1998 to 2005. All these meetings were to determine either drug marketing approval or withdrawal. Of the fifty questions put to a vote, twenty-seven – that is, 57 percent – resulted in unanimity. Of the remaining twenty-three, there was one tie vote (eight yes, eight no) and three majority votes of 58, 67, and 70 percent, respectively; all the others resulted in qualified majorities of more than 70 percent. The average majority vote (not including the twenty-seven cases of unanimity and the one tie) was 79 percent.

---

[22] Information from committee members active at the time.

[23] The time elapsed between the submission of a drug company's application and the agency's decision regarding the application cannot exceed 210 days.

For the second sounding, we considered the entire set of votes for all joint committee meetings of the Drug Safety and Risk Management Advisory Committee plus another specialized committee, from the time the Safety Committee was created in 2002–2007. We chose joint committee meetings because they are more likely than other meetings to produce divergence.[24] Votes were held in nine of these meetings. In contrast to Zuckerman, we took into account all votes, not just those bearing directly on drug approvability; this gave a total of thirty questions voted on. Eleven of the thirty instances of voting – that is, 37 percent – resulted in unanimity. The other nineteen produced majorities ranging from 53 to 97 percent (not including abstentions); the average majority score (yes or no) was 77 percent. This means that on even the most sensitive questions, advisory committees reach a significant percentage of unanimous decisions (37 percent) and, in general, strong qualified majorities.

Despite the use of voting, then, it is fair to say that opinions of FDA advisory committee experts often strongly converge. Of the total of seventy votes for the two studies, thirty-eight were unanimous, while only 10 percent were below a 70 percent majority.

These results shed light on the French case, showing that even with a technique that facilitates the expression of a variety of opinions – that is, voting – sharp evaluation divergence is unlikely and complete or strong convergence is quite probable. It is worth citing the Zuckerman figures for the same kinds of decisions as those made by the French drug approval committee, namely decisions on whether to authorize marketing:[25] 57 percent unanimity and numerous strong supermajorities. But if these results are projected onto the French committee, we see that it would not have been able to reach a decision in 43 percent of cases. Such a projection is invalid, of course, because the French committee examines all marketing applications, whereas advisory committees study only medicines that are particularly difficult to evaluate.[26] Still, we can only wonder how the French committee systematically manages to reach decisions despite a method that requires exhausting all objections.

Conditions for Reaching Decisions by Exhausting Objections. In addition to the fact demonstrated by the U.S. case – namely, that regardless of how complex medicine evaluation may be, it can produce a strong convergence of expert opinions – three other observations will explain how it is that the French committee manages to reach a decision in all cases.

1. Decision making by exhausting objections gives the committee chair strong influence of the sort that facilitates convergence.

---

[24] My thanks to Pascaline Costa for the following analysis of advisory committee voting and vote-related discussions, all based on meeting transcripts available on the FDA Web site.

[25] In France, a different committee decides whether to maintain or withdraw a medicine already on the market.

[26] This suggests that if advisory committees were called in to evaluate all prospective drugs submitted for approval, the rate of unanimous recommendations would be higher still.

2. This form of decision making allows for a division of labor: having highly specialized experts for each of the applications tends to diminish the number of objections from other members.
3. The way experts are appointed, together with the length of the chairmanship over the 1978–2000 period, worked to promote a relatively high degree of evaluation homogeneity.

As explained, silence amounts to approval of the proposal made at a given moment by the chair. But silence can mean that silent members have not yet formed a clear opinion on the question just as easily as it can mean that they approve the proposal (we will leave aside the silence of members who are not persuaded but do not have a good argument on which to base an objection). In fact, the norm by which silence is interpreted as approval actually allows for a kind of judgment delegation. Some members may simply "rest" their judgment on that of colleagues they deem better informed about certain aspects of the drug in question, or on the seriousness and reliability of the committee chair and his team, who almost always run the meetings. Given the possibility that some members will delegate judgment to other members, there are two corollaries to adopting and maintaining this mode of decision making.

First, the chair plays an essential role in the decision-making dynamic since he is the one to formulate the successive synthesizing proposals. The chair has to be able to elicit opinions and reactions to objections, and to integrate them into a new decision proposal. The scope of this role was increased by the personalities and particular competence of successive drug approval committee chairs from 1978 to 2000.[27] All committee members recognized how completely the two chairs in place between 1984 and 2000 mastered the applications the committee was called on to evaluate, and this necessarily meant those chairs had great influence on the proceedings overall, as two experts made clear in the interviews. One of them stated:

In my opinion they were hyper-professional and got carried away by their enthusiasm. The commission had to debate; they let it debate. But they had an answer to everything, all the weak points, all the positive ones – it often seemed we were dealing with a foregone conclusion.[28] (E5)

Second, decision making by exhausting objections allows for the adjustment of members' workloads. Once again, these experts are not state administrators and they all have heavy responsibilities elsewhere, often in hospitals. They are paid very little for their committee work. Often, then, they do not devote the

---

[27] There were only three chairs in this period: Legrain, Alexandre, and Caulin. As mentioned, while this mode of decision making is still in effect, the study on which my arguments are based here ran from 1978 to 2000.

[28] These two interviewees were specialists in pathologies for which there were then no recognized effective remedies. They were therefore never in a position to bring their particular competence to bear. They were the only experts to suggest that the committee might actually be considered useless in some instances.

same amount of study to all the applications, and it is worth mentioning that they receive the application file only a few weeks before the meeting. Members who feel less competent to judge certain applications or who have done no more than peruse the application to be evaluated do not participate as much as others in the deliberation and do not voice objections; they are likely to rally to the chair's or certain colleagues' proposals rather than really approve them.

Too much delegation of judgment will, of course, affect the value attributed to one feature of collective committee deliberation and decision making, that is, the enrichment of discussion afforded by multiple views of different individuals. Decision making by exhausting objections can in fact deteriorate into another form of collective decision making, in which a limited team of highly specialized, motivated experts presents evaluation proposals to a larger group of less engaged colleagues, hoping thereby to elicit a few additional useful points and corrective adjustments. This situation is in turn less likely to produce irreducible differences of opinion.

Third, from 1978 to 2000, the committee had a total of three chairs: strong personalities enjoying great medical authority. Each headed the committee for at least six consecutive years; the last two had been members from the time of its founding. Chairs were consulted on all appointments. Committee members were changed or reappointed every three years, meaning that the committee was actually made up of members co-opted from a small circle of physicians interested in evaluating medicine. This practice facilitated the convergence of ways of conceiving such evaluation.

The need for a certain homogeneity in how medicine evaluation is conceived is suggested by the early history of the European Union's Agency for the Evaluation of Medicinal Products. In 1995, Professor Alexandre was appointed chair of the drug approval committee of this newly created European agency, a committee made up of experts from all EU countries. He tried to implement the rules of decision making by exhausting objections, which he had seen applied by Professor Legrain in the French committee and which he himself had practiced as chair of that committee for eleven years. But after a while he was forced to abandon his preferred mode of decision making. Frequent cases of persistent divergence made it necessary to turn regularly to majority voting, to the point that this became the only collective decision-making method used in the European agency.

The European approval committee was made up of thirty members; each of the fifteen member states of the time appointed two experts. The aforementioned history of the agency's first months shows that despite real international homogenization and standardization of evaluation procedures and the diffusion of fixed evaluation procedures (double-blind clinical trials, risk–benefit balancing), there are still significant variations in evaluation approaches. These are only partially explained by differences among countries' medical histories (Daemmerich 2004; Hauray 2006); they can also be linked to different and even diametrically opposed "evaluation philosophies."

Reaching consensus, if only negatively by an absence of objections, thus implies using shared criteria. Assuming those criteria are in place (which is almost always the case), consensus requires having the same way of comparatively weighting them (which is not always the case). Without a community-shared conception, the real danger is not any unmanageable increase in the number of objections, but rather that it will be impossible to agree on the status of the objections, despite a strict observance of argumentative discipline.

What led the EU medicine evaluation agency to adopt voting was the fact that there were several conceptions of evaluation. A diversity of conceptions is also probably what explains the observed divergences in FDA-appointed advisory committees, whose members are recruited from throughout the United States. In contrast, member co-optation and the influence of the chair, combined with the practice of delegating judgment to others, explain how decision making by exhausting objections was able to work in the French drug approval committee from 1978 to 2000.

VI. CONCLUSION

This essay focuses on the collective decision-making processes of a particular type of deliberating group: committees of the wise, or what I have called areopagi. One of the conditions for producing collective wisdom in these groups lies in the nature and quality of the way they reach decisions. The difficulty of collective decision making in such groups is that merely aggregating member preferences – voting – does not seem to satisfy the demand for *justification* of the choices made by individuals and the group as a whole. Thus, an areopagus has to both count and weigh votes.

Throughout the Middle Ages, the Catholic Church was concerned to take both the numerical majority and the "sounder part" into account in the assemblies that were in charge of electing the heads of its various institutions. I sought to identify the general ideas and practices of the Church that might shed light on how contemporary committees of the wise operate. Three characteristics gradually became clear: specific weight is granted to reasons alongside votes; the collective decision-making process is divided into two parts; and the notion of hierarchy is always relevant.

In this essay I have also described the decision-making modes used in two modern-day instances of the areopagus, the medicine evaluation committees of France and the United States, showing that their decision-making rules, though very different, offer two original combinations of precisely the three characteristics identified in the medieval use of *sanior pars* and *maior pars*.

To test the relevance of my definition of the areopagus and the general validity of the three features involved in the composite concern for numbers and wisdom, we would have to undertake detailed studies of numerous other contemporary committees of the wise, in particular constitutional courts.

References

Bodéüs, Richard (1992), "Des raisons d'être d'une argumentation rhétorique selon Aristote," *Argumentation*, 6, pp. 297–305.

Callender, Steven (2007), "Bandwagons and Momentum in Sequential Voting," *Review of Economic Studies*, 74, pp. 653–84.

Coleman, James (1990), *Foundations of Social Theory*, Cambridge, MA: Harvard University Press.

Colomer, Josep, and McLean, Iain (1998), "Electing Popes: Approval Balloting and Qualified-Majority Rule," *Journal of Interdisciplinary History*, 29, no. 1, pp. 1–22.

Daemmerich, Arthur (2004), *Pharmacopolitics: Drug Regulation in the United States and Germany*, Chapel Hill: University of North Carolina Press.

El-Hakim, Sherif (1978), "The Structure and Dynamics of Consensus Decision-Making," *Man*, 13, pp. 55–71.

Elster, Jon (2007), *Explaining Social Behavior: More Nuts and Bolts for the Social Sciences*, Cambridge: Cambridge University Press.

Food and Drug Administration (2007), *Draft Guidance for FDA Advisory Committee Members and FDA Staff: Voting Procedures for Advisory Committee Meetings*, http://www.fda.gov/oc/advisory/VotingGuidance.html.

Gaudemet, Jean (1990), *Les élections dans l'Eglise latine. Des origines au XVIe siècle*, Paris: Fernand Lanore.

Hauray, Boris (2006), *L'Europe du médicament. Politique, expertise, intérêts privés*, Paris: Presses de Sciences Po.

Hauray, Boris, and Urfalino, Philippe (2009), "Mutual Transformation and the Development of European Policy Spaces: The Case of Medicine Licensing," *European Journal of Public Policy*, 16, no. 3, pp. 431–49.

Holmes, Stephen (1988), "Gag Rules and the Politics of Omission," in Jon Elster and Rune Stalgstad (eds.), *Constitutionalism and Democracy*, pp. 19–58, Cambridge, Cambridge University Press.

Hurlet, Frédéric (2002), "Le consensus et la concordia en Occident (Ier–IIIe siècles apr. J.-C.)," in Hervé Inglebert (éd.), *Idéologies et valeurs critiques dans le monde romain. Hommage à Claude Lepelley*, pp. 163–78, Paris: Picard.

Llull, Ramon (2001), *De arte eleccionis*, in G. Hägel and F. Pukelsheim, "Llull's Writings on Electoral Systems," *Studiana Lulliana*, 41, pp. 3–38, online: http://www.math.uni-augsburg.de/stochastik/pukelsheim/2001a.html.

McLean, Iain, Lorrey, Haidee, and Colomer, Josep M. (2008), "Social Choice in Medieval Europe," *Electronic Journal for History of Probability and Statistics*, 4, no. 1, pp. 1–23 (www.jehps.net).

Moulin, Léo, (1958a), "Sanior et maior pars. Note sur l'évolution des techniques électorales dans les ordres religieux du VIe au XIIIe siècle," *Revue Historique de Droit Français et Étranger*, 35, pp. 367–97.

—— (1958b), "Sanior et maior pars. Note sur l'évolution des techniques électorales dans les ordres religieux du VIe au XIIIe siècle (suite)," *Revue Historique de Droit Français et Étranger*, 36, pp. 490–529.

Pasquino, Pasquale (2007), "Voter et délibérer," *Revue Européenne des Sciences Sociales*, 45, no. 136, pp. 35–47.

Peltzer, Jörg (2008), *Canon Law, Careers and Conquest: Episcopal Elections in Normandy and Greater Anjou, c. 1140– c. 1230*, Cambridge, Cambridge University Press.

Przeworski, Adam (2006), "Consensus and Conflict in Western Thought on Representative Government," Paper presented at the Beijing Forum, October 20, available at politics.as.myth.edu/docs/10/2008/beijing-ba.pdf.

Sherman, Linda Ann (2004), "Looking Through a Window of the Food and Drug Administration: FDA's Advisory Committee System," *Preclinica*, 2, no. 2, pp. 99–102.

Urfalino, Philippe (2007), "La décision par consensus apparent. Nature et propriétés," *Revue Européenne des Sciences Sociales*, 45, no. 136, pp. 34–59. (An earlier version of this text in English is available at http://cespra.ehess.fr/docannexe.php?id=551.)

Vermeule, Adrian, "The Moral Force of Majority Rule," Oxford University Press blog, http://oup.com/2007/07/law.

Zukerman, Diana M. (2006), *FDA Advisory Committees: Does Approval Mean Safety?* Washington, DC: National Research Center for Women and Families.

9

Collective Wisdom

Lessons from the Theory of Judgment Aggregation

Christian List

INTRODUCTION

Can collectives be wise? The thesis that they can has recently received a lot of attention. It has been argued that in many judgmental or decision-making tasks, suitably organized groups can outperform their individual members. In particular, it is said, groups are good at meeting what I call the *correspondence challenge* (as in *correspondence with the facts*): by pooling information that is dispersed among the individual members, a group can arrive at judgments that accurately track some independent truths or make decisions that maximize an independent objective function (for a popular discussion, see Surowiecki 2004).

One of the best-known illustrations of this effect is given by Condorcet's Jury Theorem. If each member of a jury has an equal and independent chance better than random, but worse than perfect, of making a correct judgment on whether a defendant is guilty, the majority of jurors are more likely to be correct on the matter of guilt than each individual juror, and the probability of a correct majority judgment approaches certainty as the jury size increases (e.g., Grofman et al. 1983). Many generalizations and extensions of this result have been obtained, and a lot can be said about the conditions under which information pooling is truth-conducive and those under which it isn't (see, among many others, Boland 1989; Estlund 1994; List and Goodin 2001).

While the ability to make judgments that correspond with the facts is an important dimension along which a group's claim to wisdom can be assessed,

This essay reviews the lessons about collective wisdom that can be learned from recent work on the theory of judgment aggregation. It draws significantly on earlier work of mine in List (2005, 2008). Some of the ideas discussed here also draw on joint work with Philip Pettit on group agency in List and Pettit (2011); chapters 2 and 4, in particular, develop some related issues in greater detail. I wish to record my debt to Philip Pettit as well as to my other regular coauthor, Franz Dietrich, who has also significantly influenced my thinking on the present themes. I am very grateful to Karen Croxson, Jon Elster, Hélène Landemore, and the other participants in the Colloquium on Collective Wisdom at the Collège de France, May 2008, for helpful comments and discussion.

it is not the only one. The group's ability to come up with a coherent body of judgments also matters; let me call this the *coherence challenge*. A necessary condition for wisdom, it seems, is that one is able to organize one's judgments in a coherent manner. Minimally, this requires forming a body of judgments that is free of inconsistencies – or at least free of blatant inconsistencies. More strongly, it may require forming a body of judgments that satisfies certain closure conditions – for instance, closure under logical consequence. Expert panels or multimember courts, for example, would hardly be regarded as wise if they were unable to deliver judgments that were at least minimally coherent. Even a good factual accuracy of some of their judgments would not seem to be enough to compensate for certain violations of coherence. Correspondence and coherence both matter.[1]

In this essay, I discuss the lessons we can learn about collective wisdom from the emerging theory of judgment aggregation (originally formulated in List and Pettit 2002, 2004), as distinct from the literature on Condorcet's Jury Theorem. While the large body of work inspired by Condorcet's theorem has been concerned with how groups can meet the correspondence challenge, much of the recent work on judgment aggregation focuses on their performance with regard to the coherence challenge.[2] Furthermore, while the Jury Theorem and its extensions are usually taken to support a largely optimistic picture of collective wisdom, the literature on judgment aggregation is now so replete with negative results that it may give the impression that collective wisdom is impossible to attain. As with many pairs of opposite extremes, the truth lies

---

[1] Inspired by a discussion with Goldman (2004), I have previously discussed these two challenges under the labels "rationality challenge" and "knowledge challenge" (List 2005). The present terminology is inspired by the coherence and correspondence theories of truth or knowledge.

[2] A detailed review is beyond the scope of this essay, but I would like to mention some key contributions. The interest in the problem of judgment aggregation was originally sparked by the so-called *doctrinal paradox* in jurisprudence, concerning decision making in collegial courts (Kornhauser and Sager 1986, 1993), which was later generalized beyond the judicial context under the name *discursive dilemma* (Pettit 2001; List and Pettit 2002). The differences between the doctrinal paradox and the discursive dilemma are discussed in a later note. List and Pettit (2002) developed a formal model of judgment aggregation, combining Arrovian social choice theory (Arrow 1951/1963) and propositional logic, and proved a first impossibility theorem. Following this original theorem, stronger or refined impossibility results were proved, e.g., by Pauly and van Hees (2006), Dietrich (2006), and Dietrich and List (2007a). Moreover, necessary and sufficient conditions on the agenda of propositions leading to such impossibility results were identified by Nehring and Puppe (2002, 2010), Dokow and Holzman (2010a), Dietrich (2007), and Dietrich and List (2007a). Some of these results have precursors in abstract aggregation theory (Wilson 1975; Rubinstein and Fishburn 1986; Nehring and Puppe 2002). An even earlier precursor is Guilbaud's (1966) discussion of theories of the general interest. Although much work has focused on proving impossibility results, the literature also contains a number of possibility results (e.g., List 2003, 2004; Dietrich 2006; Pigozzi 2006; Dietrich and List 2010; Dietrich 2010). For an informal survey, see List (2006); for more formal surveys, see List and Puppe (2009) and List (forthcoming). The precise relationship between judgment aggregation and Arrovian preference aggregation is discussed in List and Pettit (2004) and Dietrich and List (2007a).

somewhere in the middle, and my suggestion is that insights from both the work on judgment aggregation and the work on Condorcet's Jury Theorem are needed to provide a nuanced assessment of a group's capacity to attain wisdom.

CONCEPTUAL PRELIMINARIES

When does it make sense to describe an entity as wise? Obviously, we wouldn't describe rocks, sofas, or power drills as wise. Human beings, by contrast, are paradigmatically capable of wisdom. Might the concept of wisdom also apply to nonhuman animals or to robots? There seems to be no conceptual barrier to describing a complex computational system such as HAL 9000 in Arthur C. Clarke's *Space Odyssey* as wise. Similarly, an intelligent and experienced nonhuman animal such as a primate who plays an important role in the social organization of his or her group may well qualify as wise. What makes the concept of wisdom in principle applicable in all these cases is the fact that the entities in question are agents.[3] Human beings, nonhuman animals, and sophisticated robots, unlike rocks, sofas, or power drills, can all be understood as having cognitive and conative states – which encode beliefs and desires, respectively – and as acting systematically on the basis of these states.

While wisdom is usually taken to be a property of agents, I shall here interpret wisdom more weakly as a property of entities that are at least *proto-agents*, defined as entities with cognitive states, which encode beliefs or judgments. In particular, I use the concept of wisdom to refer to a proto-agent's capacity to meet the correspondence and coherence challenges previously defined. This thin, pragmatic interpretation of wisdom contrasts with thicker, more demanding interpretations, which require richer capacities of agency. Solomonic wisdom, for example, clearly goes beyond an agent's performance at truth tracking and forming coherent judgments, but I shall set aside these more demanding issues here.

In order to assess the wisdom of collectives in the present, deflationary sense, we must therefore begin by asking whether groups can count as proto-agents. The answer depends on how a given group is organized. A well-organized expert panel, a group of scientific collaborators, or the monetary policy committee of a central bank, for example, may well be candidates for proto-agents – perhaps even candidates for fully fledged agents (following the account of group agency in List and Pettit, 2011) – whereas a random crowd of pedestrians in the town center is not; it lacks the required level of integration. In particular, the group must have the capacity to form collective beliefs or judgments, and for this it requires an organizational structure for generating them. This may take the form of a voting procedure, a deliberation protocol, or any other mechanism by which the group can make joint declarations or deliver a joint

---

[3] The notion of agency employed here is developed in List and Pettit (2011: ch. 1). It is inspired by Dennett (1987) and Pettit (1993).

Input (individual beliefs or judgments)

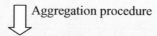
Aggregation procedure

Output (collective beliefs or judgments)

FIGURE 9.1. An aggregation procedure.

report. Such procedures are in operation in expert panels, multimember courts, policy advisory committees, and groups of scientific collaborators.

I will follow the literatures on judgment aggregation and on Condorcet's Jury Theorem in focusing on the formation of binary "acceptance/rejection" judgments, as opposed to nonbinary degrees of beliefs. Specifically, I will assume that a group seeks to form collective "acceptance/rejection" judgments on a given set of propositions and their negations – called the *agenda* – on the basis of the group members' individual judgments on them.

Although the case of nonbinary beliefs, which typically take the form of subjective probability assignments to propositions, is also important (e.g., Lehrer and Wagner 1981; Genest and Zidek 1986; Dietrich and List 2007d), many real-world judgmental or decision-making tasks by groups or committees require the determinate acceptance or rejection of certain propositions – say, on the guilt of a defendant or the viability of some policy – and this gives particular significance to the binary case.

The propositions on the agenda are formulated in propositional logic, which can express *atomic* propositions without logical connectives, such as 'p,' 'q,' 'r,' and so on, and *compound* propositions with logical connectives, such as 'p and q,' 'p or q,' 'if p then q,' and so on.[4] In a simple example, the agenda might contain just a single proposition and its negation, such as 'the defendant is guilty' versus 'the defendant is not guilty,' but later I will consider more complex cases.

The group's organizational structure will now be modeled as an aggregation procedure. As illustrated in Figure 9.1, an *aggregation procedure* is a function that assigns to each combination of the group members' individual "acceptance/rejection" judgments on the propositions on the agenda a corresponding set of collective judgments. A simple example is majority voting, whereby a group judges a given proposition to be true whenever a majority of group members does so. Later I will discuss several other aggregation procedures.

Of course, an aggregation procedure captures only part of a group's organizational structure, and there are also various ways in which a group might implement such a procedure. Just think of all the ways in which the group members may reveal their judgments to the procedure. They might do so through

---

[4] For an extension of the model to more general logics, see Dietrich (2007).

TABLE 9.1. *A Majoritarian Inconsistency*

	'p'	'If p then q'	'q'
Individual 1	True	True	True
Individual 2	True	False	False
Individual 3	False	True	False
Majority	True	True	False

explicit voting, which in turn can take a number of forms (e.g., open or anonymous), through discussion, or through their actions. However, as I will subsequently argue, the question of whether a group deserves to be called wise depends crucially on the nature of its aggregation procedure – as well as on the performance of its individual members.

Thus, the task is to investigate what properties a group's aggregation procedure must have for the group to meet the coherence challenge and what properties it must have for the group to meet the correspondence challenge. The next two sections are devoted to these questions. By combining insights from the theory of judgment aggregation with insights from the work on Condorcet's Jury Theorem, I hope to shed light on the conditions for collective wisdom.

MEETING THE COHERENCE CHALLENGE

Suppose, then, a group seeks to form collective judgments on some agenda of propositions. Can the group ensure the coherence of these judgments? Let me begin with two examples.

First, consider an expert panel that has to give advice on the health consequences of air pollution in a big city, especially pollution by very small particles. The experts have to make judgments on the following propositions (and their negations):

'p':   The average particle pollution level exceeds 50 micrograms per cubic meter air.

'if p then q': If the average particle pollution level exceeds this amount, then residents have a significantly increased risk of lung disease.

'q':   Residents have a significantly increased risk of lung disease.

All three propositions are complex factual propositions on which there may be reasonable disagreement among experts. What happens if the panel uses majority voting as its aggregation procedure? Suppose, as an illustration, that the experts' individual judgments are as shown in Table 9.1. Then a majority of experts judges 'p' to be true, a majority judges 'if p then q' to be true, and yet a majority judges 'q' to be false. The set of propositions accepted by a majority – 'p,' 'if p then q,' and 'not q' – is incoherent in two senses here. First, it violates *consistency*, defined as the requirement that it must be possible for the propositions in the set to be simultaneously true. And second, it fails to be *deductively closed*, where deductive closure is the requirement that, if the set of accepted propositions entails another proposition that is also on the agenda, then that other proposition should be accepted as well. In the present example, although 'p' and 'if p then q,' which are both collectively accepted, logically entail 'q,' the latter proposition is not accepted. Clearly, the expert panel fails to meet the coherence challenge in this example.

The second example is a historical one, reported by Elster (2007: 410–11), concerning the debates in the French Constituent Assembly of 1789 on whether the country should introduce a bicameral or a unicameral system.[5] In very simplified terms, the members of the Assembly had to make judgments on three propositions (and their negations):

'p':   It is desirable to stabilize the regime.
'q':   Bicameralism (as opposed to unicameralism) will stabilize the regime.
'r':   It is desirable to introduce bicameralism (as opposed to unicameralism).

The background assumption is that 'r' is to be accepted if and only if both 'p' and 'q' are accepted. As Elster reports, the Assembly was divided into three groups of roughly equal size. The reactionary right wanted to destabilize the regime but thought that bicameralism would stabilize it, and therefore opposed bicameralism. The moderate centrists wanted to stabilize the regime and thought that bicameralism would do so, and therefore supported bicameralism. The radical left, finally, wanted to stabilize the regime but thought that bicameralism would have the opposite effect, and hence opposed bicameralism. Thus, the individual judgments were as shown in Table 9.2.

The overall majority judgments in this example – the acceptance of 'p' and 'q' and the rejection of 'r' – are clearly inconsistent relative to the background assumption that 'r if and only if p and q.' As Elster observes, bicameralism was defeated because the Assembly ultimately voted on proposition 'r.' However, he also argues that if the Assembly had explicitly voted on each of 'p' and 'q' and none of the groups had strategically misrepresented their opinions – which he recognizes to be big ifs – then the outcome might have been the opposite one. In any case, the example suggests that the Constituent Assembly failed to meet the coherence challenge.[6]

---

[5] I am grateful to Jon Elster for drawing my attention to this example.

[6] In Elster's presentation of the example, the members of the Assembly hold *preferences* on whether or not to stabilize the regime and on whether or not to introduce bicameralism, while they hold *beliefs* on whether or not bicameralism will stabilize the regime. Thus, he casts the aggregation problem as a mixed preference–belief aggregation problem. In principle, this interpretation can be made consistent with my formalization as well, but to simplify the exposition I have translated the agents' preferences into judgments of desirability, thus interpreting their attitudes as cognitive rather than conative ones. Although there are very important differences between single-attitude

TABLE 9.2. *The French Constituent Assembly*

	'p'	'q'	'r'
Reactionaries	False	True	False
Moderates	True	True	True
Radicals	True	False	False
Majority	True	True	False

Both examples are instances of the so-called *discursive dilemma* (Pettit 2001; List and Pettit 2002), which shows that majority voting does not generally secure collective wisdom, understood in terms of coherence. The problem consists in the fact that simultaneous majority voting on some suitably connected propositions may lead to a logically inconsistent set of judgments.[7] However, the examples do not undermine the possibility of attaining collective coherence through some other aggregation procedure, distinct from proposition-by-proposition majority voting. (Indeed, the French Constituent Assembly avoided an overt instance of inconsistent majority judgments by *not* taking explicit votes on all propositions; rather, it voted only on whether or not to introduce bicameralism.) For all we can infer at this point, the problem might be an isolated artifact of majority voting.

A General Impossibility Theorem

Let us therefore set aside the specific aggregation procedure of majority voting and investigate the logical space of possible aggregation procedures more

aggregation problems (such as pure judgment aggregation) and mixed aggregation problems (such as combined preference–belief aggregation), a discussion of these issues is beyond the scope of this essay.

[7] This generalizes the earlier *doctrinal paradox* concerning judicial decisions (Kornhauser and Sager 1986, 1993). To illustrate the earlier problem, suppose a multimember court seeks to make a decision on whether a defendant is liable for breach of contract (the conclusion) on the basis of two jointly necessary and sufficient conditions (the premises): first, there was a valid contract in place, and second, the defendant's action was such as to breach a contract of this kind. If one judge holds both premises to be true, a second judge holds the first premise but not the second to be true, and a third judge holds the second premise but not the first to be true, then the majority judgments on the two premises seem to support a liable verdict, while a majority of judges individually consider the defendant not to be liable. The doctrinal paradox consists in the fact that majority voting on the premises (the premise-based or issue-by-issue procedure) may lead to a different outcome than majority voting on the conclusion (the conclusion-based or case-by-case procedure). The *discursive dilemma*, more generally, consists in the fact that simultaneous majority voting on *any* set of suitably connected propositions – whether or not they can be partitioned into premises and conclusions – may yield a logically inconsistent set of judgments. To be precise, the problem of majority inconsistency can arise as soon as the agenda of propositions (and their negations) on which judgments are to be made has at least one minimally inconsistent subset of three or more propositions (for a proof, see Dietrich and List 2007b).

generally. That logical space is truly vast: even if an "acceptance/rejection" judgment is to be made just on a single proposition – a rather simple agenda – there are 2^n possible combinations of individual judgments in an n-member group to which corresponding collective judgments must be assigned, and thus there are 2^{2^n} logically possible aggregation procedures (for further discussion, see List 2011). This number not only grows exponentially in the group size n, but even for small groups it exceeds the estimated total number of particles in the universe.

Surely, one would expect, there must exist some aggregation procedures in this large logical space that allow a group to meet the coherence challenge. To find these procedures, let us introduce some minimal conditions that an aggregation procedure might be expected to satisfy.

> **Universality:** The aggregation procedure admits as input any possible combination of consistent and complete individual judgments on the propositions on the agenda, where completeness is the requirement that for each proposition–negation pair on the agenda, either the proposition or its negation is accepted.

> **Decisiveness:** The aggregation procedure generates as output complete judgments on the propositions on the agenda.

> **Systematicity:** The collective judgment on each proposition on the agenda depends only on the individual judgments on it, and the pattern of dependence is the same across propositions.

These conditions are intended to be minimal in the sense that they are satisfied by a whole range of familiar aggregation procedures, including majority voting or even a dictatorship of a single individual. Ideally, we would like a good aggregation procedure to satisfy conditions that go beyond them. But what are the aggregation procedures that satisfy the present three conditions *and* guarantee consistent collective judgments? Surprisingly, there are only rather degenerate such procedures.

> **Theorem** (Dietrich and List 2007a): If the propositions on the agenda are nontrivially interconnected, an aggregation procedure satisfies universality, decisiveness, and systematicity and generates consistent collective judgments *only if* it is a dictatorship or inverse dictatorship of one individual.[8]

---

[8] The notion of *nontrivial interconnections* between the propositions on the agenda can be made precise. In the present theorem, it requires that (1) the agenda have at least one minimally inconsistent subset of three or more propositions, and (2) it have at least one minimally inconsistent subset with the additional property that, by negating an even number of propositions in it, it becomes consistent. The agenda in the expert-panel example meets both of these conditions. It is easy to verify that a minimally inconsistent subset of the agenda with the properties required in both (1) and (2) is the set containing the propositions 'p,' 'if p then q,' and 'not q.' The theorem stated here generalizes the original theorem in List and Pettit (2002) and a subsequent result in

Under such an aggregation procedure, the collective judgments are fully determined by a fixed single individual. In short, majority voting is not the only aggregation procedure that runs into problems like the ones in the earlier examples of the expert panel and the French Constituent Assembly. *Any* nondictatorial (and non-inverse-dictatorial) procedure satisfying universality, decisiveness, and systematicity does so.

If these three conditions were regarded as indispensable requirements on an aggregation procedure, one would have to conclude that the wisdom of a group collapses, at best, into the wisdom of some dictatorial group member or chairperson. Collective wisdom would not be possible in any interesting way. This conclusion, however, would be too quick. It is instructive to see what happens if we relax one of the three conditions.

Relaxing Universality

Universality requires the aggregation procedure to admit as input any possible combination of consistent and complete individual judgments on the propositions on the agenda. An aggregation procedure with this property exhibits a certain kind of "robustness": it works not only for special inputs, but for all possible inputs that may be brought to it. But suppose we require the formation of collective judgments only when there is sufficient agreement among the individuals. Then it becomes possible for majority voting to generate consistent group judgments.

Suppose, in particular, that the group members can be aligned from left to right – this may represent their positions on some cognitive or ideological dimension – such that the following pattern holds: for every proposition on the agenda, the individuals accepting the proposition are either all to the left, or all to the right, of those rejecting it. (This pattern is called *unidimensional alignment.*) It is then guaranteed that majority voting generates consistent collective judgments, assuming that individual judgments are consistent (List 2003; for generalizations, see Dietrich and List 2010).

To illustrate this result, consider the following example. Suppose a five-member group seeks to form attitudes toward propositions 'p,' 'if p then q,' 'q,' and their negations, as in the earlier expert-panel example, and suppose the individual judgments are as shown in Table 9.3. Here the individuals accepting any given proposition are either all to the left, or all to the right, of those rejecting it.

What are the resulting majority judgments? It is easy to see that they coincide with the judgments of the median individual on the left–right alignment – here individual 3 – since no proposition can be accepted by a majority without being accepted by the median individual. So long as the median individual holds

Pauly and van Hees (2006). Closely related results, stated in "abstract aggregation" frameworks and using slightly different conditions on the agenda and on the aggregation procedure, have been obtained by Nehring and Puppe (2002, 2010) and Dokow and Holzman (2010a).

TABLE 9.3. *Unidimensionally Aligned Judgments*

	Individual 1	Individual 2	Individual 3	Individual 4	Individual 5
'p'	False	False	False	False	True
'If p then q'	True	True	True	True	False
'q'	True	True	False	False	False

consistent judgments, the majority judgments are guaranteed to be consistent as well. (Notice that this arrangement is by no means dictatorial, since the median individual may differ from case to case.)

In short, if universality is relaxed to the requirement that the aggregation procedure admit as input only those combinations of individual judgments that satisfy a structure condition like the one just illustrated, then majority voting ensures consistent collective judgments while also satisfying decisiveness and systematicity.

Nonetheless, this solution cannot work in general. Even in an idealized expert panel making judgments on factual matters without any conflicts of interests, disagreement may still be profound, and there is no guarantee that individual judgments will neatly fall into any cohesive pattern. Moreover, in situations of significant conflicts of interests such as in the French Constituent Assembly of 1789, the level of cohesion required for consistent majority judgments may not generally be present. A best-case scenario is perhaps the situation in which the formation of group judgments is preceded by a sufficiently intense and effective period of group deliberation. Such deliberation may move individual judgments toward a more cohesive pattern, as hypothesized by theorists of deliberative democracy (Miller 1992; Knight and Johnson 1994; Dryzek and List 2003). Elsewhere, I have obtained some empirical evidence in support of an effect of this kind (List et al. 2000/2006). Still, in many collectives the empirical fact of pluralism may require the use of an aggregation procedure satisfying universality.

Relaxing Decisiveness

Decisiveness requires the aggregation procedure to generate as output complete judgments on the propositions on the agenda. Suppose a group is willing not to be opinionated on some proposition–negation pairs; it is willing to accept neither the proposition nor its negation. The group may then be able to generate consistent collective judgments in accordance with the other conditions previously introduced. It may use a supermajority or unanimity rule, for example, under which any given proposition is accepted if and only if a particular supermajority of group members – say, two-thirds, three-quarters, or all of them in the case of unanimity rule – does so. If the required supermajority threshold is sufficiently high – in the example above, any threshold above two-thirds would work – this aggregation procedure guarantees consistent collective judgments, while satisfying universality and systematicity (List 2001; Dietrich and List 2007b).[9]

Groups with stringent requirements of consensus, such as the UN Security Council or the EU Council of Ministers, often take this approach, with the result that they frequently have to suspend judgment (for a general discussion of supermajoritarian decision making, see Goodin and List 2006). But many collectives cannot afford indecisiveness; they are expected to make up their minds on the propositions brought to them on the agenda. The expert panel giving advice on air pollution may simply be required to come up with firm judgments on all proposition–negation pairs; incompleteness may not be acceptable here.

Moreover, the escape route from the impossibility theorem via relaxing decisiveness becomes even more limited if we understand coherence as requiring not only the consistency of the group judgments but also its deductive closure. It turns out that if we keep the earlier theorem's assumption about the agenda, the only aggregation procedures that generate consistent and deductively closed collective judgments and satisfy universality as well as systematicity (and do not overrule individual judgments in the special case of unanimity) are the so-called *oligarchic* ones (Dietrich and List 2008).[10] Under such a procedure, there exists a fixed subset of the individuals – possibly including everyone, possibly singleton, possibly some other subset – such that the group accepts all and only those propositions that are unanimously accepted by the individuals in the given subset. Both unanimity rule and dictatorships are special cases of oligarchic procedures under this definition, with the relevant subset including either all individuals (in the case of unanimity rule) or just one individual (in the case of a dictatorship). Since every individual in the relevant subset can veto the acceptance of any proposition, there is likely to be a stalemate, as soon as there is the slightest diversity of opinion among these individuals.

Relaxing Systematicity

The limited appeal of the previous escape routes from the impossibility theorem suggests that we may need to relax systematicity, by treating different propositions differently in the process of forming collective judgments. A group may do so, for example, by designating some propositions as *premises* and others as *conclusions* and assigning priority either to the premises or to the conclusions.

---

[9] Formally, let k be the size of the largest minimally inconsistent subset of the agenda. Then a supermajority above a proportion of $(k - 1)/k$ of the individuals must be required for the acceptance of any proposition in order to ensure collective consistency.

[10] For closely related results, see also Gärdenfors (2006) and Dokow and Holzman (2010b).

If the group assigns priority to the premises, it may use the so-called *premise-based procedure*, whereby the group first makes a collective judgment on each premise by taking a majority vote on that premise and then derives its collective judgments on the conclusions from these collective judgments on the premises. In the expert-panel example, propositions 'p' and 'if p then q' might be designated as premises (perhaps on the grounds that they are more fundamental than 'q'), and proposition 'q' might be designated as a conclusion. The panel might then take majority votes on 'p' and 'if p then q' and derive its judgment on 'q' from its majority judgments on the first two propositions.[11] Similarly, in the example of the French Constituent Assembly, propositions 'p' and 'q' might be designated as premises and proposition 'r' as a conclusion. The premise-based procedure would then amount to what Elster (2007: 410–11) describes as a hypothetical "double aggregation" procedure, according to which the Assembly would have voted, first, on whether stabilizing the regime is desirable (a normative premise) and, second, on whether bicameralism is a way to achieve stability (a causal-empirical premise), before deriving its collective judgment on whether or not to introduce bicameralism (the overall conclusion).

Alternatively, if a group assigns priority to the conclusions, it may use the so-called *conclusion-based procedure*, whereby it takes majority votes only on the conclusions and makes no collective judgments on the premises. This is the procedure that the French Constituent Assembly actually used. In addition to violating systematicity, this aggregation procedure also violates decisiveness, by producing no judgments on the premises. But sometimes the conclusions are the only propositions that matter from a practical perspective, and in such cases the lack of any collective judgments on the premises may be defensible.

The premise- and conclusion-based procedures are not the only aggregation procedures violating systematicity. The group might not only assign priority to the premises, but also assign different such premises to different subgroups, thereby introducing a division of cognitive labor. Under the so-called *distributed premise-based procedure*, different individuals specialize on different premises and express their individual judgments only on these premises. The group then makes a collective judgment on each premise by taking a majority vote on that premise among the relevant "specialists" and derives its collective judgments on the conclusions from the specialists' majority judgments on the premises. I will come back to this procedure in my discussion of the correspondence challenge.

For many cognitive tasks performed by groups, giving up systematicity and using a premise-based or conclusion-based procedure may be an attractive way to avoid the impossibility result explained earlier. Each of these procedures

---

[11] In the present example, the truth-value of 'q' is not always settled by the truth-values of 'p' and 'if p then q'; so the group may need to strengthen its premises in order to make them sufficient to determine its judgment on the conclusion.

allows the group to produce consistent collective judgments. In the case of the premise-based procedure (in either the regular or the distributed form), the group further ensures the deductive closure of its judgments. The group can then be interpreted as a "reason-driven" proto-agent that derives its collective judgments on conclusions from its collective judgments on relevant premises. Pettit (2001) speaks of the *collectivization of reason* in this context.

Still, relaxing systematicity has a price. Aggregation procedures that violate it are vulnerable to various types of strategic manipulation. As should be apparent, their outcomes can be potentially manipulated by agenda setters who have control over the choice of premises. Further, such procedures may give individuals incentives to misrepresent their premise judgments so as to lead the group to adopt conclusion judgments they prefer (Dietrich and List 2007c). For example, if the French Constituent Assembly had used the premise-based procedure, the outcome under truthful voting would have been the endorsement of bicameralism. For this reason, both the reactionaries on the right and the radicals on the left, who each opposed bicameralism (albeit for different reasons), would have had incentives to strategically misrepresent their opinions on the premises so as to prevent this outcome. The reactionaries would have been able to prevent a bicameralist outcome by expressing an insincere causal-empirical judgment that bicameralism would *not* stabilize the regime, contrary to their real opinion; and the radicals would have been able to do the same by expressing an insincere normative judgment that stabilizing the regime would *not* be desirable, contrary to their real attitude.

Lessons to be Drawn

I have shown that a group's capacity to meet the coherence challenge depends on its aggregation procedure. In general, a group can ensure the consistency of its judgments only if it uses a procedure that violates one of universality, decisiveness, or systematicity – or if it is willing to install a dictatorship (or, even more perversely, an inverse dictatorship) of one individual. Moreover, different aggregation procedures may lead to different outputs for the same inputs. As an illustration, Table 9.4 shows the collective judgments for the individual judgments in Tables 9.1 and 9.2 under different aggregation procedures.

If we were to use collective coherence as the only criterion of wisdom – disregarding correspondence with any relevant external facts – this would give us insufficient grounds for selecting a unique aggregation procedure. As illustrated, there are many possible procedures that produce consistent collective judgments, and even if we require deductive closure as a criterion of coherence in addition to consistency, several of these procedures remain. It is therefore time to turn to the correspondence challenge. At this point, however, I can safely conclude that, contrary to what the impossibility results on judgment aggregation may seem to suggest, the possibility of collective coherence is not ruled out.

TABLE 9.4. *Different Aggregation Procedures Applied to the Individual Judgments in Tables 9.1 and 9.2*

	Expert Panel			French Assembly		
	'p'	'If p then q'	'q'	'p'	'q'	'r'
Majority voting[a]	True	True	False	True	True	False
Premise-based procedure with 'p,' 'if p then q' as premises	True	True	True	True	True	True
Conclusion-based procedure with 'q' as conclusion	No judgment	No judgment	False	No judgment	No judgment	False
Distributed premise-based procedure with individual 1 specializing on 'p' and individual 2 specializing on 'if p then q'	True	False	False	False	True	False
Unanimity rule	No judgment	No judgment	No judgment	No judgment	No judgment	No judgment
Dictatorship of individual 3	False	True	False	True	False	False

[a] Inconsistent.

216

MEETING THE CORRESPONDENCE CHALLENGE

We have seen that there are several routes by which a group can ensure the coherence of its judgments. Can a group also ensure the correspondence of those judgments with the relevant facts? In order to address this question, I must first define the notion of correspondence with the facts more carefully.

Consider some proposition 'p,' which is factually true or false, such as the proposition that the average particle pollution level exceeds a certain amount in the expert-panel example or the proposition that the defendant in a criminal trial did a particular action. An agent's judgment on 'p' *corresponds with the facts* just in case the agent judges that 'p' if and only if 'p' is true. Since most agents are fallible, however, their judgments correspond with the facts at best approximately. To quantify how well they do, I will consider two conditional probabilities (List 2006): first, the conditional probability that the agent judges that 'p,' given that 'p' is true; and, second, the conditional probability that the agent does not judge that 'p,' given that 'p' is false. Call these two conditional probabilities the agent's *positive* and *negative reliability* on 'p,' respectively. In some cases these two probabilities coincide; in others they differ. An agent may be better at identifying the truth of 'p' than its falsehood, or the other way round. A doctor performing a diagnostic test on a patient, for example, may be better at detecting the presence of some disease if the patient has the disease than its absence if the patient does not. Or an expert advisory committee may be better at detecting the presence of some risk if there is such a risk than its absence if there is not. To meet the correspondence challenge with respect to a given proposition 'p,' I will assume that an agent must have a high positive and negative reliability on 'p.'[12]

By considering a group's positive and negative reliability on various propositions under different aggregation procedures and different scenarios, I will now identify conditions under which the group succeeds at meeting the correspondence challenge. It turns out that three principles of designing an aggregation procedure may promote collective wisdom: the principles of *democratization*, *decomposition*, and *decentralization*.

The Effects of Democratization

Suppose, to begin with, that a group seeks to make a judgment on a single factual proposition, such as the proposition that air pollution is above a particular threshold or that a defendant is guilty. As originally suggested by Condorcet

---

[12] A simple illustration shows that one of the two alone is not enough. Consider a medical advisory panel that always judges that a particular chemical is safe – call this proposition 'p' – regardless of how dangerous the chemical is. This committee would thus have a positive reliability of 1 on 'p': if the chemical were truly safe, the committee would certainly say so. But it would have a negative reliability of zero: even if the chemical were extremely dangerous, the committee would still deem it safe. The committee's judgments would not covary at all with the truth.

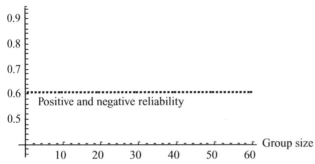

FIGURE 9.2. The group's positive and negative reliability under a dictatorship.

(1785), suppose, further, that the group members' individual judgments on proposition 'p' satisfy two favorable conditions:

Competence: Each group member has a positive and negative reliability *r* above a half, but below 1, on proposition 'p,' so that individuals are fallible in their judgments but biased toward the truth. For simplicity, all individuals have the same reliability, for example, $r = .6$.

Independence: The judgments of different group members are mutually independent.

These conditions are highly idealized, and a lot could be said about scenarios in which they are violated.[13] What is the group's positive and negative reliability on 'p' under various aggregation procedures? Consider three aggregation procedures: first, as a degenerate baseline case, a dictatorship of one individual, where the group's judgment on 'p' is always determined by the same fixed individual group member; second, the unanimity rule, where agreement among all group members is necessary and sufficient for reaching a collective judgment on 'p'; and third, majority voting on 'p.' Figures 9.2, 9.3, and 9.4 show the group's reliability on 'p' under these three aggregation procedures. The group size is plotted on the horizontal axis, the group's positive and negative reliability on 'p' on the vertical one.

Under a dictatorship, the group's positive and negative reliability on 'p' equals that of the dictator, which is .6 in the present examples. Here the group performs no better and no worse at meeting the correspondence challenge than any of its members. Not surprisingly, a dictatorial collective is no wiser than its dictator taken individually.

Under the unanimity rule, the group's positive reliability on 'p' approaches zero as the group size increases; it equals r^n. In a ten-member group with an individual reliability of .6, for example, this is .006. But the group's negative

---

[13] Indeed, Franz Dietrich (2008) goes so far as to argue that there are no situations in which Condorcet's two conditions are *simultaneously* justified.

Tracking rel.

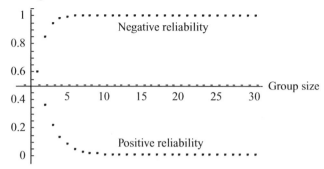

FIGURE 9.3. The group's positive and negative reliability under unanimity rule.

reliability on 'p' approaches 1 as the group size increases: it equals $1 - (1 - r)^n$. In the same example of a ten-member group, this is .999. Moreover, a determinate group judgment on 'p' – that is, a judgment that 'p' or that 'not p' – is reached only if all individuals agree on the truth-value of 'p.' If they do not, no group judgment on 'p' is made. In a large group, the unanimity rule is almost certain to produce no group judgment on 'p' at all, which makes it rather useless in many judgmental or decision-making tasks. This observation echoes my earlier remarks about the risk of indecision under unanimitarian or supermajoritarian aggregation procedures.

Finally, and most strikingly, under majority voting, the group's positive and negative reliability on 'p' exceeds that of any individual group member and approaches 1 as the group size increases. This is, of course, Condorcet's Jury Theorem.

Why does the theorem hold? By the competence condition, each individual has a probability r above a half of making a correct judgment on 'p,' and by the independence condition different individuals' judgments are independent of each other. So each individual's judgment is like an independent coin toss, where one side of the coin, say heads, corresponds to a correct judgment, which

Prob. all correct

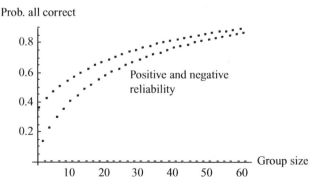

FIGURE 9.4. The group's positive and negative reliability under majority voting.

comes up with a probability of r, say .6, and the other side, tails, corresponds to an incorrect judgment, which comes up with a probability of $1 - r$, say .4. How often would you expect the coin to come up heads when it is tossed many times? Statistically, given the independence of different tosses, you expect heads in 6 out of 10 cases and tails in 4 out of 10 cases. In the case of just ten tosses, of course, the actual heads–tails pattern may still deviate from the expected one of 6–4: it may be 7–3, or 5–5, or sometimes 4–6. But now consider the case of a hundred tosses. Here the expected heads–tails pattern is 60–40. Again, the actual pattern may deviate from this; it may be 58–42, or 63–37, or 55–45. But it is less likely than in the case of ten tosses that we get heads less often than tails. Now in the case of a thousand, ten thousand, or a million tosses, it is less and less likely, by the law of large numbers, that the coin comes up heads less often than tails, given the expected frequency of .6. Translated back into the language of judgments, the probability of a majority of individuals making a correct judgment approaches 1 as the group size increases, as required by the Condorcet Jury Theorem.[14]

What lesson can be drawn from this? If group members are independent, fallible, but biased toward the truth in their judgments, majority voting outperforms both dictatorial and unanimity rules in terms of maximizing the group's positive and negative reliability on a given proposition 'p'; the only strength of unanimity rule is that it is good at avoiding false positive judgments, but at the expense of many false negative ones. Hence, when a group seeks to meet the correspondence challenge, there may be epistemic gains from democratization, that is, from adopting a majoritarian democratic structure.

The Effects of Decomposition

Suppose now a group seeks to make a judgment not just on a single factual proposition, but on an agenda of several interconnected ones (for detailed analyses on which the present discussion draws, see Bovens and Rabinowitz 2003; List 2006). For example, the group could be a university committee deciding on whether a junior academic should be given tenure, with three relevant propositions involved: first, the candidate is excellent at teaching; second, the candidate is excellent at research; and third, the candidate should be given tenure, where excellence at both teaching and research is necessary and sufficient for tenure. More generally, there are $k \geq 2$ premises and a conclusion

---

[14] The competence and independence conditions are crucial for this result. If individual reliability falls below .5, the mechanism leading to a likely majority of coin tosses on the correct side ceases to apply; in fact, then the probability of a majority of tosses on the wrong side approaches 1 with increasing group size. Similarly, if different individuals' judgments are not independent, but instead highly correlated with each other, then aggregating them will not significantly enhance overall reliability. Whether or not majoritarian aggregation is truth-conducive in the presence of less extreme interdependencies among individual judgments depends on the precise nature of these interdependencies (e.g., Boland 1989; Ladha 1992; Dietrich and List 2004; Berend and Sapir 2007).

that is true if and only if all the premises, and thereby their conjunction, are true. Alternatively, the conclusion could be true if and only if at least one premise, and thereby their disjunction, is true; the analysis would be very similar to the one given here for the conjunctive case. The French Constituent Assembly discussed earlier provides another example of the conjunctive case, although here some complications arise from the fact that one of the premises is a normative proposition that does not, on all accounts, have an independent truth value.

The first thing to note is that, in this case of multiple propositions, individuals do not generally have the same reliability on all propositions. The members of a tenure committee, for example, may be better at making correct judgments on the separate premises about teaching and research than on the overall conclusion about tenure. More generally, if each individual has the same positive and negative reliability $r > \frac{1}{2}$ on each premise and makes independent judgments on different premises, then his or her positive reliability on the conclusion is r^k, which is below r and can easily be below a half,[15] while his or her negative reliability on the conclusion is above r and thus always above a half. Here individuals are worse at detecting the truth of the conclusion than the truth of each premise, but better at detecting the falsehood of the conclusion than the falsehood of each premise. Other scenarios can be constructed, but it remains the case that individuals typically have different levels of reliability on different propositions (for further discussion, see List 2006). Condorcet's competence assumption cannot generally be sustained once we are dealing with multiple interconnected propositions.

What is the group's positive and negative reliability on the various propositions under different aggregation procedures? As before, assume that the group members' judgments are mutually independent. Majority voting performs well only on those propositions on which individuals have a positive and negative reliability above a half. In other words, majority voting performs well on a given proposition if the individuals satisfy Condorcet's competence condition on it, assuming they also satisfy the independence condition. But as just argued, individuals may not be sufficiently competent on every proposition. In addition, majority voting may fail to ensure coherent group judgments on interconnected propositions, as already shown. Let me therefore set majority voting aside and compare dictatorial, conclusion-based, and premise-based procedures. Again, dictatorships are discussed mainly in order to provide a baseline case for comparison.

Suppose, as an illustration, there are two premises, as in the university committee example, and individuals have a positive and negative reliability of .6 on each premise and are independent in their judgments across different premises. Figures 9.5 and 9.6 show the group's probability of judging all propositions correctly under a dictatorship and under the premise-based procedure,

---

[15] The latter happens whenever r is below the kth root of a half.

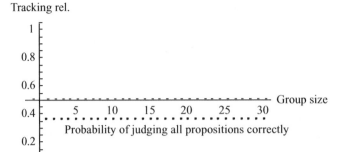

FIGURE 9.5. The group's probability of judging all propositions correctly under a dictatorship.

respectively. Figure 9.7 shows the group's positive and negative reliability on the conclusion under the conclusion-based procedure. As in the earlier figures, the group size is plotted on the horizontal axis and the probabilities in question on the vertical one.

Generally, under a dictatorship of one individual, the group's positive and negative reliability on each proposition equals that of the dictator. In particular, the probability that all propositions are judged correctly is r^k, which may be very low, especially when the number of premises k is large. Under the conclusion-based procedure, unless individuals have a very high reliability on each premise,[16] the group's positive reliability on the conclusion approaches zero as the group size increases. Its negative reliability on the conclusion approaches 1. Under the premise-based procedure, finally, the group's positive and negative reliability on every proposition approaches 1 as the group size increases. This result holds because, by the Condorcet Jury Theorem, the group's positive and negative reliability on each premise approaches 1 with increasing group size, and therefore the probability that the group derives a correct judgment on the conclusion also approaches 1 with increasing group size.

What lessons can be drawn from this second scenario? Under the assumptions made, the premise-based procedure outperforms both dictatorial and conclusion-based procedures in terms of simultaneously maximizing the group's positive and negative reliability on every proposition. Again, a dictatorship is bad at pooling the information contained in the judgments of multiple individuals. And the conclusion-based procedure, like the unanimity rule in the single-proposition case, is good at avoiding false positive judgments on the conclusion but usually bad at reaching true positive ones (Bovens and Rabinowitz 2003). For instance, even if there are only two premises and individual reliability r on each premise is above .5 but below the square root

---

[16] To secure this result, each individual's positive and negative reliability on each premise must exceed the kth root of a half, e.g., .71 when $k = 2$ or .79 when $k = 3$.

Prob. all correct

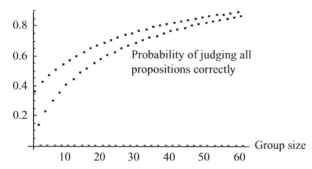

FIGURE 9.6. The group's probability of judging all propositions correctly under the premise-based procedure.

of .5, for example, $r = .65$, each individual's probability of detecting the truth of the conclusion, if it is true, is r^2, which is below .5. Thus, by the reverse of Condorcet's Jury Theorem, the probability of a correct majority judgment on the conclusion, if it is true, converges to zero as the group size increases.

Hence, if a large judgmental task, such as making a judgment on some conclusion, can be decomposed into several smaller ones, such as making judgments on certain relevant premises from which the conclusion-judgment can be derived, this decomposition can promote collective wisdom.

The Effects of Decentralization

When a group is faced with a complex judgmental task involving several propositions, different group members may have different levels of expertise on different propositions. This is an important characteristic of many collectives, such as expert panels, groups of scientific collaborators, multimember courts,

Tracking rel.

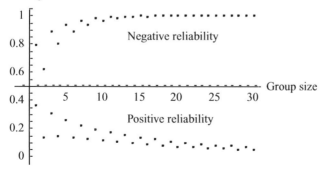

FIGURE 9.7. The group's positive and negative reliability on the conclusion under the conclusion-based procedure.

central banks, firms, organizations, and governments. Even in a group as small as a tenure committee, the representatives of the university's teaching and learning center may be better qualified to assess the candidate's teaching than some of the other committee members, whereas the latter may be better qualified to assess the candidate's research. Individuals may simply lack the resources to become sufficiently well informed on every proposition. If we take this problem seriously, can we improve on the premise-based procedure?

Suppose, as before, a group seeks to make collective judgments on an agenda containing k different premises and a conclusion, which is true if and only if all the premises are true. Instead of requiring every group member to make a judgment on every premise, the group may divide itself into several subgroups, for simplicity of roughly equal size: one for each premise, where the members of each subgroup specialize on their assigned premise and make a judgment on it alone. In the tenure committee example, one subgroup may consist of the teaching assessors and the other of the research assessors. Instead of using a regular premise-based procedure as in the previous scenario, the group may now use a distributed premise-based procedure, as defined earlier. Here, the collective judgment on each premise is made by taking a majority vote within the subgroup specializing on the given premise, and the collective judgment on the conclusion is then derived from the specialists' majority judgments on the premises.

Can the distributed premise-based procedure outperform the regular one at maximizing the group's reliability? Two effects pull in opposite directions here. On the one hand, there may be *epistemic gains from specialization*: individuals may become more reliable on the propositions on which they specialize. But on the other hand, there can also be *epistemic losses from lower numbers*: each subgroup voting on a particular proposition is smaller than the original group; it is only roughly $1/k$ of the size of the original group when there are k premises, and this may reduce the information-pooling benefits of majority voting on that proposition.

Whether or not the distributed premise-based procedure outperforms the regular one depends on which of these two effects is stronger. If there were no epistemic gains from specialization, the distributed premise-based procedure would suffer only from losses from lower numbers on each premise and would thus perform worse than the regular premise-based procedure. On the other hand, if the epistemic losses from lower numbers were relatively small compared with the epistemic gains from specialization, then the distributed premise-based procedure would outperform the regular one.

To give a simple example, suppose there are twenty individuals making judgments on two premises, where each individual's reliability on each premise is .6 without specialization. And suppose further that if we subdivide the group into two halves specializing on one premise each, then each individual's reliability on the assigned premise goes up to .7. At first sight, these gains from specialization seem relatively modest. However, it turns out that the group is better off by opting for the decentralized arrangement and using the distributed

TABLE 9.5. *Reliability Increase from r to r* Required to Outweigh the Loss from Lower Numbers*

	$k = 2, n = 50$			$k = 3, n = 51$			$k = 4, n = 52$		
r	.52	.6	.75	.52	.6	.75	.52	.6	.75
r^*	.5281	.6393	.8315	.5343	.6682	.8776	.5394	.6915	.9098

premise-based procedure. Each ten-member subgroup with an individual reliability of .7 will make a more reliable judgment on its assigned premise than the twenty-member group as a whole with each individual's reliability at .6. In the present numerical example, the original group's positive and negative reliability on each premise will be .7553, while each specialist subgroup will have a reliability of .8497 on its assigned premise. The following theorem generalizes this point:

> **Theorem** (List 2005, 2008): For any group size n (divisible by k), there exists an individual reliability level $r^* > r$ such that the following holds. If, by specializing on proposition 'p,' individuals achieve a positive and negative reliability above r^* on 'p,' then the majority judgment on 'p' in a subgroup of n/k specialists, each with reliability above r^* on 'p,' is more reliable than the majority judgment on 'p' in a group of n nonspecialists, each with reliability r on 'p.'

Hence, if, by specializing, individuals achieve a reliability above r^* on their assigned premise, the distributed premise-based procedure outperforms the regular one. How great must the increase in reliability from r to r^* be in order to have this effect? Surprisingly, a relatively small increase is enough. Table 9.5 shows some illustrative calculations. For example, when there are two premises, if the original individual reliability in a fifty-member group was .52, a reliability above .5281 after specialization is sufficient; if it was .6, a reliability above .6393 after specialization is enough.

Figure 9.8 shows the group's probability of judging all propositions correctly under regular and distributed premise-based procedures, where there are two premises and individuals have positive and negative reliabilities of .6 and .7 before and after specialization, respectively. Again, the group size is plotted on the horizontal axis, and the relevant probability on the vertical one.

The lesson from this third scenario is that, even when there are only relatively modest gains from specialization, the distributed premise-based procedure may outperform the regular one in terms of maximizing the group's positive and negative reliability on every proposition. Decentralization may therefore promote collective wisdom. If a group seeks to meet the correspondence challenge, it may thus benefit from subdividing its judgmental tasks into several smaller ones and distributing them among multiple subgroups. Plausibly, such division of cognitive labor is the mechanism underlying many of the successes of

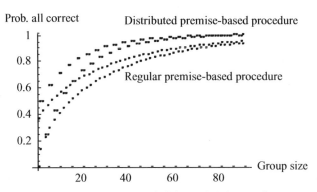

FIGURE 9.8. The group's probability of judging all propositions correctly under the distributed and regular premise-based procedure.

collective wisdom in science and in suitably structured organizations (Knorr Cetina 1999; Giere 2002; Page 2007).

CONCLUDING REMARKS

I have discussed the lessons we can learn about collective wisdom by combining insights from the emerging theory of judgment aggregation with insights from Condorcet's Jury Theorem. I have discussed two dimensions of wisdom – wisdom as coherence and wisdom as correspondence – and have asked under what conditions a group can attain wisdom on each of these dimensions.

With regard to the achievement of collective coherence, I have discussed an impossibility theorem by which we can characterize the logical space of aggregation procedures that ensure coherent collective judgments. When the propositions on which judgments are to be made are nontrivially interconnected, no nondictatorial (and non-inverse-dictatorial) aggregation procedure generating consistent collective judgments can simultaneously satisfy universality, decisiveness, and systematicity. To find a nondegenerate aggregation procedure that produces coherent collective judgments, then, it is necessary to relax one of these three conditions. Which relaxation is most defensible depends on the group and the cognitive task it faces.

With regard to the achievement of collective judgments that accurately correspond to the facts, I have identified three principles of organizational design that can promote collective wisdom: there may be benefits from democratization, from decomposition, and from decentralization. The applicability and magnitude of each benefit depend on the group and cognitive task in question, and there may not be a "one size fits all" aggregation procedure that is best for all groups and all cognitive tasks. But the possibility of each of these benefits underlines the potential for collective wisdom.

Overall, the present results paint a fairly optimistic picture of collective wisdom, contrary to the negative picture that the impossibility results on judgment aggregation seem to suggest at first sight. Of course, the details of this picture depend on a number of assumptions and favorable conditions and may change with changes in them. However, possibility results such as the ones discussed here can be illuminating, and I hope to have illustrated the usefulness of the present theoretical approach in identifying the conditions that promote collective wisdom and those that undermine it.

References

Arrow, K. (1951/1963). *Social Choice and Individual Values.* New York, Wiley.

Berend, D., and L. Sapir (2007). "Monotonicity in Condorcet's Jury Theorem with Dependent Voters." *Social Choice and Welfare* 28(3): 507–28.

Boland, P. J. (1989). "Majority Systems and the Condorcet Jury Theorem." *Statistician* 38: 181–89.

Bovens, L., and W. Rabinowitz (2003). "Complex Collective Decisions: An Epistemic Perspective." *Associations* 7: 37–50.

Condorcet, M. de (1785). *Essay sur l'application de l'analyse à la probabilité des décisions rendue à la pluralité des voix.* Paris.

Dennett, D. (1987). *The Intentional Stance.* Cambridge, MA, MIT Press.

Dietrich, F. (2006). "Judgment Aggregation: (Im)possibility Theorems." *Journal of Economic Theory* 126(1): 286–98.

  (2007). "A Generalised Model of Judgment Aggregation." *Social Choice and Welfare* 28(4): 529–65.

  (2008). "The Premises of Condorcet's Jury Theorem Are Not Simultaneously Justified." *Episteme: A Journal of Social Epistemology* 5(1): 56–73.

  (2010). "The Possibility of Judgment Aggregation on Agendas with Subjunctive Implications." *Journal of Economic Theory* 145: 603–38.

Dietrich, F., and C. List (2004). "A Model of Jury Decisions Where All Jurors Have the Same Evidence." *Synthese* 142: 175–202.

  (2007a). "Arrow's Theorem in Judgment Aggregation." *Social Choice and Welfare* 29(1): 19–33.

  (2007b). "Judgment Aggregation by Quota Rules: Majority Voting Generalized." *Journal of Theoretical Politics* 19: 391–424.

  (2007c). "Strategy-Proof Judgment Aggregation." *Economics and Philosophy* 23(3): 269–300.

  (2007d). "Opinion Pooling on General Agendas." London School of Economics.

  (2008). "Judgment Aggregation without Full Rationality." *Social Choice and Welfare* 31: 15–39.

  (2010). "Majority Voting on Restricted Domains." *Journal of Economic Theory* 145: 512–43.

Dokow, E., and R. Holzman (2010a). "Aggregation of Binary Evaluations." *Journal of Economic Theory* 145: 495–11.

  (2010b). "Aggregation of Binary Evaluations with Abstentions." *Journal of Economic Theory* 145: 544–61.

Dryzek, J., and C. List (2003). "Social Choice Theory and Deliberative Democracy: A Reconciliation." *British Journal of Political Science* 33(1): 1–28.

Elster, J. (2007). *Explaining Social Behavior: More Nuts and Bolts for the Social Sciences.* Cambridge, Cambridge University Press.

Estlund, D. (1994). "Opinion Leaders, Independence, and Condorcet's Jury Theorem." *Theory and Decision* 36: 131–62.

Gärdenfors, P. (2006). "An Arrow-like Theorem for Voting with Logical Consequences." *Economics and Philosophy* 22(2): 181–90.

Genest, C., and J. V. Zidek (1986). "Combining Probability Distributions: A Critique and Annotated Bibliography." *Statistical Science* 1(1): 113–35.

Giere, R. (2002). "Distributed Cognition in Epistemic Cultures." *Philosophy of Science* 69: 637–44.

Goldman, A. (2004). "Group Knowledge versus Group Rationality: Two Approaches to Social Epistemology." *Episteme: A Journal of Social Epistemology* 1(1): 11–22.

Goodin, R. E., and C. List (2006). "Special Majorities Rationalized." *British Journal of Political Science* 36(2): 213–41.

Grofman, B., G. Owen, and S. L. Feld (1983). "Thirteen Theorems in Search of the Truth." *Theory and Decision* 15: 261–78.

Guilbaud, G. T. (1966). "Theories of the General Interest, and the Logical Problem of Aggregation." In *Readings in Mathematical Social Science*, ed. P. F. Lazarsfeld and N. W. Henry, 262–307. Cambridge, MA, MIT Press.

Knight, J., and J. Johnson (1994). "Aggregation and Deliberation: On the Possibility of Democratic Legitimacy." *Political Theory* 22(2): 277–96.

Knorr Cetina, K. (1999). *Epistemic Cultures: How the Sciences Make Knowledge.* Cambridge, MA, Harvard University Press.

Kornhauser, L. A., and L. G. Sager (1986). "Unpacking the Court." *Yale Law Journal* 96: 82–117.

    (1993). "The One and the Many: Adjudication in Collegial Courts." *California Law Review* 81: 1–59.

Ladha, K. (1992). "The Condorcet Jury Theorem, Free Speech and Correlated Votes." *American Journal of Political Science* 36: 617–34.

Lehrer, K., and C. Wagner (1981). *Rational Consensus in Science and Society.* Dordrecht, Reidel.

    (2001). *Mission Impossible: The Problem of Democratic Aggregation in the Face of Arrow's Theorem.* D Phil thesis, University of Oxford.

    (2003). "A Possibility Theorem on Aggregation over Multiple Interconnected Propositions." *Mathematical Social Sciences* 45(1): 1–13 (with correction in *Mathematical Social Sciences* 52 [2006]: 109–10).

    (2004). "A Model of Path-Dependence in Decisions over Multiple Propositions." *American Political Science Review* 98(3): 495–513.

    (2005). "Group Knowledge and Group Rationality: A Judgment Aggregation Perspective." *Episteme: A Journal of Social Epistemology* 2(1): 25–38.

    (2006). "The Discursive Dilemma and Public Reason." *Ethics* 116(2): 362–402.

    (2008). *Distributed Cognition: A Perspective from Social Choice Theory.* Scientific Competition: Theory and Policy, Conferences on New Political Economy, vol. 24, ed. M. Albert, D. Schmidtchen, and S. Voigt. Tübingen, Mohr Siebeck.

    (2011). "The Logical Space of Democracy." *Philosophy and Public Affairs* 39: 262–97.

List, C. (forthcoming). "The Theory of Judgment Aggregation: An Introductory Review." *Synthese.*

List, C., and R. E. Goodin (2001). "Epistemic Democracy: Generalizing the Condorcet Jury Theorem." *Journal of Political Philosophy* 9: 277–306.

List, C., R. C. Luskin, J. S. Fishkin, and I. McLean (2000/2006). *Deliberation, Single-Peakedness, and the Possibility of Meaningful Democracy: Evidence from Deliberative Polls.* London, London School of Economics.

List, C., and P. Pettit (2002). "Aggregating Sets of Judgments: An Impossibility Result." *Economics and Philosophy* 18: 89–110.

    (2004). "Aggregating Sets of Judgments: Two Impossibility Results Compared." *Synthese* 140: 207–35.

    (2011). *Group Agency: The Possibility, Design and Status of Corporate Agents.* Oxford, Oxford University Press.

List, C., and C. Puppe (2009). "Judgment Aggregation: A Survey." In *Oxford Handbook of Rational and Social Choice*, ed. P. Anand, P. K. Pattanaik, and C. Puppe, 457–82. Oxford, Oxford University Press.

Miller, D. (1992). "Deliberative Democracy and Social Choice." *Political Studies* 40 (special issue): 54–67.

Nehring, K., and C. Puppe (2002). "Strategyproof Social Choice on Single-Peaked Domains: Possibility, Impossibility and the Space Between." Davis, University of California.

    (2010). "Abstract Arrovian Aggregation." *Journal of Economic Theory* 145: 467–94.

Page, S. E. (2007). *The Difference: How the Power of Diversity Creates Better Groups, Firms, Schools, and Societies.* Princeton, NJ, Princeton University Press.

Pauly, M., and M. van Hees (2006). "Logical Constraints on Judgement Aggregation." *Journal of Philosophical Logic* 35: 569–85.

Pettit, P. (1993). *The Common Mind: An Essay on Psychology, Society and Politics* (paperback ed. 1996). New York, Oxford University Press.

    (2001). "Deliberative Democracy and the Discursive Dilemma." *Philosophical Issues* (suppl. to *Nous*) 11: 268–99.

Pigozzi, G. (2006). "Belief Merging and the Discursive Dilemma: An Argument-Based Account to Paradoxes of Judgment Aggregation." *Synthese* 152: 285–98.

Rubinstein, A., and P. Fishburn (1986). "Algebraic Aggregation Theory." *Journal of Economic Theory* 38: 63–77.

Surowiecki, J. (2004). *The Wisdom of Crowds: Why the Many Are Smarter Than the Few.* London, Abacus.

Wilson, R. (1975). "On the Theory of Aggregation." *Journal of Economic Theory* 10: 89–99.

10

Democracy Counts

Should Rulers Be Numerous?

David Estlund

In this essay I want to consider the moral significance of numbers in normative democratic theory. In Section I, I suggest that the element of generality in liberal approaches to political justification leaves open many questions about how numerous the rulers should be. Even once democracy itself is assumed, the question of numbers is far from settled. All democracies employ subsets of the citizenry for much of the work of legislation and policy. Even supposing that they must be somehow democratically authorized, that says nothing yet about how numerous they should be. In Section II, I consider a handful of expanding and shrinking factors in order to make several observations about how these countervailing considerations might be thought to interact. There are no practical conclusions in the offing. My modest aim is only to exhibit some of the complexity about numbers that remains even when the principle of democracy, or inalienable popular sovereignty, is taken for granted.

I. FROM LIBERAL REPUBLICANISM TO REPRESENTATIVE DEMOCRACY

A. Sovereignty and Numbers

The idea of democracy is partly about numbers and partly about class. The term *demos* in ancient Greece referred to the class of ordinary people with no special qualifications to rule. Those with special qualifications were thought to be small in number as well, but that is a separable point. The main appeal of rule by

Previous versions of some of these ideas were presented and discussed at a conference entitled "Referenda and Direct Democracy: Moral and Legal Dilemmas," at Tel Aviv University, June 5–6, 2000; at the Colloquium on Law, Economics, and Politics, convened by Lewis Kornhauser and Lawrence Sager in 2001; at a workshop at Australia University in 2002; and at the conference on collective wisdom at Collège de France in 2008. I am grateful to participants on all of those occasions for comments and suggestions. I thank Andrew Rehfeld for instructive comments on a draft of this essay.

230

the experts was certainly not that they were few but that they were expert. The appeal for democrats of rule by the demos, the many who, by definition, have no special ruling expertise, can easily look puzzling framed in this way. What do they have going for them other than their numbers, and yet how could that possibly be a reason for them to rule? Plato raised this question repeatedly.[1] In the *Protagoras* he considers the suggestion that no elite should rule because in matters of political wisdom no one is much better than anyone else, but this is highly implausible (and Plato does not himself accept it).[2] It conflicts directly with the obvious fact that some are so much *worse* than others. It is doubtful that this could have been behind many people's democratic convictions. So perhaps there is something to the numbers themselves.

But Athenian democracy, while direct in its way, was small in comparison with the democracy of modern states, provinces, and even many cities. Not only did it restrict participation to a subset of subjects; even if it had enlarged the franchise to all resident adults, the numbers would not have been very large. Assuming, for simplicity, that enfranchising nonresidents is out of the question, if democracy is preferable to oligarchy partly because of the larger number of rulers (we don't yet know why this is an advantage), we might expect partisans of democracy to recommend that political communities be larger rather than smaller. Of course, traditionally they have recommended just the opposite. Rousseau is exemplary when he insists that even though every subject ought to share equally in sovereignty, democracy requires that political communities remain small, like Athens. And yet Rousseau unequivocally opposed reducing the number of active legislators by having some smaller set represent the others. Should the rulers be numerous or not?

Rousseau's deeper principle, of course, was generality, not numerosity. Society, he insisted, must be governed in accordance with a general will, roughly the shared contents of every member's particular will. Here generality is the crucial thing, not numbers. The principle that should guide government must be in accordance with the will of each citizen (at least so long as that will respects the same status for each other person's will; call this constraint *reasonableness*). I'll call this principle of justifiability to each *liberal republicanism*. I will call the status of being owed such a justification the status of *citizen*.

Liberal republicanism involves a kind of general will. The requirement that an arrangement be justifiable to each citizen, insofar as the arrangement is reasonable, will typically rule out a lot of arrangements. An arrangement meets this standard only if some part of what is justifiable to me overlaps with what is justifiable to you, and this overlap also overlaps with what is justifiable to the next person, and so on for every single citizen. If there is anything that meets

---

[1] The point occurs throughout the *Gorgias*. For a discussion of several related passages, see R. W. Sharples, "Plato on Democracy and Expertise," *Greece & Rome*, 2d Ser., 41, no. 1 (April 1994): 49–56.

[2] Hobbes also thought people were relatively equal in political wisdom, and so his undemocratic views have a very different basis than Plato's.

this demanding standard, it will be a certain shared content of every citizen's "acceptability set," or a kind of general will. Without saying a lot more than can be said here about the content of the proviso by which rejection is counted only if it is "reasonable," it is impossible to say whether there is any hope of any arrangement ever meeting the standard set by liberal republicanism. On the other hand, the word "reasonable" should not be assumed to mean what it means in ordinary language. It is a placeholder, with its content to be filled in by substantive moral argument about what sorts of grounds of rejection ought morally to be decisive in scuttling a proposal's legitimacy. A reasonable rejection, as I'm using the term here, is simply any rejection with this moral status. Proposals simply to use certain others for our own benefit as if they were tools clearly violate this requirement, but beyond a few simple cases like this the requirement would need more interpretation.

Liberal republicanism precludes justification in terms that any citizen could reasonably reject. I will call the set of considerations acceptable to all reasonable citizens as counting for or against a law or policy the domain of *public reason*.[3]

I believe, and will simply assume here, that Plato's claim that certain people ought to be sovereign (as individuals or an elite) owing to their superior wisdom is precluded by public reason. There is no criterion or indicator of the moral wisdom required of the sovereign that must be accepted by all who recognize the equal citizenship of others. Epistemic arguments for political arrangements are not necessarily all ruled out, but invidious comparisons (as I will call them) are. This leaves what we might call "structural" epistemic arguments, since at least these do not involve invidious comparisons. By a "structural" argument, I mean an argument that supports the epistemic value of some institutional arrangement in a way that does not depend on the use of any criterion by which the wiser citizens can supposedly be identified. For example, institutions protecting and encouraging freedom of expression might be held to promote the epistemic value of democracy in certain conditions, but this does not imply any invidious comparisons.

The question is whether structural epistemic arguments within public reason support popular sovereignty. The move to structural epistemic argument by no means guarantees this. Suppose that there were publicly convincing arguments independent of any invidious comparisons among citizens that justice would be best promoted by a dictatorship. The question of how many rulers there should be could be said to arise, in the first instance, at the level of determining the location of sovereignty. It seems best, though, not to refer to this as a point about *rulers* at all. The reason is that it conceals the step from popular sovereignty to a principle of democracy, a step that requires an argument of its own. I will address that later, but first let me propose some more terminology that will be useful in focusing our attention on this crucial step. By the *sovereign body* I mean the set of individuals whose actual acts of authorization

---

[3] This is approximately the same as Rawls's use of the term in *Political Liberalism*, New York, Columbia University Press, 1993.

are required for legitimate rule. *Liberal republicanism*, recall, is the requirement that justification be acceptable to every reasonable citizen (let *generic republicanism* mean the weaker thesis that justification requires appeal to the good of the governed, not necessarily one by one). It is important to note that liberal republicanism does not logically imply popular sovereignty.

By *popular sovereignty* I mean that no citizen has a greater share of sovereignty than any other, and only citizens are sovereign. It is perfectly consistent (though entirely contestable) to say that the general will (as we might call it), implied by liberal republicanism, might best be ascertained and promoted by some form of elite rule – rule by those most expert at ascertaining and implementing the general will. The set of *citizens*, understood as those to whom justification is owed, may or may not all be among the legitimate *members of the sovereign body*, understood as those whose actual wills are equally weighted in authorizing law and policy.

It is a substantive question, not settled by the concepts, whether only popular sovereignty could be justifiable to every (reasonable) individual. Hobbes, for example, accepts the need for justification to each individual (and is proto-liberal in this sense), but the justification he offers yields only elite sovereignty.[4] Plato, by contrast, is only a generic rather than a liberal republican and shows no sign of accepting either liberal republicanism or popular sovereignty.

An important question, then, is whether liberal republicanism – the requirement of justification to each person who will be subject to the authority in question – can (contra Hobbes) be met only by popular sovereignty (even though they are two different things).

But the next important point is that, in any case, popular sovereignty does not entail democracy. The reason is that the bare idea of popular sovereignty would seem to allow each individual to autonomously alienate or transfer her share of authority on all political matters to some other person or group. This does not reduce the idea of popular sovereignty to nothing. The crucial question would constantly arise as to whether the authoritative act of transferring authority had actually occurred as the principle of popular sovereignty would, at a minimum, require. But *democracy* would be the stronger principle that no individual's share of sovereignty can successfully be alienated in this global way. This is so far vague, since I assume the concept of democracy doesn't preclude democratic authorization of representatives or delegates in certain circumscribed ways. I will suppose that *alienation* of one's sovereignty is the irrevocable authorization of another person or body, whereas (certain kinds of) revocable or responsive authorization of another is not alienation of sovereignty. Government by representatives should not, in this day and age, be precluded by a definition of democracy, since it would be obtuse to hold that "representative democracy" is an oxymoron. The substantive questions

---

[4] Although Hobbes, in *Leviathan*, normally speaks of the sovereign by way of the singular terms such as "he" and "his," he allows that as "assembly of men" might be made sovereign. Nowhere, however, does he allow that all subjects jointly constitute the sovereign.

are not about whether representative democracy is democracy, but when, if ever, governance through representatives is legitimate or advisable. If we see the requirement of democracy as the conjunction of popular sovereignty with inalienable sovereignty, and add that sovereignty is alienated in the prohibited sense only when the transfer of authority is irrevocable, then we have begged no questions about the legitimacy of all institutions in which there are representatives. The legitimacy and advisability of revocable representation remain open.

Who are the rulers? If sovereignty is alienable, the members of the sovereign are not guaranteed to be the rulers, since it is a status they could transfer irrevocably. If sovereignty is inalienable, members of the sovereign are also the ultimate rulers. If sovereignty is also popular – equally possessed by every citizen – every citizen is equally and inalienably a ruler.

B. Representation

Election means the (revocable or responsive) sovereign authorization, by voting, of a person or body to make certain choices on behalf of, or in the name of, the sovereign body (which we are supposing is the whole body of citizens). Distinguish appointment from election so that an *appointment* is the authorization of a person or body not directly by the sovereign body, but by some other person or body authorized to do so. Let *policy* mean all collective decisions that are not elections or appointments. (A special case is legislation, which will be discussed later.)

Once popular sovereignty is accepted, there is no avoiding representation in some form. Even Athenian democracy could not entirely govern through the general assembly.[5] Even if all policy questions could be brought before the sovereign body, there must still be implementation, and the implementers must somehow be chosen. Either they are chosen by the sovereign body, which would be representation, or they are chosen by someone else so authorized by the sovereign body, in which case that person is the representative. Either way there is representation. (Nothing, by the way, is implied here about any relation between the representative and the represented other than that the one authorizes the other.)

If popular sovereignty is inalienable, as the principle of democracy says, then not only must there be representation, but it must be revocable or responsive to the will of the sovereign body. It is tempting to call this "representative democracy," but there is an ambiguity in this term that will come up shortly.

It may seem as though the implementers could, for all the principle of democracy says, be chosen without any democratic authorization, such as by a hereditary scheme, or by lot, or by some other method provided for constitutionally. Constitutions are themselves limitations on the exercise of popular sovereignty,

---

[5] See Bernard Manin, *Principles of Representative Government*, Cambridge University Press, 1997, p. 5.

but they are not inconsistent with it so long as they do not create any alternative sovereign for any purpose. A constitution may have provisions that are not open to sovereign revision, but there might still be no sovereign other than the body of citizens. If the constitution instituted a hereditary line for certain positions, the holders of those positions would not be popularly authorized, and so would be parallel or alternative sources of sovereignty. Whether or not this is a decisive argument against heredity depends on whether there are decisive reasons for insisting on popular sovereignty, a question I will not take up. I leave aside the question of how far the constitution must be popularly authorized. My question concerns when an authority arrangement, possibly including a constitution, itself incorporates popular sovereignty. The question becomes pointed when we concentrate on the inevitability of a relatively small number of policymakers for at least a sizable fraction of policy decisions.

Some might say that the question of direct versus representative democracy is not about whether every policy is somehow democratically authorized, but only whether *legislation* must be made by the whole sovereign body or whether it might instead be made by elected or appointed intermediaries. Perhaps then it would be unnecessary to resort to smaller numbers. In truth, though, the emphasis on legislation would not change matters much. Technology may well allow everyone to vote from his home computer or cellular phone, but the amount of time that would be required to run a legislature that consists of all citizens would be wildly infeasible if it is even possible in principle. (Don't think just of time spent voting when bills make it to a final vote. How could the whole body of citizens run the deliberations that would bring the bill to this point? And keep in mind the combined burden of all legislative activities that are constantly occurring at local, state, and national levels of government.)

Even if the time problem were solved, it is not clear that there is a relevant principled distinction between law and all other policy anyway. It is unavoidable that much policy be made by intermediaries rather than by the sovereign body as a whole. And we are taking for granted (by the principle of democracy) that these decisions must be authorized at least indirectly by the popular sovereign body as a whole. They are made either by authorized representatives or by those duly appointed by representatives. Only a small fraction of the necessary decisions could possibly be made by the sovereign body as a whole, and it is a cheap route to direct democracy simply to define any decision made by representatives or appointees as nonlegislative.

If the question arises as to whether representatives count as rulers, there is no reason to deny it. I do not mean only that, as citizens, they too have equal membership in the sovereign group. In addition to this, their status as authorized representatives gives them ruling powers that other citizens lack, and so they are rulers in a further sense. But it would be important to distinguish between authorized rulers and ultimate rulers. The ultimate rulers under inalienable popular sovereignty would still be the set of all citizens, since any other ruler must be authorized by acts of theirs.

C. Regency, Representative Assembly, or Referendum?

Pure direct democracy, then, is wildly infeasible. So the question is not whether democracy can legitimately employ representatives, but when it would be good to do so and when not. Not all decisions can be made by direct democracy, but since some can, there is the question of which ones should and which ones should not. Compare two positions on this question, both available within the commitment to democracy. The first, *pure representative democracy*, is the view that the sovereign body ought not to make any decisions except the election of representatives. The second view, *mixed representative democracy*, holds that while the election of representatives is necessary and legitimate (so long as the arrangements don't amount to an alienation of sovereignty), the sovereign body may also make some nonelective or directly democratic decisions. We might call directly democratic decisions other than elections *referenda*. (Consider here all and only referenda whose passage would constitute legally binding policy.)

Pragmatic reasons preclude pure direct democracy, but it is not clear that it would be desirable anyway. We are assuming popular sovereignty, but the connection between that and numerous rulers requires argument. We can grant inalienable popular sovereignty (democracy) and constitutional limits on its authority (somehow imposed), and even grant that pure direct democracy is wildly infeasible and either pure or mixed representative democracy is required on at least pragmatic grounds. But none of this lends any support to the idea that the representative body must have more than one member, an authorized and legally limited representative legislator. Hobbes had no trouble with the idea that a whole people could be represented by a single person, so nothing about the idea of representation provides the rationale for a large number of legislators rather than a single individual or a small ruling body. In an important sense, this would be a representative democracy, but it would be misleading to let that name, which invariably connotes a large number of representatives, cover it. I will refer to this possible office as *regent*, which connotes derivative authority and also the possibility of either an individual or a small board.[6]

Carl Schmitt noticed this point:

If for practical and technical reasons the representatives of the people can decide instead of the people themselves, then certainly a single trusted representative could also decide in the name of the people. Without ceasing to be democratic, the argumentation would justify an antiparliamentary Caesarism.[7]

---

[6] "Regent, 1. One who rules or reigns; a governor; a ruler. – Milton. 2. Especially, one invested with vicarious authority; one who governs a kingdom in the minority, absence, or disability of the sovereign. 3. One of a governing board; a trustee or overseer; a superintendent; a curator; as, the regents of the Smithsonian Institution." *Webster's Revised Unabridged Dictionary*, 1998.

[7] Carl Schmitt, *The Crisis of Parliamentary Democracy*, Cambridge, MA, MIT Press 1988, p. 34. Schmitt's reference to "Caesarism" shouldn't distract us from the fact that the office that I prefer to call "regent" wouldn't be a dictator but would be constitutionally limited as well as elected.

It may seem that this is precluded by the logistical problem of time that counted against pure direct democracy. No individual, even a professional, could do all that must be done by a legislature. However numerous, elected representatives are expected to closely attend to all legislation. They can do so only with staffs of their own and various appointed agencies to assist. But these devices of assistance could be made available to the regent too. She or they could have extensive powers of appointment constrained by a constitution.

My point is not to recommend the institution of a regent, but to ask what, if anything, is wrong with it from the standpoint of democracy. It is representative, democratically authorized without any alienation of sovereignty, and constitutionally limited. Citizens would not vote for laws, but nor do they do so if the legislature has five hundred members in a society of 200 million citizens.

I believe it is a critical challenge for normative democratic theory to explain what, if anything, would be wrong with a single-member legislature.

II. SHRINKING AND EXPANDING FACTORS

A. No Expansion without Quality

In the remainder of this essay, we will look at several factors that might be thought to press toward larger numbers and several that might press toward smaller numbers. The aim is only to make a beginning toward comparing the significance of these factors when taken together. There are bound to be other factors that bear on the question of numbers and other points to be made even about the ones I consider here. I emphasize this in order to guard against construing any of the arguments here as intended support for any practical proposal. The points I make here are far too preliminary and incomplete for that purpose.

Before looking at particular expanding or shrinking factors, it will help to lay out a simplified picture of how these countervailing considerations might be usefully compared. The primary simplifying device I propose is to imagine only three sizes, to be vaguely construed as regency, representative assembly, and referendum. This framework yields two places where an expanding or a shrinking factor might apply: between regency and representative assembly, or between assembly and referendum. We can leave the numbers involved fairly vague for our purposes, but let us assume that the referendum size is in the millions and the representative assembly size is between, say, a hundred and a few thousand. Figure 10.1 summarizes these points. Before looking at the specific shrinking and expanding factors, notice that countervailing factors have no general tendency to resolve in a middle space between the polar extremes.

In Figure 10.1 consider range A, the choice between small and medium numbers, or between regency and assembly. Suppose the shrinking and expanding factors resolve so as to push to the medium numbers. But then what would prevent them from resolving in the same direction in range B, the choice between

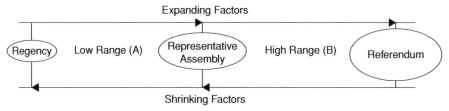

FIGURE 10.1. Expanding and shrinking factors.

medium and large numbers? What would stop the expanding factors from out-
weighing the shrinking factors? The same question can easily be put starting
from the other direction. If shrinking factors outweigh expanding factors in
range B, pushing toward assembly as against referendum, why wouldn't they
continue to prevail in range A, pressing all the way to regency?

Of course, we will have to look more closely at the factors to see how they
might resolve. The point here is just an introductory one: there is no general
reason to assume that countervailing factors will resolve somewhere between
the poles. Sometimes they do. If I have some reason to bring a large suitcase,
in order to fit more clothes, and some reason to take only a small suitcase,
which is easier to carry, these might resolve in favor of taking a middle-sized
suitcase, compromising between the countervailing factors. But in other cases,
the stronger factor might simply prevail. The stronger team in a tug of war
might be only slightly stronger, but that will not prevent it from pulling the
other team all the way over the goal line. Countervailing reasons can operate
this way as well: there might be some reasons to write a long book, but some
reasons to write a short book. It is by no means guaranteed that these will
resolve in favor of a middle-length book.

Consider, then, a list of several considerations that might be offered in favor
of larger numbers:

Fair deliberation: fairness to all views. Apart from any tendency to produce
   good deliberations or outcomes, each person is owed a hearing.
Coverage: representation of all interest perspectives. Each person's interests
   should be entered into deliberations if voters are to make an informed
   decision.
Condorcet: aggregative knowledge. Other things equal, if voters are better
   than random on the choice at hand, under majority rule voters will make
   correct decisions more often if they are more numerous, apart from any
   benefits of discussion.
Collective wisdom: inclusion of all reason perspectives. Different people
   bring different perspectives to public discussion, enhancing the epistemic
   quality of the process.

Three of these four, excepting only fair deliberation, suggest that larger numbers of participants are supported by the higher quality this would lend to the

outcomes or at least to the content of the deliberation. The first, fair deliberation, is put forward by Waldron as a nonepistemic account of the rationale for large numbers in the assembly, and I criticize his argument shortly.

Incidentally, there is no institutional necessity that the voters and deliberators be the same set of people, and some interesting questions arise if we contemplate distinguishing them. But here, in order to focus on certain points, we will assume that they are identical.

It is hard to think of expanding factors that do not rely on quality considerations. The familiar idea of procedural fairness to all participants makes no reference to quality of deliberations or outcomes, but nor does it have any apparent tendency to support larger numbers. There is no reason a regency could not be procedurally fair to all members of the larger polity. Suppose the members were chosen by lot, for example. Who does this unfairly favor? If that is a fair procedure but an objectionable one, the objections must be on grounds other than procedural fairness alone.

It might be argued that larger numbers than regency can be supported on the grounds that they are required in order to get a statistically representative assembly and that this rationale requires no appeal to the idea that this improves the content of the deliberations or the outcomes. But if that is so, what *is* the reason for having a statistically representative legislative body? To ensure that no quality considerations are moving us, suppose that we happen to know that, as it happens, even in the statistically representative body no outcomes or arguments will arise beyond those that would have arisen in a regency. Now, with those quality considerations out of the picture, what reason is there to have a representative assembly? At this point it is natural to say that people have a right to have their point of view represented, even apart from whether this improves the content of the deliberations or the outcomes. This, I take it, is Waldron's rationale, a kind of fairness to views.

B. Waldron's Fairness to Views

Waldron directly considers the question of why representative assemblies should be large.[8] He thinks discussion is central to the explanation, but not because of any tendency of discussion to promote wise decisions.[9] For Waldron, *large assemblies air a wide range of citizens' concerns, and this is important as a form of fairness to citizens whose disagreements run deep.* Individual rulers or small boards of regents would not air as broad a range of views, unfairly privileging the views of the powerful few.

---

[8] Jeremy Waldron, "Speech: Legislation by Assembly," *Loyola Law Review* 46 (2000): 507–34.

[9] In *Law and Disagreement*, Oxford University Press, 2001, Waldron gives a number of reasons for avoiding the appeal to epistemic value, especially his claim that no account of this value could be widely enough accepted by citizens with such deep and wide disagreements. I discuss this argument in "Waldron on *Law and Disagreement*," *Philosophical Studies* 99, no. 1 (May 2000): 111–28.

For Waldron, the point is not the sheer number of views represented, but the institutional effort to let *more of the people* have their views represented, whatever those views might be. It is a kind of respect to take people into account "as active intelligences and consciences."[10] Waldron is clear that he is contrasting the fairness of a large assembly to any emphasis on the epistemic value of such a process. He explicitly puts aside Aristotle's idea that a large number of people can come together to achieve a better understanding than any could have alone. The fairness embodied in large assemblies is, in Waldron's view, an explicitly nonepistemic kind of fairness.

Certainly, it would be plausible to say that a procedure is unfair if participants have *unequally accurate views of their own convictions or interests* when the vote is taken, and deliberation before the vote might be held to reduce this kind of unfairness. One problem with this approach is that it has not avoided epistemic claims for the process after all. On this view, a fair majoritarian process is one that aggregates expression of informed preferences, not simply brute preferences, and *the process transforms brute preferences to informed ones*. More precisely, the process has two phases: deliberation and voting. The deliberation phase is not recommended on grounds of its fairness but on grounds of its ability to transform the inputs in a valued way. The voting phase is one way of giving each person an equal chance of determining the outcome (though not the only way) and could be called fair on this basis. Since Waldron's recommendation of large assemblies on grounds of fairness appeals crucially to the airing of a wide variety of views, the deliberative phase is crucial to his conception of the process. If he explains the value of that phase in terms of people becoming better informed, this is an epistemic function and so not a matter of the kind of nonepistemic fairness that he hopes is a sufficient explanation for large assemblies.

A second problem for this fairness-based approach is that what is normally troubling about unequally accurate interest views or unequally informed preferences is not mainly the unfairness this might involve. Fairness alone would seem only to require that no one's view of his interests be more accurate than another's; it cannot tell us whether we should rectify the erroneous views or instead reduce the accuracy of the more accurate. The unfairness of the process, distinguished carefully from any more epistemic or instrumental value, would be removed either way. It is not fairness, then, that underlies the impulse in favor of a process in which voters are well informed about their interests. Having pointed this out, though, we might still ask whether a plausible account has to appeal to the epistemic value of the procedure with respect to the quality of the outcomes, rather than (or in addition to) only with respect to the quality of the inputs.

On Waldron's view, after the wide range of views have been given a fair hearing, a vote is taken in the assembly, and a majority or plurality of some specified size prevails. Even if we allowed that a fair process of social decision

---

[10] Waldron, "Speech," p. 529.

must involve public deliberation, why then proceed by majority rule rather than a random choice from all post-deliberation views, or even from all possible social choices, or some randomly generated list? A procedure in which the outcome is randomly chosen in one of these ways looks, on its face, not to treat any participant unfairly in the procedure. It seems objectionable only for its epistemic irrelevance.

Giving a person the chance to enter her views into public deliberation prior to a majoritarian procedure can certainly be, as Waldron says, a way of expressing a certain kind of *respect* for the person. And giving everyone something approaching an equal chance of this kind can express a kind of equal respect. This in turn may seem to be more accurately described as a form of fairness than as a device of collective wisdom. The question is whether this strikes us as any valuable form of respect even if we purge the scene of all traces of epistemic value. The idea of fairness to views is difficult to understand without assuming that the goal is a deliberation or outcome that is more responsive to the genuine balance of applicable reasons. It is crucially different, then, from other appeals to procedural fairness in which these quality issues are left completely aside.[11]

C. Quality Grounds for Expansion

I doubt, then, that there is any plausible account of why the numbers should be larger than a regency that refrains from any claims about the salutary effect of the larger numbers on the deliberations or decisions. Without defending the more quality-based rationales, I will simply suppose for expository purposes that they succeed in supporting a preference for larger numbers than regency. We will later turn to the question of whether there are shrinking factors that countervail this support.

Several questions arise if we look at range B in Figure 10.1, the larger range involving the choice between representative assembly and referendum. One question is whether there are new expanding factors at that level. I will simply assume that there are not. Another question is whether the expanding factors in the small range are still expanding factors in the large range. We are not yet asking whether they are countervailed by other factors, but only whether there is a *pro tanto* or defeasible quality advantage in large over medium numbers. Another way of asking this is to inquire whether the advantages of large numbers somehow run out or precipitously fade away above the middle range. Consider three quality arguments for middle rather than small numbers:

1. Coverage: Representation of All Interest Perspectives. The idea of a regency naturally prompts the objection that only a small subset of relevant points of view are given any political influence. Middle-sized numbers (assembly size)

---

[11] For more discussion of these matters see David Estlund, *Democratic Authority*, Princeton University Press, 2008, pp. 93–96.

will tend to represent a larger subset, which seems to be an improvement that would tend to result in less injustice. Now the question is whether it would still be a further improvement of the same kind to move from the middle numbers of an assembly to the large numbers of rule by referendum (so far as feasible, in a mixed system).

Clearly no further improvement would be possible if all relevant interests were already represented by a body of the assembly size. This would not be guaranteed by size alone and might require further arguments about the value of elections or of statistical representation. However, it is implausible in any case to think that the number of relevant interest perspectives is smaller than the number of people. The idea that, for some balance of reasons, we should settle for a representation of only a subset of relevant points of view is not at all the same as the far less plausible idea that the interest perspectives that are not represented are not relevant.[12]

Suppose there is a diminishing marginal value of the following kind: for each representative added, fewer people get their relevant interest perspective thereby represented. This might be so under some arrangements, although it would require some mechanism whereby the largest constituencies get represented first. While both election and lot might be argued to have this effect, I will not pursue the question here. In any case, if the number of relevant perspectives is equal or close to the number of citizens, the goal of representing as many relevant interest perspectives as possible does remain an expanding factor even in the high range. Whether or not it is countervailed by some shrinking factor is a question taken up later.

2. Condorcetian Aggregation.

The expanding factor based on Condorcet's Jury Theorem,[13] consisting in the epistemic value (under certain conditions) of larger numbers of voters, has a similar profile. There is no reason to think of it as dramatically weaker in either the large or the small range. There is a diminishing marginal epistemic value of extra votes, but in our simplified model we cannot say that the marginal extra voter matters significantly less in the high range than in the low range. We can be sure it matters very little in the higher parts of the high range, since the closer the group competence gets to 1 the less difference there is to be made even by a very large number of additional voters. It follows that the marginal value must diminish, but how fast it diminishes will apparently depend on how close the average individual competence is to .5. For example, if it is far above .5, the group competence will get very close to 1 even at the moderate size we're calling the assembly. So marginal votes cannot be worth a great deal above that size. But if the average

---

[12] The cases of interest perspectives and reason perspectives might be different on this score. See Jon Elster's discussion of this in Chapter 7, this volume.

[13] For explanations of the basics of the Jury Theorem and some applications to democratic theory see Estlund, *Democratic Authority* (which includes a critique), and Robert Goodin, *Reflective Democracy*, Oxford University Press, 2003.

competence is only slightly above .5, the group competence might still be a long way from 1 even at a size far above the assembly level. I doubt there is any basis for supposing the average competence to be, say, .6 rather than .501. Since we are simplifying to only two ranges, we might summarize this uncertainty, combined with the fact that there must be some diminishing value, by saying this expanding factor is only modestly weaker in the high range. It remains an expanding factor.

3. Collective Wisdom: Deliberation among All Reason Perspectives. The expanding factor of the value of public reasoning among a large and diverse set of participants seems again to operate in the large as well as in the small range, leaving aside for now whether there are countervailing factors. The reason is similar to that in the case of coverage. Just as the number of relevant interest perspectives approximates the number of citizens, why think that the number of relevant reason perspectives is any smaller? Again, there may be some institutional arrangement in which the marginal representative brings to the table the reason perspectives of fewer citizens. Still, this remains an expanding factor unless, above middle numbers, marginal representatives failed to bring in any new reason perspectives at all. This is extremely doubtful. Whether or not there are good reasons on balance for sticking to the assembly size, it is hard to see what basis there could be for thinking there are significantly fewer reason perspectives than there are citizens. I count this as a (*pro tanto*) expanding factor even in the high range.

D. Shrinking Factors

We turn now to several candidates for shrinking factors: considerations that support smaller numbers. Something might be a shrinking factor in one range but not the other, so the two ranges require separate consideration in the case of each factor. First, though, we will see that most of the candidates fail to count as shrinking factors after all. In considering the shrinking factors, I will consider not only whether they are indeed shrinking factors, but also, if they are, how they might weigh up against the quality-based expanding factors we allowed earlier.

1. Pragmatic: Pure Direct Democracy Fails Utterly, on Pragmatic Grounds. We have seen that pure direct democracy is infeasible in its demands on citizens' time and productive energy. This might seem to suggest that referendum sets the number or fraction of the citizenry who participate in legislation too high. But all it really shows is that referendum can feasibly be used only in a mixed system in which some fraction of questions is handled by other means. Once that is assumed, the pragmatic problem with deciding some appropriate fraction of issues by referendum evaporates. It turns out that the problem is not too many people, but too many issues. We will assume, then, that pure direct democracy is not an option and that only a feasible number of issues will be put to referendum if referendum is used at all. The pragmatic shrinking factor disappears.

If we are assuming a mixed system, and supposing referendum were to be used for some fraction of issues, there would remain the other issues to be handled by some smaller number. The question would remain whether those issues should be decided by assembly or by regency.

A distinct pragmatic consideration that might seem to favor shrinking is the idea that in a larger assembly the incentives to inform oneself and participate become so small as to outweigh the expected value. If so, this would encourage free-riding on informed others, leading to a decline in participation and in individual competence.[14] Notice, however, that the picture is different for members of an assembly than for ordinary voters in several respects. First, assemblies fall within a fairly narrow range of sizes (as Elster shows in Chapter 7, this volume). The choice of assembly size may not make an appreciable difference on the voter's incentives to participate, the chance of casting a deciding vote being very small in any case. Second, once you are already a member of the assembly, voting itself is almost costless. Third, the size of the group doesn't obviously affect the incentives to become an informed and effective speaker. Such a speaker might have just as much chance of swaying a decisive fraction of voters in a large assembly as in a small one. If everyone wanted to speak all the time, there would be reduced chances to speak in a large assembly. But this is normally not the case, and there might be ample time for anyone who wishes to speak to do so even in a large assembly (even if not in an imaginary enormous one of many thousands).

I conclude that shrinking the size of the assembly within the normal range has no obvious advantages with respect to encouraging either the participation or the competence of the members.

2. Preeminence: Some Few Are Significantly Wiser. The idea of preeminence reflects the familiar thought that a well-selected smaller number of rulers is likely to rule more wisely than a larger number of ordinary people. It is surely the most important traditional antidemocratic idea, but even if democracy is assumed there is a need for representation on at least some issues for pragmatic reasons. Then the question can arise, without any antidemocratic implications, as to whether a small number of expert representatives will do better than a large number of less expert representatives.

The *Federalist* papers relied heavily on the idea that legislators would be the best and brightest among us, or at least to the maximal extent possible. This *preeminence* argument (alongside the pragmatic and professionalism arguments) for elected representatives provides a reason to stem the expansion from representative assembly to direct democracy.

This raises a difficult question. Since, as I have argued, invidious comparisons of the political wisdom of citizens are precluded by liberal republicanism's

---

[14] Jon Elster discusses this in Chapter 7, this volume.

constraint of public reason, we must decide whether the claim that election produces an epistemically superior set of representatives involves precluded invidious comparison. (All we need to mean by "superior" here is that they have epistemic features that more than compensate for the presumed epistemic loss involved in the drastically smaller number of participants as compared with direct democracy.) Is the preeminence argument available within public reason? Public reason precludes our identifying any given features that make them superior, but it does not obviously preclude our saying that voters will tend to select superior people. Still, we would need some basis for this that did not appeal to any invidious bases of comparison.

Elections may tend to choose social superiors. But the idea that social superiors have superior moral and political wisdom is a central example of the kind of invidious comparison that I have claimed is open to reasonable rejection.

Manin argues on a priori grounds that election produces representatives who are perceived by voters to have, to a rare degree, some set of features that are deemed by voters to be desirable in a representative.[15] He calls this an "aristocratic" implication of elections that distinguishes them from certain other methods such as lottery. But the argument gives us no reason to suppose that the features being sought have any epistemic value, and in any case it claims only that elected representatives will be perceived to have the rare and desirable features, not that they will actually have them, as Manin clearly notes. So Manin's argument would be no basis for thinking that election produces representatives with sufficient epistemic advantages to offset the epistemic loss involved in the smaller number of participants in a representative body.

On the other hand, if, as we are supposing, the point of having a numerous assembly is that collective deliberation has some epistemic value, and this claim is supposed to be available to public reason, then it would be initially plausible to suppose in parallel fashion that collective deliberation about who would be an epistemically superior representative is itself epistemically effective, at least under certain favorable conditions, and available to public reason. This avoids identifying any nonepistemic feature of candidates, which is selected for by elections, and then claiming, invidiously, that people with that trait are morally or politically wiser than others. Yet it would still suggest that elections have some tendency to select the better candidate. However, this idea leads to a puzzle that reduces its plausibility.

If a set of people can select a subset that is epistemically better despite the loss in numbers (and possibly also a loss of epistemically valuable diversity), the subset could presumably do the same. They could select a smaller subset yet. This sub-subset could do better than the subset, but they could also select a further subset (a sub-sub-subset) that could do even better, and so on. In the end, there would result a regent with a strong claim to epistemic superiority. Call this the *problem of the shrinking assembly*.

---

[15] Manin, *Principles of Representative Government*, 132–49.

The idea that deliberative bodies have epistemic value cuts both ways: they have some epistemic advantages over smaller groups or single individuals, but they presumably would then also have the ability to select epistemically good smaller groups or individuals. Which epistemic effect is greater so far as can be determined within public reason? Notice that an argument that prevents the shrinking assembly will also tend to count against using an assembly at all rather than the larger body of sovereign citizens as a whole. It is hard to see, then, how a preeminence argument for elected representative bodies could be contained to prevent it from justifying the unattractive institution of regency instead. There may be other considerations that allow the first shrinkage but not the second, but so far it is not clear what they would be.

If things have the general structure I have described, either we should think that electoral preeminence favors regency or we should conclude from the implausibility of the supposition that the successively elected regency would rule best, that there was no effect of electoral preeminence even at the first stage, shrinking from referendum to assembly. It is important not to confuse preeminence with professionalism, the very different factor that emphasizes the epistemic benefits of being a legislator as a full-time job. I turn to that factor next. But if we put professionalism aside by supposing that everyone would have the same time and experience to devote to legislation, is it so clear that election would select significantly wiser people than a random selection? That is what electoral preeminence, by itself, supposes. Since, so far as I can see, it would also give rise to the shrinking assembly, I am tentatively inclined to doubt that there is any shrinking factor in the idea of electoral preeminence. Nonelectoral grounds for preeminence are bound to rely on invidious comparisons of a kind that are precluded by the liberal conception of political justification.

3. Professionalism: Time and Experience Promote Quality.

Professionalism is the idea that those who can develop experience in the job and devote themselves full time to it will rule significantly more wisely as a result. This could be a shrinking factor, since it is plain for pragmatic reasons that not everyone could fully acquire the epistemic advantages of professionalism. Leaving legislation to those who can might more than compensate for the epistemic loss from smaller numbers by the increased ability of the smaller number of professional legislators.

There is no problem of a shrinking assembly in this case, since the maximal benefits of professionalization would seem to be available to numbers in the middle range (or more) rather than to only some very small number. So professionalization might be a shrinking factor in the high range, though apparently not in the low range. In the high range, it is countervailed by the quality-based value of larger numbers. The question, then, is whether the lost value of numbers is outweighed by the increased value of professionalization.

On the other hand, there are difficult questions about whether the supposed epistemic value of professionalization relies on invidious comparisons of the kind that are precluded by a liberal conception of justification. The analogy is quite close to the suggestion that those with more education (of some specified kind) are more capable of ruling wisely, a consideration that led no less of an egalitarian liberal than John Stuart Mill to recommend giving extra votes to the educated (among others).[16] The reasons for rejecting Mill's scheme apply reasonably directly to the claim that professional rulers are sufficiently wiser to outweigh the disadvantage of their smaller numbers. I can sketch those reasons only briefly here.

Consider, then, a literacy criterion for voting. From the set of the literate, pull a demographically representative sample, removing the sample error with respect to race and class. Now give double voting power to everyone in the repaired sample, and so half as much to all illiterate citizens (and also to others who were excluded as a consequence of repairing the sample with respect to race and class). In this case, the cognized and demonstrable sample biases are removed, and the beneficial trait of literacy remains. The scheme strikes me as objectionable, but on what grounds? My contention is that objections to this scheme on the grounds that there may remain important sample errors of which we are unaware are not so unreasonable that they should be disqualified. That is, they are decisive against the appeal to a supposed overall epistemic benefit, from the standpoint of the wisdom required for good political rule, of being among the literate portion of the general citizenry. If this seems right in the case of a literacy criterion, why not also for any educational criterion? And if education cannot publicly be held to ground superior ruling wisdom, is professionalization different in any way that would allow it to escape the problem? More argument is required on this point, but for reasons of this kind I doubt that professionalization is available as a public basis for attributing greater political wisdom. In that case, professionalization is not available as a shrinking factor at all.[17]

4. Pathologies of Deliberation: Large Numbers Disrupt Rational Deliberation.
The final candidate for a shrinking factor is the idea that the epistemic benefits of public political deliberation are lost when the number of participants gets too large. A lack of space prevents our looking at any specific pathological mechanisms or processes in any detail. It is commonly pointed out that, in direct democracy, voters face too many issues to deal with them rationally. That objection is out of place here, though, since we are assuming the system must mix some direct democracy with some rule by smaller bodies, precisely to limit the demands on the time and rational attention of voters. So the number of issues they have to face can be modulated pragmatically.

One more pertinent common complaint about large numbers of participants is the claim that civility diminishes with the social distance between interlocutors, so it will be very thin indeed in large mass deliberations. Another worry

[16] Mill, *Considerations on Representative Government*, 1862, ch. 8.
[17] For more see Estlund, *Democratic Authority*, ch. 11.

about large numbers is that the expense of communicating to the whole electorate gives an unwarranted advantage to those who control wealth or media access. I return to this point shortly.

Stepping back from the specific pathologies that might accompany large numbers, let us consider the stakes. Suppose that pathologies of deliberation outweighed the benefits of expanding factors in the high range, and so on balance the assembly size is to be preferred to the referendum size. This would count against having a mixed system, since it counts against having any referenda at all.

Elections are, in effect, referenda themselves on the question of who shall be a representative. If the balance of considerations shows that referenda are seriously impaired by deliberative pathologies, the lesson might also be applied to the context of election as well. These considerations might, then, offer some support for a pure representative system with the assembly chosen by lot, to avoid the pathologies in the deliberations around election contests. On the other hand, there might, in principle, be pathologies about voting on issues that are less pronounced when the decision is between candidates.

Elections of members to representative assemblies have a mitigating feature: typically, the larger polity is divided into numerous sectors or districts so that voters in one district do not face the same slate of candidates as voters in other districts. As a result, the number of participants in any single election is much smaller than the community at large. It might seem, then, that it has been misleading to associate direct democracy with large numbers. Representatives can be directly chosen with only a fraction of the overall citizenry participating in any single choice.

The idea of districting is certainly important for our topic since it has the potential to mitigate any pathologies of large numbers even in a direct democratic procedure. Still, it does not automatically inoculate assembly elections from whatever deliberative pathologies come along with very large numbers. In modern states there are many millions of voters. The number involved in each election to an assembly seat is roughly equal to the number of voters divided by the number of assembly seats. We are, somewhat arbitrarily of course, considering the assembly size to be no larger than around a thousand members. Simplifying again, let us suppose the deliberative pathologies are not significant at that size, which is why assembly is initially favored over referendum with respect to deliberative pathologies. But suppose the pathologies are serious in larger sizes. This means that the pathologies would still be serious in districted assembly elections in polities with more than a million voters: a thousand assembly races decided by a thousand voters each. A larger community than that has too many voters per race, but dividing such a community into more districts increases the size of the assembly to levels where the deliberative pathologies are triggered. These numbers themselves are not to be taken seriously, since we have no clear account of the alleged deliberative pathologies or the numbers of participants required to trigger them, and to what degree, and under what institutional conditions, and so on. But the more abstract point does not depend on the actual numbers: the fact that assemblies are chosen from districts is by no means a way of avoiding whatever deliberative pathologies are involved in large numbers. They would have that value only in political communities that are very small by modern standards.

It would be natural next to consider nested levels of decision so that small groups select representatives to join with other representatives, still partitioned into small groups, to select the next level of representative. To take just one example: Suppose 1,000,000 voters are carved into 10,000 districts, yielding 100 voters per district. This in turn yields 10,000 representatives. But divide them into, say, 100 groups of 100 representatives per group. Have each of these 100 groups select several of their members, say 3, to serve in the final assembly. This yields an assembly size of 300, without any race having been decided by more than 100 voters. Such a nested arrangement has obvious interest for avoiding any pathologies of races involving too many voters. On the other hand, there are innumerable other issues about how such a scheme would operate, and so this single virtue is not any significant basis for recommending such an arrangement.

The idea of nested levels of deliberation suggests a possible reply to the very idea that there are pathologies of deliberation at large numbers. It might be argued that actual deliberations in large communities informally assume a nested structure. Very few participants are actually on the national stage. The image of each citizen deliberating with all other citizens on national questions is misleading in this context. Some citizens do speak to all others, as when they publish their opinions in a nationally accessible way. Still, only a tiny fraction of citizens participate in public deliberation at this level. Most citizens do deliberate with others about political matters, but in contexts ranging in size from a small circle of friends, to neighborhood or community groups, to publications at the level of a city newspaper. Above this size, the number of participants is very small, very possibly falling short of a size at which deliberative pathologies are serious. And at any of the lower levels, too, the numbers may be small enough to avoid the pathologies.

Again, this point is of obvious importance when it comes to evaluating the pros and cons of large numbers. But even if it is true as far as it goes, it leaves out an important sense in which these informally nested deliberators are all in the same boat. In the districting case, the smaller nested groups in districts were not deliberating on the same issue as voters in other districts, since the candidates would be different across districts. In the informal nesting case, we ought to be assuming that the issues are common to all the voters across the nation. After all, the informal nesting point is offered as a reason to deny that there is any need to break the issues up in the way that districting does. So we are imagining national referenda addressed in common by all citizens, even if the number of people addressed by most citizens is far smaller than the number of voters in the nation. The implication, I think, is that while some deliberative pathologies may yet be avoided, others will still be in play.

One sort of pathology that arises when a large number of voters are addressing the same choice is that it is very expensive and yet very effective to advertise one's point of view to the whole large group of voters. This can tend to give an unwarranted advantage to individuals or groups that control either great wealth or access to large communications media. There are empirical complexities about this, since groups with broad support might turn out to be the best at raising money. Still, other things being equal, it seems clear that groups with support among rich people have an additional advantage. I leave aside the empirical questions in order to consider what the implications of this would be if it were true. One implication is that the informal sort of nesting just described would still present one large mass audience for advertising one side or the other on the issue of the national referendum. The advantage of wealth, if there is one, would not be diluted by that kind of nesting. It would be somewhat diluted by the kind of nesting characteristic of assembly districts, since there is no national contest but only hundreds of local contexts. On the other hand, the existence of political parties blurs this distinction somewhat, since assembly elections are often partly framed as contests between national parties, in which case a mass audience for mass advertising of the party's point of view reinstates the advantages of controlling wealth or media access.

III. CONCLUSION

I do not want to impose too tidy a conclusion, since the exercise has not been of that nature. Instead, let me put forward two propositions that I hope receive some support, albeit inconclusive, from the miscellaneous points that have been made in this essay.

First, the (attractive) principle that no individual is morally more important than another from a political point of view is at some argumentative distance from the (dubious) principle that none ought to have more formal political power or influence than another (evidently precluding even rule by assembly). And neither of these is the principle of democracy, which holds (as I understand it) that political power is to be authorized by (not necessarily always exercised by) a sovereign body in which each citizen has an equal and inalienable role.

Second, democratic citizens face complex choices about how numerous the authorized rulers should be, although pure direct democracy is and always has been out of the question. If we wish to criticize the institution of, say, regency, we will need to do without the indefensible charge that it is simply undemocratic.

11

Democratic Reason

The Mechanisms of Collective Intelligence in Politics

Hélène Landemore

INTRODUCTION

Traditional justifications for democracy emphasize procedural or intrinsic arguments such as those based on the ideas of freedom, equality, justice, and fairness. Democracy is supposed to be a good thing because its procedures – deliberation and voting in particular – express values we care about. In this essay,
I explore an alternative, instrumental argument for democracy, which defines
democracy as a collective decision method that is valuable in part because it
channels citizens' collective wisdom or, as I will call it, "democratic reason."
This argument takes seriously the old Aristotelian idea that "many heads are
better than one" and that a party to which the many contribute is better than
a party organized by one person only. In the same vein as recent work done
in philosophy (e.g., Estlund 1997, 2008),[1] social epistemology (e.g., Anderson
2006), political science (e.g., Goodin 2005, 2008; Martí 2006; Ober 2009), and
legal philosophy (e.g., Sunstein 2006, 2009), I thus offer and analyze theoretical
reasons for considering the possibility that democracy has epistemic properties
that make it an instrumentally valuable decision mechanism (see Landemore in
press). More ambitiously perhaps, I propose that, in theory at least, the epistemic properties of democracy make it superior to dictatorship and any plausible variant of the rule of the few. The boldness and originality of the hypothesis
presented here derive in part from the systematic comparison between rule of
one, few, and many and also from the fact that I interpret both dictatorship
and oligarchy in the best possible light, granting that the idealized dictator and
oligarchs pursue the common good as opposed to their self-interest.[2]

---

[1] David Estlund is one of the first contemporary political theorists to have shifted the emphasis
from the intrinsic value of the democratic decision process to its instrumental value, arguing
that the normative authority of democracy is also in part "epistemic," that is, determined by the
tendency of democratic procedures to deliver "correct" or "right" results overall (Estlund 1997,
2008).

[2] I emphasize the originality of the claim because in Estlund's approach, for example, the epistemic
comparison between rule of the many and rule of the few is precluded by the requirement that

While the results of a comparison between the rule of many and the rule of one should be fairly intuitive (if, indeed, many heads are better than one), the second part of the claim is more controversial. If the idea of collective intelligence or collective wisdom applies to the many, it applies to the few as well. How could a group of oligarchs not outsmart the rest of the people if the oligarchs are carefully selected? This is the very thought behind the ideal of aristocracy: the rule of the best and brightest ought to be superior to the rule of regular citizens. In this essay I surmise that this might not be the case. However counterintuitive that claim may sound, an oligarchy of even the best and brightest need not be generally smarter than the many. This is so because of the crucial role of one component of collective wisdom, namely "cognitive diversity," or the existence within the group of multiple ways to see the world and interpret it. Applying the theoretical findings of Lu Hong and Scott Page about the relative importance of cognitive diversity and individual ability for collective problem solving and predictions (Hong and Page 2001, 2004, 2009; see also Chapter 3, this volume; Page 2007), I argue that since an ideal oligarchy of even very smart rulers can be assumed to display less cognitive diversity, at least over the long term, than an ideal democracy (direct or indirect), the few can in general and in the long run not match the epistemic competence of many moderately smart but diversely thinking individuals. In other words, to the extent that cognitive diversity is more likely to exist in the larger than the smaller group, I argue that democracy is more conducive to collective wisdom than any version of the rule of the few.

The power of the hypothesis formulated here is that, if it is true, democracy would be preferable to oligarchy on epistemic grounds *even if one could identify in advance the smartest and most virtuous individuals in a given population.* On the view presented here, in other words, even assuming that we could agree on who the best and brightest are and design what would be the perfect aristocracy, we would still be better off making the decision as a group than delegating the group's political decisions to this subset of best and brightest. To put it yet another way, the reason to include everyone in the collective decision process is not because we cannot know who the knowers are. The reason is that there are good theoretical grounds for believing that, in politics, the best knower is the group itself.

In order to support the view that democracy is, in theory at least, epistemically superior to any version of the rule of the few, I examine two of the decision mechanisms that can be said to give democracy an epistemic edge: maximally inclusive deliberation and majority rule. I argue that, to the extent that cognitive diversity can be assumed to be correlated with the number of participants,

---

any claim to authority satisfy a "general acceptability requirement." According to Estlund, even if an oligarchy of knowers were probably more epistemically reliable than democracy, it would never pass the "general acceptability" test. The hypothesis presented here is not committed to a Rawlsian framework for legitimate political authority and pursues the comparison between all forms of rule on purely epistemic grounds.

deliberation among the many is more likely to be epistemically fruitful than deliberation among the few. I also argue that, given the same assumption of cognitive diversity afforded by numbers, aggregation of judgments among the many can be epistemically as good as aggregation of judgments among the few, even if one makes unrealistic assumptions about the intelligence of the few. Taken together, the epistemic properties of those democratic decision procedures theoretically give democracy an epistemic edge over any variant of the rule of the few.

A caveat about the limitations of the argument presented here is in order. This essay deliberately operates in a simplified and idealized epistemic framework. In particular, I do not dwell on the possibility of epistemic failures in deliberative settings, such as the well-documented problems of polarization, hidden profiles, informational influences, social pressures, and informational cascades.[3] Similarly, I do not address the theoretical problems raised in social theory by the case of multiple, logically connected binary decisions, to which the impossibility results on judgment aggregations apply (e.g., List and Pettit 2002; Pauly and van Hees 2006). Instead, I restrict the analysis to situations where the choice is between two options only. One reason for sticking to a simplified framework is that before adding complicating factors, I must first be able to propose a clear and intelligible model of democratic decision making. Moreover, some of the problems that arise in a more complicated framework would presumably afflict all decision makers, whether few or many, so they are not properly discriminating in the comparison attempted here. For reasons of limited space, I focus here on the positive side of the argument. Finally, let me emphasize that the claimed epistemic properties of democracy defended here are only probable, which is to say that the argument makes room for and recognizes the possibility of democratic mistakes. The question of the proper institutional answers to bring to democratic epistemic failures – actual and probable – is important. I will not, however, address them here.[4]

This essay has five remaining sections. In the first, I develop the concept of "democratic reason" as a label for the distributed collective intelligence of the people and even, occasionally, their collective wisdom. The second section turns to deliberation as the first mechanism of democratic reason and the theoretical reasons that can be adduced for its epistemic properties. The third briefly addresses the problem of deliberation on a large scale and the relation between representation and democratic epistemic performance. The fourth focuses on majority rule and considers successively three plausible theoretical accounts of

---

[3] For an overview of these problems and references to a representative literature, see Sunstein (2006: ch. 3); for a more nuanced assessment of these problems, see Mackie (2009).

[4] I do not address the problem of potentially "tyrannical majorities" either. Popular as an argument against democracy since Tocqueville first articulated it, the problem of tyrannical rulers applies to minorities as well as majorities. It raises the liberal issue, orthogonal to the epistemic question addressed in this essay, of the proper limits of any collective decision method and any form of government (see, e.g., Rehfeld 2008: 266 for a similar and more developed point).

its epistemic properties: the Condorcet Jury Theorem, the "miracle of aggregation," and a model based on cognitive diversity (Page 2007; see also Hong and Page, Chapter 3, this volume). The fifth section provides a long answer to Caplan's (2007a) objection that voters are "rationally irrational," which should make it impossible for what I call democratic reason to emerge. The conclusion recapitulates the epistemic advantages of the rule of the many over versions of the rule of few.

DEMOCRATIC REASON AND EPISTEMIC COMPETENCE

I define "democratic reason" as a certain kind of distributed collective intelligence specific to democratic politics.[5] In what follows I will use the terms "collective intelligence" and "collective wisdom" interchangeably, even though the concept of wisdom is richer than that of intelligence and includes notions of experience, time-tested knowledge, and perhaps even virtue, which certainly ought to be part of democratic reason but which I cannot address in this essay.[6] The only diachronic aspect of intelligence that I touch on is that introduced by the institution of representation, which creates some temporal mediation between the input of citizens and its translation into actual policies.

Democratic reason is also meant in part to contrast with the less inclusive concept of public reason in Rawls, which works as a standard of liberal justification, and perhaps as a theory of limited government, but has little to do with the reason of the public at large, being in effect the reason of representatives, supreme justices, and the like (Rawls 1993). The concept of democratic reason is, by comparison, meant to be maximally inclusive and not a priori limited as to its substance. Similarly, I do not place a particular emphasis on the public dimension of democratic deliberation, preferring to focus on a more open-ended definition of democratic deliberation that may or may not be public in the Rawlsian sense of filtering out certain arguments and involving only "reasonable" people.

Borrowing from the cognitive sciences and suitably modifying for my purposes the concepts of distributed intelligence and cognitive artifact,[7] I call democratic reason the kind of collective intelligence distributed across citizens and a certain number of institutions and practices that can be seen as specific to democratic politics. As I mentioned earlier, in this essay I focus on the synchronic properties of groups of one, few, and many and leave aside the temporal dimension of democratic reason that makes it a variety of collective wisdom.[8]

[5] Democratic reason is in my view an instantiation of the larger phenomenon of "collective wisdom" studied in this volume.

[6] For a broader reflection on the notions of collective wisdom and collective intelligence, see Daniel Andler, Chapter 4, this volume.

[7] See my introduction to this volume for a proper presentation of those concepts.

[8] I do believe, however, that over time democracies are more likely to accumulate collective wisdom than are oligarchies or dictatorships, even though I will not defend this idea here.

I also propose to interpret decision procedures such as collective deliberation and majority rule as cognitive artifacts that help individuals perform a social calculus beyond their individual abilities.

The conceptual gain of an approach to democratic institutions as part of a system for intelligent collective decision making is that it allows us to explain how individual citizens cognitively unburden themselves by letting others, as well as the environment, process parts of the social calculus. Against political scientists worried that individual citizens lack the capacity for self-rule, which arguably places the right of the people to self-rule on shaky foundations, the concept of democratic reason allows one to reply that what matters is not just what individuals can do on their own, but what they can do with the help of political cognitive artifacts such as inclusive deliberation and majority rule (as well as other political cognitive artifacts that I am not considering).[9] Another way to say this is that democratic decision procedures are societal ways of making collective decisions that economize on individual epistemic competence. Notice that this is a distinct argument from the traditional idea that democracies economize on virtue.[10]

Closely related to the idea of democratic reason is the notion of epistemic competence, which is the competence one has by virtue of knowing something or having a certain kind of knowledge. I distinguish it from moral competence or virtue. Virtue ensures that a ruler wants to promote the common good rather than her private interest or that of a subset of the citizenry. Ideally we want rulers who are both smart and virtuous. One might be smart and morally evil – see the common good and refuse to choose it. In order to keep things simple here, I will assume that all rulers – whether one, few, or many – want the same thing, namely the common good. As already noted, by doing so I deliberately stack the deck in favor of oligarchy and dictatorship.

I also distinguish epistemic competence from the mere possession of information. Information is the raw data about political facts that citizens are supposed to need in order to form enlightened judgments. The relationship between

---

[9] The fact that collective intelligence can be distributed not just through space but also over time introduces an important temporal dimension into the concept of democratic reason. Democracies should be able to learn, particularly from their own mistakes, how to immunize themselves against the worst forms of individual and collective cognitive failures. It seems to me that democracies have the capacity to learn over time, as was recently evidenced, in my view, by the fact that a woman could run for president in France in 2007 and a black man in the United States in 2008.

[10] In the following, I will use the term "epistemic mechanism," or "mechanism" for short, rather than "cognitive artifact," but by "mechanism" I mean essentially the same thing as a cognitive artifact, namely a device – institution, practice, etc. – that helps us facilitate a calculus or a task. Deliberation and majority rule supplement each other in producing democratic reason. Of course, to the extent that deliberation and majority rule are epistemic mechanisms available to oligarchs and even, in a degenerate form, to dictators, I will explain why the combination of democratic deliberation and majority rule with universal suffrage is superior to the combination of deliberation among the few and majority rule among the few.

information and enlightened judgment is often reduced to a simple equation by political scientists, as if the level of information were all that mattered to establish and predict epistemic competence. It is generally assumed that to the extent that citizens do not know a set of facts – the name of their senator, the capital of Japan, which candidate supports which economic platform, the meaning of "welfare" or "liberalism" – they are epistemically incompetent. This assumption, however, rests on an empirical claim that is in my view not fully established.

For the sake of analytical clarity, I will therefore bracket the information question until the last section, where I deal with Caplan's critique of the miracle of aggregation and his more general point about the fact that democracy creates disincentives in voters to become properly informed, which is a problem if low levels of information correlate with bad choices. For now, I will simply assume that the same level of information is made available to all types of rulers (one, few, or many), be it through polls, information markets, or boards of advisers. In my view, what matters for collective epistemic competence is not so much the level of individual information as the collective level of information, as well as the existence of institutions that work as mechanisms gathering and processing this information for the group. I suspect that democratic institutions do not reduce the collective level of information, and I doubt that democratic citizens on average individually fall below the threshold that allows them to vote competently anyway, at least on most important issues. I should emphasize that I also draw a distinction between available information – which I assume is the same for all the regimes compared – and actually processed information and the additional, refined knowledge that this may produce – which may vary from one decision procedure to the next.[11]

Finally, I distinguish between collective epistemic competence and individual epistemic competence. As I said earlier, collective epistemic competence might be more than just the sum of individual epistemic competences, and indeed a property emerging from the right mix of individual epistemic competence and some other factors. Controlling for virtue and information available at the level of the group, collective epistemic competence is essentially a function of two things: individual epistemic competence and the cognitive diversity of the group.

Once we have an answer to the question of which decision procedure has, in theory, the highest collective epistemic competence, given an equal amount of information and virtue in the rulers, it will be easier to reintroduce the (raw) information and virtue components and see whether doing so modifies the conclusions reached.

---

[11] Hence, when I argue later that deliberation contributes to pooling and bringing out relevant information, I am not reintroducing something I bracketed initially. I simply point out that, based on an identical pool of raw data, deliberation allows for the identification of relevant knowledge and occasionally produces additional knowledge or information. I further argue that inclusive deliberation is better at doing this than less inclusive deliberation.

DELIBERATION: THE FORCELESS FORCE OF THE BETTER ARGUMENT

The first mechanism that arguably makes democracy an epistemically reliable collective decision rule is inclusive deliberation – that is, deliberation that involves, directly or indirectly, all the members of the group.[12] In what follows, I embrace a relatively classical notion of deliberation as an exchange of arguments for or against something (Aristotle, *Rhetoric*, I, 2). I also follow many contemporary deliberative democrats in adding to that definition the goal of a rational agreement or consensus on the better answer or argument (e.g., Cohen 1989: 21; Thompson 2008; for a dissenting view, see Mansbridge et al. 2010). Similarly, I embrace the distinction between deliberation and bargaining or negotiating (e.g., Elster 1986). On my view, deliberation, whether it is used among democrats or oligarchs, is not supposed to involve threats, promises, sophistry, or any form of "strategic" rather than "communicative" action. The better argument is supposed to triumph through what Habermas famously calls its "unforced force," that is, its obvious epistemic superiority.[13] The ideal of deliberation I have in mind is characterized by its emphasis on arguments and the search for a consensus of epistemically high quality for the sake of an impending decision.

Deliberation is generally credited with having three properties arguably conducive to its epistemic properties. Deliberation is supposed to

1. enlarge the pool of ideas and information;
2. weed out the good arguments from the bad; and
3. lead to a consensus on the "best" or most "reasonable" solution.

The first effect would seem to be irrelevant to the comparison attempted here among ideal competing decision-making procedures (rule of one, few, and many) to the extent that I have assumed an initially identical pool of information. Notice, though, that I did not assume that this identical pool amounts to full information. What I will ask in this section, therefore, is whether deliberation, used among few or many, can enlarge that initial pool of information by refining the available raw data or producing new knowledge on the basis of such data. The other two effects, I suppose, are self-explanatory.

In order to illustrate such alleged effects of deliberation, let me consider two stylized situations of what occurs in a deliberative process. I borrow the first example from the film *Twelve Angry Men*. The beauty of that example is that, among other things, it easily lends itself to an epistemic reading, since the jury deliberation assumes a procedure-independent standard of truth to be figured out: the defendant is either guilty or not guilty.

In the film, one brave dissenting jury member – number 8, played by the actor Henry Fonda – manages to persuade the other eleven jurors to reconsider the

---

[12] I leave outside the discussion of this essay the boundary question (of who belongs to the group), even though it is a central question for democratic theory.

[13] I summarize here a huge literature on the subject, following a recent survey by Martí (2006).

guilty sentence they are about to pass on a young man charged with murder. Asking the other jurors to "talk it out" before making up their mind, juror number 8 takes the group on a long deliberative journey, which ultimately ends in unanimous acquittal. *Twelve Angry Men* can be seen as illustrating the phenomenon of collective intelligence emerging from deliberation. Juror number 8, left to his own devices, would have been unable to demonstrate that the sentence was beyond reasonable doubt. Only by harnessing the intelligence of the other members, occasionally against their own passions and prejudice, does the group ultimately reach the truth.

The contributions to the deliberation vary and complement each other. Juror number 5, a young man from a violent slum, notices that the suspect could not possibly have stabbed his victim with a switchblade. Not only is the perspective of juror number 5 unique (no other juror is acquainted with the proper way to use a switchblade), it is crucial to the progress of the group's reasoning, putting in doubt the validity of a key eyewitness's report. Juror number 9, an old man, then questions the plausibility of the time it took another key witness (an invalid) to limp across his room and reach the door just in time to cross the murderer's path as he fled the building. He, too, contributes to changing the collective perspective on the way the crime took place. One of the most difficult jurors to convince, a stockbroker left unmoved by any of the other arguments, finally has to admit that a nearsighted woman is not credible when she pretends to have seen the murderer from her apartment across the street, through the windows of a passing subway, while she was lying in bed, most likely without her glasses. The deliberation process in this scenario nicely idealizes real-life deliberative processes in which participants contribute a perspective, an argument, an idea, or a piece of information and the group can reach a conclusion that no individual by himself could have reached.

Notice that in this scenario deliberation among several people has the three properties of good deliberation. First, deliberation enlarges the pool of information and ideas for all jurors, bringing to the surface knowledge about the proper use of a switchblade and a contradiction between this proper use and the eyewitness's description of the way the victim was supposedly stabbed. It also brings to the surface a fact that many in the group had noticed – the red marks on the sides of the nose of the woman who claimed to have witnessed the murder from her room – but did not know how to interpret or use. Here the proper interpretation of the fact is that the witness wears glasses and is most likely nearsighted, and the conclusion that this leads to is that the testimony cannot be trusted.

Second, deliberation allows the group to weed out the good arguments from the bad. Once they reach the conclusion that the witness is nearsighted, knowing that she reported having witnessed the murder while lying in bed, what is most likely: that she was, or was not, wearing her glasses? Even the most stubborn juror has to admit that the argument that she was not wearing her glasses is stronger than the argument that she was wearing them.

Finally, deliberation in this example leads to a unanimous consensus on the "better" answer, namely the decision to consider the young convict "not guilty" given the doubts raised by deliberation.

Now let us turn to an even more stylized situation, which should bring out the logic of collective intelligence in deliberation even more clearly.[14] Imagine that the French government is choosing a city in which to experiment with a new program. Three *députés* are deliberating, one from Calvados, one from Corrèze, one from Pas de Calais. They have the following respective local optima (by which I mean the best options they can think of for different local contexts), with the value in parentheses being the objective value of the city for the experiment on a scale from 0 to 10:

Calvados: Marseille (7), Caen (10)
Corrèze: Paris (8), Grenoble (9), Caen (10)
Pas de Calais: Grenoble (9), Caen (10)

Each député has a higher probability of getting stuck at his or her lowest optimum than at the highest one. Thus, even though Caen is the better choice, the député from Calvados is not likely to think of it first, because she thinks that only big cities like Marseille will work, or perhaps because she is subconsciously prevented from choosing the capital of her own department. Similarly, suppose that the député from Corrèze is pushing Paris, which has a value of 8, over his other two local optima, Grenoble and Caen, and that the député from Pas de Calais is pushing Grenoble (9) over her other optimum, Caen. For whatever reasons, none of the députés thinks of his or her highest optimum first. Here is where deliberation can help.

The député from Calvados might start by saying, "This program should be implemented in a big city, so I propose Marseille (7)." The député from Corrèze says, "Good idea, but then Paris (8) is better." The député from Calvados has to agree, forceless force of the better argument obliging. Then the député from Pas de Calais interjects, "Actually, Paris is really an expensive location for the project; we would be better off with a moderate-sized city, which would be just as good a test bed. How about Grenoble (9)?" The député from Corrèze agrees, but the one from Calvados then says, "Fine, but as far as moderate-sized cities go, Caen (10) is even better than Grenoble (9), and less polluted too." In the end, they can only go with Caen.

Here again deliberation among several people has the three properties of good deliberation. The pool of information is enlarged, as the député from Calvados, who is familiar with only two local optima (Marseille and Caen), ends up knowing about the qualities of Paris and Grenoble as well. The député from Corrèze learns about one other local optimum (Marseille), and the député from Pas de Calais about two others (Marseille and Paris). Notice that even if the information gained is sometimes of lesser objective quality than that which the person already held, nonetheless, only by acquiring it can the members

---

[14] I thank Scott Page for helping me with this example.

of the group reach the highest local optimum with certainty. The député of Calvados might never have considered an option she knew about, Caen (10), had she not been persuaded to abandon her initial choice (of value 7) by the other two députés, who still offered suboptimal solutions (of respective values 8 and 9).

Deliberation also allowed the group to weed out the good arguments from the bad. While it seemed at first a good argument to look for a big city (Marseille, Paris), it turned out that it was better to consider moderate-sized cities (Grenoble, Caen).

Finally, deliberation led to a consensus on the "best" solution, namely the solution that allowed the group to reach the optimum of 10, when the pre-deliberative beliefs about the best solution could have been respectively 7, 8, and 9.

According to Lu Hong and Scott Page's results on the components of collective intelligence (Hong and Page 2001, 2004; Page 2007), what matters most for the quality of collective problem solving of the type illustrated by the preceding two examples is "cognitive diversity." Cognitive diversity is the difference in the way people approach a problem or a question. It denotes more specifically a diversity of perspectives (the way of representing situations and problems), diversity of interpretations (the way of categorizing or partitioning perspectives), diversity of heuristics (the way of generating solutions to problems), and diversity of predictive models (the way of inferring cause and effect) (Page 2007: 7). Cognitive diversity is not diversity of values or goals, which would actually harm the collective effort to solve a problem. Because of the importance of cognitive diversity thus defined, given four specific conditions, "a randomly selected collection of problem solvers outperforms a collection of the best individual problem solvers" (Page 2007: 163).[15]

The general point illustrated by these two examples is that it is often better to have a group of cognitively diverse people than a group of very smart people who think alike. This is so because whereas very smart people sharing local optima will tend to get stuck quickly on their highest local common

---

[15] The four conditions are fairly reasonable. The first one requires that the problem be difficult enough, since we do not need a group to solve easy problems. The second condition requires that all problem solvers be relatively smart. In other words, the members of the group must have local optima that are not too low; otherwise the group would get stuck far from the global optimum. The third condition simply assumes a diversity of local optima such that the intersection of the problem solvers' local optima contains only the global optimum. The fourth condition requires that the initial population from which the problem solvers are selected be large and that the group of problem solvers working together contain more than a handful of people. This assumption ensures that the randomly chosen group of problem solvers in the larger pool is diverse, and in particular more cognitively diverse, than a group of the best of the larger pool – which would not necessarily be the case for too small a pool relative to the size of the subset of randomly chosen problem solvers or for too small a subset of problem solvers in absolute terms. Notice that the first part of this fourth condition can be thought of as Madison's requirement in *Federalist* 10 that the pool of candidates for the position of representative be large enough. For more on this, see Page (2007: 159–62).

optimum, the members of a more cognitively diverse group have the possibility of guiding each other beyond that local optimum toward the global optimum. We can imagine that in the scenario of *Twelve Angry Men*, if the jury had been composed of clones of juror number 8, the smartest person in the lot, they might have been stuck with the initial suspicion but would have been unable to turn it into the firm conviction of not guilty reached by the group. Similarly, if all three députés were thinking exactly alike – say, like the député of Calvados, who thought of her lower local optimum first – no matter how long they might have deliberated, the group would have remained stuck on the local optimum of Grenoble (9) and would never have been able to reach the higher local optimum of Caen (10). If all thought like the député of Calvados or Corrèze, they would still have had a given probability of reaching the global optimum, but not the certainty of the deliberating group described earlier.[16]

Deliberation, however, is not by itself democratic. In effect deliberation can theoretically occur within one person (degenerate case) or among a few oligarchs. The two examples I gave occur among twelve people or fewer. What is the gain in involving large numbers? Further, isn't there a point beyond which large numbers can worsen the quality of deliberative outcomes?

The gain in involving large numbers is that it automatically ensures greater cognitive diversity. In that sense, more is smarter.[17] I thus propose to generalize Scott Page's "Diversity Trumps Ability Theorem" into a "Numbers Trump Ability Theorem," by which what matters most for the collective intelligence of a problem-solving group is not so much individual ability as the number of people in the group. Thus, if 3 députés are more cognitively diverse and thus smarter than just 1, then 500 should be even more cognitively diverse, and thus smarter, than 3. Similarly, if 12 jurors are smarter than 1, then so would be 41 or 123 jurors. Of course, this assumption that cognitive diversity correlates with numbers will not always be verified, but it is more plausible than the reverse assumption.

A crucial problem, however, which might dampen our enthusiasm for numbers, is a question of threshold. Deliberation involving all members of the group is not always feasible (for a defense of a national holiday that would allow the entire nation to deliberate once a year across smaller subgroups, however, see

---

[16] Each member is defined by a set of local optima and a probability of getting stuck at each of his local optima. So if the deliberating group is made up of exactly the same people who have a nonzero probability of getting stuck at the nonglobal optimum, the group probability of finding the global optimum might be higher than that of any individual in the group, but it won't be 100%.

[17] Notice that to the extent that (and if it is the case that) cognitive diversity is correlated with other forms of diversity, such as gender or ethnic diversity, the argument suggests that positive discrimination is a good thing, not just on fairness grounds but also for epistemic reasons. I will not enter that complicated debate here, but it is clearly one of the potential implications of an argument advocating the epistemic properties of cognitive diversity. (For a defense of cognitive diversity as being in fact the "only" reason to support affirmative action, see the conclusions of the French sociologist Sabbagh 2003.)

James Fishkin and Bruce Ackerman's Deliberation Day proposal (Fishkin and Ackerman 2004)). In practice, past a certain numerical threshold, deliberation turns into a chaotic mess, in which case the epistemic superiority seems to go by default to deliberation involving a smaller number of people, preferably the smarter or more educated ones.

This is where the institutional device of political representation comes into play. Representation allows the indirect or mediated involvement of the many in a decision taken by the few. In other words, representation makes democratic decision making possible when numbers are too large. Let me for now turn to a detailed analysis of how and under which conditions representation allows the reconciliation of the manageability of a small assembly and the cognitive diversity of a large one.

REPRESENTATION AS A PROJECTION OF COGNITIVE DIVERSITY ON A SMALL SCALE

I propose in what follows a nonorthodox reading of representation as an institutional device allowing for democratic deliberation on a feasible scale while preserving at least some of the cognitive diversity of the group in its entirety. I do not make the optimistic, elitist hypothesis that representation ensures rule by an aristocracy of merits and talents, that is, an oligarchy of virtuous knowers.[18] In order to defend this democratic view of representatives as simply reproducing on a smaller scale the cognitive diversity of the larger group, I need to establish two things. First, I must demonstrate that an assembly of representatives is actually distinct from a group of oligarchs. Second, I must show why an assembly of representatives can in theory be epistemically superior to an assembly of oligarchs.

According to Bernard Manin's historical interpretation, periodic elections and accountability are the two principles that ensure the democratic nature of representatives' functions (Manin 1997). First, representatives are distinct from an oligarchy in that they are elected to the positions of decision makers and legislators, as opposed to born into them, as aristocrats are, or appointed by one or a few persons only, as might be the case of nonelected magistrates or experts. Representatives also differ from a class of oligarchs in that they are held accountable to the people not only at the end of their mandate, but, one might say, throughout, in informal ways. They are under the scrutiny of their constituents, who can write, call, and criticize them in ways other than voting them out.[19]

---

[18] It might have been, and might still historically be, the case that elections of representatives are seen as a way to select the "most virtuous" and "smartest," but one could also see the function that representatives fulfill as that of reproducing the cognitive diversity of the larger group on a smaller scale rather than elevating the average individual ability of the decision makers.

[19] I thus do not mean here the possibility of representatives being liable to be recalled at any time but simply the internalized pressure, in representatives' behavior, to act as if they were constantly under the public eye and could be held accountable to the people at any time.

Of course, in order for this descriptive account to be normatively compelling, one has to assume that elections are not meant, as they unfortunately tend to do in practice, to select people on criteria that give chances only to the most educated and/or the richest members of society.[20] Otherwise, the representatives would not be so different from a class of oligarchs, and other selection mechanisms might become more appealing (e.g., lotteries).[21] Similarly, one has to assume that the periodicity of the elections does in fact foster a certain turnover of elites, so that the same persons do not remain in power for too long. As to the claim that representatives are accountable, this must be combined with a properly democratic (as opposed to Burkean) understanding of their function (e.g., Urbinati 2006). Representatives are supposed to take into account their constituents' interests and judgments, not act and decide entirely on their own. Without advocating bound mandates, one can thus see the representatives' judgment as being regularly checked against the opinion of their constituency and factoring the latter in.[22] All in all, the idea is that, on a genuinely democratic normative ideal of representation, representatives are not meant to be an immutable elite of decision makers, the way the best oligarchs ought to be.

Now, how does a group of representatives theoretically compare, epistemically speaking, with an equivalent group of oligarchs? Compare the democratic solution of an elected assembly of, say, five hundred congresspersons with the oligarchic solution of five hundred individuals. Those numbers approximate the reality of the Republic of Venice in the fifteenth century, which was governed by a few hundred aristocrats. Historically it is doubtful that oligarchies were made up of the best and brightest. Imagine for the sake of the argument that the five hundred oligarchs of our example are extremely smart and knowledgeable, as well as virtuous, and, on top of this, cognitively diverse as a group. It might then seem that an oligarchy of five hundred such individuals

---

[20] For a compelling critique of and solution to the problems of representative democracy in America, see O'Leary (2006).

[21] See, e.g., Elster (1989: 78–103), Mulgan (1984: 539–560), Goodwin (1992), Duxbury (1999), Stone (2007), and Sintomer (2007). Notice that not only are lotteries arguably more just and representative than existing election mechanisms, but while they would certainly not elevate the level of individual ability – by definition, the expected individual ability of those selected would be average – they would preserve the cognitive diversity of the group. Another question is, if we stick with elections, what kind of (s)election mechanism is most conducive to cognitive diversity. In selecting, say, a hundred representatives, a system of proportional representation may produce more cognitive diversity than majority voting in single-member districts. This invites an epistemic comparison among alternative democratic selection mechanisms, some of which can produce more cognitive diversity with fewer additional members. See Elster, Chapter 7, this volume.

[22] Nadia Urbinati puts it in eloquent terms, arguing that, on her normative conception, and contra elitist definitions that pit against each other representation and participation (if not representation and democracy altogether), "representative democracy...is intrinsically, and necessarily, intertwined with participation and the informal expression of 'popular will'" (Urbinati 2006: 10).

is likely to be smarter than an assembly made up of individuals chosen by regular citizens. The problem is that such ideal circumstances, regardless of how
implausible they are initially, could not be maintained over time, for at least
two reasons. One is that absent periodic renewal of their members, the group
of oligarchs is stuck with a given level and type of cognitive diversity. Second,
absent democratic accountability, the oligarchs have no incentive to inform
themselves about the larger, changing cognitive diversity of the larger group.
In effect, no matter how smart the group of oligarchs is at the beginning, it is
unlikely to remain so over time. The group of oligarchs may be characterized
by high average individual competence, but ultimately not enough cognitive
diversity.

In the case of representative democracy, cognitive diversity of the assembly
is preserved over the long run thanks to periodic elections that renew the
pool of members. Further, an elected and accountable parliament, which is
at least minimally shaped by a larger public opinion, is more likely to stay
cognitively diverse than a body of oligarchs that can count only on the discipline
of its members to avoid the trap of "groupthink," self-serving biases, and
isolation from popular input. So while there might be times when a large
enough oligarchy might temporarily epistemically be equal, and perhaps even
superior to, a democratic assembly of representatives, I think that over the long
run this is highly implausible.[23]

On that reading of representation, the epistemic argument for deliberation
among the many presented earlier translates to representative democracy as
well, provided that representation effectively reproduces the cognitive diversity
of the larger group in the smaller one. The claim remains the same: deliberation involving the many, in a direct form (where feasible) or an indirect form
(through representation – regardless of the selection mechanism), is superior
to deliberation among the few, because to the extent that cognitive diversity
is correlated with numbers and provided that citizens are at least moderately
smart on average, the more numerous the deliberating group, the smarter it is.

MAJORITY RULE WITH UNIVERSAL SUFFRAGE

Deliberation is far from a perfect or complete decision mechanism, in part
because it is time-consuming and rarely produces unanimity. In most cases, it
has to be supplemented by another decision procedure: majority rule. While
majority rule is more efficient timewise, it does not allow for solving problems.
It does allow, however, for choosing among predetermined options, ideally

---

[23] A contemporary example of an oligarchy whose epistemic success arguably compares with those
of democratic regimes, at least so far as economic policies and public education are concerned,
would be the Communist regime in China. Because the label "communist" in fact now covers
ideological positions ranging from the far right to the far left – the only common ideology being
nationalism – one can argue that the policies pursued in China compare to those that would
be produced by the (democratic) rule of the median voter. I owe this provocative suggestion to
Pasquale Pasquino.

defined in the deliberation period. I argue in this section that far from being just a fair way to settle disagreement about the choice of an option, majority rule is also a reliable way to improve the chances that the group will pick the right one, where the "right" one is simply that which is better than the other options. Majority rule aggregates individuals' judgments about the best course of action to take or the right candidate to elect. In other words, majority rule is not only a fair way to settle on a decision when time is running out for deliberation, but a way to turn imperfect individual predictions into accurate collective ones. Again, since majority rule is available to the lone tyrant, who is the majority by himself, and a group of oligarchs, I will further need to consider whether majority rule under universal suffrage is superior to majority rule used by a minority within the larger group.

There exist at least three related but distinct theoretical arguments for the epistemic properties of majority rule: the Condorcet Jury Theorem, the "miracle of aggregation," and Scott Page's "The Crowd Beats the Average Law."[24]

The Condorcet Jury Theorem

The Condorcet Jury Theorem (CJT) demonstrates that among large electorates voting on some yes or no question, majoritarian outcomes are virtually certain to track the "truth," so long as three conditions hold: (1) voters are better than random at choosing true propositions; (2) they vote independently of each other; and (3) they vote sincerely or truthfully. To briefly illustrate, let us consider 10 voters, each of which has a .51 probability of being correct on any yes or no question. With such a small number of voters, a majority of 6 will have only a 40 percent chance of being right (assuming ties are counted as incorrect). However, if one expands the group to 1,000 people, a majority of 501 is almost 73 percent sure to be right.[25] If one expands the group to 10,000, a majority of 5,001 is almost 100 percent sure to be right. As the number of people grows infinitely large, the majority is virtually certain to be right so long as people have just a slightly higher chance of being right than wrong on any binary question. The CJT, first formulated by the Marquis de Condorcet in 1785 and rediscovered by Duncan Black in the 1950s, has spawned many formal analyses in recent decades (to name a very few, Grofman, Owen and Feld 1983; Ladha 1992; List and Goodin 2001; Bovens and Rabinowicz 2006). While the CJT has its advocates (e.g., Goodin 2005;

---

[24] Adrian Vermeule (Chapter 14, this volume) and others consider the CJT a mere variant of the miracle of aggregation. This might well be the case, in which case the CJT would probably correspond to what I call the democratic version of the miracle of aggregation, but to the extent that the relevant literature still treats them separately, I will address each account as autonomous.

[25] Notice that a majority of 501 means that at least 501 persons voted a certain way (i.e., a probability of .73 represents the sum of probabilities corresponding to the possibility that exactly 501, 502, 503, etc. all the way to 1,000 persons vote in the same way). See List (2004) for a discussion of the relevant statistical facts.

Sunstein 2009), some democratic theorists argue that the assumption that voters are on average better than random at making decisions on any political
questions is far-fetched and renders the theorem largely "irrelevant" (Estlund
2008: ch. 13). Another problem is the assumption of independence, which
seems to imply that voters do not share any source of information or deliberate among each other (e.g., the controversy between Grofman and Feld 1988;
Estlund, Waldron, Grofman, and Feld 1989; Estlund 1994). This assumption
is empirically highly implausible, because in reality people do not pick up independent signals about the world but make up their minds on the basis of a
limited and highly dependent range of cues and sources of information. Even
if the assumptions could be shown to be mathematical idealizations of a more
complicated reality, it is true that the theorem has nothing to say about what
is going on in actual judgment aggregation.

The "Miracle of Aggregation"

The miracle of aggregation (e.g., Converse 1990; Page and Shapiro 1992;
Wittman 1995; Caplan 2007a) is another explanation of collective intelligence
distinct from the Jury Theorem, although it also involves the law of large
numbers. The "miracle" is typically illustrated by the weight-guessing game
observed by the nineteenth-century statistician Francis Galton at a country fair,
in which the average answer of eight hundred participants' guesses regarding
the weight of an ox once slaughtered and dressed turned out to fall within
one pound of the right answer.[26] Many other anecdotes, recounted in both
Surowiecki (2004) and Sunstein (2006), vividly illustrate the same "miracle"
of group intelligence.

Unlike the CJT, the miracle of aggregation does not apply specifically to
majority rule but explains why the average guess of large groups of people
on matters with a factual answer tends to be uncannily accurate. It applies to
majority rule only to the extent that majority rule is conceptualized as expressing the vote of the median voter. Furthermore, the miracle of aggregation
generally applies to cases where different individuals submit their own individual estimates of some continuous quantity (e.g., the weight of an ox). The
options here are the different possible values of the quantity in question, and
there are thus more than two options. Nonetheless, to the extent that a continuum of options may be reduced to a choice between two ranges of values,
say, and with the proper qualifications, it can be considered to be an account
of majority rule's epistemic properties.

The most established version of the miracle of aggregation explains it as
the statistical phenomenon by which a few informed people in a group are
enough to guide the group to the right average answer, so long as the mean

---

[26] Some versions of the story present Galton as taking the median (which eliminates the problem
of extreme outliers). We will assume in what follows that the distinction between mean and
median does not matter in the cases that interest us.

of uninformed people's answers is zero.[27] Here collective intelligence actually depends on extracting the information held by an informed elite from the mass of noise represented by other people's opinions. So long as a sizable minority of the crowd (the minority must be pivotal) knows the right answer and everyone else makes mistakes that cancel each other out, the right answer is still going to rise to the surface, so to speak. Applied to the experiment of Galton, this explanation would imply that several persons in the crowd knew the right answer and all the others made mistakes that canceled each other out.[28]

A more democratic version of the miracle of aggregation presents things slightly differently. This time everyone has an opinion that is roughly correct, and the distribution of errors around each individual's blurry judgment is such that individual errors cancel each other out in the aggregate and the collective judgment is fairly accurate. In the example of the weight contest, this means that most people were not that far off the right weight, although none of them knew it exactly. Page and Shapiro apply this model to account for the rationality of public opinion.[29]

A third version of the miracle of aggregation assumes that the right answer is dispersed in bits and pieces among many people. So long as people express a judgment that contains one accurate piece of information and a random opinion about the piece of knowledge that they lack, the same logic of cancellation of random errors will still produce the right prediction in the aggregate. This explanation is unlikely to apply to the weight contest example, but if it did, it would require that some people in the group knew the weight of the cow's tail, some other people the weight of the ears, and so on, and that they randomized their guess about the other parts. On average all the pieces of information would aggregate to the right answer.

The miracle of aggregation, in its elitist, democratic, or distributed version, is an appealing way to account for the epistemic properties of majority rule. In effect, Galton himself, though he did not think very highly of democracy, was prompted by his own result to compare the gambling situation with democratic voting and to conclude: "The result seems more creditable to the trustworthiness of democratic judgment than might have been expected" (Galton

---

[27] This elitist version probably goes back to Berelson, Lazarsfeld, and McPhee (1954).

[28] This explanation is not very convincing in the case of the weight-guessing contest, as Scott Page (2007: 179) remarks. This inadequacy does not seem to have struck Surowiecki or Sunstein.

[29] According to them, people have meaningful opinions surrounded by noise, and aggregation across individuals produces an aggregation of those real opinions. For example, some citizens underestimate and others overestimate the benefits of immigration. "Even if individuals' responses to opinion surveys are partly random, full of measurement error, and unstable, when aggregated into a collective response – for example the percentage of people who say they favor a particular policy – the collective response may be quite meaningful and stable" (Page and Shapiro 1992). What Page and Shapiro thus suggest, without saying it in so many words, is that the public is epistemically more knowledgeable as a whole than any of the individuals who make it up, which is why politicians are right to promote immigration policies based on the public's judgment (a reasoning extended to foreign policy by Page and Bouton 2006).

1907: 246). For some, the miracle of aggregation is an even better explanation of collective intelligence and why, possibly, democracy works than the more traditional explanation in terms of deliberation and the pursuit of rational consensus.[30]

Two main objections can be raised to the miracle of aggregation.[31] First, one can deny the empirical plausibility of the hypothesis of random or symmetrical distribution of errors. Caplan points out that it is much more likely that people are cognitively biased in the same direction, so that majority rule will amplify individual mistakes, not correct for them (Caplan 2007a). I address that objection in the last section of this essay. More problematically, the miracle of aggregation relies on the same assumption of statistical independence of individual judgment as the CJT. While the assumption of independence may perhaps be interpreted as a mathematical idealization of what is really going on in judgment aggregation and might ultimately be relaxed in some sophisticated versions of both the CJT and the miracle (e.g., Boland, Proschang, and Tong 1989 for the CJT), in what follows I consider a third account of collective intelligence that is not statistical but cognitive: it opens the black box of voters' decision-making process.

Cognitive Diversity

In a book (2007) and a series of articles with Lu Hong (2001, 2004, 2009), Scott Page proposes a different account of why large groups of people can make good judgments and, in particular, accurate predictions. Unlike commentators who dismiss Page's model as less compelling than a Deweyan account of democracy's epistemic virtues based on deliberation (Anderson 2006), I think this model provides a fine-grained and empirically plausible account of the epistemic properties of judgment aggregation. Although Page's model generally applies to numerical predictions that are not of a binary form (e.g., predicting sales figures), it can be applied to scenarios where judgments are binary as well (e.g., predicting whether a candidate is competent or incompetent). In my view, Page's model can be used as a nicely tailored account of majority rule's epistemic properties to be combined with, rather than pitted against, an account of deliberation's distinct epistemic properties.

---

[30] Cass Sunstein, e.g., sees it as a "Hayekian challenge to Habermas" (Sunstein 2006). In fact, it is unclear both that the miracle of aggregation is the same thing as the invisible-hand mechanism at work in the emergence of the prices of goods or information in markets and that democratic deliberation is made superfluous by information aggregation through majority rule, polls, or markets.

[31] An additional, practical objection is that majority rule generally involves a choice between discrete options but rarely allows for the kind of "quantitative" and continuous voting observed in the ox-weight guessing game or information markets. This is not a very powerful objection, since the logic of the miracle of aggregation theoretically works even with the reduced choices offered in elections.

Unlike the miracle of aggregation, Page's account does not rely on the assumption of an infinity of independent signals or on the idea of random or symmetric mistakes canceling each other out.[32] What matters for collective intelligence is the existence of negative correlations among people's predictive models, which tends to lower the collective error and make the group smarter than the average individual within it. Negative correlations are themselves the result of cognitive diversity in the group (Hong and Page 2009).[33] Cognitive diversity is, roughly, the fact that people make predictions based on different models of the way the world works or should be interpreted. Cognitive diversity should be distinguished from both its symptoms (a different set of viewpoints or opinions) and its possible root causes (gender or ethnic diversity), as well as a diversity that is actually epistemically harmful, namely a diversity of goals or values (in an epistemic framework, as in Page's cognitive model, all the members of the group are supposed to pursue the same goal and want the same thing, namely to make an accurate prediction).

The good thing about negative correlations among individuals' predictive models is that they guarantee that where one voter makes a mistake, another is more likely to get it right and vice versa. In the aggregate, therefore, mistakes cancel each other not randomly, but systematically. The result is expressed by Page's "The Crowd Beats Average Law": the accuracy of the group's prediction is systematically better than the average accuracy of its members. In other words, the group necessarily predicts better than its average member. Further, the amount by which the group outpredicts its average member increases as the group becomes more diverse (Page 2007: 197).

To illustrate briefly, consider the case of an election between two candidates, and assume that the point of voting in that election is, among other things, to identify who is the fittest candidate for office. Individually, each of us will make a prediction based on a limited number of factors. Some of us will base our judgment on how competent in handling social issues a candidate is likely to be. Others will make a prediction based on both how fiscally conservative she is and the presumed state of the economy in the coming years. Still other people

---

[32] Scott Page in fact dismisses both the CJT and the miracle of aggregation because, in his view, they both implausibly presuppose that voters receive an infinity of independent signals that they pick up in order to make a prediction. In reality, he argues, people make up their minds on the basis of a limited and highly dependent range of cues and sources of information. The infinity of signals assumption presupposes more cognitive diversity than is empirically plausible. It is, according to Page, a "heroic assumption" (Page 2007: 192).

[33] Hong and Page (2009) demonstrate that using independent *interpretations* (not predictions) entails negatively correlated predictions. More specifically, the gist of their article consists in demonstrating that "seeing the world independently, looking at different attributes, not only does not imply, it is inconsistent with, both conditional independence of signals and independently correct signals" (Hong and Page 2009: 18). In other words, Hong and Page's model does not require that people make uncorrelated predictions but that they make up their minds independently. Except in the very implausible scenario where reasonably informed individuals each ignore a different piece of information, their predictions will not be independent but negatively correlated.

will make a prediction based on a mix of factors: the candidate's charisma, the current price of oil, and the prospect of Iran building a nuclear bomb. When examining the candidates, we will thus look at different dimensions of the same quality (or in Page's vocabulary "perspective"), which is in this case competence for office. This produces what Page calls "non-overlapping projection interpretations," that is, interpretations of the candidate's competence that do not contain any of the same variables or dimensions (e.g., competence on social or economic issues).[34]

The beauty of having such different predictive models in a group is that because of the negative correlations among predictions that they entail, the group makes even better predictions than the CJT or the miracle of aggregation would predict (for binary choices). In the example of voters deciding whether candidates are competent or incompetent, the idea is that Republicans will be more likely to be right when Democrats are more likely to be wrong and vice versa. When a Republican and a Democrat disagree, the tie can be broken by a third cognitive perspective, for example that of an Independent. When the Republican and the Democrat agree, however, the candidate is likely to be correctly described as either competent or incompetent (see Landemore 2009 for a more detailed analysis).

Let me now reformulate in more general terms the epistemic argument for majority rule that can be extracted from Hong and Page's model. The argument is that in order to maximize our chances of picking the better of two options, we are better off taking the median answer of a sufficiently cognitively diverse group of people than letting a randomly selected individual in that group make the choice for the group. This is so because, for a given group of people using different predictive models, the predictions will be negatively correlated and mistakes will cancel each other, not randomly but systematically. As a result, the average mistake of the group will be less than the average mistake of a randomly selected voter, and in fact even less so as the difference among the predictive models used by those voters increases (i.e., as there is more cognitive diversity in the group).

Hong and Page's account of the logic of group intelligence is in my view extremely promising for an epistemic justification of majority rule, at least when majority rule is used by a group of voters who make predictions based on different variables.[35] The superiority of Hong and Page's account over the CJT

---

[34] Page formalizes the "Projection Property" as follows: "If two people base their predictive models on different variables from the same perspective (formally, if they use non-overlapping projection interpretations), then the correctness of their predictions is negatively correlated for binary projections" (Page 2007: 203).

[35] A caveat must be added, lest the result seem too optimistic. You cannot have an infinity of variables or dimensions associated with a given perspective (say, competence for office). As the number of voters grows very large, the number of variables that people use to make a prediction may remain proportionally quite small (on top of social and economic issues, voters may look at personal charisma and foreign policy variables, but they might disregard variables such as the breed of the candidate's dog or the candidate's sense of humor). To avoid positive

or the miracle of aggregation is at least twofold. First, their account circumvents the problematic assumption of judgment independence, which rendered both the CJT and the miracle of aggregation somewhat unrealistic. As I understand it, the independence assumption is now applied, more plausibly, not to people's actual judgments (their outputs) but to the cognitive processes leading to those judgments (i.e., the predictive models people use to generate judgments and predictions about the world). In other words, by internalizing the independence constraint, Hong and Page's model makes it possible for citizens to share information, premises, and even conclusions, while remaining independent in terms of the cognitive processes that treated the shared information and generated the shared conclusions.

Second, Hong and Page's model supports the epistemic reliability of majority rule used among small groups.[36] Unlike what happens with the CJT or the miracle of aggregation, there need not be an infinity of voters for majority rule to guarantee 100 percent predictive accuracy. Because cognitive diversity can exist as soon as there is more than one person making the prediction, the magic can work for as small a group as three people (as in the admittedly contrived example given earlier) and is substantially increased for any addition of a person with a sufficiently diverse predictive model to the group. In the CJT, by contrast, the major payoff of majority rule occurs only with large numbers, and adding one person to the group does not make much difference.

The flip side of this, however, is that in Hong and Page's model there is a theoretical limitation on the extent to which including more and more people improves collective judgment. Cognitive diversity in judgment aggregation is not a linear function of numbers, and there are in fact diminishing returns to adding more people past a certain point. The reason, in brief, is that there are only so many different variables associated with a given perspective (e.g., competence for office) that people can use when trying to make a prediction. In trying to predict who the most competent candidate is, some people will use as a variable the candidate's charisma, others his ideological affiliation, and some others still his record as a politician. As the number of voters grows very large, however, the number of variables that people use to make a prediction may remain proportionally quite small. To avoid positive correlations as the number of people in the crowd becomes larger, either people must use cluster interpretations – for example, using both personal charisma and political record as variables – or they must base their interpretations on different perspectives – for example, by trying to predict a candidate's ability to win the elections rather

correlations as the number of people in the crowd becomes larger, people must either use cluster interpretations or base their interpretations on different perspectives. The interpretation used by someone who would judge a candidate on both her competence on social issues and competence on fiscal issues is an example of cluster interpretation.

36 In fact, their account is more optimistic for small groups than very large ones. I do not have sufficient space to address this concern here. It seems to be the case, though, that majority rule used in representative assemblies is more likely to have epistemic properties than majority rule used in referendums.

than her competence for office. What the cognitive model suggests here is that it is probably better to aggregate the views of a limited number of representatives than those of millions of voters. At the scale of an assembly of representatives, aggregating more judgments can be expected to have increasing returns in terms of cognitive diversity, which may be lost when we aggregate the views of millions of citizens. Further analyses of the implications of Hong and Page's model are certainly necessary. Suffice it to say here that their account of group competence provides, in my view, a fairly compelling epistemic argument for majority rule.[37]

What are the implications of those considerations for the idea of democratic reason? I have argued that majority rule and, in fact, any democratic mechanism that aggregates individual judgments into collective judgments have epistemic properties. Since the group's prediction is epistemically superior to that of the average citizen in the group, we have an argument for the superiority of the rule of the many to the rule of one (when the one is randomly chosen). That does not give us a maximal argument for majority rule, though, since majority rule among the many does not systematically beat majority rule among a few smart people. It is the superiority of democratic deliberation over oligarchic deliberation that allows us to derive the more ambitious claim.

THE PROBLEM OF VOTERS' "RATIONAL IRRATIONALITY" AND SYSTEMATIC COGNITIVE BIASES

According to Bryan Caplan, the main problem with the optimistic conclusions about group intelligence that I have derived is that, in some way or another, they rely on the assumption that there is a symmetrical distribution of errors around the right answer so that the mean of these errors is zero ("miracle of aggregation") or that errors are negatively correlated (Hong and Page's model), when they might in fact be positively correlated. In economic matters, at least, Caplan argues that voters are systematically biased in the same wrong direction. How does that argument affect the hypothesis proposed here that democracy is the epistemically superior collective decision method?

First, empirical observations of the way U.S. democracy functions or fails to function are not enough to falsify a more general claim about the epistemic properties of a model democracy. The empirical problems Caplan points out may be due to the fact that democracy in the United States is not a real democracy in the sense used in this essay, lacking too many of the features I have insisted on (e.g., a representative system preserving the cognitive diversity of the larger group). Caplan, however, backs up his observations with a theory of

---

[37] Owing to a lack of space, I do not address another fascinating result by Hong and Page, the "Crowd's Possibly Free Lunch Theorem" (Page 2007: 221). This theorem demonstrates that groups in which individuals make predictions based not just on different variables of the same perspective but on multiple perspectives can occasionally be as accurate in their prediction as complex regressions by experts.

the rationally irrational voter, which seems much more worrying. I will take both objections seriously and will address them in turn.

The theoretical objection is powerful if one accepts Caplan's conceptualization of the voter as rationally irrational. There are, however, many problems with this theory (see Elster and Landemore 2008 for a critique). In particular, I would emphasize here that Caplan assumes in voters a form of self-interest, incompatible with the epistemic framework of this essay. Even when they vote ideologically (for the "common good") as opposed to "rationally" (for their pocketbook), as in, for example, the case of the rich Hollywood actor who votes for higher taxes, voters do so, on Caplan's account, only because of the unlikely prospect that their votes will be pivotal. So, in effect, voters are still first and foremost preoccupied with voting their self-interest (in the form of a warm-glow effect when the impact of their vote is too low to make a difference) rather than promoting something like the common good.[38] Arguably, on Caplan's account, if their vote mattered at all, they would revert to voting their pocketbook. This perspective is utterly incompatible with the epistemic framework of the argument presented in this essay, which assumes that people are voting what they think is right for the common good, no matter how unpleasant it is for them, whether ideologically or economically. The theoretical divergence runs so deep that it is hard to see any point of intersection between these two models, which leads to drastically different predictions about the epistemic quality of democratic output.

Regardless of that theoretical divergence, however, what about the objection that even an epistemic framework may be challenged by the existence of systematic biases in voters, whether these biases are based on ignorance, irrationality, or anything else? It is true that an account of collective intelligence based on cognitive diversity is no more immune to the problem of systematic biases than is the CJT or the miracle of aggregation. If citizens share a number of wrong views – racist prejudices or systematic economic biases – majority rule will simply amplify these mistakes and make democratic decisions worse, if anything, than the decisions that could have been reached by a randomly chosen citizen. In the account of collective intelligence that I embrace, however, which emphasizes cognitive independence, the risk of systematic mistakes can arise only if the group lacks both individual predictive accuracy (i.e., people are not sufficiently intelligent) and diversity in the way they make predictions. Assuming minimally sophisticated voters relative to the questions at hand and a liberal society encouraging dissent and diverse thinking, however, Caplan's worst-case scenario of a situation in which the average error is high and diversity low – the condition for the worst-case scenario of an abysmally unintelligent majority decision – is not very plausible. In other words, it is not very plausible that there will be systematic biases on a majority of political issues.

---

[38] There is, in fact, an incoherence in the description of the "rational purchase of altruism" (see Elster and Landemore 2008).

Furthermore, deliberation can play a role in the epistemic argument for democracy developed in this essay that it cannot play in Caplan's model. When it comes to majorities making mistakes, my argument at least allows for the possibility of self-correction over time and through the means of public deliberation, whereas Caplan, it seems, would bring in the experts or exit politics altogether (for the market). In actual democracies, it is interesting to see that where systematic biases have been historically observed to exist, on race issues for example, most changes had to come from evolving majorities themselves, through a democratic process of collective self-reflection and public deliberation.[39] Democratic deliberation, which includes the experts as welcome but nonexclusive voices, is a central part of the argument put forth in this essay and offers a possible solution to the problem of the occasional systematic mistakes that the public can make.

Let me now turn to the empirical challenge based on the measurement of systematic biases in actual U.S. democratic citizens. Answering that challenge will take us on what may seem to be something of a detour in light of the larger argument. It will allow us, however, to address the question of the relationship between information and political epistemic competence.

Using empirical evidence borrowed from the literature on "enlightened preferences" (essentially Althaus 2003), the Survey of Americans and Economists on the Economy (SAEE),[40] and the results of his own comparison between the public's preferences and those of an "enlightened public" virtually endowed with a PhD in economics, Caplan diagnoses four main misconceptions in the average U.S. citizen with respect to economic questions: an antimarket bias, a protectionist bias, a pessimistic bias, and a job-oriented bias. Assuming that economists are right that, all things being equal otherwise, market mechanism is a good thing, free trade creates more riches than it destroys, growth is more likely than stagnation, and an increase in GDP matters more than job preservation, then the people are wrong to hold opposite views and ask for policies based on those views. The problem is not solved, or solved only to an insufficient degree, by the fact that policies are made by a priori slightly more competent representatives. To the extent that representatives are held accountable to the citizens, they have only limited leeway to improve the course of things. Consequently, Caplan concludes that, on economic questions at least, we would

---

[39] In that deliberation, some may want to see key Supreme Court decisions as a part of, and some others as an alternative to, the democratic dialogue, which somewhat complicates the equation. But one could always argue that the way in which a constitution can tie the hands of the people on some issues was itself initially decided democratically by a people in order to protect themselves against their own predictable irrationality, by creating constitutional safeguards for minorities, for example (Elster 1977).

[40] The survey is based on interviews with 1,510 randomly selected members of the U.S. public and 250 economic PhDs and designed to test for systematic differences in the beliefs of laypeople and experts by asking questions such as whether various factors are a "major reason," "minor reason," or "no reason at all" that "the economy is not doing better than it is."

be better off with less democratic input. He himself seems to suggest more delegation to economists and, wherever possible, letting the market run free.

Here, I will raise three criticisms. First, I question the elitist premises of Caplan's book and the method used to measure citizens' incompetence. Second, even granting that Caplan is right about the economic incompetence of the average voter, I would argue that the implications for democracy are not nearly so bad as Caplan would like to suggest. Finally, I object to the alternatives implicitly offered by Caplan. It is indeed unclear that the oligarchy of experts that Caplan sometimes seems to advocate would necessarily do much better overall than a democracy. As to the market mechanism, it is not in my view a political alternative to any form of government but a mere allocation tool in the hands of one, few, or many – thus leaving untouched the question of who should rule.

Let me start by addressing the methodological question. The first benchmark of voters' bias is knowledge of objective facts. As Caplan observes, "The simplest way to test for voter bias is to ask questions with objective quantitative answers, like the share of the federal budget dedicated to national defense or Social Security" (2007a: 25). Caplan, however, does not dwell on that first standard, acknowledging that "the main drawback of these studies [which measure the mastery of factual knowledge] is that many interesting questions are only answerable with a degree of ambiguity" (25). Indeed, one could argue that *no interesting political question* can be answered without such a degree of ambiguity, which raises the general issue of the relevance of a great deal of public opinion research that measures the ability to answer textbook political questions. Since the standard of objective facts reappears through the backdoor of the notion of "individuals with a high political IQ," let me say a few more words about why this standard is unsatisfying.

For one thing, information is distinct from competence, and the causal link between the holding of a certain type of information measured by surveys and the competence to make political choices is not easy to establish (however "intuitive" it is sometimes argued to be). In fact, most existing studies (e.g., Luskin 1987; Delli Carpini and Keeter 1996) fail to demonstrate a causal link between the inability of people to answer certain types of political quizzes and their alleged political incompetence, namely the inability to make the right choices or hold the "right" policy preferences. This is so in part because the design of factual political questionnaires smacks of elitism, measuring a type of knowledge relevant for policy analysts and journalists, but not necessarily the only one conducive to smart political choices (Lupia 2006).

The difficulty of establishing a causal link between low information level and political competence also derives from the fact that it is hard to find a good empirical benchmark for political competence that would be distinct from a good benchmark for information level. The fact that educated people are good at answering political quizzes does not entail (1) that the policy preferences of the educated are better as a result (unless you take such policy preferences as the standard, but then you are begging the question) or (2) that the policy preferences of "know-nothings" or people with low political IQs (as defined by such tests) are wrong.[41] The kind of factual knowledge measured by public opinion surveys is as crude a measurement of political competence, and there is no reason that the burden of proof should be on people who deny the connection between political IQ as it is measured by existing empirical surveys and actual political competence.

Let us now turn to the second standard: the "enlightened preferences" of a hypothetical educated public – that is, a group of people who are demographically representative but also as politically knowledgeable as possible. The method used by Althaus (2003) consists in administering a survey of policy preferences combined with a test of objective political knowledge to a group, estimating individuals' policy preferences as a function of their objective political knowledge on factual matters (e.g., how many senators each state has) and their demographics (income, race, gender), and, finally, simulating what policy preferences would look like if all members of all demographic groups had the maximum level of objective political knowledge. In other words, the goal is to compare the policy preferences of regular citizens with those of their "more educated" selves, controlling for race, gender, income, and the like.

The "enlightened-preference" approach permits testing the plausibility of the theory of the "reasoning voter," according to which people vote roughly with little knowledge what they would vote if they had maximal information thanks to cognitive shortcuts, heuristics, and online processing. The major result of this approach is to show that, no, people would probably not vote the same way, since they at least do not have the same preferences when they are little informed and very informed. They tend to be more socially liberal and economically conservative in the second case (Althaus 2003: 143). Scott Althaus uses the discrepancy between the public's preferences and those of its more "enlightened" self to criticize the representativity of opinion surveys and their usefulness in assessing the public's voice. Caplan goes one step further, using those results to suggest that democracy itself, which follows more or less the unenlightened policy preferences of the many, is flawed.

Consider, however, that the definition of "enlightened preferences" hinges on a concept of education that is correlated with the ability to score well on political IQ tests ("a test of objective political knowledge"). The standard of "enlightened preferences" is thus not much different from the knowledge of objective facts (since it is highly correlated with it). But we just saw that knowledge of objective facts might well be both an elitist measure of political knowledge and potentially irrelevant to the ability to pass a politically competent vote. So what this approach does is take as the standard of "enlightened" judgments preferences correlated with an elitist and possibly irrelevant form

---

[41] After all, even the scenarists of the TV show *The West Wing* know that you can be a competent director of communication at the White House and be unable to say three correct things about the history of the White House (*West Wing*, episode 1).

of knowledge and then argue that the discrepancy between the actual public's preferences and those "enlightened preferences" is meaningful and, in fact, an embarrassment for democracy. Such conclusions, however, merely reflect a belief present in the premise, namely that regular people are wrong and the elites are right. How is that not begging the question of who has epistemic authority in the first place?

The third standard consists of the economic preferences of a simulated public that is both demographically representative and endowed with the knowledge of a holder of a PhD in economics. The key difference between Caplan's approach and the previous approach is that "political scientists usually measure knowledge directly, while my approach proxies it using educational credentials" (2007a: 55). So, in effect, whereas the second type of approach boils down more or less to using the standard of objective facts (through the notion of political IQ) to assess the public's preferences, Caplan's approach takes as the ultimate standard the knowledge of experts. Another difference is that the competence that Caplan is trying to assess is slightly narrower than that measured by political scientists, since Caplan is interested only in political questions with an explicitly economic dimension, for which economic knowledge such as that measured by a PhD diploma might seem directly relevant (more so at least than "objective political knowledge" with respect to political competence).

So let us consider why the fourth standard – experts' knowledge – is problematic. First, Caplan constantly writes as if there were no difference between questions of economics (the science) and economic questions, which are political questions with an economic dimension. Just because PhD holders in economics are the best at answering questions in the science of economics does not make them the most competent at answering political questions with an economic component (although their input is most likely of value). In fact, if you deny that economists' political beliefs are absolute truths, the discrepancy between these beliefs and those of the public does not necessarily say much.

Despite initially acknowledging that political questions cannot be answered without a degree of ambiguity, Caplan does write as if the beliefs of economists were on a par with mathematical truths. Here is a typical example. Caplan argues that "elitist though it sounds, [inferring the existence of systematic biases in the public from the existence of systematic differences between economists and noneconomists] is the standard practice in the broader literature on biases" (52). Caplan goes on to appeal to the authority of no less than Kahneman and Tversky, who describe their own method this way: "The presence of an error of judgment is demonstrated by comparing people's responses either with an *established fact* . . . or *with an accepted rule of arithmetic, logic, or statistics*" (52, my emphasis).[42] Caplan thus draws a clear parallel between the consensual

---

[42] Caplan further comments: "'Established' or 'accepted' by whom? By experts of course" (2007a: 52). Notice, however, that unlike mathematical truths, which can be accepted by everyone, not just experts, economic truths are never as universally endorsed.

beliefs of economists, on the one hand, and objective facts or the rules of arithmetic, logic, or statistics, on the other. This parallel, however, is highly misleading. To the extent that economic beliefs are about facts (the share of foreign aid in the federal budget) or about mathematical theorems, they are not necessarily relevant, or not directly so, to political decisions. To the extent that these beliefs are more "political" – even the least controversial ones, like "free trade is good" or "people are not saving enough" – they are much more contingent on a shifting cultural and possibly ideological consensus among experts than Caplan allows for. By playing on this ambiguity between pure questions of textbook economics and political questions with an economic dimension, and by misleadingly identifying the beliefs of economists at a given time with factual truth or mathematical principles, Caplan in fact begs the question of who has authority in the first place. In his view, on anything remotely economic, economists know better. If you deny that premise, however, none of Caplan's conclusions follow.

Both the "enlightened-preference" approach and Caplan's "enlightened-public" approach beg the question of who is politically competent in the first place, whether it is people with a high political IQ or economists. Caplan supports that way of proceeding by arguing that "the burden of the proof should be on those who doubt the common sense assumption that we should trust the experts" (2007a: 82). One might reply, however, that democracy is premised on the very rejection of that "commonsense" assumption. For democrats since at least the Sophist Protagoras,[43] politics is the realm where no one is to be trusted more than others to begin with. This is why, as Socrates could observe, the Athenian Assembly behaves very differently when the problem is to build an edifice or a ship than when the question is to figure out the good of the city. In the first scenario, the Assembly calls in architects and shipbuilders, and if someone who is not considered a competent technician in the relevant field speaks up to give his opinion, the crowd boos and shames him into silence. By contrast, Socrates goes on:

When the question is an affair of state, then everybody is free to have a say – carpenter, tinker, cobbler, sailor, passenger; rich and poor, high and low – anyone who likes gets up, and no one reproaches him, as in the former case, with not having learned, and having no teacher, and yet giving advice. (*Protagoras* 319d)

For Athenian democrats, the real test of competence and expertise in politics is the ability to convince others in the Assembly. This is why, even if ultimately only the best arguments and information are supposed to triumph, everyone has the right to speak up.

I just criticized Caplan for begging the question of who is right in politics when defining the benchmark of competent answers as those of people who

---

[43] According to Cynthia Farrar, "Protagoras was, so far as we know, the first democratic political theorist in the history of the world" (1988: 77).

think like economists. Aren't democrats begging the question the other way around by denying that there are experts in the first place?

The positions are not exactly symmetrical. In Caplan's case, the question of who knows best and what the right answers are is a priori locked and determined. The economists know better, their answers are the right ones, and thus any deviation from their position must be measured as a bias. On the democratic view, there is genuine agnosticism as to who knows best and what is the right answer, at least at the outset. Who knows best and what the right answers are can be determined, in the short term, only on the merits of different claims competing in the public space and later, in the much longer term, by a retrospective look at how well the country did overall, given that such and such policies were implemented, or even by a comparison between expected and actual results for every chosen policy. At the moment of decision making, when such hindsight is not available, the benchmark of right political answers is, for Caplan, whatever economists say, whereas for democrats the benchmark is only the "unforced force of the better argument" (which does not mean that the best argument will always triumph) and/or majority outcomes (which does not mean that the majority is always right).

Of course, when we look at certain resilient discrepancies between what the public thinks and what economists think, there are cases where experts are probably right and the public probably wrong. For example, people tend to think that "taxes are too high" or that "foreign aid spending is too high" (Caplan 2007a: 57), whereas economists and the "enlightened public" sensibly differ. A lot hinges here on what is meant by "too high" and the point of comparison implied in these judgments, so I am not entirely conceding that these are clear-cut examples of biases on the part of regular citizens. Still, one might plausibly argue that, on certain questions, an oligarchy of knowers would make more enlightened decisions than a democracy. There are, however, a few reasons that granting topical incompetence here and there does not affect the general argument for democracy developed in this essay.

First, topical incompetence does not establish global incompetence, and in particular the meta-incompetence to recognize one's topical incompetence. Even if we accept that citizens are bad at answering political questions of an economic nature, that does not mean that they are not reasonable enough – that is, minimally competent – to acknowledge that fact and accept institutional arrangements that compensate for it, such as the delegation of some decisions to acknowledged experts.

Second, the delegation of some choices to experts does not imply the failure of democracy. Democracies that delegate some decisions to a few unelected individuals do not ipso facto turn into oligarchies. The fact that the consent of the people was initially obtained for this delegation to take place (directly or through their representatives) still makes the decisions of those experts "democratic" in a larger sense. To the extent that the independence of central banks itself was a democratic choice, it should testify to democratic intelligence on Caplan's view, since his story is supposedly voter-driven. Conversely, the decision power of democratically authorized experts on some economic questions does not prove the superiority of oligarchy over democracy but simply establishes the necessity of having some efficient technocratic cogs in a larger and complex democratic structure of governance.[44] The relevant comparison for my purpose in this essay is not between democracy and that technocratic branch of the government, but democracy and oligarchy when both are equipped with a competent technocracy of that kind. John Stuart Mill thought that the only virtue of a monarchy was its bureaucracy, whereas the virtue of a democracy was its bureaucracy plus the intelligence that goes into overseeing it (Mill 1991: chs. 5 and 6). Similarly, my argument leads me to conclude that when both democracy and oligarchy are equipped with a competent cadre of experts, democracy will still, on average and in the long term, outperform oligarchy.

Third, even if Caplan is right about voters' topical incompetence, particularly in economic matters, why does he not consider the possibility that such topical incompetence might be solved over time through education and public debates? I have already mentioned that deliberation might be a solution to systematic biases. But Caplan seems to equate observed ideological preferences with deeply entrenched cognitive biases and heuristics. In the same way that people are known to suffer from base-rate neglect[45] or to be subject to framing effects,[46] Caplan suggests that they are systematically anti–free trade and pro–job security. But an antimarket or a pro–job bias is of a different nature than an inability to calculate probabilities correctly or see a glass as equally half-full and half-empty. Such economic biases are due less to the limits of human cognitive abilities than to cultural factors. After all, while all human beings may suffer from some form of base-rate neglect, Americans are actually much less obsessed with job security than Europeans. Bill Clinton during his presidential campaign could thus warn the U.S. public that they would have to change jobs seven to eight times in a lifetime – a discourse utterly unthinkable in a French context. Racial and sexist prejudices have noticeably diminished in most Western democracies over just a few generations. These facts suggest that some biases can be corrected, at least partially. Maybe economic biases are of a more enduring nature, but Caplan does not demonstrate this for a fact. Education and a more deliberative democracy, however trite that may sound, may well be the answers to (at least some) of the flaws of our existing democracy in the West.

The final objection I will raise is to an apparent implication of Caplan's indictment of democracy – that we would be better off with an oligarchy of

[44] In fact, this voluntary delegation of technical economic questions to experts might be all that Caplan ultimately advocates.

[45] The base-rate neglect or fallacy consists in neglecting the prior probability of some hypothesis H when one is trying to assess the conditional probability of this hypothesis given some evidence E.

[46] They give different answers to questions that are the same but that frame things differently.

experts[47] – is that groups of experts are not foolproof either. Philip Tetlock (2005) showed in his study of "political judgment" that when it comes to assessing a problem and making political predictions, political "experts" hardly do better than laypeople and, on the purely predictive side, are in general outperformed by simple statistical regressions. Striking what should seem to be a deadly blow against the idea that politics is a matter of expertise, Tetlock concludes that it does not really matter *who* the experts are (economists or political scientists or philosophers or the like) or *what* they think (ideologically, i.e., whether they tend to be pro-market or socialist). What matters is the *way* political experts think, namely whether they think as "foxes" or as "hedgehogs."

Borrowing Isaiah Berlin's ideal-types, Tetlock characterizes "foxes" as eclectic thinkers with an ability to use different frameworks and theories. By contrast, "hedgehogs" are dogmatic thinkers with a one-size-fits-all theory of the world. From what Tetlock could empirically observe, foxes are almost always better forecasters than hedgehogs. Tetlock also shows that both foxes and hedgehogs are generally outperformed by statistical regressions. If political experts – pundits, political campaign leaders, diplomats, and so on – tend to overestimate their knowledge, analytical skills, and ability to predict what will happen, it is probable that economists – who tend to fit the model of the "hedgehog" or dogmatic thinker described by Tetlock – suffer from the same cognitive failures.

Do Tetlock's results imply that there is no added value to expert advice compared with the judgment of well-informed laities? Concludes Tetlock:

> In this age of academic hyperspecialization, there is no reason for supposing that contributors to top journals – distinguished political scientists, area study specialists, economists, and so on – are any better than journalists or attentive readers of the *New York Times* in "reading" emerging situations." (Tetlock 2005: 223)

In reply to this, Caplan argues that one should not misinterpret the meaning of Tetlock's results. According to him, all that Tetlock shows is that experts are bad at answering difficult questions, not easy ones, which does not imply that laypeople would do much better on either type of question (Caplan 2007b). Fair enough, but that still not does give us a decisive argument as to why we should ultimately trust economist experts more than laypeople (or their representatives) when it comes to making political decisions, even when those decisions have an economic component. In fact, the argument from diversity presented earlier implies that lack of cognitive diversity among experts can offset the advantage represented by their individual expertise, while, on the contrary, the cognitive diversity of large groups of nonexperts can to a degree compensate

---

[47] Caplan would deny that this is the solution he advocates, yet everything, from the cover of his book to many assertions in it, invites an antidemocratic reading. Caplan could have tried harder to dissuade the reader from thinking that what he ultimately advocates is the rule of experts, in the same way as he would have liked to see Tetlock be clearer about the fact that his book does not establish the superiority of the layperson over the expert (Caplan 2007b).

for their lack of individual expertise. In terms of predictive accuracy, large groups of laypeople and small groups of experts may well draw a tie.

There are at least four standards in Caplans' book that serve as benchmarks of citizens' biases: objective facts with a verifiable answer, the simulated "enlightened preferences" of a public with a high political IQ, the simulated preferences of an "enlightened public" with the knowledge of a PhD in economics, and finally the policy preferences of economists themselves. The problem is that objective facts are not a conclusive standard (the relationship between the possession of factual knowledge and epistemic competence being too shaky), that taking economists' knowledge as the standard begs the question of who has authority in politics in the first place, and that the other two – "enlightened preferences" or "enlightened public" – are actually facts of expert knowledge in disguise.

CONCLUSION

I have defended the view that, as a collective decision procedure, democracy is more epistemically reliable than oligarchy. This is so because, even assuming that we could identify the best few, either they would not be numerous enough, and therefore cognitively diverse enough, to compete with many average smart people (in a direct democracy), or they would not be cognitively diverse enough over the long run (in a representative democracy).

I have proposed arguments supporting the hypothesis that deliberation and majority rule have epistemic properties of their own, which are maximized when their use is most inclusive, because of the key factor of cognitive diversity. Combining the epistemic properties of deliberation and majority rule, I conclude that democracy – in theory – is superior to any version of the rule of the few, including when we make unrealistic assumptions about the intelligence of the few. On that view, the good thing about democracy is that it naturally economizes on individual intelligence, while maximizing through sheer numbers the key factor of cognitive diversity.

Remember now that we neutralized the impact of two other factors of collective epistemic competence, namely virtue and information level, stacking the deck against democracy in the first case and, to some perhaps, for democracy in the second case. Holding both the virtue and information factors constant, we find that the rule of the many is epistemically superior to the rule of the few. What happens when we (theoretically) reintroduce those two variables?

If we reintroduce the virtue dimension, all other things being equal, it should be obvious that it harms dictatorship and oligarchy more than it harms democracy. It would take saints in a dictatorship or an oligarchy not to abuse an unchallenged power to do what can best serve the ruler(s), even if they have to make some concessions to the masses to keep them quiet. By contrast, it is a long-standing argument that the rule of the many, which is structurally designed to rule for the greatest number, economizes on virtue. To the extent that collective epistemic competence is also a function of the decision makers' virtue, democracy is a fortiori preferable to the rule of the few when we reintroduce the virtue component.

If we now reintroduce the factor of (raw) information, what happens? On the one hand, democratic citizens have arguably fewer incentives to become informed than oligarchs, since each of their votes matters less to the outcome and since they have to bear only an infinitesimal cost for their decisions. Notice that this does not, however, necessarily apply to the decisions of representatives, whose votes can be pivotal and who are judged by their ability to deliver good results. For these reasons, representatives need to become informed and, conversely, to inform their constituencies. Further, it remains an open question whether low levels of information directly translate into low epistemic competence, especially if the relevant epistemic competence consists only in identifying competent representatives or answering general questions on referenda. The democratic mechanisms of deliberation and voting might be precisely why citizens need not become more informed individually, if those mechanisms are able, as I hypothesize, to turn their relatively weak input into a much better output.

On the other hand, we saw that the great advantage of deliberation among many diversely thinking individuals is that the available information is processed more efficiently than deliberation among the few like-minded, and thus additional, refined information becomes available. So long as voting occurs after sufficient public debate, one can argue that democracy is at least as well off in terms of the information available at the level of the group as an oligarchy would be. Whether the amount of information made collectively available through democratic deliberation more than compensates for voters' disincentives to become informed remains an open question. To what extent this problem of information really matters is not at all clear either. All in all, I do not think that reintroducing the information variable harms democracy or gives oligarchy an advantage.

The argument put forward in this essay forms a theoretical, autonomous argument in favor of democracy, distinct from arguments relying on theories of consent or equality or justice. This is not the place to defend the superiority of an epistemic justification of democracy over other justifications. Let me just suggest that whatever might be, or might have been, the initial reasons to prefer democracy over dictatorship or oligarchy, collective wisdom (democratic reason) might help explain why we keep it. Josiah Ober (2009; see also Chapter 6, this volume) argues on the basis of historical evidence that the superiority of Athens over rival city-states derived from the epistemic properties of its democratic institutions, in particular the deliberative institution of the Council of 500 and the nondeliberative practice of "ostracism." I see his contribution as providing historical evidence supporting the theoretical claim presented here.

Let me add a final word on the conditions for democratic reason to emerge. I have insisted on the importance of cognitive diversity for the emergence of the phenomenon of collective intelligence. Without it, the mechanisms of deliberation and majority rule risk producing democratic unreason. I have assumed throughout this essay that more people bring in more cognitive diversity. In order for this correlation between numbers and cognitive diversity to remain plausible, though, one must be considering a specific kind of society, characterized, among other things, by the existence of a free market of ideas, ensuring that the constant conflict of points of view and arguments renews perspectives, interpretations, heuristics, and predictive models – the toolbox of democratic reason. The emergence of democratic reason is thus conditional on the existence of a social and cultural context that nurtures and protects, among other differences, cognitive differences.

Although I cannot substantiate that claim here, my guess is that to the extent that the epistemic argument for democracy is true, it shows that democratic reason and liberalism go together. In other words, democracy is more likely to be smart if it is also liberal and applies to an "open society." Illiberal or authoritarian democracies that foster conformism of views and stifle dissent risk turning both deliberation and majority rule into dangerous mechanisms for collective unreason, depriving themselves in particular of the possibility of coming up with efficient solutions to collective problems, accurate information aggregation, and reliable predictions. Other key factors are probably the independence of the media, as well as an educative system that nurtures cognitive differences and the ability to express them.

Bibliography

Althaus, Scott L. 2003. *Collective Preferences in Democratic Politics: Opinion Surveys and the Will of the People.* Cambridge: Cambridge University Press.

Anderson, Elizabeth. 2006. "The Epistemology of Democracy." *Episteme: A Journal of Social Epistemology* 3 (1): 8–22.

Austen-Smith, David, and Jeffrey S. Banks. 1996. "Information Aggregation, Rationality and the Condorcet Jury Theorem." *American Political Science Review* 90 (1): 34–45.

Berelson, Bernard R., Paul F. Lazarsfeld, and William N. McPhee. 1954. *Voting: A Study of Opinion Formation in a Presidential Campaign.* Chicago: University of Chicago Press.

Black, Duncan. 1958. *Theory of Elections and Committees.* Cambridge: Cambridge University Press.

Bohman, James. 2007. "Political Communication and the Epistemic Value of Diversity: Deliberation and Legitimation in Media Societies." *Communication Theory* 17 (4): 348–55.

Boland, Philip J., Frank Proschan, and Yung Liang Tong. 1989. "Modelling Dependence in Simple and Indirect Majority Systems." *Journal of Applied Probability* 26: 81–88.

Bovens, Luc, and Wlodek Rabinowicz. 2006. "Democratic Answers to Complex Questions – An Epistemic Perspective." *Synthese* 150: 131–53.

Breton, Philippe. 2006. *L'incompétence démocratique. La crise de la parole aux sources du malaise (dans la) politique.* Paris: La Découverte.

Caplan, Bryan. 2007a. *The Myth of the Rational Voter: Why Democracies Choose Bad Policies*. Princeton, NJ: Princeton University Press.

    2007b. "Have the Experts Been Weighed, Measured, and Found Wanting?" *Critical Review* 19 (1): 81–91.

Cohen, Joshua. 1989. "Deliberation and Democratic Legitimacy." In A. Hamlin and P. Pettit (eds.), *The Good Polity*, 17–34. (Oxford: Blackwell).

    1986. "An Epistemic Conception of Democracy." *Ethics* 97 (1): 26–38.

Condorcet, Marquis J. A. C. 1875. *Essai sur l'application de l'analyse à la probabilité rendue à la pluralité des voix*. Les Archives de la Révolution Française. Oxford: Pergamon Press.

Condorcet, Marie Jean Antoine Nicolas de. 1976. *Selected Writings*. Ed. Michael K. Baker. Indianapolis: Bobbs-Merrill.

Converse, Philip E. 1990. "Popular Representation and the Distribution of Information." In J. A. Ferejohn and J. H. Kuklinski (eds.), *Information and Democratic Processes*, 369–88: Urbana: University of Illinois Press.

Cox, Gary. 2006. "The Organization of Democratic Legislatures." In B. Weingast and D. Wittman (eds.), *The Oxford Handbook of Political Economy*, 141–61. Oxford: Oxford University Press.

Dekel, Eddie, and Michele Piccione. 2000. "Sequential Voting Procedures in Symmetric Binary Elections." *Journal of Political Economy* 108 (1): 34–55.

Delli Carpini, Michael X., and Scott Keeter. 1996. *What Americans Know About Politics and Why It Matters*. New Haven, CT: Yale University Press.

Dowding, Keith, and Martin Van Hees. 2007. "In Praise of Manipulation." *British Journal of Political Science* 38: 1–15.

Duxbury, Neil. 1999. *Random Justice: On Lotteries and Legal Decision-Making*. Oxford: Oxford University Press.

Elster, Jon. 2008. *Le désintéressement. Critique de l'homme économique*. Paris: Le Seuil.

    1989. *Solomonic Judgments: Studies in the Limits of Rationality*. Cambridge: Cambridge University Press; Paris: Éditions de la Maison des sciences de l'homme.

    1986. "The Market and the Forum: Three Varieties of Political Theory." In J. Elster and A. Aanund (eds.), *The Foundations of Social Choice Theory*, 103–32. Cambridge: Cambridge University Press.

    1977. "Ulysses and the Sirens: A Theory of Imperfect Rationality." *Social Science Information* 1977 (16): 469–526.

Elster, Jon, and Hélène Landemore. 2008. "Ideology and Dystopia." *Critical Review* 20 (3): 273–89.

Estlund, David. 2008. *Democratic Authority: A Philosophical Framework*. Princeton, NJ: Princeton University Press.

    1997. "Beyond Fairness and Deliberation: The Epistemic Dimension of Democratic Authority." In James Bohman and William Rehg (eds.), *Deliberative Democracy*, 173–204. Cambridge, MA: MIT Press.

    1994. "Opinion Leaders, Independence, and Condorcet's Jury Theorem." *Theory and Decision* 36: 131–62.

Estlund, David, Jeremy Waldron, Bernard Grofman, and Scott L. Feld. 1989. "Democratic Theory and the Public Interest: Condorcet and Rousseau Revisited," *American Political Science Review* 83 (4): 1317–40.

Farrar, Cynthia. 1988. *The Origins of Democratic Thinking: The Invention of Politics in Classical Athens*. Cambridge: Cambridge University Press.

Fauré, Christine. 1989. "La pensée probabiliste de Condorcet et le suffrage féminin." In Pierre Crépel and Christian Gilain (eds.), *Colloque international. Condorcet: mathématicien, économiste, philosophe, homme politique*, 349–54. Paris, Minerve.

Feddersen, Timothy, and Wolfgang Pesendorfer. 1998. "Convicting the Innocent: The Inferiority of Unanimous Jury Verdicts under Strategic Voting." *American Political Science Review* 92 (1): 23–35.

——— 1997. "Voting Behavior and Information Aggregation in Elections with Private Information." *Econometrica* 65 (5): 1029–58.

Fishkin, James. 2009. *When the People Speak: Deliberative Democracy and Public Consultation*. Oxford: Oxford University Press.

Fishkin, James, and Bruce Ackerman. 2004. *Deliberation Day*. New Haven, CT: Yale University Press.

Galton, Francis. 1907. "Vox Populi." *Nature* 75 (March 7): 450–51.

Goodin, Robert. 2008. *Innovating Democracy: Democratic Theory and Practice After the Deliberative Turn*. Oxford: Oxford University Press.

——— 2005. *Reflective Democracy*. Oxford: Oxford University Press.

Goodwin, Barbara. 1992. *Justice by Lottery*. Chicago: University of Chicago Press.

Gottfredson, Linda S. 1997. "Why g Matters: The Complexity of Everyday Life." *Intelligence* 24 (1): 79–132.

Grofman, Bernard, and Scott L. Feld. 1988. "Rousseau's General Will: A Condorcetian Perspective." *American Political Science Review* 82: 567–76.

Grofman, Bernard, Guillermo Owen, and Scott L. Feld. 1983. "Thirteen Theorems in Search of the Truth." *Theory and Decision* 15: 261–78.

Hong, Lu, and Scott Page. 2009. "Interpreted and Generated Signals." *Journal of Economic Theory* 144 (5): 2174–96.

——— 2004. "Groups of Diverse Problem Solvers Can Outperform Groups of High-Ability Problem Solvers." *Proceedings of the National Academy of Sciences*, 101 (46): 16385–89.

——— 2001. "Problem Solving by Heterogeneous Agents." *Journal of Economic Theory* 97 (1): 123–63.

Hutchins, Edwin. 1995. *Cognition in the Wild*. Cambridge, MA: MIT Press.

Karotkin, Drora, and Jacob Paroush. 2003. "Optimum Committee Size: Quality-versus-Quantity Dilemma." *Social Choice and Welfare* 20 (3): 429–41.

Kemp, Simon. 2007. "Psychology and Opposition to Free-Trade." *World Trade Review* 6 (1): 25–44.

Kruger, J., and D. Dunning. 1999. "Unskilled and Unaware of It." *Journal of Personality and Social Psychology* 77: 1121–34.

Ladha, Krishna. 1992. "The Condorcet Jury Theorem, Free Speech, and Correlated Votes." *American Journal of Political Science* 36 (3): 617–34.

Lamberson, P. J., and Scott Page. Forthcoming. "Optimal Forecasting Groups," *Management Science*; see http://mansci.journal.informs.org/content/early/2011/10/28/mnsc.1110.1441.abstract.

Landemore, Hélène. In press. *Democratic Reason: Politics, Collective Intelligence, and the Rule of the Many*. Princeton, NJ: Princeton University Press.

——— 2009. "Majority Rule and the Wisdom of Crowds: The Task-Specificity of Majority Rule as a Predictive Tool." Paper Presented at the Paris International Conference on Majority Rule, Collège de France, May 13–15.

Lave, Jean. 1988. *Cognition in Practice: Mind, Mathematics, and Culture in Everyday Life*. New York: Cambridge University Press.

List, Christian. 2004. "On the Significance of the Absolute Margin." *British Journal for the Philosophy of Science* 55 (3): 521–44.

List, Christian, and Robert E. Goodin. 2001. "Epistemic Democracy: Generalizing the Condorcet Jury Theorem." *Journal of Political Philosophy* 9 (3): 227–306.

List, Christian, and Philip Pettit. 2006. "Group Agency and Supervenience." *Southern Journal of Philosophy* 44 (1): 85–105.

2005b. "On the Many as One." *Philosophy and Public Affairs* 33 (4): 377–90.

2002. "Aggregating Sets of Judgments: An Impossibility Result." *Economics and Philosophy* 18: 89–110.

Lupia, Arthur. 2006. "How Elitism Undermines the Study of Voter Competence." *Critical Review* 18 (1–3): 217–32.

Luskin, Robert C. 1987. "Measuring Political Sophistication." *American Journal of Political Science* 31: 856–99.

Mackie, Gerry. 2009. "Astroturfing Infotopia." *Theoria* 56 (119): 30–56.

2003. *Democracy Defended*. Cambridge: Cambridge University Press.

2002. "Does Democratic Deliberation Change Minds?" Prepared for the workshop *Democratic Theory: The Canberra Papers*, March 27.

Mansbridge, Jane, James Bohman, Simone Chambers, David Estlund, Andreas Føllesdal, Archon Fung, Christina Lafont, Bernard Manin, and José Luis Martí. 2010. "The Place of Self-Interest and the Role of Power in Deliberative Democracy." *Journal of Political Philosophy* 18 (1): 64–100.

Manin, Bernard. 1997. *Les principes du gouvernement représentatif*. Paris: Flammarion.

Mansbridge, Jane. 2009. "Deliberative and Non-Deliberative Negotiations" (April 6): HKS, Working Paper No. RWP09-010. Available at SSRN: http://ssrn.com/abstract=1380433.

2003. "Rethinking Representation." *American Political Science Review* 97 (4): 515–28.

1999. "Should Blacks Represent Blacks and Women Represent Women? A Contingent 'Yes.'" *Journal of Politics* 61: 628–57.

Martí, José Luis. 2006. "The Epistemic Conception of Deliberative Democracy Defended." In Samantha Besson and José Luis Martí, *Democracy and Its Discontents: National and Post-national Challenges*, 27–56. Burlington, VT: Ashgate.

Mill, John Stuart. 1991. *Considerations on Representative Government*. Amherst, NY: Prometheus Books.

Mulgan, Richard G. 1984. "Lot as a Democratic Device of Selection." *Review of Politics* 46: 539–60.

Norman, D. A. 1991. "Cognitive Artifacts." In J. M. Carroll (ed.), *Designing Interaction: Psychology at the Human–Computer Interface*, 17–38. New York: Cambridge University Press.

Ober, Josiah. 2009. *Democracy and Knowledge*. Princeton, NJ: Princeton University Press.

O'Leary, Kevin. 2006. *Saving Democracy: A Plan for Real Representation in America*. Stanford, CA: Stanford University Press.

Page, Benjamin, and Marshall M. Bouton. 2006. *The Foreign Policy Disconnect: What Americans Want from Our Leaders but Don't Get*. Chicago: University of Chicago Press.

Page, Benjamin, and Robert Y. Shapiro. 1992. *The Rational Public: Fifty Years of Trends in Americans' Policy Preferences*. Chicago: University of Chicago Press.

Page, Scott. 2007. *The Difference: How the Power of Diversity Creates Better Groups, Firms, Schools, and Societies*. Princeton, NJ: Princeton University Press.

Panning, William H. 1986. "Information Pooling and Group Decisions in Nonexperimental Settings." In Bernard Grofman and Guillermo Owen (eds.), *Information Pooling and Group Decision Making*, 159–66. Greenwich, CT: JAI Press.

Pauly, Marc, and Martin van Hees. 2006. "Logical Constraints on Judgment Aggregation." *Journal of Philosophical Logic* 35 (6): 569–85.

Pettit, Philip. 2004. "Groups with a Mind of Their Own." In Frederick Schmitt (ed.), *Socializing Metaphysics*, 167–93. Lanham, MD: Rowman & Littlefield.

Popkin, Samuel. 1994. *The Reasoning Voter*. Chicago: University of Chicago Press.

Popkin, Samuel, and Michael Dimock. 1999. "Political Knowledge and Citizen Competence." In Stephen Elkin and Karol Soltan (eds.), *Citizen Competence and Democratic Institutions*, 117–46. University Park: Pennsylvania State University Press.

Rawls, John. 1993. *Political Liberalism*. New York: Columbia University Press.

Rehfeld, Andrew. 2010. "On Quotas and Qualifications for Office." In Ian Shapiro, Susan Stokes, Elisabeth Woods, and Alexander Kirschner (eds.), *Political Representation*, 236–70. New York: Cambridge University Press.

——— 2009. "Representation Rethought." *American Political Science Review* 103 (2): 214–30.

——— 2008. "Extremism in the Defense of Moderation: A Response to My Critics." *Polity* 40 (2): 254–71.

——— 2006. "Towards a General Theory of Political Representation." *Journal of Politics* 68 (1): 1–21.

——— 2005. *The Concept of Constituency: Political Representation, Democratic Legitimacy and Institutional Design*. Cambridge: Cambridge University Press.

Rumelhart, D. E., P. Smolensky, J. L. McClelland, and G. E. Hinton. 1986. "Schemata and Sequential Thought Processes in PDP Models." In J. L. McClelland, D. E. Rumelhart, and the PDP Research Group (eds.), *Parallel Distributed Processing: Explorations in the Microstructure of Cognition*, vol. 2: *Psychological and Biologieal Models*, 7–57. Cambridge MA: MIT Press.

Sabbagh, Daniel. 2003. *L'égalité par le droit. Les paradoxes de la discrimination positive aux Etats-Unis*. Paris: Economica.

Schofield, Norman. 2002. "Madison and the Founding of the Two-Party System." In Samuel Kernell (ed.), *James Madison: The Theory and Practice of Republican Government*, 302–27. Stanford, CA: Stanford University Press.

Sintomer, Yves. 2007. *Le pouvoir au peuple: Jury citoyens, tirage au sort et démocratie participative*. Paris: La Découverte.

Stone, Peter. 2010. *The Luck of the Draw: The Role of Lotteries in Decision-Making*. Oxford: Oxford University Press.

——— 2009. "The Logic of Random Selection." *Political Theory* 37: 375–97.

——— 2007. "Why Lotteries Are Just?" *Journal of Political Philosophy* 15 (3): 276–95.

Sunstein, Cass R. 2009. *A Constitution of Many Minds: Why the Founding Document Doesn't Mean What It Meant Before*. Princeton, NJ: Princeton University Press.

——— 2006. *Infotopia: How Many Minds Produce Knowledge*. Oxford: Oxford University Press.

Surowiecki, James. 2004. *The Wisdom of Crowds: Why the Many Are Smarter Than the Few*. New York: Doubleday.

Tetlock, P. 2005. *Expert Political Judgment*. Princeton, NJ: Princeton University Press.

Thompson, D. F. (2008). "Deliberative Democratic Theory and Empirical Political Science." *Annual Review of Political Science* 11: 497–520.

Urbinati, Nadia. 2006. *Representative Democracy: Principles and Genealogy.* Chicago: University of Chicago Press.

Wertsch, J. V. 1998. *Mind as Action.* New York: Oxford University Press.

Wittman, Donald. 1995. *The Myth of Democratic Failure: Why Political Institutions Are Efficient.* Chicago: University of Chicago Press.

Young, H. P. 1988. "Condorcet's Theory of Voting." *American Political Science Review* 82: 1231–44.

12

Rational Ignorance and Beyond

Gerry Mackie

INTRODUCTION

An economist would be "embarrassed to be seen at the voting booth" (Dubner and Levitt 2005). Although most citizens vote, the standard view in rational choice theory is that it is irrational to do so. It is extremely unlikely that any one vote would break a tie, and when a single vote does not break a tie it does not cause the outcome. Since voting is costly, almost any single vote would be instrumentally irrational. And if it is irrational to vote, it is at least as irrational to know anything about the candidate or issue voted on. "Economists have long argued that voter ignorance is a predictable response to the fact that one vote doesn't matter. Why study the issues if you can't change the outcome? Why control your knee-jerk emotional and ideological reactions if you can't change the outcome?" (Caplan 2007: 2). Although many citizens have some political knowledge, the standard view in rational choice theory is that voters are "rationally ignorant."

I begin this essay by briefly tracing the discourse of the folly of crowds from Plato through Le Bon to Schumpeter, who is critical to its establishment in U.S. political science. Postwar survey research revealing the weak knowledge of voters about political facts was explained by Downs with reference to the paradox of nonvoting, the idea that it is irrational for any one material egoist to vote unless he is pivotal to bringing about the outcome. The pivotalist model of voter turnout is misconceived, I argue. In its place I offer what I call the "contributory model." First, the empirical evidence is that many voters tend to vote for the general interest, not for their self-interest. Second, many voters are motivated not only by the winning value of voting, being pivotal, but also by its mandate value, advancing the tally of one's side in one election and beyond. Contributing to the advance of a great public good is sufficient to motivate

I thank conference participants and the volume editors for advice. This essay borrows some of its ideas from Mackie (2008a, b, 2009).

voting for many, I suggest. Unlike the pivotalist model, the contributory model is consistent with two observations. First, many citizens do vote. Second, those voters say in scientific surveys that they vote in order to do their duty and to influence the outcome.

Next, with the contributory model in hand, I challenge the economic model of information acquisition and the idea of rational ignorance. For economists, the wisdom of crowds does apply, quite nicely, to the marketplace. Some even infer that market actors must be perfectly informed. For many economists, however, the voter is perfectly uninformed, due to rational ignorance. Hence, democratic decision should be minimized and formerly political decisions transferred to the marketplace. I claim that the supposed contrast between consumer knowledge and voter ignorance is theoretical speculation, not empirical fact, and I illustrate with some instances of weak consumer knowledge and strong voter knowledge. The public choice school of thought derives two further analyses from the pivotality account, each damaging to democracy. Brennan and Lomasky accept the pivotalist model of voting, accept the fact that people do vote, and conclude that since voters almost never vote for instrumental reasons, they must vote for expressive reasons: they desire to express a desire. I respond that the contributory model of voting restores primacy to instrumentality in the voting decision, and I dissect a widely cited analogization of voting to cheering and booing at a football game. The expressive theory claims that voters undisciplined by instrumental consequence would express their emotions and that often such expression would be irresponsible and harmful in the aggregate. I comment that the contributory account restores the discipline of consequence to voting. Caplan, following up on Schumpeter, argues that voters are both ignorant and irrational – irrational in that sometimes they hold beliefs they should know to be false, particularly in politics. I respond that his thesis of rational irrationality depends on the pivotalist model of voting and does not apply should the contributory model of voting be a more accurate description of reality. I also offer an alternative explanation for why a generally rational individual would retain an apparently false belief.

The wisdom of crowds is the idea that the aggregation of the judgments of the less informed many may be as good as or better than the judgments of the more informed few or one. In its weaker form the idea is that, if error is randomly distributed, then in the aggregation of multitudinous judgments, error cancels out and truth remains. In its stronger form, as in the Condorcet Jury Theorem, if judgments of the many are on average better than random, then aggregation of those judgments approaches truth quickly as the number of independent judgments increases. My guess is that the wisdom of crowds helps make democracy a success but that its scope and its power are much weaker than indicated by the pure models. However, if error is not random, but biased, or if judgments are on average worse than random, then the wisdom of crowds turns viciously into the folly of crowds. The pivotalist model of voting implies the concept of the rational ignorance of citizens, and rational ignorance underwrites both Brennan's idea that voters are expressive, and hence more emotional than rational, and Caplan's idea that voters are rationally irrational. If citizens are perfectly ignorant or, worse, systematically biased, there can be no wisdom of crowds in a democracy.

FROM PLATO TO DOWNS

In the Western tradition of political thought, the claim that citizens are woefully ignorant about politics goes back as far as Plato's aristocratic disgust at the fact that the democratic assembly listens to persons of all ranks and professions without distinction, rather than consulting the noble and the rich as they should (Plato 1978). It is well known that in the democratic polity citizens praise insolence, anarchy, extravagance, and shamelessness; not only the slaves, but even the dogs and the donkeys, are too full of freedom (Plato 1992: 560e). Although no democrat, Aristotle had friendlier views about the wisdom of crowds. He observed that it is possible (but not necessary) that the many, who are not excellent as individuals, are better when they come together than the few best. True, some crafts are best judged by their few expert practitioners, but others are best judged by their many intended beneficiaries: the guests, for example, are better judges of the feast than the cook. Aristotle's arguments were repeated and embellished by Marsilius of Padua, among other scholastics, and later by some republicans, including Machiavelli. As cities swelled, industry proliferated, and the liberal democratic state consolidated in the later nineteenth century, a reactionary panic gripped the upper classes. Mob psychology was generalized by Le Bon into a pseudo-scientific theory of the crowd. Every individual, including voters in democratic elections and deputies in democratic assemblies, partakes of a normal civilized self and an abnormal uncivilized self – atavistic, antirational, and dangerous – incarnated by group action. Elsewhere, Lenin knew what had to be done: a revolutionary vanguard must lead the masses, who otherwise would languish in spontaneity. Hitler proposed that truly Germanic democracy required a leader of genius to take power away from the majority of ignoramuses and incompetents: a hundred empty heads do not make one wise man, he counseled (Hitler 1999: 75–91).

Schumpeter (1942: 256–64) spritzed up with economics Le Bon's wilted theory and transplanted it to American soil. He said that individual will is more definite with respect to consumer choice, because consumers directly experience the consequences of their choices, but it is indefinite with respect to democratic choice because voters do not. Individual will is not independent in politics, because it is formed mostly by the propaganda of leaders and their parties, again because there is no relation between voter choice and consequence.

Every parliament, every committee, every council of war composed of a dozen generals in their sixties, displays, in however mild a form, some of those features that stand out so glaringly in the case of the rabble, in particular a reduced sense of responsibility, a lower level of energy of thought and greater sensitiveness to nonlogical influences.... Newspaper readers, radio audiences, members of a party even if not physically gathered together are terribly easy to work up into a psychological crowd and into a state of frenzy. (257)

Schumpeter holds that the judgment of a qualified leader is generally better than the pooled judgment of lesser beings, which is one reason he so emphasizes individual leadership.

Another sort of irrationality is exemplified by advertising, which relies on repetition and association of the targeted product with basic needs such as sex and social approval. There is a check on commercial advertising, says Schumpeter, in that the consumer accumulates favorable and unfavorable experiences with products, improving evaluation. Thus, she is rational about "most of the decisions of daily life that lie within the little field which the individual citizen's mind encompasses with a full sense of its reality . . . the things which are familiar to him independently of what his newspaper tells him" (258–59). Individual will might be definite and genuine with respect to local politics or with respect to "many national issues that concern individuals and groups . . . directly and unmistakably" (260), but less so than within the familiar field.

Otherwise, with respect to national and international affairs unlinked to personal concerns the sense of reality is . . . completely lost. . . . [T]he great political questions take their place in the psychic economy of the typical citizen with those leisure-hour interests that have not attained the rank of hobbies. . . . One has one's phrases, of course, and one's wishes and daydreams and grumbles; especially one has one's likes and dislikes. (261)

There are two further ominous consequences, he says. First, in political matters the typical citizen would yield to extrarational or irrational prejudice and impulse, and relax his usual moral standards. Second, the absence of the rationalizing influence of experience and responsibility in political affairs means that the typical citizen is vulnerable to advertising by groups with an ax to grind, and "they are able to fashion, and within very wide limits, even to create the will of the people. . . . [W]e are confronted with . . . not a genuine but a manufactured will" (263). Unlike the consumer, the citizen does not accumulate favorable and unfavorable experiences with political products.

Survey research in the 1950s by political scientists associated with the University of Michigan found that citizens are variably informed and that many know little about the not so obvious facts of politics (Campbell et al. 1960, although Bryce 1995/1889 reported the same finding seventy years earlier, and with a more charitable and astute interpretation, in my view). In the same tradition, Converse (1964) claimed to find little understanding of ideology in the electorate (but his data are suspect; see Popkin 2006).

The paradox of nonvoting was first stated by Downs (1957: 244–46) and is often formulated as follows: B is the individual's benefit from a winning election outcome, C is the cost of the individual voting, and p is the probability that an individual's vote is pivotal in causing the winning election outcome. An individual would vote, then, when $pB - C > 0$. The probability of being

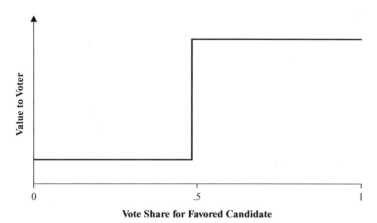

FIGURE 12.1. Voting: only value winning.

pivotal, however, is minuscule, effectively zero; for any individual, the act of voting is all cost and almost no benefit, and hence no one should vote. Downs (1957: 244–46, 266–71) premised rational ignorance directly on the paradox of nonvoting (298): if one has no incentive to cast a costly vote, one has no incentive to gather costly political information. Deductive theory's necessity claim seemed to explain the data indicating the absence of knowledge.

THE PARADOX OF NONVOTING

Elsewhere, in response to the alleged paradox of nonvoting, I more fully develop a contributory theory of voting (Mackie 2008b). Its argument can be summarized with a simple example. Suppose, reasonably, that one likes playing basketball for the sake of winning, winning by the largest margin, and losing by the smallest margin. The paradox, however, insists that only winning counts, and thus it would be irrational to play on the team if one expected to lose or to win by more than one point. Past responses to the paradox say: Who cares about the score? It's stupid to play, or one is paid to play, or it's one's duty to play. Or one expresses a desire for victory in play.

The paradox of nonvoting assumes that voters value only the winning of an election. Their utility function would look like that in Figure 12.1. It can be seen that unless one's additional vote pivotally causes the outcome, it is of no marginal value. It would be futile or redundant. If 39 voters out of 100 vote for a cause, a 40th vote for the cause changes nothing. If 51 out of 100 vote for a cause, a 52nd vote for the cause changes nothing. The claim that voting is irrational often confounds two logically independent claims: redundancy and imperceptibility.

It is likely that many voters value both winning and how much their cause wins or loses by, the latter termed the "mandate value of voting." Their utility functions are shown in Figure 12.2. Each voter's contribution is pivotal to

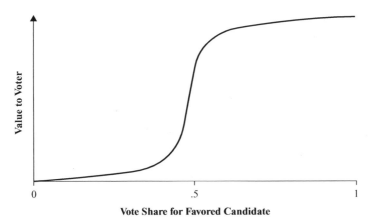

FIGURE 12.2. Voting: value winning and mandate.

the mandate value. None is futile or redundant. If 39 out of 100 vote for a cause, a 40th advances its mandate value. If 52 out of 100 vote for a cause, a 53rd advances the mandate value. In a mass democratic election involving two major parties, for example, a large mandate for the left party in the last election would in the present term of office shift the party's governing policies left and, assuming no change among voters, shift the policies of both parties left in the next election (Fowler and Smirnov 2007). Now the objection is that a voter's contribution is not redundant, but imperceptible. Before addressing the imperceptibility objection, let us consider that voters are oriented mostly to the public interest rather than to simple self-interest (see Mackie 2008b and references therein). Voters are most strongly motivated by duty and by a desire to influence the social outcome (see Mackie 2008b and references therein).

The American Citizen Participation Study, for example, asked an instructive series of questions about citizens' motivations to vote (Table 12.1). Prosocial motivation dominates: half the respondents said at least one particular problem motivated them to vote, and for 9 percent of them myself, family, or others were affected by the problem, for 46 percent all the community was affected, and for 45 percent all the nation was affected. Most intend to influence the outcome: 97 percent say the chance to make the community or nation a better place to live is somewhat or very important, 91 percent say the chance to influence public policy is somewhat or very important, 65 percent say that furtherance of party goals is somewhat or very important, and 22 percent say that getting help from an official on a family problem is somewhat or very important. Most are morally motivated to vote: 96 percent say that my duty as a citizen is somewhat or very important; 86 percent that to do my share is somewhat or very important. Given that so many voters name both influence and duty, someone who says that she has a duty to vote most likely means that she has the consequentialist duty to advance the public good; that is, she is instrumentally motivated. Side payments for voting are not very

TABLE 12.1. *Self-Reported Reasons to Vote*

Reasons People Give for Voting	Not Very Important (%)	Somewhat Important (%)	Very Important (%)
Direct instrumental			
Chance to make community or nation a better place to live	3	14	83
Chance to influence public policy	10	26	65
Chance to further party goals	35	30	35
Way to get help from official on family problem	79	14	8
Moral			
My duty as a citizen	4	18	78
Doing my share	14	41	45
Indirect instrumental			
Recognition from people I respect	71	18	11
Didn't want to say no to someone who asked	88	9	3
Intrinsic			
Exciting to vote	63	23	14

Source: American Citizen Participation Study, 1990.

important: 71 percent say so about obtaining recognition from people I respect, 88 percent about not wanting to say no to someone who asked. Finally, few vote because they find it exciting to do so.

These responses are consistent with the contributory theory. Label the number of citizens N, the number of voters for one of the causes n, a voter's contribution to that cause roughly $1/n$, and his discounting of benefit to any other individual α ($0 < \alpha < 1$), and a citizen will vote when $1/n$ ($B_{\text{self}} + \alpha NB_{\text{society}}) - C > 0$ (adapted from Edlin, Gelman, and Kaplan 2007). The term for benefit to self, B_{self}, is small compared with the term for benefit to society, B_{society}, and, when each is multiplied by $1/n$ contribution, benefit to self usually goes to almost nothing, leaving benefit to society as the principal motivation for voting. If so, then, just as deliberation may operate as a filter to exclude unjustifiable preferences, voting may operate as a filter to exclude self-interest and include public interest as input to collective decisions.

Is an "imperceptible" contribution to the benefit of society irrational (Olson 1971: 64), even if the benefit exceeds the cost of the contribution? Parfit (1994: 75–82) argues that it is mistaken to ignore imperceptible harms and benefits, and I do not know of reasons to reject his arguments. Suppose Fatima wants to become a champion gymnast. Her friends correctly tell her that any one day of practice only imperceptibly advances her toward that goal, but incorrectly tell her that for that reason she should skip every practice. My contribution of $25 is imperceptible in comparison with UNICEF's $100 million budget, but its comparative smallness does not reduce its value from $25 to $0. Empirical studies show that humans strongly contribute to low-cost continuous public goods (Pellikaan and van der Veen 2002; Frey and Meier 2004). Voting in an election is more vivid in process and result than is contributing to many other such public goods, and voter turnout is high in developed democracies (although in the United States and Switzerland, it is exceptionally low).

RATIONAL IGNORANCE

Downs (1957: 244–46, 266–71) premised rational ignorance directly on the paradox of nonvoting: if one has no incentive to cast a costly vote, one also has no incentive to gather costly political information (298). Downs recognizes "future-oriented" voting (49), what I have called its "mandate value." He also assumes that citizens are motivated to pursue any economic or political goal, not only egoistic ones (6, 37). These two points are compatible with the contributory account. Yet Downs lapses into egoistic logic in concluding rational ignorance ("it is individually irrational to be well-informed," 246). Having to explain the fact of robust turnout, he then retreats, stating that "[r]ational men in a democracy are motivated to some extent by a sense of social responsibility relatively independent of their own short-run gains and losses" (267), because collapse of the democracy due to regular nonvoting would be catastrophic. In a final implausible pirouette (269–71), he adds that nonetheless citizens (excepting those lobbyists who happen to have the opportunity to pivotally influence policy) would be irrational to acquire political information (298). If all voters were necessarily ignorant, then elected officials would be unconstrained, there would be no democratic accountability, and catastrophe would follow. Downs's ad hoc explanation for voter turnout should also predict rational knowledge of politics, not rational ignorance.

The pivotal voter model has difficulty explaining why voters turn out in large numbers, and its companion, rational ignorance, I shall argue, has difficulty explaining why voters seem to be about as well informed as consumers.

Do Voters Know Enough to Make Good Decisions?

If there is one thing that many people know about political science, it is that citizens are woefully uninformed about politics. We are hearing a lot about the topic these days – from, among others, Bryan Caplan (2007), *The Myth of the Rational Voter: Why Democracies Choose Bad Policies*; Rick Shenkman (2008), *Just How Stupid Are We? Facing the Truth About the American Voter*; and Ilya Somin (forthcoming), *Democracy and the Problem of Political Ignorance*. These authors (each affiliated with George Mason University) emphatically relate many poignant instances of citizen ignorance. Caplan and Somin are libertarians who believe it would be beneficial to reduce the scope of democratic government in favor of market exchange. Majority agreement or disagreement has nothing to do with the truth and rightness of libertarian claims, which should be evaluated directly on their merits. Libertarians, though, like

Marxists of yore with their concept of false consciousness, need a theory about why the majority fail to accept their doctrines, and the ignorance and irrationality of the democratic voter is one such theory.

Empirical findings about the imperfection of knowledge in actual democratic politics are compared with theoretical assumptions about the perfection of knowledge in idealized market exchange. Neoclassical economics, for modeling convenience, assumes that humans are perfectly informed. That is the default, and sometimes one or another departure from perfect information is modeled. One hopes it is true that everyone understands that perfect information is a modeling assumption and not a fact. The efficient markets hypothesis further holds that prices of traded items accurately reflect all publicly known information at all times. Although the market must be somewhat efficient, crashes and bubbles suggest that it is not entirely so: people do engage in herding behavior (Shiller 2005) – for example, someone copying her neighbor, who has big paper gains on his house, by taking out an interest-only adjustable-rate mortgage to speculate on a home purchase, or a pension fund buying opaque mortgage-backed securities only because other pension funds do. Citizens do tend to lack encyclopedic discursive information about politics in the survey setting, an observation that prompted several programs of research in political science.

What does democratic theory expect of citizens? Schumpeter invented a classical doctrine of democracy, attributing it to the utilitarians, which supposedly assumed that democracy requires a fully informed citizenry (Mackie 2009). However, John Stuart Mill, the intellectual avatar of liberal democracy, worried considerably about the ignorance and incapacity of the citizens (and of any other controlling body in a government). That is why he wrote in 1861 that "it is essential to representative government that the practical supremacy in the state should reside in the representatives of the people" (1977: 423), that those representatives should depend on an expert bureaucracy for advice, and that the citizenry should become better educated both by publicly funded education and by civic participation. James Bryce (1995/1889: chs. 76–87), another influential early theorist of representative democracy, in his 1888 study of the American regime, provided quite a realistic account of how a weakly informed general population could nevertheless control its representatives for the benefit of all. Althaus (2006) details how modern democratic thought generally has not demanded a highly informed citizenry.

Humans lack perfect information about all aspects of their lives. Any individual faces a hard-biting constraint on knowledge acquisition: a limited number of hours in a day and in a lifetime, not to mention forgone opportunities. People begin from complete ignorance, not from complete knowledge, and use a variety of devices to approximate competence. To buy a car one does not need to know who is in charge of the Chevrolet division or the Corolla division, or how the firms make their decisions. One compares the final products, not as zealously as would a geeky academic, but with reference to easily obtained information from advertising, personal experience, word of mouth, and scattered bits of expert opinion. Voters don't need to know how the government kitchen is organized. They each can judge whether they have more or less liberty, safety, peace, and prosperity since the last election and, like the guests at Aristotle's feast, switch chefs when meals worsen. There is one thing that each of them does know well, how government policy affects her life, and the aggregation of those judgments is more authoritative than the judgment of any panel of expert chefs. Enns and Kellstedt (2008) provide evidence to support the view that "even the least politically sophisticated segment of society receives messages about the economy and uses this information to update attitudes about political issues."

The low-information rationality school of political cognition holds that humans are cognitive misers who use quick heuristics, information shortcuts, to make decisions. (Lupia, McCubbins, and Popkin 2000 is slightly dated but an excellent introduction that contains contrary views.) Lupia and McCubbins (1998) study in depth whether citizens can learn what they need to know. They distinguish *information*, the abyss of possible facts, from *knowledge*, the ability to make accurate predictions. More information is not necessarily better in order to make a better prediction and, given budget constraints, usually would cost more than it's worth. For voters to make a reasoned choice requires sufficient knowledge, not the Wikipedia of information tested in survey research and retailed in stories about how stupid voters are.

The ignorance finding is due to uncharitable research design in some cases. Gibson and Caldeira (2007) mention that the 2000 American National Election Study had an open-ended question as to who William Rehnquist is and coded as correct only the answer "Chief Justice of the Supreme Court" (when in fact his official title is Chief Justice of the United States), with the result that 10.1 percent gave a "correct" answer. The study revealed that 72 percent of answers coded as incorrect (excluding don't-know answers) were in fact nearly correct. A conventional survey takes a respondent by surprise, asking for an immediate answer to a question the respondent is unlikely to have recently considered. Prior and Lupia (2005) gave respondents a dollar for a correct answer, twenty-four hours to answer the questions, or both, and correctness increased from 11 percent to 24 percent.

The miracle of aggregation – in the thinner sense that aggregate public opinion and voting about broad and important issues change sensibly in response to events and to changing government policies, and that government in turn responds to changing opinions and votes of the citizens – is well supported. Page and Shapiro (1992) survey the policy preferences of Americans from the 1930s to 1990. They conclude that aggregated American opinions on public policies are rational, in the sense that they are stable, coherent, and make sense in terms of underlying values and available information. Most important for the argument here, public opinions change in understandable and predictable ways in response to changing events, and changes of opinion are sensible adjustments to new information and conditions. Examples are rife. World War II increased support for military spending, wage and price controls, long working days, high taxes, and the prohibition of strikes, and the end of the war increased support for the reversal of those policies (332). And so on. Wlezien's (1995; Soroka and Wlezien 2004, 2005) thermostatic model is supported by evidence that the public responds to certain general categories of public expenditure. When the level of policy is greater than the public prefers, the public favors less, and when the level of policy is lower than the public prefers, the public favors more. In turn, budgetary decisions follow public preferences. Erikson, MacKuen, and Stimson (2002), in their sophisticated and richly detailed analyses, argue that election results are influenced by "macropartisanship," roughly, accountability for past economic and other government performance, and by "public mood," roughly, the public's demand for future policy change. They also argue that public opinion does not respond to policy at the individual level (342–51), but "when we turn to aggregates, the nation as a whole, the public *does* react (and react appropriately) to policy making by the national government" (351).

Is the Marginal Costs Model of Information Acquisition Plausible?

The economic theory of knowledge acquisition holds that an individual seeks new information up to the point where the marginal cost of new information equals its marginal benefit. The proposition has always had a whiff of paradox about it, or confusion perhaps. Since the individual by definition lacks information concerning a possible decision, how could he know what information is worth obtaining and what not? By its market price? The more it costs the more it is worth having? That means that the purchaser has perfect information that the seller of the information is trustworthy, that unknown information is exactly relevant to the decision problem at hand, and that it is worth as least as much as it costs. Maybe that describes buying an issue of the U.S. monthly magazine *Consumer Reports* containing vehicle reliability reports, but sadly most ignorance is not so easily tamed. What if the information is not for sale on the market, but must be discovered directly by the individual? Would the effort and opportunity cost of obtaining the information measure its worth? No: Suppose the person studies astrology for a month to learn how to better assess the reliability of alternative automobile purchases. Studying astrology for two months wouldn't make the decision better. Consider: How is it that I know that astrology wouldn't help? Did I test that belief in an experiment? Can I cite any experiment carried out by others on the question? I shall return to this point.

The marginal costs model assumes that an individual otherwise has perfect information or, somehow, sufficient information to calculate the acquisition decision. It applies now and then, here and there, but it could never be a general model of information acquisition. Assume a person with no information. How does she proceed? She doesn't know whether it is worth having any kind of knowledge; she doesn't know the truth or falsity of any possible belief; maybe she doesn't even know that she has desires. The marginal costs model is necessarily parasitic on some other more general theory of learning and knowledge. The model does not warrant any sweeping, or even any modestly general, account of knowledge acquisition, not by *Homo sapiens*, not by *Homo economicus*, and not by *Homo democraticus*.

The pivotalist model and the marginal costs model together imply that acquiring political knowledge is almost never instrumentally beneficial. Some instrumentally valuable political knowledge comes at no effort or opportunity cost, what Downs (1957: 221) called the "free information system." It is acquired incidentally in pursuit of some other purpose; for example, watching an entertaining television show exposes one to a political advertisement. Other than paid advertisement or accidental personal encounters with lobbyists, however, no other incidental knowledge would appear, I infer. The idea that at a poker game one learns about a political candidate, or that there is a frequency of political buttons among one's friends, depends on the presence of contributory actors, whose existence the pivotalist would deny. In contrast, a contributory voter or activist would be instrumentally motivated to obtain political knowledge, up to a point.

Much knowledge acquisition is intrinsically beneficial, a pleasure in itself to discover, whether it is knowledge of wars and elections, baseball stats, Pokemon trading cards, geography and history, wedding planning, daily news, child development, handgun types, and so on. Surely the overall levels of individuals' curiosity vary, and the targets of their curiosity vary even more, but a thirst for knowledge is ordinarily part of the human experience. The interest emotion motivates exploration and learning, globally and locally (Silvia 2008). It is generally adaptive, because a creature lacking perfect information does not know whether the unknown is harmful and to be further avoided or whether the unknown is helpful and to be pursued. To speculate, it may, like other positive emotions, be evolutionarily adaptive: negative emotions such as fear motivate avoidance of threat, but positive emotions such as interest function during times when individuals are able to consolidate and expand their resources. Interest, which motivates people to try new things, people, places, and experiences, is distinct from happiness, which motivates attachment to what is known to be enjoyable (Gallagher and Lopez 2007; Kashdan and Silvia 2002; Silvia 2008).

Caplan (2007, 120–21) considers history, philosophy, religion, astronomy, geology, politics, and the like to be impractical knowledge. Erring in any of these disciplines is costless, except perhaps for the social consequences of being thought ignorant by others. Practical knowledge involves getting out of bed, driving to work, eating lunch, going home, having dinner, watching television, and going to sleep. Here, an error in one's beliefs is far more likely to have adverse consequences, he says. If Caplan is correct, then the marginal costs model of information acquisition would advise one to forgo such impractical knowledge. I join John Stuart Mill, however, in thinking it better to be Socrates dissatisfied than a fool satisfied. An economics that accepts preferences as sovereign has no authority to criticize me for obtaining satisfaction from the rhapsodic application of my impractical knowledge as I wander the Cathedral of Our Lady of Chartres. Not only is "impractical" knowledge intrinsically valuable, as in the preceding example, it is of instrumental value as well. In a complex and largely unknown world, to possess a magpie's nest of useless knowledge is instrumentally valuable in obtaining goods and avoiding losses. Serendipity, the discovery of things by accident, has brought us Velcro, penicillin, x-rays, Teflon, dynamite, the Dead Sea Scrolls, and thousands of other benefits (R. Roberts, 1989, ix). The economist Jevons, the physicist Mach, and the scientist Priestley are, according to sociologist of science Merton (Merton and Barber 2004: 158–62), just a few of those who say that accidents more often than design propel the advance of discovery. Louis Pasteur, according to Merton, taught his overly practical students that "[t]heory alone can bring forth and develop the spirit of invention." Pasteur, one of the greatest benefactors of humankind, also said that "chance favors only the prepared mind" (R. Roberts 1989: 244), but what is preparation? Kekule did not calculatively learn the image of the ouroboros, the snake swallowing its tail, in order to discover the structure of benzene years later; presumably, he just happened to know it out of natural curiosity. Caplan neglects the value of supposedly impractical knowledge in obtaining gains, but it helps avoid losses as well. In the U.S. television series of the same name, the hero MacGyver repeatedly applies seemingly useless knowledge in devising escapes from looming catastrophes, and apparently useless knowledge is serendipitously beneficial in our more mundane lives.

Much novel knowledge, including local social and political knowledge, as well as national political knowledge, is not obtained from dubious testimony or costly experiment, but is immediately inferred from theory at no cost. I shall elaborate on this point in the section on rational irrationality. In summary, I have suggested three types of costless information acquisition: the incidental, the inquisitive, and the inferential. Costless information acquisition might create a sufficient background of knowledge in which a marginal cost model of information acquisition could operate. The contributory theory of voting allows for instrumental turnout and it allows for instrumental information acquisition, up to a point. Given the many demands of his life, the citizen would seek the minimum costly knowledge needed for reasoned choice, in politics, in the market, and in other life activities.

Rational Ignorance Applies to Both Voters and Consumers

A recent pilot study by Mat McCubbins, with my participation, compared student respondents' knowledge of issues of concern to voters and issues of concern to consumers. Large majorities know about national political issues, and few (including me) know much about important but obscure state political issues. As to consumer issues, people don't know which sports activities are more or less likely to cause injury, the content of toothpaste, the market costs of health insurance, which common foods have greater or fewer calories, which common grocery items cost more or less, or that acetaminophen is the most common cause of liver failure, or that you're more likely in your home to die of a fall rather than in a fire, among other things. They do know some details about their most beloved consumer items such as iPods. Voters and consumers each showed a wide range of knowledge and ignorance on factual questions.

A response may be to concede that consumers are rationally ignorant about trivial purchases but become fully informed when the stakes are high. How about the typical consumer's biggest transaction, with the direst economic consequences: the purchase of a home? A quantitative survey by the U.S. Federal Trade Commission of 819 recent mortgage customers asked them to examine and compare hypothetical loan documents (Lacko and Pappalardo 2007: ES-6, ES-7). The study disclosed the following:

The failure to convey key mortgage costs was evident across a wide range of loan terms and among substantial proportions of study participants.

- About a fifth of the respondents viewing the current disclosure forms could not correctly identify the APR [annual percentage rate] of the loan, the amount of cash due at closing, or the monthly payment (including whether it included escrow for taxes and insurance).
- Nearly a quarter could not identify the amount of settlement charges.
- About a third could not identify the interest rate or which of two loans was less expensive, and a third did not recognize that the loan included a large balloon payment or that the loan amount included money borrowed to pay for settlement charges.
- Half could not correctly identify the loan amount.
- Two-thirds did not recognize that they would be charged a prepayment penalty if in two years they refinanced with another lender (and a third did not even recognize that they "may" be charged such a penalty).
- Three-quarters did not recognize that substantial charges for optional credit insurance were included in the loan.
- Almost four-fifths did not know why the interest rate and APR of a loan sometimes differ.
- Nearly nine-tenths could not identify the total amount of up-front charges in the loan.

The results were confirmed and broadened by thirty-six in-depth interviews with recent mortgage buyers about their actual loan experiences: "Many had loans that were significantly more costly than they believed. . . . Many of these borrowers did not learn of these costs and terms until at or after the loan settlement, and some appeared to learn for the first time during the interview. Some of these borrowers reported that they had spent considerable time shopping and comparing loan offers, but still experienced problems or misunderstandings" (Lacko and Pappalardo 2007). In a review article on consumer knowledge, Alba and Hutchinson (2000: 123) conclude that "[c]onsumers are overconfident – they think they know more than they actually do."

In contrast, according to Delli Carpini and Keeter (1996), 91 percent of survey respondents could locate Texas on a map (1988), 76 percent the Soviet Union (1988), 63 percent Grenada (1983), and 61 percent Peru (1988);

59 percent knew which state had the largest population (1988), 55 percent could name one Central American country (1988), and so on. In history, 91 percent knew that the United States dropped atomic bombs on Japan (1990), 84 percent why Pearl Harbor is important (1981), 81 percent who Andrew Jackson was (1955), 74 percent who gave the Statue of Liberty to the United States (1986), 58 percent who Napoleon Bonaparte was (1975), and so on. In politics (all 1989), 96 percent knew the length of a presidential term, 89 percent could define "veto," 74 percent know who the vice president was, 73 percent the governor, 55 percent which party controlled the Senate, and so on. The range of knowledge and ignorance of political facts is much wider on the ignorance side than indicated in this exercise, but the point about comparing consumer and voter knowledge is made.

The notion that consumers are necessarily better informed than voters is a theoretical speculation, not an empirical fact.

THE EXPRESSIVE THEORY OF VOTING

The expressive theory of voting (Brennan and Lomasky 1993) is probably the modally endorsed model these days. Market and ballot choices are each composed of both instrumental and expressive elements, it says. Individuals may value expression of a preference through a market exchange or a vote; in other words, they desire to express a desire. The expressive aspect of voting is "action that is undertaken for its own sake rather than to bring about particular consequences" (25). The formula becomes $pB - C + E > 0$, where E is the expressive value of voting; the instrumental value of pB is approximately zero, and an individual votes if and only if the expressive value of the act exceeds its cost. The expressive theory holds that there is almost never a causal connection between an individual's vote and the associated electoral outcome; that expressive considerations disproportionately influence the ballot in comparison to the market; and that a divergence between individuals' expressive preferences and their instrumental preferences perversely distorts the aggregate outcome.

Comparing Market and Ballot

The expressivists (Brennan and Lomasky 1993: 20) compare exchange in the market to voting in a democracy. Their analysis is intended to show that in market exchange there is a causal connection between choice and outcome, but in democratic voting there is not; that exchange is disciplined by opportunity cost but voting is not; and that market choice is primarily instrumental but voting choice is almost purely expressive. For economists, whatever an individual actually chooses is, *by definition*, rational, so long as preferences are consistently rank-ordered. An individual is assumed to have full information, to enjoy costless deliberation, to make no mistakes, to suffer from no weakness of the will, and to be free of systematically biased judgments. The economic actor is a unitary individual or a unitary collective such as a business firm, rational by assumption. The consistent choices of such an actor in a market are rational, setting up one side of the market: ballot comparison. Public choice theory initially made its mark by analogizing voters to consumers and by applying the tools of economics to political questions. The enterprise is fruitful to an extent, but the analogy is far from perfect. When a citizen votes for health insurance for all children, she does not choose that outcome in the same way that she chooses an Orange Mocha Frappuccino Blended Coffee at Starbucks. Rather, I would say, she contributes to a collective decision. The expressivists emphasize the disanalogy but analyze it differently.

The expressivists say that market choice is always pivotal, but voting choice is almost never pivotal, and this contrast grounds their judgment that voting is "pseudorational" (21). When I buy an Orange Mocha Frappuccino Blended Coffee my action is *pivotal*: I choose alternative *a* over alternative *b*. The final benefit of the choice is the net benefit of *a* (the benefit of the beverage minus its direct cost) minus the opportunity cost of *a*. The opportunity cost of *a* is the net benefit of the next-best alternative *b* (the benefit of the next-best alternative minus its direct costs). If I fail to choose better *a*, and instead choose worse *b*, then my interests are set back. The consequence of being set back by choosing *b* disciplines me to choose *a*. If I prefer the outcome of state health insurance for all children, when I vote for that alternative, call it *a*, the final benefit is the net benefit of voting for it minus the net benefit of voting against it, call that *b*. However, my vote is not *pivotal* to either choice, except in the one in a million or worse chance that my single vote changes a loser to a winner. Whether I vote for the insurance or against it, the outcome is the same; thus, if I fail to choose *a* and instead choose *b*, my interests are not set back. Market exchange is disciplined by consequences; voting is not. Many people vote in elections even though they know that their vote is not pivotal; hence, some other value must motivate their action. The expressivist holds that they vote almost entirely in order to *express* a preference for, say, state health insurance for all children. The expressivists also provisionally assume *Homo economicus*, that both consumers and voters are instrumentally motivated by egoistic aims.

Say that an actor's choice is motivated by both instrumental value and a narrowly defined expressive value. The consumer instrumentally values the possession and consumption of the Orange Mocha Frappuccino, and also perhaps values expressing a preference for it through the act of exchange. The voter's valuation of state health insurance for all children is discounted by the minuscule chance of pivotality, say one in a million: instrumental value is nil and thus the value of *expressing* the preference for state health insurance for all children becomes supreme. Say that for individual *i*, R is the *instrumental* value of alternative *a* and L is its *expressive* value. Then, in market choice, an individual chooses alternative *a* over alternative *b* if and only if

$$R_a^i + L_a^i > R_b^i + L_b^i$$

Empirically, I surmise, the value of merely expressing a desire for a market good is usually quite small. A bit of caution here: by "expressive value" the expressivist means only the value of expressing a desire for the good, and nothing more. The otherwise expressive value of possessing, treasuring, flaunting the good is outside the analysis (Brennan and Lomasky 1993: 34). To fairly make a comparison with voting by secret ballot, we would add the additional assumption that it is only the value of expressing to oneself a desire for the market good by exchanging for it, not expressing to others such a desire.

And in voting choice, when h is the minuscule chance of i's being pivotal to the outcome, an individual chooses a over b if and only if

$$h R_a^i + L_a^i > h R_b^i + L_b^i$$

In market choice, instrumental value generally exceeds narrow expressive value, and in voting choice, narrow expressive value almost completely dominates instrumental value. It is important to understand that the broad expressive values associated with realizing a particular public good would *also* be discounted by h; only narrow expressive value motivates the voter. An actor motivated by narrow expressive value is more emotional in his choices than an actor motivated by instrumental value, and it is possible that voters motivated by expressive interests in the aggregate would choose an outcome contrary to their instrumental interests. Thus, "preferences revealed in electoral settings do not possess the same normative authority as those revealed in the ideal market context" (Brennan and Lomasky 1993: 28).

What Is Expressive Value?

The expressivists' main example of intrinsically valued preference revelation or expression of desire is the cheering and booing at a football game. Cheering and booing declare which team the fan prefers to win, although the fan does not cheer or boo as a means to bring about her team's success. She desires to express a desire for its victory but does not choose its victory, the expressivists say. However, spectators at a live game do believe that their cheering and booing, although neither individually pivotal toward victory nor perceptible toward advance, influence the team's performance. Home advantage is an established phenomenon in sports science, although the evidence as to whether crowd support furthers it is inconclusive. A survey of English football fans, however, shows that they believe that crowd support is the most likely cause of home advantage. Moreover, 93 percent endorse the statement that "the more supportive the crowd, the better its team will play," and 80 percent endorse the statement that "a quiet home crowd will discourage the home players" (Wolfson, Wakelin, and Lewis 2005). Such evidence, along with simple introspection, suggests that it is false that members of the audience do not intend to influence the outcome. Moreover, fans cheer not only final victory and loss, but also each increment of the game's progress; and they can cheer their losing team after it has lost (what does that have to do with expressing a desire for victory?). Fans cheer and boo a band's musical performance, even though it has nothing to do with victory or loss in team competition. It is somewhat an involuntary expression, difficult to suppress, like laughing. Cheering and booing, though, express approval and disapproval and are in some sense intended to motivate a performer in this and future performances; laughter is more involuntary and seems more remote from an intention to influence the performance. We cheer and boo games on radio and television even though the players cannot hear us, and we laugh at Seinfeld and Colbert even though they cannot hear our response: the mediated response is plainly parasitic on the live response, however.

Cheering at a football game is not like voting; rather, it is like cheering at a presidential debate or cheering the vote tally on the television at a neighborhood election-night party (doubly "expressive," in that none of the candidates can hear our cheers, and all the votes are already cast). Voting is not like cheering a football team; rather, it is like playing on a football team. A player values the team's winning the game, its losing by the smallest margin, and its winning by the largest margin. The pivotalist says it is only rational for an individual to play in a game if he will be pivotal to its victory; if the team would lose or would win by more than one point, participation would be futile or redundant and hence instrumentally irrational. Since people do play on teams that lose or that win by more than one point, the pivotalist searches for an act-contingent value of playing: one plays because one is paid to play, or because one considers it a duty to play, or, as the expressivist would have it, because one wishes by playing to satisfy a desire to express a desire for victory. There is nothing irrational, however, about wanting to contribute instrumentally to a team's tally, short of victory, or beyond it. Sports bookmakers take bets both on victory and on point spread, as do political prediction markets. For some, to play football is fun regardless of the score (although note that practice is usually not as fun as a real game), but I doubt that there are many who value the act of voting mostly because it is fun (Table 12.1 shows that few find it "exciting").

Market versus Ballot, or Individual Action versus Collective Action?

The expressivists' real contrast is not between market and ballot, but between action caused by one individual and action caused by an aggregate or collective of individuals. If I choose to buy a cup of fair-trade coffee on the market, I pivotally obtain caffeine and sugar, but I do not in terms of the expressive theory pivotally bring about fair trade. A boycott or a "buycott" (buying a product to promote its ethical value) is an individual consumer action that is part of a larger collective action, subject to pivotality and perceptibility objections. A survey of U.S. respondents by Zukin et al. (2006) shows that voting is the most frequently performed civic activity (51 percent), followed by deciding not to buy a product in protest (38 percent), next by buying a product in order to support a company (35 percent), then by trying to persuade others how to vote (33 percent). That some consumers are willing to pay more for fair-trade goods is shown in field experiments (Prasad et al. 2004; Hiscox and Smyth 2005). The expressivist would have to say that the fair-trade aspect of a coffee purchase is undisciplined by opportunity cost. That would mean that if the consumer learned that her brand of fair-trade coffee were fraudulent, she would continue to pay a higher price for it anyway, in order to express her support for fair trade, since her act has almost no instrumental value. The contributory theory says that her contribution advances the goal of fair trade and that if she learned it was fraudulent she would choose her next-best alternative.

Voting Is Disciplined by Consequences

Suppose that each citizen values his contribution to the advancement of a great public good, whether it is a program to eliminate basic poverty, avoidance of confiscatory taxation that would make the most disadvantaged worse off, or avoidance of a foolishly self-destructive war, and suppose that voters are those citizens for whom the benefit of advancing the public good exceeds the cost of voting. Such voters are disciplined by opportunity costs. The net mandate-and-winning value of alternative a exceeds that of alternative b. When that great public good declines due to ruinous policies, the voter is directly motivated to remedy the error by voting for better policies at the next election. The expressivists' main point is that noninstrumental voters are not disciplined by outcomes and that democratic choice is suspect compared with market choice for that reason. The pivotal model of voting implies not only rational ignorance, but also, say the expressivists, only an expressive value to voting. Moreover, that expressive value is determined by emotions, which could be benevolent but could also be distorted by envy, malice, belligerence, narcissism, or frivolity. Systematically biasing emotions add up to the folly of crowds, not the wisdom of crowds. The contributory theory says that the citizen directly values the public good and is thereby disciplined by consequences.

RATIONAL IRRATIONALITY

Downs predicts that citizens will be rationally ignorant. Brennan predicts that the emotionalism of expressive voters can aggregate to collective outcomes far contrary to their instrumental interests. Caplan (2007: 137–40) considers his work complementary to Brennan's. Expressive voters, says Caplan, care more about how policies sound than how they work, but know that the feel-good policies they favor are mistaken. In contrast, his rationally irrational voters don't know that the policies they favor are mistaken (although they should). In emphasizing not only the ignorance but also the irrationality of the democratic citizen, he is truer to Schumpeter than is Downs. The basic idea is that people are more likely to discard false beliefs concerning practical pursuits like doing their job and driving their car than to discard false beliefs concerning what he calls impractical pursuits like politics and religion. Irrational beliefs are probably found in all types of human activity but are especially prominent in politics, he says (115). "If people are rational as consumers but irrational as voters," he concludes, "it is a good idea to rely more on markets and less on politics" (114).

In one formulation, Caplan's simple model of rational irrationality posits that an agent desires two goods: more egoistic material wealth and more irrationality (123). In another formulation, that same agent desires personal wealth and loyalty to her ideology (18). If the utility gain of holding a false belief (or of remaining loyal to the ideology that entails the false belief) is less than the utility loss of reduced wealth consequent to the holding of the belief, she abandons the false belief. If the utility gain of holding a false belief is greater than the utility loss of reduced wealth consequent to the holding of the belief, she holds onto the false belief (or remains loyal to the entailment of his ideology). Caplan observes that people with worldviews sometimes have motivated beliefs; that is, they wrongly let their desires influence their beliefs. He ascribes this loyalty to a political ideology (17); pride (17); the passions of comfort, flattery, or excitement (116); beliefs that make one feel better about oneself (116); the need to esteem oneself and one's worldview and to despise others (116); a liking for believing that one is right (117); the desire for hope and illusion (118); the wish to believe (118); and active avoidance of truth (123). The general idea, I think, is that for someone with a worldview, hot emotion distorts cold cognition. The emotional attachment to the worldview causes the agent to wrongly believe as true something he would rightly believe as false in the absence of the emotion.

Caplan appeals to a 1996 survey, which shows that the opinions of ordinary Americans on the economy differ somewhat from the opinions of economists; he concludes that ordinary Americans hold irrational beliefs about the economy and that their defective economic worldview resembles that of religious believers (19). Neither the survey technique nor the comparison to experts is cognitively charitable. You are at home thinking of your mother's hospitalization and making a grocery list when a surveyor telephones and asks you to evaluate 137 statements about the U.S. economy all in one quick phone call. Your answers are compared with those of an employed PhD economist, who thinks about these issues almost every day. Even still, in 18 out of 37 issues considered in Caplan's comparison, popular and expert opinion point in the same direction. In about 11 questions where opinion points in opposite directions, there is a severe framing effect. First, for example, respondents are told, here is a list of reasons, having to do with businesses, that some people have given to explain why the economy isn't doing better than it is. Seven reasons follow. All of them are endorsed by ordinary respondents, but only two of them are endorsed by economists. The question frame invites a hurried nonexpert to endorse all the statements. Second, many of the statements are true even if according to economists they have nothing to do with economic health: technology *is* displacing workers, companies *are* sending jobs overseas, and companies *are* downsizing. When asked separately whether technological change, outsourcing, and downsizing are *good in the long run* (of twenty years), on average ordinary Americans, consistent with economic theory, think them to be good, just not as confidently as do the economists. Some are downright trick questions: Has *family income* for *average* Americans kept pace with the cost of living? Ordinary Americans say no, economists say yes. Individual income can go down as family income goes up if more family members enter the economy, as they have; income is a superset of wages; and if inequality increases, then mean income can go up as median income goes down. Both ordinary Americans and economists endorsed other statements that inequality has increased, that average individual wages are lower, and that a family needs two full-time wage earners.

The pivotal voter model, premised on the assumption that voters value only their own private good and not the public good, and on the assumption that voters value only the winning aspect of voting and not the mandate aspect of voting, concludes that the instrumental consequences of any individual vote are approximately zero. If the pivotal voter model were true, the rational irrationality model would predict that false beliefs about issues decided by democratic voting would almost never face the test of consequence. Thus, voters would almost never discard false beliefs about democratic issues. "Voters' lack of decisiveness changes everything. . . . Shoppers have incentives to be rational. Voters do not" (Caplan 2007: 140). Shoppers' choices do face the test of consequence, according to Caplan (negative externalities of a shopper's choice, such as an SUV endangering smaller cars, would not constrain an egoistic shopper, I'm sure Caplan would agree). Hence, decisions should be removed from the forum to the market.

Caplan does not say so, but if the logic were correct, a similar abundance of false beliefs would be associated with any human collective action involving more than a few people, including the pursuit of policies that would replace democracy with market exchange. Is it true that people in pursuit of individual goals have fewer false beliefs than people in pursuit of collective goals? Do javelin throwers have fewer false beliefs about the javelin throw than U.S. baseball players have about playing the game of baseball? Do sole proprietorships outperform partnerships, and partnerships corporations?

If humans value only material wealth, irrationality, and the trade-offs between them, then Caplan's model is indisputable. If, however, the contributory voter model were more accurate, such that many voters care about advancing a great public good, then Caplan's irrationality model would find instead that false beliefs related to democratic decisions would encounter the test of consequence and hence, to some extent, would be discarded, just as in individual consumer action. People in pursuit of individual goals would not necessarily have fewer false beliefs than people in pursuit of collective goals. Baseball players would have roughly the same degree of true belief about the game of baseball as javelin throwers would have about the javelin throw. Caplan is one of the few in rational choice theory to recognize and acknowledge the robust empirical findings that voters tend not to vote on the basis of self-interest but rather vote for what they believe to be in the general interest of the nation (19). Thus, it is a surprise that his account of the ignorance and irrationality of voters depends entirely on the assumption that they are egoists: "Voter ignorance is a product of natural human selfishness" (5; see

also 17, 102 for similar statements). The assumption that voters are naturally selfish contradicts the fact that they are known to vote for the general
interest.

He contrasts practical action, disciplined by consequences ("how many people believe they can catch bullets in their teeth?" 137), with impractical action,
such as politics and religion, which are not. In response, first, consider supposedly impractical politics. I say that the citizen does suffer the consequences of
bad government: depression, unemployment, corrupt officials, military draft,
uninsured medical crisis, confiscatory regulation, air pollution, you name it.
One does not need practical experience with fascism or communism in order
to disfavor such alternatives. But the citizen would be irrational to act on any
of these problems of collective action, or even to think about them, according
to the rational ignorance conception.

From Schumpeter to Caplan, economists argue that voters are not motivated
by political consequences to vote and to learn about issues that could come to
a vote. Rather than an enlightenment doctrine of reason, the Schumpeterian
literature more closely resembles a revival of peasant suspicion and fatalism,
with all the illiberal consequences bound to follow from wider adoption of
such attitudes. By the contributory account, it is rational for me to advance
the challenge against such fatalism, but by the pivotalist account, because a
successful defense requires sustained collective action, it is irrational for any
one egoist to waste time on it.

Second, consider supposedly impractical religion. The adherent of a religion
is likely to consider it quite practical, perhaps providing a way to eternal life
and certainly providing guidance in right action, both for its own sake and
for its consequences for self and others. It may be objected that the faithful's
calculation is premised on *believed* consequences of action, but the same is
true in the "practical" realm: individuals act not in anticipation of actual
consequences but rather in anticipation of believed consequences, and such
beliefs can be fatally mistaken. Here is an example. Some people *do* believe they
are immune to bullets, and they *do* suffer the consequences of their false beliefs.
In the Maji Maji war of 1905–1907, by locals in what is now Tanzania against
German colonialists, the locals believed that water talismans would protect
them from harm by turning bullets into water. *Maji* is Swahili for "water,"
and a similar belief that properly applied water talismans provide immunity to
bullets, grenades, and rockets is also found among Mayi Mayi rebel warrior
bands in today's Congo (Jourdan, n.d.). This is no isolated anomaly, but a
startlingly false belief stable across hundreds of miles of territory and a hundred
years of known duration. As one might guess, apparent falsifications of the
belief are easily accounted for. If one breaks any of the rules, the charm won't
work. These are the rules in one locality, according to a firsthand report:
one must scream "mayi-mayi" as one fights, not steal, not look at blood, not
wash or use soap, not eat manioc leaves, not eat foods cooked with peel,
not eat bones, and not have sexual intercourse. The rules, especially the last
one, are impossible to satisfy. The Maji Maji suffer not from a false belief

in isolation, but from an inadequately predictive worldview. The economic theory of knowledge, by considering a belief in isolation from other attitudes, commits what I call the analytic fallacy. Beliefs and desires are not falsified or devalued one by one; instead they are located within networks of attitudes, or call them worldviews, which themselves are evaluated holistically one against another by how coherent each is in accounting for the variety of beliefs and desires.

This is not to say that one worldview is as good as another – far from it. Some are much better than others at prediction, for example. Some are hypercoherent, too strongly linking a variety of attitudes into a single principle; adherents follow them faithfully, but too many anomalies accumulate and deconversion quickly occurs, as seen in the rapid turnover of membership in Leninist and Randian groups. The Maji Maji accept that water talismans make their wearer immune to bullets, and tests showing otherwise are rationally explained away. Someone of my background infers immediately, with no effort or opportunity cost, that the talisman claim is implausible, and there is no need to test empirically the instantaneous judgment. The economic theory of knowledge acquisition does not account for this variety of knowledge.

Why would people sometimes appear to value beliefs they should know to be false? Caplan is alert to the fact that irrationality is selective. His theory is that, for one who holds a worldview, hot passion distorts cold cognition and that the irrationality is outright. I offer the sketch of an alternative theory, which claims both to better preserve rationality and to be more true to reality.

He provides examples of motivated beliefs in three religions and in Stalinism. I would like to add a fifth and perhaps more powerful secular example of the phenomenon. According to Murray Rothbard (1972):

The all-encompassing nature of the Randian line may be illustrated by an incident that occurred to a friend of mine who once asked a leading Randian if he disagreed with the movement's position on any conceivable subject. After several minutes of hard thought, the Randian replied: "Well, I can't quite understand their position on smoking." Astonished that the Rand cult had any position on smoking, my friend pressed on: "They have a position on smoking? What is it?" The Randian replied that smoking, according to the cult, was a moral obligation. . . . The official justification for making smoking a moral obligation was a sentence in *Atlas* where the heroine refers to a lit cigarette as symbolizing a fire in the mind, the fire of creative ideas. . . . One suspects that the actual reason, as in so many other parts of Randian theory, from Rachmaninoff to Victor Hugo to tap dancing, was that Rand simply liked smoking and had the need to cast about for a philosophical system that would make her personal whims not only moral but also a moral obligation incumbent upon everyone who desires to be rational.

Caplan cites Rand as an authority on avoiding rational irrationality. She "calls it 'blanking out': 'the willful suspension of one's consciousness, the refusal to think – not blindness, but the refusal to see; not ignorance, but the refusal to know'" (14–15). I can testify from personal experience that it is easier to spot the inconsistencies in another's worldview than in one's own.

Human judgment does not and cannot proceed from the repeated aggregation of thousands of atomistic evaluations (see Mackie 2006). Individuals and groups seek radical shortcuts, among them tacit or express theories that conveniently relate holistically and summarize those thousands of atoms. Social scientists, for example, don't just list data; rather, they seek the simplest useful theory capable of explaining the data. Individuals aspire to coherent moral codes. A prevailing theory is unique if constrained by observations that are multitudinous, less ambiguous, and less inconsistent. Ordinary perception, walking into the yard in the daylight and seeing a tree, is strongly constrained by observations. Wittgenstein's duck-rabbit or the Necker Cube, where perception flips back and forth from one conclusion to the other, permits two theories consistent with the observations. A multitude of observations permits the unique conclusion that the earth circles the sun. At one point in our history, observations were fewer and permitted for a time two coherent theories, the Ptolemaic and the Copernican.

Textbook physical science, not on the frontiers of investigation, pretty much settles on one theory coherent with the observations. Even so, anomalous observations crop up, and as they accumulate, one theory can displace another. Social science and social policy are built on fewer, more ambiguous, less consistent observations; and, as with the duck-rabbit, although many theories and policies are unacceptable because not coherent with the observations, it may be that more than one is acceptable because each of them is coherent with observations. Unaccepted theories are almost inaudible, but the clash of the few acceptable theories is noisily conspicuous. When observational constraints are strong, a consensus theory prevails. When constraints are weaker, several theories are rationally acceptable, such as left and right in U.S. electoral politics or the several liberal theories of justice in political philosophy.

Why would a Jain, or a Muslim, or a Hindu, or a Stalinist, or a Randian hold onto a belief that in isolation seems to be unsupported? For the same reason that an established scientific theory would dismiss as suspect an observation inconsistent with the theory. The apparently false belief is supported by connections to other attitudes more confidently held. A worldview is the ultimate heuristic. A worldview is generally useful, but none can be universally useful; each encounters anomalies, some far more than others.

Why would an individual remain loyal to what an outsider would consider a weakly predictive worldview? In the rational choice spirit, we should consider the counterfactual: someone would choose a weakly predictive worldview in order to avoid some worse choice. What would be worse? To have no worldview at all, to confront a random onslaught of isolated facts and valuations with no relations among them, each requiring costly independent assessments. One would not give up a weakly predictive worldview for a nonpredictive lack of a worldview. One would give up a weakly predictive worldview only for the sake of a more strongly predictive one. Moreover, the choices are analogous to a coordination game with ranked equilibria (Mackie 1996). In Sweden, the convention was to drive on the left, but that arbitrary convention became an inferior one as traffic increased with right-driving continental Europe. Individual Swedes could not change from left to right on their own, because of the interdependence of their choices. In the absence of a coordinated convention shift, the Swedes would be stuck (as the British are to this day) in the inferior convention. A weakly predictive worldview, made up of an interdependent network of attitudes, cannot be given up one attitude at a time. Many of its interdependent elements must be challenged together, and many of the interdependent elements of the more strongly predictive worldview must be appreciated together, before a shift in worldview is possible.

Cognition and affect are always intermingled. Emotion is as much the handmaiden of reason as reason is of emotion. Quiet background emotions direct attention during daily routines, an emotion of interest motivates general exploration, and disruptive emotions (the affect program theory; see Kovach and de Lancey, 2005) such as surprise, anger, fear, disgust, sadness, joy, lust, and agapic care focus the individual on issues potentially crucial to survival and reproduction.

Consider the phenomenology of truth and error. When someone aggressively denies something you know to be true, anger can result. Long ago I was on the Oregon coast watching the winter sunset with a group of friends. I said that the wind-twisted shore pine around us was the same species as the straight lodgepole pine, traditionally used for teepee poles, we had seen the previous spring in Montana. My friend Gino stubbornly disagreed, but he was totally wrong, and I still remember my frustration with him thirty years on. I never performed genetic tests to determine the truth of the identity; rather, I relied on a worldview that for a web of reasons assigns high credence to the testimony of botanists. When working on a difficult paper one constantly strives for correctness, but in revision after revision one finds errors, and one feels sorrow and shame upon uncovering them. Such hot emotions are associated with being *actually* right or wrong, not just with being mistakenly right or wrong. Affect may be appropriate or inappropriate. Passion about an entire worldview and dismissal of isolated threats to it are rational given the alternative of no worldview.

Biased assimilation is a variety of motivated belief discussed in political science. People evaluate new evidence in light of their prior convictions, and are likely to accept evidence in agreement with their views and to reject evidence that is not. Gerber and Green (1999) discuss how these phenomena can be consistent with rational Bayesian updating. If one receives ten pieces of evidence in support of a proposition, an eleventh against it would make very little difference. That is considering a single belief in isolation. As I have said, a belief can be even more embedded by its interdependence with other beliefs and desires in a much larger attitude network. Considering the single belief in isolation, it may appear to be irrationally persistent, but considered within its network it is rational to persist in it.

CONCLUSION

The folly of crowds is a standard theme in an antidemocratic discourse of at least 2,400 years' duration (J. Roberts 1994), stated ever more desperately in the folly of crowds literature at the turn of the twentieth century as mass representative democracy became a reality. A line runs from Le Bon to Schumpeter to Downs to Brennan to Caplan, and Caplan (2007: 19) quotes approvingly from Le Bon, for instance, "The masses have never thirsted after truth. They turn aside from evidence that is not to their taste, preferring to deify error, if error seduce them." The aristocratic economist Schumpeter extended the contrast of competent aristocrat against incompetent commoners to competent market against incompetent democracy. The pivotal model of voting, mistaken from its inception, nevertheless implied the academically popular and ostensibly scientific concept of rational ignorance. The pivotal model and rational ignorance in turn gave birth to the expressive model of voting and its emotionally irresponsible citizens, and then the purely irrational citizens of Caplan's. I have tried to take out the tree at its roots, by challenging the pivotal model of voting and then working through the implications.

I wish citizens were better informed, but we do live in a representative democracy, and they have better things to do with their time. The economic theories of democracy often model modern political democracy as if it were direct rather than representative in nature. This error raises citizen competence requirements to a superhuman level. Standard arguments about division of labor, principal–agent delegation, and competitive elections account for campaign discourse, parties, legislatures, and bureaucracies as information-improving devices.

Citizens know enough to make good enough decisions, I argue, and that knowledge combined with the institutions of representative democracy promotes outcomes better for most than would rule by experts or unregulated market exchange.

References

Alba, Joseph W., and J. Wesley Hutchinson. 2000. "Knowledge Calibration: What Consumers Know and What They Think They Know." *Journal of Consumer Research* 27(2): 123–56.

Althaus, Scott L. 2006. "False Starts, Dead Ends, and New Opportunities in Public Opinion Research." *Critical Review* 18(1–3): 75–104.

Brennan, Geoffrey, and Loren Lomasky. 1993. *Democracy and Decision: The Pure Theory of Electoral Preference.* Cambridge: Cambridge University Press.

Bryce, Viscount James. 1995/1889. *The American Commonwealth*, 2 vols. Indianapolis: Liberty Fund.

Campbell, Angus, et al. 1960. *The American Voter.* New York: John Wiley.

Caplan, Bryan. 2007. *The Myth of the Rational Voter: Why Democracies Choose Bad Policies.* Princeton, NJ: Princeton University Press.

Converse, Philip E. 1964. "The Nature of Belief Systems in Mass Publics." In D. E. Apter, ed., *Ideology and Discontent*, 206–61. London: Free Press of Glencoe.

Delli Carpini, Michael X., and Scott Keeter. 1996. *What Americans Know About Politics and Why It Matters.* New Haven, CT: Yale University Press.

Downs, Antony. 1957. *An Economic Theory of Democracy.* New York: Harper & Row.

Dubner, Stephen J., and Steven D. Levitt. 2005. "Why Vote?" *New York Times Magazine,* November 6.

Edlin, Aaron, Andrew Gelman, and Noah Kaplan. 2007. "Voting as a Rational Choice: The Effect of Preferences Regarding the Well-Being of Others." *Rationality and Society* 19(3): 293–314.

Enns, Peter K., and Paul M. Kellstedt. 2008. "Policy Mood and Political Sophistication: Why Everybody Moves Mood." *British Journal of Political Science* 38(3): 433–54.

Erikson, Robert S., Michael B. MacKuen, and James A. Stimson. 2002. *The Macro Polity.* Cambridge: Cambridge University Press.

Fowler, James H., and Oleg Smirnov. 2007. *Mandates, Parties, and Voters.* Philadelphia: Temple University Press.

Frey, Bruno, and Stephan Meier. 2004. "Pro-Social Behavior in a Natural Setting." *Journal of Economic Behavior and Organization* 54: 65–88.

Gallagher, Matthew W., and Shane J. Lopez. 2007. "Curiosity and Well-Being." *Journal of Positive Psychology* 2(4): 236–48.

Gerber, Alan, and Donald Green. 1999. "Misperceptions about Perceptual Bias." *Annual Review of Political Science* 2: 189–210.

Gibson, James L., and Gregory A. Caldeira. 2007. "Knowing about Courts." Paper presented at the Annual National Conference of the Midwest Political Science Association, April 12–15, Chicago.

Hiscox, Michael J., and Nicholas F. B. Smyth. 2005. "Is There Consumer Demand for Improved Labor Standards? Evidence from Field Experiments in Social Labeling." Unpublished manuscript, Harvard University. http://www.people.fas.harvard.edu/~hiscox/SocialLabeling.pdf.

Hitler, Adolf. 1999. *Mein Kampf.* Translated by Ralph Manheim. New York: Houghton Mifflin.

Jourdan, Luca. n.d. "Mayi-Mayi: Young Rebels in Kivu." University of Bologna.

Kashdan, Todd B., and Paul J. Silvia. 2002. "Curiosity and Interest: The Benefits of Thriving on Novelty and Change." In Shane J. Lopez, ed., *Handbook of Positive Psychology,* 2d ed., 367–75. Oxford: Oxford University Press.

Kovach, Adam, and Craig de Lancey. 2005. "On Emotions and the Explanation of Behavior." *Nous* 39(1): 106–22.

Lacko, James M., and Janis K. Pappalardo. 2007. "Improving Consumer Mortgage Disclosures: An Empirical Assessment of Current and Prototype Disclosure Forms." Bureau of Economics Staff Report. Washington, D.C.: Federal Trade Commission, June.

Lupia, Arthur, and Mathew D. McCubbins. 1998. *The Democratic Dilemma: Can Citizens Learn What They Need to Know?* Cambridge: Cambridge University Press.

Lupia, Arthur, Mathew D. McCubbins, and Samuel L. Popkin. 2000. *Elements of Choice: Cognition, Choice, and the Bounds of Rationality.* Cambridge: Cambridge University Press.

Mackie, Gerry. 1996. "Ending Footbinding and Infibulation: A Convention Account." *American Sociological Review* 61: 999–1017.

⎯⎯⎯ 2006. "Does Democratic Deliberation Change Minds?" *Philosophy, Politics and Economics* 5(3): 279–303.

2008a. "An Examination of the Expressive Theory of Voting." Unpublished manuscript, University of California, San Diego.

2008b. "Why It's Rational to Vote." Unpublished manuscript, University of California, San Diego.

2009. "Schumpeter's Leadership Democracy." *Political Theory* 37: 128.

Merton, Robert K., and Elinor Barber. 2004. *The Travels and Adventures of Serendipity*. Princeton, NJ: Princeton University Press.

Mill, John Stuart. 1977. Considerations on Representative Government. In *Collected Works of John Stuart Mill*, edited by John M. Robson. vol. 19. Toronto: University of Toronto Press.

Olson, Mancur. 1971. *The Logic of Collective Action*. Cambridge, MA: Harvard University Press.

Page, Benjamin I., and Robert Y. Shapiro. 1992. *The Rational Public: Fifty Years of Trends in Americans' Policy Preferences*. Chicago: Chicago University Press.

Parfit, Derek. 1994. *Reasons and Persons*. Oxford: Oxford University Press.

Pellikaan, Huib, and Robert J. van der Veen. 2002. *Environmental Dilemmas and Policy Design*. Cambridge: Cambridge University Press.

Plato. 1978. *Protagoras*. Translated by John Stuart Mill, in his *Collected Works*, vol. 11, 43–45. Toronto: University of Toronto Press.

1992. *The Republic*. Translated by G. M. A. Grube. Indianapolis: Hackett.

Popkin, Samuel L. 2006. "The Factual Basis of 'Belief Systems': A Reassessment." *Critical Review* 18(1): 233–54.

Prasad, Monica, et al. 2004. "Consumers of the World Unite: A Market-Based Approach to Sweatshops. *Labor Studies Journal* 29(3): 57–79.

Prior, Markus, and Arthur Lupia. 2005. "What Citizens Know Depends on How You Ask Them: Political Knowledge and Political Learning Skills." http://mpra.ub.uni-muenchen.de/103/.

Roberts, Jennifer Tolbert. 1994. *Athens on Trial: The Antidemocratic Tradition in Western Thought*. Princeton, NJ: Princeton University Press.

Roberts, Royston M. 1989. *Serendipity: Accidental Discoveries in Science*. New York: John Wiley.

Rothbard, Murray. 1972. "The Sociology of the Ayn Rand Cult." http://www.lewrockwell.com/rothbard/rothbard23.html.

Schumpeter, Joseph. 1942. *Capitalism, Socialism and Democracy*. New York: Harper.

Shenkman, Richard. 2008. *Just How Stupid Are We? Facing the Truth about the American Voter*. New York: Basic Books.

Shiller, Robert J. 2005. *Irrational Exuberance*, 2d ed. Princeton, NJ: Princeton University Press.

Silvia, Paul J. 2008. "Interest: The Curious Emotion." *Current Directions in Psychological Science* 17(1): 57–60.

Somin, Ilya. Forthcoming. *Democracy and the Problem of Political Ignorance* (Ann Arbor: University of Michigan Press).

Soroka, Stuart N., and Christopher Wlezien. 2004. "Opinion Representation and Policy Feedback: Canada in Comparative Perspective." *Canadian Journal of Political Science* 37(3): 531–59.

2005. "Opinion–Policy Dynamics: Public Preferences and Public Expenditures in the United Kingdom." *British Journal of Political Science* 35: 665–89.

Wlezien, Christopher. 1995. "The Public as Thermostat: Dynamics of Preferences for Spending." *American Journal of Political Science* 39(4): 981–1000.

Wolfson, Sandy, Delia Wakelin, and Matthew Lewis. 2005. "Football Supporters' Pre-
    dictions of Their Role in Home Advantage." *Journal of Sports Sciences* 23(4):
    365–74.
Wright, Richard W. 1985. "Causation in Tort Law." *California Law Review* 73: 1375.
Zukin, Cliff, et al. 2006. *A New Engagement? Political Participation, Civic Life, and
    the Changing American Citizen.* Oxford: Oxford University Press.

13

The Myth of the Rational Voter and Political Theory

Bryan Caplan

INTRODUCTION

My *Myth of the Rational Voter: Why Democracies Choose Bad Policies* (Caplan 2007) argues that aggregation is overrated. There turn out to be important subjects – especially economics – about which the average citizen is not merely ignorant, but systematically mistaken. I add that if social scientists had reflected on their models more carefully, these findings would not have surprised them. Researchers should never have expected the public's beliefs about politics and policy to be rational, because, selfishly speaking, political rationality does not pay.

This essay has two goals. The first is to sketch the main arguments from *The Myth of the Rational Voter*, with a focus on aggregation, "the wisdom of crowds," and why they have been oversold. The second is to respond to challenges to my approach raised by some of the contributors to this volume.

WHEN AGGREGATION FAILS

Sometimes aggregation works – the many are smarter than the few, the average guess is better than the best individual guess, and random errors harmlessly cancel out. James Surowiecki's *The Wisdom of Crowds* (2004) is full of vivid examples. What happens, though, if we look for counterexamples? Are they hard to find? Are they important?

Before we can begin to answer these questions, we need to know something more basic: How can you empirically test the wisdom of a crowd? There are three main approaches (Caplan 2007: 25–28, 50–56):

1. *Objective quantitative comparisons.* Ask the public questions with objective quantitative answers, and see if the average response is correct. For example, if foreign aid is 1 percent of the U.S. federal budget, you could ask people to guess the fraction of the budget that goes to foreign aid, then test whether the *average* response equals 1 percent.

2. *Enlightened preferences.* Give the public a "political IQ" test *plus* a survey about policy preferences. Then test whether – holding everything else constant – *average* policy preferences stay the same as political IQ rises (Althaus 2003).
3. *Lay–expert comparisons.* Ask laypeople and experts identical questions, then test whether their *average* answers are equal. Whenever one of these tests fails, we have a potential counterexample to the wisdom of crowds.

But where should we begin our search for counterexamples? *The Myth of the Rational Voter* points to economics as a promising starting place. Economists often assert that the public has misconceptions about their subject. Correcting these misconceptions is one of the main goals of introductory economics. Indeed, economists have spent centuries bemoaning the public's systematically biased beliefs about their field (Caplan 2007: 30–40). As Simon Newcomb wrote in an 1893 *Quarterly Journal of Economics*:

> The fact that there is a wide divergence between many of the practical conclusions of economic science, as laid down by its professional exponents, and the thought of the public at large, as reflected in its current discussion and in legislation, is one with which all are familiar. (1893: 375)

Of course, economists' complaints are only a lead. To put public opinion on trial – much less secure a conviction – requires serious empirical study. What happens if we actually test the public's economic beliefs for systematic bias?

First, it is easy to find objective quantitative questions to which the public's average response is wrong. For example, the public grossly exaggerates government spending on foreign aid and welfare, and sharply underestimates government spending on Social Security and health (Washington Post et al. 1997).

Second, people with high political IQs favor markedly different economic policies than otherwise identical people with low political IQs. As a rule, the better-informed are more pro-market than the rest of the population (Althaus 2003).

Third, laypeople and experts have large systematic disagreements about how the economy works. Many studies present suggestive evidence to this effect (Caplan 2007: 50–52). The main weakness of this literature, though, is that surveys rarely ask laypeople and experts the *same questions*. This makes it hard to tell how much of the disagreement is real and how much is just a question-wording effect. To handle this concern, *The Myth of the Rational Voter* turns to the Survey of Americans and Economists on the Economy (Washington Post et al. 1996, henceforth SAEE; Blendon et al. 1997). Constructed in 1996 by the Kaiser Family Foundation, the Washington Post, and the Harvard University Survey Project, this data set compiles the responses of 1,510 random Americans and 250 PhD economists to a long and diverse list of questions about how the economy works.

If the wisdom of crowds functions as advertised, we would expect laypeople and experts to have the same *average* beliefs. They do not; systematic disagreement between economists and the public is the rule, not the exception. The SAEE's raw belief gaps are statistically significant for thirty-three out of thirty-seven questions. They are also of very large magnitude: Caplan (2008: 406) calculates that, in the SAEE, the disagreement between laypeople and experts is more than 70 percent larger than the disagreement between America's extreme Left and extreme Right.

A defender of the wisdom of crowds could object, "Maybe the public is wise, and the economists aren't." Maybe. But a general presumption in favor of experts is almost unavoidable; the burden of proof lies on those who question experts' reliability. What specific reasons are there to distrust economists?

Critics of the economics profession have two standard answers. The first is *self-serving bias*: economists are rich and tenured, and imagine that whatever is good for them is good for the world. The second is *ideological bias*: economists are a cult of far-right ideologues posing as scientists. Unfortunately for the critics, the SAEE contains enough details about its respondents to test and reject both of these hypotheses. After controlling for a long list of measures of self-interest – income, income growth, job security, race, sex, and age – more than 80 percent of the average belief gap remains. After controlling for ideology and party identification, the average belief gap actually gets *bigger* – because contrary to what critics claim, the typical economist is a moderate Democrat.

In sum, important counterexamples of the wisdom of crowds are easy to find. Economics is an important subject, and not just to economists: the public almost always says "the economy" is its greatest concern (Abramson, Aldrich, and Rohde 2002). But when economics comes up, aggregation breaks down. Public opinion about economics fails every major test of the wisdom of crowds. Instead of praising aggregation, social scientists should try harder to draw the border between the wisdom of crowds and the folly of masses.

WHY AGGREGATION FAILS

When rational choice scholars see my empirics, they often grant that systematic errors occur in practice, but wonder, "How are they possible in theory?" I take this question seriously. Rational choice analysis of human behavior has been most useful, and we should be reluctant to dismiss the whole approach in the face of a few anomalies.

It turns out, however, that there is a simple way to reconcile rational choice theory and widespread systematic bias. Consider: Why do rational choice theorists expect beliefs to be unbiased in the first place? To the best of my knowledge, no one has gone much beyond the main argument in John Muth's (1961: 330) seminal article on rational expectations: "[I]f expectations were not moderately rational there would be opportunities for economists [or anyone else who had rational expectations] to make profits in commodity speculation, running a firm, or selling the information to current owners."

On reflection, this argument hardly implies that beliefs will be unbiased (or "rational") *all the time*. When the private cost of error is high, Muth has a point. But there are many subjects where the private cost of error is low or zero. On subjects like the Civil War, the origin of the human species, or the age of the earth, you can believe whatever you like without risking a penny. The same goes for most beliefs about politics and policy. Precisely because one vote makes little difference, a person can safely believe in – and vote for – even the most disastrous of policies.

You could admit that some biases are available free of charge, but still object: Why would anyone actually *want* to be biased? My main response is that people sometimes have *preferences over beliefs*. Especially in areas like religion, philosophy, and politics, many feel a strong sense of attachment to their views. They do not experience them merely as "leading hypotheses." They identify with their conclusions and want to keep believing them.

If you have preferences over beliefs, objectivity can hurt you deep inside. The worldview that doesn't fit the facts could be your own. One effective way to shield your beliefs from reality is to lower your intellectual standards. This is an especially attractive option when the cost of being wrong is zero – or if other people pay the price of your mistakes.

I call this model of belief formation "rational irrationality" to distinguish it from the more familiar model of "rational ignorance" (Caplan 2007: 94–141). Both models assume that cognition responds to incentives and reach pessimistic conclusions about the average voters' beliefs about politics and policy. But rational ignorance puts a lower bound on voter error. When he knows nothing about a subject, the rationally ignorant voter is agnostic and happily leaves decisions in wiser hands. In contrast, the rationally irrational voter "knows what ain't so." He doesn't need to study economics for years to conclude, for example, that protectionist policies are the path to prosperity. If voters are rationally irrational, counterproductive policies can easily win by popular demand.

Perhaps the main complaint about the rational irrationality model is that it is psychologically implausible. Do people really figure out the truth, then consciously cast it aside in favor of comforting error? But as *The Myth of the Rational Voter* (2007: 125–31) explains, the model is open to a range of psychological interpretations. The only crucial assumption of the model is that the demand for irrationality is downward-sloping; when the price of irrationality goes up, people "buy" less.

REPLY TO ESTLUND

The remainder of this essay is a response to three of my critics, beginning with oral comments made by David Estlund at the conference on which this volume is based (which echo our earlier exchange on the blog Cato Unbound; Caplan 2006; Estlund 2006).

My disagreement with Professor Estlund is fairly limited. In fact, he says (perhaps slightly tongue in cheek) that he accepts all of my arguments and rejects only my conclusions. The crux of our dispute seems to be what Estlund calls the "expert/boss fallacy." As he explains in his *Democratic Authority* (2007: 3):

It is important to see that authority does not simply follow from expertise. Even if we grant that there are better and worse political decisions (which I think we must), and that some people know better what should be done than others (we all think some are much worse than others), it simply does not follow from their expertise that they have authority over us, or that they ought to. This expert/boss fallacy is tempting, but someone's knowledge about what should be done leaves completely open what should be done about who is to rule. You might be correct, but what makes you boss?

Estlund makes his point with the aid of several analogies, but one is particularly striking: Suppose it could be shown that parenting experts know more about how children should be raised than the average parent. Does this imply that parenting experts, not parents, should make our decisions about child rearing?

Estlund's parenting example suggests that he is raising a concern about autonomy (Caplan 2009; Paul et al. 2003). Don't people have a right (within limits) to make the wrong choice about how to raise their kids? However, in his comments Estlund explicitly distances himself from autonomy-based arguments.[1]

Once we set aside autonomy concerns, though, Estlund's expert/boss "fallacy" makes sense. Given the claim that "the experts are more likely to be right about X than us," it is hard to deny that "we should do what the experts think about X." If economists are better than laypeople at weighing the merits of free trade and protection, there has to be a *presumption* that we should adopt the trade policy that economists think best. Of course, you could deny that economists know better; but once you grant that premise, it is hard to see why you shouldn't heed their judgment.

So suppose we grant that we should heed experts' judgments. This admission quickly raises the next question: What should experts do if someone violates the moral imperative to heed their advice? In a democratic context, this question becomes: Would it be justifiable for experts to overrule the majority for its own good – i.e., for experts to act as "bosses"? Once we set aside arguments from autonomy, as Estlund seems to do, it is hard to see any principled objection to this expert/boss inference (not "fallacy"). Think about it this way: By assumption, an expert knows more than you do, and you won't listen.

---

[1] See Caplan (2009) for a critique of autonomy-based defenses of democracy: "[A]utonomy-based defenses of deference to democracy fall short because there are conflicting autonomies at stake. Group autonomy can, and usually does, violate individual autonomy. Furthermore, since arguments about group autonomy normally *build upon* intuitions about individual autonomy, it is difficult for group autonomy to prevail in this conflict."

Without challenging these premises, how could you block the expert/boss inference *other than* by saying, "I have a right to make the wrong decision"?

My defense of the expert/boss inference does not imply that expert rule is *always* an improvement. First, even assuming that experts are overruling the majority for its own good, pragmatic objections to rule by experts remain. The public might resist, and the costs of the ensuing conflict might outweigh the benefits of improved policy. In a similar vein, experts might be more influential if they avoid the appearance of arrogance. By refraining from overtly overruling the public, they might enjoy greater public trust and find it easier to get good results.

Second, just because experts say they are overruling the majority for its own good, it does not follow that they really are. We can question experts' motivation: for all their knowledge, they might lie, abuse their power, or ignore concerns outside their area of expertise. We can also question their expertise itself: maybe the experts know as little as the public they seek to overrule; maybe they know less.

So, yes, it is *possible* for Estlund to accept all of my arguments without embracing my conclusions about improving upon democratic outcomes. But as an economist as well as a human being, I'm not very interested in what's *possible*; I'm interested in what's *plausible*. At least at the current margin in Western democracies, none of the aforementioned reservations are plausible.

Yes, it is possible to question the experts' expertise, but all of the main empirical approaches show that knowledge effects are real and large (Caplan 2007: 24–28; 50–93).[2] It is possible to question experts' motives, but at our current margin in Western democracies, such worries seem fairly remote. To take a particularly clear case, economists have almost complete control over monetary policy, but there is little evidence that they are using this autonomy to take advantage of the public. Indeed, there is good evidence that insulating central bankers from popular influence is a free lunch: independence reduces inflation without reducing employment or output (see, e.g., Alesina and Summers 1993). Finally, it is possible for experts to stir up public resistance and resentment, but in modern Western democracies, these are mild problems. A few people advocate a substantial decrease in the independence of the Federal Reserve, but this is no more than a fringe movement. The fear that moderate,

---

[2] Estlund worries that economists suffer from a "pro-market bias." I find this concern implausible given the biography of the typical economist. Most economists lean left before they study economics; during the course of their economic education, they reject many antimarket views, but typically remain liberal or moderate Democrats. If economists really had a pro-market bias, I would expect them to either (1) be pro-market before they studied economics or (2) distance themselves from the ideological left during the course of their studies. In my experience, the typical economist embraces the mindset of Alan Blinder's *Hard Heads, Soft Hearts* (1987): we should use economics to figure out the best *means* for advancing moderately leftist *ends*. It is dedication to these ends that often leads even leftist economists to reluctantly embrace further use of the market mechanism.

gradual increases in expert influence would spark a populist backlash is far-fetched.

The takeaway is that Estlund should accept not only my arguments, but my conclusions as well. Unless he wants to switch to an autonomy-based defense of democracy, he has good reason to support the kind of reforms explored in *The Myth of the Rational Voter*. Let me add that I am open to modifications of my admittedly exploratory reform proposals. If the narrow-mindedness and groupthink of experts are serious concerns – and I suspect they are – it is unwise to give experts *unchecked* control over important policies. Fortunately, "experts are only advisers" and "experts have complete control" are just two end points on a continuum with infinite intermediate possibilities. If you worry about giving the Council of Economic Advisers plenary power to overturn economic legislation, for example, one simple solution would be to allow Congress to overrule the CEA with a two-thirds vote.

Estlund's final objection might be, "None of these eccentric reforms are going to happen." If he said this, I would agree. If I am right about voters, institutional fixes will normally suffer from a catch-22; if voters were reasonable enough to accept them, you probably wouldn't need them in the first place (Caplan 2007: 199). In practice, those who recognize the defects of democracy have to settle for the less glamorous approach: using persuasion and political slack to nudge policy in a better direction.

REPLY TO LANDEMORE

In her essay "Democratic Reason: The Mechanisms of Collective Intelligence in Politics" (Chapter 11, this volume), Hélène Landemore defends the strong thesis that democracy has greater epistemic properties than dictatorship and any variant of the rule of the few. The essay explores several mechanisms that might give democracy an epistemic edge. Unfortunately, I do not see that she goes any further than this. Landemore rejects all of the main approaches for empirically testing her views on methodological grounds, has no specific suggestions for improving these approaches, and offers no alternative empirical approach to support her conclusion. Her arguments may appeal to readers who already sympathize with her conclusion, but she needs to try harder to persuade the skeptics.

Voter Knowledge and Epistemic Competence

A large empirical literature finds that voters know little about politics and policy (Somin 2004; Delli Carpini and Keeter 1996; Dye and Zeigler 1996; Bennett 1996; Smith 1989; Neuman 1986). Landemore does not dispute these basic facts, but denies their importance, on the grounds that information, as she argues, is distinct from competence, and the causal link between the holding of a certain type of information measured by surveys and the competence to make political choices is not easy to establish.

She then turns to the three major empirical approaches – objective quantitative comparisons, enlightened preferences, and lay–expert comparisons – that try to link information level to political competence. She rejects all three.[3]

Objective Quantitative Comparisons. As I admit in my book, the main problem with this approach is that it is inapplicable to many interesting questions. Landemore amplifies my concern by insisting that objective quantitative comparisons are irrelevant to *all* interesting questions. If a political question is sufficiently clear-cut to apply this approach, it is not interesting since, according to her, no interesting political question can be answered without such a degree of ambiguity.

Landemore's blanket rejection is puzzling. If someone thinks that we spend ten times as much money on foreign aid as we really do, isn't this error likely to affect her spending and budget preferences? If many people make this error, isn't the position of the median voter likely to shift? Landemore protests that there is no reason the burden of the proof should be on people who deny the connection between political IQ as it measured by existing empirical surveys and actual political competence. But there is a burden of proof on people who make counterintuitive claims, and the claim that large misconceptions about spending have *no effect* on policy preferences is highly counterintuitive.

Enlightened Preferences. Landemore ably explains the essence of the enlightened-preference approach. She admits that we can use this approach to test the "cognitive shortcuts" hypothesis that the uninformed vote as if they were highly informed. She adds that the cognitive shortcuts hypothesis badly fails this empirical test and that the major result of this approach is to show that, no, people would probably not vote the same way since they at least do not have the same preferences when they are little informed and very informed.

Nevertheless, Landemore largely rejects the enlightened-preference approach. Why? Because, according to her, knowledge of objective facts might well be both an elitist measure of political knowledge and potentially irrelevant to the ability to pass a politically competent vote. In her view, the enlightened-preference approach begs the question by merely reflecting a belief present in the premise, namely that regular people are wrong and the elites right.

---

[3] There are at least two other measures of epistemic competence that Landemore might have considered:

  (a) *Education.* A large literature examines the effects of education on politically relevant beliefs and preferences. The findings parallel those in the enlightened-preference literature. In *The Myth of the Rational Voter* (2007: 154–56), for example, I show that as education goes up, the large systematic belief gaps between economists and noneconomists noticeably shrink.

  (b) *IQ.* The literature on IQ (Jensen 1998) and public opinion is admittedly much smaller than the literature on education and public opinion, but it also finds systematic effects. Caplan and Miller (2007) show that IQ makes people "think like economists" on a wide variety of positive and normative economic questions – even controlling for education.

Landemore's complaint about "elitist measures of political knowledge" verges on tautology. Suppose an approach is willing to test the hypothesis that "a regular group of human beings" supports the wrong policy. Is this approach "elitist" by definition? If so, elitism is virtually a synonym for questioning Landemore's epistemic defense of democracy.

Her complaint that political IQ is *potentially* irrelevant to the ability to pass a politically competent vote is also puzzling. After all, the whole point of the enlightened-preference approach is to empirically test whether political IQ affects policy preferences. The method *specifically allows* for the possibility that political IQ doesn't matter; it could have a regression coefficient of zero. When you actually run the regression, however, that is rarely what you see.

But doesn't this just beg the question, as Landemore alleges? It depends on what the question is. If the question is "Are regular people right?" then the enlightened-preference approach does not prejudge. If the question is "Are elites right?" the enlightened-preference approach *still* does not prejudge; it allows for the possibility that elite opinion is a product of noncognitive characteristics.

What if the question is "When poorly informed people disagree with well-informed people who are otherwise identical to themselves, are the well-informed right?" *Then*, it is question-begging to appeal to evidence based on enlightened preferences. But to the best of my knowledge, no prominent defender of the approach ever said this. Instead, the standard response would be "That is the key *assumption* on which the enlightened-preference approach depends. It seems highly plausible. Do you have some specific objection to it?" That is how progressive empirical research works: people find reasonable starting points and solicit specific criticisms. As far as I can tell, Landemore has no specific criticisms of the enlightened-preference approach to offer.

Lay–Expert Comparisons. The final standard that Landemore considers and rejects is expert judgment in general, and economists' judgment in particular.[4] Her reasons? First, she reminds us that there is a difference between "questions of economics (the science) and economic questions, which are political questions with an economic dimension."[5] Second, she points out that economists' judgments are not "absolute truths" and not comparable to "the rules of arithmetic, logic or statistics." By assuming that "on anything remotely economical, economists know better," I am once again "begging the question."[6]

Strangely, though, my book explicitly accepts both of Landemore's claims. I recognize the difference between "questions of economics" and "economic

---

[4] Landemore splits the lay–expert comparison approach into two standards: my enlightened-public standard (where we see what the average person would think if she had expert credentials) and the simpler standard of average expert judgment. Since Landemore uses the same arguments against both positions, I consider them under a single heading.

[5] Landemore, Chapter 11, this volume. Economists use slightly different terminology for the same concepts: we say "positive economics" instead of "questions of economics" and "normative economics" instead of "economic questions" (Friedman 1953).

[6] Landemore, Chapter 11, this volume.

questions." In fact, the whole point of chapter 6 of *The Myth of the Rational Voter* is to explore the *connection* between these two logically distinct subjects:

Economists have spent more time criticizing the public's misconceptions than precisely explaining *how* they cause bad policies. They take the connection largely for granted. . . .
  In theory, it is conceivable that the public's biases spin the wheels of democracy with little effect on policy. In a variant of the Miracle of Aggregation, different delusions might mutually annihilate. Maybe each voter who overestimates the social benefits of protectionism also overestimates his ability to thrive under free trade. With selfish voters, free trade would still prevail, enriching a population convinced that "Free trade hurts everyone but me." (Caplan 2007: 142–43; footnotes omitted)

Landemore similarly misstates my position on expertise. I repeatedly say that experts are fallible and grant that the public might be right to disagree with them (e.g., Caplan 2007: 52, 53). I do not mention "mathematicians, logicians, and statisticians" in order to praise economists by association. I mention them to highlight economists' credibility deficit, and I empirically test whether it is deserved:

In principle, experts could be mistaken instead of the public. But if mathematicians, logicians, or statisticians say the public is wrong, who would dream of "blaming the experts"? Economists get a lot less respect. (Caplan 2007: 53)

If Landemore and I agree about the "questions of economics" / "economic questions" distinction and the fallibility of experts, where do we really disagree? First, although "questions of economics" and "economic questions" are conceptually distinct, I think the two are empirically closely connected. Most people vote for the policies they consider best for society as a whole (Caplan 2007: 148–51). Most people consider economic prosperity a major component of social well-being (Abramson et al. 2002). Given these two empirically verified premises, beliefs about the most effective ways to promote prosperity (questions of economics) readily translate into economic policy preferences (economic questions). How many people support protectionist policies *despite* their belief that free trade makes society richer?
  Second, although I never claim that economists are in possession of "absolute truth," this is an absurd benchmark. When two people disagree, we do not have to imagine that one person has "absolute truth" in order to take a side. Reasonable people side with whoever is *more likely* to be right. Furthermore, if one side accuses the other of "bias" but the accusations do not check out, reasonable people respond by trusting the accused more than the accuser.
  Finally, contrary to Landemore, lay–experts comparisons do not beg the question of epistemic competence. My empirical approach does not rule out the possibility that the public is right; nor does it rule out the possibility that the experts are wrong. Its key assumption is simply that after controlling for a long list of possible confounding variables, any *remaining* lay–expert belief gaps are evidence of public bias.

Landemore's dismissal of multiple empirical literatures relevant to her thesis highlights a paradox in her position. She strongly believes in the epistemic superiority of democracy. But she also laments the near impossibility of judging political competence. No standard is good enough to marginally reduce her confidence, and she proposes no alternative standard. But without a standard of competence, how can Landemore begin to judge the epistemic quality of democracy, much less make the extreme claim that "rule of the many epistemically beats any variant of the rule of the few"?

The Enlightenment Assumption and Binary Choices

To make her case, Landemore appeals to the Condorcet Jury Theorem and defends its key assumptions of enlightenment, independence, and sincerity. I have no serious qualms about independence and sincerity, but enlightenment (specifically, that the average voter is right more than half the time) is another matter. As I have already discussed, this assumption is inconsistent with all of the main literatures that empirically test it. Raising knowledge levels is often enough to turn the majority position into the minority position. If Condorcet's assumptions were satisfied, this would almost never happen.

Even if we limit our attention to what Landemore, following Lupia (2006), calls "big choices,"[7] it is easy to produce counterexamples. The American National Election Study asks respondents to say which of the following views is closer to their own: "One, we need a strong government to handle today's complex economic problems; or two, the free market can handle these problems without government becoming involved." The actual distribution of opinion on this "big choice" is 62/38 in favor of strong government. But Althaus (2003: 111) estimates that the majority position would flip to 53/47 in favor of free markets if respondents were highly informed. The same holds for other arguably big choices, such as deficit reduction and abortion on demand.

In any case, even if the enlightenment assumption holds up empirically, it only shows that the *better* of the two leading choices will prevail. But where do the two leading choices come from? They are in large part a *function of the public's level of understanding.* Suppose that two candidates compete in terms of their competence and their position on trade. If the majority is protectionist, both candidates will endogenously embrace protectionism in order to win. As a result, the public will have a "big choice" between two protectionist candidates. Condorcet's assumptions only imply that the more competent protectionist will win.[8]

---

[7] According to Landemore, who follows Lupia, "big choices" have three properties: (1) they are generally binary (yes or no, or a choice between two candidates); (2) simple and widely available pieces of information (or cues) help people vote as they would if they knew more about the choices in question; and (3) their salience makes it easier for ordinary people to use cues effectively.

[8] In a similar vein, consider the following. Empirically, information effects are much larger for policy views than for voting or party identification. Holding candidates' platforms constant, you

Landemore closes her defense of Condorcet's enlightenment assumption by discussing my view that the public suffers from "topical incompetence," especially in the area of economics. She does not actively dispute the charge, but tries to mitigate it by saying that even if we assume that this topical incompetence is a fact, that still does not establish that (1) democratic citizens are incompetent across the board; (2) experts would systematically do better; (3) there is no democratic solution to that democratic problem.

Given the strength of Landemore's thesis that the rule of the many epistemically beats any variant of the rule of the few, though, these arguments are not on point. If there are important topics where experts are competent and the public is not, it is highly unlikely that the "rule of the many" will epistemically beat *any* variant of the rule of the few. (How about the variant where experts get 1.1 votes?) Furthermore, the feasibility of eliminating the public's topical incompetence is a red herring. If the public is even *temporarily* topically incompetent, her thesis is overstated.

Later in her essay, Landemore argues for optimism about democracy's capacity for self-improvement and criticizes me for overlooking it. In support of her case, she suggests that economic biases may be due less to the limits of human cognitive abilities than to cultural factors and gives as an example the difference in attitudes toward job security between Americans and Europeans. She also asks why I do not entertain the possibility that voters' topical incompetence might be solved over time through education and public debates. These criticisms puzzle me. An explicit goal of chapter 8 of my book is to explore ways to improve the public's economic competence. I emphasize the value of education and communication, and discuss ways to raise the quality of both. Solving the problem of topical incompetence is very much on my mind.

Unfortunately, I have to doubt that a solution is *likely*. Changing cultures is notoriously difficult, and democracies rarely try to change their cultures in unpopular ways. It is hard to root out students' protectionist thinking in a college classroom, and harder still to convince the protectionist majority that we need to root out protectionist thinking.

Expertise and Diversity

Landemore is troubled by what she sees as an apparent implication of my indictment of democracy – the rule of experts – and objects that groups of experts are not foolproof either. Perhaps I should have made myself clearer, but this is not an accurate statement of my view. *The Myth of the Rational Voter* suggests greater reliance on expert judgment, not oligarchic rule. I certainly

would conclude that information has little effect on political outcomes. But precisely because there are large information effects on policy views, it is a mistake to "hold candidates' platforms constant." If voters knew more, both candidates would respond by adjusting their platforms so that they had greater appeal to the well informed.

never claim to have a "foolproof" alternative. I merely point out an array of bad policies and consider ways to mitigate them. As I explain in my reply to Estlund, the danger of delegating total control to a small group of experts is obvious, but there is a continuum of options between giving experts no more than advisory powers, on the one hand, and absolute control, on the other.

Let me close by addressing Landemore's concern about experts' alleged lack of cognitive diversity, which, according to her, can offset the advantage represented by their individual expertise, while, on the contrary, the cognitive diversity of large groups of nonexperts can to a degree compensate for their lack of individual expertise. She argues that in terms of predictive accuracy, large groups of laypeople and small groups of experts may well draw a tie. I agree that this is possible. But is it plausible? Let us return to economics. By what standard does the "diverse" public have a more accurate understanding of the subject than the "nondiverse" economics profession?[9] At best, worries about experts' "diversity deficit" are plausible until you examine specific issues. Consider the strict labor market regulation that has given many European economies – most obviously France, Germany, and Italy – decades of high unemployment (Gersemann 2005). These policies enjoy the support of the "diverse" masses and strong criticism from "nondiverse" economists. Does Landemore really think laypeople and experts are likely to "draw a tie" on this question? If not here, then where?

REPLY TO MACKIE

Last, I turn to Gerry Mackie's careful and thought-provoking "Rational Igno-rance and Beyond" (Chapter 12, this volume). In this essay, Mackie criticizes what he sees as a crucial building block of the economic approach to poli-tics: the pivotal voter model. He then extends his critique to several different economic models of voting – including mine.

Implications of the Failure of the Pivotal Voter Model

Mackie spends a lot of time pointing out the inferiority of the pivotal voter model to his "contributory model." But he never quite nails economists' core intuition about voter participation: a rational selfish actor will not vote in large-N elections because the expected selfish benefits (using "expectation" in its statistical sense and "selfish" in its nontautological dictionary sense) are markedly smaller than the expected selfish costs. Given this starting point, most economists deduce that people who *do* vote in large-N elections are either less than fully rational, less than fully selfish, or both.

---

[9] Incidentally, economics does seem to be the most *ideologically* diverse of the social sciences (Klein and Stern 2005).

From this perspective, Mackie's detailed comparison of the pivotalist model and the contributory model is a long walk for a short drink. The pivotalist model focuses on a very small probability of making a substantial difference; the contributory model focuses on a substantial probability of making a very small difference. In both cases, economists' core intuition about voting applies: the expected selfish benefits of voting in a large-N election are markedly smaller than the expected selfish costs.[10] And in both cases, observed turnout rates show that voters are less than fully rational, less than fully selfish, or both.

I suspect that Mackie would grant that rational egoists would not vote. But once we find this common ground, where do we go next? Mackie sounds like he wants to drop the whole economic approach to politics. I see this as premature. Before we shift paradigms, we should consider *how much* we have to relax the standard economic assumptions of rationality and selfishness in order to reconcile theory and observation.

If voting cost 99 percent of our average annual income, but half of us still voted, it would be time for economists to admit that our "results" have been wildly oversold. In reality, though, we need only slightly weaken standard economic assumptions to fit the facts. The act of voting takes perhaps an hour per year. That is an hour more than a perfectly rational, perfectly selfish agent would spend, but it is only 0.05 percent of a full-time worker's annual income. *Homo economicus* would not vote, but someone vanishingly close to *Homo economicus* easily could.

Of course, there is more to political participation than voting. If you add the cost of following the news, one hour per year understates the total. (On the other hand, you shouldn't naively tally the total number of hours people spend reading and watching the news. After all, news also has entertainment and social networking value.) Counting higher-strata information sources (political magazines, academic journals, works of history, etc.) does little to boost the average level of political effort. After all, the population of the United States

---

[10] Mackie is, however, incorrect to conclude that economists' intuition applies to *all* large-N activities: "[I]f the logic were correct, a similar abundance of false beliefs would be associated with any human collective action involving more than a few people, including the pursuit of policies that would replace democracy with market exchange. Is it true that people in pursuit of individual goals have fewer false beliefs than people in pursuit of collective goals? Do javelin throwers have fewer false beliefs about the javelin throw than U.S. baseball players have about playing the game of baseball? Do sole proprietorships outperform partnerships, and partnerships corporations?" (Chapter 12, this volume). The flaw in Mackie's analysis is that, in business and sports, financial rewards and penalties heavily depend on *individual* performance. For any given individual, then, the benefits of rationality about the subject at hand normally exceed the costs. If you push the question further and ask, "Yes, but *why* do such incentives exist?" I will appeal to the standard economic argument that firms and teams, unlike governments, are normally run by people ("residual claimants") with strong financial stakes in the performance of their organizations. On the important question of why democratic governments make little use of performance-based incentives, see Caplan (2001).

is more than a *thousand* times as large as the circulations of even well-known political magazines like *National Review*, *The New Republic*, and *The Nation*.[11]

What about political scientists' finding, which both Mackie and I accept, that voters tend to vote not for their self-interest but rather for what they believe to be in the general interest of the nation? This looks like a large deviation from standard economic assumptions. Mackie presents it as a serious weakness, if not an outright contradiction, in my position: "Thus, it is a surprise that his [Caplan's] account of the ignorance and irrationality of voters depends entirely on the assumption that they are egoists."[12] However, as I explain in *The Myth of the Rational Voter* (2007: 150–51), the standard economic approach specifically predicts that a small degree of unselfish motivation will lead to *highly* unselfish voting. After all, according to both the pivotalist and the contributory models of voting, the expected effect of one vote on policy is very small. This makes it is very cheap to indulge altruistic preferences (or any preferences at all) at the voting booth.

Mackie's strategy is to use the fact that people vote as a lever to overturn the vast literature that builds on the pivotalist model of voting. What he overlooks, though, is that a mild deviation from the standard economic model of voting can accommodate the realities of voter turnout without a paradigm shift.

For example, while the act of voting takes about one hour per year, the act of voting *intelligently* requires hundreds of hours of study of economics, political science, environmental science, and so on. A slightly toned down version of the economic model that Mackie rejects correctly predicts that many people will spend one hour to vote, but very few will spend hundreds of hours to vote intelligently.

To the best of my understanding, Mackie's strategy is to argue from the premise of voter participation to the conclusion of *high-quality* voter participation.[13] If this indeed is his plan, then I have to object, "You can't get there from here." Yes, a rational, selfish agent would not participate at all. And yes, a rational, unselfish agent would participate in a high-quality way. But an agent who slightly deviated from the standard economic assumptions of rationality and selfishness could easily participate in a very low quality way. That is precisely what most voters do.

By analogy, from the premise that people attend church, it would be absurd to deduce that churchgoers carefully scrutinize religious doctrines or actually live the Sermon on the Mount. People happy to take the time to attend a weekly church service balk at the prospect of reading a comparative religion textbook

---

[11] Google.com reports circulations of 155,000 for *National Review*, 60,000 for *The New Republic*, and 184,000 for *The Nation*.

[12] Mackie, Chapter 12, this volume.

[13] I believe that Gerry Mackie said this at the conference on which this volume is based, but I cannot find an explicit statement to this effect in the text of his paper.

or giving all their possessions to the poor. They care enough to participate, but not enough to participate in a high-quality way.

Rationality: Empirics and Theory

Mackie objects that the notion that consumers are necessarily better informed than voters is a theoretical speculation, not an empirical fact. He then describes his fascinating preliminary research with Mathew McCubbins that empirically compares human's epistemic competence qua consumer and qua voter. So far, he reports, there is little evidence that consumer cognition dominates voter cognition.

I applaud this line of research. It is the next logical step to take in the conversation. My primary concern, though, is figuring out how to determine that two sets of questions are of roughly equal difficulty. Almost no one can name all the ingredients in ice cream, and almost everyone can name the president, but this hardly shows that consumers know less than voters.

It is important to emphasize that we cannot use accuracy as our measure of difficulty; that would be circular. To make progress, we need to devise some other metric of difficulty. I am open to suggestions, but here is my best so far: get researchers from a wide range of perspectives to vouch for questions' "equal difficulty" *before* running the survey. As I explain in an exchange with Donald Wittman, a well-known defender of voter rationality:

Another approach is for scholars who disagree about consumer rationality to join forces to write a mutually acceptable survey. Perhaps it is naive to hope for a meeting of the minds, but it is easier to reach a consensus *ex ante* than *ex post*. A test of consumer rationality jointly written by Donald Wittman and Bryan Caplan would have more credibility than two studies of this question that we ran independently. (Caplan 2005: 176)

For example, I suggest we compare voters' knowledge of the federal budget with consumers' knowledge of their own budgets. These seem like questions of intrinsically comparable difficulty. My bet is that people's consumer beliefs will be much less biased than their voter beliefs, but I am open to correction by data.

Still, I would be disingenuous to claim that I am agnostic on this question until new empirical studies arrive. Daily experience has long since convinced me that ordinary consumers are pretty shrewd. I can't give them perfect marks; no matter how bad a movie is, many consumers cling to the sunk-cost fallacy and refuse to walk out. Nevertheless, my years of talking to noneconomists about their market behavior – and eavesdropping in the grocery store – bear out Bastiat's (1964: 84) observation:

[E]ach man is *in practice* an excellent economist, producing or exchanging according as he finds it more advantageous to do the one or the other. Everyone gains a knowledge of this science through experience; or rather, the science itself is only this same experience accurately observed and methodically interpreted.

In contrast, when I discuss economics and politics with noneconomists – or simply listen in on their conversations – I find *most* of what they say to be shockingly irrational. The content is usually terrible, riddled with the biases I discuss in *The Myth of the Rational Voter*. Even worse, though, is the method: emotional, dogmatic, and hasty. Mackie may say that the Schumpeterian literature seems like a revival of peasant suspicion and fatalism, rather than "an enlightenment doctrine of reason." But it is not "unenlightened" to say that most people are unenlightened.

Given his "peasant suspicion and fatalism" remark, it is odd that Mackie follows up with a qualified defense of the rationality of religious dogmas, Stalinism, and the Randian position on smoking. To me, Rand's pro-smoking view is a valuable warning that even people officially committed to rationality fail to live up to their ideals. But Mackie has a different take. He asks why a Jain, Muslim, Hindu, Stalinist, or Randian would hold onto a belief that in isolation seems to be unsupported, and his answer is that they would do so for the same reason that an established scientific theory would dismiss as suspect an observation inconsistent with the theory.

Mackie distances himself from relativism, accepting that not all worldviews are as good as others, and even that some are much better than others, at prediction. He also recognizes that any given worldview is generally useful, although none can be universally useful, since they each encounter anomalies, some far more than others, But in the end, his charitable interpretation of the worldviews I stigmatize as "irrational" is unconvincing. Almost every worldview *claims* to be good at prediction and free of serious anomalies. Aren't some worldviews nevertheless more justified in claiming these epistemic virtues than others? If Mackie says no, he ends up being a relativist after all. If he says yes, he will probably end up with a view similar to mine: when their cherished beliefs don't measure up, people often selectively relax their intellectual standards to shield their beliefs from the facts. Indeed, isn't that how most worldviews survive?

References

Abramson, Paul, John Aldrich, and David Rohde. 2002. *Change and Continuity in the 2000 Elections*. Washington, DC: CQ Press.

Alesina, Alberto, and Lawrence Summers. 1993. "Central Bank Independence and Macroeconomic Performance: Some Comparative Evidence." *Journal of Money and Credit* 25(2): 151–62.

Althaus, Scott. 2003. *Collective Preferences in Democratic Politics: Opinion Surveys and the Will of the People*. Cambridge: Cambridge University Press.

Bastiat, Frédéric. 1964. *Economic Sophisms*. Irvington-on-Hudson, NY: Foundation for Economic Education.

Bennett, Stephen. 1996. "'Know-Nothings' Revisited Again." *Political Behavior* 18(3): 219–33.

Blendon, Robert, John Benson, Mollyann Brodie, Richard Morin, Drew Altman, Daniel Gitterman, Mario Brossard, and Matt James. 1997. "Bridging the Gap Between the Public's and Economists' Views of the Economy." *Journal of Economic Perspectives* 11(3): 105–88.

Blinder, Alan. 1987. *Hard Heads, Soft Hearts: Tough-Minded Economics for a Just Society*. Reading, MA: Addison-Wesley.

Caplan, Bryan. 2009. "Majorities Against Utility: Implications of the Failure of the Miracle of Aggregation." *Social Philosophy and Policy* 26(1): 198–211.

———. 2008. "Reply to My Critics." *Critical Review* 20(3): 377–413.

———. 2007. *The Myth of the Rational Voter: Why Democracies Choose Bad Policies*. Princeton, NJ: Princeton University Press.

———. 2006. "The Myth of the Rational Voter." *Cato Unbound*, November 6. http://www.cato-unbound.org/2006/11/06/bryan-caplan/the-myth-of-the-rational-voter.

———. 2005. "Rejoinder to Wittman: True Myths." *Econ Journal Watch* 2(2): 165–85.

———. 2001. "Rational Irrationality and the Microfoundations of Political Failure." *Public Choice* 107 (3/4): 311–31.

Caplan, Bryan, and Stephen Miller. 2007. "Intelligence Makes People Think Like Economists: Evidence from the General Social Survey." Unpublished manuscript. http://www.gmu.edu/departments/economics/bcaplan/iqbeliefej.doc.

Delli Carpini, Michael, and Scott Keeter. 1996. *What Americans Know About Politics and Why It Matters*. New Haven, CT: Yale University Press.

Dye, Thomas, and Harmon Zeigler. 1996. *The Irony of Democracy: An Uncommon Introduction to American Politics*. 10th ed. New York: Wadsworth.

Estlund, David. 2007. *Democratic Authority: A Philosophical Framework*. Princeton, NJ: Princeton University Press.

———. 2006. "Outsmarting Democracy?" *Cato Unbound*, November 6. http://www.cato-unbound.org/2006/11/08/david-estlund/out-smarting-democracy.

Friedman, Milton. 1953. "The Methodology of Positive Economics." In Friedman, *Essays in Positive Economics*, 3–43. Chicago: University of Chicago Press.

Gersemann, Olaf. 2005. *Cowboy Capitalism: European Myths, American Reality*. Washington, DC: Cato Institute.

Jensen, Arthur. 1998. *The g Factor: The Science of Mental Ability*. Westport, CT: Praeger.

Klein, Daniel, and Charlotta Stern. 2005. "Political Diversity in Six Disciplines." *Academic Questions* 18(1): 40–52.

Lupia, Arthur. 2006. "How Elitism Undermines the Study of Voter Competence." *Critical Review* 18(1–3): 217–32.

Muth, John. 1961. "Rational Expectations and the Theory of Price Movements." *Econometrica* 29(3): 315–35.

Neuman, W. Russell. 1986. *The Paradox of Mass Politics: Knowledge and Opinion in the American Electorate*. Cambridge, MA: Harvard University Press.

Newcomb, Simon. 1893. "The Problem of Economic Education." *Quarterly Journal of Economics* 7(4): 375–99.

Paul, Ellen Frankel, Fred Miller, and Jeffrey Paul (eds.). 2003. *Autonomy*. Cambridge: Cambridge University Press.

Smith, Eric. 1989. *The Unchanging American Voter*. Berkeley: University of California Press.

Somin, Ilya. 2004. "Political Ignorance and the Countermajoritarian Difficulty: A New Perspective on the 'Central Obsession' of Constitutional Theory." *Iowa Law Review* 89(4): 1287–1372.

Surowiecki, James. 2004. *The Wisdom of Crowds*. New York: Doubleday.

Washington Post, Kaiser Family Foundation, and Harvard University Survey Project. 1997. "Survey of Americans' Knowledge and Attitudes about Entitlements." http://www.kff.org/medicare/loader.cfm?url=/commonspot/security/getfile.cfm& PageID=14513.

    1996. "Survey of Americans and Economists on the Economy." October 16, no. 1199. http://www.kff.org/kaiserpolls/1199-econgen.cfm.

14

Collective Wisdom and Institutional Design

Adrian Vermeule

Recent years have seen an outpouring of work on the wisdom and folly of crowds, on mechanisms of judgment aggregation, and on many-minds arguments in legal and political theory. The next task is to bring these ideas down to the level of institutional design, and I will attempt to do so here. After clarifying the conceptual issues and the mechanisms of collective wisdom, I will outline a framework for cashing out those mechanisms at the institutional level, detailing the trade-offs and institutional variables that are most critical.

My purpose is to examine the institutional implications of collective wisdom, not the intrinsic persuasiveness of the mechanisms said to produce it. I believe that the proper attitude toward those mechanisms is one of qualified skepticism; in important cases, they turn out to be both ill-defined and fragile, applying only under relatively narrow conditions (Vermeule 2009). Nothing in this essay, however, turns on the validity of that claim, which I bracket insofar as possible. Instead I ask a different question: Under conditions in which collective wisdom can exist, how should institutions be structured to generate and exploit that wisdom?

Section I evaluates several competing conceptions of both wisdom and collective wisdom. I argue for a reductionist approach that equates wisdom with epistemic accuracy, and collective wisdom with collective epistemic accuracy. Section II explains the major mechanisms of collective wisdom. Section III asks how lawmaking authority should be allocated across institutions and how those institutions should be designed, if the social goal is strictly to maximize the epistemic quality of governmental decision making. I argue that epistemic considerations suggest a shift of lawmaking authority from courts to legislatures; design reforms of the courts, such as the appointment of nonlawyer

Thanks to Karen Croxson, Jon Elster, Jacob Gersen, Hélène Landemore, Dan Meltzer, and Eric Posner for helpful comments and to Joel Peters-Fransen for helpful research. Some portions of this essay are adapted from Vermeule, "Many-Minds Arguments in Legal Theory," *Journal of Legal Analysis* 1 (2009): 1–45.

judges; and an increase in the number of congressional seats. Section IV asks not how collective wisdom can be maximized, but how it can be optimized. I examine trade-offs between and among collective wisdom and other welfarist values, such as the costs of decision making, the aggregation of preferences, and the perceived legitimacy of the legal system.

I. WISDOM AND COLLECTIVE WISDOM

A small question: What is wisdom? In what I will call the *baseline conception*, "wisdom" is just a synonym for epistemic accuracy in judgment, or truth-tracking capacity (Goodin 2003: 91); the "wisdom of crowds" is the epistemic accuracy of crowds. Several alternative conceptions of collective wisdom reject this view, however. I will canvass these alternatives and argue that each is even more problematic than the baseline conception. For lack of a better alternative, therefore, the baseline conception prevails. And on pragmatic grounds, it is the best conception with which to analyze questions of institutional design, or so I will argue.

There are two parts to each of these conceptions: an account of individual wisdom and an account of collective wisdom. It is always an open question whether the collective version can in a valid way be generated from the individual version. As we will see, certain conceptions of wisdom at the level of individuals cannot be translated to the collective level without falling into a fallacy of composition.

A. The Baseline Conception

In the simplest conception, wisdom is just a fancy synonym for judgment, and judgment is the ability to give all factors their due weight (Elster 1983: 16) and (therefore) to reach epistemically accurate conclusions. Wisdom, in short, is judgment that tracks the truth. This conception is entirely agnostic about the content of the relevant truths. They may be factual, causal, moral, or legal. To be sure, in each of these domains, someone or other denies that there are any truths to be tracked. Some postmodernists and defenders of the "strong program" in the sociology of science sometimes seem to deny that there are factual or causal truths, while moral and legal skeptics of various sorts deny that there are moral or legal truths. These controversies affect the size of the domain within which epistemic accuracy gets purchase but do not undermine the baseline conception itself. Whatever truths there are, a decision procedure that tracks them is accurate to that extent.

On this account, a given institution might have more than one task. A legislature, for example, will sometimes be engaged in an epistemic task involving the aggregation of judgments where there is a fact of the matter and sometimes be engaged in a nonepistemic task involving the aggregation of preferences. The result is a difficult question of institutional design. If an institution has both epistemic and nonepistemic tasks, its structure cannot be chosen so as to strictly maximize the performance of one task or the other; the aim must be some optimal combination. In Section III, I will bracket this issue by assuming that the task is strictly to maximize epistemic performance, but I offer some remarks on the design of multipurpose institutions in Section IV.

A disadvantage of defining wisdom as truth-tracking judgment is that it collapses wisdom and accuracy. The implication, which some will find jarring, is that an algorithm can be wise, because it gives all decision-making factors their due weight and thus makes highly accurate judgments.[1] As we will see, alternative conceptions of wisdom hold that wisdom involves something more than accurate judgment. However, there is no agreement among those other conceptions as to the nature of the extra element. Allied in rejecting the baseline conception, they come to blows over what should replace it.

An advantage of the baseline conception is that it transposes in a straightforward way from the individual level to the group level; collective wisdom is just collective epistemic capacity to track the truth. Although we will see various mechanisms that can cause a group to track the truth more or less successfully than the individuals it comprises, there is no conceptual problem with the move to the aggregate level. As we will also see, some other conceptions fail to make that move successfully.

B. Wisdom as Impartial Rationality

Jon Elster advances a conception of collective wisdom that combines two elements: (1) impartial motivation and (2) rational belief formation. This conception treats individual wisdom as synonymous with the "reason" of the French moralists and of Hume. In this sense, reason, and hence individual wisdom, is opposed to both interest and passion. In parallel fashion, collective wisdom describes decision making that is both politically impartial, in the sense that it takes into account all affected interests, and also rational, in the sense that decision makers are not subject to wishful thinking or other emotional influences on cognition.[2]

The picture of a decision maker that is both benevolent and rational is attractive, and it undoubtedly captures the moralists' conception of reason. Yet it may pack too much into the idea of wisdom, at least for purposes of discussing institutional design. Elster implicitly appeals to the unity of the virtues, the idea being that a wise decision maker must be not only rational but also motivated by the common interest. But why should the latter stipulation be added? The leader of a criminal gang might surely be described as wise,

---

[1] For the superiority of simple algorithms over expert judgment, see Dawes, Faust, and Meehl (1979). For their superiority even in matters of complex political judgment, see Tetlock (2005: 76–77).

[2] Elster observes that emotions can also promote rational decision making (1999: 283) and can motivate desirable action in everyday life and in politics. See also Damásio (1994: 173–74) and Rubenfeld (2001: 129).

although his wisdom is put to the service of a self-interested private group. Even if wisdom is something more or different than truth tracking, it need not be directed toward public-spirited ends.

C. Wisdom as Truth Plus Coherence

Christian List accepts that truth tracking – what he calls "correspondence" – is an element of wisdom but adds that "coherence" is as well. These are not necessary conditions for wisdom, but rather two separate desiderata that interact in complex ways and that may trade off against one another. The trade offs can be illustrated with reference to the "doctrinal paradox," in which a majority of a multimember court votes on an interconnected set of propositions. A majority votes that 'p' is true, a different majority votes that if 'p' is true then 'q' is true, and a yet different majority votes that 'q' is false, despite the fact that the truth of 'q' follows from the earlier majority votes. This outcome, which is incoherent at the group level, can be avoided if the ultimate judgment or conclusion, rather than each interconnected proposition, is voted on. Voting only on conclusions rather than on premises fits with the theory of judicial "minimalism" (Sunstein 1999), which generates consensus by allowing judges to reach "incompletely theorized agreements" (Sunstein 2000). However, as List shows, voting on the antecedent propositions has offsetting epistemic virtues; as compared with conclusion-based voting, it improves both positive reliability, or the chance of getting the truth, and negative reliability, or the chance of avoiding untruth.

List does not make clear, however, why coherence should be an element of collective wisdom. Why is group-level coherence even a value?[3] Even if coherence is a desirable property of individual judgments, it is not obvious that it is a desirable property of collective ones. If the multimember court were a big person, like Ronald Dworkin's (1977: 105–30) mythical judge, Hercules, the pattern of judgments that creates the doctrinal paradox would raise a serious problem of coherence. But the court is not a big person; why should anyone care that its judgments would be incoherent if it were?

There are several possible answers, none of which is very satisfactory. First, one might posit a connection between coherence and legal certainty, which is undoubtedly a systemic benefit. The intuition is that regulated parties who must implement or comply with the court's directives or predict the court's future decisions will do better if they are given a theory that is coherent at the group level than if they are not. Yet the connection between coherence and certainty is at best highly contingent. Certainty results from the breadth of

---

[3] Marmor (2006) discusses this point, confining his skeptical arguments to legislative voting rather than judicial voting. The suggestion in the text is that there is reason for skepticism about whether group-level coherence is ever a value, in any collective decision-making body. In a similar vein, Kornhauser (2008) argues that "aggregate rationality" is too demanding for either courts or legislatures.

the court's conclusions, not the theoretical depth of its premises. In a system of conclusion-based voting, the scope of the rules on which the court settles may be very broad, making many questions highly predictable. Conversely, in a system of premise-based voting, the court's deeply coherent views may be narrowly defined, leaving open many questions for the future and producing a great deal of uncertainty.

Second, suppose the court is embedded in a society where many citizens view "The Court" as a personified entity. Even if this view is irrational, the incoherence of the court's group-level judgments might discredit the court and even, in the extreme, bring its sociological legitimacy into question. This possibility seems highly speculative, however. It requires imagining a public that not only observes and cares about judgments rather than sheer results, but that observes and cares about a collective pattern of judgments over a series of propositions or cases. As List explains, as the set of propositions (cases) that must be consulted to observe incoherence grows, these possibilities become all the more attenuated.

Finally, Ronald Dworkin famously objects to "checkerboard" systems of legal rules, which he condemns for lack of integrity – meaning that "there is not a conceivable single rational moral agent whose moral point of view could justify the entire set of prescriptions under consideration" (Marmor 2006: 127). Abortions should not be available only to women born on even-numbered days of the month. However, even if Dworkin's objection is correct, it need not have anything to do with aggregate coherence as such. Rather the objection is best understood as a complaint that, in checkerboard systems of law, the particular legal rule at issue has no conceivable rational basis (Marmor 2006). Despite Dworkin's reference to a "set of prescriptions," this is a complaint that can be lodged against a single rule, not a complaint that can arise only given the interrelation of a series of judgments. The form of group-level incoherence that List discusses, by contrast, presupposes a connected set of propositions. Dworkin and List are talking about different things.

Overall, then, it is not obvious why group-level coherence is even desirable. To apply Dworkin's terms to this setting, there may not be a conceivable single agent whose moral point of view could justify the entire set of rules; but if we are dealing with a multimember decision-making body in any event, why should that matter? Absent a better answer to this question, coherence across a set of propositions drops out as a component of collective wisdom, and we are left with correspondence, or the truth-tracking tendency of the collective decision-maker's operative conclusion, as the only desideratum. Suppose that on a three-member court, a majority votes that there was a contract, a different majority votes that if there was a contract it was breached, and another majority votes that the contract was not breached, so that the defendant wins. From an epistemic perspective, the only thing we ought to care about is whether, assuming there is a right answer to the question of which party should win, the group has in fact gotten the answer right. If it has, it is unnecessarily demanding to ask for anything more (Kornhauser 2008).

D. Wisdom as Experience

Burkeans of various stripes advance a conception of wisdom as lived experience. This has the virtue of capturing ordinary usage better than several of the other conceptions. It explains why, as to individuals, wisdom is typically associated with old age. On this conception, wisdom is a richer idea than epistemic accuracy; an algorithm can be accurate, whereas an algorithm cannot be wise.

However, problems arise when wisdom as lived experience is transposed to the collective case. What exactly is the collective analogue of individual wisdom? Burkeans tend to assume that the analogue is tradition – rules, norms, and practices that have stood the test of time. However, as Pascal and Bentham pointed out, this idea rests on a fallacy of composition (Pascal 1910: 449; Bentham 1824: 69–79). In the individual case, those born earlier have lived longer and are thus wiser than the young, whereas in the collective case generations born earlier are the generations of humankind's infancy. Lived experience favors "younger" or newer generations, who have accumulated more knowledge than generations past. In Bentham's phrase, the "wisdom of the ancestors" is really the "wisdom of the cradle" (Bentham 1824: 71).

E. Pragmatics

I will opt for the baseline conception on pragmatic grounds. The issues surrounding the concept of wisdom and its competing conceptions, in both the individual and collective case, are multifarious and complex. The baseline conception is simplistic; it arguably fails to capture richer dimensions of wisdom. This very simplicity, however, is also its major advantage. Few doubt that truth tracking or epistemic accuracy is part of wisdom, if not the whole of it. And the rival conceptions of wisdom cannot agree on a candidate for the additional component. The very multiplicity of those candidates – impartial motivation, theoretical coherence, and lived experience, among others – suggests that taking the lowest common denominator allows us to say something of interest to proponents of all the richer conceptions of wisdom, even if it is not wholly satisfying to any of them. Finally, epistemic accuracy transposes in a straightforward way from the individual case to the collective case, a property that it shares with wisdom-as-impartial-rationality but that other conceptions of wisdom do not possess.

II. MECHANISMS OF COLLECTIVE WISDOM

Suppose that wisdom is defined as epistemic accuracy. How do collective decision-making bodies compare with individuals in producing it? I will offer a brief and selective catalogue of the mechanisms of collective wisdom – brief because most of these mechanisms, such as Condorcet's Jury Theorem, are well known; selective because I examine only mechanisms that have useful

implications for institutional design and are thus relevant for my purposes in
Sections III and IV.

A. Statistical Aggregation

The best-known mechanisms of collective wisdom rest on the statistical principle known as the law of large numbers.[4] As the size of a sample group increases,
the expected frequency of an event and the actual frequency will tend to converge; it becomes less and less likely that, by chance, actual outcomes will
deviate from expected outcomes. If a coin has a .6 chance of coming up heads,
we might easily get more tails than heads after ten tosses, but we are extremely
unlikely to do so after one thousand tosses.[5]

The law of large numbers powers the famous Condorcet Jury Theorem.
The theorem states, in its simplest form, that where a group votes on two
alternatives, one of which is correct, and the members of the group are even
slightly more likely to be right than wrong, then as the number of members in
the group increases, the probability that a majority[6] vote of the group is correct
tends toward certainty. Given certain conditions, the group's chance of being
correct will necessarily exceed that of its average member and may even exceed
that of its best member – hence the association with collective wisdom.

The principal conditions embedded in this definition are that voters address
a common question, vote sincerely, are of sufficient competence that they are
more likely to be right than wrong, and vote independently. The first condition says that all voters address the same question; the second that they
attempt to get the answer right; the third that voters are better than random
at doing so; the fourth that voters' votes are statistically independent of one
another, although not necessarily causally independent (Estlund 1994). The

---

[4] The distinction between statistical and perspectival aggregation is adapted from Hong and Page;
see Chapter 3, this volume.

[5] This is a standard illustration; note, however, that it assumes a particular model of probability
that is not inherent in the operation of the Jury Theorem (Edelman 2002: 329).

[6] The Jury Theorem can be extended to qualified majority ("supermajority") rules, but only with
restrictions. It has been shown that a qualified majority rule maximizes the probability of making
a correct decision, with the requisite majority depending, among other things, on the relative
payoffs of rejecting and approving projects (Ben-Yashar and Nitzan 1997). If the costs of error in
either direction are symmetric, individuals' competence is uniform, and there is no prior reason
to think one answer or the other more likely, then simple majority rule is optimal (Ben-Yashar
and Nitzan 1997: 183). I return to the issue of voting rules weighted by asymmetric error costs
in Section IV. The main result holds only if the status quo is stipulated to prevail in the event that
no alternative garners the requisite supermajority. This is, of course, a democratically suspect
condition. If the status quo preference is abandoned, a weaker result holds: "[F]or sufficiently
large electorates . . . if the average competence of the voters is greater than the fraction of the
votes needed for passage," a group decision is more likely to be correct than the decision of a
single randomly chosen individual (Fey 2003: 28). This condition is rather demanding; if the
decision-making group uses a two-thirds majority rule, for example, average competence must
be at least .67. Nothing in my claims here turns on whether the group voting rule is a simple or
qualified majority, so I will refer to "majority" voting for simplicity.

last condition is critical; its implication is that epistemic diversity is as important as competence (Page 2007). Given reasonable assumptions, the chance of a majority selecting the right answer varies inversely with the correlation of bias across the decision-making group (Ladha 1992: 632). Where voters in the group have biases that are uncorrelated or negatively correlated, their errors are more likely to wash out, allowing the correct votes to become decisive. If, however, voters' biases are highly correlated, the "miracle of aggregation" will likely fail (Caplan 2007: 5).

The Condorcet theorem can be extended in several directions. The competence condition can be relaxed to require merely that the average competence be better than random.[7] The set of possible answers can be larger than two, in which case the option that receives a plurality of votes is most likely to be correct (although not necessarily more likely to be correct than all the incorrect answers combined) (List and Goodin 2001: 285). Finally, the theorem has been extended to show that where each voter asks only which collective choice best promotes her individual interests and is better than random at doing so, as the size of the voting group increases, a majority is increasingly likely to correctly choose the option that does in fact maximally satisfy the preferences of a majority. In this extension, there is no true common question – each voter asks which option benefits herself, a question that may have different answers for different people – and "correct" means correct in light of the voters' preferences, not correct altogether.

It is often said that the Jury Theorem requires an exogenous right answer, and the last extension I mentioned seems to contradict this. But the question turns out to be semantic, not substantive. The law of large numbers that powers the Jury Theorem also yields the preference-based extension; as numbers increase, it becomes increasingly unlikely that a majority will vote, by mistake, against the interests of the majority. We can if we like restrict the label "Condorcet Jury Theorem" to cases with exogenous right answers, but nothing in the nature of the mechanism requires this.

B. Perspectival Aggregation

A very different class of models involves the aggregation of multiple perspectives (Page 2007: 185–88). These models are not Condorcetian. It is not that each individual gets an imperfect signal about the correct answer to a common question, as when each member of a crowd guesses the number of beans in a jar. Rather, each individual has information about *part* of the answer to the question, as in the story of the blind men and the elephant. None of the blind men can possibly deduce the shape of the whole elephant just by touching the leg or trunk; that is why one thinks the elephant is a tree, another that it is

---

[7] So long as the distribution of competence is symmetric around the mean. See Bernard Grofman et al. (1983: 273–74).

a snake, and so on. To arrive at the truth, the blind men must compose their separate perspectives.

Despite this difference, perspectival aggregation and statistical aggregation share a critical feature. In either case, the major determinants of the group's epistemic performance are *numbers*, (average) *competence*, and *diversity* (see Hong and Page, Chapter 3, this volume). Whereas competence is a property of individuals, diversity is an emergent property of the group. Holding numbers constant, a group will be more likely either to vote for the right answer or to achieve an accurate composite perspective, as the group's members possess more information or as they hold more diverse perspectives. The relevant type of diversity is cognitive, but cognitive diversity may be correlated with diversity along other margins, such as race, class, or profession.

C. Evolutionary Aggregation

The foregoing mechanisms of collective wisdom have two main features: (1) they are intentional mechanisms in which each participant aims to produce the correct collective decision; (2) they are synchronic mechanisms in which the whole group makes its decision at a given time. Either condition can be relaxed. Synchronic nonintentional aggregation, in which only the first condition is relaxed, is illustrated by the neoclassical economic model of a perfect market that instantaneously reaches equilibrium, with all Pareto-improving trades consummated in decentralized transactions. Diachronic intentional aggregation, in which only the second condition is relaxed, involves decision makers who deliberately draw on the information embodied in past decisions. An example is the judicial practice of following precedent, which I will consider in Section III.

Evolutionary models go further by dispensing with *both* conditions. They are necessarily diachronic; rather than comparing a crowd voting simultaneously at time T with an individual at time T, they compare the result of a sequence of decisions with the result of an individual making a single decision at any given time in the sequence. Furthermore, they do not presuppose that the group's members intentionally seek an accurate collective decision. Rather, they offer invisible-hand mechanisms (Nozick 1994; Ullmann-Margalit 1997) in which collective wisdom arises as a "result of human action, but not the execution of any human design" (Ferguson 2000: 187).

Thus, a standard evolutionary model in law-and-economics describes conditions under which the common law will evolve to efficiency. This is an invisible-hand model, in which the process of adjudication produces efficient rules even though individual judges do not aim to supply efficient rules. The mechanism is, roughly, that where prospective litigants decide either to settle cases or else to challenge precedents through litigation and where the stakes are equally distributed, precedents that inflict deadweight losses will be challenged more frequently and will thus be more likely to be overturned, moving the common law toward efficiency (Rubin 1977: 53). Nothing in this model, however, is unique to the common law. A structurally analogous model shows conditions under which legislation will evolve to efficiency, as interest groups press legislatures to overturn statutes that inflict deadweight losses (Becker 1985). Conversely, either legislation or common law will be inefficient if stakes are asymmetrically distributed across groups. Where that is so, rent-seeking groups can influence legislators so as to obtain concentrated benefits while imposing larger diffuse costs on others, resulting in welfare losses, but this is equally possible by means of rent-seeking litigation in the courts (Elhauge 1991: 66).

The relationship of efficiency to wisdom or collective wisdom is just that invisible-hand processes of legal evolution, if they obtain, can help the legal system accurately identify efficient rules, even if no actor in the system has sufficient information to do so on his own. The invisible-hand mechanism substitutes for intentional efficiency-seeking action on the part of judges; even if judges lack the information necessary to produce efficient rules, such rules emerge spontaneously, just as, in Hayek's view, invisible-hand mechanisms in explicit economic markets aggregate dispersed information about optimal production and exchange, information that is embodied in prices (Hayek 1948).

More recently, economists Nicola Gennaioli and Andrei Shleifer (2007) have explored hybrid evolutionary models in which the common law converges on rules that are informationally efficient, meaning that the rules incorporate all available information. In the basic model, the common law evolves through the distinguishing of earlier cases by politically biased judges, who are constrained to use only legally relevant distinctions; if a prior case held that all dogs must be leashed, the judges may hold that only dogs that are able to bite must be leashed, but they may not hold that dogs need be leashed only on Tuesdays. Under certain conditions, the process of distinguishing will yield rules that incorporate all information held by the judges, although no judge is motivated to adopt such rules. By contrast, where judges are allowed to overrule cases rather than distinguish them, the common law may lurch between opposing views without convergence on any stable rule, let alone an informationally efficient one.

D. Deliberation

How do the foregoing mechanisms relate to the processes of group deliberation? The relationships are contingent and causal, not analytic. Nothing in statistical aggregation, perspectival aggregation, or evolutionary aggregation requires deliberation to make them work (to whatever extent they do work). Whether deliberation promotes or retards the operation of the mechanisms depends upon context.

Under the models of evolutionary aggregation previously canvassed, deliberation is usually irrelevant by stipulation. The agents are black boxes who react mechanically to the decisions of other agents, as when judges in the classic law and economics models are modeled as ciphers who overrule decisions with some probability. Deliberation could be built into such models, but it is unclear why one would want to do so; the whole point of the models is to illustrate that invisible-hand processes can produce efficiency or full information even if none of the agents involved aim to do so.[8]

What about statistical and perspectival aggregation? It was thought, at one point, that deliberation would necessarily undermine the operation of the Jury Theorem by producing highly correlated biases, and thus compromising independence (Grofman and Feld 1988: 569).[9] If so, the ideal aggregation procedure might actually bar mutual discussion among the voters prior to voting, as Rousseau suggested for mass elections (Rousseau 2002: 173). However, the theorem requires only statistical independence, not causal independence (Estlund 2008: 225). The views of voters may be causally influenced by the views of other voters; so long as positive correlation does not grow too high – so long as deliberation does not create too much groupthink – statistical aggregation can still work, depending on the precise degree of correlation and the precise size and competence of the group. The lesson for institutional design is not that deliberation should be banned, but that the group and its procedures should be well structured to preserve epistemic diversity.

While deliberation need not undermine the operation of statistical aggregation, by the same token it is unnecessary for the mechanism to work; purely notional groups can have good Condorcetian credentials. Deliberation is also unnecessary for the operation of perspectival aggregation. Consider Aristotle's idea of the "Wisdom of the Multitude" (Waldron 1995), in which "the many are better judges than a single man of music and poetry; for some understand one part, and some another, and among them they understand the whole" (Aristotle 1988: 66). Although some theorists seem to assume that this idea has a necessary connection to deliberation,[10] it does not. Perspectival aggregation can be accomplished just by having each participant unilaterally reveal a bit of dispersed information to the group, without discussion.[11] One can define "deliberation" so expansively as to subsume this case, but nothing of substance is gained by doing so.

Overall, then, different aggregation mechanisms can be combined with deliberation, or not, in different ways. The benefits and costs of deliberation, and their interaction with the relevant mechanisms, are contextual questions about which it is difficult to say anything general. In what follows, I will generally assume for simplicity that the agents do not deliberate unless their doing so would affect the analysis in a given context.

---

[8] However, such agents could deliberate in the thin sense of exchanging information about how to promote their self-interested goals, where those happen to overlap. For this thin sense of deliberation, see Fearon (1998: 44–47).

[9] For a critique of this view, see Estlund et al. (1989: 1320).

[10] Waldron himself holds this view (1995: 568–70). Waldron's assumption may stem from conflating exegesis of Aristotle, who himself assumes a connection to deliberation, and the analytic structure of the perspectival aggregation mechanism Aristotle discusses, a mechanism that is not intrinsically deliberative.

[11] Page (2007) provides examples of this.

III. MAXIMIZING COLLECTIVE WISDOM

I now turn to cashing out the baseline conception of collective wisdom, and the mechanisms that generate it, for the design of legal institutions and the allocation of lawmaking authority among those institutions. Assuming that the goal is to maximize the epistemic quality of the laws – to maximize the extent to which the laws are premised on truths, whether factual, causal, moral, or legal – how should lawmaking be structured? (Section IV relaxes this assumption and examines trade-offs between and among epistemic quality and other values.)

I will take up three questions of interest to legal theorists, focusing on the United States so as to minimize my own blunders. I hope that at least some of the analysis will transpose, mutatis mutandis, to other settings. The questions are these:

(A) Given institutions as they are currently designed, how should the authority to develop "constitutional common law" be allocated between courts, on the one hand, and the legislative-executive lawmaking process, on the other?

(B) How should the Supreme Court be designed to maximize the epistemic quality of its decisions?

(C) How should Congress be designed to maximize the epistemic quality of its decisions?

My conclusions are, broadly speaking, Benthamite. As to the first question, I suggest that the goal of maximizing epistemic quality requires a large-scale reallocation of lawmaking authority from courts to legislatures. More specifically, courts should defer to Congress's efforts to liquidate, through statutes, the meaning of vague, ambiguous, or aspirational constitutional provisions. The resulting regime is one of *deference for courts, common-law constitutionalism for legislatures*. As to the second question, I suggest that at least some nonlawyers should be appointed as justices of the Supreme Court. As to the third question, I suggest very tentatively that Congress's membership should be expanded, by statute, to bring it into line with the representation ratio that prevails in other liberal democracies.

Four caveats should be kept in mind throughout the following analysis. First, to isolate the epistemic issues, I assume that all relevant agents are good-faith truth seekers; for example, I assume that both legislators and judges attempt in good faith to determine the constitutionality of proposed or enacted statutes, according to whatever theory of constitutional meaning they hold. Where I relax this assumption, it is only to skew the playing field *against* the claims I wish to make.

Second, my analysis addresses only a subset of the relevant issues; although I discuss these questions to illustrate the sort of institutional analysis that can be done within an epistemic framework, I am unable to do all of it here. For example, I will ask what is the epistemically optimal composition of the

Supreme Court, holding its current size fixed; by contrast, I will ask how large the Congress should be. These choices are somewhat arbitrary, but I believe that posing the questions that I do is more realistic than asking, for example, whether a Court of a hundred members would be desirable. In any event, a degree of arbitrariness is inevitable, because realistically speaking not all margins of design can be explored simultaneously; some features of institutions must be held constant in order to say anything at all.

Third, I will ignore the presidency in this section, except to the extent that the president is the legislator in chief and thus a participant in the legislative process. The main arguments for unilateral presidential authority, not shared with Congress, are not epistemic; they involve competing goods such as the speed of action. I take up the resulting trade-offs in Section IV.

Finally, and most broadly, the tasks of institutional design and the allocation of lawmaking authority should in principle be pursued simultaneously. Conclusions on either margin should be adjusted until a kind of reflective equilibrium arises, in which institutions are designed in an epistemically optimal manner, given the allocation of lawmaking authority, and in which authority is allocated in an epistemically optimal manner, given the institutional design. In reality, however, one is forced to discuss these issues piecemeal, seriatim, and in a partial rather than comprehensive fashion, as I will do here for the most part. At the end of the discussion, however, I will briefly examine some interactions among the separate components of the analysis.

A. Common-Law Constitutionalism

Common-law constitutionalism is a family of views rather than a crisply defined position. For my purposes, a rough but useful definition is this: common-law constitutionalism holds that constitutional law should be developed primarily through judicial precedents, which themselves may draw on larger social traditions. Common-law constitutionalism has several antonyms and targets. One antonym is originalism, or the idea that the main source of constitutional law should be the original public understanding of the constitutional text. A different antonym is some form of moral perfectionism, in which individual judges develop constitutional law in accordance with their best moral understandings. And there are an indefinite number of possible combinations, hybrids, and shadings. Dworkin's theory of adjudication, which combines moral justification with precedential fit, is a hybrid of perfectionism and common-law constitutionalism. Antonin Scalia's theory, which admits precedent as a side constraint on original understanding,[12] is a hybrid of common-law constitutionalism and originalism.

Although common-law constitutionalism can be given several justifications, the only one relevant here is epistemic. The claim is that the constitutional common law embodies a latent form of collective wisdom. In a neo-Burkean

---

[12] Scalia describes himself as a "faint-hearted originalist" (1989: 864).

version, precedents generate collective wisdom that exceeds what any individual judge could generate through her own moral reasoning; more judicial heads are better than one, or so the argument runs.

What mechanisms of collective wisdom underpin epistemic arguments for the constitutional common law? Here the theorists tend to be vague. Sometimes there is a gesture toward the "evolutionary" properties of the constitutional common law; this idea might be cashed out through either the models of evolution to efficiency or the models of informational evolution already described. More explicitly, it has been argued that the constitutional common law embodies the aggregate information of many judges, over time, in a way that can be modeled by the Condorcet Jury Theorem (Sunstein 2006: 372; Sunstein 2009). On this view, precedent embodies the information of past judges. By drawing on that information, current judges can do as well as a notional voting group composed of all past and present judges who considered the issue.

It is, I believe, highly contestable that the aggregation mechanisms canvassed in Section II accurately describe the processes of the constitutional common law. As I have discussed the issues at length elsewhere (Vermeule 2007b), however, I will restrict myself to one major point about the *comparative epistemic competence of institutions*: even if the constitutional common law embodies a form of collective wisdom, the same mechanisms suggest that legislation will do as well or even better. Strikingly, the very mechanisms that are said to generate the latent wisdom of the constitutional common law are the same mechanisms that democratic theorists have recently invoked to support the epistemic quality of legislation (Estlund 2008; see also Landemore, Chapter 11, this volume). In my view, the democratic theorists have the better argument. Common-law constitutionalism errs by slipping from one claim – that many judicial heads are better than one – to the very different claim that many judicial heads are better than many legislative ones.

I begin with the Jury Theorem. In the crucial case, imagine that there is an ambiguous constitutional provision, a line of Supreme Court precedent interpreting the provision to mean A rather than B, and a recent statute that attempts to "liquidate" the constitutional ambiguity by interpreting it, explicitly or implicitly, to mean B rather than A. Suppose also that there is an exogenous right answer to this question, from the standpoint of an infallible interpreter akin to Dworkin's Hercules. (If the Jury Theorem applies at all, the comparative epistemic analysis does not depend on the content of the relevant answer or the nature of the theory that generates it.) Which view, the judicial or the legislative, is more likely to be correct?

Standard constitutional theory emphasizes the legal expertise and political impartiality of the judges. The standard theory implicitly pictures highly biased legislators and relatively unbiased judges. In a Condorcetian framework, the expertise and impartiality of judges tend to raise the justices' average competence, whereas the electoral connection subjects legislators to political forces that compromise their epistemic performance.

Even if we focus solely on competence – shortly I will turn to numerosity and diversity, the other determinants of epistemic performance – it is not clear that the judges' average competence exceeds that of legislators. The problem is that there is an *information–bias trade-off*: the very political insulation that creates judicial neutrality, and thus pushes the judges' competence up, also tends to deprive the judges of information, which pushes it down (Komesar 1994: 141–42). The judicial system uses a structured adversary process with strict constraints on ex parte contacts and independent investigation, which tends to equalize the production of information and thus to reduce skew or bias, at the cost of generating less information overall. Conversely, legislative fact finding uses a relatively unstructured hybrid process, part adversarial and part administrative or inquisitorial, which generates more information overall, at the cost of greater bias or skew.

Put differently, the task of generating information trades off against the epistemic efficiency of its use. Although political forces may cause legislators to use the information they possess in distorted ways, they may, by the same token, possess so much more information as to more than compensate for the epistemic inefficiency. Precisely because they are less insulated, legislators are more likely to possess information about changing political, social, and economic conditions and changing public values, all of which are indispensable to common-law constitutionalism.

However, to slant the assumptions against the view I want to suggest, let us suppose that the average competence of the judges is indeed superior to that of legislators. From the Condorcetian perspective, however, competence is only one factor and can easily be dominated by numerosity and diversity, both of which legislatures tend to possess in greater degree than courts. The traditional view implicitly points to one element of the Condorcetian framework, over-looking that other elements of the framework, which are equally integral to the operation of the theorem, have a very different valence.

Numerosity and Precedent. The standard view overlooks the mathematical power of legislative numbers. Suppose that each justice has a .75 chance of hitting the right answer, even in the hardest case. Under majority rule, the group's competence is noticeably higher, at .95. However, in an institutional comparison, numbers will tell. If the average competence of the legislators is a mere .6, and there are 301 legislators – about two-thirds of the modern House of Representatives – the chance that a majority of legislators will get the answer right is vanishingly close to 1 (List and Goodin 2001: 287). These are only sample figures, but they illustrate the sheer power of numbers as against the expertise of small groups.

Common-law constitutionalism objects that examples like this assume a one-off decision, whereas a practice of precedent allows current judges to draw on the information held by the justices of the past, in effect expanding the size of the Court. The problems with this suggestion are legion; I will mention several, in increasing order of gravity. (1) Only a few dozen justices, at most, have considered any given issue, so the gap between judicial and legislative numbers is too great to be bridged by precedent. (2) Legislators, too, can read the judicial precedents for whatever information they contain, in effect expanding the size of the legislature by the same number. (3) Legislatures also sometimes draw on their own precedents when fashioning new statutes, albeit in a less formalized way than courts. If judicial precedent makes judicial decisions better informed, then legislative precedent makes legislative decisions better informed. (4) If past judges were themselves common-law constitutionalists, basing their decisions on precedent, then the precedents they generated were not independent for purposes of the Jury Theorem; they added no new information to the sequence of common-law decisions. At the limit, only the first decision in a series contains any information, with all the rest following it in an information cascade (Bikchandandi et al. 1998: 162).

Of these, the fourth point is the most critical. The *Burkean paradox* is that an epistemic strategy of relying on precedent or tradition for its embodied collective wisdom works only if, or to the extent that, past decision makers were not themselves Burkeans and thereby contributed independent information to the stream of decisions.[13] The Burkean paradox is a sliding scale, not an all-or-nothing affair. Perhaps some judges in the stream of precedent or tradition have contributed independently, while some have not, in which case the informational value of that stream must still be discounted appropriately, but not to zero. Moreover, individual judges might adopt an intermediate approach, according to which they give some but not complete deference to the views of the past. This will alleviate the paradox, but only at the price of diluting the benefits of following tradition in the first place.

It is fair to point out, however, that the third and fourth points trade off against one another. To the extent that legislatures draw on their own precedents, they too are subject to the Burkean paradox. In either the judicial or legislative setting, there is a trade-off: drawing on precedent exploits the information of the past, thereby improving decisions in the present, but adds nothing to the institution's informational stock for future use – a stock that is continually depreciating as circumstances change. It is unclear whether, and under what conditions, legislatures or courts strike the optimal balance between the short-run benefits of exploiting extant information and the long-run benefits of generating new information. There is no basis for confidence, however, that the judicial balance is systematically superior. The upshot is that legislatures are far more numerous, which gives them clear epistemic advantages under

---

[13] Moore (1996: 269) makes a similar point. To be sure, if decision makers were unboundedly rational, the best strategy of all would simply be to combine one's current information with whatever information precedent or tradition contains, giving all sources of information their due weight. However, the Burkean view itself assumes that imperfect decision makers, with limited cognitive capacity, cannot do so; they are constrained to substitute tradition for independent reason, to a greater or lesser extent, rather than simply to add the two together. I follow that assumption in order to engage with Burkeanism's internal logic; I also believe the assumption to be correct, although I need not defend that belief here.

the Condorcetian model if competence is minimally adequate, while the use of precedent by either legislatures or courts has ambiguous effects and thus cannot offset the inherent advantage of legislative numbers.

Diversity. The standard theory, which emphasizes the judges' competence, also overlooks the idea that under a robust range of conditions "diversity trumps ability" (Page 2007). It has been shown that adding group members whose competence is *worse* than random can actually improve overall group performance, if their biases are negatively correlated to a sufficient degree with those of experts (Ladha 1992: 629). From a Condorcetian perspective, then, the counterintuitive conclusion is that under plausible conditions a decision-making group that is professionally diverse will outperform a group of specialists. Professional diversity is correlated with epistemic diversity; conversely, a major source of correlated biases is common professional training, which raises individual competence but which can also induce common blind spots and groupthink. Lawyers in particular have been shown to share traits that are distinctive compared with those of both the general population and other professionals (Daicoff 2004).

Most legislatures are professionally far more diverse than most courts. Congress, for example, is much more professionally diverse than the Supreme Court. Between 1960 and 2004, about 45 percent of Congress's members were former lawyers (Kraus and Suarez 2004: 2125–29); the rest were former businesspeople, teachers, physicians, soldiers, and so forth. All elected legislators are professional politicians, but for almost all that is a second career, whereas judging is typically a second job within the legal career. The bench is professionally continuous with the bar, whereas the legislature is a place where many different types of professionals assemble.

Legislators sometimes defer to other legislators, as when the floor defers to specialized committees or when partisanship causes legislators to vote in blocs. Deference reduces epistemic independence and thus detracts from group accuracy, all else equal. Yet the overall epistemic effects are ambiguous, because all else is not equal. Deference to opinion leaders, while reducing independence, raises overall group performance if the opinion leaders are of sufficiently high average competence (Estlund et al. 1989: 1318); that is the very point of having an epistemically specialized committee system, which assumes that there are net epistemic gains from the trade of independence for competence. Moreover, intragroup deference and bloc voting is routine within multimember courts as well. Justices develop informal specialties in particular subjects and tend to vote in blocs in an important subset of cases.

One cannot prove a claim, either way, about how all these factors net out. What is clear is that legislatures are more numerous and, along many margins, more diverse than courts, and those factors plausibly overwhelm the judges' superior average competence, if it exists. At a minimum, traditional theory is wrong to focus myopically on competence alone. Legislatures do not obviously fare worse, and quite possibly fare better, within the very epistemic framework that the Condorcetian case invokes. Similar points obtain if we understand aggregation in perspectival rather than statistical terms. While judicial expertise in law ensures high competence, the sheer number of legislators and their comparatively high diversity along professional and other dimensions ensure that legislatures have many more bits of dispersed information to aggregate and more perspectives to contribute.

What about an evolutionary case for common-law constitutionalism? Common-law constitutional theory refers to evolution in vague terms, which makes it difficult even to pin down the relevant questions. However, I will offer an observation that holds as to all evolutionary models of adjudication. Those models say nothing, so far, about the *rate* at which precedent evolves to efficiency or informational efficiency. If the political, social, and economic environment changes rapidly, then the location of the optimum is a moving target;[14] the constitutional common law may be far from the optimum at any given point, even if it is continually evolving toward it.

By contrast, in a rapidly changing environment, inefficient or ill-informed legislation may be closer to the optimum at any given time than is the constitutional common law, even if the latter is converging on the optimum (Ponzetto and Fernandez 2008). Any system of precedent is path-dependent, meaning for these purposes that there is a positive cost for judges to coordinate on switching to a new rule.[15] As that cost increases, precedent takes longer to adjust to the new environment. Because of this, the more rapidly the environment changes, the greater the *comparative* efficiency or informational content of statute law, even if statute law is poorly informed or inefficient due to the limits of legislators' foresight or interest-group pressures. If statutes can innovate more rapidly than the common law when circumstances change, "the fundamental trade-off is between evolution towards efficiency when the social optimum does not change, and rapid legal innovation when it does.... This price [i.e., the cost of inefficient legislation] is only worth paying when social change is sufficiently intense" (Ponzetto and Fernandez 2008). Casual observation supports this model; as the pace of social change has increased in Anglo-American jurisdictions, the common law has been largely supplanted by statutes and area-specific codes, continually revised.

If these points are correct, the overall problem with epistemic justifications of common-law constitutionalism is that they are self-undermining as theories of judicial review – of the power of courts to invalidate contrary legislation. If the antonym of common-law constitutionalism is a kind of solipsistic moral perfectionism on the part of individual judges, then it may be useful to point out that many judicial heads are better than one. By the same token, however, many legislative heads are better still. The very mechanisms of collective wisdom to which common-law constitutionalism appeals suggest that legislative constitutionalism will be of yet higher epistemic quality. On epistemic grounds,

---

[14] I adapt this point from Elster (1987: 714).

[15] For this and other senses of path dependence, see Hathaway (2001: 622–49).

the best regime would be one in which courts defer to legislative efforts to liquidate or disambiguate constitutional provisions and to adjust constitutional law to changing circumstances over time. The resulting regime would be one of deference by courts, common-law constitutionalism by legislatures.

An alternative view is that the best regime of all would be one of *cumulative epistemic competence*. On this view, even if legislatures have epistemic advantages relative to courts, one might nonetheless hold that adding courts to the mix improves the overall epistemic capacities of the system. Giving some weight to judicial decisions would reduce the correlation of biases, raise the average competence of decision makers, and add even more numbers to the system.

It is not clear, however, that this system would be epistemically superior to a regime of deferential courts. Legislators who anticipate constitutional review by judges may rationally invest less in gathering and processing information, producing a kind of epistemic free-riding or moral hazard: anticipating that the judges will catch their mistakes, legislators will for that very reason commit more mistakes. The epistemic free-riding might even be mutual, in a case of "after you, Alphonse." Legislators and judges might then reach fewer right answers than would either institution acting alone.

More important, the cumulative approach is not possible in the most testing cases, whether or not it is desirable. The most testing cases are those in which courts engaged in constitutional review decide whether to invalidate – not merely supplement or interstitially improve – legislative action. In such cases, the institutional designer must choose whether the legislative or the judicial view will eventually prevail. Given this choice, I suggest that on epistemic grounds the legislative view is likely to be superior on average.

This broad suggestion is not a well-specified proposal, but only a first approximation – a framework for thinking about proposals. It leaves important details obscure, such as exactly how much deference is due and whether there is material variation of comparative epistemic competence across different areas or legal questions. If this variation can be captured in a more nuanced allocation of institutional authority, it should be. However, the standard view that favors common-law constitutionalism by judges is also a loose framework rather than a well-specified decision rule. My main point, at the same level of generality, is that epistemic arguments for the general superiority of judicial common-law constitutionalism are self-undermining.

B. The Design of the Supreme Court

So far I have held constant the current design of both legislatures and courts. If we relax this assumption, interesting possibilities emerge. I will begin with a judicial example, which involves the composition of the Supreme Court. My suggestion is that the Court should have more than zero lay or non-lawyer members (Vermeule 2007a: 1569). There is no legal barrier to this proposal in the U.S. case; no legal rule requires the Court's members to be lawyers at all, although the untheorized practice has been to stock the Court solely with lawyers. By contrast, nonlawyers serve on the French Conseil Constitutionnel.

The basic intuition behind the proposal is that the epistemic gains of including more than zero nonlawyers outweigh the epistemic losses. What are the gains? The Court's docket is highly heterogeneous: it includes not only cases in which law is autarkic, or strictly inward-looking, but many cases in which law itself incorporates factual, causal, or moral claims from other disciplines and spheres of life. Consider the explicit or implicit scientific issues that arise when the Court discusses global warming, the accounting issues in many financial and tax cases, the historical issues pertinent to originalist constitutional adjudication, and the penological issues in prison-conditions cases. These examples involve nonlegal specialized knowledge, but there is also a domain of highly salient cases in which the Court opines on matters not subject to specialized professional knowledge at all, such as the "mystery of human life" (*Planned Parenthood v. Casey*, 505 U.S. 833, 851 (1992)).

In this environment, adding nonlawyers would produce benefits in terms of both competence and group diversity. As to competence, nonlawyers will on average do better than lawyers where rules of constitutional law are themselves premised on nonlegal specialized knowledge, such as economics, environmental science, or psychology. As to diversity, adding nonlawyers can improve the Court's overall performance even in cases outside the nonlawyer's domain of expertise, by reducing the correlation of biases across the group. Recall that adding decision makers who are worse than random can improve group decision making, under conditions in which "diversity trumps ability." Because lawyers display correlated biases, diversifying the professional composition of the Court will produce epistemic gains.

Which nonlawyers should be added, if any are, depends on the Court's docket. If the Court is facing a steady stream of complex business cases, a financial accountant would be desirable; if the stream involves the regulation of carbon emissions, an environmental scientist would be preferable. And, of course, more than one nonlawyer might be optimal. Appointments of this sort have a dual advantage, both reducing the correlation of biases and increasing the Court's average competence in the relevant class of cases. By contrast, appointing an astrologer would produce only the diversity benefit and thus be strictly inferior to appointing a professional with relevant expertise. To be sure, the Court's membership itself partly determines the docket, but only partly; events outside the courthouse and the pool of available cases also shape the Court's agenda.

The cost side is that nonlawyers will predictably make more blunders in cases where law is purely autarkic, incorporating no specialized or unspecialized outside knowledge. The cost is real, as are the benefits; the problem is that their magnitudes are uncertain. Under uncertainty, I suggest, it is a poor strategy of institutional design to adopt an extreme solution, filling all nine slots with lawyers. Rather, on marginalist grounds, the safest guess is that the epistemic gains of adding the first nonlawyer will exceed the epistemic costs of subtracting the ninth lawyer. Zero nonlawyers is itself a contestable choice with no natural priority.

For those who are unpersuaded by this proposal, a weaker version is simply that the Court should at least have more than zero members with *dual competence*: members who possess well-defined expertise in some profession besides law. Even that weaker proposal would effect a large change from the status quo. Although a dual-competence approach would still require that all members be lawyers, it would not require that they be lawyers alone, which is overwhelmingly the case on the current Supreme Court.

Although the dual-competence approach would be an improvement, I believe that having lay justices would be better still. From the standpoint of epistemic diversity, the problem with the dual-competence approach is that it does nothing to reduce the positive correlation of lawyerly biases. The dual-competence approach begs a crucial question of design: should dual competence be built in at the level of individuals or at the aggregate level? A set of justices containing both pure lawyers and pure nonlawyers would be dual-competent *as a group* even if none of its members were dual-competent, taking them one by one. By building in dual competence at the group level rather than at the level of individuals, the institutional designer can obtain the same level of competence with a greater degree of epistemic diversity.

C. The Design of Congress

When discussing the Court's design, I held the number of judges constant and suggested diversifying their composition. In the case of Congress, I will focus on the epistemic effects of varying the number of legislators. My basic suggestion is that, on epistemic grounds, there are reasonable grounds to think that Congress is too small, although there are several crosscutting considerations in play (see Estlund, Chapter 10, this volume).

I will begin with the epistemic benefits of increasing legislative size. The representation ratio for Congress has fallen steadily over the course of U.S. history, from 1 representative for every 30,000 inhabitants in 1792, to 1 for more than 611,000 inhabitants in recent years (Auriol and Gary-Bobo 2007: 3). Increasing the number of representatives would increase the total amount of information held by the legislature overall. On a perspectival analysis, Madison suggested that representatives bring with them local information that can be combined into an overall view of national conditions (Rossiter 1961: *Federalist* 56). On a Condorcetian analysis, numbers have an exponential power that pushes group performance higher so long as average competence is better than random to begin with. Because the increase is exponential, further increases in numbers produce diminishing marginal epistemic gains; but the total gain may still be appreciable, depending on how many are added and the starting level of competence. Where average competence is .51 and there are two options, a move from 101 voters to 601 raises group accuracy from .58 to .69 (List and Goodin 2001: 287). Finally, and most important, increasing the number of legislators will tend to increase the epistemic diversity of the group.

There are at least three possible countervailing factors, however. First, to increase legislative numbers might require that individual competence be diluted. Because members of the current Congress are selected from a much larger pool than were members in 1789, if elections have any tendency to select those of higher than average epistemic competence the falling ratio should tend to raise the average epistemic competence of the modern legislator; conversely, raising the ratio would yield lower competence. By the same token, Madison also claimed (echoing Condorcet) that "the larger the number [of representatives], the greater will be the proportion of members of limited information and of weak capacities" (Rossiter 1961: *Federalist* 58, p. 360).

Second, there is the problem of epistemic free-riding among legislators. Bentham argued that although "with a larger number there is also a larger probability of a good rather than a bad decision," the problem is that "the greater the number of voters [in the legislature] the less the weight and the value of each vote, the less its price in the eyes of the voter, and the less of an incentive he has in assuring that it conforms to the true end or even in casting it at all" (translated by Elster, Chapter 7, this volume). Larger legislative size creates a group that is potentially capable of generating more information but that exploits its potential less efficiently. If, however, legislators bring a great deal of information with them rather than generating it while in office, this effect is diluted; recall that Madison's point about the epistemic benefits of representation was based on legislators' preexisting knowledge of local conditions.[16]

Finally, the issue of legislative numbers is hard to disentangle from the organization of Congress. As Machiavelli put it, "[A] multitude without a head is useless" (Machiavelli 1996: 92); a group of hundreds of legislators must be organized hierarchically in order for anything to get done. The epistemic effects of legislative organization are crosscutting, as mentioned earlier. On the one hand, a system of specialized committees increases the average competence of the committee members, and by deferring to the committees, members on the floor in effect increase their own competence (Krehbiel 1991: 61–104). On the other hand, deference reduces the number of independent votes. Fewer independent votes of greater average competence might be either better or worse, depending on the precise numbers (Estlund 1994: 158–59).

The net force of these countervailing considerations is unclear in the abstract; one must obtain detailed evidence with respect to particular legislatures. One might, however, use an indirect strategy for determining the optimal number of representatives, by using the average representation ratio of liberal democracies

---

[16] In Chapter 7, this volume, Elster provides a full argument that representation supplies the assembly with knowledge of local interests.

as the normative benchmark. On this criterion, Congress should have more than eight hundred members, summing the House and Senate together (Auriol and Gary-Bobo 2007: 4). Congress is a striking international outlier on the low side, which implies that its membership should be increased.

This indirect strategy, however, assumes that there is some mechanism – either intentional or evolutionary – causing liberal democracies to converge on an epistemically optimal legislative size. Although the validity of such an assumption is an open question, I note the striking discovery that, across liberal democracies, the size of a unicameral legislature or of the lower house in a bicameral legislature shows a strong tendency to approximate the cube root of the national population (Lutz 2006: 227–34). This fact might be a statistical artifact, but it might also result from constitutional designers' attempts to trade off the costs and benefits of size, expanding the legislature until the marginal costs and benefits of the last legislative seat are equal. I return to this issue in Section IV.

D. Interactions

To show how collective wisdom might be cashed out at the level of institutional design, I have suggested that common-law constitutionalism should, on epistemic grounds, be the province of legislatures rather than courts; that the Supreme Court should contain more than zero nonlawyers; and that Congress may possibly be too small, although the issues are complex. As I mentioned, the ideal would be to adjust these claims in reflective equilibrium, combining institutional design and the allocation of lawmaking authority into an overall epistemic optimum. Although I will not attempt that daunting task here, I will briefly discuss how the claims interact.

The claim about common-law constitutionalism and the claim about non-lawyer justices are substitutes. If legislatures excel on the very margins proposed by epistemic defenses of common-law constitutionalism, it is in part because of their greater diversity, which often trumps competence. Increasing the Court's epistemic diversity would then dilute the force of the argument. However, the substitution relationship does not entail that we must choose between the two claims altogether. The epistemic optimum might require that a balance be struck, in which some constitutional authority is transferred to the legislature while some epistemic diversity is introduced into the Court.

By contrast, the epistemic argument for increasing Congress's membership is a complement, not a substitute, for the argument about common-law constitutionalism. If Congress were to become more numerous and diverse, and by doing so increased its epistemic capacities, the argument for legislative jurisdiction over common-law constitutionalism is all the stronger. Moreover, subject to the cost–benefit qualification I will set out in Section IV, it is desirable to increase the absolute epistemic competence of both Congress and the judiciary, whatever the calculus of relative epistemic competence at any given time.

IV. OPTIMIZING COLLECTIVE WISDOM

In Section III, I assumed for simplicity that the social goal is to maximize the epistemic quality of lawmaking. Relaxing that assumption, we may ask how the goal of maximizing epistemic quality trades off against other social goals. On this perspective, epistemic quality should be optimized, not maximized. Where aggregate welfare[17] would be increased by sacrificing, at the margin, some epistemic quality for greater gains in other goods, the legal system should do so.

A. Collective Wisdom and Asymmetric Error Costs

Arranging institutions so as to maximize the simple probability of getting the right answer is a bad idea if there are asymmetric harms from erring in one direction or another. In List's terms, the right decision rule will maximize, not the sum of positive and negative reliability (the chance of avoiding type I and type II errors), but rather a sum weighted by the costs of error. Majority voting maximizes the sum of positive and negative reliability, but qualified majority or "supermajority" rules have higher negative reliability; they tend to block changes that are not truly good, even if they also block changes that truly are good.

Of course, qualified majority rules have many collateral costs. For one thing, they must either favor the status quo or else risk indeterminacy if none of the alternatives can gain the requisite supermajority. For another, qualified majority rules block more bad changes but make the bad changes that do occur more sticky. In a long-run perspective, simple majority rule makes it easier for a coalition of legislators in future periods to overturn the bad decisions of previous periods (McGann 2006: 202). In particular settings, however, those costs may be worth incurring in order to block more bad changes in the current period; here the social rate of time discounting is critical.

Although the proper solutions vary across contexts, the general implications for institutional design are straightforward. In legislatures, qualified majority voting rules are ubiquitous and can be defended in terms of their negative epistemic reliability. Judicial review of statutes for constitutional validity, which is similar in effect to a supermajority voting rule within the legislature, has been defended on the ground that the costs of erroneously allowing unconstitutional legislation to become law are greater than the costs of erroneously invalidating legislation (Cross 2000: 1576; Fallon 2008: 1714). In other arenas, Karen Croxson and others have begun to explore similar points in the design of epistemic mechanisms, such as prediction markets within firms. The designer of a prediction market or indeed any epistemic mechanism may well

---

[17] Although I phrase this point in welfarist terms, a parallel point could be made in other moral idioms as well. Any criterion of successful institutional design that admits a plurality of goods, including but not limited to epistemic quality, must face the question of how to combine, arrange, or trade off those goods against one another where they conflict.

have reason to maximize, not the simple epistemic accuracy of the mechanism, but its weighted accuracy.

B. Collective Wisdom and the Costs of Decision Making

The goal of maximizing epistemic quality systematically trades off against the costs of decision making. Epistemic or cognitive diversity tends to be correlated with other differences that make collective action more costly. Members of an epistemically diverse group may hold fewer common premises, raising the costs of mutual comprehension; they may lack a common language, raising the costs of communication. At the limit, maximizing epistemic diversity might produce, not collective wisdom, but a Tower of Babel.

Where this sort of trade-off obtains, a straightforward optimization problem arises. Increasing epistemic diversity will increase the epistemic quality of decisions, but it will also raise the costs of reaching the decisions that are made and increase the risk that the group will reach no decision at all. Buchanan and Tullock's analysis of the optimal size of the representative assembly (1999: 113–14), which trades off externalities against decision costs, thus has a straightforward epistemic analogue. As Madison put it, in determining the size of the assembly, the constitutional designer must consider not only the benefits of "free consultation and discussion" that come from adding members, but also the costs of "the confusion and intemperance of a multitude" (Rossiter 1961; *Federalist* 55).

There is some evidence suggesting, though hardly proving, that constitutional designers do reason this way. Earlier, I mentioned the finding that legislative size tends to track the cube root of national population. If there is any mechanism that makes this regularity a real phenomenon rather than a statistical artifact, it is that constitutional designers intentionally trade off the benefits of legislative size against the costs (Lutz 2006: 229–30). Some of those benefits and costs are epistemic, but some involve decision costs and (I will shortly suggest) the efficient aggregation of preferences rather than the accurate aggregation of judgments. An ideal institutional designer will take all these considerations into account.

C. Collective Wisdom and Executive Action

An important special case of the trade-off between epistemic quality and decision costs is the trade-off between the epistemic qualities of legislative deliberation and the relative speed and force of executive action. Although the executive, like Congress, is a they, not an it, executive decision making is on average more centralized, hierarchical, and swift than legislative decision making. Where the president acts as legislator in chief, his capacities simply add to Congress's epistemic quality at the margin. By contrast, where the issue is how to allocate exclusive decision-making authority between Congress and the president, an approach based on cumulative epistemic competence is not possible. One must compare the possible allocations and optimize in light of the twin risks that executive decision making will be ill-informed or rash and that legislative decision making will be slow, feeble, or incoherent. I will not attempt to answer such questions here; the subject is already canvassed in an enormous literature.[18]

D. Collective Wisdom and Expressive Harms

In some cases, the goal of maximizing epistemic quality bumps up against expressive commitments and deep normative premises of the legal system. Consider the question, much debated in U.S. legal theory of late, whether U.S. courts should consult the law of foreign jurisdictions when fashioning legal rules. A powerful argument in favor of this practice rests on a kind of epistemic cost–benefit analysis (Posner and Sunstein 2006: 142). On the benefit side, the argument invokes the Jury Theorem to suggest that foreign courts can be viewed as a notional voting group whose majority judgment will converge on correct legal answers to common problems. On the other hand, the U.S. legal system will face higher costs of decision making when consulting the law of multiple foreign jurisdictions. So far as these factors go, reasonable minds can differ about whether the benefits exceed the costs.

However, there is a further problem that becomes clear when we ask exactly which foreign jurisdictions should be included in the notional voting group. Bracketing the increased costs of decision making, should the reference group include only standard liberal democracies, or should it also include (say) North Korea and Zimbabwe? Solely on epistemic grounds, there are plausible arguments that such nations should be included. The political distortions rampant in the background political and legal systems of these nations can be understood either as violations of the sincerity condition of the Jury Theorem or as factors that reduce the average epistemic competence of the relevant judges. As against this, however, including nonliberal or nondemocratic nations would certainly do a great deal to reduce the correlation of biases across the notional voting group. This is epistemic diversity with a vengeance.

But something has gone wrong here. The obvious reason not to include those nations is that doing so would violate deep normative and expressive commitments of the U.S. legal system. Whatever the epistemic calculus, U.S. courts will not and ought not afford a kind of tacit recognition or endorsement to the practices of despotic regimes. The example underscores that neither epistemic diversity nor epistemic quality is to be maximized at all costs; they must be balanced against, and sometimes overbalanced by, nonepistemic normative considerations about the composition of the relevant decision-making groups. I can offer no general insights into the shape of these normative and expressive constraints on epistemic considerations – I can only plead in mitigation that the relevant issues are too heterogeneous and fact-bound – but there is no doubt that some such constraints exist.

---

[18] For one view, see Posner and Vermeule (2007).

E. Multipurpose Institutions

I mentioned in Section I that some institutions have multiple purposes or tasks: they are sometimes engaged in epistemic tasks involving the aggregation of judgments, sometimes engaged in nonepistemic tasks involving the aggregation of preferences. The resulting problem for institutional design is that the institutional structure that maximizes performance on one task need not maximize performance on the other. For multitask institutions, the optimal structure is one that trades off the two margins.

Consider the information–bias trade-off that affects judicial institutions. The political insulation of the judges, arising from legal protections for salary and tenure and from thick norms of judicial independence, improves the judges' epistemic performance by reducing political distortions. Where the judicial task is to find right answers to questions of law or fact, political insulation allows judges to pursue "the ways of the scholar" (Bickel 1962: 25–26). On the other hand, the same insulation makes judges poor democratic representatives and thus poor aggregators of political preferences in domains where constitutional law in effect requires preference aggregation. A possible fix for the latter problem is to appoint politicians to the bench (Peretti 2007: 122), leavening the other judges' scholarly ways with an instinctive understanding of public preferences. This solution, however, trades off against the strictly epistemic dimensions of the Court's mission, because the politician-judge will be technically less skilled. The question is how the trade-off should be struck at the margin; on a multimember high court, it seems highly plausible that at least one member should be a politician rather than a legal technocrat. Here again, the model is the Conseil Constitutionnel, which includes former presidents of the Republic and other statespersons.

V. CONCLUSION

Ideas have a life cycle that begins with a generation phase and moves to an exploitation phase. In recent years, theorists from various disciplines have generated many novel ideas about collective wisdom. My suggestion is that it is time to move to the exploitation phase, cashing out the conceptions and mechanisms of collective wisdom by applying them to concrete problems of institutional design. How much utility the mechanisms will have, and where, is an open question. However, the applications I have offered may at least indicate some of the major problems and possible solutions.

References

Aristotle (1988), *The Politics*, ed. S. Everson, Cambridge: Cambridge University Press.
Auriol, E., and Gary-Bobo, R. (2007), "On the Optimal Number of Representatives," http://idei.fr/doc/wp/optimal_number.pdf.
Becker, G. (1985), "Public Policy, Pressure Groups, and Dead Weight Loss," *Journal of Public Economics* 28: 329–47.

Bentham, J. (1824), *The Book of Fallacies*, London: John & H. L. Hunt.

Ben-Yashar, R., and Nitzan, S. (1997), "The Optimal Decision Rule for Fixed-Size Committees in Dichotomous Choice Situations: The General Result," *International Economic Review* 38, 175–86.

Bickel, A. (1962), *The Least Dangerous Branch: The Supreme Court at the Bar of Politics*, Indianapolis: Bobbs-Merrill.

Bikchandandi, S., et al. (1998), "Learning from the Behavior of Others: Conformity, Fads, and Informational Cascades," *Journal of Economic Perspectives* 12: 151–70.

Buchanan, J., and Tullock, G. (1999), *The Calculus of Consent*, Indianapolis: Liberty Fund.

Caplan, B. (2007), *The Myth of the Rational Voter: Why Democracies Choose Bad Policies*, Princeton, NJ: Princeton University Press.

Cross, F. (2000), "Institutions and Enforcement of the Bill of Rights," *Cornell Law Review* 85: 1529–1608.

Daicoff, S. (2004), *Lawyer, Know Thyself: A Psychological Analysis of Personality Strengths and Weaknesses*, Washington, DC: American Psychological Association.

Damásio, A. (1994), *Descartes' Error: Emotion, Reason and the Human Brain*, New York: Putnam.

Dawes, R., Faust, D., and Meehl, P. (1979), "Clinical versus Actuarial Judgment," *Science* 243: 1668–74.

Dworkin, R. (1977), *Taking Rights Seriously*, Cambridge, MA: Harvard University Press.

Edelman, P. (2002), "On Legal Interpretations of the Condorcet Jury Theorem," *Journal of Legal Studies* 31: 327–49.

Elhauge, E. (1991), "Does Interest Group Theory Justify More Intrusive Judicial Review?" *Yale Law Journal* 101: 31–110.

Elster, J. (1983), *Sour Grapes: Studies in the Subversion of Rationality*, Cambridge: Cambridge University Press.

(1987), "Comments on van der Veen and Van Parijs," *Theory and Society* 15: 709–22.

(1999), *Alchemies of the Mind: Rationality and Emotions*, New York: Cambridge University Press.

Estlund, D. (1994), "Opinion Leaders, Independence, and the Condorcet Jury Theorem," *Theory and Decision* 36: 131–62.

(2008), *Democratic Authority: A Philosophical Framework*, Princeton, NJ: Princeton University Press.

Estlund, D., et al. (1989), "Democratic Theory and the Public Interest: Condorcet and Rousseau Revisited," *American Political Science Review* 83: 1317–40.

Fallon, Jr., R. (2008), "The Core of an Uneasy Case for Judicial Review," *Harvard Law Review* 121: 1693–1736.

Fearon, J. (1998), "Deliberation as Discussion," in J. Elster (ed.), *Deliberative Democracy*, 46–68. Cambridge: Cambridge University Press.

Ferguson, A. (2000), *An Essay on the History of Civil Society*, New York: Georg Olms.

Fey, M. (2003), "A Note on the Condorcet Jury Theorem with Supermajority Voting Rules," *Social Choice and Welfare* 20: 27–32.

Gennaioli, N., and Shleifer, A. (2007), "The Evolution of Common Law," *Journal of Political Economy* 115: 43–68.

Goodin, R. (2003), *Reflective Democracy*, New York: Oxford University Press.

Grofman, B., and Feld, S. (1988), "Rousseau's General Will: A Condorcetian Perspective," *American Political Science Review* 82: 567–76.

Grofman, B., Owen, G., and Feld, S. L. (1983), "Thirteen Theorems in Search of the Truth," *Theory and Decision* 15: 261–78.

Hathaway, O. (2001), "Path Dependence in the Law: The Course and Pattern of Legal Change in a Common Law System," *Iowa Law Review* 86: 601–65.

Hayek, F. (1948), "The Use of Knowledge in Society," in F. Hayek, *Individualism and Economic Order*, Chicago: University of Chicago Press.

Komesar, N. (1994), *Imperfect Alternatives: Choosing Institutions in Law, Economics, and Public Policy*, Chicago: University of Chicago Press.

Kornhauser, L. (2008), "Aggregate Rationality in Adjudication and Legislation," *Politics, Philosophy and Economics* 7: 5–28.

Kraus, C., and Suarez, T. (2004), "Is There a Doctor in the House? . . . or the Senate? Physicians in the U.S. Congress, 1960–2004," *Journal of the American Medical Association* 292: 2125–29.

Krehbiel, K. (1991), *Information and Legislative Organization*, Ann Arbor: University of Michigan Press.

Ladha, K. (1992), "The Condorcet Jury Theorem, Free Speech, and Correlated Votes," *American Journal of Political Science* 36: 617–34.

List, C., and Goodin, R. (2001), "Epistemic Democracy: Generalizing the Condorcet Jury Theorem," *Journal of Political Philosophy* 9: 277–306.

Lutz, D. (2006), *Principles of Constitutional Design*, Cambridge: Cambridge University Press.

Machiavelli, N. (1996), *Discourses on Livy*, trans. H. Mansfield and N. Tarcov, Chicago: University of Chicago Press.

Marmor, A. (2006), "Should We Value Legislative Integrity?" in R. Bauman and T. Kahana (eds.), *The Least Examined Branch: The Role of Legislatures in the Constitutional State*, 125–38. Cambridge: Cambridge University Press.

McGann, A. (2006), *The Logic of Democracy*, Ann Arbor: University of Michigan Press.

Moore, M. (1996), "The Dead Hand of Constitutional Tradition," *Harvard Journal of Law and Public Policy* 19: 263–73.

Nozick, R. (1994), "Invisible-Hand Explanations," *American Economic Review* 84: 314–18.

Page, S. (2007), *The Difference*, Princeton, NJ: Princeton University Press.

Pascal, B. (1910), "Preface to the Treatise on Vacuum," in Pascal, *Thoughts, Letters, and Minor Works*, ed. C. Eliot, New York: P. F. Collier.

Peretti, T. (2007), "Where Have All the Politicians Gone? Recruiting for the Modern Supreme Court," *Judicature* 91: 112–22.

Ponzetto, G., and Fernandez, P. (2008), "Case Law vs. Statute Law: An Evolutionary Comparison," *Journal of Legal Studies* 38, http://www.people.fas.harvard.edu/~ponzetto/PF.pdf.

Posner, E., and Sunstein, C. (2006), "The Law of Other States," *Stanford Law Review* 59: 131–79.

Posner, E., and Vermeule, A. (2007), *Terror in the Balance*, New York: Oxford University Press.

Rossiter, C. (ed.) (1961), *The Federalist Papers*, New York: Mentor.

Rousseau, J.-J. (2002), *The Social Contract and the First and Second Discourses*, ed. S. Dunn, New Haven, CT: Yale University Press.

Rubenfeld, J. (2001), *Freedom and Time*, New Haven CT: Yale University Press.

Rubin, P. (1977), "Why Is the Common Law Efficient?" *Journal of Legal Studies* 6: 51–63.

Scalia, A. (1989), "Originalism: The Lesser Evil," *University of Cincinnati Law Review* 57: 849–65.

Sunstein, C. (1999), *One Case at a Time*, Cambridge, MA: Harvard University Press.

(2000), "Practical Reason and Incompletely Theorized Agreements," in E. Ullman-Margalit (ed.), *Reasoning Practically*, 98–119. New York: Oxford University Press.

(2006), "Burkean Minimalism," *University of Michigan Law Review* 105: 353–408.

(2009), *A Constitution of Many Minds*, Princeton, NJ: Princeton University Press.

Tetlock, P. (2005), *Expert Political Judgment*, Princeton, NJ: Princeton University Press.

Ullmann-Margalit, E. (1997), "The Invisible Hand and the Cunning of Reason," *Social Research* 64: 181–98.

Vermeule, A. (2007a), "Should We Have Lay Justices?" *Stanford Law Review* 59: 1569–1612.

(2007b), "Common Law Constitutionalism and the Limits of Reason," *Columbia Law Review* 107: 1482–1532.

(2009), "Many-Minds Arguments in Legal Theory," *Journal of Legal Analysis* 1: 1–45.

Waldron, J. (1995), "The Wisdom of the Multitude: Some Reflections on Book 3, Chapter 11 of Aristotle's *Politics*," *Political Theory* 23: 563–84.

15

Reasoning as a Social Competence

Dan Sperber and Hugo Mercier

Groups do better than individuals at reasoning tasks and, in some cases, do even better than *any* of their individual members. Here is an illustration. In the standard version of the Wason selection task (Wason 1966), the most commonly studied problem in the psychology of reasoning, only about 10 percent of participants give the correct solution, even though it can be arrived at by elementary deductive reasoning.[1] Such poor performance begs for an explanation, and a great many have been offered. What makes the selection task relevant here is that the difference between individual and group performance is striking. Moshman and Geil, for instance (1998), had participants try to resolve the task either individually or in groups of five or six participants. While, not surprisingly, only 9 percent of the participants working on their own found the correct solution, an astonishing 70 percent of the groups did. Moreover, when groups were formed with participants who had first tried to solve the task individually, 80 percent of the groups succeeded, including 30 percent of the groups in which none of the members had succeeded on his or her own. How are such differences between individual and group performance to be explained?

Reasoning is quite generally viewed as an ability aimed at serving the reasoner's own cognitive goals. If so, the contribution of reasoning to "collective wisdom" – for instance, to the collective discovery of the correct solution to the Wason selection task in the study of Moshman and Geil – should be seen

---

[1] In the standard Wason selection task (of which there are a great many variants), participants are presented with four cards that have a number on one side and a letter on the other. Two of the cards are shown with the number side up displaying, say, a 4 and a 7, and two with the letter side up displaying, say, an A and a K. Participants are asked: "Which of these four cards is it necessary to turn over in order to ascertain whether the following claim is true or false: If a card has a vowel on one side, it has an even number on the other side?" Whereas the correct answer is "A and 7," most of the participants answer "A" or "A and 4" (for an analysis and explanation of the task consistent with the approach to reasoning presented here, see Sperber, Cara, and Girotto 1995).

as a side effect, a by-product of its proper function. We want to argue, on the contrary, that the function of reasoning is primarily social and that it is the individual benefits that are side effects. The function of reasoning is to produce arguments in order to convince others and to evaluate arguments others use in order to convince us. We will show how this view of reasoning as a form of social competence correctly predicts both good and bad performance in the individual and in the collective case, and helps explain a variety of psychological and sociological phenomena.

It is easy enough to adduce examples of impressive, mediocre, or abysmal collective performance: think of teamwork in science, television games such as "Family Feud," and lynching. One might explain this variety of cases in different ways. The simplest explanation – but clearly an inadequate one – would be that, in each case, performance results from the aggregation of the contributions of individuals endowed to various degrees with an all-purpose general intelligence or, if you prefer, "rationality" and that the differences in the quality of the outcomes is what you should expect assuming a normal distribution (the best and worst examples being selected at both ends of the bell-shaped curve). A somewhat more plausible explanation would take into account the institutional articulation of individual contributions and help explain the fact that collective performances of a given type (e.g., scientific work vs. mob "justice") tend to cluster at one or another end of the distribution. In a typical social science fashion, such explanations involve an idealized assumption about rationality but no serious consideration of actual mental mechanisms.

It would be preferable, for the sake of simplicity, if a sophisticated understanding of social phenomena could be achieved with little or no psychology, but, we would argue (see Sperber 2006), this is as implausible as achieving a deep understanding of epidemiological phenomena without a serious interest in pathology – and for similar reasons. We explore rather the possibility that explaining different kinds of collective cognitive performances requires paying attention to the individual psychological mechanisms and dispositions involved.

The common view of human thinking as a relatively homogeneous process governed by intelligence or reason and interfered with by passions is based on conscious access to our thoughts and on our ability to integrate our conscious thoughts in discursive form. Conscious access to our thoughts, however, tells us little about thinking proper, that is, about the processes through which we produce these thoughts. The discursive integration of our thoughts tells us little about their articulation in the mind. Empirical research in cognitive psychology strongly suggests that, actually, conscious access to thought *processes* is extremely poor; that there is no unified, domain-general mechanism to which "reason" or "intelligence" would refer; that thought processes are carried out by a variety of autonomous mental mechanisms (often described as "modules"); and that many of these mechanisms use as input or produce as output a variety of intermediate-level mental representations that are not accessible to consciousness (see, e.g., Dennett 1991; Marr 1982; Sperber 2001).

Is reasoning, then, the output of a single mental mechanism or of several, and if so of which? In psychology of reasoning, the search had initially been for *the* underlying mechanism, in the singular. The most debated question was, did this mechanism use logical rules (Rips 1994), mental models (Johnson-Laird 1983), or pragmatic schemas (Cheng and Holyoak 1985)?

More recently, many researchers have argued that reasoning can be carried out through two distinct cognitive systems. System 1 processes are typically described as unconscious, implicit, automatic, associative, or heuristic. They are seen as fast, cheap, and generally efficient in ordinary circumstances but prone to mistakes when the conditions or the problems are nonstandard. System 2 processes are described, on the contrary, as conscious, explicit, rule-based, or analytic. They are seen as slow and effortful but as more systematically reliable and as better at handling nontrivial cases. Actually, such "dual-system theories," according to which mental processes can be divided into two broad types, are common or even dominant in many fields of psychology. Within cognitive psychology, they started in the fields of attention (Posner and Snyder 1975) and memory (Schacter 1987), soon followed by learning (Berry and Dienes 1993; Reber 1993), before expanding toward reasoning (Evans and Over 1996; Sloman 1996; Stanovich 2004) and decision making (Kahneman 2003; Kahneman and Frederick 2002). They are present in nearly every domain of social psychology, most notably in persuasion and attitude change (Chaiken, Liberman, and Eagly 1989; Petty and Cacioppo 1986), but also in attitudes (Wilson, Lindsey, and Schooler 2000), stereotypes (Bodenhausen, Macrae, and Sherman 1999), and person perception (Uleman 1999). They are also found in moral (Haidt 2001) and developmental (Klaczynski and Lavallee 2005) psychology.

A good illustration of the speed and apparent effectiveness of system 1 processes is provided by a study of Todorov et al. (2005) on judgments of competence. Participants were shown for just one second the pictures of two faces unknown to them and were asked which of the two individuals looked more competent. One might think that, in order to judge an individual's competence, a variety of evidence would be needed and that facial appearance would be of limited relevance. Still, participants showed no qualms about answering the question. This reliance on a quasi-immediate first impression is a perfect example of system 1 inference. Actually, the faces were those of candidates who had competed for election to the U.S. Senate. The participants' answers predicted the result of the elections with 67.6 percent accuracy. As the authors note:

Actual voting decisions are certainly based on multiple sources of information other than inferences from facial appearance. Voters can use this additional information to modify initial impressions of political candidates. However, from a dual-system perspective, correction of intuitive system 1 judgments is a prerogative of system 2 processes that are attention-dependent and are often anchored on intuitive system 1 judgments. Thus, correction of initial impressions may be insufficient. In the case of voting decisions, these decisions can be anchored on initial inferences of competence from facial appearance. From this perspective, in the absence of any other information, voting preferences should be closely related to such inferences. In real-life voting decisions, additional information may weaken the relation between inferences from faces and decisions but may not change the nature of the relation. (Todorov et al. 2005: 1625)

The Wason selection task (mentioned earlier) provides the most common example of fast and unconscious system 1 mental processes yielding an answer that happens to be false. Another clear and simpler example is provided by the bat and ball problem (Frederick 2005): "A bat and a ball together cost $1.10. The bat costs $1.00 more than the ball. How much does the ball cost?" For most of us, when we are first presented with the problem, an answer springs to mind: the ball costs 10 cents. Presumably, this answer comes somehow from an instantaneous realization that the first amount mentioned ($1.10) equals the second amount mentioned ($1.00) plus 10 cents and from the implicit and unexamined presupposition that this directly provides an answer to the problem. We are able, however, but with more effort, to understand that if the ball costs 10 cents and therefore the bat 1 dollar, the difference between the two items is not 1 dollar as stipulated, but 90 cents. Our initial answer cannot be right! More careful system 2 reasoning reveals the correct answer: the ball costs 5 cents (and the bat $1.05, with a total of $1.10 and a difference of 1 dollar). These two successive answers illustrate the duality of processes involved.

While much evidence has accumulated in favor of a dual-system view of reasoning (Evans 2003, 2008), the contrast between the two postulated systems is left vague, and explanations of why the mind should have such a dual organization are at best very sketchy. We have suggested a more explicit and principled distinction between "intuitive" and "reflective" inferences (Mercier and Sperber 2009) that can be seen as a particular version of dual-system theories, provided that they are broadly characterized, or else as an alternative to these theories, drawing on much of the same evidence and sharing several fundamental hunches. We argue that system 1, or intuitive, inferences are carried out by a variety of domain-specific mechanisms. Reflective inference, which corresponds to reasoning in the ordinary sense of the term, is, we claim, the indirect output of a single module. A distinctive feature of our approach, relevant to the discussion of "collective wisdom," is the claim that the main function of reflective inference is to produce and evaluate arguments occurring in interpersonal communication (rather than to help individual ratiocination).

INTUITIVE INFERENCE

In dual-system theories of reasoning, "reasoning" and "inference" are used more or less as synonyms. We prefer to use "inference" in a wider sense common in psychology, and "reasoning" in a narrower sense common in ordinary language and in philosophy. An inference, as the term is used in psychology, is a process that, given some input information, reliably yields as output further information that is likely to be true if the input information is. Inference is involved not only in thinking but also in perception and in motor control. When you see a three-dimensional object, a house or a horse, for instance, you have sensory information only about the part of its surface that reflects light to your retina, and perceiving it as a house or as a horse involves *inferring* from this sensory information about a surface the kind of three-dimensional object it is. When you decide to grasp, say, a mug, you use your perception of the mug and of your own bodily position in space to infer at each moment throughout the movement the best way to carry out your intention. Inferences so understood are performed not only by humans but also by all species endowed with cognitive capacities. They are an essential ingredient of any cognitive system.

Even if we restrict "inference" – as we will do from now on – to refer to processes that have conceptual representations both as input and as output (in contrast to perceptual inferences that have sensory input and to motor control inferences that have motor command output), we have grounds to assume that a vast number of conceptual inferences are unconsciously performed all the time in human mental life. Here are some instances:

1. You hear the sound of steps growing louder, and you assume that someone is coming closer.
2. Joan suddenly turns and looks in a given direction, and you assume that she is looking at something of possible relevance to her.
3. You feel a few drops of rain falling, and you assume that it is beginning to rain.
4. You feel nauseated, and you assume that you have eaten something bad.
5. You hear the doorbell ring, and you assume that someone is at the door.
6. Having heard the doorbell ring and assumed that someone is at the door, you take for granted that it probably is the person whom you were expecting at that moment.
7. You are told that Bill is eight years old and that Bob is six, and you immediately realize that Bill is older than Bob.

In all these cases, there may be a reluctance to concede that some inference has taken place. From a cognitive point of view, however, the fact is that some new assumption has been arrived at on the basis of previous information that warrants it. Some process must have occurred, even if rapid, automatic, and unconscious. Whatever the particular form of such a cognitive process, its function is to produce new assumptions warranted by previous ones, and this is enough to make it an inferential process. In our examples, the conceptual output of a perception process (1 to 5) or of a wholly conceptual process (6 and 7) provides premises for a further inference that may be warranted inductively (1 to 6) or deductively (7). Of course, it is possible to draw such inferences in a conscious and reflective manner, but typically, the output of inferential processes of this kind is arrived at without any awareness of the process itself and comes to mind as self-evident. In other words, much inference is just something that occurs in us, at a subpersonal level, and not something we, as persons, do.

How are such spontaneous, mostly unconscious inferences achieved? One possible view is they are all drawn by a general inferential mechanism that has access to a wide base of encyclopedic data with much general information that can be represented in conditional form, such as "if movement sounds are growing louder, then the source of these sounds is getting nearer," or "if the doorbell rings, someone is at the door." These serve as the major premise in inferences from a general proposition to a particular case where a specific assumption (e.g., "movement sounds are now growing louder"; "the doorbell is ringing") serves as the minor premise. In other words, unconscious inference would resemble conscious reasoning with conclusions following from premises in virtue of quite general deductive or inductive warrant relationships.

Assuming that unconscious inference works like conscious reasoning except for the fact that it is unconscious raises the following puzzle: Why would we ever bother to perform in a conscious and painstaking manner what we would be quite good at doing unconsciously and almost effortlessly? Even assuming some satisfactory solution to this puzzle, we would still be left with two more substantial problems, one having to do with relevance and the other with efficiency.

Here is the relevance problem: For any minor premise such as "the doorbell is ringing," there is a vast array of encyclopedic information that could provide a major premise (e.g., "if the doorbell is ringing, electricity is working properly"; "if the doorbell is ringing, pressure is being exerted on the bell button"; "if the doorbell is ringing, air is vibrating"). In a given situation very few, if any, of these possible major premises are used to derive a conclusion, even though these conclusions would all be similarly warranted. What happens is that only contextually *relevant* inferences tend to be drawn (Van der Henst 2006; Van der Henst, Sperber, and Politzer 2002). A general inferential ability is not, by itself, geared to homing in on such relevant inferences.

Here is the efficiency problem: Inferences in many specific domains could be more efficient if tailored to take advantage of the specificity of the domain and to employ dedicated procedures rather than have that specificity be represented in propositional form and used by general procedures such as conditional inferences. For instance, we expect not only humans but also other animals to be able to draw inferences about the movement of looming objects from their increasing loudness. Presumably, animals do not draw these inferences by using propositional generalizations as premises in conditional inference. More plausibly, they take advantage of the regular correlation between noise and movement. This regular correlation has allowed the evolution of an ad hoc procedure that directly yields an assumption about relative nearness of a moving object from a perception of increasing or decreasing movement noises, without a general assumption about the relationship between the two being represented as a piece of encyclopedic knowledge and used as a major premise in some form of general conditional reasoning. For humans, too, it would be advantageous to have the same kind of ad hoc, automatic procedure. Similarly, understanding that someone is at the door when the doorbell rings is better left to an ad hoc kind of cognitive reflex than to general knowledge and inferential capacities. In the case of the doorbell, the "cognitive reflex" is obviously acquired and is preceded by the acquisition of the relevant encyclopedic knowledge, whereas in the case of looming sources of sound, it might well be innate (and the relevant encyclopedic knowledge is acquired later, if at all). What both examples suggest, in spite of this difference, is that many inferences may be more effectively carried by specialized domain-specific mental devices or "modules" than by a general ability drawing on a single huge database.

Assuming that the efficiency problem is, at least in part, solved by the existence of many specialized inferential modules contributes to solving the relevance problem. Presumably, those inferences that become modularized either in evolution or in cognitive development are those that are the most likely to be relevant and to be performed spontaneously (for other and subtler ways in which modularity contributes to relevance, see Sperber 2005).

The image of spontaneous inference that emerges through these remarks (and that we have developed elsewhere; see Mercier and Sperber 2009) is not one of a single system but of a great variety of narrowly specialized modules. Several dual-system theorists have similarly argued that so-called "system 1" is in fact a medley of diverse procedures (see, e.g., Stanovich 2004). But what about system 2?

METAREPRESENTATIONAL INFERENCES: INTUITIVE AND REFLECTIVE

Humans have the "metarepresentational" ability to represent representations: mental representations such as the thoughts of others and their own thoughts and public representations such as utterances. They draw intuitive inferences about representations just as they do about other things in the world, for instance:

8. Seeing Joan open the fridge with an empty beer mug in her hand, you infer that she wants *to drink beer*.
9. From the same behavioral evidence, you also infer that Joan believes that *there is beer in the fridge*.
10. Knowing that Joan wants *to drink beer* and believes *there is beer in the fridge*, you infer that she will look for beer in the fridge.
11. You are asked whether Joan is expecting *Bill to come to the party*, and knowing that she believes that *Jill is coming to the party* and that *Jill always brings Bill to parties*, you immediately answer, "Yes!" On what basis? You infer Joan's expectation from her beliefs.
12. Asked whether she would like to go for a walk, Joan answers, shaking her head, "I am tired" and you infer her to mean that, no, *she does not want to go for a walk because she is tired*.

In 8 to 12, the italicized words represent not (or at least not directly) a state of affairs but the content of a mental representation. As in cases 1 to 7, an inference takes place without, usually, being noticed as such. In 8 and 9, a mental state is inferred from an observation of behavior. In 10, an expectation of behavior is arrived at on the basis of knowledge of mental states. In 11, a mental state is inferred from knowledge of other mental states. In 12, the content of a very specific type of mental state, a communicative intention, is inferred from verbal behavior.

We now look at an example similar to 12 but with an interesting twist:

13. You ask Steve whether he believes that Joan would like to go for a walk, and he answers, shaking his head, "She is tired."

As Joan is in 12, Steve, in 13, is describing a state of affairs from which you can infer – and he intends you to infer – that Joan would not want to go for a walk. When Joan is herself speaking, as in 12, given that people are, in such matters, reliable authorities on their own wants, you are likely to trust her and to believe that indeed she doesn't want to go for a walk (you may be more skeptical about her excuse, but this is beside the present point). In 13, Steve is less an authority on Joan's wants, and hence you are less likely to accept his opinion on trust. On the other hand, let us assume, you trust and believe him when he says that she is tired, something easier for him to ascertain. In saying that Joan is tired, Steve provides you with an argument for the conclusion he wants you to draw: you may yourself conclude that Joan, being tired, is unlikely to want to go for a walk.

You might have been wholly trustful and have accepted both Steve's explicit meaning – that Joan is tired – and his implicit meaning – that she does not want to go for a walk – without even paying attention to the fact that the former is an argument for believing the latter. We are, however, considering the case where, not being wholly disposed to take Steve's word for it, you pay attention to the argument. Only if you find the argument good enough in the circumstances will you then accept its implicit conclusion.

If you ponder Steve's argument, if you consider whether accepting that Joan is tired is a good reason to believe that she would not want to go for a walk, then what you are engaged in is reflective inference; you are reasoning, in a quite ordinary sense of the term. You are paying conscious attention to the relationship between argument and claim, or premises and intended conclusions. Unlike what happens in intuitive inference, you may end up accepting a conclusion *for a reason represented as such*.

Reasoning so understood involves paying attention to the relationship between claims and reasons to accept them. While accepting or rejecting the claim is done reflectively, the relationship between claim and reasons is intuitively assessed: you intuitively understand, say, that the fact that Joan is tired constitutes a good reason to believe that she wouldn't want to go for a walk. You then, or so it seems to you, decide to accept Steve's conclusion.

It could be argued that when one consciously reasons and sees oneself as involved in a series of personal epistemic decisions, one is mistaking the visible tip of a mental iceberg for its largely invisible structure. Actually, what happens is that a series of inferences is taking place unconsciously. These inferences deliver as their output conscious representations about relationships between reasons and claims. The conscious self's grasp of these relationships is just the intuitive awareness of the output of mental work performed at a subpersonal level. The conscious self builds a narrative out of formal relationships. It sees itself as making epistemic decisions to accept or reject conclusions, when in fact these decisions have been all but made at this subpersonal level. True, one can engage in higher-order reasoning, that is, reason about reasons, rather than just accept them or reject them as intuitively strong or weak. You may, for instance, ponder the extent to which Joan's tiredness provides a good reason to believe she would not want to go for a walk; after all, being tired may sometimes motivate one to go for a walk rather than, say, keep working. Such higher-order reasoning is relatively rare and, ultimately, cannot but be grounded in intuitions about even higher order relationships between reasons and claims. Reasoning as we consciously experience it, that is, as a series of conscious epistemic assessments and decisions, may well be, to a large extent, a cognitive illusion (just as may be making practical decisions; see, e.g., Soon et al. 2008). In challenging the Cartesian sense of reasoning as an exercise of free will guided by reasons rather than compelled by causes, we challenge also the sense of reasoning as a higher form of *individual* cognition.

Here is a real-life example of reasoning in the sense intended. During the 2008 primaries of the U.S. presidential election, the organization Move On ran a competition for the best thirty-second video ad for Barack Obama. One of the winners was entitled "They Said He Was Unprepared. . . . "[2] This is what you saw and heard:

[*A succession of still pictures of Obama campaigning.*]
    A man from Illinois was running for president.
    His opponents ridiculed him as inexperienced and woefully unprepared.
    His only government experience had been service in the Illinois State legislature plus two years as an obscure member of Congress.
    He had never held an executive or management position of any kind.
    Yet THIS man [*now a picture Abraham Lincoln*] was elected President. Twice. And [*now pictures of Lincoln and Obama side by side*] they said he was unprepared!

Until you saw the picture of Lincoln, you assumed that the "man from Illinois" said to be unprepared was Obama, and you thought you recognized arguments that were indeed being used against him at the time by his rivals for the Democratic nomination. When the picture of Lincoln appeared and you heard that "this man was elected President. Twice," you understood that all these arguments had been used to claim that Lincoln would not be a good president. Well, he was a great president. So these arguments against Lincoln were not good ones. By parity of reasoning, you were given to understand, the same arguments were not good ones against Obama.

---

[2] By Josh Garrett, at http://www.youtube.com/watch?v=LuVNZPoVPYg.

Note the cognitive complexity involved in comprehending such an ad. Viewers had to correct their first impression that the target of the arguments quoted was Obama and understand that it was Lincoln. They had to realize that what these arguments were intended to show had been refuted by Lincoln's career. They had to focus on the fact that almost identical arguments were now used against Obama (a step made easy by their initial misidentification of the target). Finally, they had to conclude that, by parity of reasoning, these arguments were flawed when leveled at Obama. Watching this ad, viewers don't just end up with the conclusion springing unannounced to the mind as in intuitive inference that Obama's relative unpreparedness need not stand in the way of his becoming a good president. To come to this conclusion, they have to be aware of the intermediary steps. Like most real-life complex arguments, this one was enthymematic, so most of these steps had to be reconstructed. Still, viewers had little difficulty doing all this in thirty seconds (as evidenced by the fact that they voted this ad the best in the competition). The almost exhilarating sense of cognitive control provided by understanding and accepting (or rejecting) such a complex argument is based, we suggest, on the efficacy of the unconscious processes involved and on the fact that the conscious self is given the grand role of undersigning their output.

It is contentious whether other animals have any metarepresentational ability, in particular the ability to infer what another animal wants or believes from observations of its behavior. In any case, no one has ever suggested that the metarepresentational abilities of other animals, if they have any, might extend to metarepresenting not just mental representations but also public representations such as utterances or, even more implausibly, logical and evidential relationships among representations as in reasoning. Reasoning is specifically human. It is clearly linked to language (Carruthers 2009). Reasoning takes as input and produces as output conceptual representations that typically can be consciously represented and verbalized.

WHY DO HUMANS REASON?

Most philosophical and psychological approaches to reasoning seem to take for granted that the role or the function of reasoning is to enhance individual cognition. There is no doubt that it often does so. There also is plenty of evidence that reasoning is fallible (see Evans 2002 in the case of deductive reasoning) and that reasoning sometimes lowers overall cognitive performance (Dijksterhuis 2004; Dijksterhuis et al. 2006; Wilson et al. 1989). Moreover, reasoning is a costly mental activity. To assess its efficiency, not only benefits but also costs have to be taken into account. When this is done, it ceases to be self-evident that reasoning is just a "Good Thing" for which there would necessarily have been selective pressure in the evolution of the species.

More specifically, cognitive mechanisms are likely to have evolved so as to be well adapted to a species' environment and to the kinds of information that environment provides (Sterelny 2003, in press). In this respect, the human environment is unique: much of the information available to humans is provided by other humans.

Ordinarily, in a natural environment, most information is provided by the very items the information is about. Material objects, for instance, reflect or emit a variety of waves (e.g., sound or light) that facilitate their identification. The information provided by many items – such as stones, stars, water, fire – whether it is rich or poor, is unbiased: it is not geared to misleading organisms endowed with the cognitive capacities to exploit this information. A species' cognitive mechanisms are likely to have evolved so as better to exploit information provided by items of importance to members of that species. This is likely to have resulted, as we suggested, in the evolution of many specialized cognitive mechanisms or modules that are each adjusted to a specific part or aspect of the environment.

There are, however, items in the environment that have evolved so as to mislead some of the organisms that might interact with them. This is in particular the case, across species, of predators and prey, which, for complementary reasons, may gain from not being properly identified and may use, for this, various forms of camouflage or mimicry. It is also the case, within species, of potential mates that may gain from giving an exaggerated image of their qualities and of competitors that may gain from giving an exaggerated image of their strength. In many cases, such misinformation may succeed: edible viceroy butterflies are generally mistaken for poisonous monarchs by birds who would otherwise eat them, and that's that. The conflict of interests between source and target of information may, in other cases, have led to an evolutionary arms race, with the target becoming better and better at seeing through misleading information and the source producing in response information that is more and more misleading. In such cases, what we should expect to find, on the target's side, are quite specialized cognitive mechanisms aimed at quite specific and repetitive forms of misinformation.

Other sources of information in the environment may be neither neutral nor misleading but on the contrary helpful, as in the relationships between nurturing mothers and offspring or among social insects. In such cases, one may find communication abilities evolving, with organisms providing honest information not only about themselves but also about their environment. Typically, the information communicated is very specific – about the location of nectar among honeybees, for instance – and the cognitive mechanisms used to exploit it are quite specialized coding and decoding mechanisms. Whereas misinformation, mimicry, or camouflage, say, works only if the targets do not have mechanisms dedicated to recognizing it, cooperative information, as among social insects, works only if the recipients have dedicated mechanisms to recognize and decode it.

Human communication stands apart not only because of its incomparable richness and importance for individual cognition and for social interaction, not only because it is not a mere matter of coding and decoding (Sperber and

Wilson 1995), but also because it is routinely used both honestly to inform and dishonestly to mislead. In other terms, humans, who stand to gain immensely from the communication of others, incur a commensurate risk of being deceived and manipulated. How could, notwithstanding this risk, communication evolve into such an essential aspect of human life? To appreciate the evolutionary significance of the problem, we compare it to the well-known dilemma of cooperation.

Cooperation is another "Good Thing" that, at first blush, should be widespread in nature. In fact, it is quite rare, and there is a simple evolutionary explanation for this. While cooperators stand to gain from participating honestly, that is from paying the cost and sharing the benefits of cooperation, they stand to gain even more from cheating – that is, sharing the benefits without paying the cost. Cheating undermines cooperation and makes it evolutionarily unstable unless it is in some way prevented or circumscribed. Cheating may be controlled if cooperators recognize cheaters and deny them the benefits of cooperation. For instance, if cooperators adopt a tit-for-tat strategy, formal models have shown, the evolutionary instability of cooperation may in principle be overcome (Axelrod 1984).

Communication among the members of a group can be seen as a form of cooperation, and deception as a form of cheating. So, then, why not just apply models of the evolution of cooperation to the special case of communication and have, for instance, an ad hoc version of the for tit-for-tat strategy: you lie to me, I lie to you, or you lie to me, I stop believing you (see Blais 1987 for a more sophisticated "epistemic tit for tat")? Well, whereas in standard cooperation, unsanctioned cheating is always advantageous, the goals of communicators are very often better achieved by honest communication. We communicate in particular to coordinate with others, to make requests of them, and, for this, honest information best serves our goal. So if I were to lie to you or to refuse to believe you in retaliation for your having lied to me, I might not only punish you but also harm myself. More generally, to get as much benefit as possible from communication while minimizing the risk of being deceived requires a kind of "epistemic vigilance" (Sperber et al. 2010) that filters communicated information in sophisticated ways. Systematically disbelieving communicators who have been deceitful about one topic would, for instance, entail ignoring the fact that they may nevertheless be uniquely well informed and often reliable about other topics (e.g., about themselves). Well-adjusted trust in communicated information must then take into account the character and circumstances of the communicator and the contents of communication.

Communication is so advantageous to human beings, on the one hand, and makes them so vulnerable to misinformation, on the other, that there must have been, we suggest, strong and ongoing pressure for developing mechanisms of epistemic vigilance geared at constantly adjusted well-calibrated trust. Much of epistemic vigilance focuses on the communicator: whom to believe, when, and on what topic and issue. Recent experimental work shows that children develop, from the age of three, the ability to take into account evidence of the competence or benevolence of the communicator in deciding whom to trust (Harris 2007; Mascaro and Sperber 2009). Though it would still deserve more extensive empirical study, this ability is well in evidence in adults (Petty and Wegener 1998).

Judging the trustworthiness of the source of information is not the only way to filter communicated information. The content of that information may itself be more or less believable, independent of its source. What might make it more or less believable is the effect that accepting it would have on the overall consistency of our beliefs. To take cases at the two extremes, believing a contradiction would introduce an inconsistency in our beliefs, and so would disbelieving a tautology, whatever their sources. Even in less extreme cases, the very content of a claim may weigh in favor of believing or disbelieving it. If a claim is entailed by what we already believe, this is a reason to believe it (and since we may not have considered this entailment of our beliefs before, it may well be novel and relevant). This, however, may not be a sufficient reason. Realizing that our previous beliefs entail some implausible consequence we had not thought of before may give us a reason to revise our beliefs rather than accept this consequence. If a claim contradicts what we already believe, this is a reason to reject it. It may not be a sufficient reason either. By rejecting such a claim, we may miss an opportunity to appropriately revise beliefs that may have been wrong from the start or that need updating.

Believability of a content and reliability of its source may interact. If we deem trustworthy a person who makes a claim that contradicts our beliefs, then some belief revision is anyhow unavoidable: if we accept the claim, we must revise the beliefs it contradicts; if we reject the claim, we must revise our belief that the source is trustworthy.

In a nutshell, although attending to its consistency with previously held beliefs is highly relevant to filtering newly communicated information, this cannot rationally determine an automatic acceptance or rejection heuristic. Inconsistency of a claim with our beliefs on its subject matter or with our trust in its source calls for reflection (see Thagard 2005). This is true not just of logical inconsistency but also of a probabilistic form of inconsistency where, in the light of what we already believe, a novel claim is just highly improbable.

Checking inconsistency may be a powerful way to help decide what new beliefs to accept or reject and what old beliefs to revise, but it is not a simple and cheap procedure. At least from an evolutionary point of view, it would not make much sense for an organism to make the effort to check the mutual consistency of beliefs that wholly and purely result from its own perceptions and inferences.[3] Perceptual and inferential mechanisms have evolved to serve the cognitive need of the organism. Of course, these mechanisms may occasionally err, and their errors might be revealed by some form of consistency

---

[3] Note that socialized human beings, even when alone, never have perceptions and inferences that are wholly and purely their own, since their human perception and inference make use of conceptual tools acquired through cultural transmission.

checking. However, not only would this procedure be costly, it would itself not be error-proof. Checking, on the other hand, the consistency of communicated information makes much more sense because communicators serve their own ends, which may differ from those of their audience and are often best served by misinforming the audience. We suggest that the cost of consistency checking is worth incurring only in order to filter communicated information.

Imagine, then, in the evolution of human communication, a stage where people do not argue but make factual claims that are often highly informative and relevant but that may also be dishonest. When trust in the communicator is not sufficient to accept what is being communicated, addressees consider the content and check both its internal consistency and its consistency with what they already believe. When they hit an inconsistency, they have to take an epistemic decision – or so it seems subjectively – and either reject the new information or else "bet on its truth" (De Sousa 1971) and revise their beliefs.

The same people who, as addressees, use consistency checking to sift what they are told often find themselves in the position of communicator, now addressing other consistency checkers. One way to persuade one's addressees is to help them check the consistency of what one is claiming with what they believe or, even better if possible, to help them realize that it would be inconsistent with what they already believe not to accept one's claim. The communicator is better off making an honest display of the very consistency addressees are anyhow checking. This amounts to, instead of just making a claim, *giving reasons* it should be accepted, *arguing* for it. Once communicators resort to giving reasons, they have a use for an ad hoc logical and argumentative vocabulary ("if…then," "therefore," etc.) that is of no use, on the other hand, for making plain factual claims. This vocabulary helps display, for the examination of the addressees, the reasons they should accept claims they are unprepared to accept just on trust.

Reasoning can be defined as the ability to produce and evaluate reasons. It is a costly ability: it involves special metarepresentational capacities found only among humans, it requires practice to reach proficiency, and exerting it is relatively slow and effortful. Reasoning, we argue, evolved because of its contribution to the effectiveness of human communication, enhancing content-based epistemic vigilance and one's ability to persuade a vigilant audience. The reasons reasoning is primarily about are not solipsistic. They are not for private appreciation. They are arguments used, or at least rehearsed, for persuading others.

What we are proposing, then, is an argumentative theory of reasoning. We are not the first to do so. Others (Billig 1996; Perelman 1949; Perelman and Olbrechts-Tyteca 1969; Toulmin 1958) have maintained that reasoning is primarily about producing and evaluating arguments. They have done so mostly on introspective grounds and in a philosophical perspective. We may be more original in doing so on empirical grounds and in a naturalistic and evolutionary perspective (see also Dessalles 2007).

EMPIRICAL EVIDENCE FOR THE ARGUMENTATIVE THEORY
OF REASONING

The argumentative theory of reasoning we have briefly sketched, though still too vague in many respects, has experimentally testable consequences. More specifically, claiming that reasoning is a social competence aimed at producing arguments to convince others and evaluating such arguments makes it possible to engage in "adaptive thinking": inferring structure and performance from function. The theory predicts when reasoning should be efficient and when it should lead us astray, and how. These predictions can be pitted against relevant results from different areas of psychology – social psychology, psychology of reasoning and decision making, and developmental psychology. We briefly do so here (for a richer review, see Mercier and Sperber 2009, 2011).

The first and most straightforward prediction of the argumentative theory is that people should be good at arguing. Any evolved mechanism should be good at performing the task it evolved for – otherwise it would not have evolved in the first place. And indeed, researchers studying persuasion and attitude change have repeatedly shown that when people are interested in the conclusion of an argument, they are much more influenced by a strong argument than by a weak one (see Petty and Wegener 1998 for a review). Participants are also able to spot argumentative fallacies and to react appropriately to them (Hahn and Oaksford 2007; Neuman, Weinstock, and Glasner 2006; Rips 2002). They can recognize the larger, macrostructure of arguments, keep track of the commitments of different speakers, and correctly attribute the burden of proof – all these being skills needed to follow or take part in an argument (Bailenson and Rips 1996; Ricco 2003; Rips 1998). When it comes to production, people have no problems generating arguments supporting their views or counterarguments attacking an alternative (Kuhn, Weinstock, and Flaton 1994; Shaw 1996). Blanchette and Dunbar (2000, 2001) have demonstrated that people use deeper analogies when they aim at convincing someone. More generally, researchers who have looked at actual arguments and debates, even among untrained participants, are often "impressed by the coherence of the reasoning displayed" (Resnick et al. 1993: 362).

The developmental evidence is even more striking. Nancy Stein and her colleagues have shown that children as young as three are perfectly able to engage in argumentation (Stein and Albro 2001; Stein and Bernas 1999; Stein and Miller 1993). Preschoolers can even spot argumentative fallacies such as circular reasoning (Baum, Danovitch, and Keil 2007). By contrast, standard reasoning problems have been found not to be even worth testing until relatively late in adolescence – and even then, performance tends to be abysmal (see, e.g., Barrouillet, Grosset, and Lecas 2000).

As we mentioned earlier, the general conclusion most commonly drawn from the psychology of reasoning is that people are not very good at it. The second and more specific prediction of the argumentative theory is that people should reason much better in argumentative contexts. Reasoning should be more naturally triggered when people have to convince other people or to evaluate arguments aimed at convincing them. Moreover, reasoning should be specifically adjusted to these goals and good at achieving them, just as, say, a corkscrew, being specially designed to pull out corks, is likely to be better at doing so than at performing other odd tasks it may occasionally be used for. There is much evidence to confirm this prediction. For instance, when people want to attack alternative views, they are very good at making use of *modus tollens* arguments (Pennington and Hastie 1993). On the other hand, half of the people tested in standard reasoning tasks lacking an argumentative context fail on *modus tollens* tasks (Evans, Newstead, and Byrne 1993).

Even more persuasive are experiments in which exactly the same tasks are used in individual and in group settings. As we mentioned, when a task has a demonstrably correct answer that most individual participants fail to give, groups generally do much better – sometimes dramatically so (Bonner, Baumann, and Dalal 2002; Laughlin and Ellis 1986; Moshman and Geil 1998). This is not an effect of enhanced motivation to perform well in group situations, since monetary incentives, which have, if anything, stronger motivating force, have no comparable effect (see Camerer and Hogarth 1999, in the general case, and Jones and Sugden 2001, for the Wason selection task). Discussion, on the other hand, is crucial for group performance (see Schulz-Hardt et al. 2006). In a discussion, participants are able both to produce good arguments and to select the best among those produced by the group. It is not surprising, therefore, that learning methods that rely on peer discussions have been found to be extremely effective (see Slavin 1995 for review) and are now being adopted at all levels of education, from elementary school up to MIT (Rimer 2009).

The next prediction of the argumentative theory may seem paradoxical: human reasoning may owe part of its effectiveness to what, from a strictly epistemic point of view, should be seen as a flaw. When people are engaged in a debate, what they look for, what is useful to them, are arguments that support their views or undermine those of their interlocutor. Finding arguments for the opposite view (unless it is in order to anticipate and refute them) is counterproductive. Reasoning, as a mechanism that allows us to find arguments in such contexts, *should* therefore be biased. More specifically, it should – and does indeed – display a confirmation bias. Across a vast range of experiments, people have repeatedly shown a tendency to look only for arguments that support their views, their hypotheses (see Nickerson 1998 for review). It has also been shown that people search mostly for new information that supports their opinions (S. M. Smith, Fabrigar, and Norris 2008). In psychology of reasoning, the confirmation bias has been blamed for participants' failures in most tasks, including conditional reasoning tasks (Evans 1996), hypothesis testing (Poletiek 1996; Tweney et al. 1980), and syllogistic reasoning (Evans et al. 1999; Newstead, Handley, and Buck 1999). The confirmation bias is not something that people can easily suppress; it is a ubiquitous feature of reasoning. Instructions putting a special emphasis on objectivity fail to diminish the bias. On the contrary, in an experiment by Lord, such instructions caused participants to reason more, but doing so with an intact bias, they provided responses that were *even more biased* (Lord, Lepper, and Preston 1984).

Is the confirmation bias, therefore, an aspect of reasoning that may be effective from a practical point of view but that makes reasoning epistemically defective? Not really. People are quite able to falsify ideas or hypotheses... *when they disagree with them*. When a hypothesis is presented by someone else, participants are much more likely to look for falsifying evidence (Cowley and Byrne 2005). When, for instance, people disagree with the conditional statement to be tested in the Wason selection task, a majority are able to pick the cards that can effectively falsify the statement, thereby successfully solving the task (Dawson, Gilovich, and Regan 2002). Similarly, when people believe that the conclusion of a syllogism is false – if it conflicts with their beliefs, for instance – they look for counterexamples, something they fail to do otherwise (Klauer, Musch, and Naumer 2000).

Even useful biases can have excessive consequences, especially when at work in nonstandard contexts. The ability to "find or make a reason for everything one has a mind to do," to use Benjamin Franklin's apt characterization (Franklin 1799), can lead to a biased assessment of arguments when they are encountered outside of an actual discussion (Cacioppo and Petty 1979; Edwards and Smith 1996; Klaczynski and Lavallee 2005). Sometimes the bias is so strong as to make people change their mind in a direction opposite to that of the argument they are presented with and that has a conclusion opposite to their own views (Lord, Ross, and Lepper 1979; Pomerantz, Chaiken, and Tordesillas 1995; Taber and Lodge 2006). A similar polarization can occur when people are reasoning on their own on some topic: finding only arguments that support their initial intuition, people end up with, if anything, a stronger view (Chaiken and Yates 1985; Sadler and Tesser 1973). The same mechanism leads to overconfidence in the correctness of one's answers: "Surely it must be right, given all the supporting evidence I can think of" (Koriat, Lichtenstein, and Fischhoff 1980). Participants also use reasoning to salvage a belief they hold dear even if it is shown to be erroneous (Guenther and Alicke 2008). Finally, by finding handy excuses and justifications, reasoning can allow us to bypass our own moral intuitions (e.g., Bandura 1990; Valdesolo and DeSteno 2008). With alarming frequency, reasoning on our own leads to a distortion of our beliefs, something one would not predict if the function of reasoning were to guide us toward the truth.

How should reasoning affect decision? According to the standard view, reasoning should help us take better decisions. For the argumentative theory, however, reasoning is more likely to bring us toward decisions that we can justify to others, that is, decisions for which we easily find arguments. The correlation between the ease with which a decision can be justified to an audience and its rationality is at best a weak one. Often, easy justifiability may favor a worse decision. Researchers working within the framework of reason-based choice have demonstrated that participants often choose a particular alternative because it is easy to find reasons for it (Shafir, Simonson, and Tversky 1993).

More often than not, this leads participants toward a choice that does not truly satisfy them. We would argue that the overuse of reasoning in search of justifications helps explain many errors and biases such as the sunk cost fallacy (Arkes and Ayton 1999), the attraction and compromise effects (Simonson 1989), the disjunction effect (Tversky and Shafir 1992), or preference inversion (Hsee et al. 1999) (for a more exhaustive list, see Mercier and Sperber, in press). Participants tend, for instance, to choose a bigger chocolate in the shape of a cockroach over a smaller heart-shaped one because it is easy to justify picking a bigger chocolate and hard to justify the "irrational" feeling of disgust its shape may elicit – and they end up not enjoying at all the roach-shaped chocolate (Hsee 1999).

SOME SOCIAL CONSEQUENCES OF A SOCIAL COMPETENCE

Reasoning, we have argued, is a specialized metarepresentational competence with a primarily social cognitive function. It is both structurally and functionally quite different from intuitive inferential mechanisms that have a primarily individual cognitive function. Collective cognitive performance may be based on the aggregation of individual intuitions or on argumentative interaction, with quite different outcomes. Individual intuitions are not aimed at collective aggregation, and when some aggregation does take place, it is typically through some quite artificial mechanism. Individual opinion on some numerical value may, for instance, be collected, and the mean computed. Provided that individual opinions depart randomly from the true value, the aggregation process turns out to be remarkably efficient (see Hogarth 1978 and, for a recent review, Larrick and Soll 2006).

When people in a group must come to some collective judgment or decision and cannot argue to do so, the group typically converges on the average of the opinions of its members (Allport 1924; Farnsworth and Behner 1931). When people argue, however, the direction the group takes depends on the strength, the number, and the direction of the arguments that are used (Isenberg 1986; Vinokur 1971; Vinokur and Burnstein 1978). When the questions debated are relatively simple – as in many experimental settings – one argument often wins and determines the decision of the group (see, e.g., McGuire, Kiesler, and Siegel 1987). The efficiency of reasoning is evidenced by the fact that when a demonstrably correct answer is defended within the group, the arguments that support this answer tend to be accepted (Bonner et al. 2002; Laughlin and Ellis 1986; Moshman and Geil 1998).

When argumentation and hence reasoning are at work, they shape the outcomes of group processes. In many cases, this is for the best – more information is shared, superior arguments are granted more weight. Sometimes, however, reasoning creates a *polarization* of the group (Sunstein 2002). This happens mostly when people are forced to debate an issue on which they already agree. In this case, group members submit different arguments all supporting the same position. Other group members, agreeing with the conclusions of these arguments, do not examine them thoroughly. People thus end up with even more reasons to hold their initial view or with reasons to hold an even stronger view of the same tenor. Various disasters – most famously, the Bay of Pigs (Janis 1982) – have been blamed on this kind of process. It is important to note that, in these cases, reasoning is *not* used in its normal context. There may be a discussion, but it is a forced one: people do not spontaneously argue when they agree. These results are nonetheless relevant because such situations are quite common in a modern environment. Often, groups – committees or courts, for instance – charged with making a decision have to justify it, and therefore to produce arguments. When they agree on the decision in the first place, this may result in overbiased arguments.

The phenomenon of group polarization helps explain another cognitively and socially relevant feature of reasoning: its potential creativity. Intuitive mechanisms for aggregating information never lead to an answer that is outside the range of the initial answers. Reasoning often does. In many cases, this will lead a group to an answer that is better than any of those that were initially entertained (Blinder and Morgan 2000; Glachan and Light 1982; Laughlin et al. 2006; Michaelsen, Watson, and Black 1989; M. K. Smith et al. 2009; Sniezek and Henry 1989). In other cases, however, this may lead to an answer worse than any of the initial ones. In the right institutional environment, however, such excesses can themselves be turned to good. Consider, for instance, different scientific groups (labs or schools of thought), each following with utter conviction a different idea. Each group is likely to suffer from a form of polarization. When, however, there is a process of selection going on at a higher level – when, for instance, the ideas coming from these different groups are evaluated and tested by a larger community – the polarization may have allowed for a much broader exploration of the space of ideas. Many will have been wrong, but hopefully some may have been even "more right than they thought," and polarization will have allowed them to dig into new and otherwise unreachable territory.

It is common to think of science as epitomizing the power and creativity of human reasoning. Of course, it is well understood that science is a collective enterprise, but still, individual scientists are seen as contributing to it through the exercise of a faculty aimed at individually seeking the truth. Seeing reasoning as primarily a social competence aimed at persuading and at being persuaded only by good reasons suggests another way of articulating reason and science and, more generally, the cognitive and the social.

A proper understanding of group performance – of "collective wisdom," for instance – requires attending equally to cognitive and to social mechanisms.

References

Allport, F. (1924). *Social Psychology*. Boston: Houghton Mifflin.

Arkes, H. R., and Ayton, P. (1999). The sunk cost and Concorde effects: Are humans less rational than lower animals? *Psychological Bulletin, 125*(5), 591–600.

Axelrod, R. (1984). *The Evolution of Co-operation.* New York: Basic Books.

Bailenson, J. N., and Rips, L. J. (1996). Informal reasoning and burden of proof. *Applied Cognitive Psychology, 10*(7), 3–16.

Bandura, A. (1990). Selective activation and disengagement of moral control. *Journal of Social Issues, 46*(1), 27–46.

Barrouillet, P., Grosset, N., and Lecas, J. F. (2000). Conditional reasoning by mental models: Chronometric and developmental evidence. *Cognition, 75*(3), 237–66.

Baum, L. A., Danovitch, J. H., and Keil, F. C. (2007). Children's sensitivity to circular explanations. *Journal of Experimental Child Psychology, 100*(2), 146–55.

Berry, D. C., and Dienes, Z. (1993). *Implicit Learning.* Hillsdale, NJ: Lawrence Erlbaum.

Billig, M. (1996). *Arguing and Thinking: A Rhetorical Approach to Social Psychology.* Cambridge: Cambridge University Press.

Blais, M. J. (1987). Epistemic tit for tat. *Journal of Philosophy, 84*(7), 363–75.

Blanchette, I., and Dunbar, K. (2000). How analogies are generated: The roles of structural and superficial similarity. *Memory & Cognition, 28*(1), 108–24.

(2001). Analogy use in naturalistic settings: The influence of audience, emotion, and goals. *Memory & Cognition, 29*(5), 730–35.

Blinder, A. S., and Morgan, J. (2000). Are two heads better than one? An experimental analysis of group vs. individual decision making. NBER Working Paper.

Bodenhausen, G. V., Macrae, C. N., and Sherman, J. W. (1999). On the dialectics of discrimination: Dual processes in social stereotyping. In S. Chaiken and Y. Trope (eds.), *Dual-Process Theories in Social Psychology* (pp. 271–91). New York: Guilford Press.

Bonner, B. L., Baumann, M. R., and Dalal, R. S. (2002). The effects of member expertise on group decision making and performance. *Organizational Behavior and Human Decision Processes, 88,* 719–36.

Cacioppo, J. T., and Petty, R. E. (1979). Effects of message repetition and position on cognitive response, recall, and persuasion. *Journal of Personality and Social Psychology, 37*(1), 97–109.

Camerer, C., and Hogarth, R. M. (1999). The effect of financial incentives on performance in experiments: A review and capital–labor theory. *Journal of Risk and Uncertainty, 19,* 7–42.

Carruthers, P. (2009). An architecture for dual reasoning. In J. S. B. T. Evans and K. Frankish (eds.), *In Two Minds* (pp. 109–28). New York: Oxford University Press.

Chaiken, S., Liberman, A., and Eagly, A. H. (1989). Heuristic and systematic processing within and beyond the persuasion context. In J. S. Uleman and J. A. Bargh (eds.), *Unintended Thought* (pp. 212–52). New York: Guilford Press.

Chaiken, S., and Yates, S. (1985). Affective–cognitive consistency and thought-induced attitude polarization. *Journal of Personality and Social Psychology, 49*(6), 1470–81.

Cheng, P. W., and Holyoak, K. J. (1985). Pragmatic reasoning schemas. *Cognitive Psychology, 17,* 391–416.

Cowley, M., and Byrne, R. M. J. (2005). When falsification is the only path to truth. Paper presented at the Twenty-Seventh Annual Conference of the Cognitive Science Society, Stresa, Italy.

Dawson, E., Gilovich, T., and Regan, D. T. (2002). Motivated reasoning and performance on the Wason selection task. *Personality and Social Psychology Bulletin, 28*(10), 1379.

Dennett, D. C. (1991). *Consciousness Explained*. Boston: Little, Brown.

De Sousa, R. B. (1971). How to give a piece of your mind: Or, the logic of assent and belief. *Review of Metaphysics, 25*, 52–79.

Dessalles, J.-L. (2007). *Why We Talk: The Evolutionary Origins of Language*. Oxford: Oxford University Press.

Dijksterhuis, A. (2004). Think different: The merits of unconscious thought in preference development and decision making. *Journal of Personality and Social Psychology, 87*(5), 586–98.

Dijksterhuis, A., Bos, M. W., Nordgren, L. F., and van Baaren, R. B. (2006). On making the right choice: The deliberation-without-attention effect. *Science, 311*(5763), 1005–1007.

Edwards, K., and Smith, E. E. (1996). A disconfirmation bias in the evaluation of arguments. *Journal of Personality and Social Psychology, 71*, 5–24.

Evans, J. S. B. T. (1996). Deciding before you think: Relevance and reasoning in the selection task. *British Journal of Psychology, 87*, 223–40.

(2002). Logic and human reasoning: An assessment of the deduction paradigm. *Psychological Bulletin, 128*(6), 978–96.

(2003). In two minds: Dual-process accounts of reasoning. *Trends in Cognitive Sciences, 7*(10), 454–59.

(2008). Dual-processing accounts of reasoning, judgment and social cognition. *Annual Review of Psychology, 59*, 255–78.

Evans, J. S. B. T., Handley, S. J., Harper, C. N. J., and Johnson-Laird, P. N. (1999). Reasoning about necessity and possibility: A test of the mental model theory of deduction. *Journal of Experimental Psychology: Learning, Memory, and Cognition, 25*(6), 1495–1513.

Evans, J. S. B. T., Newstead, S. E., and Byrne, R. M. J. (1993). *Human Reasoning: The Psychology of Deduction*. Hillsdale, NJ: Lawrence Erlbaum.

Evans, J. S. B. T., and Over, D. E. (1996). *Rationality and Reasoning*. Hove: Psychology Press.

Farnsworth, P. R., and Behner, A. (1931). A note on the attitude of social conformity. *Journal of Social Psychology, 2*, 126–28.

Franklin, B. (1799). *The Autobiography of Benjamin Franklin*.

Frederick, S. (2005). Cognitive reflection and decision making. *Journal of Economic Perspectives, 19*(4), 25–42.

Glachan, M., and Light, P. (1982). Peer interaction and learning: Can two wrongs make a right? In G. Butterworth and P. Light (eds.), *Social Cognition: Studies in the Development of Understanding* (pp. 238–62). Chicago: University of Chicago Press.

Guenther, C. L., and Alicke, M. D. (2008). Self-enhancement and belief perseverance. *Journal of Experimental Social Psychology, 44*(3), 706–12.

Hahn, U., and Oaksford, M. (2007). The rationality of informal argumentation: A Bayesian approach to reasoning fallacies. *Psychological Review, 114*(3), 704–32.

Haidt, J. (2001). The emotional dog and its rational tail: A social intuitionist approach to moral judgment. *Psychological Review, 108*(4), 814–34.

Harris, P. L. (2007). *Trust. Developmental Science, 10*, 135–38.

Hogarth, R. M. (1978). A note on aggregating opinions. *Organizational Behavior and Human Performance, 21*, 40–46.

Hsee, C. K. (1999). Value seeking and prediction–decision inconsistency: Why don't people take what they predict they'll like the most? *Psychonomic Bulletin and Review, 6*(4), 555–61.

Hsee, C. K., Loewenstein, G. F., Blount, S., and Bazerman, M. H. (1999). Preference reversals between joint and separate evaluations of options: A review and theoretical analysis. *Psychological Bulletin, 125*(5), 576–90.

Isenberg, D. J. (1986). Group polarization: A critical review and meta-analysis. *Journal of Personality and Social Psychology, 50*(6), 1141–51.

Janis, I. L. (1982). *Groupthink* (2d ed.). Boston: Houghton Mifflin.

Johnson-Laird, P. N. (1983). *Mental Models.* Cambridge: Cambridge University Press.

Jones, M., and Sugden, R. (2001). Positive confirmation bias in the acquisition of information. *Theory and Decision, 50*(1), 59–99.

Kahneman, D. (2003). A perspective on judgment and choice: Mapping bounded rationality. *American Psychologist, 58*(9), 697–720.

Kahneman, D., and Frederick, S. (2002). Representativeness revisited: Attribute substitution in intuitive judgement. In T. Gilovich, D. Griffin, and D. Kahneman (eds.), *Heuristics and Biases: The Psychology of Intuitive Judgment* (pp. 49–81). Cambridge: Cambridge University Press.

Klaczynski, P. A., and Lavallee, K. L. (2005). Domain-specific identity, epistemic regulation, and intellectual ability as predictors of belief-based reasoning: A dual-process perspective. *Journal of Experimental Child Psychology, 92,* 1–24.

Klauer, K. C., Musch, J., and Naumer, B. (2000). On belief bias in syllogistic reasoning. *Psychology Review, 107*(4), 852–84.

Koriat, A., Lichtenstein, S., and Fischhoff, B. (1980). Reasons for confidence. *Journal of Experimental Psychology: Human Learning and Memory and Cognition, 6,* 107–18.

Kuhn, D., Weinstock, M., and Flaton, R. (1994). How well do jurors reason? Competence dimensions of individual variation in a juror reasoning task. *Psychological Science, 5,* 289–96.

Larrick, R. P., and Soll, J. B. (2006). Intuitions about combining opinions : Misappreciation of the averaging principle. *Management Science, 52,* 111–27.

Laughlin, P. R., and Ellis, A. L. (1986). Demonstrability and social combination processes on mathematical intellective tasks. *Journal of Experimental Social Psychology, 22,* 177–89.

Laughlin, P. R., Hatch, E. C., Silver, J. S., and Boh, L. (2006). Groups perform better than the best individuals on letters-to-numbers problems: Effects of group size. *Journal of Personality and Social Psychology, 90,* 644–51.

Lord, C. G., Lepper, M. R., and Preston, E. (1984). Considering the opposite: A corrective strategy for social judgment. *Journal of Personality and Social Psychology, 47,* 1231–43.

Lord, C. G., Ross, L., and Lepper, M. R. (1979). Biased assimilation and attitude polarization: The effects of prior theories on subsequently considered evidence. *Journal of Personality and Social Psychology, 37*(11), 2098–2109.

Marr, D. (1982). *Vision: A Computational Investigation into the Human Representation and Processing of Visual Information.* San Francisco: Freeman.

Mascaro, O., and Sperber, D. (2009). The moral, epistemic, and mindreading components of children's vigilance towards deception. *Cognition, 112,* 367–80.

McGuire, T. W., Kiesler, S., and Siegel, J. (1987). Group and computer-mediated discussion effects in risk decision making. *Journal of Personality and Social Psychology, 52*(5), 917–30.

Mercier, H., and Sperber, D. (2009). Intuitive and reflective inferences. In J. S. B. T. Evans and K. Frankish (eds.), *In Two Minds* (pp. 149–70). New York: Oxford University Press.

(2011). Why do humans reason? Arguments for an argumentative theory. *Behavioral and Brain Sciences*, 34(2), 57–74.

Michaelsen, L. K., Watson, W. E., and Black, R. H. (1989). A realistic test of individual versus group consensus decision making. *Journal of Applied Psychology*, 74(5), 834–39.

Moshman, D., and Geil, M. (1998). Collaborative reasoning: Evidence for collective rationality. *Thinking and Reasoning*, 4(3), 231–48.

Neuman, Y., Weinstock, M. P., and Glasner, A. (2006). The effect of contextual factors on the judgement of informal reasoning fallacies. *Quarterly Journal of Experimental Psychology*, 59(2), 411–25.

Newstead, S. E., Handley, S. J., and Buck, E. (1999). Falsifying mental models: Testing the predictions of theories of syllogistic reasoning. *Memory and Cognition*, 27(2), 344–54.

Nickerson, R. S. (1998). Confirmation bias: A ubiquitous phenomena in many guises. *Review of General Psychology*, 2, 175–220.

Pennington, N., and Hastie, R. (1993). Reasoning in explanation-based decision-making. *Cognition*, 49, 123–63.

Perelman, C. (1949). Philosophies premieres et philosophie regressive. *Dialectica*, 11, 175–91.

Perelman, C., and Olbrechts-Tyteca, L. (1969). *The New Rhetoric: A Treatise on Argumentation*. Notre Dame, IN: University of Notre Dame Press.

Petty, R. E., and Cacioppo, J. T. (1986). The elaboration likelihood model of persuasion. In L. Berkowitz (ed.), *Advances in Experimental Social Psychology* (vol. 19, pp. 123–205). Orlando, FL: Academic Press.

Petty, R. E., and Wegener, D. T. (1998). Attitude change: Multiple roles for persuasion variables. In D. Gilbert, S. Fiske, and G. Lindzey (eds.), *The Handbook of Social Psychology* (vol. 1, pp. 323–90). Boston: McGraw-Hill.

Poletiek, F. H. (1996). Paradoxes of falsification. *Quarterly Journal of Experimental Psychology*, 49A, 447–62.

Pomerantz, E. M., Chaiken, S., and Tordesillas, R. S. (1995). Attitude strength and resistance processes. *Journal of Personality and Social Psychology*, 69(3), 408–19.

Posner, M. I., and Snyder, C. R. R. (1975). Attention and cognitive control. In R. L. Solso (ed.), *Information Processing and Cognition: The Loyola Symposium* (pp. 55–85). Hillsdale, NJ: Lawrence Erlbaum.

Reber, A. S. (1993). *Implicit Learning and Tacit Knowledge*. New York: Oxford University Press.

Resnick, L. B., Salmon, M., Zeitz, C. M., Wathen, S. H., and Holowchak, M. (1993). Reasoning in conversation. *Cognition and Instruction*, 11(3/4), 347–64.

Ricco, R. B. (2003). The macrostructure of informal arguments: A proposed model and analysis. *Quarterly Journal of Experimental Psychology A*, 56(6), 1021–51.

Rimer, S. (2009, January 13). A new formula for teaching introductory physics. *International Herald Tribune*.

Rips, L. J. (1994). *The Psychology of Proof: Deductive Reasoning in Human Thinking*. Cambridge, MA: MIT Press.

(1998). Reasoning and conversation. *Psychological Review*, 105, 411–41.

(2002). Circular reasoning. *Cognitive Science*, 26, 767–95.

Sadler, O., and Tesser, A. (1973). Some effects of salience and time upon interpersonal hostility and attraction during social isolation. *Sociometry*, 36(1), 99–112.

Schacter, D. L. (1987). Implicit memory: History and current status. *Journal of Experimental Psychology. Learning, Memory, and Cognition*, 13(3), 501–18.

Schulz-Hardt, S., Brodbeck, F. C., Mojzisch, A., Kerschreiter, R., and Frey, D. (2006). Group decision making in hidden profile situations: Dissent as a facilitator for decision quality. *Journal of Personality and Social Psychology, 91*(6), 1080–93.

Shafir, E., Simonson, I., and Tversky, A. (1993). Reason-based choice. *Cognition, 49*(1/2), 11–36.

Shaw, V. F. (1996). The cognitive processes in informal reasoning. *Thinking & Reasoning, 2*(1), 51–80.

Simonson, I. (1989). Choice based on reasons: The case of attraction and compromise effects. *Journal of Consumer Research, 16*(2), 158–74.

Slavin, R. E. (1995). *Cooperative Learning: Theory, Research, and Practice*. London: Allyn & Bacon.

Sloman, S. A. (1996). The empirical case for two systems of reasoning. *Psychological Bulletin, 119*(1), 3–22.

Smith, M. K., Wood, W. B., Adams, W. K., Wieman, C., Knight, J. K., Guild, N., et al. (2009). Why peer discussion improves student performance on in-class concept questions. *Science, 323*(5910), 122.

Smith, S. M., Fabrigar, L. R., and Norris, M. E. (2008). Reflecting on six decades of selective exposure research: Progress, challenges, and opportunities. *Social and Personality Psychology Compass, 2*(1), 464–93.

Sniezek, J. A., and Henry, R. A. (1989). Accuracy and confidence in group judgment. *Organizational Behavior and Human Decision Processes, 43*(1), 1–28.

Soon, C. S., Brass, M., Heinze, H. J., and Haynes, J. D. (2008). Unconscious determinants of free decisions in the human brain. *Nature Neuroscience, 11*, 543–45.

Sperber, D. (2001). In defense of massive modularity. In E. Dupoux (ed.), *Language, Brain and Cognitive Development: Essays in Honor of Jacques Mehler* (pp. 47–57). Cambridge, MA: MIT Press.

   (2005). Modularity and relevance: How can a massively modular mind be flexible and context-sensitive? In P. Carruthers, S. Laurence, and S. Stich (eds.), *The Innate Mind: Structure and Contents* (pp. 53–58). New York: Oxford University Press.

   (2006). Why a deep understanding of cultural evolution is incompatible with shallow psychology. In N. J. Enfield and S. Levinson (eds.), *Roots of Human Sociality* (pp. 441–49). Oxford: Berg.

Sperber, D., Cara, F., and Girotto, V. (1995). Relevance theory explains the selection task. *Cognition, 57*, 31–95.

Sperber, D., Clément, F., Heintz, C., Mascaro, O., Mercier, H., Origgi, G., and Wilson, D. (2010). Epistemic vigilance. *Mind & Language, 25*(4), 359–93.

Sperber, D., and Wilson, D. (1995). *Relevance: Communication and Cognition*. Oxford: Blackwell.

Stanovich, K. E. (2004). *The Robot's Rebellion*. Chicago: Chicago University Press.

Stein, N. L., and Albro, E. R. (2001). The origins and nature of arguments: Studies in conflict understanding, emotion, and negotiation. *Discourse Processes, 32*(2/3), 113–33.

Stein, N. L., and Bernas, R. (1999). The early emergence of argumentative knowledge and skill. In J. Andriessen and P. Coirier (eds.), *Foundations of Argumentative Text Processing* (pp. 97–116). Amsterdam: Amsterdam University Press.

Stein, N. L., and Miller, C. A. (1993). The development of meaning and reasoning skill in argumentative contexts: Evaluating, explaining, and generating evidence. In R. Glaser (ed.), *Advances in Instructional Psychology* (vol. 4, pp. 285–335). Hillsdale, NJ: Lawrence Erlbaum.

Sterelny, K. (2003). *Thought in a Hostile World*. Oxford: Blackwell.

(in press). *The Fate of the Third Chimpanzee*. Cambridge, MA: MIT Press.

Sunstein, C. R. (2002). The law of group polarization. *Journal of Political Philosophy*, 10(2), 175–95.

Taber, C. S., and Lodge, M. (2006). Motivated skepticism in the evaluation of political beliefs. *American Journal of Political Science*, 50(3), 755–69.

Thagard, P. (2005). Testimony, credibility, and explanatory coherence. *Erkenntnis*, 63, 295–316.

Todorov, A., Mandisodza, A. N., Goren, A., and Hall, C. C. (2005). Inferences of competence from faces predict election outcomes. *Science*, 308, 1623–26.

Toulmin, S. (1958). *The Uses of Argument*. Cambridge: Cambridge University Press.

Tversky, A., and Shafir, E. (1992). The disjunction effect in choice under uncertainty. *Psychological Science*, 3(5), 305–309.

Tweney, R. D., Doherty, M. E., Worner, W. J., Pliske, D. B., Mynatt, C. R., Gross, K. A., et al. (1980). Strategies of rule discovery in an inference task. *Quarterly Journal of Experimental Psychology*, 32(1), 109–23.

Uleman, J. (1999). Spontaneous versus intentional inferences in impression formation. In S. Chaiken and Y. Trope (eds.), *Dual-Process Theories in Social Psychology*. New York: Guilford Press.

Valdesolo, P., and DeSteno, D. (2008). The duality of virtue: Deconstructing the moral hypocrite. *Journal of Experimental Social Psychology*, 44(5), 1334–38.

Van der Henst, J.-B. (2006). Relevance effects in reasoning. *Mind & Society*, 5(2), 229–45.

Van der Henst, J.-B., Sperber, D., and Politzer, G. (2002). When is a conclusion worth deriving? A relevance-based analysis of indeterminate relational problems. *Thinking and Reasoning*, 8, 1–20.

Vinokur, A. (1971). Review and theoretical analysis of the effects of group processes upon individual and group decisions involving risk. *Psychological Bulletin*, 76(4), 231–50.

Vinokur, A., and Burnstein, E. (1978). Depolarization of attitudes in groups. *Journal of Personality and Social Psychology*, 36(8), 872–85.

Wason, P. C. (1966). Reasoning. In B. M. Foss (ed.), *New Horizons in Psychology* (vol. 1, pp. 106–37). Harmondsworth: Penguin.

Wilson, T. D., Dunn, D. S., Kraft, D., and Lisle, D. J. (1989). Introspection, attitude change, and attitude–behavior consistency: The disruptive effects of explaining why we feel the way we do. In L. Berkowitz (ed.), *Advances in Experimental Social Psychology* (vol. 19, pp. 123–205). Orlando, FL: Academic Press.

Wilson, T. D., Lindsey, S., and Schooler, T. Y. (2000). A model of dual attitudes. *Psychological Review*, 107(1), 101–26.

Conclusion

Jon Elster

The contributions to this volume draw on philosophy, economics, political science, legal theory, history, and evolutionary psychology. It is, indeed, a diverse collection. Since the value of diversity is a recurring theme in many of the chapters, the editors hope, of course, that the volume illustrates the idea that the whole is more than the sum of its parts. At the same time, the diversity makes it impossible to summarize and synthesize the arguments and claims put forward in the various chapters. Instead, I shall simply make some interrelated comments on some of the recurrent themes. As the chapters speak very well for themselves, I will not try to summarize them or deal with them in anything like a representative manner.

The general proposition defended – or questioned – throughout the volume is the idea that under suitable conditions *many heads are better than one*. To illustrate the controversy, we may look at two different evaluations of Athenian democracy. In his eulogy of Athens, Pericles is reported to have said:

Our public men have, besides politics, their private affairs to attend to, and our ordinary citizens, though occupied with the pursuits of industry, are still fair judges of public matters; for, unlike any other nation, we regard the citizen who takes no part in these duties not as unambitious but as useless, and we are able to judge proposals even if we cannot originate them; instead of looking on discussion as a stumbling-block in the way of action, we think it an indispensable preliminary to any wise action at all. (Thucydides, II.40)

Although I have already cited Madison's comment on the Athenian assembly in Chapter 7, I reproduce it here for the reader's convenience:

Sixty or seventy men may be more properly trusted with a given degree of power than six or seven. But it does not follow that six or seven hundred would be proportionally a better depositary. And if we carry on the supposition to six or seven thousand, the whole reasoning ought to be reversed. The truth is that in all cases a certain number at least seems to be necessary to secure the benefits of free consultation and discussion, and to guard against too easy a combination for improper purposes; as, on the other hand, the number ought at most to be kept within a certain limit, in order to avoid the confusion and intemperance of a multitude. In all very numerous assemblies, of whatever character composed, passion never fails to wrest the sceptre from reason. Had every Athenian citizen been a Socrates, every Athenian assembly would still have been a mob. (*Federalist 55*)

Joshua Ober, in Chapter 6, seems to side with Pericles. It is worth noting, though, that his view may not be that different from Madison's. Ober emphasizes the crucial role of the Council of 500 in generating the epistemic virtues of Athenian democracy. Following Pericles, we may distinguish between the ability of a collective body to originate proposals and the ability to judge them (see also the more extensive discussion later in the present chapter). Even if the six thousand citizens that made up a typical Athenian assembly were too numerous to debate among themselves, the sheer force of their number might still impart wisdom to their choice among the proposals offered to them. This is indeed a central issue in this volume, where many contributors discuss Condorcet's Jury Theorem and its relevance to collective wisdom. In our contributions, David Estlund and I also discuss some other factors that may shape the optimal size of decision-making bodies. I say more about this question shortly.

The idea of collective wisdom is not limited to assembly decision making. In this volume, the contributors examine numerous other institutions from this perspective, including elections, prediction markets, the World Wide Web, courts, and expert committees. Before I discuss and elaborate on some of their arguments, some comments on the idea of wisdom might be useful. In Chapter 4, which focuses on this issue, Daniel Andler distinguishes among intelligence, rationality, and wisdom as (somewhat) independent attributes of individuals as well as of groups. In addition, perhaps controversially, he includes creativity as a component of intelligence.

For most of the contributors, wisdom means ability to track the truth. Any process whereby a numerous body is more likely, ceteris paribus, to make true statements or correct predictions than a smaller body (or an individual) exemplifies collective wisdom in this epistemic sense. This idea is, of course, consistent with the proposition that an even larger body would be *less* likely to reach the truth. I shall return to that issue.

One might want, however, to extend the idea of wisdom beyond that of tracking the truth. First, wisdom may be seen as creativity or *problem solving*, "thinking outside the box." In some cases this process involves finding the right answer to an epistemic problem, an instance being the Wason selection task discussed by Sperber and Mercier in Chapter 15. As they show, groups do much better than individuals on this task. In other cases, however, it is a question of finding a good solution to a practical problem. A tool designed for one task may be used for another, as when, lacking a hammer, one uses a wrench to drive in a nail. A group of individuals is more likely than a single person to develop this idea, assuming that it will occur to each of them with the same probability. This mechanism, although important, does not involve the *interaction* that we intuitively associate with collective wisdom. Nor would it make sense to talk about collective wisdom when the task requires widely different capacities that no single individual could possess, as in the Manhattan Project. A better example might be the Internet-mediated task of reaching a target individual in a foreign country by passing the message to a social acquaintance who is considered "closer" than oneself to the target (Dodds, Muhamad, and Watts 2003). Origgi, in Chapter 2, touches on similar mechanisms.

Next, one might want to extend the idea of wisdom to cover *normative rightness*. At the level of an individual, this includes the ability to make decisions that make her life as a whole go better. The ability to defer gratification is a case in point. Similarly, the ability to "bracket" risky decisions rather than face them one at a time can enhance welfare (Read, Loewenstein, and Rabin 1999). A collective, too, will be better off over time if it is able to make investments that require a temporary sacrifice ("one step backward, two steps forward") and to avoid the "Dutch disease" by saving a large fraction of boom revenues. Similarly, it will be better off if it is able to respond to expected risk in a rule-based way ("you win some, you lose some") rather than on a case-by-case basis. To my knowledge, little is known about the mechanisms that might make societies wiser, in these respects, than the individuals who make them up.

As Adam Smith (1759/1976: 189) noted, the ability to defer gratification is a form of *impartiality over time*. For the impartial spectator, "the pleasure which we are to enjoy a week hence, or a year hence, is just as interesting as that which we are to enjoy this moment." The demand for normative rightness might also be taken to include the idea of *impartiality across persons*. In Chapter 7, I suggest that wisdom might be a matter of (doubly!) impartial motivations conjoined with epistemic rationality. Vermeule, in Chapter 14, demurs, on the grounds that this conception is too moralized. Although in matters of definition nobody is right or wrong, I might reply that his example of the wise gang leader might be understood as wisdom in the impartial service of all gang members. In practice, the norm of impartiality is in fact usually defined with reference to some proper subgroup of humanity as a whole.

The epistemic understanding of wisdom is no doubt more robust and less controversial than normative interpretations. Yet in thinking about political institutions, I believe it would be a mistake to ignore the need to foster or reflect a concern for the general interest. A small elite may be superior on epistemic grounds but inferior on normative grounds. In his comparative analyses of aristocracy and democracy, Tocqueville (2004: 284) first observes that "the moral ascendancy of the majority rests in part on the idea that there is more enlightenment and wisdom in assembly of many than in the mind of one, or that the number of legislators matters more than the manner of their selection." In this passage, he neither endorses nor refutes the idea of the "wisdom of crowds." His insistence elsewhere on the value of two-stage elections and on the superiority of the Senate over the more numerous House of Representatives suggests, however, that in his view the manner of selection *was* important and that the few *could* be wiser than the many. The wisdom of the many is part of the ideology of democracy, not of its reality. As he also states (263), "an aristocratic body is too numerous to be ensnared yet not numerous enough to yield to the intoxication of mindless passion.... Democracy's resources are therefore more imperfect than those of aristocracy."

When Tocqueville goes on to observe that "the moral ascendancy of the majority also rests on the principle that the interests of the greater number ought to be preferred to those of the few" (285), it is an idea that he unambiguously *does* endorse. In general, "the aim of legislation in a democracy is more useful (*utile*) to humanity than that of legislation in an aristocracy" (265). As an objection to the aristocratic mode of government, he cites the fact that "society is often sacrificed to the individual and the prosperity of the greater number to the grandeur of a few" (823). The class interest of aristocratic leaders will encourage them "to work together to achieve a result that is not necessarily the happiness of the greater number" (267). By contrast, democracies will tend to promote the general interest because the majority of citizens "may be mistaken but cannot be in conflict with themselves" (265). Although democratic officials "may often betray their trust and commit grave errors, they will never *systematically* adopt a line hostile to the majority" (267; my emphasis). No group or class can expect a cumulative and sustained advantage from the workings of democracy in the way elites in aristocratic societies can.

Tocqueville believed that, on the whole, the normative wisdom of democracy outweighed its lack of epistemic wisdom. He did not ask, as James Harington had done before him, whether one might, by proper institutional design, combine the virtues of both systems. In a famous "divide-and-choose" argument for bicameralism, Harrington (1656/1992: 173) argued for a strict division of political labor between the few and the many. The senate would have to "divide," that is, to debate and propose.

The senate then having divided, who shall choose? [There is no remedy] but to have another council to choose. The wisdom of the few may be the light of mankind; but the interest of the few is not the profit of mankind nor of a commonwealth. Wherefore . . . they must not choose lest it put out their light. But as the council dividing consists of the wisdom of the commonwealth, so the assembly or council choosing should consist of the interest of the commonwealth: as the wisdom of the commonwealth is in the aristocracy, so the interest of the commonwealth is in the whole body of the people. And whereas this, in case the commonwealth consist of a whole nation, is too unwieldy a body to be assembled, this council is to consist of such a representative as may be equal, and so constituted, as can never contract any other interest than that of the whole people.

Harrington (1656/1992: 177) also offered historical examples meant to show the need to keep the two functions – *debating and then proposing* versus *deciding without debating* – strictly separate. In his opinion, Athens was ruined by the fact that the Assembly took it upon itself to debate the proposals put to it by the Council of 500. By contrast, the long life of Sparta was due to the fact of the people "resolving only, and never debating." (Levy (2003: 210–16) argues, however, that the people's assembly was probably allowed to *debate* the proposals but not to *modify* them.) To these examples, we may add that of the large Athenian juries, whose members were also, according to Aristotle (*Politics* 1268 b), discouraged from communicating among themselves and from modifying the sentences proposed by the one or the other side.

One may perhaps, by a stretch of the imagination, consider the ban on debates as anticipating the independence condition of Condorcet's Jury Theorem. Although through discussion "one learn facts that one ignored and is made aware of objections one had not foreseen, . . . one is also seduced and worked up by the voice of an orator, led into error by clever sophistry without having the time to subject to the empire of those sudden movements which excite the assembly" (Condorcet 1789/1847: 344). Condorcet goes on to claim that unless there is a need to inform oneself concerning recent events, "it would be easy to prove that spoken discussion harms the truth more than serving it, and that the preference [*voeu*] of the majority would more often conform to the truth if one deduced it, without discussion, from votes given separately." In fact, he adds, the same result could be obtained if the vote took place after a "written discussion, which would perhaps be less impractical, long and costly than usually believed."

In Chapters 4 and 14, respectively, Andler and Vermeule discuss *tradition*, *precedent*, and *culture* as possible repositories of collective wisdom. To their observations I would add the idea that *proverbs*, "the wisdom of the ages," can be seen from this perspective. Many proverbs and maxims encapsulate robust insights with the quality of "ex post obviousness" that might be used as a defining property of wisdom. Let me cite a few:

The best swimmers drown.
Honesty is the best policy, but he who is governed by that maxim is not an honest man.
Love is blind and believes itself to be invisible.
Each believes easily what he fears and what he hopes.
Who loves himself has no rivals.
Whoever has offended never forgives.
A small loan makes a friend, a big one an enemy.
Blackening others doesn't make you white.
The great and the rich have everything, except someone to tell them the truth.
Many guards make a poor watch.
The more cooks, the more salty the broth.
The more cooks, the thinner the soup.
Too many masters govern badly.
One man's dog lives, two men's dog dies.
What's everybody's business is nobody's business.
Two heads are better than one.

The last seven proverbs are *about* collective wisdom, all but the very last in a somewhat dismal tenor. Several suggest that increasing the number of agents dilutes attention or responsibility. If there had been only a few people watching Kitty Genovese being beaten to death, rather than thirty-eight, there might have been a better chance that one of them would have called the police. The idea harks back to Aristotle's criticism of Plato's ideal of communal property: "That which is common to the greatest number has the least care bestowed upon it" (*Politics* 1261 b). Two of the proverbs suggest that multiple principals might have bad effects due to a lack of coordination, and one that they might eat of the public trough so that less is left for distribution. Whereas these sayings point to causal mechanisms, the sole positive affirmation does not.

One might question, however, the *wisdom* of proverbs on several grounds. First, some proverbs are simply false. In Chapter 15, Sperber and Mercier point to the costs of "systematically disbelieving communicators who have been deceitful about one topic." Many proverbs, nevertheless, enjoin us to do precisely this, because "Who tells one lie, will tell a hundred." Second, proverbs often form *contradictories*. "Rumors often lie" may be contrasted with "Rumors seldom lie." There are many pairs like this, and they are obviously useless. Third, proverbs often form *contraries*. "Out of sight, out of mind" may be contrasted with "Absence makes the heart grow fonder." As I have argued elsewhere (Elster 1999: ch. 1), pairs like these can be deeply illuminating. Pascal's statement "The opposite of a truth is the opposite truth" has, in fact, achieved quasi-proverbial status. (In Niels Bohr's version: "The opposite of a profound truth is another profound truth.") Hence, we may take the idea of wisdom in a sense that is broad enough to include contraries. In many situations, the epistemic ideal of a *unique truth* may be too demanding. The collective wisdom embodied in proverbs suggests that we lower our sights.

In terms of often-cited writings on the topic, under what conditions does the "madness of crowds" (Mackay 1841/1980) dominate the "wisdom of crowds" (Surowiecki 2004)? Is it true, as Lord Chesterfield (1774/1992: 225) wrote to his son, that "every numerous assembly is *mob*; let the individuals who compose it be what they will" and that "understanding they have collectively none"? Or could it be the case that "the many, of whom each individual is but an ordinary person, when they meet together may very likely be better than the few good, if regarded not individually but collectively" (Aristotle, *Politics* 1281 a–b)?

Although the question has no general answer, one may be able to suggest some sufficient conditions for the one or the other effect to be more likely to occur. Before I discuss some of them, it may be appropriate to point out that the reference to "crowds" tends to prejudge the question. Although a "crowd" is not necessarily a "mob," in Madison's language, there is a tendency to assume that crowds are governed by their emotions and that interaction among their members is likely to have negative rather than positive consequences. Arguably, the events of 1789 and 1989 show that this assumption is far from always justified. The more important point, however, is that the unstructured crowd is not the generic form of collective behavior. Elections, assemblies, and committees are highly elaborate institutions whose effects – positive or negative – depend heavily on their internal structure. This is the main topic of my own contribution.

Let me first address some of the paradoxes and pathologies of collective decision making. Generally speaking, collective decisions may involve the aggregation of individual preferences, of individual beliefs, or both. Since Condorcet in 1786 pointed out the possibility of cyclical majorities and Arrow generalized his result in 1950, it has been known that preference aggregation may yield an incoherent outcome. Although the empirical importance of the phenomenon has been questioned (Mackie 2004), there is little doubt that it sometimes does occur (see Hylland 2006 for a compelling example). Even when it occurs, however, there is no reason to think that it shows a *lack* of collective wisdom. Folly is a meaningful concept only when that of wisdom is well defined. Although any decision that is eventually taken in the presence of cycling majorities will be an artifact of agenda setting, that fact renders it *arbitrary* rather than unwise.

In the present volume, the paradox of preference aggregation takes second place to the paradox of belief aggregation, first stated by Poisson (1837: 21n.) and rediscovered by Vacca (1921). In its modern form, discussed in Chapters 5, 9, and 14 by Ferejohn, List, and Vermeule, respectively, it is variously called "the doctrinal paradox" (Kornhauser and Sager 1986) or the "discursive dilemma" (Pettit 2001).

Suppose that the members of the relevant body state their beliefs concerning an unconditional statement **p**, a conditional statement 'if p then q,' and the unconditional statement **q**. The paradox arises when a majority believes **p**, another majority believes 'if p then q,' and a third majority believes non-q. Hence, first aggregating premises and then drawing the conclusion from them leads to the acceptance of **q**, whereas a direct vote on **q** leads to its rejection. In a variant of the paradox that involves preferences as well as beliefs, a majority desires that **p**, another majority believes that **q** is the best means to realize **p**, and a third majority rejects **q** in favor of **r**. Again, separate aggregation of desires and beliefs leads to a different recommendation than a direct vote on policy. (In all cases, individual rationality and sincerity is assumed.)

Whereas the paradox of cyclical social preferences arises when there is *no* way of aggregating individual preferences, the doctrinal paradox arises because there are *two* ways of aggregating individual attitudes. In practice, aggregating conclusions in a one-step operation is probably more common than first aggregating premises and then drawing the conclusion from the aggregated premises. In legislatures, it might be very difficult to assemble a majority if one had to include reasons for the decision (Bentham 1999: 121–23). This fact probably explains the resolution adopted by the House of Commons on December 2, 1882, asserting that any vote on the reasons for a piece of legislation had to be taken *after* the vote on the law itself (Pierre 1893: 1007). By contrast, smaller bodies such as courts or central bank committees (Claussen and Røisland 2010) sometimes aggregate premises.

Independently of this factual question, it has been argued that collective wisdom requires the use of the one or the other procedure or, more radically, a reconsideration of the premises to ensure coherence between them. As Vermeule notes in his chapter, advocates of judicial minimalism (Sunstein 1999) might favor aggregation of conclusions. Pettit (2001) argues for aggregation of premises. In his chapter, Ferejohn argues in favor of reconsidering the premises to ensure coherence between the premise-based and the conclusion-based recommendations. In the legislative context, he argues, "[t]he aim is to produce an outcome that is acceptable to a majority and is coherent, and to accomplish this each member is deliberatively disposed to reconsider his own judgments as to the premises and the result, and so each is engaged in a process of reflective equilibrium." (By analogy, one might respond to the problem of cyclical majorities by requiring members to reconsider their preferences so that the decision will appear as rationally grounded in the preferences of the majority rather than as the arbitrary result of agenda setting.) As Ferejohn also notes, however, the reconsideration and hence the public justification could take several forms, and hence some arbitrariness would remain.

The *paradoxes* of aggregation are deep and, in a sense, irresolvable. By contrast, the *pathologies* of collective decision making can in some cases be overcome by skillful institutional design (Vermeule 2007). In Chapter 8, Urfalino notes the dangers of sequential voting. Whether by irrational conformism or by rational herding, those who vote later in the sequence may be unduly influenced by those who cast their vote before them. Urfalino reports that in 2007 the U.S. Federal Drug Administration implemented voting by the raising of hands to reduce this danger. Hand raising is rarely simultaneous, however: it is usually possible to "peek" at the behavior of some influential member before casting one's vote. Following Bentham (1999: ch. XIV) it can be argued that, in assembly voting, the twin dangers of hypocrisy and conformism can be reduced by ensuring that votes are public ex post but unobservable ex ante. If each member, unobserved by others, casts his vote on a ballot and signs it, the secretary making the tally can read out loud who voted how.

Rational herding occurs when each person in a sequence forms a conclusion based on her own private evidence and on the conclusions of those who preceded her in the sequence. As Vermeule emphasizes in his chapter, this process often prevents the aggregation of information because the earlier signals tend to swamp the later. To overcome this problem, one might either let each person remain ignorant about what the others think, as suggested in the preceding paragraph, or let him have access to the private information of his predecessors in the chain. Suppose that your doctor advises you to have surgery. Generally speaking, it is a good idea to seek a second opinion. Because of the problem of rational herding, you should then either not tell the second doctor what the first said, or ask the first to communicate the full medical dossier to the second.

As I note in my chapter, Bentham also identified another potential pathology of collective decision making, namely informational free-riding. Following Condorcet, we might want an assembly to have as many members as possible. Bentham argued, however, that in a large assembly, the incentive of the members to gather additional information would be diluted. To determine the optimal size of the assembly, one would have to take account of both effects. As argued by Vermeule (2007), the problem of informational free-riding can also be attenuated if the members of the assembly precommit themselves by creating a legally enforceable obligation to gather certain kinds of information before legislating. As an example, he cites the Unfunded Mandates Reform Act of 1995, which obligates Congress to determine the obligations that a federal law would impose on states, municipalities, and tribes, and indicate which of them would not be funded by the federal government.

In Chapter 10, Estlund offers a *catalogue raisonné* of factors that favor either expansion or contraction of the assembly, without reaching a definite conclusion about its optimal size. I discuss some of the same factors in my own chapter. Here I want only to add a further consideration, also mentioned in Vermeule's chapter, in favor of contraction. As the size of the assembly increases, the competence of each additional member may go down, thus invalidating one of the assumptions of Condorcet's Jury Theorem. (Condorcet was, of course, aware of this fact.) In this case, the decreasing average competence of individual members is exogenous, due to the distribution of natural talent in the population pool, whereas in the argument from informational free-riding it is an endogenous effect of assembly size.

A further pathology is created by the risk that a representative assembly might turn into a self-perpetuating oligarchy. In Chapter 6, Ober notes that because the Athenian councilors served for only one year, they "never developed a self-serving identity or a corporate culture." The early American states also imposed short tenure on their assemblies, for the same reason. An additional reason, especially important in the case of juries, is that their ephemeral existence makes it difficult to bribe or threaten the members.

At the same time, rapid turnover is an obstacle for learning and professionalism. Tocqueville (2004: 237) asserted that "[i]n America, men remain in power for but an instant before fading back into a crowd which itself changes from day to day, so that the record of society's actions there is often scantier than that of an ordinary family's action." Hence, "[i]t is very difficult for American administrators to learn from one another" (238). In this dimension, too, one could draw up a list of factors favoring contraction and expansion, yet it would probably be as difficult to determine the optimal length of tenure for representatives as to determine their optimal number. Moreover, the two optima would have to be determined simultaneously (in terms of cross-derivatives) rather than separately.

Many of the chapters argue for the value of *diversity* in generating collective wisdom. Although this effect has been known in a general way since Aristotle, the work of Hong and Page (including Chapter 3 in the present volume) offers the first rigorous discussion. To achieve diversity in the decision-making body, one might proceed in several ways. In my chapter, I argue for the superiority of *proportional voting* over majority voting in electing deputies to a constituent assembly. Other bodies have achieved diversity by selecting members *by lot.* The Athenians used this method to choose the members of the Council of 500, jurors, and lawgivers (*nomothetai*). In recent years, it has also been used to choose members of citizens' assemblies in British Columbia (Lang 2007), in modern Greece (Fishkin et al. 2008), and in China (Fishkin et al. 2010). In most of these cases, however, the lottery has been used to *choose among self-selected individuals* – those who came forward as candidates for the lottery or who accepted to serve once chosen by the lottery. To ensure sufficient diversity, one might have to *make participation compulsory* for those chosen by the lottery. In principle, this is the case for jury service in many countries, although the scope for peremptory challenges in jury selection tends to reduce diversity (Sommers 2008). Alternatively, one could *mandate diversity* along certain dimensions. In Norway, the law calls for equal representation of men and women on juries and for at least 40 percent representation of women on corporate boards.

The value of diversity is twofold, as is illustrated by two comments by Alan Blinder on central bank committees. On the one hand, diversity tends to reduce conformism. In the Federal Open Market Committee under Alan Greenspan, conformism was a real obstacle – of which we are currently seeing the results – to collective wisdom. "Real benefits – such as the avoidance of group-think – accrue from bringing fresh, diverse points of view into the committee room" (Blinder 2008). While the avoidance of groupthink is a purely negative virtue, diversity can also have a more positive function. In another article, Blinder (2007: 110) refers to the demonstration by Hong and Page (2004) "that what they call 'diverse' groups can outperform individuals or more homogeneous groups in solving complex problems. Their operational definition of diversity is that the members of the group employ different decision making heuristics." In his argument for appointing nonlawyers to the Supreme Court, Vermeule also relies on the positive value of diversity. As he notes, such appointments have already been made to the French Conseil Constitutionnel.

Mechanisms for collective wisdom may be compared to alchemy – they turn lead (mediocre individual judgment) into gold (good collective judgment). Yet the individual judgments have to be at least mediocre rather than poor. Formally, this requirement is reflected in the competence condition of the Condorcet Jury Theorem. In the present volume, the issue of epistemic voter competence is at the core of the chapters by Caplan, Landemore, and Mackie. Landemore and Mackie (Chapters 11 and 12, respectively) offer critical discussions of the claim made by Caplan (2007) that voters are massively biased, notably in matters pertaining to the economy, to which Caplan offers a spirited response in Chapter 13. Readers will make up their own minds.

I conclude by raising a question concerning the relation between epistemic and normative wisdom. Tocqueville claimed, as we saw, that even unenlightened voters in a democracy had "better" preferences – more responsive to the general interest – than the members of an aristocratic elite. In his view, a Pareto-inefficient outcome more in line with popular views about distributive justice is generally superior to an efficient outcome at odds with those views. Hence, even epistemically incompetent voters might produce collective wisdom.

References

Bentham, J. (1843), "Radical reform bill," in J. Bowring (ed.), *The Works of Jeremy Bentham*, vol. 3, Edinburgh: William Tait.

(1999), *Political Tactics*, Oxford University Press.

Blinder, A. (2007), "Monetary policy by committee," *European Journal of Political Economy* 23: 106–23.

(2008), "Making monetary policy by committee," CEPS Working Paper No. 167.

Caplan, B. (2007), *The Myth of the Rational Voter: Why Democracies Choose Bad Policies*, Princeton, NJ: Princeton University Press.

Chesterfield, Earl of (1774/1792), *Lord Chesterfield's Letters*, Oxford University Press.

Claussen, C., and Røisland, Ø. (2010), "The discursive dilemma in monetary policy," Bank of Norway Working Paper 2010/05.

Condorcet, Marquis de (1789/1847), "Examen sur cette question: Est-il utile de diviser une assemblée nationale en plusieurs chambres?" in Condorcet, *Oeuvres*, vol. 9, Paris: Firmin Didot.

Dodds, P., Muhamad, R., and Watts, D. (2003), "An experimental study of search in global, social networks," *Science* 301: 827–29.

Elster, J. (1999), *Alchemies of the Mind*, Cambridge University Press.

Fishkin, J., et al. (2008), "Returning deliberative democracy to Athens: Deliberative polling for candidate selection," paper presented at the Annual Meeting of the American Political Science Association.

(2010), "Deliberative democracy in an unlikely place: Deliberative polling in China," *British Journal of Political Science* 40: 435–48.

Harrington J. (1656 /1992), *Oceana*, Cambridge University Press.

Hong, L., and Page, S. (2004), "Groups of diverse problem solvers can outperform groups of high-ability problem solvers," Proceedings of the National Academy of Sciences 101 (46), 16385–89.

Hylland, A. (2006), "The Condorcet paradox in theory and practice," in J. Elster et al. (eds.), *Understanding Choice, Explaining Behavior: Essays in Honour of Ole-Jørgen Skog*, Oslo Academic Press.

Kornhauser, L., and Sager, L. (1986), "Unpacking the Court," *Yale Law Journal* 96: 82–117.

Lang, A. (2007), "But is it for real? The British Columbia citizens' assembly as a model of state-sponsored citizen empowerment," *Politics and Society* 35: 35–69.

Levy, E. (2003), *Sparte*, Paris: Étude.

Mackay (1841/1980), *Extraordinary Popular Delusions and the Madness of Crowds*, New York: Wilder.

Mackie, G. (2004), *Democracy Defended*, Cambridge University Press.

Pettit, P. (2001), "Deliberative democracy and the discursive dilemma," *Philosophical Issues* (suppl. to *Nous* 11), 268–99.

Pierre, E. (1893), *Traité de politique électorale et parlementaire*, Paris: Librairies-Imprimeries Réunies.

Poisson, S. (1837), *Recherches sur la probabilité des jugements*, Paris; also available as a Google Book.

Read, D., Loewenstein, G., and Rabin, M. (1999), "Choice bracketing," *Journal of Risk and Uncertainty* 19: 171–97.

Smith, A. (1759/1976), *A Theory of Moral Sentiments*, Oxford University Press.

Sommers, S. (2008), "Determinants and consequences of jury racial diversity," *Social Issues and Policy Review* 2: 65–102.

Sunstein, C. (1999), *One Case at a Time*, Cambridge, MA: Harvard University Press.

Surowiecki, J. (2004), *The Wisdom of Crowds*, New York: Doubleday.

Tocqueville, A. de (2004), *Democracy in America*, New York: Library of America.

Vacca, R. (1921), "Opinioni individuali e deliberazione collettive," *Rivista Internazionale di Filosofia del Diritto* 52: 52–59.

Vermeule, A. (2007), *Mechanisms of Democracy*, Cambridge, MA: Harvard University Press.

Index

Made in the USA
Middletown, DE
19 June 2018